D1606587

ity onlap, one updip pinch-out, and one anticline. Mene Grande field contains traps that are Miocene sandstone updip porosity pinch-outs and an anticlinal nose with Eocene sandstone porosity pinch-outs. The Miocene sandstones are distributary channels in a deltaic complex and the Eocene sandstones are primarily fluvial. The huge trap of Lima-Indiana is a complex combination of updip porosity pinch-out, regional anticline, and fractured reservoir. The much smaller trap found at Richardton/Taylor is a combination of a lateral porosity loss in the sandstone reservoir draped across the upthrown block of a faulted anticline.

Another aspect described in each field study is the history of the field's exploration and development. What seems obvious today usually was not obvious when these fields were discovered. Many times what was expected was not what was found. Geologists discovered these fields by creating concepts based on information limited by the technology available at the time. Drilling and discovery show how closely concept matches reality. Knowing the history of discovery may help explorationists realize that problems, seemingly insoluble at one time, were eventually solved. It is also instructive to learn of the sequence of thinking that solved these problems.

Careful study of these fields will enhance the prospect generator's knowledge base, and consequently, his or her ability to apply that knowledge toward future prospecting.

Norman H. Foster
Edward A. Beaumont, Editors

AAPG TREATISE OF PETROLEUM GEOLOGY

_____

The American Association of Petroleum Geologists
gratefully acknowledges and appreciates the leadership and support
of the AAPG Foundation in the development of the
Treatise of Petroleum Geology

STRATIGRAPHIC TRAPS III

COMPILED BY
NORMAN H. FOSTER
AND
EDWARD A. BEAUMONT

TREATISE OF PETROLEUM GEOLOGY
ATLAS OF OIL AND GAS FIELDS

PUBLISHED BY
THE AMERICAN ASSOCIATION OF PETROLEUM GEOLOGISTS
TULSA, OKLAHOMA 74101, U.S.A.

ISBN: 0-89181-587-2
ISSN: 1043-6103

Available from:
The AAPG Bookstore
P.O. Box 979
Tulsa, OK 74101-0979

Phone: (918) 584-2555
Telex: 49-9432
FAX: (918) 584-0469

Association Editor: Susan Longacre
Science Director: Gary D. Howell
Publications Manager: Cathleen P. Williams
Special Projects Editor: Anne H. Thomas
Science Staff: William G. Brownfield
Project Production: Custom Editorial Productions, Inc.

TABLE OF CONTENTS

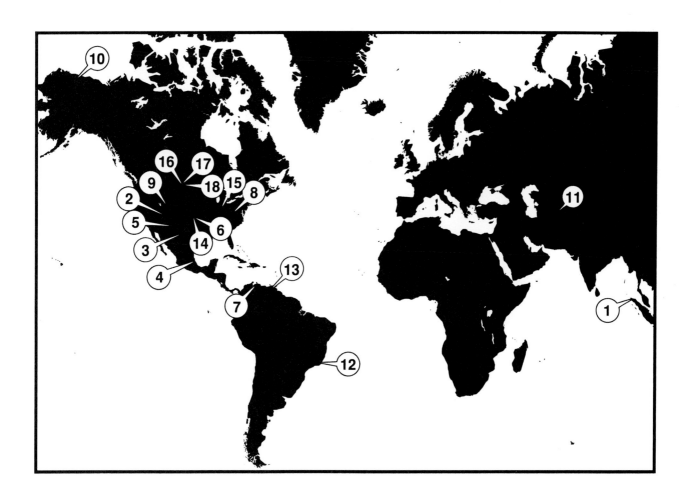

TREATISE OF PETROLEUM GEOLOGY
ADVISORY BOARD

John M. Parker
Dallas L. Peck
William H. Pelton
Alain Perrodon
James A. Peterson
R. Michael Peterson
Max Grow Pitcher
David E. Powley
William F. Precht
A. Pulunggono
Bailey Rascoe, Jr.
Donald L. Rasmussen
R. Randy Ray
Dudley D. Rice
Edward P. Riker
Edward C. Roy, Jr.
Eric A. Rudd
Floyd F. Sabins, Jr.
Nahum Schneidermann
Peter A. Scholle
George L. Scott, Jr.
Robert T. Sellars, Jr.
Faroog A. Sharief
John W. Shelton
Phillip W. Shoemaker

Synthia E. Smith
Robert M. Sneider
Stephen A. Sonnenberg
William E. Speer
Ernest J. Spradlin
Bill St. John
Philip H. Stark
Richard Steinmetz
Per R. Stokke
Douglas K. Strickland
James V. Taranik
Harry Ter Best, Jr.
Bruce K. Thatcher, Jr.
M. Ray Thomasson
Jack C. Threet
Bernard Tissot
Donald F. Todd
Harrison L. Townes
M. O. Turner
Peter R. Vail
B. van Hoorn
Arthur M. Van Tyne
Kent Lee Van Zant
Ian R. Vann
Harry K. Veal*

Steven L. Veal
Richard R. Vincelette
Cecil von Hagen
Fred J. Wagner, Jr.
William A. Walker, Jr.
Anthony Walton
Douglas W. Waples
Harry W. Wassall, III
W. Lynn Watney
N. L. Watts
Koenradd J. Weber
Robert J. Weimer
Dietrich H. Welte
Alun H. Whittaker
James E. Wilson, Jr.
John R. Wingert
Martha O. Withjack
P. W. J. Wood
Homer O. Woodbury
Walter W. Wornardt
Marcelo R. Yrigoyen
Mehmet A. Yukler
Zhai Guangming
Robert Zinke

* Deceased

American Association of Petroleum Geologists Foundation
Treatise of Petroleum Geology Fund*

Major Corporate Contributors
($25,000 or more)

Amoco Production Company
BP Exploration Company Limited
Chevron Corporation
Exxon Company, U.S.A.
Mobil Oil Corporation
Oryx Energy Company
Pennzoil Exploration and Production Company
Shell Oil Company
Texaco Foundation
Union Pacific Foundation
Unocal Corporation

Other Corporate Contributors
($5,000 to $25,000)

ARCO Oil & Gas Company
Ashland Oil, Inc.
Cabot Oil & Gas Corporation
Canadian Hunter Exploration Ltd.
Conoco Inc.
Marathon Oil Company
The McGee Foundation, Inc.
Phillips Petroleum Company
Transco Energy Company
Union Texas Petroleum Corporation

Major Individual Contributors
($1,000 or more)

John J. Amoruso
Thornton E. Anderson
C. Hayden Atchison
Richard A. Baile
Richard R. Bloomer
A. S. Bonner, Jr.
David G. Campbell
Herbert G. Davis
George A. Donnelly, Jr.
Paul H. Dudley, Jr.
Lewis G. Fearing
Lawrence W. Funkhouser
James A. Gibbs
George R. Gibson
William E. Gipson
Mrs. Vito A. (Mary Jane) Gotautas
Robert D. Gunn
Merrill W. Haas
Cecil V. Hagen
Frank W. Harrison
William A. Heck
Roy M. Huffington
J. R. Jackson, Jr.
Harrison C. Jamison
Thomas N. Jordan, Jr.
Hugh M. Looney
Jack P. Martin
John W. Mason
George B. McBride
Dean A. McGee
John R. McMillan
Lee Wayne Moore
Grover E. Murray
Rudolf B. Siegert
Robert M. Sneider
Estate of Mrs. John (Elizabeth) Teagle
Jack C. Threet
Charles Weiner
Harry Westmoreland
James E. Wilson, Jr.
P. W. J. Wood

The Foundation also gratefully acknowledges the many who have supported this endeavor with additional contributions.

*Based on contributions received as of March 31, 1992.

PREFACE

The Atlas of Oil and Gas Fields and the Treatise of Petroleum Geology

The *Treatise of Petroleum Geology* was conceived during a discussion held at the annual AAPG meeting in 1984 in San Antonio, Texas. This discussion led to the conviction that AAPG should publish a state-of-the-art textbook in petroleum geology, aimed not at the student, but at the practicing petroleum geologist. The textbook gradually evolved into a series of three different publications: the Reprint Series, the Atlas of Oil and Gas Fields, and the Handbook of Petroleum Geology. Collectively these publications are known as the *Treatise of Petroleum Geology*, AAPG's Diamond Jubilee project commemorating the Association's 75th anniversary in 1991.

With input from the Advisory Board of the Treatise of Petroleum Geology, we designed this set of publications to represent, to the degree possible, the cutting edge in petroleum exploration knowledge and application: the Reprint Series to provide useful and important published literature; the Atlas to comprise a collection of detailed field studies that illustrate the many ways oil and gas are trapped and to serve as a guide to the petroleum geology of basins where these fields are found; and the Handbook as a professional explorationist's guide to the latest knowledge in the various areas of petroleum geology and related disciplines.

The Treatise Atlas is part of AAPG's long tradition of publishing field studies. Notable AAPG field study compilations include *Structure of Typical American Fields*, published in 1929 and edited by Sidney Powers; and Memoir 30, *Giant Fields of 1968-1978*, published in 1981 and edited by Michel T. Halbouty. The Treatise Atlas continues that tradition but introduces a format designed for easier access to data.

Hundreds of geologists participated in this first compilation of the Atlas. Authors are from all parts of the industry and numerous countries. We gratefully acknowledge the generous contribution of their knowledge, resources, and time.

Purpose of the Atlas

The purpose of the Atlas is twofold: (1) to help exploration and development geologists become more efficient by increasing their awareness of the ways oil and gas are trapped, and (2) to serve as a reference for both the petroleum geology of the fields described and the basins in which they occur.

Imagination is the primary tool of the explorationist. Wallace E. Pratt once said that the unfound field must first be sought in the mind. In part, what is imagined is based on what is remembered; memory is the direct link to what is created in the mind. To create ideas that lead to the discovery of new fields, the mind of the geologist builds from its knowledge of petroleum geology. To that end, the Atlas of field studies will be a primary source for locating much of the information necessary for creating prospects and will provide a connection to the phenomenon of oil and gas traps.

Next to the firsthand experience of having prospects tested with the drill bit, studying the many facets and concepts of developed fields is perhaps the best way for the geologist to develop the ability to create plays and prospects. Also, familiarity with the many ways oil and gas are trapped allows the geologist to see through the noise inherent to exploration data and to close gaps in that data.

Format of the Atlas

To facilitate data access, all field studies in the Atlas follow the same format. Once users become familiar with this format, they will know where to look for the information they seek. Different fields from different parts of the world can be easily compared and contrasted.

The following is a generalized format outline for field studies in the Atlas:

Location
History
   Pre-Discovery
   Discovery
   Post-Discovery
Discovery Method
Structure
   Tectonic History
   Regional Structure
   Local Structure
Stratigraphy
Trap
   General Description
   Reservoir(s)
   Source(s)
Exploration Concepts

Criteria for Inclusion of a Field

Fields described in the Atlas are selected using two main criteria: (1) trap type, and (2) geographic distribution. Our ultimate goal for the Atlas is to include a field study from each major petroleum-producing province and to include an example of each known trap type. Size or economic importance are not, of themselves, criteria. Many fields that are not giants are included because they are geologically unique, because they are significant examples of geological investigation and original thinking, or because they are historically important, having led to the discovery of many other fields.

Grouping of Fields into Separate Volumes

We considered several ways to group fields in these volumes. We chose trap type because the purpose of the Atlas is to make exploration geologists more effective oil and gas trap finders, regardless of where they search for traps.

Grouping oil and gas field studies into separate volumes by trap type is a difficult exercise. We decided to group the fields into volumes by designating them as structural or stratigraphic traps. Most traps are a combination of both structure and stratigraphy. Some traps are obviously more a consequence of one than the other, but many are not. The continuum that exists between purely stratigraphic and purely structural traps is what makes grouping difficult. A further complication is that many fields contain more than one trap type.

Papers Selected for *Stratigraphic Traps III*

This volume in the Atlas of Oil and Gas Fields series contains studies of fields with traps that are mainly stratigraphic in nature. Structure is an important element in the traps of several fields, but overall, the main trapping features are stratigraphic in the group of fields in this volume.

Distribution of the fields of this volume is worldwide. Thirteen are found in the United States and five are outside the United States. In a volume dedicated to stratigraphic traps, one should not be too surprised that most of the fields described in the volume are located in the United States, where basins have, on average, been penetrated by orders of magnitude more wells than basins outside the United States. Therefore, the number discovered to date of these more-difficult-to-find traps is greater in the United States because of its high density of subsurface control. In fact, of the 41 fields described in the three volumes of the atlas devoted to stratigraphic traps, only eight occur outside the United States.

The oil and gas explorationist investigating only non-U.S. basins still has every reason to be interested in field studies of stratigraphic traps found in U.S. basins. As the quality of good structural prospects diminishes and as subsurface data increase for basins outside the United States, stratigraphic prospects will become increasingly important worldwide. Lessons learned in the United States may help to provide more efficient exploration in the rest of the world.

We classify as a stratigraphic trap any trap that exists solely as a result of stratigraphic elements, such as an updip loss of porosity. In this volume, the traps in the fields of Arun, Aneth, Stanley, Chicontepec, Pecos Slope, Glenn Pool, Burbank, Quiriquire, and Cacão easily fit into the stratigraphic category. Arun and Aneth have carbonate buildups, Chicontepec has a giant submarine canyon trap, Pecos Slope has an updip loss of porosity due to diagenetic effects, and Glenn Pool and Burbank have traps caused by updip losses of porosity in multi-storied alluvial and deltaic sandstones. The trap of Cacão is a paleogeomorphic high. Quiriquire's trap is an updip loss of porosity due to asphalt plugging of pores in an outcropping alluvial fan.

Some of the fields in this volume illustrate the difficulty of classifying traps as either stratigraphic or structural. For example, the trap of Rojo Caballos, South consists of an allochthonous block of carbonate rock embedded in a basinal shale. The block of Paleozoic carbonate rock became detached from a carbonate platform edge and slid into the basin center. Is it more structural or stratigraphic? One could argue that the gravity sliding that moved the carbonate block to the basin center is a structural process and therefore the trap is structural. Conversely, one could argue that gravity sliding is a sedimentological process and that no deformation ever occurred in any part of the rocks that make up the trap; therefore, the trap is stratigraphic. We decided to call it stratigraphic but would not argue with anyone who would label it structural.

Another field with a trap that is difficult to classify as either structural or stratigraphic is Elkhorn Ranch field. The author, William DeMis, presents compelling evidence showing it to contain a hydrodynamic trap on an anticlinal nose. This field study probably best belongs in a volume dedicated to hydrodynamic traps, but we did not have enough such fields to constitute a separate volume. There are examples of fields in various basins of the world with stratigraphic or structural traps that are modified by hydrodynamics. The trap of Dauletabad-Donmez, a Soviet field also described in this volume, has a trap that is a combination of stratigraphic porosity pinch-out and faulting modified by hydrodynamics.

Six other fields in this volume have traps possessing some degree of structural control. The trap of Red Wash field is controlled by the distribution of porosity caused by facies changes in a lacustrine deltaic complex across an anticlinal nose. Most of Elk-Poca's trap is a result of an updip pinch-out of nearshore marine sandstones; however, the southern end of the field is broadened by the presence of an anticline. Kuparuk River field contains several traps: two unconformity truncation traps, one unconform-

Arun Field—Indonesia
North Sumatra Basin, Sumatra

CLIFTON F. JORDAN, JR.
Mobil Research and Development Corporation
Dallas, Texas

MARDHAN ABDULLAH
Mobil Oil Indonesia
Jakarta, Indonesia

FIELD CLASSIFICATION

BASIN: North Sumatra
BASIN TYPE: Backarc
RESERVOIR ROCK TYPE: Limestone
RESERVOIR ENVIRONMENT OF DEPOSITION: Patch Reef Complex
TRAP DESCRIPTION: Shale-Encased Patch Reef

RESERVOIR AGE: Miocene
PETROLEUM TYPE: Oil
TRAP TYPE: Reef

LOCATION

The Arun field is located near the northern tip (Figure 1) of the island of Sumatra, Indonesia, approximately 140 mi (225 km) northwest of Medan, the capital of Aceh Province. Arun, the largest gas field in the North Sumatra basin, with an estimated initial dry gas in place of over 16 tcf (Alford et al., 1975), ranks as the 104th largest oil and gas field in the world (Carmalt and St. John, 1984). The field occupies a central portion of Mobil's "B" Block contract area (Figure 2). Arun is an onshore field situated 3 mi (5 km) south of the Andaman Sea shoreline, at the northwestern entrance to the Strait of Malacca. The topography of the field area is gently sloping coastal plain (Figure 3), comprised mainly of terraced rice paddies. The Arun field produces from four clusters to minimize disturbance to this prolific farmland. Foothills of the Barisan Mountains that form the backbone of Sumatra lie only 6 mi (10 km) south of the field.

HISTORY

Pre-Discovery

Exploration rights in the North Sumatra basin were first acquired by Asamera Oil Company in the "B" Block of northern Sumatra in November 1966. Mobil Oil Indonesia acquired the block from Asamera in July 1968 in a production-sharing agreement with Pertamina, the Indonesian national oil company; Asamera had done essentially nothing with the block to that date.

Earliest exploration activity in this part of Sumatra consisted of surface studies led by Indonesian geologists during the early 1900s. Subsequent field work by Shell and Stanvac geologists resulted in the drilling of several wildcat wells in the North Sumatra basin to test post-Baong sandstones and the discovery of one small oil field (Pase field) in such deposits 13 mi (20 km) west of Arun.

Discovery

Initial exploration by Mobil Oil Indonesia in the "B" Block began in 1968, consisting primarily of reflection seismic surveys that defined the basement high upon which the Arun reef (i.e., reef facies of the Arun Limestone) is situated. Gravity surveys had also been gathered during early exploration phases to better outline basement blocks. In 1970 a Raytheon/Westinghouse side-looking airborne radar (SLAR) survey, one of the first such surveys ever contracted commercially, was flown over North Sumatra. Structure and stratigraphy were spectacularly displayed on the SLAR images. A prominent drainage anomaly in the Keureutu and Pase River patterns was mapped, roughly over the present site of the Arun field, which was discovered in 1971. The discovery was based on a loose grid (21 lines) of relatively poor quality seismic data with three- and sixfold stacking. The Arun reef was evident on these lines, especially east-west lines, and confirmed a large, deep closure near suspected basement levels and also provided the basis for positioning the Arun discovery well.

The Arun A-1 discovery was drilled into the crest of the Arun structure and encountered nearly 1100 ft (335 m) of reefal limestone with gas shows and

1

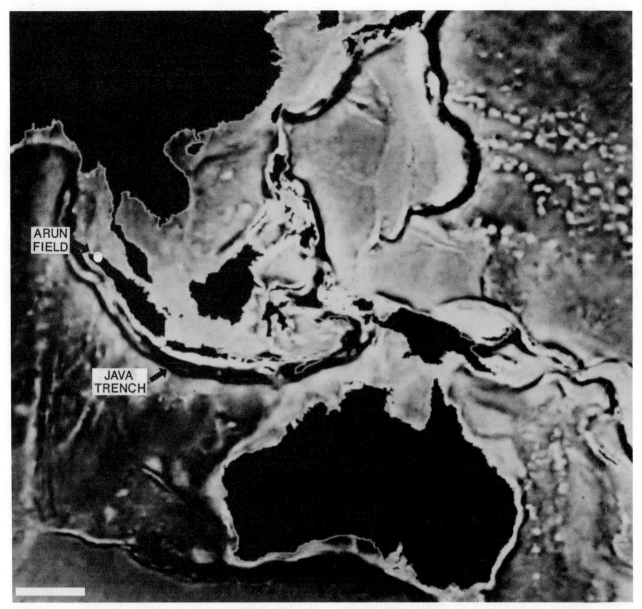

Figure 1. Regional location map of the Arun gas-condensate field; note its backarc position behind the Java trench. Seasat gravity map is from Haxby (1987). Scale bar, 620 mi (1000 km).

good indications of liquid hydrocarbons (Figure 4). Three tests were conducted that flowed gas and condensate at a maximum rate of 14.07 mmcf of gas per day and 472 BCPD (56° API) on a ½-in. diameter choke. Formation evaluation in the gas zone indicated porosity of 6–30% with an average of 16% and water saturations of 10–60% with an average of 10.7%.

Following the gas-condensate discovery, additional seismic coverage in the form of 12- and 24-fold CDP stacked lines was obtained as infill over the Arun reef. Ten appraisal wells were drilled in the first two years to delineate the basic outline of the reservoir. Important tests included the following wells (Figure 5): (1) the A-4 well, which was drilled far to the northeast but was abandoned owing to

mechanical problems; (2) the A-8 well, which encountered a thin, off-reef carbonate section of nonreservoir quality; and (3) the A-9 well, which was drilled far to the south where the Arun reservoir is structurally low and water wet.

Post-Discovery

The Arun field began production in March 1977. As of March 1989, a total of 77 wells has been drilled, of which 47 are gas producers, 10 are gas injectors, and 20 are abandoned (Figure 5). Development of the field was based on a cluster concept: Production wells

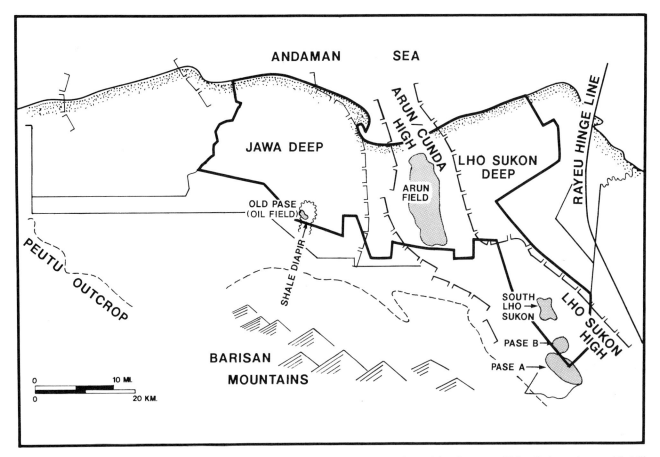

Figure 2. Major tectonic elements associated with the Arun field include the basement ridge formed by the Arun-Cunda and Lho Sukon highs, which is flanked by subbasins of the Jawa and Lho Sukon deeps. Mobil's "B" Block contract area is indicated by the heavy outline. Shaded areas are oil fields.

are drilled along the crest of the Arun reef from four clusters, each with a maximum of 16 wells. Most directional holes are drilled eastward, fanning out into the thickest and most porous part of the Arun reservoir, a pattern dictated by the distribution of reef facies, i.e., coral algal boundstones.

Average reservoir pressure at a datum of 10,050 ft (3200 m) subsea has declined from the original pressure of 7100 psig to 4330 psig (48.95 to 29.85 MPa) as of January 1989 (Figure 6). Material balance analysis of pressure-production data indicates that the reservoir produces by means of a volumetric depletion drive mechanism. No movement of the gas-water contact is evident to date. The dew-point of the original reservoir gas is estimated to be 4300 psig (29.6 MPa).

The condensate is 56° API and is swept from the reservoir by gas reinjected along the margins of the field. A pipeline 18 mi (29 km) long transmits gas and liquids from the field to a coastal LNG plant and terminal (Figure 7). Six trains for gas processing are currently in operation at P. T. Arun, and Arun LNG is shipped to Japan, supplying nearly half their annual gas consumption.

Previous studies of the Arun field were conducted by Graves and Weegar (1973, 1974), Alford et al. (1975), Houpt and Kersting (1976), Soeparjadi (1982), and Nelson et al. (1982). The present study presents results of detailed correlations within the Arun reservoir, allowing a systematic mapping of selected depositional features and reservoir properties. At the time of this study, wells A-1 through A-77 were drilled. Computer mapping, however, is based only on the first 54 wells drilled, of which 15 were cored.

Recent reserve-determination procedures were summarized by Humphreys (1986); however, no updated reserve estimates were published at that time. Previous estimates of Alford et al. (1975) place reserves of initial dry gas in place at 16.1 tcf. As such, the giant Arun field is Indonesia's largest gas field and has been one of Mobil Oil Corporation's largest operations since the late seventies. The current reservoir management plan is to control injection gas distribution, implement a balanced production scheme, selectively complete producing and injection wells, develop the steep eastern flank of the reef, and continually update the geological description of the reservoir.

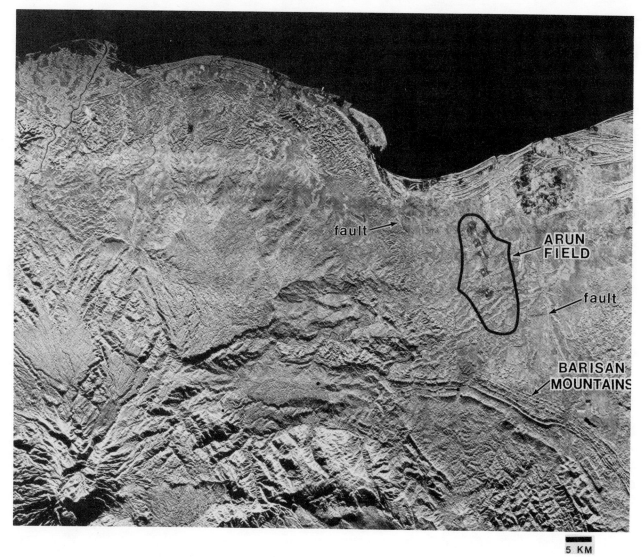

5 KM

Figure 3. Synthetic aperature radar image of the Arun field. The two northwest-southeast faults that flank the basement ridge over which the Arun reef grew are apparent. Also to be seen are thrust faults along the Barisan Mountains front south of the field and the large volcano with lava flows.

DISCOVERY METHOD

Discovery of oil and gas in Miocene reefs during the 1950s in Irian Jaya (Visser and Hermes, 1962) provided the impetus for exploration in the early 1970s in several basins across Indonesia, including the North Sumatra basin. Basement highs, recognized both by reflection seismic and gravity surveys, were drilled as likely foundations for thick reef sequences. A marked velocity contrast between the Arun reef and the shales that encase it enabled seismic definition of the reef in the first reflection surveys (Figures 8 and 9).

STRUCTURE

Tectonic History

Tectonically, the Arun field rests on a basement ridge trending north-northwest–south-southeast (Figure 2) in a backarc setting north of one of the earth's longest subduction zones, the Java trench, which runs parallel to the southern coast of Java and Sumatra and eastward into the Banda Sea (Figure 1). Strong structural movement along a bounding fault between the Barisan Mountains and

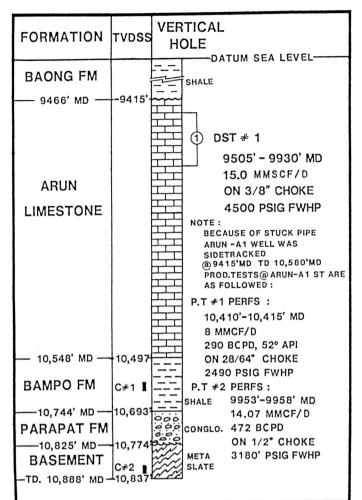

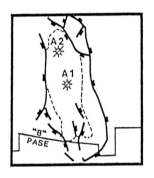

SPUDDED · : 12 AUGUST 1971
SUSPENDED : 4 DECEMBER 1971
KB : 51 FEET

PRELIMINARY RESERVOIR PARAMETERS :

	ARUN LS.
AVG. NET PAY FT	494
AVG. $\emptyset$ (%)	16
AVG. SW (%)	10.7
HYDROCARBON GAS (%)	84.5

Figure 4. Summary statistics of the discovery well, the Arun A-1, "B" block. MD, measured depth. TVDSS, true vertical depth subsea. Map shows location of the well in the field.

the North Sumatra basin occurred as a slab overlying the plate approaching from the south passed through three distinct tectonic phases: (1) a slab dipped northward in a homocline that underwent mild uplift prior to 30 Ma, (2) a sag developed in the overriding slab that experienced mild subsidence rates from 7 to 30 Ma, and (3) a backarc basin with extreme subsidence occurred along bounding faults in the downwarped slab during the last 7 m.y.

Regional Structure

Basement composition, as observed in core samples from the A-8 well to the northeast of the field, is gray phyllite of probable Triassic age (Soeparjadi, 1982). Seismic mapping indicates relief of 1000–2000 ft (305–610 m) from the top of the basement ridge into the adjacent Lho Sukon deep to the east and 1000 ft (305 m) into the Jawa deep to the west.

A radar image of the Arun field (Figure 3) reveals the traces of north-northwest to south-southeast bounding faults on the east and west sides of the basement ridge upon which the Arun reef grew, as well as the structural complexity of the Barisan Mountain front to the south of the field. Thrust faults are observed south of the field toward the Barisan Mountain uplift. Volcanic activity of Holocene age is also apparent in this photo: the large volcano southwest of Arun field and numerous lava flows that obscure older structural features. A zone of thrust faulting south of the A-9 well is considered by some to provide an exit for formation waters flowing out of the Arun reef.

Local Structure

Maps of the top of the Arun structure (Figures 10 and 11) show a prominent north-south ridge with

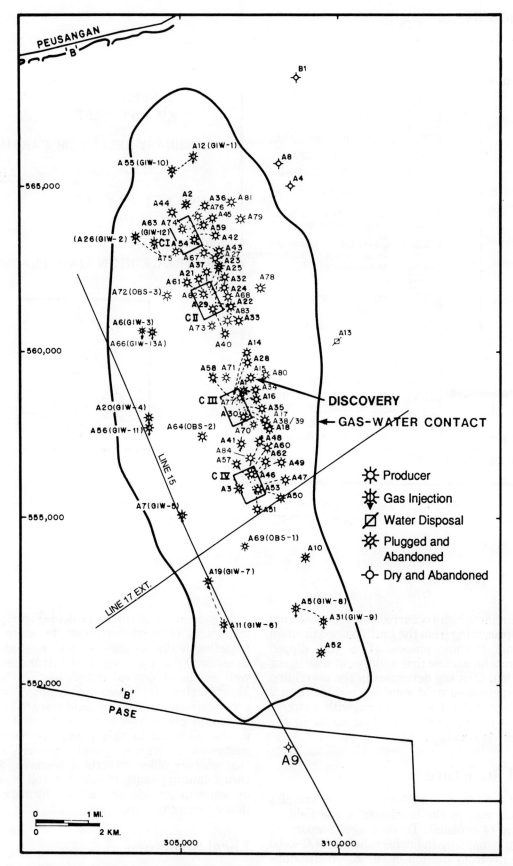

Figure 5. Arun field well location map. Seismic lines 15 and 17 ext. are shown by Figures 8 and 9.

6

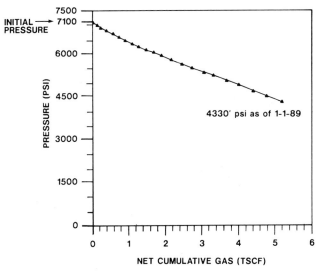

Figure 6. Arun field reservoir pressure decline curve.

small, second-order highs occurring along the ridge axis. Regional dip is to the south with east and west dips indicating the basic shape of the Arun reef mass. The gas cap (Figure 11B) is best developed to the north and is rimmed by a thin gas-water transition zone. The water leg was encountered in the A-9 well, which was drilled at the southern end of the field. The possibility of a tilted gas-water interface at Arun cannot be resolved with existing data.

STRATIGRAPHY

Tertiary Formations

The first sediments to be laid down on the basement were thin, localized Oligocene sandstones of the Parapat Formation, followed by shales of the

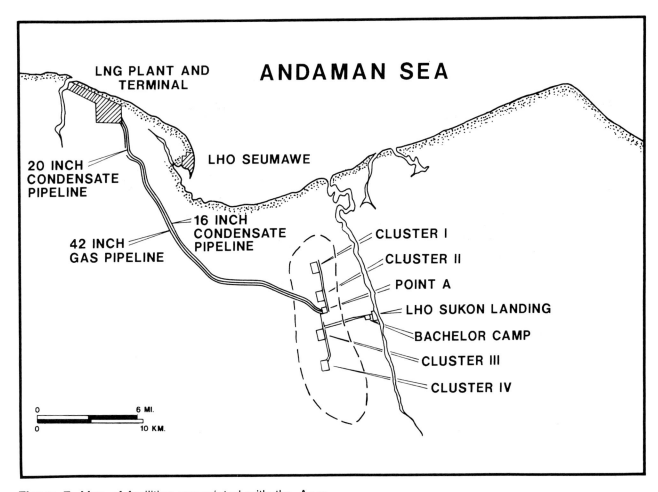

Figure 7. Map of facilities associated with the Arun field.

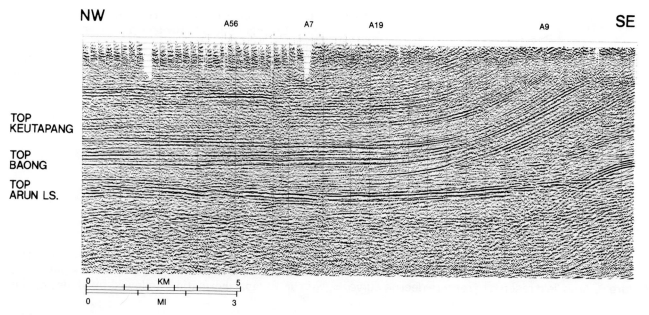

NW   SE
                    A56   A7   A19   A9

TOP
KEUTAPANG

TOP
BAONG

TOP
ARUN LS.

Figure 8. Northwest-southeast "B" Block seismic line 15 across the Arun field. The location of the line is shown on Figures 5 and 10. (From Graves and Weegar, 1973.)

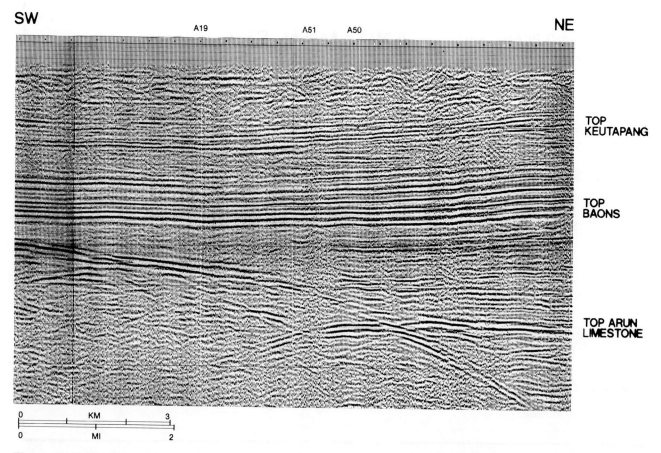

SW   NE
              A19   A51   A50

TOP
KEUTAPANG

TOP
BAONS

TOP ARUN
LIMESTONE

Figure 9. Northeast-southwest "B" Block seismic line 17-extension across the Arun field. The location of the line is shown on Figures 5 and 10. (From Graves and Weegar, 1973.)

8

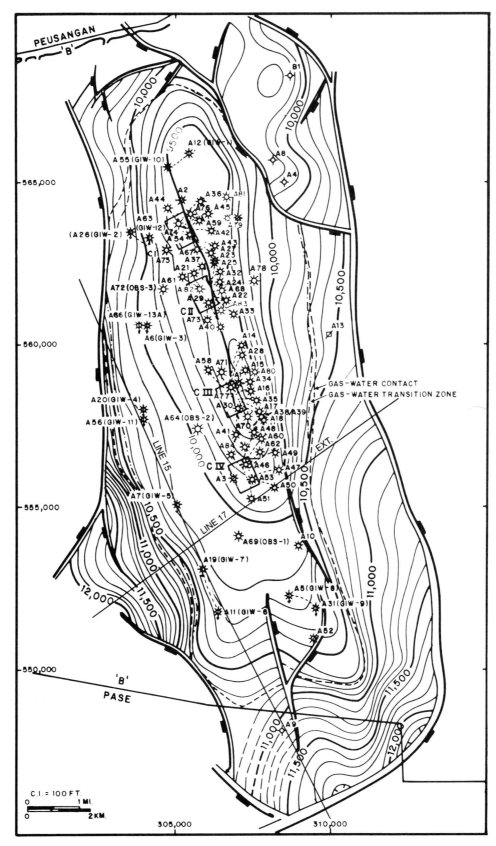

Figure 10. Structure contour map on the top of the
Arun Limestone. Seismic lines 15 and 17 ext. are shown
by Figures 8 and 9. (Axial measures in meters.)

9

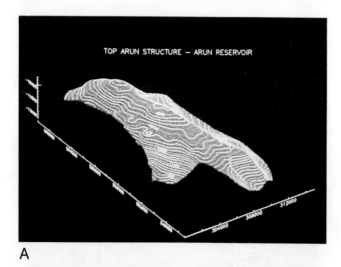

A

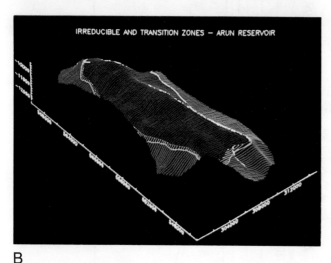

B

Figure 11. Isometric diagrams of the Arun reservoir. (A) Top Arun structure, 100 ft (30.5 m) contour interval. (B) Top Arun structure with gas cap in red, a thin gas-water transition zone in green, and the water leg in blue. (Horizontal axes in meters, each tick 2000 m; vertical axes in feet subsea, each major division 1000 ft.)

Bampo Formation (Figure 12). Microfossils from the Bampo indicate normal marine conditions of a transgressive sequence that draped over the basement ridge and thickened into adjacent basins. The average thickness of the Bampo and the Parapat formations ranges from 300 to 600 ft (90–180 m) over the basement ridge and becomes several hundred feet thicker off the high into either flanking basin. New paleontologic information indicates the presence of a late Oligocene to early Miocene unconformity at the top of the Bampo Shale.

Deposition of Tertiary limestones began in the early Miocene on top of the Bampo Shale. At this time, a period of regional tectonic quiescence occurred, with calcareous shales rich in planktonics

(i.e., the Peutu Formation) being deposited in deep off-reef shelf areas; meanwhile, reef growth (the Arun Limestone) flourished in clear shallow waters over topographic highs in the North Sumatra basin. Other carbonate bodies, such as the Pase field and the South Lho Sukon field, also occur along the axis of the basement ridge underlying the Arun field, demonstrating the strong relationship between Miocene tectonics and carbonate deposition.

A major unconformity occurs at the top of the Arun Limestone, following which a 1200 ft thick (366 m thick) sequence of marine shales, the Baong Shale, was deposited on top of the Arun Limestone. The overlying Keutapang, lower Seurula, upper Seurula, Julu Rayeu, and unnamed Quaternary units represent a coarsening-upward megacycle of clastic deposition that fills in this Tertiary basin with some 8000 ft (2440 m) of terrigenous sediments in just 9 m.y. Shales dominate in the lower to middle part of the Keutapang Formation where the top of the geopressured zone occurs. Conversely, conglomerate beds are common in upper Seurula through Quaternary beds.

Age relationships, based on recent paleontological studies and on strontium isotope age-dates, are plotted on the Cenozoic cycle chart of Haq et al. (1987) to show the deposition of Tertiary sediments in the North Sumatra basin since the late Oligocene (Figure 13). Three major periods of erosion or nondeposition have taken place during the Tertiary in the North Sumatra basin. Evidence is presented for the recognition of each unconformity. These data were used in later Thermat determinations of the geothermal gradient in this area.

The unconformity at the base of the Tertiary section lies on top of a metamorphosed terrain that (as cored in the A-1 and A-8 wells) consists of greenish-gray phyllite. This rock forms the faulted basement ridge that the Arun reef is founded upon. Basement is considered to be of probable Triassic age (Soeparjadi, 1982). If that is correct, a period of approximately 160 m.y. elapsed in which relief on the basement must have been considerably subdued. As seen in seismic lines across the Arun field, the Parapat Sandstone onlaps this basement ridge on both the east and west sides.

A paraconformity occurs at the top of the Bampo Shale, and apparently a minimum of 7.3 m.y. is not represented by sedimentation. This has not been previously documented and is based on the following evidence. (1) The oldest Arun Limestone, dated using larger foraminifera, is middle early Miocene, i.e., upper zone N5? or N6 of Blow (1969). These samples were from the A-54 and A-7 wells, less than 75 ft (23 m) above the top of the Bampo Shale. (2) The youngest Bampo Shale encountered is late Oligocene, i.e., zone NP24 of Martini (1971). These samples were from the A-13 well in uppermost Bampo Shale beds. Furthermore, planktonic foraminifera from the A-13 and A-54 wells, again from uppermost Bampo beds, indicate a late Oligocene age (N2–N3); the qualifier "possible" is a result of poor preservation of the

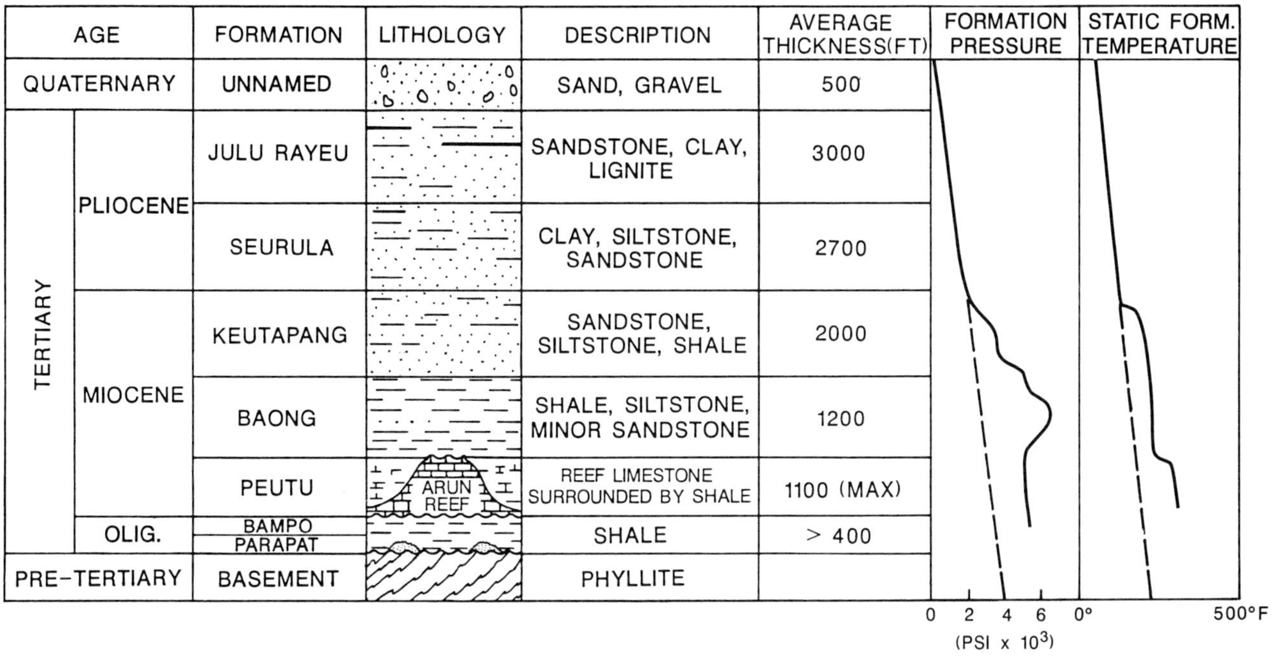

Figure 12. Stratigraphic column and temperature/ pressure profiles at the Arun field (6 × 10³ psi ~40 MPa.)

foraminifera in the A-54 because of pyritization, a phenomenon typical of the Bampo Shale.

The most economically important unconformity occurs at the top of the Arun Limestone, most significant since this was a period of dissolution porosity development within the exposed Arun reef. East-west seismic lines across the Arun field show beds of the Baong Shale onlapping the lower flanks of the reef, suggesting relief of well over 500 ft (150 m) (Figure 9). A minimum of 2.3–4.6 m.y. elapsed during this period of exposure.

Paleontological and strontium-isotope data indicate a lifespan for the Arun reef of 3.9–5.7 m.y., which can be used to estimate the reef's rate of sedimentation. Using a maximum thickness of 1100 ft (335 m), the growth rate of the reef falls in the range of 0.193–0.282 ft/millennium (0.0589–0.0860 m/ millennium). Since nearly the same assemblage of corals live today as in the Miocene, a good comparison should exist between Holocene and Miocene rates of reef-building. However, Holocene rates of reef growth are approximately 3 ft/millennium (0.9 m/millennium) (Wilson, 1975), an order of magnitude greater. Thus, the length of time determined for Arun reef growth must include the times represented by unconformities, during which nondeposition or erosion occurred. This would then indicate rapid, but sporadic growth patterns in Miocene reef facies.

Arun Subunits

Previous studies have not dealt with detailed correlations within the Arun reservoir; the field has always been modeled from the outside as a mound-shaped deposit. Houpt and Kersting (1976), after examining carbonate facies in the completely cored Arun sequence in the A-2 well, stated that "All of these rock types appear to have a random vertical distribution within the reef."

Log correlations within the reservoir have indeed been difficult owing to the lack of shales or other marker beds within the thick, relatively pure carbonate sequence. Based on core examination, log responses are attributed to subtle lithologic changes observed in beds of limestone as thin as 3 in. (7.6 cm).

Periodically, minor influxes of suspension-borne clays from the Lho Sukon and Jawa deep drifted across the Arun reef, depositing fine terrigenous clastics in reef flank and interreef lagoon environments. Detailed lithologic logging revealed the presence of thin (3 to 9 in.; 7.6 to 22.9 cm) marker beds within the Arun Limestone that correlate with low-level, second-order gamma-ray responses, with potassium (rather than uranium or thorium) causing the effect. These thin beds consist of wavy-laminated skeletal wackestones, commonly with abundant stylolites and/or horsetail laminations of argillaceous material. High clay contents are indicated by the gamma-ray response; some clay enrichments are concentrations of insoluble minerals along stylolites, while others are depositional wisps of terrigenous clays that were laid down below wave base along the deep margins of the reef. These argillaceous marker beds (log horizons CC, EE, HH, KK, MM, and NN in Figure 14) can be correlated to varying degrees across the field and are used to provide the

11

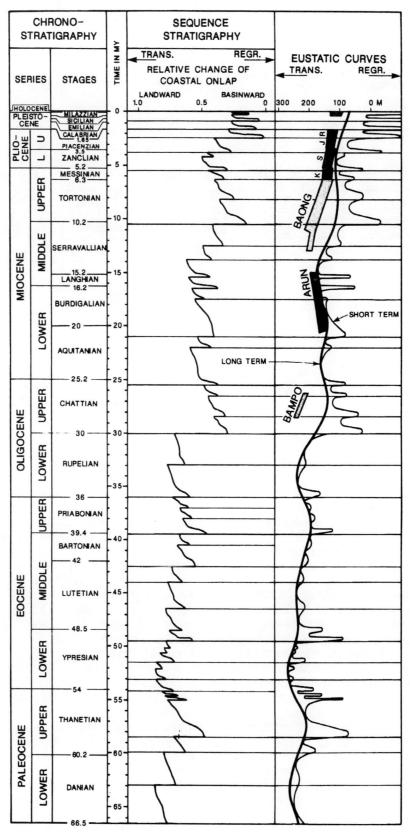

Figure 13. Cenozoic cycle chart (after Haq et al., 1987)
and Tertiary sedimentation on the Arun high.

12

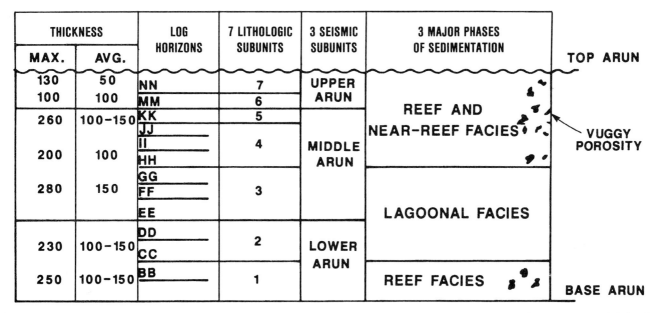

THICKNESS		LOG HORIZONS	7 LITHOLOGIC SUBUNITS	3 SEISMIC SUBUNITS	3 MAJOR PHASES OF SEDIMENTATION	
MAX.	AVG.					TOP ARUN
130	50	NN	7	UPPER ARUN	REEF AND NEAR-REEF FACIES	
100	100	MM	6			VUGGY POROSITY
260	100-150	KK JJ	5	MIDDLE ARUN		
200	100	II HH	4			
280	150	GG FF EE	3		LAGOONAL FACIES	
230	100-150	DD CC	2	LOWER ARUN		
250	100-150	BB	1		REEF FACIES	BASE ARUN

Figure 14. Field-wide correlation of seven internal zones within the Arun reef. The maximum reef thickness is about 1100 ft (335 m), averaging 700 to 850 ft (210 to 260 m).

first breakdown of the Arun reservoir into mappable Arun subunits. It is possible that some of these beds may result from light falls of volcanic ash, possibly establishing time lines through the reef.

The gamma-ray log response to these beds (Figure 15) shows a direct relation to the occurrence of thin, argillaceous marker beds within the Arun Limestone. Seven second-order gamma-ray peaks occur in the A-2 well, and all correspond to marker beds logged in the core. From the seven gamma-ray peaks in the A-54 well, five argillaceous zones were logged in the initial core examination; two subtle zones were added after referring to the gamma-ray log. It would not be unreasonable to expect poor core recovery, however, in these marker bed intervals, and every one may not be observed in core, especially not 3 in. thick beds.

Gamma-ray responses tied to core descriptions provided the only method of correlating within the reservoir. Fourteen gamma-ray horizons (Figures 14 and 15) were correlated, but none proved to be a reliable marker in all wells. Realizing that these markers occurred on a local basis, seven horizons with the most widespread and strongest responses were selected for fieldwide mapping. These seven zones form the geologic framework for the reservoir and allow a step-by-step mapping of the reef through time.

Correlations of seven Arun subunits show that subunits 1–5 occur everywhere across the field, but subunits 6 and 7 occur only in the central and southern parts of the field (Figure 16). This trend was substantiated later (1) by detailed seismic facies mapping of the field and (2) by making detailed correlations with twice as many log markers across the field.

TRAP

Trap Type

Shales on all sides and above and below the Arun reef provide an effective seal for the overpressured limestone. Basically, the Arun reef is encased in sealing shales and is a classic stratigraphic trap. Figures 10 and 11 show the structural configuration of the reservoir and the position of the gas cap.

Reservoirs

Reef growth in the Miocene flourished, as it does today, in clear, warm-water, shallow shelves found in tropical to subtropical climates. Paleoclimate studies by Savin (1977) indicate that tropical Miocene temperatures at the latitude of the North Sumatra basin warmed about 3°C (5.4°F) through the lifespan of the Arun reef.

The global distribution of known Miocene reefs is mapped as an east-west curvilinear ribbon, running as a broad belt through the tropical/subtropical latitudes of the Tethian Seaway, connecting three Miocene reef provinces (Jordan et al., 1990):

1. southeast Asia and the Indo-Pacific Ocean
2. the Mediterranean/Middle East
3. the Caribbean

The Miocene reef at the Arun field is in the Indo-Pacific province and, at 1100 ft (335 m) thick, is one of the thickest known reefs of its age. With regard to areal extent, it is also one of the largest Tertiary patch reef complexes in the world.

13

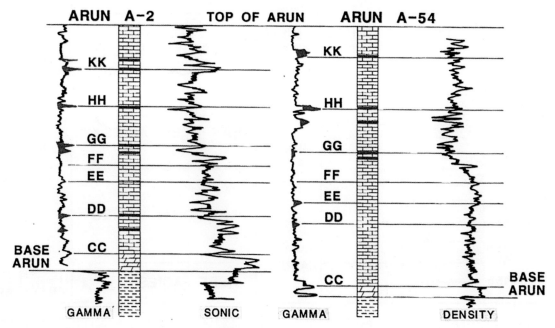

Figure 15. Detailed log correlations in which red indicates marker bed occurrences in core and in gamma-ray log responses.

Depositional Facies of the Arun Limestone

Over 6000 ft (1829 m) of core had been taken in the Arun field, following the completion of the A-54 well. The first 16 cored wells, totaling 4300 ft (1311 m) of section (Figure 17), form the database for lithofacies mapping. Five of these wells cored most of the Arun section present, while the remaining 11 were "spot checks." The contact between the Arun Limestone and the overlying Baong Shale has never been cored, mainly because of engineering considerations, and only two wells at the time (the A-54 and the A-13) were cored through the contact between the Arun Limestone and the underlying Bampo Shale.

Consistency in petrographic data collection was assured by having the same geologists (i.e., the authors of this study) examine all cores from the first 15 cored wells. Core preparation included slabbing and acid-etching. Emphasis in core logging was placed on lithology and porosity evaluations. Numerous core samples were selected for thin-section analysis as well as for several types of geochemical analyses.

Sample description and logging were carried out utilizing a concise scheme described by Jordan (1985). Figure 18 summarizes use of this procedure for Tertiary carbonate rocks of Indonesia. The basic facies equation is shown to have four elements for each carbonate facies type. Symbols used to describe features occurring in the Arun Limestone are listed, as well as three examples of reef-related facies. The comprehensive list of lithologic symbols was presented by Wilson and Jordan (1983).

The Arun Limestone is comprised of three main lithofacies (Figure 19) that are interpreted as follows

with regard to depositional environments: (1) coral encrusting–red-algal boundstones and coral boundstones indicative of reef environments; (2) mixed-skeletal packstones with branching coral fragments indicative of near-reef environments; and (3) benthonic-foraminiferal mixed-skeletal packstones to wackestones indicative of interreef lagoonal environments. The off-reef Peutu Limestone consists of benthonic-foraminiferal, planktonic-foraminiferal packstones indicative of middle-shelf environments.

Reef Facies—Reef facies include various types of boundstones, most of which are coral boundstones and coral encrusting–red-algal boundstones. These formed in shallow water by the growth and accretion of various types of coral and red algae to create a wave-resistant bathymetric feature that affected sedimentation on and around it. Basically, fossil reefs are the skeletal remains of part of a diverse marine ecosystem with an ecological complexity of several interrelated trophic levels—a complexity surpassed only by that of the tropical rain forest.

As shown in the schematic core diagram of Figure 18, not all of the reef rock consists of coral branches and red algal crusts. There is a considerable amount of interstitial sediment, consisting of skeletal packstone to wackestone deposited between frame-building elements of the reef. This composition is not unusual for boundstone textures and is understood in the definition and use of the term *boundstone* (Dunham, 1962). In Tertiary reefs, corals and red algae commonly bind together to form localized coralgal knobs that in turn coalesce to form an

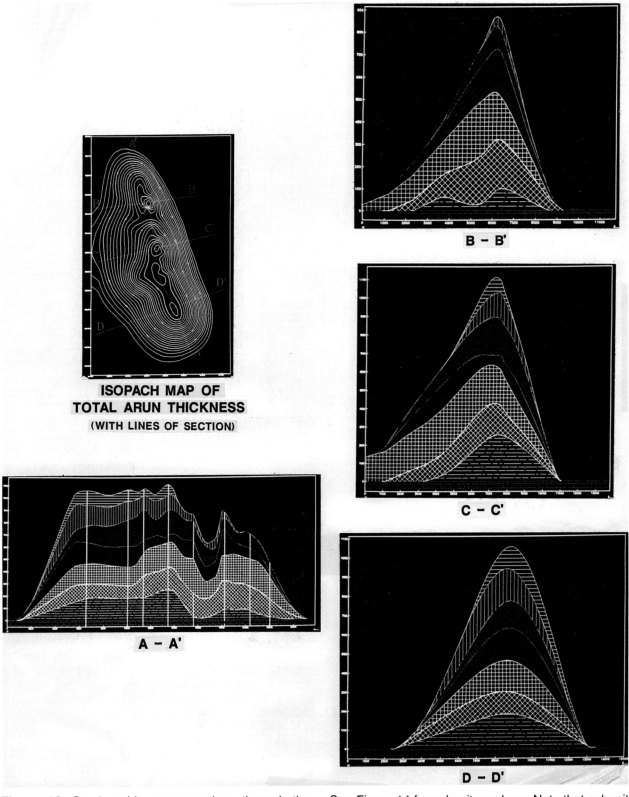

Figure 16. Stratigraphic cross sections through the Arun reservoir based on gamma-ray log correlations, core examination, and an isopach map (upper left) of the total Arun thickness. (Contour interval, 50 ft; 15.2 m.) See Figure 14 for subunit numbers. Note that subunits 6 and 7 do not occur in the northern part of the field. Profile vertical scales in feet, each tick 100 ft; horizontal scales in meters, each tick 1000 m.

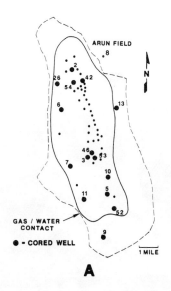

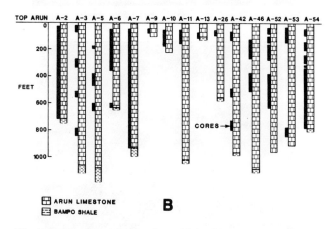

Figure 17. Core control used in lithofacies mapping of the Arun reservoir. (A) Lateral control. (B) Vertical control. Solid vertical bars are core intervals.

individual patch reef, measured on a scale of hundreds of meters across.

Just as boundstones are not 100% frame-builders, reefs are not 100% boundstones. In general, there is a large volume of reef-related skeletal debris surrounding and internally filling a reef; e.g., note the coral rudstone interval in Figure 20A. On the reef crest, sediments include large branches and plates of coral, broken off by storms and bioeroders of several varieties. Generally, when interpreting boundstone textures in carbonates, it is difficult because of the large size of coral or algal colonies to be certain that reef-building elements are truly in place (i.e., in growth position), rather than occurring in a detrital mode. Some reef specialists ("purists") would insist that none of the reef framework material in a fossil reef is truly in place, having collapsed or fallen over as the reef is subjected to continual biological and physical forces of erosion.

Evidence of subareal exposure of reef sequences includes sharp color changes parallel to bedding and irregular contacts with truncation of fossils and bedding features. These indicate that the Arun reef grew up in a discontinuous fashion, in rapid spurts, interrupted at times by subaerial exposure, a typical feature of Holocene and ancient reef systems alike (Wilson, 1975).

The problem of "taphonomic filters" acting on reef deposits has been interpreted as severe by some workers who claim that most reefs are not recognized as such owing to lack of preservation of mineralogically unstable corals (James, 1982). This appears to make good geologic sense, especially for thin, platy forms. However, some workers (e.g., Friedman, 1975) overemphasized poor textural preservation of fossil reefs to the point that he thought that "reef rock is commonly described as a biomicrite or micritic limestone." This was based on his interpretation that in reefs "bioerosion keeps pace with skeletal secretion," and corals are under-represented in that they are degraded rapidly ("anatomic dismemberment") and are only sparingly preserved in the rock record.

The recognition of a diverse coral fauna of large heads, branches, and plates in reef facies of the Arun Limestone does not support the idea of poor preservation masking obvious reef fabrics. Over 400 coral specimens were selected from slabbed Arun cores, of which 235 were identified (Table 1). Stanley H. Frost, a Tertiary coral specialist (Frost, 1988), was hired on a consultant basis to make taxonomic investigations into the rich coral fauna at Arun. Twenty-two species comprising 18 genera of Miocene corals were recognized.

Totals reveal that 37% of the Arun reef corals were medium-size head corals or encrusting corals and that 29.7% were large, massive colonies with widths of several meters across. All but one of the species of the Arun corals are living today; most can be found living on modern reefs in Indonesian waters (Jordan et al., 1985). By far the most important frame-builder of the Arun reef was *Porites* cf *P. lutea*, a large massive coral, commonly described as "buttress-forming."

Large benthonic foraminifera associated with reef and near-reef facies include robust, nearly spherical *Miogypsina* species (e.g., *M. globulina*) and *Lepidocyclina* species, the latter of which range from shallow-water environments down to intermediate depths (Hallock and Glenn, 1986; Glenn, 1988).

Judging from the persistence of muddy carbonate textures in the reef proper and in surrounding near-reef sediments, Miocene sea conditions at Arun must have maintained low- to moderate-energy levels. In addition, the diversity of the coral fauna suggests a middle-shelf patch reef complex on a well-circulating, moderately deep shelf.

In addition to the problem of preservation and recognition of boundstone textures, there remain the persistent questions of "What *is* a reef? How much of a reef actually consists of boundstone textures, or how much boundstone would have to occur in a core before a reef environment was recognized?"

A

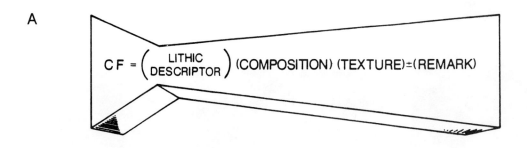

$$CF = \left(\begin{array}{c} \text{LITHIC} \\ \text{DESCRIPTOR} \end{array} \right) \text{(COMPOSITION) (TEXTURE)} \pm \text{(REMARK)}$$

B

LITHIC DESCRIPTORS

▷	BRECCIATED	≈	CRINKLY LAMINATIONS	⌇	STYLOLITE
≡	EVEN LAMINATIONS	⁄⁄	FRACTURES		

COMPOSITION

λ	BIOCLASTS	⓪	BENTHONIC FORAMS	Ⓞ	MOLLUSCS
⊗	CORAL (UNDIFF)	♋	PLANKTONIC FORAMS	ⓓ	KUPHUS
Ψ	BRANCHING CORAL	⚏	ENCRUSTING RED ALGAE		
⌢	PLATY CORAL	Ⴘ	BRANCHING RED ALGAE		

TEXTURE

M	MUDSTONE	P	PACKSTONE	B	BOUNDSTONE
W	WACKESTONE	G	GRAINSTONE		

C

REEF FACIES   NEAR-REEF FACIES   LAGOONAL FACIES

⊗ ⚏ B   Ⓞλ P+Ψ   Ⓞλ P/W

☐ = MATRIX WITH MICROPOROSITY (BC φ).

■ = MACROPOROSITY (VUG φ AND MO φ)

Figure 18. Lithologic logging of Arun facies. (A) The carbonate facies equation. (B) Common symbols and abbreviations used in Arun sample description. (C) Basic Arun lithofacies.

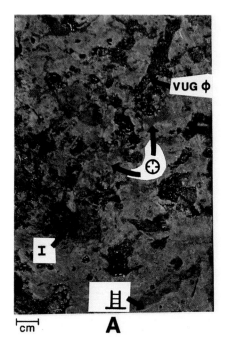

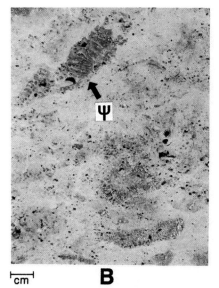

Figure 19. Depositional facies of the Arun Limestone. (A) Reef facies consisting of coral encrusting–red-algal boundstone from the Arun A-10, subunit 6, 10,232 ft (3118.7 m). Corals and red algal crusts are indicated by symbols in the photograph. Well-developed vuggy porosity shows plugging by reddish-brown Invermul drilling mud (indicated by I) and accounts for lost circulation in reef facies in this well. (B) Near-reef facies consisting of skeletal packstone with coral branches from the Arun A-7, subunit 3, 10,759 ft (3279.3 m). Admixed coral debris is from the pruning of branching finger corals from nearby reefs by storms. Symbol indicates reef rubble consisting of broken coral branches. (C) Lagoonal facies consisting of foraminiferal packstone from the Arun A-2, subunit 2, 10,049 ft (3062.9 m). Over 90% of the grains are foraminifera, most of which are species of *Lepidocyclina*. This is the most homogeneous rock type found in the Arun Limestone.

Near-Reef Facies—As implied in the name, near-reef facies are coarse, poorly sorted deposits of skeletal packstone with admixed branches and plates of corals derived from the physical and biological breakdown of reef frame-builders. Basically, this rock type consists of coral fragments floating (in the floatstone sense described by Embry and Klovan, 1971) in a muddy sand matrix of skeletal packstone, commonly rich in large benthonic foraminifera. This facies is distinguished from reef facies by a dominance of sediment over frame-builders, such as corals; the inverse is true, of course, for reef facies. Owing to the presence of large, broken coral fragments, near-reef deposits are interpreted as cavity fillings in the reef mass proper or as coarse, reef flank beds.

A typical sequence of near-reef facies logged from the A-7 core is shown in Figure 20B. Near-reef sediments contain elements of both reef and interreef lagoonal environments, and thus are treated as a transitional facies type that tends to rim or flank mappable reef masses. They may also occur as broad sheets of very poorly developed "reef facies" over the broad, bulging nose of a paleohigh, a pattern observed over the southern end of the Arun field. Volumetrically, near-reef sediments account for 14% of the total Arun reef complex.

Interreef Lagoonal Facies—Deposits of foraminiferal skeletal packstone characterize moderately deep water sedimentation occurring between patch reefs, categorized as interreef lagoons (Jordan, 1978). Within the Arun reef complex, interreef lagoonal facies account for 33% of the cored intervals studied. Such conditions also existed off the sides of the patch reef complex as a whole and serve as a transitional facies to deep, open-water middle-shelf facies. A typical sequence of lagoonal facies logged from A-53 cores is shown in Figure 20C.

Certain large benthonic foraminifera are characteristic of moderately deep, interreef lagoonal environments; these include mainly species of *Operculina* and *Cycloclypeus* (Glenn, 1988).

Middle-Shelf Facies—Thin sequences of Peutu Limestone at A-8 (19 ft; 6 m) and at A-13 (98 ft; 30 m) are regarded as condensed Arun-equivalent section, deposited in an off-reef setting. The middle-shelf facies from the A-13 core consists of benthonic-foraminiferal, planktonic-foraminiferal packstone with some reworked pebbles from the underlying Baong Shale. This facies contains both shallow- and deep-water foraminifera, representing a mix of shallow reef and deep middle-shelf faunas that is

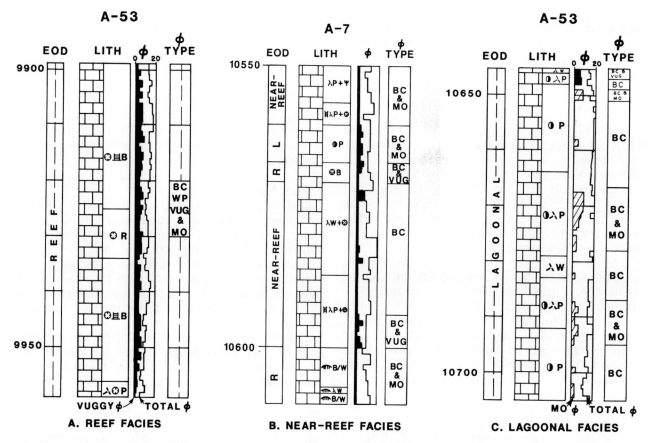

Figure 20. Typical Arun facies as determined through core examination. Porosity types are from Choquette and Pray (1970); lithologic abbreviations of B for boundstone, W for wackestone, P for packstone, and R for rudstone are from Dunham (1962) and Embry and Klovan (1971). EOD, environment of deposition.

Table 1. Corals identified in cores from the Arun Reef, listed in order of decreasing abundance; only one species is extinct.

MAJOR REEF-BUILDING CORALS
Porites cf *P. lutea*
Cyphastrea microphthalma
Astreopora myriophthalma
Stylocoeniella guentheri
Acropora spp.

ACCESSORY CORALS
Goniopora stuchburyi
Favia speciosa
Alveopora fenestrata
Leptoseris hawaiiensis
Oulophyllia aspera
Porites spp.
Diploastrea heliopora
Favia stelligeri

RARE CORALS
Anisocoenia crassisepta (extinct)
Galaxea fascicularis
Pavona varians
Montipora hispida
Platygyra spp.
Alveopora allingi
Symphyllia nobilis
Caulastrea sp.

---

characteristic of a forereef setting. This facies most likely occurs as a wedge-shaped deposit along the steep eastern side of the Arun reef that thins uniformly out into the off-reef basin. Similar deposits in the A-26 well show the same faunal mixture, but contain no gravel. The A-26 beds are interpreted as an incursion of deep-water off-reef sedimentation onto the more gentle northwestern flank of the reef complex.

Certain large benthonic foraminifera are characteristic of deep off-reef environments of the middle shelf; these include *Cycloclypeus* species and moderately convex *Amphistegina* species (Glenn, 1988).

In a regional sense, the Arun field occupies a middle-shelf position in the North Sumatra basin and was deposited as a large complex of individual patch reefs. The Arun field is the largest "carbonate anomaly" in the North Sumatra basin. It is built on a paleotopographic high in the midst of off-reef sedimentation of fines that blanketed the broad, deep, central parts of the basin with argillaceous foraminiferal packstones rich in planktonic foraminifera. The fact that there is no true "forereef" or "backreef" was recognized by Houpt and Kersting (1976). Since the reef is an elliptical-shaped middle-shelf phenomenon, it has basically a radial symmetry and pattern of sediment dispersion. Despite the occurrence of a

steep windward slope on its eastern side, mapped as a "near vertical reef edge," the Arun reef is in no way an outer-shelf barrier reef with linear facies patterns and well-developed backreef deposits.

A shelf-to-basin profile (Figure 21) shows the Arun reef as a middle-shelf patch reef complex in the center of a 150 to 200 mi wide (240–320 km wide) basin, the North Sumatra basin, which is bounded by land on three sides and is connected to the open sea only to the northwest, now the Andaman Sea. Maximum water depths on the shelf were most likely on the order of 1000 ft (310 m). The edge of the shelf sediments that filled this basin occurs to the northwest; this shelf edge is a typical setting for the possible development of a thick Miocene barrier reef system, shown conceptually in Figure 21.

An alternate interpretation would be to consider the Arun reef an "atoll," formed on an uplifted basement block in a basinal setting with water depths of 1000 ft (310 m). Kingston (1978) divided the North Sumatra basin into a broad, shallow shelf area on the eastern side of the basin (a shelf with patch reef complexes described by Mundt, 1982) and basinal facies on the western side of the basin. This paleogeographic reconstruction would treat the Arun field as an offshore, open-water atoll with its own shallow shelf area developed on the top of the atoll.

The main difference between the two interpretations is whether one considers 1000 ft (310 m) of water a deep shelf or a basin. Owing to the dominance of large benthonic foraminifera over planktonic foraminifera observed in Arun cores from the off-reef A-13 well, the authors favor a middle-shelf patch reef interpretation. In addition, the high-energy type of reef facies and the resultant linear facies patterns of an outer-shelf barrier reef or an atoll-margin system do not occur in the moderate-energy environments of the Arun reef.

Pulau Seribu is a modern patch reef complex in the West Java Sea, approximately 30 mi (50 km) northwest of Jakarta, that apparently is a living example of the Arun reef (Jordan et al., 1985). Three Holocene reef-related facies occur there, representing reef, near-reef, and interreef lagoonal environments (Figure 22); these compare well with equivalent facies of the Arun reservoir shown in Figure 19.

Facies maps of Pulau Seribu show relatively low amounts of bonafide coral boundstone facies. Coral molluscan grainstones predominate in reef top and forereef environments, and foraminiferal molluscan packstones accumulate in interreef channels approximately 100 ft (31 m) deep. Foraminifera-bearing shales occur in deeper water (about 200 ft or 62 m deep) on the eastern (windward) side of the complex, and argillaceous foraminiferal packstones occur at similar depths on the western (leeward) side. Since the islands of Pulau Seribu were formed by storms piling up reef-derived sediment, the composition and texture of island sediment is indistinguishable from nearby reef and near-reef facies. In the Arun cores, there is little physical evidence for the development of island facies other than a few surfaces of truncation that are interpreted as exposure surfaces. In general, these facies patterns compare well with those of the Arun reef, realizing that much less detail in mapping is possible at 10,000–11,000 ft (3100–3400 m) in the subsurface. In addition, both reef systems are shaped the same and are nearly the same size. Apparently, the reefs even experienced the same prevailing wind direction, with strong winds blowing east to west.

Facies Maps

Reef, near-reef, lagoonal, and middle-shelf facies were mapped for all Arun subunits (Figure 23). Reef facies occur primarily along the center spine of the build-up with flanking bodies of near-reef facies especially well developed on the wide, southern part of the complex. Lagoonal facies are found along the sides of the build-up or in large interreef channels like the one that separates the northern satellite reef from the main reef.

Considerable lumping of lithofacies was done in preparing the facies maps. It was not uncommon, for example, to encounter 20 ft (6 m) of lagoonal deposits that had to be ignored in mapping 60 ft (18 m) of reef. It must also be noted that core control is poorest in the lower three Arun subunits; thus these maps are more generalized. This is most likely why near-reef facies are not mapped in these horizons.

It is apparent from these maps that periods of most extensive reef growth occurred early in the history of the Arun reef (subunit 1) and in its last stages (subunits 4–7). During the deposition of subunits 2 and 3, reef facies clung to the center ridge of the complex with lagoonal facies, as defined previously, occurring along the broad flanks of the build-up; this represents a middle period of relatively deeper water that confined and limited reef growth to high areas. Another rapid rise in sea level took place following the deposition of subunit 5 and apparently drowned the northern satellite reef, thus depositing subunits 6 and 7 only in the middle and southern part of the complex. This interpretation is supported by the following observations: (1) a rapid global rise in sea level reported by Haq et al. (1987) for the Miocene, (2) facies patterns of Arun Limestone subunits showing a small northern satellite reef surrounded by lagoonal facies (Figure 23), and (3) an upward increase in the abundance of planktonic foraminifera in these sediments.

An alternate explanation for missing subunits 6 and 7 at the northern end of the field would be removal by erosion. An unconformity exists at the top of the Arun Limestone, occurring everywhere across the field. Localized erosion of the northern end of the reef thus could account for missing section there.

Patterns of facies distribution shown in Figure 23 include the broad sheet of lagoonal deposits of subunit 3 that represent a deepening over the reef, the development of a satellite reef to the north of

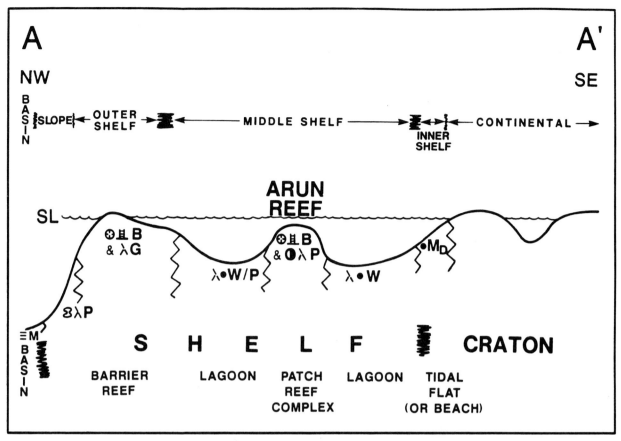

Figure 21. Depositional setting of the Arun reef, shown on a shelf-to-basin profile along line A-A', transecting the North Sumatra basin. See Figure 18 for an explanation of lithologic symbols used.

the complex (with a channel separating it from the Arun reef proper), the distribution of interreef lagoonal deposits between and around centers of reef growth, and the general proportion of reef to near-reef sediments in the system.

The form of the Arun reef is best shown by a generalized east-west lithofacies cross section (Figure 24). The overall thickening of carbonates over the paleohigh, the location of reef nuclei on the crest and upper eastern (windward) flank of the reef, and

21

Figure 22. Holocene carbonate sediments at Pulau Seribu as modern counterparts for Arun lithofacies; compare with Figure 19. (A) Holocene reef deposits of coral encrusting–red-algal boundstones of a living reef 50 km northeast of Jakarta. Platy and branching corals dominate with red algae appearing as smooth encrustations that bind corals together and create a wave-resistant biomass. Water depth is 2 m (6.5 ft). (B) Holocene near-reef sediments of skeletal grain-stone/packstone with coral branches. Reef flank or reef top sediments contain significant amounts of admixed coral debris from nearby coral encrusting–red-algal boundstones. Arrow indicates broken branches near the side of a reef mass. Water depth is 3 m (10 ft). (C) Holocene lagoonal sediments of foraminiferal molluscan packstone. An essentially flat sea floor exists off the reef in about 25 m (80 ft) of water. This is an interreef lagoon setting with numerous burrow mounds.

the steep eastern side of the reef are evident. Houpt and Kersting (1976), in preparing geophysical models of the steep eastern side of the field, pointed out that seismic lines over this steep escarpment have been interpreted as "a fault, a seismic discontinuity, and as a steep reef face implying the presence of forereef facies." Their models indicate that diffractions from a steep slope of 30–60° could readily be interpreted as primary reflections.

Porosity Types

Once a reef has been formed, one of two basic "diagenetic scenarios" occurs: (1) The reef may be subaerially exposed to porosity-creating meteoric diagenesis and then be buried in the subsurface, or (2) the reef may be buried by sediments in the marine phreatic zone and steadily subside into the subsurface without ever seeing the "light of meteoric diagenesis."

Which one occurs is important regarding diagenesis and the development of porosity in carbonate build-ups. In the first case, initially high values of primary interparticle and intraparticle porosity (some of which may be occluded by submarine cementation) and high values of permeability are enhanced by the creation and addition of dissolution porosity (moldic, vuggy, and solution-enlarged fracture porosity). In the second case, marine cements may proliferate, especially on the open-ocean side of barrier reef systems, plugging most of the reef's

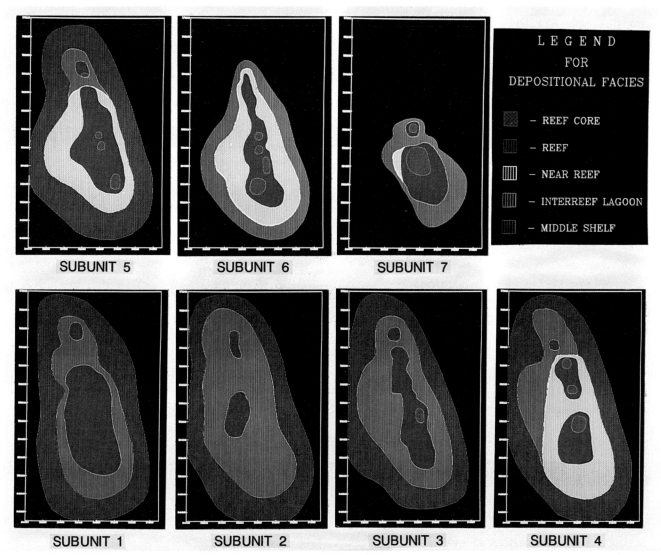

Figure 23. Depositional facies maps of Arun subunits 1–7 (oldest to youngest). Reef facies (two shades of red) are restricted to the spine of the basement ridge, forming a northern satellite reef that is missing in maps of the two youngest subunits. (Horizontal distances in 2 km increments; each map about 15 × 25 km [9 × 15.5 mi].)

original porosity; all that can be hoped for in this case would be remnant primary porosity.

Fortunately, the Arun reef experienced strong meteoric diagenesis in which several types of dissolution pores were created; one-fourth of the field's total porosity is attributed to this type of porosity. The remaining three-fourths of the porosity at Arun results from incompletely cemented, lime mud matrix material that was preserved in its present porous state by extremely rapid subsidence rates, leaving little time for complete cementation of lime mud.

Porosity types observed in cores and thin-sections of the Arun reservoir are listed in Table 2 using the nomenclature of Choquette and Pray (1970).

Macroporosity—Several types of large, visible pores are found in the Arun reservoir (Figure 25A–I). Vuggy and moldic porosity dominate over intraparticle, fracture, and breccia porosity. Of all these porosity types, only intraparticle porosity is primary, the others being dissolution or diagenetic types of porosity associated with shallow-burial formation fluids. Vugs and molds are related to the dissolution of aragonitic coral fragments and high-magnesium-calcite foraminifera, respectively, and thus the distribution of these types of porosity is controlled both by diagenetic and primary facies patterns. Evidence of dissolution porosity can be found throughout the entire mass of the Arun reef (not including flank positions of the A-13 and A-26 wells); thus, the diagenetic overprint is uniform and complete.

Approximately 25% of the reservoir's total porosity is due to this facies-controlled macroporosity. This interpretation is based on the comparison of visual

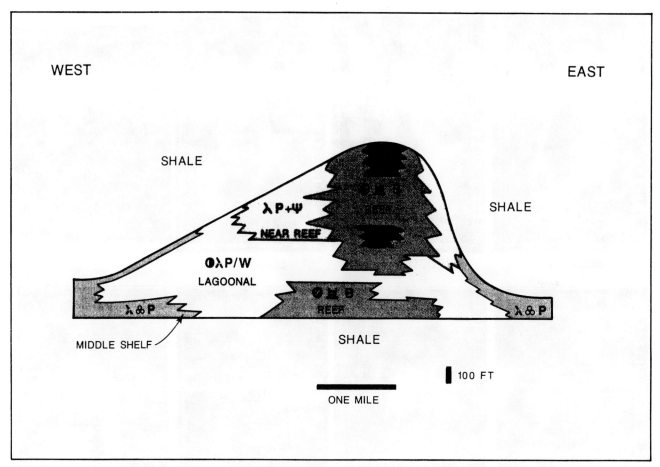

Figure 24. Generalized lithofacies cross section across the Arun reef showing lithofacies and associated depositional environments. Vertical exaggeration is about 10×.

Table 2. Porosity types in the Arun reservoir.

Porosity	Type	Distribution	Occurs as:
BC ϕ	Intercrystalline porosity	Pervasive throughout the reservoir (75% of total ϕ)	Microspar matrix of recrystallized lime mud
VUG ϕ	Vuggy porosity	Reef & near-reef facies	Dissolved aragonite fossils, especially corals
MO ϕ	Moldic porosity	Lagoonal facies	Dissolved benthonic foraminifera
WP ϕ	Intraparticle porosity	All facies	Primary living space for soft parts of corals and foraminifera
FR ϕ	Fracture porosity	All facies	Vertical fractures, commonly solution-enlarged
BR ϕ	Breccia porosity	Reef facies	Minor solution-collapse features

estimates of porosity in slabbed and whole core with total porosity measurements made on standard 1-in. diameter perm plugs and also on whole core samples. By subtracting visual porosity from total measured porosity, one can calculate microporosity.

The amount of "section with vuggy porosity greater than 5%," as determined from routine core logging throughout the reef, is 21%. This means that of the 39% of the limestone mass that is reef facies and of the 15% that is near-reef facies, 21% had significant macroporosity. Across the field, reef facies average 17.5% porosity and 189.6 md permeability. Calcite cementation of large pores in the Arun reservoir is incomplete and not a problem. Most macropores are partially cemented by coarse calcite deep-burial cements and retain most of their

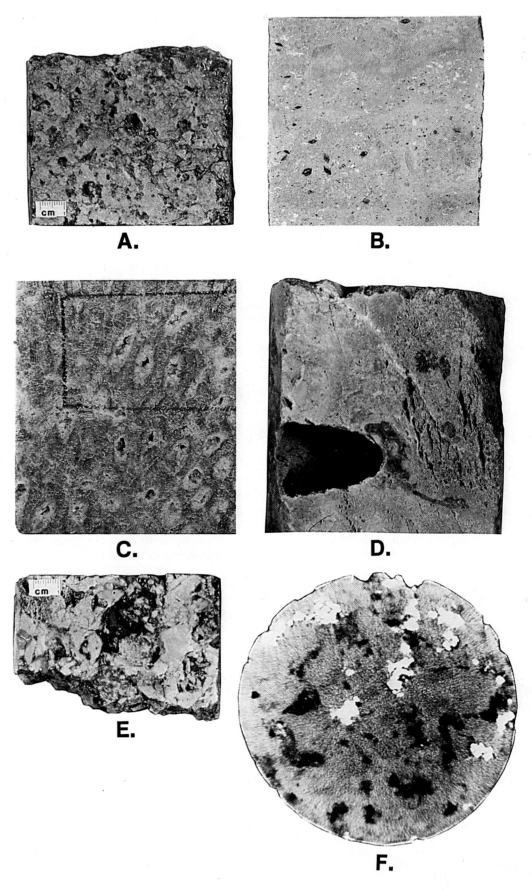

A.

B.

C.

D.

E.

F.

FIGURE 25: SEE THE FOLLOWING PAGE FOR CAPTION

Figure 25. Porosity in the Arun reservoir; A–F are in same scale; G–I are as indicated. (A) Vuggy porosity (10%) in a coral encrusting–red-algal boundstone; core slab, A-10, 10,185 ft (3104.4 m). (B) Moldic porosity in a foram branching–red-algal packstone; molds formed owing to preferential dissolution of large benthonic foraminifera; core slab, A-7, 10,266 ft (3129.1 m). (C) Intraparticle porosity, partially occluded by clear, coarse crystals of calcite that grew on the walls of individual corallites, core slab, A-7, 11,027 ft (3361.0 m). (D) Fracture porosity, solution-enlarged, is shown in a coral boundstone; core slab, A-2, 9632 ft (2935.8 m). (E) Breccia porosity in a brecciated coral encrusting–red-algal boundstone with 10% visible porosity, part of which is filled with reddish-brown Invermul drilling mud; core slab, A-10, 10,220 ft (3115.1 m). (F) CAT scan view across a whole core sample of coral boundstone; bright white areas indicate density differences associated with drilling mud; A-3, 9934 ft (3027.9 m). (G) Arun microporosity (15.1% as determined by perm plug analysis) in this skeletal packstone; arrow indicates SEM sample location; core slab, A-7, 10,799 ft (3291.5 m). (H) SEM view of microspar and the pervasive microporosity that gives the Arun Limestone its tremendous storage capacity for gas as well as its characteristic "chalkiness"; core chip from A-7, 10,799 ft (3291.5 m), sampled in G above. (I) Close-up of microspar crystals and extensive development of intercrystalline porosity within a limestone reservoir; A-7, 10,799 ft (3291.5 m), a SEM enlargement of the area framed in H above.

effectiveness. Permeabilities in facies with well-developed macroporosity (i.e., reef facies) tend to be an order of magnitude higher than those without.

Extensive microfracturing, as suggested by Houpt and Kersting (1976), is not a significant type of porosity in the Arun field. The distribution of microfractures is not as pervasive as previously thought, and many of them are healed with late-stage calcite cement.

Microporosity—The most important pore type in the Arun reservoir is pervasive microporosity, which occurs in all Arun facies and accounts for approximately 75% of the total porosity in the reservoir. Micropores are 2–4 microns across and, as seen in SEM (Figure 25G–I), have complex microrhombic shapes as a result of being enclosed by 3–4 micron-sized rhombs of calcite. In lagoonal facies, the great majority of the porosity, more than 90%, is this type of microporosity; that is, few vugs and molds occur in lagoonal facies. Fieldwide, the average porosity of lagoonal facies is 14.6%, and the average permeability is 45.6 md.

This property of tremendously well developed microporosity accounts for the difficulty in keeping the core face wet when conducting routine core examination, because the micropores act as an effective sponge. Since the pores are so small, this type of porosity cannot be estimated visually with any reliability. Consequently, visual porosity estimates were restricted to macropores.

As determined by conventional core plug analysis and by log evaluation, porosity values throughout the Arun reef are good, averaging 16% across the field and ranging as high as 33%. Porosity tends to increase toward the top of the Arun reef, with highest porosities occurring in the central part of the complex and decreasing down the flanks. This pattern of porosity distribution is the result of meteoric diagenesis, whereby the most intense dissolution of metastable carbonate minerals takes place near the surface.

Isopach Maps

Isopach maps (Figures 26 and 27) and isopach perspective diagrams (Figure 28) for seven Arun subunits indicate that each subunit grew up from three to five depocenters, each interpreted to be a cluster of patch reefs. The thickest part of each build-up consists of reef and near-reef facies. Thickness relationships show (1) that the northernmost of the individual reefs occurs as a satellite reef that does not grow upward into subunits 6 and 7, (2) that the width of the reef mass becomes wider toward the south, giving the reef a somewhat bulbous shape in plan view, and (3) that the eastern side of the Arun reef is steeper than the western flank.

Faults

Major faults with 1000–2000 ft (310–620 m) of displacement occur on both flanks of the Arun field and downdrop section to give the outline of the field a scalloped appearance in map view. Four to six minor faults with displacements on the order of a few hundreds of feet occur over the crest of the field. Since all seven Arun subunits are porous and all are in communication, these faults are of little consequence.

SOURCE AND MIGRATION OF ARUN HYDROCARBONS

Organic Richness

Prior to 1984, only 52 analyses of total organic carbon (TOC) had been made on samples from early wells, mainly the A-1 and A-2. The present study adds over 200 new TOC analyses with as good a sample coverage as the cores permit. Figure 29 summarizes sample control and lists average TOC values for various formations as analyzed in each well shown. Statistical compilations are shown in the same format for each stratigraphic unit at each well. For example, a TOC value of 1.89 is shown for the Baong Shale in the A-13 well; the standard deviation is 0.39, and 90 samples were analyzed. Most samples analyzed were shales, but a few typically lean limestone samples with TOC values in the range of 0.23–0.58 were included for comparison.

A pattern emerges in which organically rich shales occur only in off-reef locations, and organically lean shales occur over the paleohigh upon which the Arun reef is founded. Deep, anoxic off-reef waters surrounding the reef contrast with shallow, oxygenated waters associated with the position of the reef. Data from conventional TOC analyses are summarized as follows: (1) the Keutapang Formation averages 1.44 off the reef but is only 0.31 above it; (2) the Baong Shale averages 1.89 off the reef but is only 0.27 over it; and (3) the Bampo Shale averages 1.90 off the reef but is only 0.38 below it. A similar general relationship was observed by Kingston (1978) in a regional study of the North Sumatra basin.

To determine if part of this richness is due to the presence of migrated hydrocarbons, a separate set of ten samples was selected (eight shale and two limestone samples from the reef) for measuring TOC values two times per sample: one sample cut consisted of typical subsurface samples, and the other cut had the hydrocarbons extracted by soxhlet flushing. Results of these comparisons (Table 3) indicated that significant amounts of bitumen contributed to the TOC; on the average, 21.0% of the total organic material consisted of migrated hydrocarbons.

In spite of this reduction in TOC values, the shales in off-reef areas remain sufficiently rich in organics to qualify as good hydrocarbon source rocks. For example, TOC values in the Baong Formation before extraction were 3.0–3.1, whereas after extraction they were 1.7–1.8.

Organic Quality

The quality of organic material in shales surrounding the Arun reservoir has been evaluated by subjecting 36 samples from three wells (A-1, A-7, and A-13) to Rock-Eval pyrolysis. Several properties (Table 4) are measured and calculated by the following suite of organic analyses.

1. S_1—the quantity of free hydrocarbons in the rock

The property measured by the S_1 peak is roughly analogous to the solvent extractable fraction of the organic matter. This measure, and two other S values, are measured in units of mg/g of rock. S_1 ranges from 0.01 in the lower Keutapang of the A-7 well to a maximum of 30.6 from the Baong Shale of the A-13 well. The high values agree with the

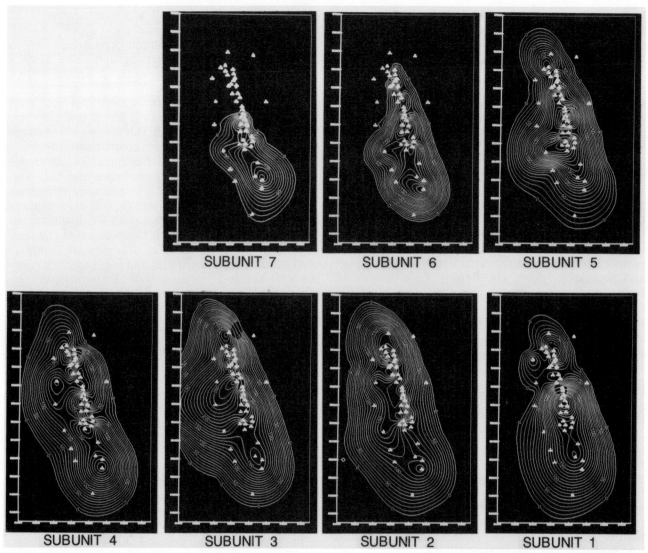

SUBUNIT 7   SUBUNIT 6   SUBUNIT 5

SUBUNIT 4   SUBUNIT 3   SUBUNIT 2   SUBUNIT 1

Figure 26. Isopach maps of Arun subunits 1–7, based on 54 wells; contour interval, 10 ft (3 m). The maps are approximately 15 × 25 km (9 × 15.5 mi). (See Figure 16 for cross sections of the reef showing the subunits.)

observed differences in measuring TOC values of shales before and after extraction and support the idea of migrated oil being present in the shale.

2. S_2—quantity of hydrocarbons released by the breakdown of kerogen during pyrolysis

S_2 values range from 0.05 for the upper Baong Shale in the A-7 well to 9.2 for the Bampo Shale in the A-13 well. Values greater than 5 indicate good source potential. No source potential is recognized from S_2 peaks for samples from wells situated on the reef; only the off-reef A-13 records S_2 values in that range.

However, part of the richness is due to migrated hydrocarbons. As already discussed for TOC values in A-13, extraction of selected samples reduced the S_2 values between 50% and 70%. Therefore, the S_2

potential values are substantially lower. Despite these reductions, the actual potential in the Baong Shale away from the reef, as represented by samples in well A-13, is considerably higher than that of shale deposited over or under the reef.

3. S_3—related to the amount of oxygen present in the kerogen

Low S_3 peak values were measured for all shale samples from wells drilled over the reef; the minimum value measured was 0.3 from lower Keutapang beds in the A-7 well. Higher values for S_3 were encountered, with the maximum for the Bampo Shale in the off-reef A-13 well.

4. S_2/S_3 ratio—a general indication of kerogen quality or type

28

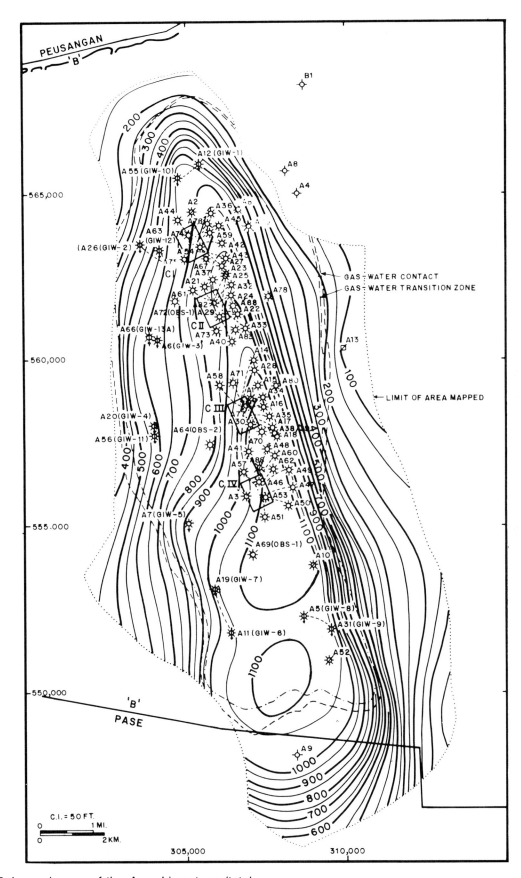

Figure 27. Isopach map of the Arun Limestone (total thickness in feet).

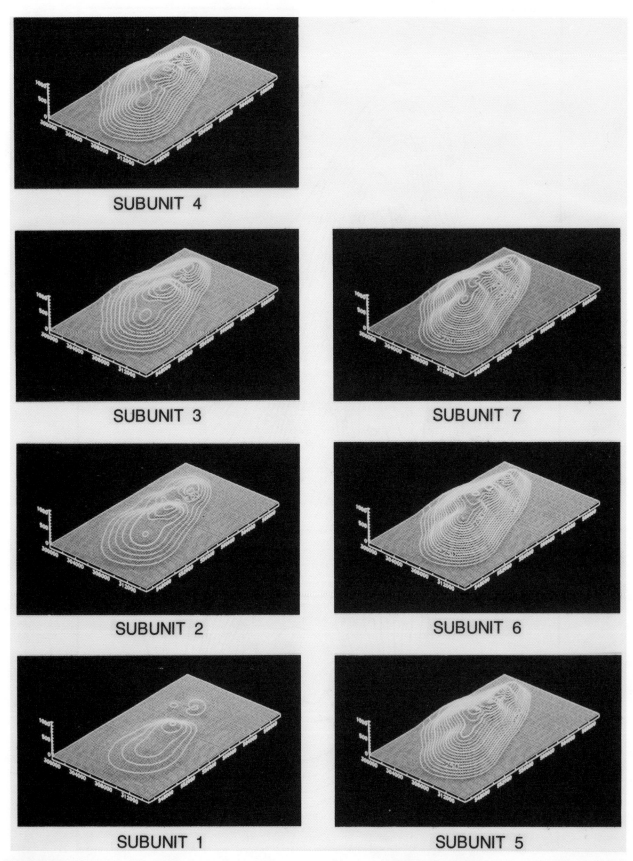

Figure 28. Isometric diagrams of isopachs of Arun subunits 1-7 and of the total Arun thickness, viewed from the southeast; contour interval, 50 ft (15.2 m). Horizontal areas approximately 15 × 25 km (9 × 15.5 m).

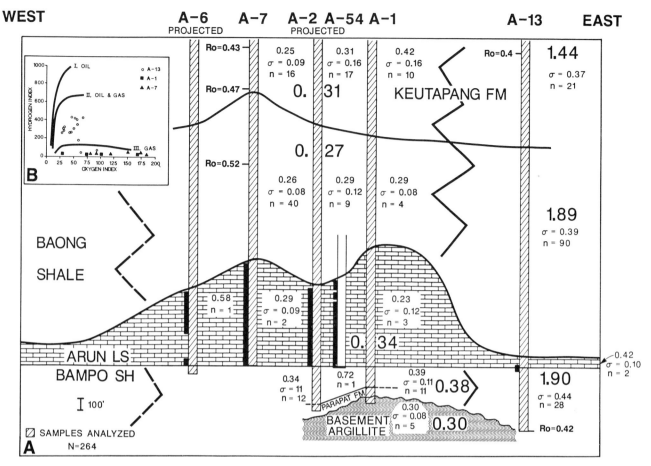

Figure 29. Source rock geochemistry of shales surrounding the Arun Limestone. (A) Summary of TOC and R_o analyses. (B) Kerogen type determination from Rock Eval prolysis data.

Calculation of this ratio indicates whether a given rock will generate oil, gas, or both. Low values from the A-1 and A-7 wells indicate a gas source, whereas most S_2/S_3 values from the A-13 well are an order of magnitude higher, indicating oil generation potential.

5. $S_1/S_1 + S_2$—the productivity index

This ratio indicates the amount of free hydrocarbons, either in situ or migrated, relative to the total hydrocarbon potential in a given sample. For the moderate maturity level of these rocks, this ratio should not exceed 0.15. In the comparison of Rock-Eval data for extracted versus nonextracted samples, all original samples exceed the 0.15 limit and attest to the abundance of migrated hydrocarbons.

6. T_{max}—the temperature in the Rock-Eval technique at which maximum rate of generation occurs

T_{max} values are used to indicate approximate levels of thermal maturity for kerogen being analyzed. T_{max} values below 430°C are considered low maturity. Values for T_{max} for most samples range from 403 to 446°C. In the shales immediately surrounding the

Arun Limestone, most values fall into the range of immature or barely mature.

7. Hydrogen index (HI) is defined as S_2/g TOC and is indicative of the hydrogen content of the organic matter in a rock.

Values less than 150 are considered poor source values (with some potential, however, for gas); 150–300 are considered gas/condensate prone; and greater than 300 are considered oil-prone source rocks. Since the apparent hydrocarbon potential was affected by migrated hydrocarbons, only the potentials of the extracted samples are meaningful. For extracted samples, the Bampo Shale from the A-13 has the best hydrogen index at 206 mg HC/g TOC. Source rocks with potentials in this range should generate a reasonable amount of condensate and gas. Keutapang and Baong Shale samples from this same well indicate a potential to generate fair quantities of gas and condensate. In contrast, the hydrocarbon potential of shale samples from wells penetrating the reef is too low to be of consequence.

8. Oxygen index—mg CO_2/g TOC

Table 3. Arun source rock data.

Before Extraction

Sample Number	Well Name	Sample Type	Formation	Depth (ft)	TOC (%)	S₁ (mg/g rock)	S₂ (mg/g rock)	Tmax (°C)	HI (mg HC/g TOC)	PI (S₁/S₁ + S₂)
1297-4-1	Arun A-6	Core	Arun LS	1076	0.58	0.26	0.39	403	67	0.40
1297-4-2	Arun A-7	Core	Arun LS	10,020–10,176	0.38	0.01	0.09	440	23	0.10
1297-4-3	Arun A-13	Cuttings	Keutapang Fm	7950–8190	1.35	0.74	0.95	422	70	0.44
1297-4-4	Arun A-13	Cuttings	Keutapang Fm	8250–8400	2.18	2.83	4.89	427	224	0.37
1297-4-5	Arun A-13	Cuttings	Baong Fm	8640–8700	2.97	11.33	6.09	435	205	0.65
1297-4-6	Arun A-13	Cuttings	Baong Fm	9840–9920	3.08	13.90	5.92	437	192	0.70
1297-4-7	Arun A-13	Core	Bampo Sh	10,558–10,559	0.68	0.41	0.20	441	29	0.67
1297-4-8	Arun A-13	Cuttings	Bampo Sh	10,610–10,700	2.04	5.38	4.18	430	204	0.56
1297-4-9	Arun A-13	Cuttings	Bampo Sh	11,040–11,070	2.54	2.47	2.63	436	103	0.48
1297-4-10	Arun A-54	Core	Bampo Sh	10,347.5	0.72	0.36	0.41	443	56	0.47
1297-3-1	Arun A-13	Cuttings	Baong Sh	9220–40 and 9340–60	2.14	8.01	7.20 (1.86)*	413	336	0.53
1297-3-2	Arun A-13	Cuttings	Baong Sh	10,142.5	0.35	0.06	0.06 (1.69)	389	17	0.50

After Extraction

Sample Number	Well Name	Sample Type	Formation	Depth (ft)	TOC (%)	S₁ (mg/g rock)	S₂ (mg/g rock)	Tmax (°C)	HI (mg HC/g TOC)	PI (S₁/S₁ + S₂)	Percent Change in TOC from Original
1297-4-1	Arun A-6	Core	Arun LS	1076	0.48	0.01	0.12	435	25	0.08	82.8
1297-4-2	Arun A-7	Core	Arun LS	10,020–10,176	0.37	0.00	0.05	442	13	0.00	97.4
1297-4-3	Arun A-13	Cuttings	Keutapang Fm	7950–8190	1.21	0.04	0.52	435	42	0.07	89.6
1297-4-4	Arun A-13	Cuttings	Keutapang Fm	8250–8400	1.66	0.14	2.78	429	167	0.05	76.1
1297-4-5	Arun A-13	Cuttings	Baong Fm	8640–8700	1.79	0.25	3.33	435	186	0.07	60.3
1297-4-6	Arun A-13	Cuttings	Baong Fm	9840–9920	1.72	0.25	3.21	437	186	0.07	55.8
1297-4-7	Arun A-13	Core	Bampo Sh	10,558–10,559	0.59	0.05	0.11	442	18	0.31	86.8
1297-4-8	Arun A-13	Cuttings	Bampo Sh	10,610–10,700	1.51	0.39	3.12	437	206	0.11	74.0
1297-4-9	Arun A-13	Cuttings	Bampo Sh	11,040–11,070	2.09	0.15	1.77	439	84	0.08	82.3
1297-4-10	Arun A-54	Core	Bampo Sh	10,347.5	0.61	0.07	0.24	447	39	0.23	84.7
1297-3-1	Arun A-13	Cuttings	Baong Sh	9220–40 and 9340–60	1.31	0.06	2.12 (1.89)	435	162	0.03	61.2
1297-3-2	Arun A-13	Cuttings	Baong Sh	10,142.5	0.34	0.05	0.05 (1.51)	349	15	0.33	97.1
										Avg.	79.0
										Std. Dev.	13.3

*Parentheses indicate replicate analyses.

32

Table 4. Rock-Eval and TOC analyses for selected samples from the Arun A-1, A-7, and A-13 wells.

Sample Identification		Data (S_1, S_2, S_3, mg/g of rock—T_{max}, °C)						Hydrogen Index (mg HC/g TOC)	Oxygen Index (mg CO$_2$/g TOC)	TOC (%)
RRUS	Depth (ft)	S_1	S_2	S_3	S_2/S_3	$S_1/(S_1+S_2)$	T_{max}			
				Rock-Eval Pyrolysis Raw Data						
				Arun A-1						
4	10,602.5	0.105	0.148	0.708	0.209	0.413	428	35	169	0.42
4	10,720.0	0.181	0.564	0.647	0.872	0.243	480	26	30	2.16
8	10,780.0	0.062	0.108	0.295	0.366	0.365	437	28	76	0.39
11	10,863.0	0.065	0.076	0.314	0.242	0.461	446	25	101	0.31
				Rock-Eval Pyrolysis Raw Data						
				Arun A-7						
504	8355	0.012	0.117	0.267	0.438	0.093	431	98	222	0.12
507	8445	0.027	0.185	0.657	0.282	0.127	426	49	173	0.38
512	8595	0.074	0.132	0.315	0.419	0.359	440	63	150	0.21
520	8835	0.023	0.052	0.292	0.178	0.307	425	33	182	0.16
531	9165	0.038	0.104	0.392	0.265	0.268	423	32	119	0.33
537	9345	0.039	0.156	0.376	0.415	0.200	433	34	82	0.46
554	10,085	0.033	0.134	0.335	0.400	0.198	440	37	93	0.36
				Rock-Eval Pyrolysis Raw Data						
				Arun A-13						
105	8070.0	0.728	0.615	0.841	0.731	0.542	433	46	63	1.33
109	8190.0	2.962	2.544	0.836	3.043	0.538	426	179	59	1.42
115	8390.0	7.855	5.869	0.595	9.864	0.572	427	322	33	1.82
123	8670.0	18.079	6.340	0.708	8.955	0.740	408	288	32	2.20
133	8870.0	18.657	8.039	0.858	9.369	0.699	416	430	46	1.87
142	9050.0	7.708	6.370	1.022	6.233	0.548	434	352	56	1.81
151	9230.0	7.296	6.784	0.837	8.105	0.518	429	421	52	1.61
163	9470.0	12.183	6.387	1.048	4.094	0.729	437	307	50	2.08
173	9650.0	14.0	5.59	0.79	7.076	0.715	407	259	—	2.22
185	9890.0	30.6	6.28	0.86	7.302	0.830	432	2	31	2.54
191	10,010.0	5.928	5.882	0.990	5.941	0.502	425	269	45	2.19
202	10,270.0	3.572	4.671	0.648	7.208	0.433	424	403	56	1.16
213	10,655.0	11.870	6.656	1.086	6.129	0.641	437	263	43	2.53
220	10,795.0	18.783	9.245	1.455	6.354	0.670	434	426	67	2.17
230	10,995.0	2.251	1.060	1.341	0.790	0.680	419	73	92	1.45

Oxygen index values for reef wells are variable and range from 30 to 222, averaging 127. On the other hand, values for off-reef wells range from 29 to 92, averaging 50.

A plot of the hydrogen index versus the oxygen index on a van Krevelen-type diagram (Figure 29B) shows that the samples from the A-13 well have a better hydrocarbon potential than those from the A-1 and A-7. The values plotted, however, are for unextracted samples and represent relative differences only. Nonetheless, source rocks from the vicinity of the A-13 well are thought to have the potential to generate gas and condensate.

9. Visual examination

Organic material in polished vitrinite blocks was examined visually, although the material consisted of very fine particles and was difficult to identify. It was interpreted as a mixture of type II (algal) and type III (woody, herbaceous) kerogen. Kingston (1978) recognized a predominance of amorphous oil-prone kerogen in the Bampo Shale and a predominance of structured, woody-herbaceous gas-prone kerogen in the Baong Shale.

Maturity

Determinations of maturity by vitrinite reflectance (R_0) techniques have been few in this study area. R_0 values are barely mature to mature for shales encasing the Arun reservoir (Table 5 and Figure 29). In the A-7 well, R_0 values range from 0.17 to 0.52, but do not increase downward in a linear fashion; minor reversals in the trend occur downhole and are due to the combined problems of caved sample materials and of reworked organic material. The source of Arun hydrocarbons is interpreted to be laterally equivalent organic-rich shales of the Bampo, Baong, or lower Keutapang that are more mature, meaning somewhat further away from the Arun reef and deeper in the section. This interpretation is supported by the data of Kingston (1978), who analyzed samples across the entire basin.

Maturation curves for the Baong and Bampo shales (Figure 30) are updated with regard to new paleontological determinations and show four unconformities in the Tertiary section, periods of sea level stillstand, most likely accompanied by minor amounts of erosion. Extremely rapid subsidence that began 7 m.y. ago placed Bampo and Baong sections occurring on the flanks of the Arun reef (i.e., at A-13) at the proper depth for generating hydrocarbons only 2.5 m.y.a. A depth-burial curve for the deep shelf areas a few tens of kilometers offshore away from the reef was constructed (Figure 30) using a theoretical approach to thermally model the Lho Sukon deep to the east of the Arun field; at a depth of 9800 ft (3100 m) in the deeper parts of the shelf, significant hydrocarbon generation occurred no earlier than 3.0 m.y.a.

To make this prediction, a two-dimensional, non-steady state heat conduction simulator, called GOLIATH, was run on a generalized cross-section of the Arun field to establish a lower limit on the average geothermal gradient away from the reef.

Potential heat refraction owing to thermal conductivity contrast and thermal blanketing effects were considered in the model. The advective fluid movement that can play a major role in the redistribution of heat within a basin was neglected because requisite data were unavailable. Thermal conductivities were assigned based on average values for the given lithologies consistent with Thamrin (1985). The results indicate that the onset of hydrocarbon generation in the deepest parts of the North Sumatra basin occurred 3.0 m.y.a. and that

Table 5. Vitrinite reflectance (R_0) values for the Arun A-7 and A-13 wells.

Arun A-7 well			Arun A-13 well		
Depth in Feet	R_0	Formation	Depth in Feet	R_0	Formation
1000–1030	0.17	Julu Rayeu	7950–8190	0.41	Keutapang
2020–2080	0.18	Julu Rayeu	8250–8400	0.44	Keutapang
3010–3070	0.18	Julu Rayeu	10,400–10,500	0.34	Baong/Arun
4000–4030	0.18	Upper Seurula	10,610–10,700	0.42	Bampo Shale
5140–5160	0.33	Upper Seurula	11,040–11,083	0.42	Bampo Shale
5750–5760	0.36	Lower Seurula			
6050–6060	0.35	Lower Seurula			
6450–6460	0.37	Lower Seurula			
6640–6660	0.44	Keutapang			
7250–7260	0.39	Keutapang			
8260–8300	0.43	Keutapang			
8620–8690	0.47	Keutapang			
8740–8810	0.36	Baong Shale			
9070–9140	0.46	Baong Shale			
9310–9380	0.52	Baong Shale			
9720–9790	0.35	Baong Shale			
10,050–10,120	0.39	Baong Shale			

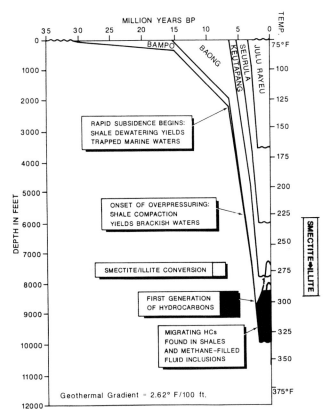

Figure 30. Shale and organic diagenesis curves for the Bampo and Baong source rocks.

reasonable levels (i.e., I, Mobil's maturation index, is 128) of maturity have been reached. The net effect of conductive heat refraction and thermal blanketing proved to be minimal compared to the rapid rate of subsidence.

Migration

Although much of the evidence is indirect, the migration setting of the Arun reservoir is ideal in that it is completely encased by shales that provide the source and seal for this stratigraphic trap and in that it is located atop a basement ridge with updip routes of migration into the reef from adjacent anoxic subbasins. In addition, the Arun high is fault-bounded on its east and west sides, thereby allowing deep-seated gas to migrate up into the reservoir along fault planes and fracture systems that were apparently active during deposition.

There are two lines of direct evidence that migration has been "caught in the act": (1) TOCs are lower in samples that have had their hydrocarbons extracted than those that have not, and (2) aqueous fluid inclusions contain about 2% dissolved gas. Analysis of this gas indicates strong similarity with gas in the Arun reservoir. Both are primarily methane with a moderate amount of CO_2.

Kingston (1978) theorized that, since the deep-seated Baong and Bampo shales had undergone dewatering via the smectite/illite clay transformation prior to maturation, the lack of water in the sediments would inhibit the generation and maturation of large oil molecules.

Considering the isolation of the Arun reservoir in a thick shale sequence, migration of gas into the reservoir must have been accompanied by a flow of water out of the limestone. Otherwise, incoming gas would not have been able to fill the reservoir. Presumably, the "drain" for exiting waters is along thrust faults in the structurally complex southern part of the field where the Barisan Mountains are uplifted.

Another effect of migration is to displace pore fluids and thereby remove the fluid medium in which late-stage pore-plugging calcite cements are precipitated. Trapped hydrocarbons in fluid inclusions in calcite cements indicate that there was a transition period in which both cement-precipitating fluids and hydrocarbons filled pores. However, significant cementation was arrested by the migration of gas into the Arun reservoir.

EXPLORATION CONCEPTS

Several lessons can be learned from the database provided by development drilling of the Arun field. The long-standing concept of drilling paleohighs is substantiated, especially those with the possibility of reef growth. A rapid rise in sea level during the Miocene accentuated reef growth and allowed thick sequences to accumulate. Diagenetic alteration during subaerial exposure added dissolution porosity to already porous lime mud in the reef. Since dissolution porosity accounts for only one-fourth of the reef's total, it is important to realize that the bulk of the porosity results from incomplete diagenesis of lime mud that was buried in a rapidly subsiding backarc basin. Thus, Arun is not a simple case of subaerial exposure of reef-related lithofacies.

ACKNOWLEDGMENTS

This study benefited from the input of several workers who provided a multidisciplined team effort to understanding the many facets of the Arun reservoir. These include the following staff of Mobil Oil Corporation: R. C. Belcher (ISM mapping), R. L. Borger (radar imagery and computer mapping), R. T. Clarke (vitrinite reflectance), W. C. Gardner (field development), J. R. Gormly (organic geochemistry), R. B. Koepnick (strontium isotopes), S. F. Percival (nannofossil zonations), M. B. Ray (thermal modeling), B. K. Rodgers (foraminiferal zonations), J. K. Sales (structural geology), J. Wallace (log analysis), and W. G. Zempolich (isotope geochemist).

35

REFERENCES CITED

Aadland, A. J., and R. S. K. Phoa, 1981, Geothermal gradient map of Indonesia, Indonesian Petroleum Association, 43 p. plus two maps.

Alford, M. E., L. L. Cargile, and M. B. Siagian, 1975, Development of the Arun gas field: Proceedings of the 4th Indonesian Petroleum Convention, v. II, p. 173-187.

Berggren, W. A., D. V. Kent, and J. A. van Couvering, 1985, The Neogene: Part 2, Neogene geochronology and chronostratigraphy, in N. J. Snelling, ed., GSA Memoir 10, p. 199-210.

Blow, W. H., 1969, Late Middle Eocene to Recent planktonic foraminiferal biostratigraphy, in R. Bronnimann and H. Renz, eds., Proceedings of the First International Conference on Planktonic Microfossils, Geneva, 1967, v. 1: Leiden, Brill Pub. Co., p. 199-421.

Burke, W. H., R. E. Denison, E. A. Hetherington, R. B. Koepnick, H. F. Nelson, and J. B. Otto, 1982, Variation of seawater Sr^{87}/Sr^{86} throughout Phanerozoic time: Geology, v. 10, p. 516-519.

Carmalt, S. W., and B. St. John, 1984, Giant oil and gas fields, in M. T. Halbouty, ed., Future petroleum provinces of the world: AAPG Memoir 40, p. 11-53.

Choquette, P. W., and L. C. Pray, 1970, Geologic nomenclature and classification of porosity in sedimentary carbonates: AAPG Bulletin, v. 54, p. 207-250.

Dunham, R. J., 1962, Classification of carbonate rocks according to depositional texture, in W. E. Ham, ed., Classification of carbonate rocks, AAPG Memoir 1, p. 108-121.

Embry, A. F., and J. E. Klovan, 1971, A Late Devonian reef tract on Northwestern Banks, Northwest Territories: Canadian Petroleum Geology Bulletin, v. 19, p. 730-781.

Friedman, G. M., 1975, The making and unmaking of limestones or the downs and ups of porosity: Journal of Sedimentary Petrology, v. 45, p. 379-398.

Frost, S. H., 1988, Miocene reef corals: a review (abs.): AAPG Bulletin, v. 72, p. 187.

Glenn, E. C., 1988, Review of Miocene larger foraminifera (abs.): AAPG Bulletin, v. 72, p. 189.

Graves, R. R., and A. A. Weegar, 1973, Geology of the Arun gas field (North Sumatra): Proceedings of the 2nd Indonesian Petroleum Convention, p. 23-51.

Graves, R. R., and A. A. Weegar, 1974, Geology of the Arun gas field: Fourth Exploration Seminar at the Egyptian General Petroleum Corporation.

Hallock, P., and E. C. Glenn, 1986, Larger foraminifera: a tool for paleoenvironmental analysis of Cenozoic depositional facies: Palios, v. 1, p. 55-64.

Haq, B. U., J. Hardenbol, and P. R. Vail, 1987; Chronology of fluctuating sea levels since the Triassic: Science, v. 235, p. 1156-1167.

Haxby, W. F., 1987, Gravity field of the world's ocean, 1:40,000,000: World Data Center A for Marine Geology and Geophysics Report MGG-3, published for the Office of Naval Research, available from Natl. Geophys. Data Center, E/GC3, 325 Broadway, Boulder, CO 80303.

Houpt, J. R., and C. C. Kersting, 1976, Arun reef, Bee Block, North Sumatra: Proceedings of the IPA Carbonate Seminar, Indonesian Petroleum Association, Special Volume, p. 42-60.

Humphreys, N. V., 1986, A synergistic approach to reservoir management: Proceedings of the Indonesian Petroleum Association, Fifteenth Annual Convention, p. 143-160.

James, S. J., 1982, Micritization and the disappearing coral reef: Joint ASCOPE/CCOP Workshop on Hydrocarbon Occurrence in Carbonate Formations, August 2-7, 1982, Surabaya, Indonesia.

Jordan, C. F., Jr., 1978, Tropical lagoonal sedimentation, in R. W. Fairbridge and J. Bourgeois, eds., The encyclopedia of sedimentology: Stroudsburg, Dowden, Hutchinson, and Ross, p. 821-828.

Jordan, C. F., Jr., 1985, A shorthand notation for carbonate facies—Dunham revisited (abs.): AAPG Bulletin, v. 69, p. 88.

Jordan, C. F., Jr., R. J. Wharton, and R. E. Cook, 1985; Holocene carbonate facies of Pulau Seribu Patch Reef Complex, West Java Sea (abs.): AAPG Bulletin, v. 69, p. 270-271.

Jordan, C. F., Jr., M. W. Colgan, S. H. Frost, E. C. Glenn, D. Bosence, and M. Esteban, 1990, An overview of Miocene reefs (abs.): AAPG Bulletin, v. 74, p. 688-689.

Kamili, Z. A., J. Kingston, Z. Achmad, A. Wahab, S. Sosromihargjo, and C. U. Crausaz, 1976, Contribution to the pre-Baong stratigraphy of North Sumatra: Proceedings of the Indonesian Petroleum Association Fifth Annual Convention, p. 91-108.

Kendall, G. C., and W. Schlager, 1981, Carbonates and relative changes in sea level: Marine Geology, v. 44, p. 181-212.

Kersting, C. C., and J. R. Houpt, 1976, Arun reef, Bee Block, North Sumatra: Indonesian Petroleum Association Carbonate Seminar, September, 1976, 26 p.

Kingston, J., 1978, Oil and gas generation, migration and accumulation in the North Sumatra Basin: Proceedings of the Indonesian Petroleum Association, Seventh Annual Convention, p. 75-104.

Martini, E., 1971, Standard Tertiary and Quaternary calcareous nannoplankton zonation: Proceedings II, Planktonic Conference, Roma, 1970, v. 2, p. 739-785.

Moore, R. C., ed., 1956, The treatise on invertebrate paleontology, Part F, Coelenterata: University of Kansas Press, p. F248 and F353.

Mundt, P. A., 1982, Miocene reefs, offshore North Sumatra: Offshore South East Asia 82 Conference, Singapore, p. 1-11.

Nelson, H. F., M. Abdullah, C. F. Jordan, A. J. Jenik, 1982, Petrography of the Arun gas field, Aceh Province, Indonesia: Joint ASCOPE/CCOP Workshop on Hydrocarbon Occurrence in Carbonates, August 2-7, 1982, Surabaya, Indonesia, 38 p.

Savin, S. M., 1977, The history of the earth's surface temperature during the past 100 million years: Annual Review of Earth and Planetary Science, v. 5, p. 319-355.

Schlager, W., 1981, The paradox of drowned reefs and carbonate platforms: GSA Bulletin, v. 92, p. 197-211.

Soeparjadi, R. A., 1982, Geology of the Arun gas field: Journal of Petroleum Technology, p. 1163-1172.

Stockman, K. W., R. N. Ginsburg, and E. A. Shinn, 1967, The production of lime mud by algae in south Florida: Journal of Sedimentary Petrology, v. 37, p. 633-648.

Thamrin, M., 1985, An investigation of the relationships between the geology of Indonesian sedimentary basins and heat flow density: Tectonophysics, v. 121, p. 45-62.

Visser, W. A., and J. J. Hermes, 1962, Geological results of the exploration for oil in Netherlands New Guinea: Koninkl Nederlands Geol. Mijnbouwkundig Genoot, Geol. Ser. v. 20, 265 p.

Walker, P., M. Maas, and M. D. Burnaman, 1986, Structure interpretation problems of a Lower Miocene reef associated with a shallow low velocity anomaly, North Sumatra: Proceedings of the Indonesian Petroleum Association, Fifteenth Annual Convention, p. 279-288.

Wilson, J. L., 1975, Carbonate facies in geologic history: New York, Springer-Verlag, 471 p.

Wilson, J. L., and C. F. Jordan, 1983, Middle shelf environments, in P. A. Scholle, D. G. Bebout, and C. H. Moore, eds., Carbonate depositional environments: AAPG Memoir 33, p. 298-343.

Appendix 1. Field Description

Field name .... *Arun field*

Ultimate recoverable reserves .... *NA**
*The only estimate available is 16.1 tscf of dry gas initially in place (Alford et al., 1975).

Field location:

    Country .... *Indonesia*

    State .... *Aceh Province*

    Basin/Province .... *North Sumatra basin*

Field discovery:

    Year first pay discovered .... *Miocene Arun Limestone (reef)   1971*

Discovery well name and general location:

    First pay .... *Arun A-1, east central part of Arun field, north tip of Sumatra,*
    140 mi (225 km) northwest of Medan, capital of Aceh Province

Discovery well operator .... *Pertamina–Mobil*

IP .... *P.T. #1 perforations (10,410–10,415 ft MD or 3173–3174.5 m MD) 8 mmcfg/d and 290 BCPD;*
P.T. #2 perforations (9953–9958 ft MD or 3033.6–3035.2 m MD) 14 mmcfg/d and 472 BCPD

All other zones with shows of oil and gas in the field:

Age	Formation	Type of Show
Lower Pliocene	*lower Seurula Formation*	*Oil*
Upper Miocene	*Keutapang Formation*	*Oil*

Geologic concept leading to discovery and method or methods used to delineate prospect
Seismic survey focused by earlier surface geology and side-looking airborne radar. Seismic data indicated a "build-up" on a basement ridge, which was later drilled and found to be a patch reef complex.

Structure:

    Province/basin type .... *Backarc basin*

    Tectonic history
    A subsiding backarc basin went through a Tertiary filling sequence dominated by coarsening-upward clastics except for a period of Miocene reef growth that occurred on paleohighs. Depth-burial curves indicate subsidence of the Arun Limestone to 3000 ft (900 m) by the end of the Miocene (5.3 m.y.a.) and rapid subsidence to 10,000 ft (3050 m) by the end of the Pliocene (1.5 m.y.a.).

    Regional structure
    A north-south basement ridge provided a paleohigh for the site of Miocene reef growth; syndepositional faulting occurred along both sides of the ridge.

    Local structure
    1100 ft (335 m) of Miocene reef growth took place along the crest of the underlying basement ridge.

Trap:

    Trap type(s) .... *Stratigraphic trap (a shale-encased reef)*

Basin stratigraphy (major stratigraphic intervals from surface to deepest penetration in field):

Chronostratigraphy	Formation	Depth to Top in ft (m)
Upper Pliocene	*Julu Rayeu*	*0–500 (150)*
Lower Pliocene	*Seurula Formation*	*4200 (1280)*
Upper Miocene	*Keutapang Formation*	*6500 (1980)*
Middle-upper Miocene	*Baong Shale*	*8700 (2650)*
Lower-middle Miocene	*Arun Limestone*	*10,050 (3060)*
Upper Oligocene	*Bampo Shale*	*11,150 (3400)*
	Parapat Sandstone	*12,150 (3700)*
Probable Triassic	*phyllite basement*	*12,750 (3890)*

Reservoir characteristics:

Number of reservoirs *1*

Formations .... *Arun Limestone*

Ages .... *Lower and middle Miocene*

Depths to tops of reservoirs .... *10,000 ft (3050 m) avg.*

Gross thickness (top to bottom of producing interval) .... *500 ft (150 m) (1100 ft; 335 m max)*

Net thickness—total thickness of producing zones

    Average .... *500 ft (150 m)*

    Maximum .... *1000 ft (305 m)*

Lithology

Coral encrusting–red-algal boundstones and foraminiferal mixed-skeletal packstones

Porosity type .... *Pervasive microporosity with moldic, vuggy, and fracture macroporosity*

Average porosity *16.0%*

Average permeability .... *13.5 md*

Seals:

Upper

    Formation, fault, or other feature .... *Baong Shale*

    Lithology .... *Shale*

Lateral

    Formation, fault, or other feature .... *Baong and Bampo shales*

    Lithology .... *Shales*

Source:

Formation and age .... *Middle and upper Miocene Baong Shale and Upper Oligocene Bampo Shale*

Lithology .... *Shale*

Average total organic carbon (TOC) *1.9%*

Maximum TOC *3.8%*

Kerogen type (I, II, or III) .... *I/II*

Vitrinite reflectance (maturation) .... $R_o = 0.45\%$

Time of hydrocarbon expulsion .... *Pliocene*

Present depth to top of source .... *8300 ft (2530 m)*

Thickness .... *1600 ft (790 m)*

Potential yield .... *NA*

Appendix 2. Production Data

Field name .... *Arun field*

Field size:

    Proved acres .... *23,240 ac (9412 ha)*

    Number of wells all years *74*

    Current number of wells .... *74 as of 11/1987*

    Well spacing .... *1000 ft (305 m)*

    Ultimate recoverable .... *NA*

    Cumulative production .... *About 5.2 tscf of gas (1/1/89); condensate NA*

    Annual production .... *NA*

    Present decline rate .... *NA*

        Initial decline rate .... *NA*

        Overall decline rate .... *NA*

    Annual water production .... *NA*

In place, total reserves .... *16.1 tcf (dry gas)*
In place, per acre foot .... *NA*
Primary recovery .... *NA*
Secondary recovery .... *NA*
Enhanced recovery .... *NA*
Cumulative water production .... *NA*

Drilling and casing practices:

Amount of surface casing set .... *2000 ft (610 m) (20-in. casing)*
Casing program .... *30-in., 20-in., 13⅜-in., 9⅝-in., 7-in. prod. tbg., 5½-in. liner*
Drilling mud .... *Water and oil-based muds*
Bit program .... *26-in., 17½-in., 12¼-in., 8½-in.*
High pressure zones .... *Baong Formation*

Completion practices:

Interval(s) perforated .... *Top 300 ft (90 m) of producing zone*
Well treatment .... *Acidizing*

Formation evaluation:

Logging suites .... *DIS-LSS-GR, DLL-BHC Sonic-GR, and LDL-CNL-GR*
Testing practices .... *DST, HRCU, PLT*
Mud logging techniques .... *Rate of penetration (ROP), gas chromatography*

Oil characteristics:

API gravity .... *56° (condensate)*
Base .... *NA*
Initial GOR .... *NA*
Sulfur, wt% .... *NA*
Viscosity, SUS .... *NA*
Pour point .... *NA*
Gas-oil distillate .... *NA*

Field characteristics:

Average elevation .... *40 ft (12 m)*
Initial pressure .... *7100 psi (48.95 MPa)*
Present pressure .... *4800 psi (33.09 MPa)*
Pressure gradient .... *0.1 psi/ft (0.69 kPa)*
Temperature .... *352°F (179°C)*
Geothermal gradient .... *0.0262°F/ft (0.0478°C/m)*
Drive .... *Gas expansion*
Oil column thickness .... *NA*
Oil-water contact .... *NA*
Connate water *10.7%*
Water salinity, TDS .... *14,000 ppm*
Resistivity of water .... *0.13 ohm-m*
Bulk volume water (%) *4.3%*

Transportation method and market for oil and gas:
Arun gas is shipped as LNG by tanker to Japan, supplying nearly one-half that country's annual gas consumption

Aneth Field—U.S.A.
Paradox Basin, Utah

JAMES A. PETERSON
U. S. Geological Survey
University of Montana
Missoula, Montana

FIELD CLASSIFICATION

BASIN: Paradox
BASIN TYPE: Foredeep
RESERVOIR ROCK TYPE: Dolomite and
   Limestone
RESERVOIR ENVIRONMENT OF DEPOSITION: Marine Shelf
TRAP DESCRIPTION: Partly dolomitized algal carbonate mound on a weak structural nose

RESERVOIR AGE: Pennsylvanian
PETROLEUM TYPE: Oil
TRAP TYPE: Carbonate Mound

INTRODUCTION

The Aneth oil field is located in southeastern Utah in the southern part of the Paradox basin, on the southwestern border of the Blanding subbasin (Figures 1-3). Most of the petroleum reserves of the basin are in carbonate reservoirs of Pennsylvanian age positioned within the shelf carbonate facies along the southwestern border of the Paradox basin. The total areal extent of the Aneth field is approximately 48,000 ac (75 mi^2; 195 km^2). Aneth is by far the largest of approximately 125 oil and gas fields in the basin. Estimated ultimate primary and secondary recovery from the field is approximately 400 MMBO (million barrels of oil), more than two-thirds of the total oil reserves of the basin.

HISTORY

The Four Corners area (Utah, Colorado, Arizona, and New Mexico) of the southwestern United States has undergone sporadic exploration activity since the early 1900s. The initial play was in the Paradox basin where the first oil (1908) was found at shallow depths in fractured clastic rocks at the Mexican Hat field near the San Juan River on the Monument uplift (Figure 3). In the early 1900s, gas was discovered in Cretaceous sandstone reservoirs in the San Juan basin of northwestern New Mexico, which later developed into the basinwide Ignacio-Blanco gas field. Between 1920 and 1940, sporadic drilling occurred in the adjoining Paradox basin, but except for some oil and gas production (1929) from Pennsylvanian reservoirs in northwestern New Mexico, little success resulted. Interest in the potential of Pennsylvanian

rocks was stimulated by the 1945 discovery of large volumes of gas in carbonate reservoirs of the Paradox Formation at Barker Creek dome in northwestern New Mexico near the Colorado border. With subsequent oil and gas discoveries at Boundary Butte in Utah (1948), the search for Pennsylvanian petroleum traps took on broader proportions. Most of the earlier discoveries had been based on exploration of surface structures, but in the early 1950s the search moved farther out into the Paradox basin where refined geophysical work was required. Most of this activity was on Navajo Indian tribal lands. Shell Oil Company et al. initiated an extensive seismic program that delineated several subsurface structural closures in southeastern Utah. Two of the better structures, Bluff and Desert Creek, were drilled by Shell in 1953 (Figure 4). Although economic failures, both of these initial wells encountered encouraging oil shows and porosity in carbonate rocks above the salt section in what later came to be known as the Desert Creek and Ismay (Bluff) zones (Figure 5). A second well was drilled downflank on the Bluff and Desert Creek structures in 1954. Each encountered improved reservoir rocks, resulting in a discovery at Desert Creek, the first in the Aneth area, and a marginal discovery at Bluff. These successes, although small, motivated a large sealed-bid sale of Navajo Indian lands. Participating in the sale were several major companies, including Shell, Texaco, Superior, Carter, Phillips, and others. The Texaco C-1 Navajo Aneth discovery was completed in the Pennsylvanian Hermosa Formation (Figure 5) at 5828 to 5879 ft (1778–1793 m) in February 1956, flowing 1700 BOPD (barrels of oil per day). Three subsequent discoveries, the Shell No. 1 North Desert Creek (September 1956, Ratherford Unit), Texaco No. 1 Navajo C (January 1957, McElmo Creek Unit), and

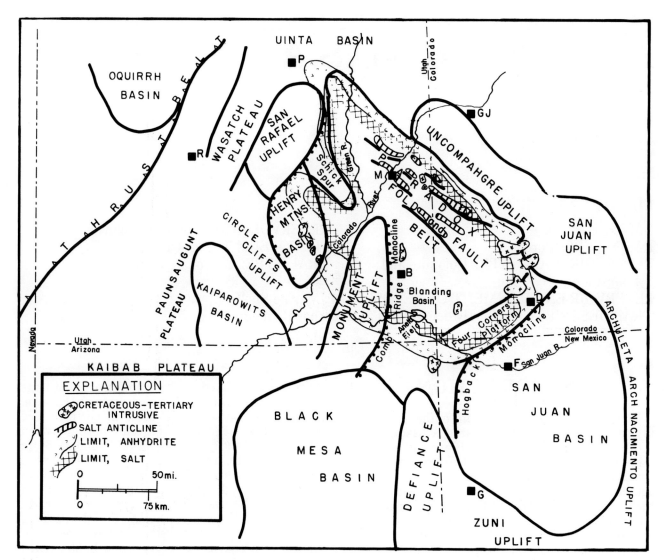

Figure 1. Major structural features, Paradox basin and adjacent region.

Davis Oil No. 1 Navajo A (February 1957, White Mesa Unit) all proved to be in the massive carbonate buildup that makes up the Greater Aneth field. The Davis discovery was drilled on a farmout from Carter Oil Co., which had drilled the White Mesa No. 1 well in 1955 on a structural closure just a short distance southeast of the edge of the main Aneth buildup.

DISCOVERY METHOD

Early exploratory drilling in the southwestern Paradox basin was based on identification of seismic structures on mappable horizons near the top of the Paradox Formation. Stratigraphic isolation of the Aneth mound complex was a major factor in the disappointing early exploration efforts in the basin. Prior to the Aneth discovery, nine abandoned

exploratory wells, in addition to the discovery wells of four nearby marginally commercial fields, had been drilled on seismic highs (Figure 4). The giant field was literally surrounded by these exploratory failures before the discovery well was drilled in a relatively low structural position on the axis of the Bluff-Aneth subsurface structural nose. The discovery was made only after most of the more significant structural closures of the area had been drilled with relatively insignificant success.

STRUCTURE AND PALEOSTRUCTURE

The Paradox basin is within the central part of the Colorado Plateau physiographic province. Regionally, the basin is bounded on the south by the

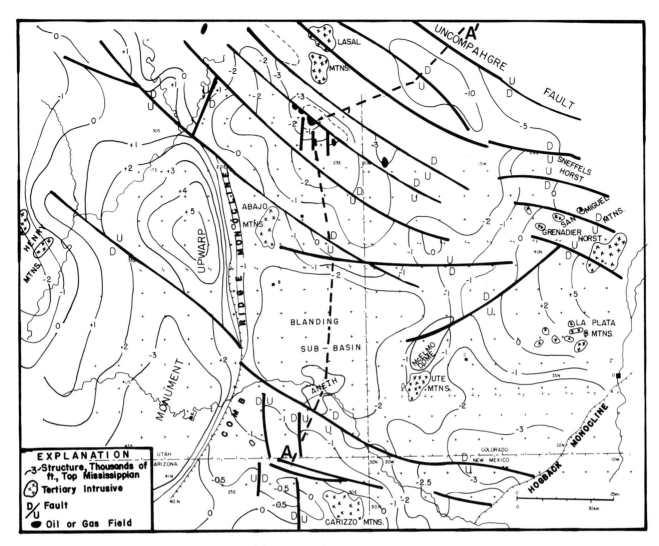

Figure 2. Structure map, in thousands of feet, top of Mississippian Leadville Limestone. Line of cross section A-A', Figure 8, is shown.

Four Corners platform and the Defiance uplift, on the west by the Monument upwarp and San Rafael swell, on the north by the confluence of the San Rafael and the northwest extension of the Uncompahgre uplift, and on the east by the Uncompahgre and San Juan uplifts (Figure 1). All these major features underwent ancestral stages of tectonic growth as early as Pennsylvanian time, with probable earlier minor growth of some of the features.

The Pennsylvanian Paradox evaporite basin was the northwestern part of an elongate northwest-trending structural-sedimentary trough, which developed as part of the crustal disturbance that created the Ancestral Rocky Mountains. Rapid subsidence of the northwestern part of the regional trough in Early Pennsylvanian time initiated semi-isolation and restriction of marine circulation between the distal northwest part of the trough and the open marine accessway to the southeast.

Continuation of this process resulted in the deposition of thick evaporites in the Paradox basin during Desmoinesian time (Figures 6-8). The complementary uplifts on the east side of the basin (Uncompahgre and San Luis) (Figures 1 and 7) rose rapidly at this time and shed large volumes of clastic debris along their borders, but the central basin areas were essentially starved of clastic material during evaporite deposition.

By early Mesozoic time, subsidence of the Paradox basin and accompanying rise of the Uncompahgre-San Luis highland (Figure 6) diminished greatly when the region became part of the Mesozoic Rocky Mountain geosyncline. In the early to middle Mesozoic, the area was covered by several thousand feet of marine and continental clastic deposits. Late Mesozoic deposition was dominated by continental and marine clastics of Late Cretaceous age, most of which have been removed by Cenozoic erosion.

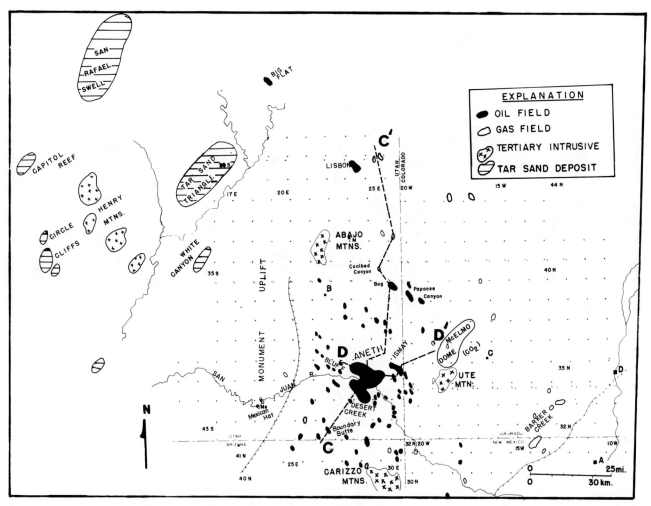

Figure 3. Pennsylvanian oil and gas fields, Paradox basin. Lines of cross sections C–C′ and D–D′ of Figures 14 and 15 and location of major tar deposits in Permian sandstone reservoirs are shown. Towns shown: Utah— B, Blanding; M, Mexican Hat; Colorado—C, Cortez; D, Durango.

During the latest Cretaceous and early to middle Tertiary, folding and faulting occurred, much of which tended to follow Paleozoic structural trends. Several igneous stocks or laccolith intrusions were emplaced at this time (Figure 1).

Kelley (1955) described three main tectonic elements of the present basin area (Figure 1). (1) The first is the Paradox fold and fault belt, adjacent to the northwest-trending Uncompahgre uplift, which is dominated by northwest-trending folds and faults, many of which are associated with prominent piercement salt anticlines in the northeastern part of the belt. The southwestern part of the belt is more mildly deformed, but folds and faults generally maintain the northwesterly trend, some associated with salt swells. (2) The second is the Monument uplift, a north-south elongated uplift bounded on the east by the steeply dipping Comb Ridge monocline. (3) The third is the Blanding subbasin, which occupies the southern part of the Paradox basin east of the Monument upwarp. Gentle folds within the Blanding subbasin trend generally west to northwest.

Several broad, open folds occupy the southern boundary of the basin.

The Four Corners platform on the southeastern margin of the Paradox basin is occupied by several gentle folds, generally northeast-trending, and is bounded on the southeast by the steeply dipping Hogback monocline.

Kelley (1955) interpreted the Paradox basin as a strong post-Mississippian sag, part of a broad belt of northwest-southeast tangential compression related to formation of the Ancestral Rockies.

Szabo and Wengerd (1975) explain the Paradox basin as the result of a regional sag between the Zuni and Front Range uplifts caused by withdrawal and lateral transfer of subcrustal material in a broad area of eastern Utah and western Colorado. In the Early Pennsylvanian, accelerated subsidence resulted in flexing and faulting in the fold and fault belt and in mid-basin arching along the Uncompahgre arch. The resulting Uncompahgre–San Luis uplift separated the initial broad basin into two half-basins, the Paradox and Eagle (Figure 7). Continued

44

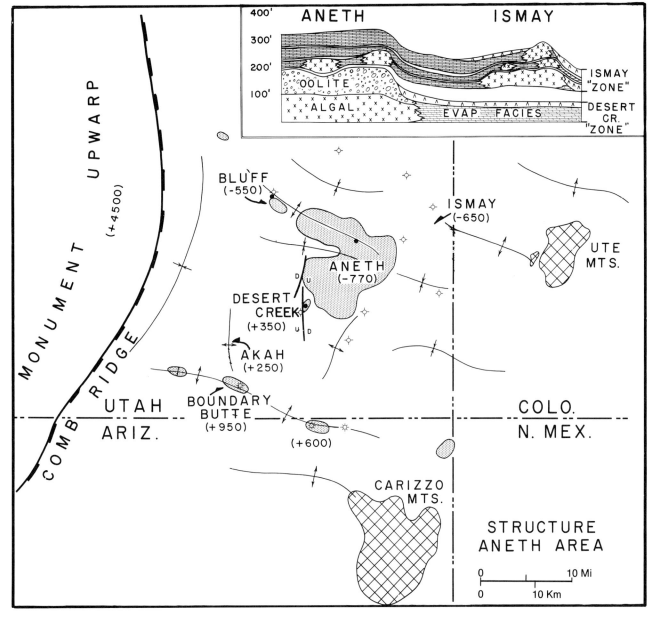

Figure 4. Generalized structure on top of Desert Creek zone, Aneth area. Exploratory failures and marginal field discoveries (solid circles) drilled prior to Aneth discovery (solid circle) are shown. Positive and negative values in parentheses are approximate elevations in feet relative to sea level. (Modified after Peterson, 1966.)

subsidence, basin expansion, rejuvenated flexing and faulting in a series of steps, along with radial folding, lasted through middle Desmoinesian time, when emergence and faulting of the Uncompahgre occurred. This activity shaped the final form of the Paradox basin.

Stevenson and Baars (1986) interpreted the Paradox basin as a complex "pull-apart" basin related to the intersection of conjugate lineaments of continental dimensions. Extensional tectonics related to growth of the Ancestral Rocky Mountains in Pennsylvanian time caused rapid subsidence of the basin along rejuvenated basement structures, some of which may be as old as the Proterozoic.

Kluth (1986) presented a plate tectonic model to explain the development of the Ancestral Rocky Mountains and associated basins. In Pennsylvanian time, during the assembly of the supercontinent, Pangea, the faults and foreland block uplifts characteristic of the Ancestral Rocky Mountains resulted from transcurrent faulting along the craton margin, with wrenching and translation, during the collision of North America and South America–Africa (Figure 9). The large fault block mountains formed when the southwestern peninsular projection of the craton (Transcontinental arch and its extension) was pushed northward by the collision. In the Early Pennsylvanian, the collision began in the Ouachita

45

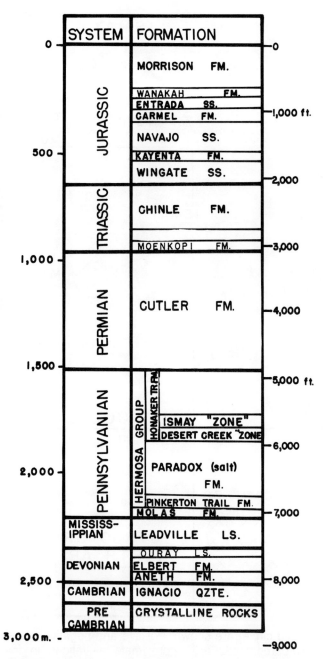

Figure 5. Stratigraphic column and average depths, Aneth oil field.

basin, according to the Klemme basin classification (Klemme, 1980; Klemme, personal communication, 1989; Halbouty et al., 1970). The concept of the "pull-apart" basin was applied by Burchfiel and Stewart (1966) to the Death Valley graben. Klemme (1980), however, applied the "pull-apart" term to large, linear basins (Klemme type V) occupying the intermediate crustal zone between thick continental crust and thin oceanic crust along the major oceanic boundaries of spreading plates (divergent margins). The Klemme type II basin and Kluth's model appear to correspond well with the geology of the Paradox-Uncompahgre couple and its regional relationships.

STRATIGRAPHY AND SEDIMENTATION

Detailed discussions of Paradox basin stratigraphy are published by several authors, including Wengerd and Strickland (1954), Wengerd (1951, 1955, 1958, 1962), Wengerd and Matheny (1958), Wengerd and Szabo (1968), Herman and Sharps (1956), Herman and Barkell (1957), Welsh (1958), Peterson (1959, 1966a, 1966b), Peterson and Ohlen (1963), Peterson and Hite (1969), Hite (1960, 1961, 1968, 1970), Hite and Buckner (1981), Fetzner (1960), Ohlen and MacIntyre (1965), Parker and Roberts (1963), Szabo and Wengerd (1975), Stevenson and Baars (1986), and others listed in the References.

The stratigraphic section in the Aneth area comprises Cambrian through Jurassic rocks approximately 8500 ft (2600 m) thick (Figure 5). Thickness of Pennsylvanian rocks in the Paradox basin ranges from approximately 1000 ft (300 m) in northeastern Arizona to 2500 ft (750 m) in the Aneth area, to more than 5000 ft (1500 m) in the basin depositional axis adjacent to the Uncompahgre uplift (Figure 7).

During most of Paleozoic time, the North American continent was located in the tropical to subtropical latitude belt where optimal conditions for carbonate deposition existed (Figure 9). The approximate position of the Pennsylvanian equator was a short distance south of the Paradox basin, approximately across present-day central New Mexico and Arizona (Figure 7). Prevailing wind direction was approximately from a present-day north-northeast direction (F. Peterson, 1988; Parrish and Peterson, 1988).

The pre-Pennsylvanian sedimentary pattern of most of the Rocky Mountain region is that of relatively stable and widespread shelf deposition of shallow-water marine carbonate and clastic sediments. Sedimentary facies were associated with regional transgressions of the early Paleozoic seas across the broad Rocky Mountain shelf lying west of the Transcontinental arch, a feature that extended from Minnesota southwest to central Colorado, northern New Mexico, and northern Arizona (Figure 6). During Mississippian time, marine shallow-water skeletal and oolitic carbonate deposits (Leadville

Mountains region of southwestern Arkansas and Oklahoma and shifted westward with time. By the Middle Pennsylvanian, continental foreland deformation reached its greatest intensity, resulting in growth of the Ancestral Rocky Mountains and associated strongly downwarped basins. Positioning of the block uplifts and basins was probably governed in part by pre-existing zones of crustal weakness along the continental margin of the time. Deformation of the craton diminished during Early Permian.

The Paradox is a hybrid basin, a type IIBa platform rift-sag followed by a type IIa foredeep and foreland

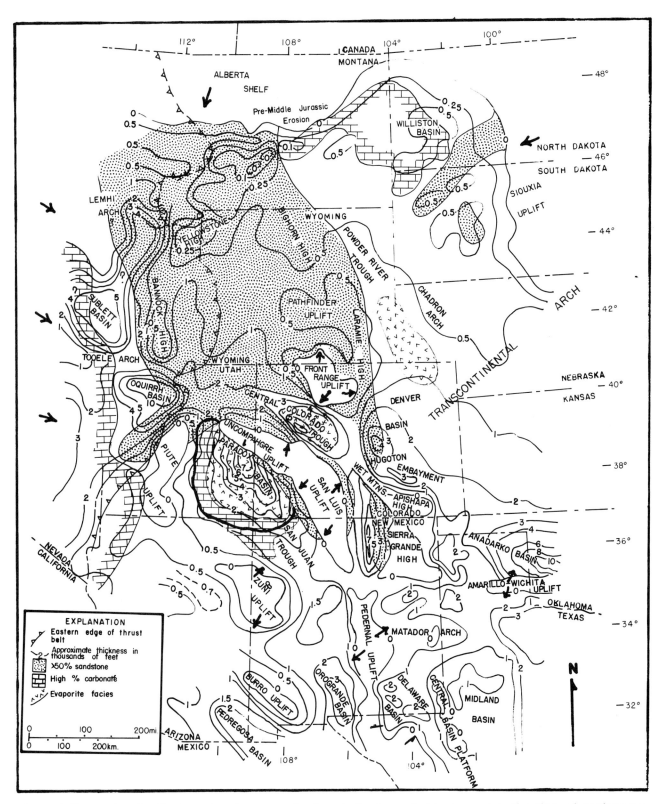

Figure 6. Pennsylvanian System, showing approximate thickness, general sedimentary facies, and main tectonic elements, Rocky Mountain region. Data are palinspastically restored in western thrust belt. Arrows indicate probable transport direction of terrigenous clastic sediments. Boundary of Paradox basin shown by heavy line. (Modified after Peterson and Smith, 1986.)

47

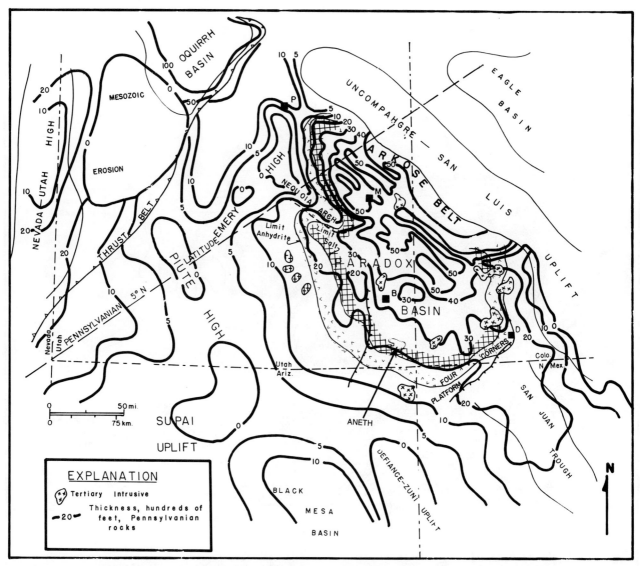

Figure 7. Thickness map, Pennsylvanian System, Paradox basin region, showing edge of Paradox basin evaporites and basins and uplifts of Pennsylvanian age. Arkose belt on east side of basin grades rapidly westward into salt and black shale facies. East edge of Mesozoic Sevier thrust belt and position of Pennsylvanian 5° north latitude are shown.

Limestone and equivalents) blanketed the entire Rocky Mountain shelf. Prolonged emergence of the shelf area during Late Mississippian and Early Pennsylvanian time resulted in regional development of karst topography with associated red regolith, weathered carbonate rubble, and extensive solution features at the top of the Mississippian carbonate section that extended from New Mexico and Arizona north into Canada.

Early in Pennsylvanian time, the broad emergent Rocky Mountain continental shelf underwent the initial stages of tectonism that intensified during Middle Pennsylvanian to Permian time with the rapid growth of the Ancestral Rocky Mountains (Oklahoma-Colorado Mountains). Active subsidence of the Paradox basin began in the early Desmoinesian and continued at an accelerated pace until approximately the middle Permian. Through most of the early and middle Mesozoic, the region became emergent and was relatively stable tectonically. Continental deposition prevailed during much of this time. During most of the Late Cretaceous, marine and intertonguing continental clastics at or near the western margin of the Cretaceous seaway were deposited across most of the region.

Pennsylvanian deposition in the Paradox basin was strongly cyclic and is represented by at least 35 to 40 complete or partial cycles, giving an average time per cycle on the order of 300,000 to 400,000 years. Development of the cycles is probably related to a combination of factors, including: (1) eustatic sea level changes caused by cycles of Carboniferous

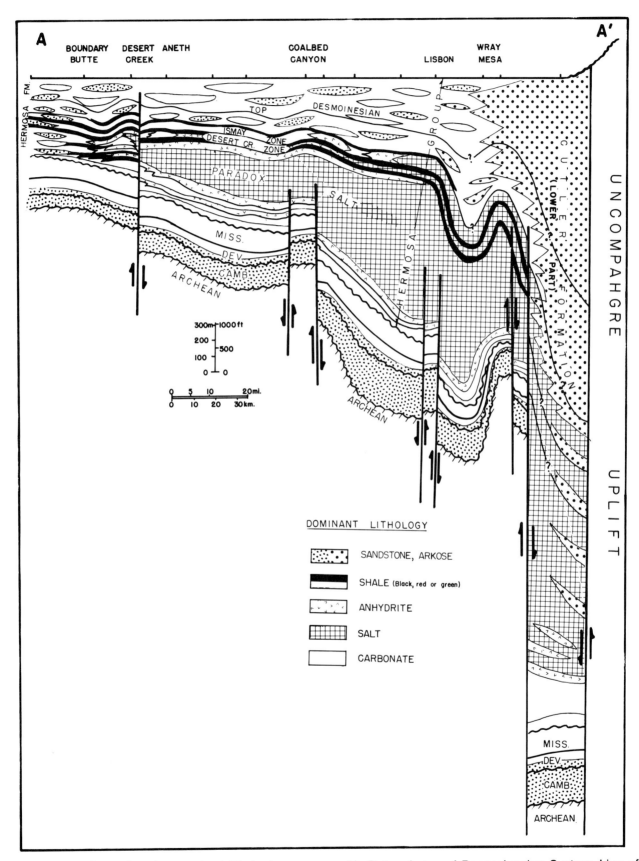

Figure 8. North-south paleostructural-lithologic cross section A–A', northeastern Arizona to Uncompahgre uplift. Datum is top of Pennsylvanian System. Line of cross section shown on Figure 2.

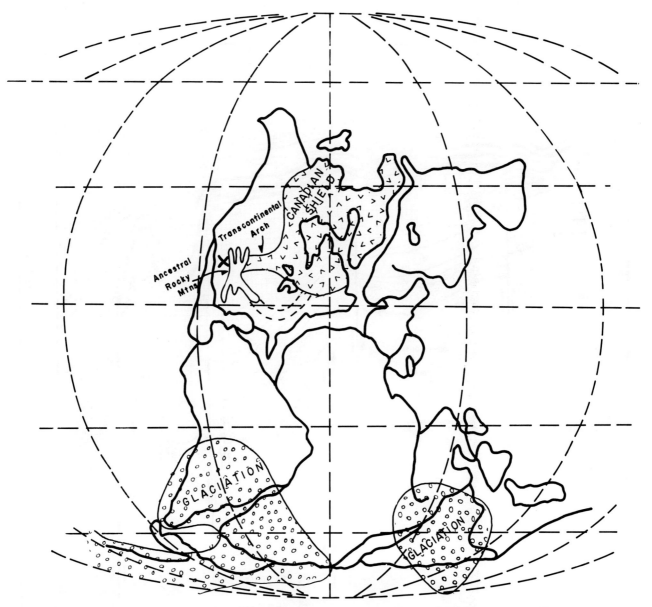

Figure 9. Paleolatitudinal position of North American continent (Larussia), Middle Pennsylvanian time. X, approximate location of Paradox basin. Approximate position of Ancestral Rocky Mountains and Transcon- tinental arch and areas of late Paleozoic continental glaciation in southern hemisphere are shown. (Modified after Bambach et al., 1980.)

glaciation in the southern hemisphere, probably in combination with ocean basin events related to sea floor spreading, (2) more localized changes in rate and type of clastic influx and its relation to submarine topography, (3) climatic effects, and (4) minor changes in rates of basin subsidence and tectonic movements.

During the Pennsylvanian and Permian, uplifts peripheral to the basin furnished clastic debris that was carried into the rapidly subsiding Paradox trough. The major source of clastic material was the Uncompahgre-San Luis uplift, which supplied more than 15,000 ft (4600 m) of coarse arkosic clastic debris along the northeast border of the basin. Minor sources for finer clastics were present on the southwest and west (Figures 7 and 8). Pennsylvanian-Permian

tectonism accompanied by cyclic eustatic sea level changes and the relative isolation of the Paradox trough from the main marine realm to the southeast and west resulted in complicated and diverse facies patterns within the basin. During Desmoinesian time, three main intertonguing sedimentary facies were deposited: (1) a coarse-clastic facies that became increasingly arkosic beginning in middle Desmoinesian time and reaching maximum thickness in a narrow belt along the northeastern border of the basin adjacent to the Uncompahgre-San Luis uplift (Figure 8); (2) an evaporite facies, mainly of early Desmoinesian age, thickest in the basin center, including salt (halite and potash), anhydrite, finely crystalline dolomite, and black organic-rich shale, and (3) a shelf carbonate facies, along the southern and southwestern shelf of the basin. The carbonate facies locally contains mound-like buildups of biogenic carbonates. A narrow belt of mound-bearing sandy to silty carbonates also is present between the clastic and evaporite facies along the western border of the San Luis uplift near the main marine accessway of the basin. The evaporite-dominated facies of the inner basin change relatively abruptly to carbonate facies across the shelf area to the southwest, where the Hermosa Group becomes predominantly cyclically deposited carbonate rocks with minor fine-grained clastics.

Time equivalents of the various facies can be correlated from the inner basin to the shelf province on the basis of basinwide black and gray shaly marker units, the most prominent of which are organic-rich. The " lower Hermosa" or Pinkerton Trail Formation demonstrates the initial development of cyclic sedimentation that resulted in repetitive deposition of clastic and carbonate units. Vertically, the cyclic section shows a progressive increase in carbonate content and ultimately grades through dolomite and black shale into the overlying Paradox Formation evaporite facies.

TRAP

The Aneth field is primarily a stratigraphic trap. The reservoir complex is an isolated carbonate mound buildup in which the oil accumulation has undergone only minor redistribution because of relatively insignificant post-mound structural growth. Oil accumulation is controlled primarily by the carbonate reservoir mound buildup trends, together with porosity-permeability discontinuities within the buildup belt. Structural influence is limited to local redistribution of earlier oil accumulation within the isolated reservoir geometry during subsequent development of the structural framework of the area. Minor localization of the original, broader accumulation may have occurred during Laramide and later structural growth.

The Aneth field is located on the "Bluff nose," a gentle fold that extends southeast off the prominent Bluff anticline (Figures 4, 10, and 11). A significant amount of structural closure on the nose at Aneth probably is related to draping and differential compaction over the underlying carbonate mound complex. Judging from restored-thickness studies of the post-Ismay stratigraphic section, oil generation probably began by Early to middle Cretaceous time. Maximum depth of burial of the Aneth reservoir beds is estimated to have been approximately 10,000–12,000 ft (3000–3500 m) and probably occurred during early Tertiary time.

Oil production from Pennsylvanian carbonate reservoirs in the Aneth area is from isolated carbonate-mound buildup reservoirs that provide the major trapping mechanism for accumulation. The primarily stratigraphic traps are commonly assisted by minor post-depositional folding. Structural influence is local within elongated mound trends, some of which are only a few miles wide but which may extend for several miles in a generally northwest direction.

Two main carbonate mound intervals or "cycles," known in the industry as the Desert Creek and Ismay zones (Figures 5 and 8), are of particular economic interest and contain the major petroleum reserves of the basin (Figures 12 and 13). Subcycles are recognized in both these zones, the lower and upper Desert Creek and the lower, middle, and upper Ismay (Figure 13). The most important porosity development within these two zones occurs basinward (i.e., northeast) from the main Pennsylvanian shelf carbonate belt along the southwest flank of the basin. The relatively basinward position and the associated lateral facies relations are of great importance in providing the prominent isolated stratigraphic trap in the Aneth carbonate mound reservoir.

Reservoirs

Desert Creek Zone

The Desert Creek zone stratigraphic section at the Aneth field consists of the following sequence, from the base upward (Figures 13–15):

1. Black, laminated, organic-rich, dolomitic, silty shale or shaly dolomite and siltstone (Chimney Rock shale of industry usage), the basal unit of the cycle. The Chimney Rock is underlain by a 10–15 ft (3–5 m) anhydrite bed, which lies above approximately 150 ft (45 m) of halite.
2. Dark brown to gray, finely crystalline or chalky dolomite or dolomitic, fossiliferous limestone.
3. Porous algal limestone or slightly dolomitic limestone, locally pelletal (Figure 16).
4. Thin anhydrite bed, present only on the fringes of the mound buildup.
5. Foraminiferal pellet limestone.
6. Porous "leached oolite," slightly dolomitic limestone, commonly fossiliferous (Figure 16).
7. Thin anhydrite bed, present only on the fringes of the buildup. This is the top of the cycle, overlain by black, organic-rich shale (Gothic shale of industry usage) similar to the basal unit of the Desert Creek cycle (Chimney Rock shale). The Gothic is the basal unit of the overlying Ismay zone.

Porosity in the Desert Creek zone at the Aneth field is in two main reservoir rock types, a calcareous phylloid (leaf-like) algal limestone in the lower part, and a "leached oolite" limestone and dolomite interval in the upper part (Figures 13–16). The algal reservoir is slightly over 100 ft (30 m) thick in the central part of the mound, and the leached oolite averages approximately 100 ft (30 m) in most of the mound area, giving a maximum mound thickness

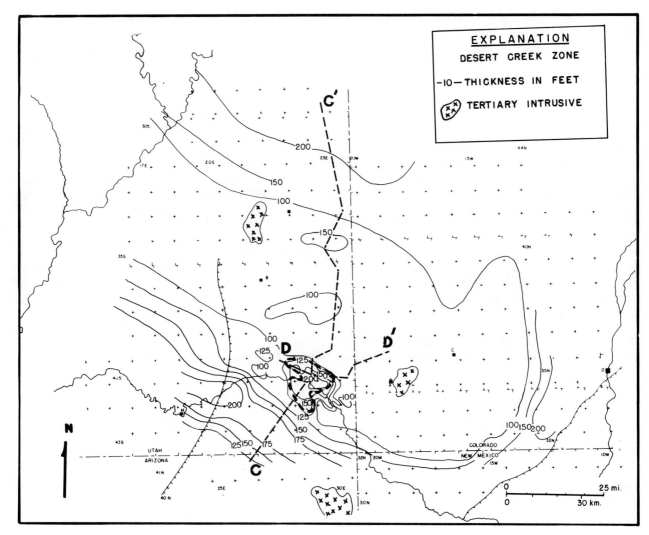

Figure 10. Thickness, Desert Creek zone. Outline of Aneth field shown by heavy dashed line. Lines of cross sections C–C′ and D–D′ of Figures 14 and 15 are shown.

of somewhat over 200 ft (60 m) (Figure 14). In plan view (Figures 10 and 12), the overall porous mound buildup is somewhat horseshoe-shaped with the major breadth and thickness in the greater Aneth field area, thinning to the northwest along two relatively narrow and irregular arms. The middle Desert Creek anhydrite unit covers the thinner part of the mound belt to the northwest. The anhydrite also covers other small individual Desert Creek mound buildups away from the Aneth field but does not cover the mound rocks in the field proper (Figures 14 and 15). The main porous rock in the lower Desert Creek mounds is composed largely of calcified remains of the green alga *Ivanovia* (Khovorova, 1946; Parks, 1958; Wray and Konishi, 1960) intermixed with pelleted mud lenses, which probably represent pockets of fine lime mud trapped during mound growth (Figure 16). Fusulinids, other small foraminifers, some brachiopods, mollusks, and *Chaetetes* corals are present but not abundant in the algal rock unit. The better porosity is almost universally

associated with pockets of maximum accumulation of leafy *Ivanovia* skeletal material, although the fine details of algal structure commonly are obscured by recrystallization, leaching, and cementation.

Thickness of the mound complex decreases rapidly to 100 ft (30 m) or less away from the mound in the surrounding evaporitic facies (Figures 10, 14, and 15). The eastern flank of the mound complex is steepest, with relief of more than 100 ft (30 m) in less than 1 mi (1.6 km) in places. The combined pay thickness of both zones averages about 50 ft (15 m) but reaches 100 ft (30 m) or more in some parts of the field. Productive limits of the field are generally determined by porosity and permeability changes related to carbonate facies changes, mound pinchouts, and anhydrite sealing near the periphery of the mound buildup. An unusual aspect of the Aneth mound is that it is almost completely filled with oil. A relatively small volume of porous, water-wet reservoir is present around the periphery of the mound (Figures 12 and 13).

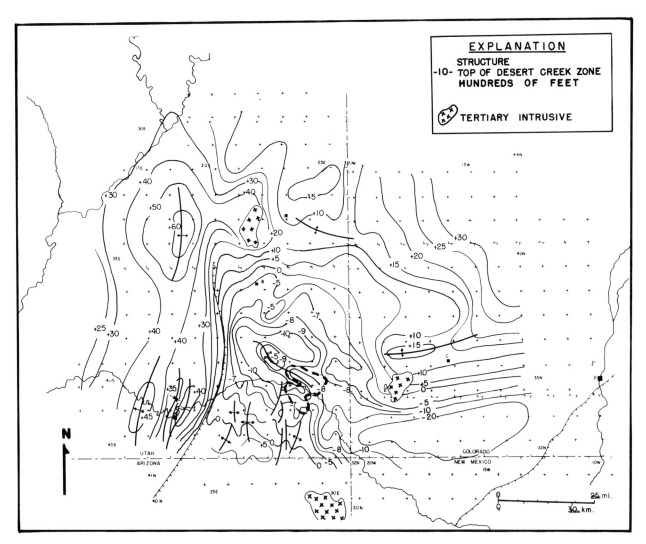

Figure 11. Structure in hundreds of feet, top of Desert Creek zone. Outline of Aneth field shown by heavy dashed line.

The upper Desert Creek "leached oolite" facies consists largely of oolites, pellets, and coated fossil fragments that have been irregularly leached, recrystallized, and partly dolomitized (Figure 16). Oolitic and pelletal rocks generally are thicker on the borders of the main mound. The inner part of the upper Desert Creek contains beds of bioclastic and recrystallized limestone mud, along with porous oolite-pelletal beds that are discontinuous in an apparent channel-like pattern. Porosity is generally associated with apparent leaching and partial dolomitization of the "oolite" and pellet-rock facies and is, on the average, higher than in the underlying algal facies. However, permeability of the "leached oolite" reservoir rock averages considerably lower than that of the algal reservoir (Table 1). The upper oolite unit attains maximum thickness in the main mound area of the Aneth field, where it represents more than half the porous section. Laterally, away from the Aneth mound complex, the oolite interval

changes rapidly to chalky dolomite and anhydrite facies and is absent in the smaller Desert Creek mound buildups of the Blanding subbasin (Figures 14 and 15). The "leached oolite" facies also is present in the upper Desert Creek in a broad belt along the southwest basin shelf (Figure 14), where it commonly contains as much as 50 ft (15 m) or more of porous oil-stained limestone. However, along this extensive belt the Desert Creek section has not been found with sufficient permeability for economic petroleum production.

Ismay Zone

Limestone mound porosity in the Ismay zone in the Aneth area is present largely in the lower Ismay, with more localized buildups in the middle and upper Ismay. Porous bodies are generally elongated northwesterly and are formed of somewhat discontinuous, irregular-shaped, narrow belts of algal limestone. This reservoir rock is similar to that of

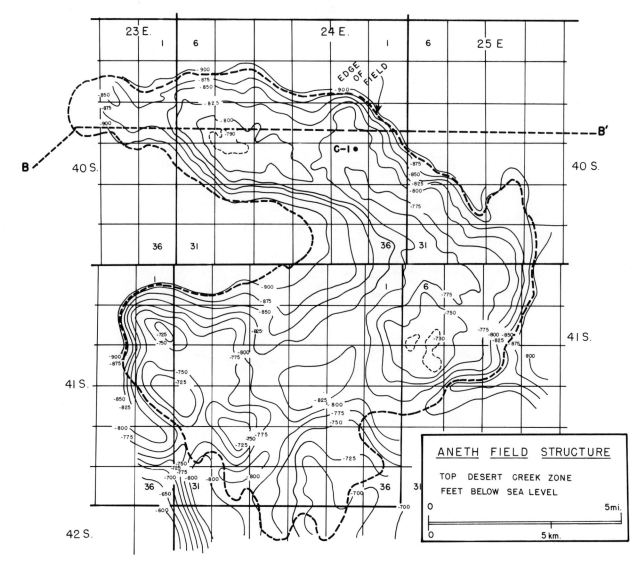

Figure 12. Structure in feet, top of Desert Creek zone, Aneth field; contour interval, 25 ft. C-1 discovery well and line of cross section B–B′ of Figure 13 are shown.

the algal and pelleted-mud reservoir rock of the lower Desert Creek zone (Figure 16). The lower Ismay mound reservoir is exposed on outcrop in the San Juan River canyon east of Mexican Hat, Utah. The outcropping beds illustrate the discontinuous nature of individual algal buildups within the southwesternmost belt of Ismay mounds. A well drilled in the mound belt may encounter a thin mound section, with small recovery of hydrocarbons, whereas one drilled a short distance away may penetrate a greatly thickened mound of reservoir quality.

In the Ismay field area east of Aneth, the lower Ismay mound buildup is at maximum thickness along the eastern borders of the Ismay zone buildup trend (Figures 3 and 15). Reservoir facies here are dominated by recrystallized algal and pelleted mud rocks similar to those of the lower Desert Creek mounds.

Source

Production from the greater Aneth field is almost entirely from the Desert Creek zone with minor production from the lower Ismay. The Desert Creek zone is underlain by the Chimney Rock shale and overlain by the Gothic shale, both of which are organic-rich black sapropelic calcareous or dolomitic shale units (Figures 15–18). Both of these units, along with similar beds intertonguing with the reservoir facies, are the probable source rocks for the Aneth oil. In the Blanding subbasin area, total organic carbon (TOC) values for the Chimney Rock shale range from approximately 1.0% to more than 3%, and values for the Gothic shale range from approximately 1.5% to near 4.0% (Hite et al., 1984; Shell Oil Co., personal communication, 1988). Organic-rich shales in the Paradox evaporite cycles below the Desert

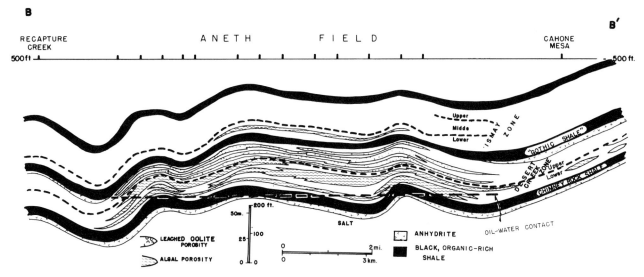

Figure 13. West-east structural-stratigraphic cross section B-B', Aneth field; datum -500 ft elevation, showing general facies, porosity intervals, oil-water contact, and organic-rich Chimney Rock and Gothic shales. Line of cross section shown on Figure 12.

Creek zone may contain TOC values as high as 13% (Hite et al., 1984). Total thickness of organic-rich Pennsylvanian rocks in the Paradox basin is as high as 1000 ft or more in the central part of the basin (Figure 19). Vitrinite reflectance (R_o) values in the limited numbers of available core samples near the Aneth field range from approximately 0.8 to near 1.5; mean vitrinite reflectance (R_o mean) values may range between 1.3 and 2.5 for the Chimney Rock shale and 0.8 and 1.2 for the Gothic shale (Shell Oil Co., personal communication, 1988). The Gothic shale is the main seal (Figures 14 and 15). The field includes two productive zones: Zone II, the lower Desert Creek algal limestone reservoir, and Zone I, the upper Desert Creek "leached oolite" limestone reservoir. Porous intervals in both zones tend to be lensing in nature with rapid lateral and vertical changes, although most are interconnected to varying degrees. Porosity in both zones has been enhanced by dissolution, recrystallization, and secondary dolomitization. On the flanks of the Aneth mound buildup, an 8–10 ft (2.5–3 m) regional bed of anhydrite occurs at the top of each zone but in each case the anhydrite pinches out around the edges of the mound.

EXPLORATION CONCEPTS

Genesis of the Aneth Carbonate Reservoir Complex

The Paradox algal leaf mounds have been studied by numerous researchers over the approximately 30 years since they were first found in the Paradox basin (Peterson, 1959, 1966a, 1966b; Elias, 1962, 1963; Choquette and Traut, 1963; Peterson and Ohlen, 1963; Pray and Wray, 1963; Peterson and Hite, 1969; Irwin, 1963, 1978; Choquette, 1983). Of the approximately 40 main Pennsylvanian depositional cycles recognized in the Paradox basin, only two, the Desert Creek and Ismay, contain significant buildups of algal leaf mounds. With few if any exceptions, reservoir development and oil production from these intervals is associated with the algal reservoir rock. The algal buildups are formed largely of the accumulated calcified skeletal phylloid structures of the alga *Ivanovia*, along with pockets of finely crystalline, pelletal lime mud lenses. Other skeletal fossil materials such as brachiopods, foraminifers, fusulinids, mollusks, and uncommon *Chaetetes* corals are also present.

The sedimentary and organic record revealed by study of subsurface and outcrop samples, cores, geophysical well logs, and thousands of thin sections indicate that the basic environmental requisites for optimum mound growth include: (1) relatively normal marine salinity, (2) shallow to intermediate water depth, (3) open marine circulation, (4) clear, nonturbid, warm waters, (5) the evolutionary stage of the dominant species occupying the appropriate environmental niche, and (6) possible scarcity of herbivorous invertebrate predators, the remains of which are relatively uncommon in the algal mound rock, perhaps because of slightly elevated salinity. However, the presence of fusulinids, other small foraminifers, brachiopods, and *Chaetetes* corals indicates that water salinity during mound growth was near normal marine. The Desert Creek and Ismay algal mounds apparently represent a combination of ecologic conditions favoring the prolific growth of this single algal species at rates sufficiently rapid to mask the accumulation of other sediment

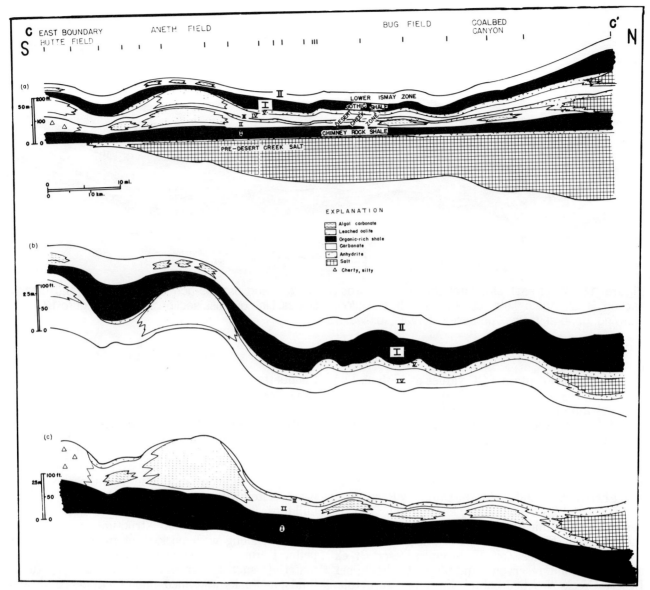

Figure 14. North-south lithofacies cross section C-C', northeastern Arizona to center of Paradox basin, Desert Creek zone and pre-Desert Creek salt. Present-day thicknesses shown by (a). Datum is base of Chimney Rock shale. Datum for cross sections (b) upper Desert Creek, and (c), lower Desert Creek, is estimated sea level during time of deposition, using estimated precompaction thicknesses of shale units. Roman numerals correspond to phases of mound growth described in text and shown on Figures 21-27. Line of cross section shown on Figure 10.

and biotic debris that may have been forming at a relatively normal rate.

The origin and positioning of the algal mounds is debatable. A question pondered by most researchers has been: Why is the Aneth algal-mound complex isolated where it is, 25-30 mi (40-50 km) basinward of the main basin shelf margin and at a substantial distance from any paleostructural features that appear to have been important at the time? Several hypotheses have been considered: (1) possible paleotectonic control (Picard, 1958; Elias, 1962, 1963),

(2) a primarily depositional mudbank origin (Peterson, 1966a, 1966b; Peterson and Hite, 1969), (3) growth downslope from tectonically induced shoals (Wilson, 1975), and (4) development because of structural instability, probably independent of prevailing winds or paleocurrent directions (Stevenson and Baars, 1986).

Detailed vertical sequence (oldest to youngest) of Desert Creek and lower Ismay cycles in the Aneth area are characterized below (Peterson, 1959; Peterson and Ohlen, 1963).

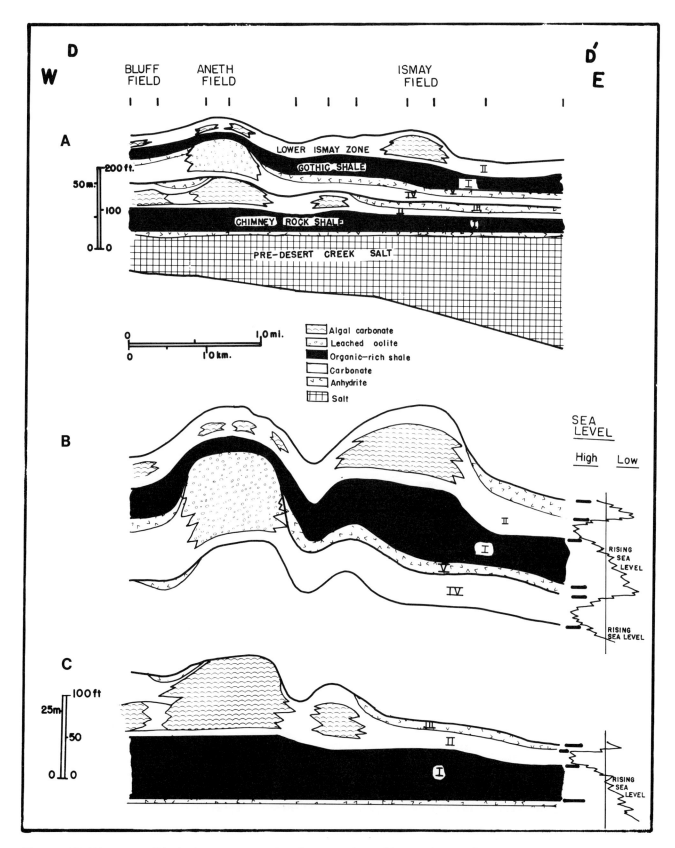

Figure 15. West-east lithofacies cross section D–D′, Bluff, Aneth, and Ismay fields, Desert Creek zone and pre-Desert Creek salt. Present-day thicknesses shown by (A). Datum is base of Chimney Rock shale. Datum for cross section (B), upper Desert Creek, and (C), lower Desert Creek, is estimated sea level during time of deposition using estimated pre-compaction thicknesses of shale units. Roman numerals correspond to phases of mound growth described in text and shown on Figures 21–27. Line of cross section shown on Figure 10.

57

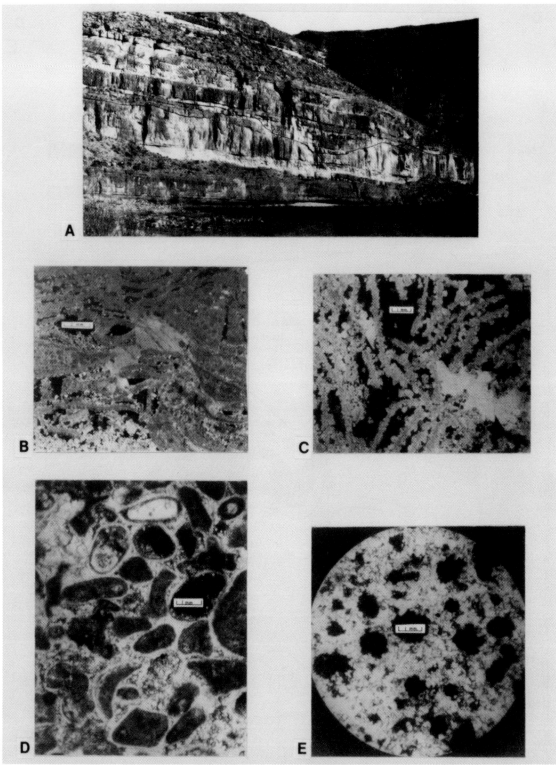

Figure 16. (A) Exposed algal mounds of oil-stained lower Ismay cycle algal leaf carbonate reservoirs in San Juan River canyon on Monument uplift east of Mexican Hat, Utah (see Figure 3). Photomicrographs of reservoir rocks in Aneth area shown by B through E. (B) Algal reservoir, Desert Creek zone, Desert Creek field. Rock is composed of elongate algal fragments of fibrous calcite, pelletal mud lenses, and some large calcite crystals. (C) Highly leached and recrystallized algal reservoir, lower Desert Creek zone, Aneth field. Pore spaces are black. (D) Bank-edge "leached oolite" reservoir of upper Desert Creek zone, southwest side of greater Aneth field. Matrix material is mostly recrystallized limestone mud and cement. (E) Highly leached, recrystallized, and partly dolomitized, "leached oolite" reservoir of upper Desert Creek zone at the center of the greater Aneth field. Pore spaces are black. (Modified after Peterson, 1966.)

Table 1. Reservoir parameters, Aneth oil field (after McComas, 1963).

	Porosity (%)		Permeability (millidarcies)		Residual Oil Saturation %		Total Water Saturation %		Connate Water Saturation %		Barrels of Oil in Place (range)	Estimated Recovery (% of oil in place)
	Range	Avg.	Range	Avg.	Range	Avg.	Range	Avg.	Range	Avg.		
Algal reservoir	3.5–26.2	9.5	0.1–932	24	4.0–26.2	9.5	13.4–54.4	31.0	10–54	28	205–766 Barrels/ acre-ft	19–23
Oomoldic (leached oolite)	7.3–23.6	11.3	0.1–31	3.4	7–35	17.0	7.2–53.4	30.0	7.0–53	30		
Dolomite (inter- crystalline porosity)	8.2–32.4	13.0	0.1–83	3.0	8.5–38.8	17.0	23.5–55.8	35.0		33.0		
Leached fossil hash	0.3–18.9	6.3	0.1–1165	5.1	0.0–43.7	9.3	18–51.6	31.0		30.0		

1. Pre-Desert Creek cycle. Anhydrite underlain by salt—the most widespread salt unit of the basin that extends farthest to the southwest on the shelf (Figures 5, 8, and 20).
2. Basal black, laminated, organic-rich, dolomitic, silty shale or shaly dolomite and siltstone, high in disseminated sulfide minerals (Chimney Rock shale). These rocks contain conodonts, bone fragments, fish teeth, phosphatic brachiopods, occasional carbonized plant stems, and other fragments and represent anoxic, reducing conditions. The unit is basinwide in extent (Figures 8 and 17).
3. Dark brown or gray, chalky dolomite or dark carbonate mudstone, moderately organic-rich, approximately 10–20 ft (3–6 m) thick. This rock commonly contains phosphatic brachiopods, bryozoans, crinoids, ostracods, conodonts, sponge spicules, and carbonaceous fragments, possibly the remains of primitive marine plants. The upper part of this unit in places contains beds of limestone with faunal content similar to that of the chalky dolomite.
4. Porous algal limestone or slightly dolomitized limestone, made up mostly of the calcified leaf-like plates of the alga Ivanovia and other leaf-like or stem-like algal fragments. This is the main mound-buildup rock, which shows considerable variation in carbonate mud content, possibly related in part to variations in the sediment-baffling effect of the growing algae. In places the rock is composed almost entirely of pelletal carbonate mud with only scattered algal and other fossil fragments. Elsewhere it is composed almost entirely of algal leaf-like fragments. The mound

rock also contains numerous pelletal mud lenses interpreted as pockets of carbonate mud that settled among the leaf-like algal framework (Figure 16). Leaching and recrystallization of the algal-rich rock are common. Associated fossils include fusulinids, other small foraminifers, productid brachiopods, red algae, mollusks, bryozoans, rare Chaetetes corals, and other fossil debris.
5. Foraminiferal-pellet limestone capping beds. These beds overlie the main algal buildup rock and form a relatively thin capping unit. The rock contains abundant small Foraminifera shells, including encrusting forms, and fusulinids intermixed with pelletal limestone beds containing simple pellets, coated pellets, and incipient oolites with nuclei of foraminiferal or other shell fragments. The unit represents shoaling conditions above the main buildup associated with falling sea level and is of probable tidal origin. Around the border of the mound, the upper Desert Creek regional anhydrite bed is present at the equivalent stratigraphic position, grading to halite farther toward the basin center.
6. "Leached oolite" rock. This rock type dominates approximately the upper one-half of the Aneth buildup, reaching a thickness of more than 100 ft (30 m) in parts of the Aneth complex (Figures 13–15). These rocks comprise a prominently oolitic and pelletal peripheral or "rim" facies and an inner bioclastic and lime-mud facies. The biotic content of the peripheral facies is dominated by skeletal remains of tubular and encrusting foraminifers; the peripheral facies grades bankward to a muddy bioclastic facies dominated by abundant fusulin-

59

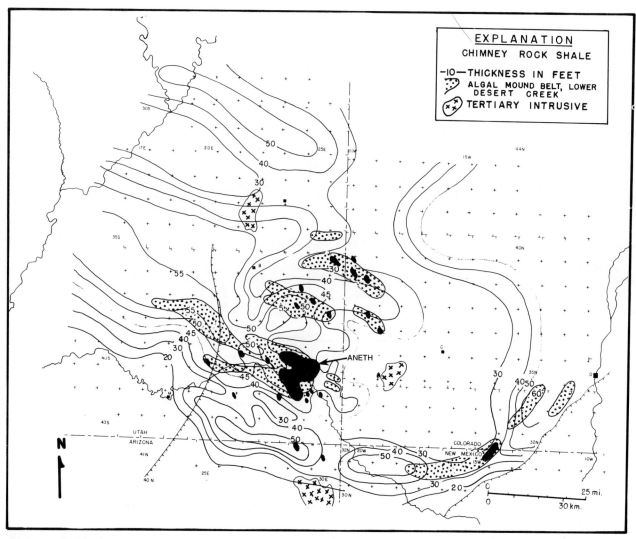

Figure 17. Thickness in feet, Chimney Rock shale, showing location and thickness of Chimney Rock mudbank, distribution of lower Desert Creek algal mound belts, and oil or gas fields (solid black) producing from lower Desert Creek algal carbonate reservoirs.

ids, small foraminifers, brachiopods, and broken algal fragments. Much of this facies has been recrystallized and partly dolomitized. Oolite particles usually contain only a single coating of carbonate rind, probably deposited around algal and other fossil fragments. Evidence of channeling, wave- and current-built banks, broken fossil debris, and some cross-bedding suggests more active wave and current activity and shallower water conditions, in contrast to the evidence for quieter-water deposition indicated by the algal leaf rock of the lower Desert Creek subcycle. The original fabric of this rock is partly obscured by excessive recrystallization and dolomitization. The irregular shapes of the particles suggest that they originally may have included pellets, tubular foraminifers, other fossil fragments, and algal stems or other algal fragments. The more oolitic

and thicker "rim" or peripheral facies suggests the prevalence of upwelling, carbonate-rich waters, and tidal current buildup around the bank edges. The upper oolite facies occurs directly above the main algal mound buildup at Aneth, but it is not present at any of the smaller algal buildups elsewhere in the vicinity where algal buildups are overlain by the basin-wide middle Desert Creek anhydrite. The off-mound facies-equivalent of the "leached oolite" beds consists of a thin sequence of finely crystalline dark dolomite or shaly dolomite interbedded with thin, organic-rich, dolomite shale beds. These rocks are also overlain by the upper anhydrite bed, which pinches out adjacent to the Aneth buildup. The upper oolite facies also occurs in a broad northwest-southeast belt along the margin of the main basin shelf southwest of Aneth (Figures 6 and 14).

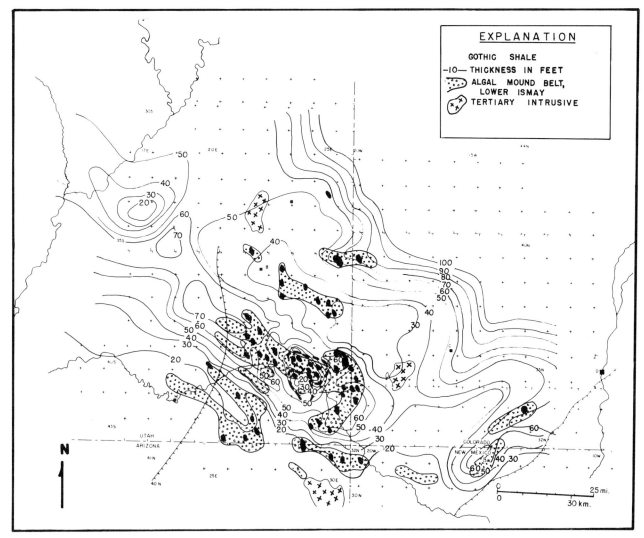

Figure 18. Thickness in feet, Gothic shale, showing location and thickness of Gothic mudbank, distribution of Ismay mound belts, and oil or gas fields (solid black) producing from lower Ismay algal carbonate reservoirs.

The upper oolite facies is overlain by the organic-rich Gothic shale, the basal unit of the overlying Ismay zone. The marked thinning of the Gothic over the Aneth buildup, compared with adjacent areas (Figures 14 and 15), reflects the topographic expression of the Aneth mound during deposition of the overlying shaly beds.

The combination of paleogeographic, eustatic, and other factors resulting in the location, nature, and unusual size of the Aneth carbonate buildup can be visualized in a sequence of environmental-ecological and depositional phases as described below (modified after Peterson, 1959; Peterson and Ohlen, 1963).

Pre-Desert Creek Evaporite Phase

Stratigraphically beneath the Aneth complex, salt beds of the pre-Desert Creek (Akah) cycle 150–200 ft (45–60 m) thick are present, overlain by a regional bed of anhydrite (Figures 8, 13, and 20). During deposition of the main pre-Desert Creek (Akah) salt facies, most of the basin area was semistarved of clastic material. Salt deposition reached its maximum areal extent in the Paradox basin during this time. Beginning with the Desert Creek cycle, clastic influx to the basin increased, mainly because of two factors: (1) progressive spreading of the marine shoreline toward the basin edges (transgression) and consequent reworking and redeposition of clastic material accumulated on the previously exposed basin shelf and (2) probable increase in uplift of the main clastic source areas, the Piute-Emery lowland to the west, Zuni-Defiance lowland to the south, and the Uncompahgre–San Luis highland to the northeast, on the west of which the Silverton delta began to form at this time. During rising sea level stages of the cycles, tongues of clastic sediment extended into the basin, partly built by longshore drift related to wind and wave action and partly by extension

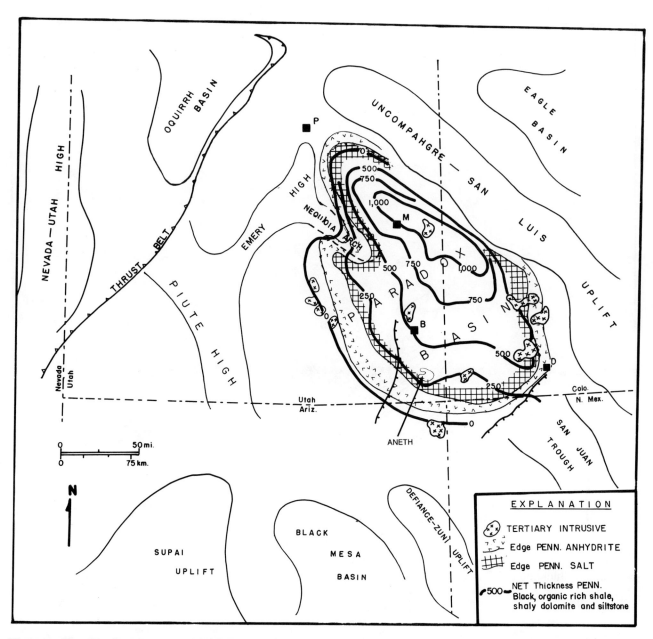

Figure 19. Composite net thickness in feet of Pennsylvanian black, organic-rich rocks, Paradox basin.

of alluvial-deltaic distributory patterns. These clastic tongues influenced greatly the nature of the sea bottom topography prior to deposition of the marine carbonate phase of each cycle or subcycle.

Phase I, Desert Creek Cycle
(Chimney Rock Shale)

Deposition of the pre-Desert Creek evaporite beds left a broad, flat surface on which the black, organic-rich, silty mud beds of the Chimney Rock shale and time-equivalent beds were deposited during the rising sea level stage of the Desert Creek cycle. With rising sea level, the inflow of normal marine waters

increased across the Four Corners platform accessway, mixing with the supersaline waters of the evaporite basin. For some time the basin waters remained abnormally saline and essentially devoid of normal marine biota. The continued influx of normal sea water across the shallow-water Four Corners sill at this time resulted in an exceptionally high nutrient supply near the basin entrance, with abnormally high production of phytoplankton and zooplankton that drifted into the basin with the incoming currents. As increasingly higher salinity was encountered in the surface waters of the inner basin, accumulating dead plankton remains in part

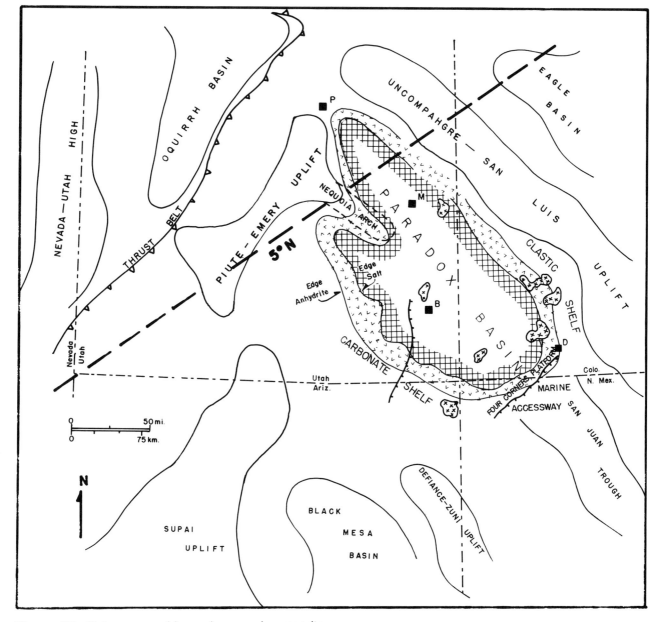

Figure 20. Paleogeographic and general evaporite facies map, pre-Desert Creek (Akah) cycle. Pennsylvanian 5° north latitude line is shown.

settled in abundance to the poorly circulated anoxic basin bottom and in part drifted toward the south part of the basin by the prevailing northerly winds of the time (Figure 21). The process is visualized as similar to that described by Kirkland and Evans (1981), who used the Paradox basin as an example for their model. At the same time, with rising sea level, the basin waters expanded areally and a wind-generated northwest to southeast longshore current system developed. Fine clastic material, derived partly from the Piute-Emery lowland area and partly from the previously exposed shelf, was transported to the southeast by longshore drift and intermixed

with wind-driven plankton remains to form the organic-rich longshore mudbank of the Chimney Rock shale. Both the plankton and the sediment supply may have been seasonal, as suggested by the laminated bedding of the Chimney Rock shale. The presence of phosphatic brachiopods in these beds indicates an adequate supply of phosphate in the waters crossing the Four Corners sill into the basin. Carbonized land plant remains in the Chimney Rock and other Paradox black shales, particularly on the east side of the basin, probably represent reworking of these materials from land areas flooded by the advancing strand line during early rising sea level

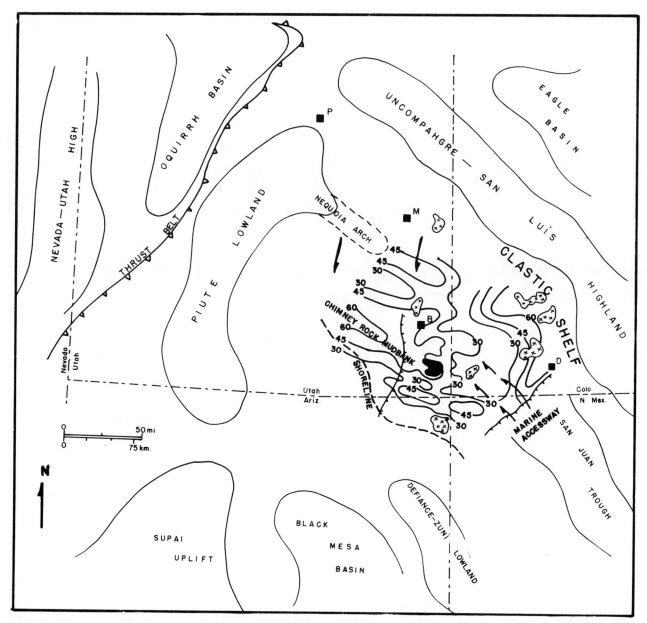

Figure 21. Paleogeographic map, Phase I of Desert Creek cycle, showing marine accessway, position and thickness in feet of Chimney Rock mudbank, and Aneth field. Wind direction shown by heavy arrows. Influxing marine waters at main basin entrance shown by lighter arrows.

stages. With continued rising of the sea level, more normal marine circulation patterns began to return to the basin, resulting in the gradation upward from the organic-rich muds into a carbonate-rich mud (the dark carbonate mudstone unit), which contains a mixture of near- or seminormal marine faunas whose remains became mixed with carbonate mud to form the substrate on which the overlying mound buildup grew. This unit, immediately above the Chimney Rock shale, is commonly dolomitized in the greater Aneth area. The Chimney Rock unit was built southeastward from the clastic source area on the northwest into a mud and silt longshore bank as far

as the Aneth area before sediment supply and increased water depth diminished the building process.

The present-day thickness of the Chimney Rock shale ranges from a maximum of more than 60 ft (17 m) to the northwest, to approximately 45 to 50 ft (13-15 m) in the immediate Aneth area, to less than 30 ft (9 m) in the main basin trough to the north and east (Figure 17). These values probably represent precompaction thicknesses on the order of 100 to 125 ft (30-38 m) and 50 to 75 ft (15-23 m), suggesting sea bottom topography or water depth differences on the order of 50 ft (15 m) or more at

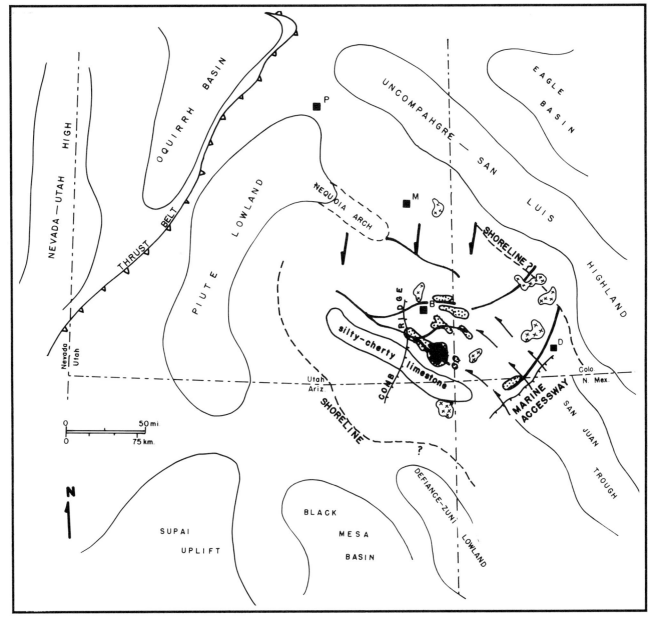

Figure 22. Paleogeographic map, Phase II of Desert Creek cycle, lower Desert Creek algal buildup, showing marine accessway, Chimney Rock shale thick trends (heavy lines), distribution of lower Desert Creek algal mound belts, and Aneth field. Wind direction shown by heavy arrows. Influxing marine waters at main basin entrance shown by lighter arrows.

the close of Chimney Rock deposition, immediately prior to the early growth stage of the Aneth carbonate mound.

Phase II, Lower Desert Creek Algal Mound Buildup

The flat surface of the Chimney Rock shallow-water mudbank left a broad, flat, subsea platform surface on which initial growth of the Aneth lower Desert Creek algal bank occurred. The carbonate bank facies occurs in a northwest-southeast belt approximately 75 mi (120 km) long and 10 to 20 mi (16–32 km) wide, extending from the immediate Aneth field area to beyond the Comb Ridge (Figure 22). Maximum build-up of algal rock is in a slightly horseshoe-shaped body about 12 mi (20 km) wide and 15 mi (25 km) long at the southeastern extremity of the mound belt where the Aneth field is located. The mound facies built up as gradually rising sea level restored more open and normal marine circulation conditions to the basin shelf. The mound grew to maximum extent at a position where influxing normal marine waters from the southeast encountered shallowing sea bottom conditions along the southeast margin of the Chimney Rock mudbank. At the same time, smaller and less extensive algal banks formed farther basinward on extensions of the Chimney Rock mudbank (Figures 21 and 22). Between the algal carbonate banks, the time-equivalent facies is primarily dark-colored, finely crystalline dolomite deposited as deeper-water carbonate mud intermixed with fine clay or silt and the remains of marine plankton. Deposition of the Aneth bank algal facies was limited on the southeast, northeast, and southwest by the deeper waters along the edge of the Chimney Rock mudbank. The algal facies is also absent farther southwest where shallower waters were present along the margin of the main basin shelf. Here, the time-equivalent facies consists of silty, cherty, argillaceous, finely crystalline carbonate deposited under turbid conditions unfavorable for optimum growth of normal carbonate-contributing organisms. The main algal buildup at Aneth grades upward to foraminiferal-pellet limestone beds, with evidence of shoaling conditions indicating lowering sea level.

Phase III, Middle Desert Creek Evaporite

To the northeast of the Aneth bank, the approximate stratigraphic position of the upper horizon of the algal buildup is represented by a basinwide anhydrite unit (middle Desert Creek anhydrite) approximately 5 to 15 ft (1.5–4.5 m) thick, which grades to halite approximately 50 to 75 mi (80–120 km) to the northeast (Figure 23). The middle Desert Creek anhydrite pinches out against the Aneth bank along the east, northeast and west flanks (Figures 13, 14, 15, and 23). These stratigraphic relationships are considered to represent the following: (1) maximum sea level fall of the subcycle; (2) subaerial exposure of the southwestern basin shelf, including the Aneth algal bank buildup, except for intermitent tidal and storm surge effects (the smaller algal banks basinward of the Aneth bank, however, probably were not emergent at this time, as evidenced by the continuation of the anhydrite bed across the top of these mounds; mound porosity in these areas may have been subjected to initial anhydrite [or gypsum] infilling at this time); (3) cessation of algal and other normal marine biotic production; and (4) near-isolation of the basin with influx of marine waters primarily confined to tidal fluctuations across the Four Corners shelf adjacent to the main marine accessway to the southeast.

During this time, the Aneth mound probably underwent the first phase of early diagenesis, including (1) leaching, recrystallization, and partial cementation of the algal fabric, (2) selective partial or complete filling of pore spaces by reprecipitated crystalline calcite or aragonite, (3) early dolomitization, partly by reflux from the main saline basin toward the elongate trough separating the Aneth bank complex from the main shelf to the southwest (Figure 23), and (4) early dolomitizatlon of the

carbonate mud unit underlying the porous algal bank by settling and concentration of heavy magnesium-rich waters in the lower parts of the mound immediately above the impermeable Chimney Rock shale beds.

Phase IV, Upper Desert Creek "Leached Oolite" Facies

The Desert Creek "leached oolite" comprises the approximately 100 ft (30 m) of the upper Desert Creek subcycle at Aneth (Figure 24). This unit was deposited during the second high sea level stage of the main cycle. The rock has been generally recrystallized and partly dolomitized. Much of the material is probably fossil fragments with a single coating of calcite. The unit is considered to have been deposited in shallow-water, nonturbid areas of the basin shelf on shallow-water sea bottom topographic features inherited from those built up during formation of the underlying lower Desert Creek subcycle. Evidence of shallow-water, tidal, and supratidal features suggests that sea-level rise was not as high as that of the preceding algal buildup subcycle. In the greater Aneth complex, distribution of the upper oolite beds is limited to the area of maximum buildup of the lower Desert Creek mound, where shallowest water conditions prevailed. The "leached oolite" facies is also present southwest of Aneth along a northwest-southeast belt approximately 100 to 125 mi (30–38 km) long, interpreted as the main basin shelf margin at this time. Porosity in the "leached oolite" rock at Aneth is variable but generally is higher than that of the algal rock. Permeability, however, of the oolite rock is characteristically lower than that of the algal reservoir (Table 1).

Phase V, Upper Desert Creek Anhydrite

To the northwest and surrounding the Aneth bank, a basinwide bed of anhydrite is present at the top of the Desert Creek zone, grading to halite in the basin center (Figure 25). The anhydrite pinches out on the flanks of the main Aneth bank and also along the northeast flank of the elongate "leached oolite" bank southwest of Aneth. This unit represents deposition during the maximum low sea level stage of the upper Desert Creek subcycle, when the southwest shelf region, including the Aneth bank, was again exposed, except for intermittent tidal and storm surge effects. A second stage of early diagenesis of the Aneth bank probably occurred at this time, including further leaching, dolomitization, and recrystallization of the mound complex.

Phases I and II, Post-Desert Creek (Lower Ismay Subcycle)

In the Aneth area, the lower Ismay subcycle in most ways represents a close repetition of the sedimentary processes that formed the lower Desert Creek subcycle. Some main differences include (1) clastic influx into the basin increased at this time and the Silverton delta adjacent to the Uncompahgre–

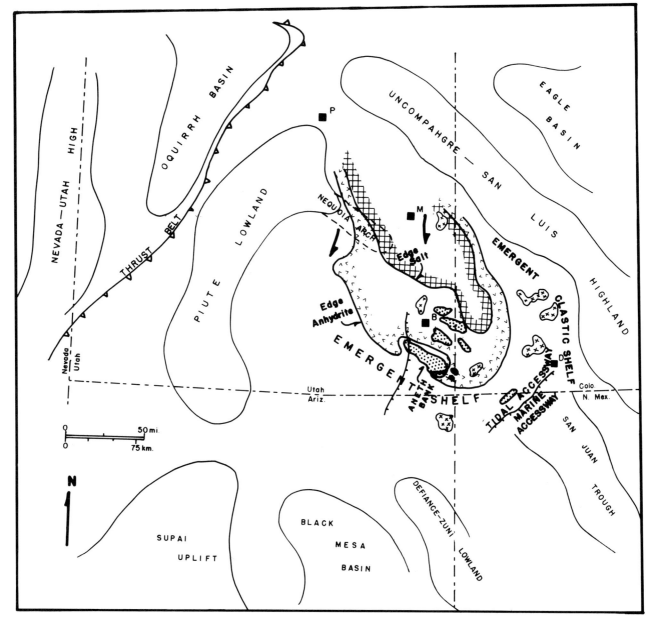

Figure 23. Paleogeographic map, Phase III of Desert Creek cycle, showing distribution of middle Desert Creek evaporites and underlying lower Desert Creek algal mound belts (stippled pattern). Wind direction shown by heavy arrows.

San Luis highland on the east side of the basin became more prominent, (2) the algal-mound buildups in the lower Ismay are smaller in comparison with the Aneth buildup and tend to be more scattered patch-like buildups than are those of the lower Desert Creek.

The basin-wide, organic-rich Gothic shale overlies the Desert Creek zone (Figure 26). The origin of this unit is interpreted as a repetition of early rising sea level processes similar to those prevalent during deposition of the Chimney Rock shale at the base of the Desert Creek zone. The northwest-southeast elongate, silty, organic-rich Gothic mudbank, sourced by processes similar to those of the Chimney Rock,

built up along almost precisely the same trend as the Chimney Rock mudbank. The growing Gothic mudbank enveloped the Aneth Desert Creek mound complex and extended approximately 35 to 40 mi (55–65 km) farther southeast than that of the Chimney Rock. The present-day Gothic shale trend is as much as 60 to 65 ft (18–20 m) thick to the northwest and sharply thins to less than 30 ft (9 m) along the southeast-facing leading edge near the Utah-Colorado border (Figure 26). Pre-compaction thicknesses probably were on the order of 110 to 135 ft (33–40 m) and 50 to 60 ft (15–18 m), representing sea bottom topographic or water depth differences of 60 to 75 ft (18–23 m) or more at the close of Gothic deposition,

67

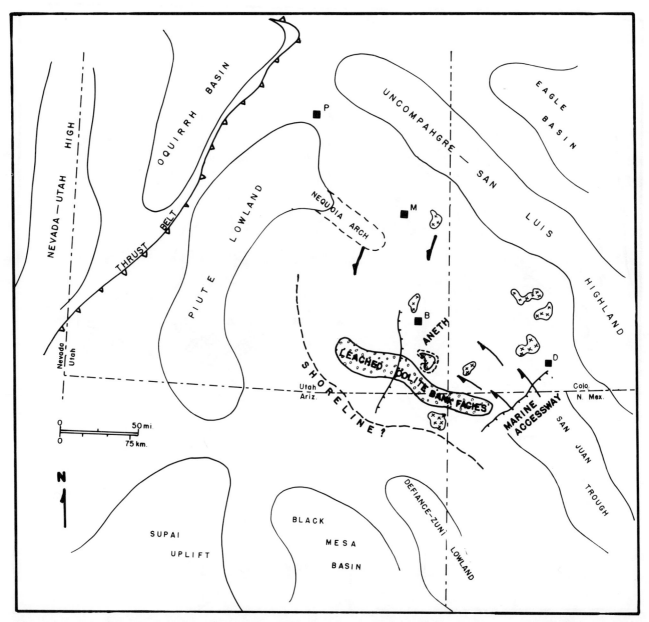

Figure 24. Paleogeographic map, Phase IV of Desert Creek cycle, upper Desert Creek "leached oolite" buildup, showing distribution of "leached oolite" facies. Wind direction shown by heavy arrows. Influxing marine waters at main basin entrance shown by lighter arrows.

immediately prior to the early growth stages of the lower Ismay algal mound belt.

The most prominent lower Ismay algal bank buildups (Ismay and other associated fields) occur along the southeast margin of the Gothic bank in a paleogeographic position similar to that of the lower Desert Creek Aneth buildup overlying the Chimney Rock mudbank. The lower Ismay algal-bank complex extends to the northwest for approximately 50 mi (80 km), roughly coincident with the thickness trend of the Gothic mudbank (Figures 26 and 27). Other northwest–southeast-trending lower Ismay algal-bank complexes are present to the southwest,

positioned along Desert Creek depositional trends that influenced water depths where Ismay mounds developed. Other generally smaller mound belts are also present basinward of the Aneth area, in most cases associated with Desert Creek buildups or thick belts of Gothic shale.

The lower Ismay cycle terminated with deposition of a basinwide anhydrite and halite unit that is absent over the main mound belts, indicating a low sea level post-mound origin (Figure 27), similar to the evaporite unit above the Desert Creek carbonate buildups.

The sequence and distribution of rock types in the lower Ismay carbonate mounds are remarkably

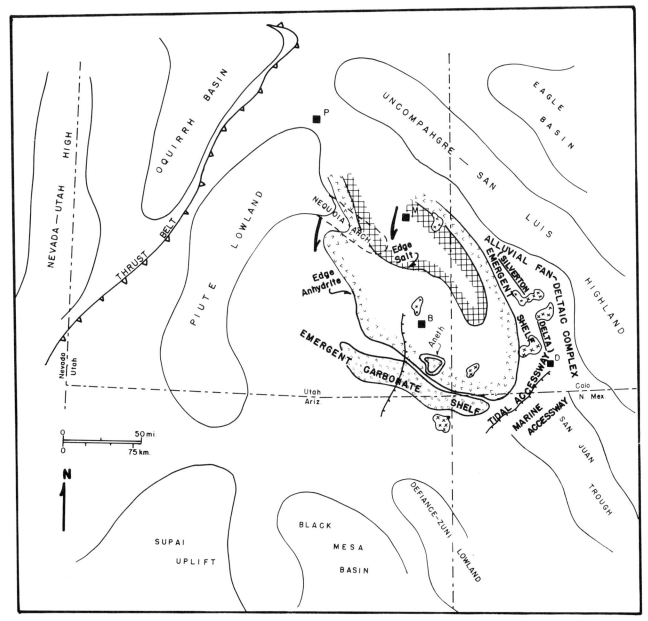

Figure 25. Paleogeographic map, Phase V of Desert Creek cycle, upper anhydrite, showing distribution of upper Desert Creek evaporites and positions of underlying "leached oolite" buildups. Wind direction shown by heavy arrows.

similar to those in the Aneth mound (Choquette and Traut, 1963; Choquette, 1983), although thickness and lateral extent of the Ismay mounds are generally less than the Aneth buildup. The discontinuous nature of individual mound buildups is demonstrated in outcrops of the lower Ismay mounds in the San Juan River canyon between Bluff and Mexican Hat, Utah (Figure 16). These exposed mounds are considerably smaller than many of those encountered in the subsurface, probably because of the detrimental effects of silt and mud influx from clastic source areas to the south and southwest on the mound-building organisms.

Paleotectonic Evidence

Detailed sedimentary analysis of the Desert Creek zone and related sedimentary facies-stratigraphic relations indicate strongly that the Aneth and related algal banks originated by sedimentary processes unrelated to penecontemporaneous local paleostructural growth. Thickness studies of the pre-Desert Creek stratigraphic section in the Four Corners area show a lack of evidence for paleostructural growth related to the Aneth trend (Figures 28–32). The thickness map of the Cambrian System shows normal thickening to the northwest across the Blanding basin region (Figure 28). Cambrian

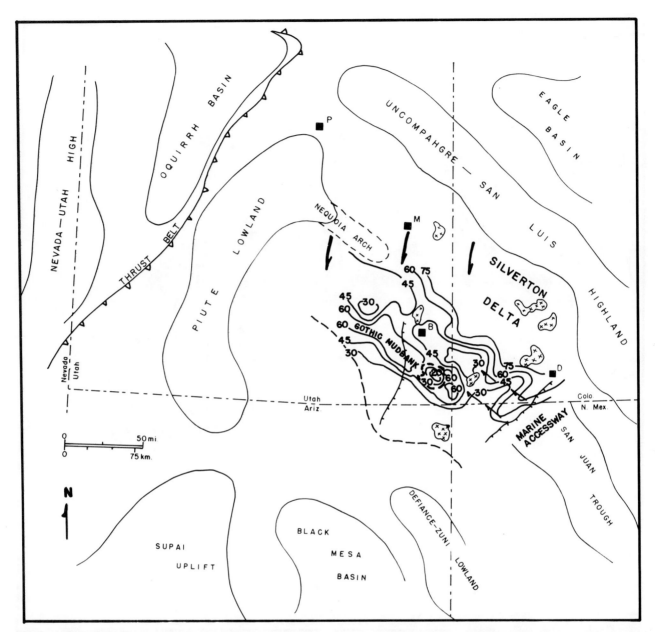

Figure 26. Paleogeographic map, Phase I of Ismay cycle (Gothic shale), showing thickness in feet and position of Gothic mudbank and location of Aneth field (heavy dashed line). Wind direction shown by heavy arrows. Influxing marine waters at main basin entrance shown by lighter arrows.

deposition was followed by a long period of erosion or nondeposition (Late Cambrian to Late Devonian time). Devonian thickness patterns show a prominent sag in the general Aneth area (Figure 29). The depositional thickness pattern in the Aneth area persists to some degree during the Mississippian (Figure 30), which was followed by regional emergence and weathering of the Leadville or Redwall Limestones. The interval between the top of the Leadville and the base of the Chimney Rock shale (top of Akah salt) shows no thickness evidence of paleostructural growth related to the Aneth area (Figure 31). Likewise, a detailed thickness map of the total Pennsylvanian indicates uniform slope to the northeast across the site of the Aneth mound buildup (Figure 32).

Summary

The Aneth oil field and other petroleum pools in Pennsylvanian carbonate reservoirs of the Paradox basin are regionally and locally isolated stratigraphic traps. By world standards, the petroleum resources of the Paradox basin are not large, although the basin is unusually rich in volume of source rock. Except for Aneth, carbonate reservoir bodies are generally small to medium in size, and all tend to be isolated

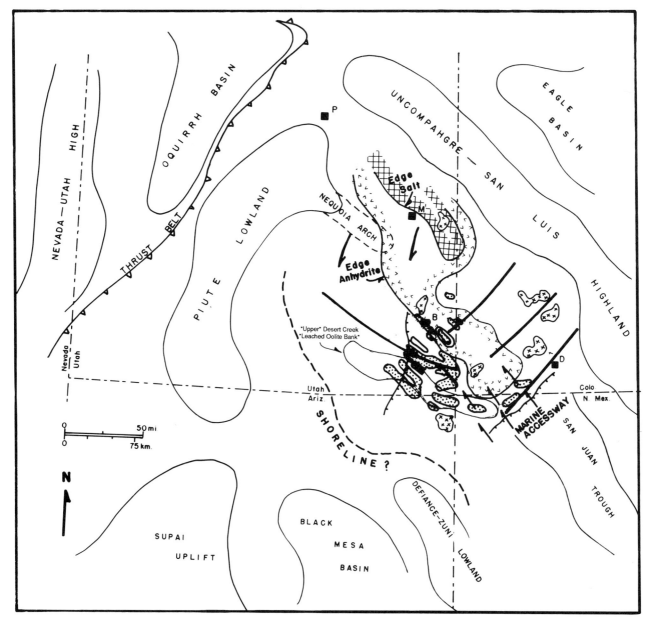

Figure 27. Paleogeographic map, Phase II of Ismay cycle (lower Ismay algal mound-bearing subcycle), showing Gothic shale thick trends (heavy lines), distribution of lower Ismay algal mound belts (stippled pattern), position of upper Desert Creek "leached oolite" bank, and distribution of evaporites at top of lower Ismay cycle. Wind direction shown by heavy arrows. Influxing marine waters at main basin entrance shown by lighter arrows.

and distinct porous bodies. Almost all the known oil resources of the basin occur in the Blanding subbasin. At least two-thirds of these resources are from the giant Aneth field.

The reasons for the heavy concentration of Paradox basin hydrocarbons in the Blanding subbasin are considered to reflect a delicate balance between the depositional and tectonic factors that combined to generate and preserve the petroleum accumulations, as follows:

1. During deposition of the Desert Creek and Ismay carbonate-evaporite cycles, the Blanding subbasin

occupied a mildly subsiding area on the broad shelf of the Paradox basin, intermediate between the slowly subsiding main shelf to the southwest and the rapidly subsiding salt basin trough to the northeast. The Aneth area was located at a position where influxing, high-nutrient marine waters spread across the subbasin from the main basin sill entrance (Four Corners Platform) on the southeast. This location was at a well-circulated, clear, marine-water position between the detrimental effects of both the turbid-water, clastic influx from the southwest and the higher salinity water environment of the basin interior. Within

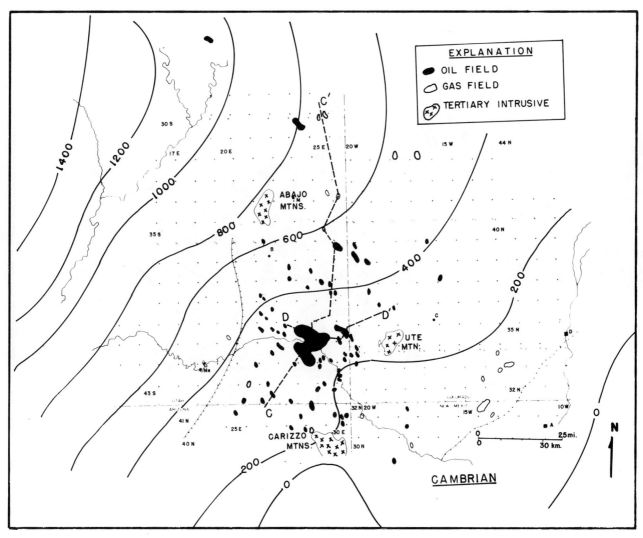

Figure 28. Thickness in feet, Cambrian System, southern Paradox basin. Main oil and gas fields of Paradox basin and lines of cross sections C–C' and D–D' of Figures 14 and 15 are shown.

the clear-water belt, algal growth and other skeletal carbonate production reached optimum efficiency in shallow-water areas on relatively subtle topographic highs, in most cases caused by the development of more localized, mainly clastic, mudbank buildups. The Aneth bank grew on the broad southeastern margin of one of these buildups (the Chimney Rock). The northwest-southeast trends of the mudbank buildups were related to increased source of clastics from the northwest and the effect of longshore drift related to the prevailing wind system of the time.

2. The Blanding subbasin was located in the optimum area for deposition of organic-rich sediments in the precarbonate stages of the cycle. Here organic-rich deposits accumulated immediately basinward of the basin shelf because of high zooplankton and phytoplankton productivity at the basin entrance to the southeast and the accompanying drift of organic material toward the northwest by inward-circulating marine waters.

Large amounts of the organic material accumulated in the longshore mudbanks because prevailing wind directions caused much of the material to drift toward the southwest and accumulate in the growing longshore mudbank deposits prior to development of the algal mound belts.

3. Eustatic sea level changes resulted in cyclic repetition of the source rock and carbonate reservoir sequences. Rising sea level conditions provided organic-rich argillaceous beds that serve as both source rocks and seals for the hydrocarbon accumulations. Subaerial exposure of carbonate buildups during low sea level stages of the eustatic cycles caused early diagenesis and leaching that improved reservoir quality in most cases, particularly at Aneth. At lowest sea level, gypsum was deposited in the Blanding subbasin area. These beds, in the form of anhydrite, now provide seals for most hydrocarbon accumulations in the smaller mound buildups away from the Aneth complex.

72

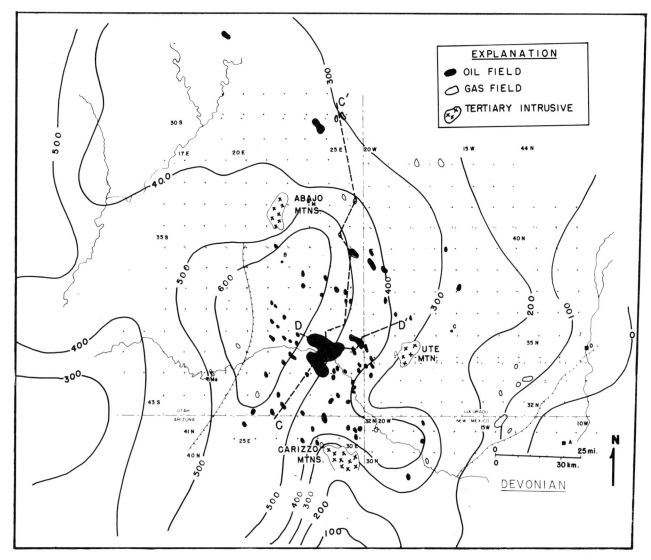

Figure 29. Thickness in feet, Devonian System, southern Paradox basin. Main oil and gas fields of Paradox basin and lines of cross sections C–C′ and D–D′ of Figures 14 and 15 are shown.

4. Post-depositional tectonic activity in the Blanding subbasin has been relatively minor. Early accumulations of hydrocarbons in the area have been preserved more or less in their original form except for mild localization by Mesozoic and later structural growth. In most cases, migration of hydrocarbons has been over short distances with source rocks immediately adjacent to or intertonguing with the reservoir beds.

5. The Blanding subbasin area is hydrodynamically stable without evidence of a currently active flow system (Thackston et al., 1981). Formation waters, which are probably connate, are generally high in NaCl and $CaSO_4$ total dissolved solids and are isolated from an active flow system. Oil fields are solution gas drive. The following additional discussion of hydrodynamic considerations is courtesy of David E. Powley (Amoco, Tulsa, Oklahoma):

Stability of the fluid system in the Aneth area is confirmed by drill-stem test (DST) data (Figure 33). Fluid pressure studies in the general Aneth area suggest that all of the formations of the lower Paleozoic in the Blanding subbasin and immediate area to the northeast exhibit a common potentiometric surface and thus are probably in hydraulic communication. In the surrounding shelf areas, however, these formations are hydraulically separated from the Blanding subbasin. The underpressured rocks (Figure 33) involve Mississippian and older rocks only in the periphery of the subbasin, whereas in the center of the subbasin younger Paleozoic rocks are in the isolated fluid system. The top of the underpressured fluid compartment appears to be at a higher elevation in the Aneth area than in adjacent areas. DST plots shown on Figure 33 are shut-in pressures

73

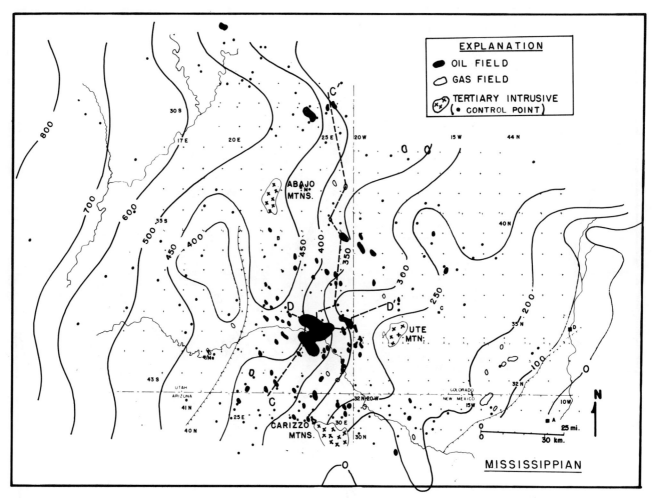

Figure 30. Thickness in feet, Mississippian System, southern Paradox basin. Main oil and gas fields of Paradox basin and lines of cross sections C-C′ and D-D′ of Figures 14 and 15 are shown.

measured in all formations. Hence, further definitive work, such as pressures/elevation cross sections east-west across the Aneth area should be constructed for further documentation. However, the plots of Figure 33 constitute a basis for demonstration that the Aneth reservoir is within a fairly large, isolated, underpressured fluid compartment. Segregation within the compartment has protected the rocks from water flushing and bacterial invasion; this factor has also been important in confining the oil generated within the Blanding subbasin and in preventing the hydrocarbons from migrating outside the subbasin. The rocks in the shelf areas around the subbasin probably were starved of migrating oil, and oil that did generate was not protected from the destructive factors of water flushing and bacterial invasion.

Lessons

On the basis of both detailed stratigraphic and paleostructural analyses, the evidence strongly indicates that the concentration of hydrocarbon deposits in the Blanding subbasin is predominantly related to the close relationship between the depositional and tectonic factors discussed. Modern-day exploration in the Paradox basin has the advantage of greatly improved technology developed during the past 35 years since the Aneth discovery. High-resolution seismic methods have significantly improved subsurface structural mapping and, in addition, have provided a means for delineation of isolated carbonate reservoir bodies such as those prevalent in the Blanding subbasin. Logging techniques have greatly improved, allowing for more refined reservoir analysis as well as stratigraphic correlation procedures. Both radiometric and paleontologic dating and correlation techniques have greatly advanced since 1954. Source rock analyses and interpretations are highly improved today. Identification of gas- versus oil-prone source rocks is now a highly refined procedure. Knowledge of depositional processes in carbonate and evaporite environments has greatly advanced in the past 35 years, allowing for more accurate predictions of positions and trends of carbonate buildups.

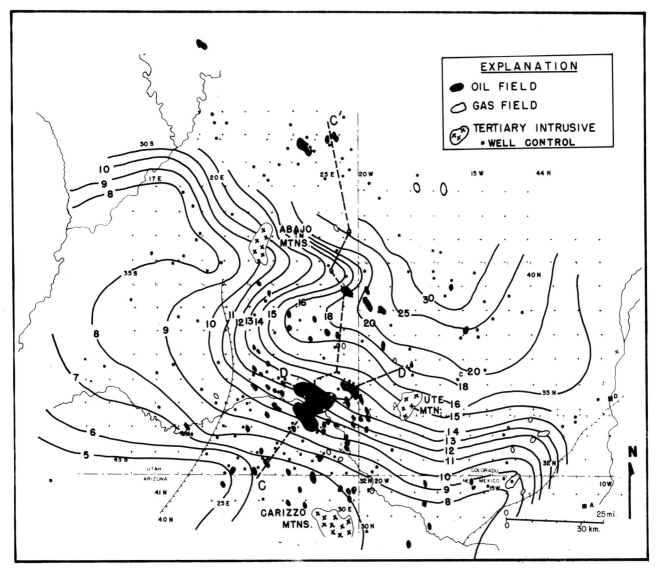

Figure 31. Thickness in hundreds of feet, base of Pennsylvanian System to base of Chimney Rock shale (top of Akah salt and anhydrite), southern Paradox basin. Main oil and gas fields of Paradox basin and lines of cross sections C–C' and D–D' of Figures 14 and 15 are shown.

The isolated, stratigraphic, and combined clastic-carbonate genetic nature of the giant Aneth carbonate mound complex may be somewhat unique among the world's carbonate provinces. However, there is mounting evidence that geologic processes similar to those responsible for the Paradox basin carbonate buildups may be involved in varying degrees with the genesis of isolated or semi-isolated carbonate buildups in many petroleum provinces. As more and more of the world's petroleum basins approach the mature stage of development, exploration geologists will logically turn to an intensified search for stratigraphic or combined stratigraphic-structural traps. As this effort progresses, more refined and detailed technical and geological approaches will become increasingly necessary in order to delineate and predict these subtle and elusive traps. Applica-

tion of principles such as those documented for the Aneth and other isolated carbonate mounds of the Paradox basin would aid greatly in this search.

ACKNOWLEDGMENTS

This paper benefitted greatly from reviews by F. Peterson, U.S. Geological Survey; P. W. Choquette, Marathon Oil Co.; C. D. Irwin, Independent; J. L. Wilson, University of Michigan; D. E. Powley, Amoco Production Co.; and E. A. Beaumont, Consultant. Useful information on the history of the Aneth discovery was provided by G. Sturgeon and L. R. Newfarmer, Shell Oil Co., retired. Certain statistical information on the Aneth field was provided by Kevin

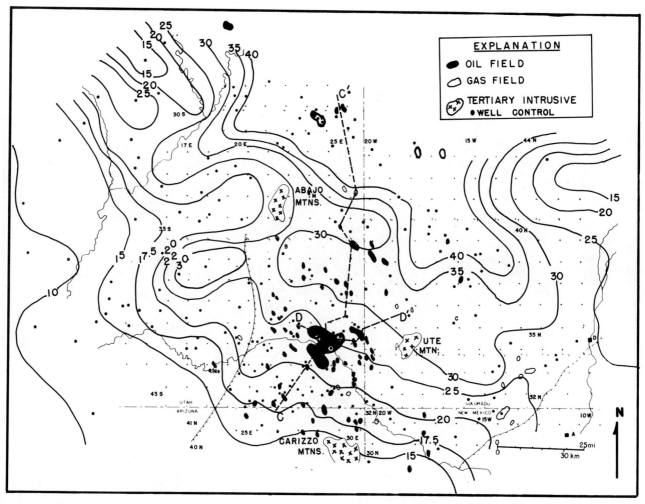

Figure 32. Thickness in hundreds of feet, Pennsylvanian System, southern Paradox basin. Main oil and gas fields of Paradox basin and lines of cross sections C-C' and D-D' of Figures 14 and 15 are shown.

Smith, Petroleum Information; Harold H. Brown, Geological Consultant; D. E. Powley; and the Utah Geological and Mineral Survey.

REFERENCES

Baars, D. L., 1966, Pre-Pennsylvanian paleotectonics—key to basin evolution and petroleum occurrences in Paradox basin: American Association of Petroleum Geologists Bulletin, v. 50, p. 2082-2111.

Barrs, D. L., and C. M. Stevenson, 1982, Subtle stratigraphic traps in Paleozoic rocks of Paradox basin, *in* M. Halbouty, ed., Deliberate search for the subtle trap: American Association of Petroleum Geologists Memoir 32, p. 131-158.

Babcock, P. E., 1978, Aneth (Aneth Unit), *in* J. E. Fassett, ed., Oil and gas fields of the Four Corners area: Four Corners Geological Society, p. 577-579.

Babcock, P. E., 1978, Aneth (McElmo Creek Unit), *in* J. E. Fassett, ed., Oil and gas fields of the Four Corners area: Four Corners Geological Society, p. 580-583.

Bambach, R. K., C. R. Scotese, and A. M. Ziegler, 1980, Before Pangea—the geographies of the Paleozoic world: American Scientist, v. 68, p. 26-38.

Berghorn, C., and F. S. Reid, 1981, Facies recognition and hydrocarbon potential of the Pennsylvanian Paradox Formation, *in* D. L. Wiegand, ed., Geology of the Paradox basin: Rocky Mountain Association of Geologists, p. 111-117.

Burchfiel, B. C., and J. H. Stewart, 1966, "Pull-apart" origin of the central segment of Death Valley, California: Geological Society of America Bulletin, v. 77, p. 439-442.

Carter, K. E., 1958, Stratigraphy of Desert Creek and Ismay zones and relationship to oil, Paradox basin, Utah, *in* A. F. Sanborn, ed., Guidebook to the geology of the Paradox basin: Intermountain Association of Petroleum Geologists, p. 138-145.

Choquette, P. W., 1983, Platy algal reef mounds, Paradox basin, *in* P. A. Scholle, D. G. Bebout, and C. H. Moore, eds., Carbonate depositional environments: American Association of Petroleum Geologists Memoir 33, p. 454-462.

Choquette, P. W., and J. D. Traut, 1963, Pennsylvanian carbonate reservoirs, Ismay field, Utah and Colorado, *in* R. O. Bass and S. L. Sharps, eds., shelf carbonates of the Paradox basin: Four Corners Geological Society, p. 149--156.

Elias, G. K., 1962, Paleoecology of lower Pennsylvanian bioherms, Paradox basin, Four Corners area: Guidebook, 27th Annual Field Conference, Kansas Geological Society, p. 124-128.

Elias, G. K., 1963, Habitat of Pennsylvanian algal bioherms, Four Corners area, *in* R. O. Bass and S. L. Sharps, eds., Shelf carbonates of the Paradox basin: Four Corners Geological Society, p. 185-203.

Fetzner, R. W., 1960, Pennsylvanian paleotectonics of the Colorado Plateau: American Association of Petroleum Geologists Bulletin, v. 44, p. 1371-1413.

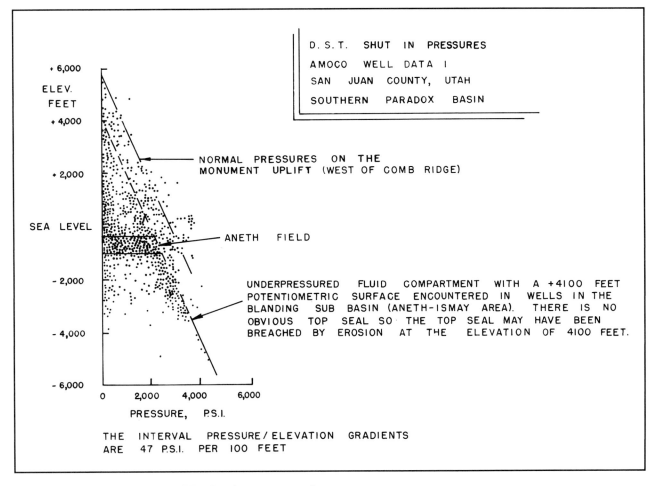

Figure 33. Drill-stem test (DST) shut-in pressures in pounds per square inch (PSI) measured in wells in the Aneth area. (Chart courtesy of D. E. Powley.)

Freeman, W. M., 1978, Aneth (Ratherford Unit), *in* J. E. Fassett, ed., Oil and gas fields of the Four Corners area: Four Corners Geological Society, p. 584–586.

Girdley, W. A., 1969, Character of part of the Hermosa Formation (Pennsylvanian), San Juan Mountains, Colorado, *in* J. Shomaker, ed., Guidebook of San Juan–San Miguel–La Plata region, New Mexico and Colorado: New Mexico Geological Society, p. 150–158.

Girdley, W. A., 1969, Character of part of the Hermosa Formation (Pennsylvanian) San Juan Mountains, Colorado, *in* J. Shomaker, ed., Guidebook of San Juan–San Miguel–La Plata region, New Mexico and Colorado: New Mexico Geological Society, p. 150–158.

Gray, R. S., 1967, Cache Field—a Pennsylvanian algal reservoir in southwestern Colorado: American Association of Petroleum Geologists Bulletin, v. 51, p. 1959–1978.

Halbouty, M. T., A. A. Meyerhoff, R. E. King, R. H. Dott, Sr., H. D. Klemme, and T. Shabad, 1970, World's giant oil and gas fields, geologic factors affecting their formation, and basin classification, *in* M. T. Halbouty, ed., Geology of giant petroleum fields: American Association of Petroleum Geologists Memoir 14, p. 502–555.

Herman, G., and C. A. Barkell, 1957, Pennsylvanian stratigraphy and productive zones, Paradox salt basin: American Association of Petroleum Geologists Bulletin, v. 41, p. 861–881.

Herman, G., and S. L. Sharps, 1956, Pennsylvanian and Permian stratigraphy of the Paradox salt embayment, *in* J. A. Peterson, ed., Geology and economic deposits of east-central Utah: Intermountain Association of Petroleum Geologists, 7th Annual Field Conference, p. 77–84.

Hite, R. J., 1960, Stratigraphy of the saline facies of the Paradox Member of the Paradox Formation of southeastern Utah and southwestern Colorado, *in* K. G. Smith, ed., Geology of the Paradox fold and fault belt, Third Field Conference Guidebook: Four Corners Geological Society, p. 86–89.

Hite, R. J., 1961, Potash-bearing evaporite cycles in the salt anticlines of the Paradox basin, Colorado and Utah, *in* Short papers in the geologic and hydrogeologic sciences: U.S. Geological Survey Professional Paper 424D, p. D135–D138.

Hite, R. J., 1968, Salt deposits of the Paradox basin, southeastern Utah and southwestern Colorado, *in* R. B. Mattox, ed., Saline deposits: Geological Society of America Special Paper 88, p. 319–330.

Hite, R. J., 1970, Shelf carbonate sedimentation controlled by salinity in the Paradox basin, southeast Utah, *in* J. L. Rau and L. F. Dellwig, eds., Symposium on salt, 3rd, v. 1: Northern Ohio Geological Society, p. 48–66.

Hite, R. J., and D. H. Buckner, 1981, Stratigraphic correlations, facies concepts, and cyclicity in Pennsylvanian rocks of the Paradox basin, *in* D. L. Wiegand, ed., Geology of the Paradox basin: Rocky Mountain Association of Geologists, p. 147–159.

Hite, R. J., D. E. Anders, and T. G. Ging, 1984, Organic-rich source rocks of Pennsylvanian age in the Paradox basin of Utah and Colorado, *in* J. Woodward, F. F. Meissner, and J. L. Clayton, eds., Hydrocarbon source rocks of the greater Rocky Mountain region: Rocky Mountain Association of Geologists, p. 255–274.

Irwin, C. D., 1963, Producing carbonate reservoirs in the Four

Corners area, *in* R. O. Bass and S. L. Sharps, eds., Shelf carbonates of the Paradox basin: Four/* Corners Geological Society, p. 144-148.

Irwin, C. D., 1978, Aneth (White Mesa), *in* J. E. Fassett, ed., Oil and gas fields of the Four Corners area: Four Corners Geological Society, p. 587-590.

Kelley, V. C., 1955, Regional tectonics of the Colorado Plateau and relationship to the origin and distribution of uranium: University of New Mexico Publications in Geology No. 5, 120 p.

Khovorova, I. V., 1946, On a new genus of algae from the Middle Carboniferous deposits of the Moscow basin: Academy of Sciences, USSR, Doklady, v. 53, n. 8, p. 737-739.

Kirkland, D. W., and R. Evans, 1981, Source-rock potential of evaporitic environment: American Association of Petroleum Geologists Bulletin, v. 65, p. 181-190.

Klemme, H. D., 1980, Petroleum basins—classification and characteristics: Journal of Petroleum Geology, v. 3, n. 2, p. 187-207.

Kluth, C. F., 1986, Plate tectonics of the ancestral Rocky Mountains, *in* J. A. Peterson, ed., Paleotectonics and sedimentation in the Rocky Mountain region, U.S.: American Association of Petroleum Geologists Memoir 41, p. 353-369.

Lessentine, R. H., 1965, Kaiparowits and Black Mesa basins: stratigraphic synthesis: American Association of Petroleum Geologists Bulletin, v. 49, p. 1997-2019.

Linscott, R. O., 1958, Petrography and petrology of Ismay and Desert Creek zones, Four Corners region, *in* A. F. Sanborn, ed., Guidebook to the geology of the Paradox basin: Intermountain Association of Petroleum Geologists, p. 146-152.

Malin, W. J., 1958, A preliminary informal system of nomenclature for a part of the Pennsylvanian of the Paradox basin, *in* A. F. Sanborn, ed., Guidebook to the geology of the Paradox basin: Intermountain Association of Petroleum Geologists, p. 135-137.

Matheny, M. L., 1978, A history of the petroleum industry in the Four Corners area, *in* J. E. Fassett, ed., Oil and gas fields of the Four Corners area: Four Corners Geological Society, p. 17-24.

McComas, M. R., 1963, Productive core analysis characteristics of carbonate rocks in the Four Corners area, *in* R. O. Bass and S. L. Sharps, eds., Shelf carbonates of the Paradox basin: Four Corners Geological Society, p. 149-156.

Molenaar, C. M., 1975, Some notes on Upper Cretaceous stratigraphy of the Paradox basin, *in* J. E. Fassett, ed., Guidebook 8th Field Conference, Canyonlands Country: Four Corners Geological Society, p. 191-192.

Molenaar, C. M., 1981, Mesozoic stratigraphy of the Paradox basin—an overview, *in* D. L. Weigand, ed., Geology of the Paradox basin: Rocky Mountain Association of Geologists, p. 119-127.

Murray, R. C., 1960, Origin of porosity in carbonate rocks: Journal of Sedimentary Petrology, v. 30, p. 59-84.

Ohlen, H. R., and L. B. McIntyre, 1965, Stratigraphy and tectonic features of Paradox basin, Four Corners area: American Association of Petroleum Geologists Bulletin, v. 49, p. 2020-2040.

Parker, J. W., and F. W. Roberts, 1963, Devonian and Mississippian stratigraphy of the central part of the Colorado Plateau *in* R. O. Bass and S. L. Sharps, eds., Shelf carbonates of the Paradox basin: Four Corners Geological Society, p. 31-60.

Parks, J. M., 1958, Plate-shaped calcareous algae in late Paleozoic rocks of Mid-continent (abs.): Geological Society of America Bulletin, v. 69, p. 1627.

Parrish, J. T., and F. Peterson, 1988, Wind directions predicted from global circulation models and wind directions determined from eolian sandstones of the western United States—a comparison: Sedimentary Geology, v. 56, p. 261-282.

Peterson, F., 1988, Pennsylvanian to Jurassic eolian transportation systems in the western United States: Sedimentary Geology, v. 56, p. 207-260.

Peterson, J. A., 1959, Petroleum geology of the Four Corners area: 5th World Petroleum Congress, Proceedings, Sec. 1, p. 499-523.

Peterson, J. A., 1966a, Genesis and diagenesis of Paradox basin carbonate mound reservoirs, *in* Symposium on recently developed geologic principles and sedimentation of the Permo-Pennsylvanian of the Rocky Mountains: Wyoming Geological Association, 20th Annual Field Conference, p. 67-86.

Peterson, J. A., 1966b, Stratigraphic vs. structural controls on carbonate-mound hydrocarbon accumulation, Aneth Area, Paradox basin: American Association of Petroleum Geologists Bulletin, v. 50, p. 2068-2081.

Peterson, J. A., and R. J. Hite, 1969, Pennsylvanian evaporite-carbonate cycles and their relation to petroleum occurrence, southern Rocky Mountains: American Association of Petroleum Geologists Bulletin, v. 53, p. 884-908.

Peterson, J. A., and H. R. Ohlen, 1963, Pennsylvanian shelf carbonates, Paradox basin, *in* R. O. Bass and S. L. Sharps, eds., Shelf carbonates of the Paradox basin: Four Corners Geological Society, p. 65-79.

Peterson, J. A., and D. L. Smith, 1986, Rocky Mountain paleogeography through geologic time, *in* J. A. Peterson, ed., Paleotectonics and sedimentation in the Rocky Mountain Region: American Association of Petroleum Geologists Memoir 41, p. 3-19.

Picard, M. D., 1958, Subsurface structure, Aneth and adjacent areas, San Juan County, Utah, *in* A. F. Sanborn, ed., Guidebook to the geology of the Paradox basin: Intermountain Association of Petroleum Geologists, p. 226-230.

Pray, L. C., and J. L. Wray, 1963, Porous algal facies (Pennsylvanian), Honaker Trail, San Juan Canyon, Utah, *in* R. O. Bass and S. L. Sharps, eds., Shelf carbonates of the Paradox basin: Four Corners Geological Society, p. 204-234.

Quigley, M. D., 1958, Aneth field and surrounding area, *in* A. F. Sanborn, ed., Guidebook to the geology of the Paradox basin: Intermountain Association of Petroleum Geologists, p. 247-253.

Roylance, M. H., 1984, Significance of botryoidal aragonite in early diagenetic history of phylloid algal mounds in Bug and Papoose Canyon fields, southeastern Utah and southwestern Colorado (abs.): American Association of Petroleum Geologists, v. 68, p. 523.

Shoemaker, E. M., J. E. Case, and D. P. Elston, 1958, Salt anticlines of the Paradox basin, *in* A. F. Sanborn, ed., Guidebook to the geology of the Paradox basin: Intermountain Association of Petroleum Geologists, p. 39-59.

Spoelhof, R. W., 1976, Pennsylvanian stratigraphy and paleotectonics of the western San Juan Mountains, southwestern Colorado, *in* R. C. Epis and R. W. Weimer, eds., Studies in Colorado field geology: Professional Contributions of the Colorado School of Mines No. 8, p. 159-179.

Stevenson, G. M., and D. L. Baars, 1986, The Paradox: a pull-apart basin of Pennsylvanian age, *in* J. A. Peterson, ed., Paleotectonics and sedimentation in the Rocky Mountain Region, United States: American Association of Petroleum Geologists Memoir 41, p. 513-539.

Stokes, W. L., 1948, Geology of the Utah-Colorado salt dome region, with emphasis on Gypsum Valley, *in* Guidebook to the geology of Utah, 2: Utah Geological Society, 50 p.

Stokes, W. L., 1956, Nature and origin of Paradox basin salt structures, *in* J. A. Peterson, ed., Geology and economic deposits of eastern Utah: Intermountain Association of Petroleum Geologists, 7th Annual Field Conference, p. 42-47.

Szabo, E., and S. A. Wengerd, 1975, Stratigraphy and tectogenesis of the Paradox basin, *in* J. R. Fassett, ed., 8th Field Conference Guidebook, Canyonland Country: Four Corners Geological Society, p. 193-210.

Thackston, J. W., B. L. McCulley, and L. M. Preslo, 1981, Ground-water circulation in the western Paradox Basin, Utah, *in* D. L. Weigand, ed., Geology of the Paradox basin: Rocky Mountain Association of Geologists, Denver, CO, p. 201-225.

Thomaidis, N. D., 1978, Stratigraphy and oil and gas production, Utah (southeast), *in* J. E. Fassett, ed., Oil and gas fields of the Four Corners area: Four Corners Geological Society, p. 62-63.

Welsh, J. E., 1958, Faunizones of the Pennsylvanian and Permian rocks in the Paradox basin, *in* A. F. Sanborn, ed., Guidebook to the geology of the Paradox basin: Intermountain Association of Petroleum Geologists, p. 153-162.

Wengerd, S. A., 1951, Reef limestones of Hermosa Formation, San Juan Canyon, Utah: American Association of Petroleum Geologists Bulletin, v. 35, p. 1038-1051.

Wengerd, S. A., 1955, Biohermal trends in Pennsylvanian strata of San Juan County, Utah, *in* Geology of parts of Paradox, Black Mesa, and San Juan basins: Four Corners Geological Society Field Conference Guidebook, p. 70-77.

Wengerd, S. A., 1958, Pennsylvanian stratigraphy, southwest

shelf, Paradox basin, *in* R. O. Bass and S. L. Sharps, eds., Shelf carbonates of the Paradox basin: Four Corners Geological Society, p. 109-134.

Wengerd, S. A., 1962, Pennsylvanian sedimentation in Paradox basin, Four Corners region, *in* Pennsylvanian system in United States, a symposium: American Association of Petroleum Geologists, p. 264-330.

Wengerd, S. A., and M. L. Matheny, 1958, Pennsylvanian system of Four Corners region: American Association of Petroleum Geologists Bulletin, v. 42, p. 2048-2106.

Wengerd, S. A., and J. W. Strickland, 1954, Pennsylvanian stratigraphy of Paradox salt basin, Four Corners region,

Colorado and Utah: American Association of Petroleum Geologists Bulletin, v. 38, p. 2157-2199.

Wengerd, S. A., and E. Szabo, 1968, Pennsylvanian correlations in southwestern Colorado, *in* J. Shomaker, ed., Guidebook of San Juan-San Miguel-LaPlata region: New Mexico Geological Society, p. 159-164.

Wilson, J. L., 1975, Carbonate facies in geologic history: New York, Springer-Verlag, 471 p.

Wray, J. L., and K. Konishi, 1960, Pennsylvanian and Permian codiacean algae (abs.): Geological Society of America Bulletin, v. 71, p. 2006.

Appendix 1. Field Description

Field name .... *Aneth field*

Ultimate recoverable reserves .... *400 million bbl*

Field location:

    Country .... *U.S.A.*

    State .... *Utah*

    Basin/Province .... *Paradox basin*

Field discovery:

    Year first pay discovered .... *Pennsylvanian Hermosa Formation, Desert Creek zones 1956*

Discovery well name and general location:

    First pay .... *Texaco, Navajo C-1, NW NE Sec. 23, T40S, R24E, San Juan County, Utah*

Discovery well operator .... *Texaco*

IP in barrels per day and/or cubic feet or cubic meters per day:

    First pay .... *1704 BOPD flowing*

All other zones with shows of oil and gas in the field:

Age	Formation	Type of Show
Pennsylvanian	*Hermosa Formation, Ismay zone*	*Oil*

Geologic concept leading to discovery and method or methods used to delineate prospect

Seismic work and surface mapping; play concept was exploration on the southwest carbonate shelf of salt basin. Evidence for the carbonate shelf was from some older wells drilled to south in Utah and in northwest New Mexico. Oil shows and a few small discoveries from carbonate reservoirs had been made in these areas.

Structure:

    Province/basin type .... *Klemme IIA, craton margin composite*

    Tectonic history

    Paradox basin sag was formed as part of southeast-northwest faulting and sagging related to Pennsylvanian-Permian growth of Ancestral Rocky Mountains. Southeast-northwest salt anticline growth in basin center became prominent in early Mesozoic. Broad Laramide uplift of region in late Mesozoic and Tertiary was accompanied by gentle folding and minor faulting, in part by rejuvenation of older structures.

    Regional structure

    Located on basin side of platform or shelf extending northwest from Four Corners platform.

    Local structure

    Structural nose extending to southeast from Bluff anticline; structural closure on field is about 150 ft, much of which may be due to draping and compaction over carbonate buildup.

Trap:

    Trap type(s)

    Primarily stratigraphic; isolated carbonate mound buildup; porosity deteriorates rapidly on edge of field due to thinning of reservoir facies, change in organic framework, and anhydrite sealing.

Basin stratigraphy (major stratigraphic intervals from surface to deepest penetration in field):

Chronostratigraphy	Formation	Depth to Top in ft (m)
Upper Jurassic	*Morrison*	*Surface to 600 (183)*
Lower Jurassic	*Navajo Sandstone*	*1200 (366)*
Upper Triassic	*Chinle*	*2100 (640)*
Permian	*Cutler*	*3100 (946)*
Pennsylvanian	*Hermosa*	*4800 (1464)*
Pennsylvanian–Desmoinesian	*Ismay zone*	*5500 (1678)*

	Desert Creek zone	5700 (1738)
Mississippian	Leadville Limestone	7100 (2166)
Devonian	Elbert	7500 (2288)
Cambrian	Ignacio	8100 (2470)
Precambrian	Crystalline rocks	8400 (2562)

Reservoir characteristics:

Number of reservoirs .... *One main reservoir, comprised of several semi-isolated intervals*
Formations .... *Hermosa Formation (Group); Desert Creek zone*
Ages .... *Pennsylvanian (Desmoinesian)*
Depths to tops of reservoirs .... *5600–5800 ft (1708–1769 m)*
Gross thickness (top to bottom of producing interval) .... *200 ft (61 m)*
Net thickness—total thickness of producing zones
    Average .... *165 ft (50.6 m)*
    Maximum .... *205 ft (62.5 m)*
Lithology
Dolomitized to lightly dolomitized algal limestone; leached and recrystallized oolitic limestone; fine to medium crystalline dolomite
Porosity type .... *Intergranular to vuggy porosity with intercrystalline and moldic porosity*
Average porosity *10%*
Average permeability .... *15 md (average ranges from 3.0 to 27 md, depending on reservoir)*

Seals:
  Upper
    Formation, fault, or other feature .... *Gothic shale*
    Lithology .... *Organic-rich dolomitic shale*
  Lateral
    Formation, fault, or other feature .... *Permeability loss due to facies change and anhydrite sealing*
    Lithology .... *Dolomite, dolomitic shale and anhydrite*

Source:
  Formation and age .... *Hermosa Formation, Chimney Rock and Gothic shales (Desmoinesian)*
  Lithology .... *Organic-rich, dolomitic shale*
  Average total organic carbon (TOC) *1–2%*
  Maximum TOC *4–5%*
  Kerogen type (I, II, or III) .... *NA*
  Vitrinite reflectance (maturation) .... $R_o = 0.8-2.5$
  Time of hydrocarbon expulsion .... *Early to middle Cretaceous*
  Present depth to top of source .... *5500–5700 ft (1678–1738 m)*
  Thickness .... *75–100 ft (22.9–30.5 m)*
  Potential yield .... *NA*

Appendix 2. Production Data

Field name .... *Aneth field*
Field size:
  Proved acres .... *48,000 ac (19,440 ha)*
  Number of wells all years .... *Approx. 850*
  Current number of wells (10/1990) *471*
  Well spacing .... *40 ac (16.2 ha)*
  Ultimate recoverable .... *400 million bbl*

Cumulative production (10/1990) .... *Oil, 364.3 million bbl; gas, 335.1 million bbl*
Annual production (1990) .... *Oil, 6.8 million bbl; gas, 3.6 million bbl*
Annual water production (1990) .... *32 million bbl*
In place, total reserves .... *1100 million bbl*
Primary recovery .... *200 million bbl*
Secondary recovery .... *200 million bbl*
Cumulative water production (10/1990) .... *482.4 million bbl*

Drilling and casing practices:

Amount of surface casing set .... *180, 550, or 1100 ft (55, 168, or 336 m)*
Casing program .... *8⅝-in. to 550 or 1500 ft (168 or 458 m); 5½-in. to TD*
Drilling mud .... *NA*
Bit program .... *NA*
High pressure zones .... *None*

Completion practices:

Interval(s) perforated .... *Intervals range from 8–51 ft (2.4–15.6 m)*
Well treatment .... *Mud acid and petrofrac*

Formation evaluation: .... *NA*

Oil characteristics:

Type .... *Paraffinic*
API gravity .... *40–42°*
Base .... *NA*
Initial GOR .... *660 ft³ gas/bbl oil (116.2 Sm³ gas/m³ oil)*
Sulfur, wt% *0.20%*
Viscosity, SUS .... *0.53–0.54 cp*
Pour point .... *10°F (–12°C)*
Gas-oil distillate .... *NA*

Field characteristics:

Average elevation .... *4750 ft (1449 m)*
Initial pressure .... *2170 psi at –800 ft MSL (14,962 kPa at –244 m MSL)*
Present pressure .... *NA*
Pressure gradient .... *Underpressured*
Temperature .... *120–125°F (48.8–51.7°C)*
Geothermal gradient .... *10–11°F/1000 ft (18.2–20.0°C/1000 m)*
Drive .... *Solution gas*
Oil column thickness .... *450 ft (137 m)*
Oil-water contact .... *–1000 ft (–305 m)*
Connate water *7–54%*
Water salinity, TDS .... *103,000 to 304,000 mg/TDS*
Resistivity of water .... *0.35 at formation temperature*
Bulk volume water (%) .... *NA*

Transportation method and market for oil and gas:
Texas-New Mexico pipeline; Four Corners pipeline to California

Rojo Caballos, South Field— U.S.A.
Delaware Basin, Texas

BERNOLD M. HANSON
Independent Consultant
Midland, Texas

MARK A. GUINAN
Independent Consultant
Midland, Texas

FIELD CLASSIFICATION

BASIN: Permian
BASIN TYPE: Foredeep
RESERVOIR ROCK TYPE: Carbonate

RESERVOIR AGE: Mississippian, Devonian, and Ordovician
PETROLEUM TYPE: Oil and Gas

RESERVOIR ENVIRONMENT OF DEPOSITION: Platform

TRAP DESCRIPTION: Production from faulted anticline masked by an overlying allochthonous block of limestone that was deposited in center of basin by gravity sliding

LOCATION

The Rojo Caballos, South field is located in northwest Pecos County, Texas, approximately 30 mi (48 km) northwest of the city of Ft. Stockton, and about 10 mi (16 km) south of the community of Coyanosa. Structurally, the field is near the east flank of the Delaware basin and adjacent to the Central basin platform (Figure 1). The Delaware basin, which is a subbasin of the Permian basin, contains the thickest sedimentary sequence within the Permian basin proper.

The Rojo Caballos and Rojo Caballos, South fields encompass 17 sections (10,880 ac or 4400 ha) of land and contain six oil- and gas-producing horizons: the Bell Canyon Formation of the Permian Delaware Mountain Group, the Permian Wolfcamp sandstone, the Pennsylvanian Atoka detrital cherty limestone, the Mississippian limestone, the Devonian chert, and the Ellenburger dolomite (Table 1).

Most of the other significant fields in the area are deep Ellenburger gas fields varying in depth from approximately 15,000 ft (4500 m) to 22,000 ft (6600 m). These fields are Gomez, Coyanosa, Toro, Waha, Northwest Hamon, and Rojo Caballos, West. Total ultimate gas recovery in the Rojo Caballos, South field from the combined Ellenburger, Devonian, and Mississippian reservoirs is estimated to be 233.5 billion cubic feet (bcf). The Rojo Caballos, South field is unique because it is overlain by a slide block that masks the underlying structure.

HISTORY

Pre-Discovery

The Rojo Caballos, South field was not discovered for some 12 years after shallower production had been established in the Rojo Caballos field. In 1960, Mobil Oil Company drilled the No. 1 Moore to a total depth of 15,300 ft (4590 m), which was the discovery well for the Rojo Caballos Pennsylvanian field (Figure 2). This well was drilled on an interpreted Ellenburger seismic closure. The well never reached the Ellenburger, but bottomed in the Pennsylvanian Atoka section and was completed in that zone for 102 million cubic feet of gas per day (102 MMCFG/day) from perforations at 15,041 ft (4512 m) to 15,147 ft (4544 m).

Subsequently, Mobil drilled three more producers to the Atoka horizon, one of which was the No. 1 Schlosser (Figures 2 and 3), which found a repeated section that included the Atoka, Barnett, and Mississippian limestone prior to penetrating the in situ Wolfcamp, Pennyslvanian Atoka, and the Upper Mississippian Barnett. The well was plugged back and completed in 1961 in the first Atoka section and was the structurally highest well in the field. The repeated section appeared to be the result of a reverse fault.

In 1963, Roden Oil Company drilled the first of two deep tests in the field area. The Roden #1 State-McIntyre was drilled to a total depth of 22,035 ft

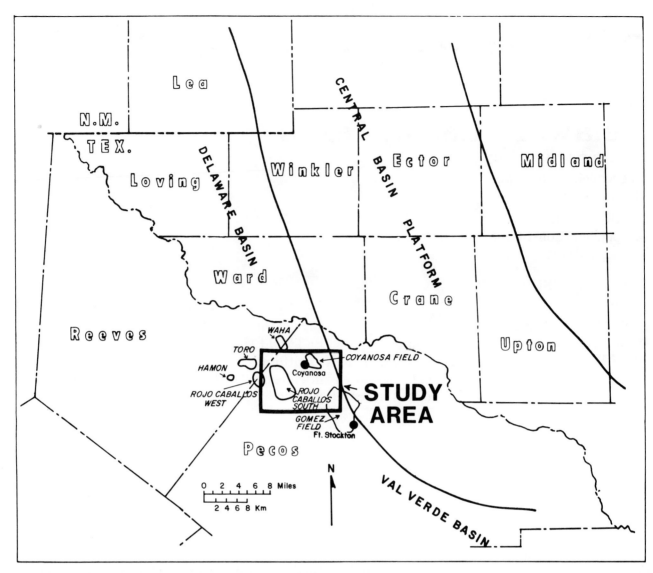

Figure I. Regional map of the Permian basin, highlighting study area.

(6677 m) in the Ellenburger Formation, from which salt water was recovered. The well was plugged back to 13,000 ft (3939 m) and was completed as the discovery well in the Wolfcamp from perforations 10,936 to 10,942 ft (3314–3316 m). When the electrical logs were released to the industry in 1964 and a comparison was made with the logs from the Mobil #1 Schlosser, it was apparent that a reverse fault would not satisfy the observed conditions. The two wells were 2 mi (3.2 km) apart, and although the Roden well lacked the Atoka pay of the Mobil well, the Mississippian limestone sections were almost identical in thickness and in character (Figure 3). The Roden well thickness was 700 ft (212 m) and the Mobil well was 672 ft (204 m). Both wells re-entered the Wolfcamp at approximately the same interval and were correlative to the Mobil well's total

depth in the lower Atoka section. The second Mississippian limestone section in the Roden well was 385 ft (117 m) thick, which was near the thickness of other wells in nearby fields such as Toro and Rojo Caballos, West. Rather than a reverse fault, a submarine slide more closely fit the observed phenomenon (Figure 4).

The second deep test to be drilled in the Rojo Caballos field was the Union Texas Petroleum—Chambers & Kennedy #1 Weatherby, which was completed in 1968 (Figure 3). The total depth was 22,193 ft (6725 m) in the Ellenburger dolomite, from which salt water was recovered on testing. The well was plugged back to 16,043 ft (4862 m) and completed in a detrital zone that the operators identified as Atoka. The well did not have the slide block that was present in the Mobil #1 Schlosser or the Roden

Table 1. Stratigraphic column West Texas–Southeast New Mexico

System	Series	Northwest Shelf	Central Basin Platform	Midland Basin & Eastern Shelf	Delaware Basin	Val Verde Basin	
Permian	Ochoa	Dewey Lake, Rustler, Salado	Dewey Lake, Rustler, Salado	Dewey Lake, Rustler, Salado	Dewey Lake, Rustler, Salado, Castile	Rustler, Salado	● □
	Guadalupe	Tansill, Yates, Seven Rivers, Queen, Grayburg, San Andres, Glorieta	Tansill, Yates, Seven Rivers, Queen, Grayburg, San Andres, Glorieta	Tansill, Yates, Seven Rivers, Queen, Grayburg, San Andres, San Angelo	Delaware Mt Group, Bell Canyon, Cherry Canyon, Brushy Canyon	Tansill, Yates, Seven Rivers, Queen, Grayburg, San Andres	● △ □
	Leonard	Yeso / Clear Fork / Wichita / Abo	Clear Fork, Wichita	Leonard, Spraberry–Dean	Bone Spring	Leonard	● △ □
	Wolfcamp	Wolfcamp	Wolfcamp	Wolfcamp	Wolfcamp	Wolfcamp	● △ □
Pennsylvanian	Virgil	Cisco	Cisco	(Absent or Thin) / Cisco	(Absent or Thin)	(Absent or Thin)	● △ □
	Missouri	Canyon	Canyon	Canyon			● △ □
	Des Moines	Strawn	Strawn	Strawn	Strawn	Strawn	● △ □
	Atoka	Atoka — Bend	Atoka — Bend	Atoka — Bend	Atoka — Bend	Atoka — Bend	● △ □
	Morrow	Morrow	(Absent)	(Absent)	Morrow	(Absent)	● △ □
Mississippian	Chester, Meremec, Osage	Chester, Meremec—, Osage	Chester, Meremec—"Barnett", Osage	Chester, Meremec—"Barnett", Osage	Chester, Meremec—"Barnett", Osage	Chester, Meremec—"Barnett", Osage	
	Kinderhook	Kinderhook, Woodford	Kinderhook, Woodford, Devonian	Kinderhook, Woodford, Devonian	Kinderhook, Woodford, Devonian	Woodford, Devonian	□
Devonian		Devonian, Silurian (Undifferentiated)	Devonian, Silurian SH, Fusselman	Devonian, Silurian SH, Fusselman	Devonian, Mid. Silurian, Fusselman	Devonian, Mid. Silurian, Fusselman	□
Silurian							△
Ordovician	Upper	Montoya	Montoya	Sylvan, Montoya	Sylvan, Montoya	Sylvan, Montoya	● □
	Middle	Simpson	Simpson	Simpson	Simpson	Simpson	
	Lower	Ellenburger	Ellenburger	Ellenburger	Ellenburger	Ellenburger	
Cambrian	Upper	Cambrian	Cambrian	Cambrian	Cambrian	Cambrian	● △ □
Precambrian							

● Reservoir Rock   △ Source Rock   □ Seal

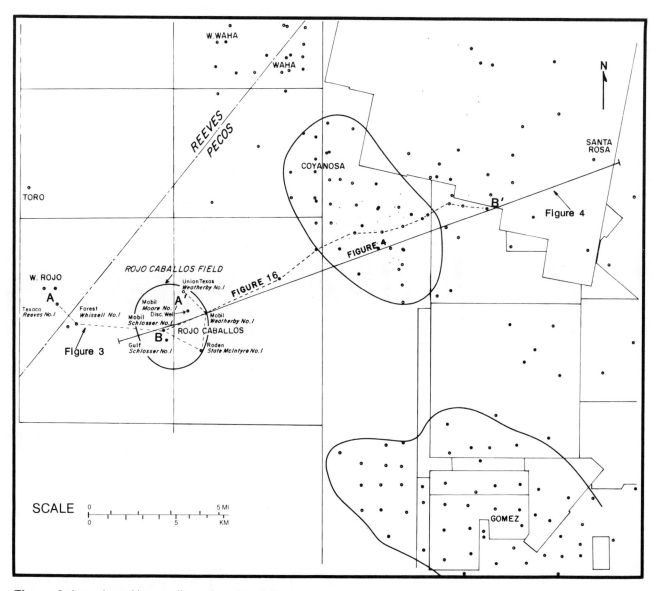

Figure 2. Location of key wells and cross sections.

#1 State-McIntyre, but the Atoka detrital section was at the same stratigraphic interval. No further deep drilling was done in the Rojo Caballos field until the drilling of the discovery well in the Rojo Caballos, South field in 1972–1973.

In 1965, the Cactus Drilling Company No. 1 McCarty was drilled and completed as a Delaware Mountain Group sandstone well at a depth of 5258 ft (1577 m). The well was put in the Rojo Caballos, Delaware field and had a potential of 35 BOPD and 23 BWPD.

Discovery

Guinan (1971a, 1971b) and Hanson agreed that a large-scale submarine slide was present in the area (Figure 4), the toe of which originated in the Coyanosa field to the east, which traversed the sea floor to Rojo Caballos, a distance of some 7 mi (11 km). The event occurred in early Wolfcamp time.

A lease block was assembled on a farmout from Mobil Oil Company et al. and a subsurface interpretation was made by the authors in an effort to get the prospect drilled. The slide block overlying the Rojo Caballos, South prospect was interpreted to be analogous to the Heart Mountain slide block in the Big Horn basin of Wyoming (Pierce, 1941, 1957; Hanson and Guinan, 1975).

The Rojo Caballos, South prospect was submitted to the Gulf Oil Corporation. The local management agreed with the slide concept and committed to a one-half interest in the prospect. A seismic shooting option was granted to Union Oil Company of California, and two seismic lines were run across the area (Figures 5, 6, and 7). Mr. Robert J. Pervinsek,

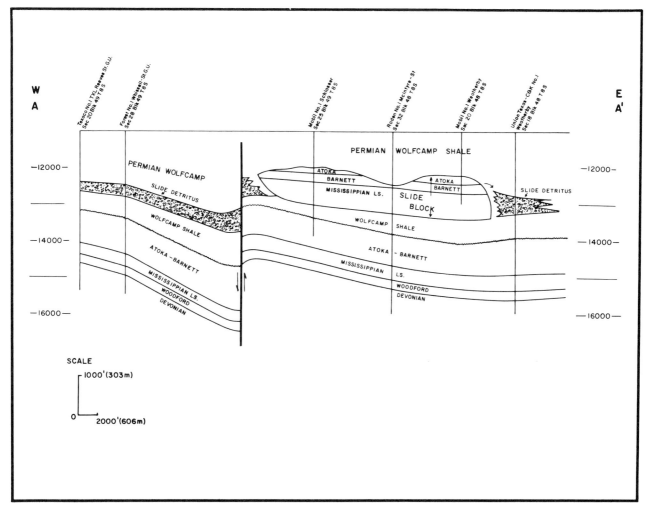

Figure 3. West to east cross section A-A' from the Rojo Caballos, West field through Rojo Caballos and Rojo Caballos, South fields. Location on Figure 2. The Mobil No. 1 Schlosser was the first well to encounter a repeat section at Rojo Caballos, interpreted at the time to be the result of reverse faulting.

geophysicist with Union Oil of California, interpreted the two seismic lines to show a slide block above an asymmetrical fold (Figures 8 and 9). The seismic interpretation also indicated a fault on the west side of the structure. Mr. Pervinsek was unable to convince Union Oil to take an interest in the prospect. The authors were given permission to use the seismic data in finding another participant. Superior Oil took the other one-half interest, after which Gulf and Superior jointly did additional seismic work.

The No. 1 Fred Schlosser located in Sec. 25 was spudded in July 1972 and was drilled to a total depth of 21,630 ft (6489 m). This was the discovery well for the Rojo Caballos, South Ellenburger field. The well was potentialed for 84 MMCFG/day from perforations from 20,791 ft (6244 m) to 21,429 ft (6435 m) and from open hole below the 5-in. liner set at 21,429 ft (6435 m) and total depth of 21,630 ft (6489 m).

Post-Discovery

A continuous development drilling program resulted in eight Ellenburger producers and no dry holes (Figure 10). In the process of drilling and establishing Ellenburger production, hydrocarbon shows were encountered in the Mississippian and the Devonian formations. The field now has ten Devonian wells (Figure 11) and one Mississippian producer (Figure 12), which is completed in the Mississippian section of the slide block. Five Pennsylvanian Atoka wells of the Rojo Caballos field are also completed in the slide block. Since the 1965 discovery of gas in the Bell Canyon Formation of the Delaware Mountain Group, 11 Bell Canyon wells have been completed in the Rojo Caballos, Delaware field.

Several types of completions have been used in the various pay horizons. Some of the Ellenburger wells

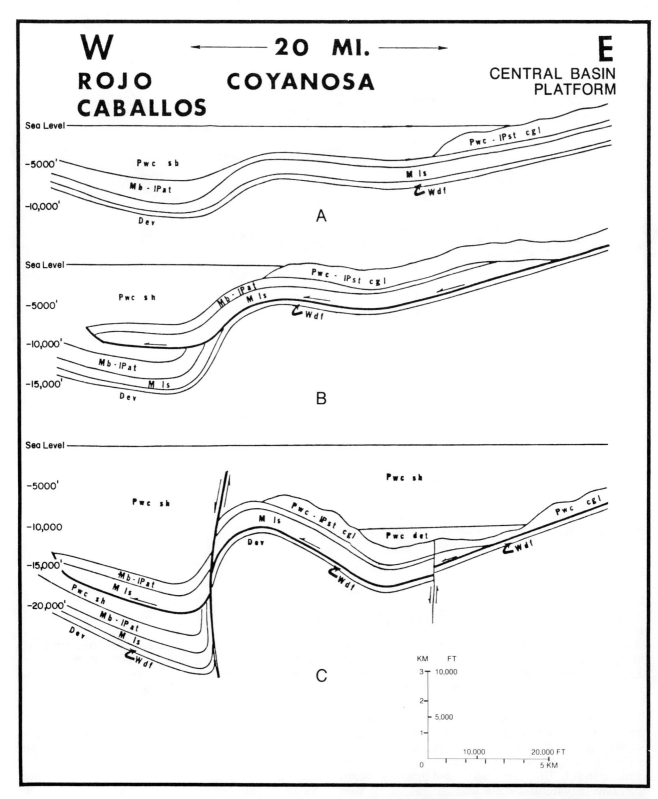

Figure 4. Progressive slide development from the Central Basin platform through the Coyanosa area into the Rojo Caballos area. The location of the diagrammatic cross section is shown on Figure 2. Length about 20 mi (32 km). (A) Early Wolfcamp prior to slide. (B) Middle Wolfcamp post slide. (C) Late Wolfcamp–early Leonard. Formation abbreviations: PWC Sh, Wolfcamp shale; PWC IPst Cgl, Wolfcamp-Strawn conglomerate; MB-IPat, Mississippian Barnett Atoka undivided; Mls, Mississippian limestone; Dev, Devonian; Pwc det, Wolfcamp detritus.

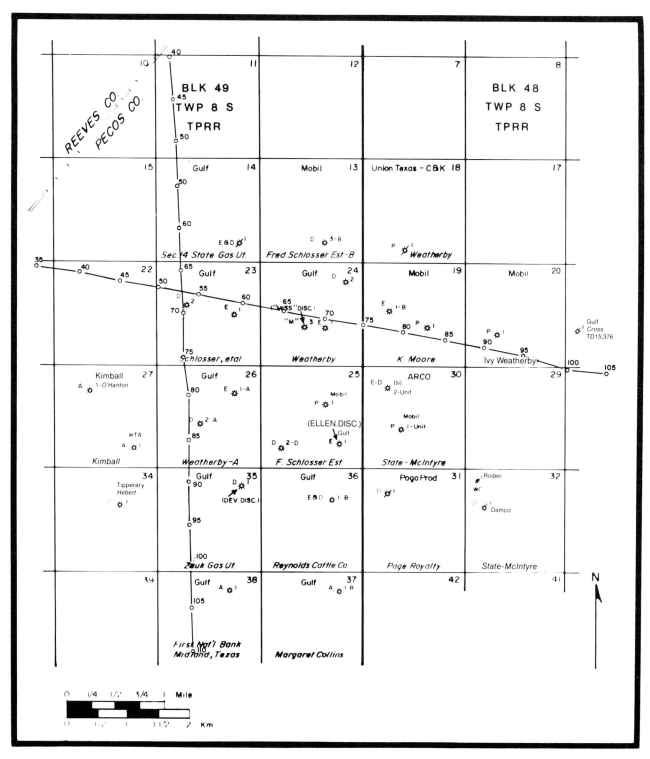

Figure 5. Locations of east-west and north-south seismic lines shown on Figures 6 and 7. This shooting was prior to the drilling of the discovery well. The interpretation that was the basis for drilling the discovery is shown on Figures 8 and 9.

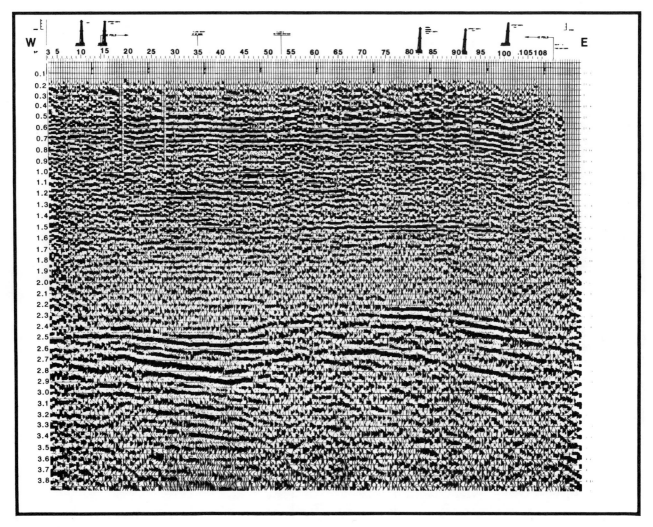

Figure 6. East-west seismic cross section, original data acquired prior to drilling the discovery. Figure 5 shows location and Figure 8 shows interpretation. From shot point 35 to 105 is about 5.8 mi (9.4 km).

have been completed open hole while others are producing through casing perforations. All of the wells have been acidized, and in some instances hydraulic fracturing was used to increase productivity. Three of the Ellenburger tests have been plugged back to the Devonian (Figure 10). Four wells were drilled only to the Devonian (Figure 11) and completed in this pay zone. One well was drilled and completed in the Mississippian (Figure 12). The Mississippian, Devonian, and Ellenburger wells are drilled on 640 ac (259 ha) proration units. There are no dual completions.

DISCOVERY METHOD

The Rojo Caballos, South field was discovered as the result of some imaginative subsurface geology that was subsequently supported by improved seismic techniques available in the 1970 decade

compared to those of the 1960 period (Figure 13). Subsurface data were obtained from three wells drilled in the development of the Rojo Caballos field: Socony Mobil #1 Schlosser Estate Sec. 25, Blk. 49, T8S, TPRR (drilled in 1961); Roden Oil Co. #1 McIntyre-State, Sec. 32, Blk. 48, T8S, TPRR (drilled in 1963); and Union Texas Petroleum #1 Weatherby, Sec. 18, Blk. 48, T8S, TPRR (drilled in 1968). These three wells furnished key information for the subsurface interpretation (Figure 3). This interpretation included, first, a slide block masking a deeper structure and, second, a strong component of east-northeast dip present at the in situ Mississippian limestone horizon (Figure 13). The Socony Mobil #1 Schlosser Estate, although it did not quite reach the in situ Mississippian limestone, was some 800 ft (240 m) high to the Union Texas well and 560 ft (168 m) high to the Roden well. (It should be noted that the Mississippian limestone is generally conformable with all the subjacent beds.) Further, a down-to-west fault or structural rollover would be

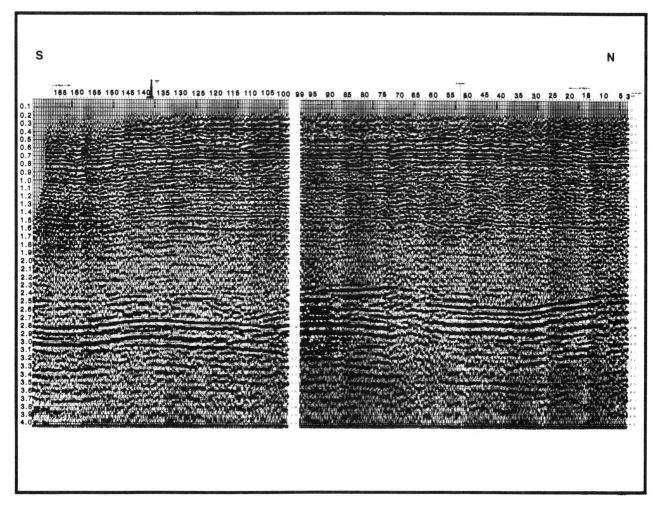

Figure 7. North-south seismic cross section original data. Location shown on Figure 5 and interpretation on Figure 9. From shot point 40 to 110 is 5.8 mi (9.4 km).

necessary from a three-point dip standpoint to accommodate the east component of dip displayed between the Texaco #1 TXL Reeves State, Sec. 20, Blk. 49, T8S, TPRR, and the Forrest Oil Company #1 Whissell-State, Sec. 27, Blk. 49, T8S, TPRR, which are on the east flank of the Rojo Caballos, West field (Figures 3 and 14).

STRUCTURE

The slide block maximum dimensions are 16 mi (26 km) from east to west, 9 mi (14 km) from north to south, and 2000 ft (600 m) thick. Apparent lateral displacement, east to west, is 7 mi (11 km) (Figure 15).

At the base of the allochthonous plate (Figure 4) was the thick, competent Mississippian limestone. The slide was triggered by the weight of the thick Permian–Pennsylvanian conglomerates shed from the Central basin uplift on the eastern side of the

Coyanosa field coupled with the subsidence of the basin on the western and southwestern flank of the Coyanosa field (Figure 4). The slide sole followed the bedding plane at the top of the Woodford in the eastern two-thirds of the area; while in the western, the arcuate toe of the slide cut-up the stratigraphic section along the western and southwestern flanks of Coyanosa and continued along the sea floor to Rojo Caballos and Rojo Coballos, South fields.

The Rojo Caballos, South field structure, which trends northwest-southeast, is bounded by a fault on the south that has a throw of 1100+ ft (330 m). Steep dip on the west side of the structure may be associated with a fault. There is approximately 1000 ft (300 m) of effective closure at the Ellenburger horizon (Figure 10). The apex of the structure on the top of the Devonian (Figure 11) and Mississippian limestone (Figure 13) appears to be conformable with the Mississippian structure map on the allochthonous block (Figure 12).

91

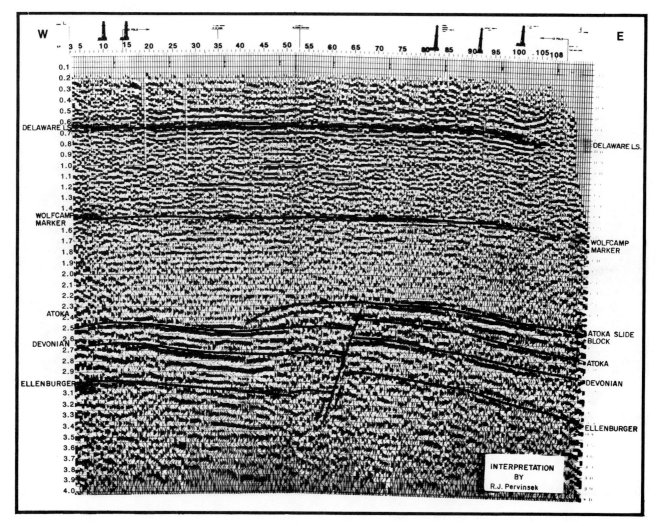

Figure 8. East-west interpreted cross section through Rojo Caballos, South prior to drilling discovery well.

This is the same cross section as that shown uninterpreted by Figure 6. Location shown on Figure 5.

The Rojo Caballos, South anticline is one of several north–south-oriented anticlines on a west-to-east–trending structural platform with major down-to-the-south faulting on the south. The fields on these anticlines are gas-producing from the Ellenburger Formation and are from west to east: West Hamon; Hamon; Rojo Caballos, West; and Rojo Caballos, South. There is a periodicity of about 4 mi (6.4 km) from apex to apex along this structural trend, with decreasing amplitude from east to west.

STRATIGRAPHY

The lower Ordovician Ellenburger dolomite, the main gas producer in the Rojo Caballos, South field, is the oldest stratigraphic unit penetrated. The deepest Ellenburger penetration in the field was 1006 ft (302 m) in the Gulf #1 Weatherby, Sec. 24, Blk. 49, T8S, TPRR. Four miles (6.4 km) to the west,

in the Rojo Caballos, West field, 1505 ft (456 m) of Ellenburger was penetrated in the Texaco #1 TXL Reeves-State, Sec. 20, Blk. 49, T8S, TPRR (Figure 16).

The Simpson shales of Middle Ordovician age (Figures 17B and 17C) are believed to be the primary source beds as well as the seal for Ellenburger production. The Simpson unconformably overlies the Ellenburger and is composed predominantly of gray shales interbedded with limestone and occasional sandstone. The average thickness of the Simpson within this area is approximately 2000 ft.

The source rock and seal responsible for oil accumulation in the Devonian reservoirs is widely believed to be the Woodford Shale, which is Upper Devonian in age and overlain by middle and Upper Mississippian limestones and dark shales (Figure 17B). The Woodford formation is predominantly a black to brown shale unit, which evolved from a transgressive marine unit, a product of a stagnant basin. The average thickness of the Woodford in the Rojo Caballos, South field is approximately 200 ft.

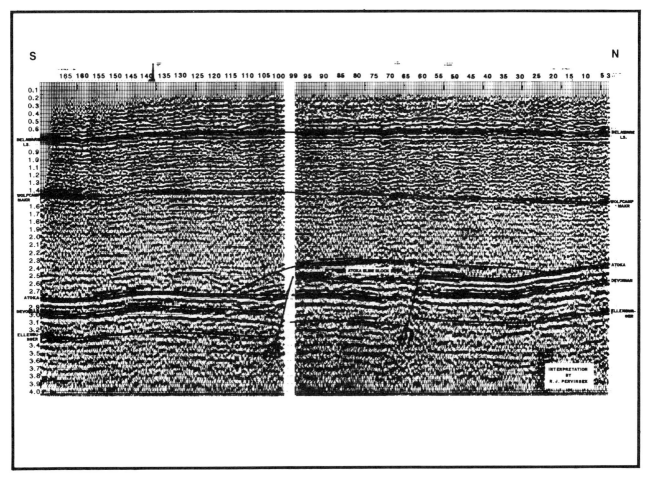

Figure 9. North-south interpreted seismic cross section through Rojo Caballos, South prior to drilling discovery well. This is the same cross section as shown uninterpreted by Figure 7. Location shown by Figure 5.

Production within the Devonian occurs in chert breccias in structural traps, generally horsts and faulted anticlines. The Woodford Shale unit is believed to be the source rock for the Mississippian limestone as well. Production within the Mississippian occurs through irregularly distributed porous beds that have low permeabilities.

Sandstone reservoirs within the Pennsylvanian are presumed to have been charged from the Morrow and Atokan basinal shales, the thin shales of the Strawn, or the shales of the Cisco and Wolfcamp age rocks. These beds may serve as lateral seals. The Wolfcamp is described as a cyclic sequence of siltstone, greenish-gray shale, thin limestone beds, and some conglomerate. The limestones are interbedded with basinal clastics, which are shales with a high content of sandstone and siltstone. The shales are most likely to be the source beds, whereas the limestone and/or the sandstones serve as the reservoir rocks. The thickness of the Wolfcamp averages approximately 5950 ft (1785 m) in the area

of interest. Hydrocarbon reservoirs within the Pennsylvanian may occur through stratigraphic or structural trapping. Oil may have migrated from the basin to the surrounding uplifts and shelves and been converted to gas through maturation.

Basinal Leonardian facies, which contains the Bone Spring formation, is its own source rock as well as reservoir. It may also be the source to some of the Delaware Mountain Group production. The entire Bone Spring unit of 7400 ft (2220 m) covers the Rojo Caballos, South field.

The Delaware Mountain Group has been divided into three formations: the Bell Canyon, Cherry Canyon, and Brushy Canyon. These units contain basinal facies of dark shales and very fine sandstones to siltstones. The group is probably the source of its own oil. There is a lack of major unconformities within the Delaware; therefore, losses from oil-bearing rocks were prevented. Production is found in stratigraphic porosity traps within the basinal sand units or in channel deposits that pinch out updip

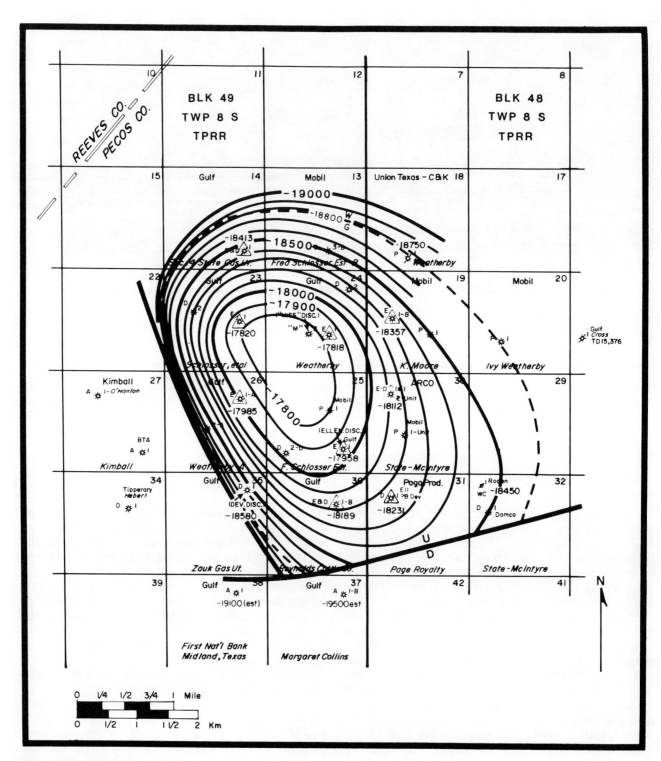

Figure 10. Structure contour map of top of Ellenburger after discovery. Triangles are locations of Ellenburger producing wells. Contour interval, 100 ft.

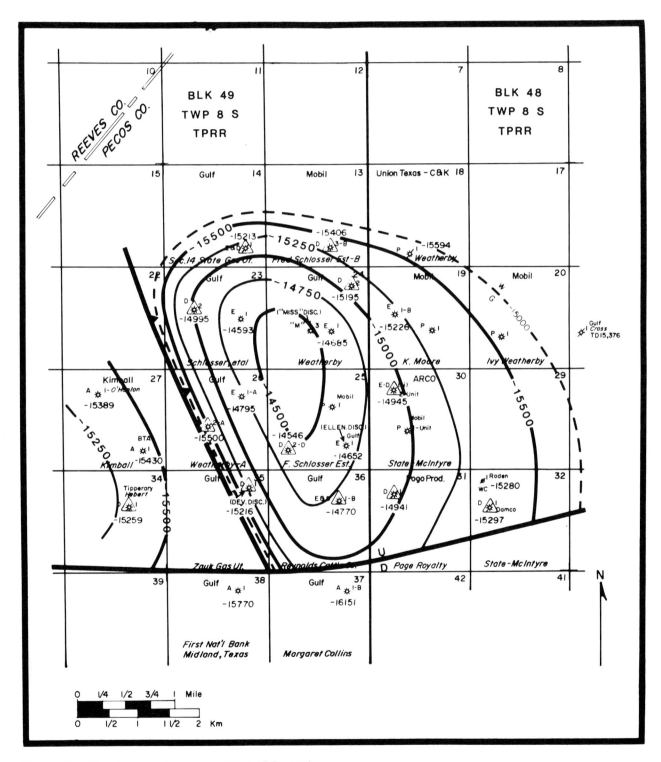

Figure 11. Structure contour map of top of Devonian. Triangles are locations of wells productive from the Devonian. Contour interval, 250 ft.

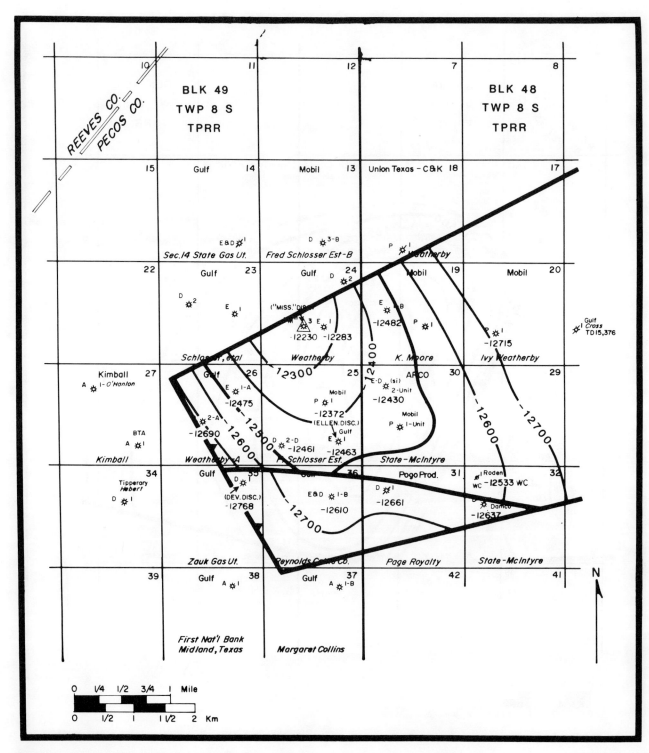

Figure 12. Structure contour map on top of allochthonous block. Triangle is location of Mississippian
producing well (discovery well). Contour interval, 100 ft.

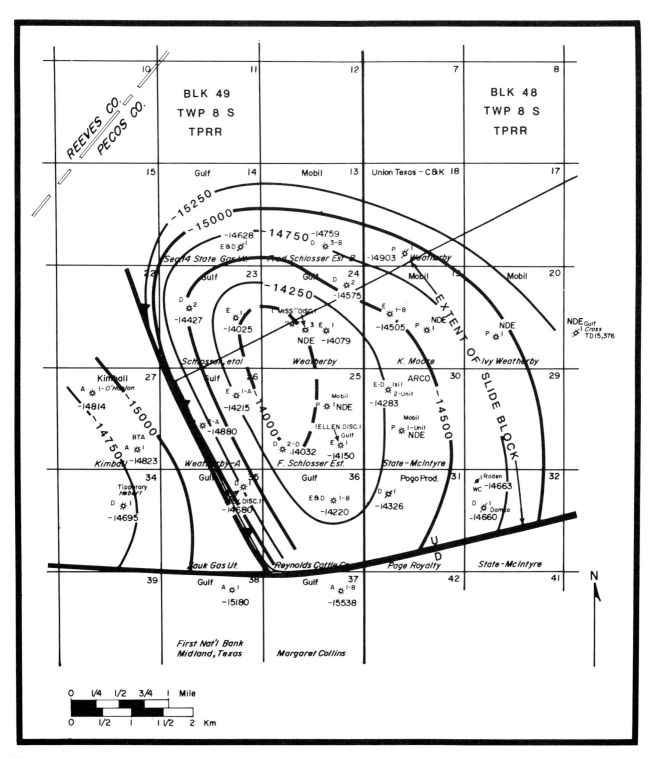

Figure 13. In place structure contour map of top of Mississippian limestone. P, Pennsylvanian producer; A, Pennsylvanian Atoka producer; M, Mississippian producer; D, Devonian producer; E, Ellenburger producer. Contour interval, 250 ft.

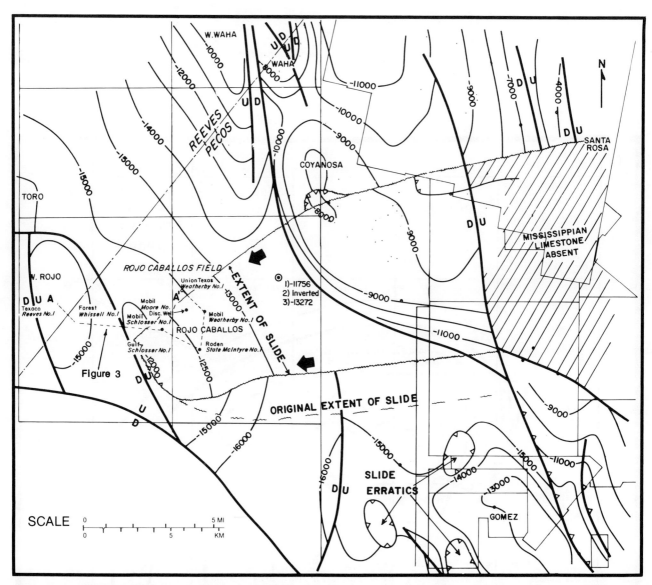

Figure 14. Structure contour map of top of Mississippian limestone showing slide block and its areal extent. Contour interval, 1000 ft.

or laterally, and also from structural traps. Open fractures are unknown because of the soft nature of the Delaware Mountain Group.

TRAP

In the Ellenburger and Devonian pools of Rojo Caballos, South, the trap below the slide block is an asymmetrical anticline with a fault on the south and west side of the fold. The Simpson shales form the seal for the Ellenburger Formation, and the Woodford Shale serves as the seal for the Devonian. The Mississippian has the Barnett Shale for its seal; however, this formation only produces in the slide

block. Within the Pennsylvanian, the trapping mechanism consists of limestone porosity zones, which are covered by organic-rich shales. In addition, the formations of this system may have structural closure. The Delaware Mountain Group oil is trapped by porosity pinch-outs on structural noses.

Reservoir

At Rojo Caballos, South, reservoir depth varies as a result of the asymmetrical folding. The top of the Ellenburger occurs at a depth of approximately 20,000 ft (6000 m) near the apex of the structure. The best porosity occurs approximately 300 ft (91 m) below the top, with a tendency for a loss of porosity

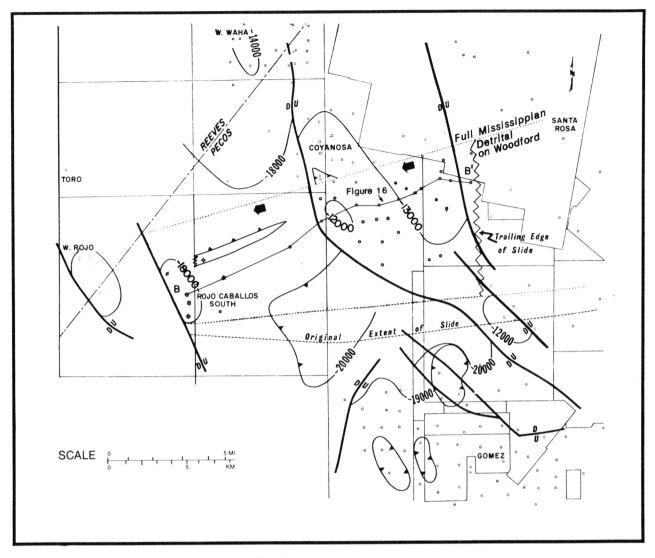

Figure 15. Interpretation of present Ellenburger structure showing wells producing from below the slide block.

on the flanks of the structure. There is approximately 1000 ft (300 m) of structural closure containing a 900 ft (273 m) gas column. The gas-water contact is at –18,800 ft (–5640 m).

The Devonian pay occurs at approximately 17,300 ft (5190 m) at the apex and has in excess of 1250 ft (379 m) of structural closure. The gas-water contact is approximately at –15,700 ft (–4788 m).

Fracturing, especially on the steep west flank of the structure, creates by far the best reservoir in the Devonian in the Rojo Caballos, South field. The Gulf #1 Zauk, Sec. 35, and the Gulf #2 D Weatherby, Sec. 26, Blk. 49, T8S, TPRR, are the structurally lowest, but the best Devonian wells in the field. The fracturing occurs in the upper 200 ft (60 m) of the Devonian.

Stratigraphy and Facies

The oil- and gas-productive horizons penetrated below the slide block in the Rojo Caballos, South field are the Pennsylvanian Atoka, the Mississippian limestone, the Devonian, and the Ellenburger. The characteristics of each are given on the gamma-ray density log (Figures 17A, 17B, and 17C).

The Ellenburger horizon, which is Lower Ordovician in age, is a dolomite, or biomicrite, ranging in color from brown to tan, to gray, and to white, having a very fine to medium crystalline texture, with some samples having coarsely crystalline texture. The porosity ranges from intercrystalline (average being approximately 4%) to cavernous. Veining has been noted, which is indicative of

99

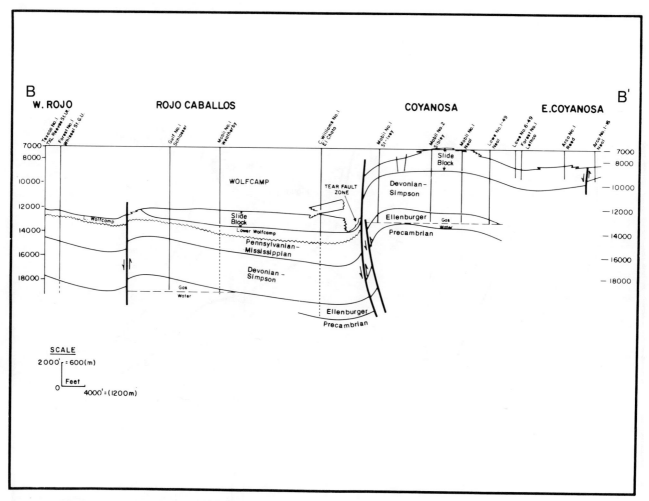

Figure 16. East to west cross section from East Coyanosa to Rojo Caballos, South and Rojo Caballos, West fields. The location of the cross section is indicated on Figure 15.

fractures being present. The top of the Ellenburger is an erosional unconformity. The lower section of the Ellenburger was deposited as a shelf facies, whereas the middle and upper portions of the section were deposited in subtidal and intertidal/supratidal channel belts (Hanson et al., 1988). The wells in the immediate area did not drill through the Ellenburger section; therefore, the total thickness of the section is not known but may be as thick as 1500 ft (450 m).

The Devonian section is approximately 500 ft (150 m) thick and consists predominantly of chert with interstratified limestone and accessory dolomite scattered throughout. The chert is smooth, speckled, and in places translucent and fractured; it occurs in an array of colors of brown, light blue, tan, and white. The limestone occurs as brown, gray, or tan, is partly siliceous, and has a fine to very fine crystalline texture. Dolomite, which is present in very small percentages, is gray or tan, partly siliceous, and finely crystalline in texture. No porosity was noted in the samples, although it has been found that porosity does occur as vugs and intercrystalline spaces and in the chert, porosity resulting from the dissolution of the carbonate constituents of the rock by the formation waters. The Devonian remains as a transgressive marine facies throughout (Hanson et al., 1988).

The Mississippian limestone section is composed of limestone, chert, dolomite, and small percentages of shale. No porosity or permeability was noted in the samples, but the limestone was found to be nonporous and to have a low permeability. The limestone is brown to tan or gray in color and is fine to very fine crystalline, micritic, and sometimes siliceous. The interstratified dolomite occurs in color from shades of tan to gray-tan and has very fine to fine grains. It is occasionally siliceous. The chert found within the Mississippian limestone occurs in a variety of colors ranging from green to brown, blue, gray, or tan. It has a smooth subgranular texture and is in places speckled or translucent. A dark gray, firm shale is interbedded with the limestone, which may also occur in colors of red, green, or brown. The darker colors of the limestone and shale are indicative

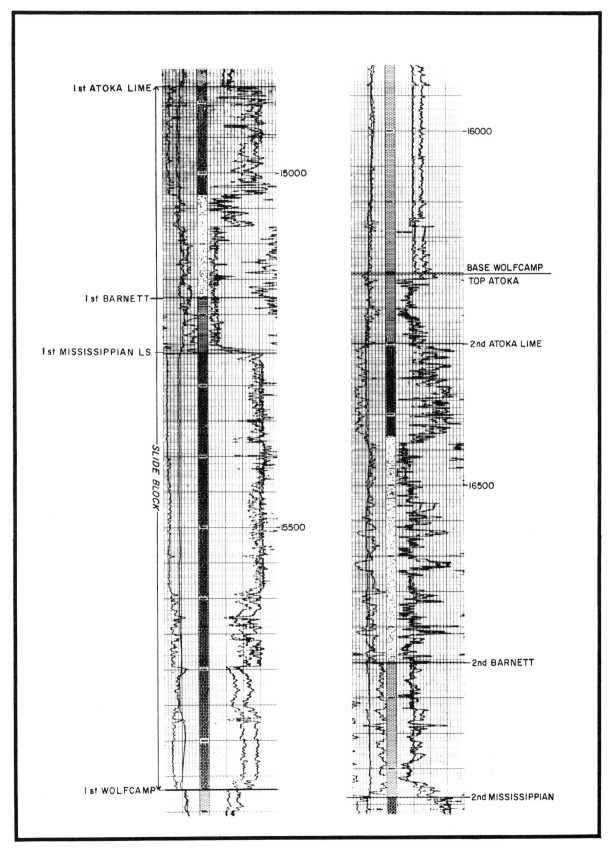

Figure 17A. GR-density log of discovery well from 1st Atoka through 2nd Barnett shale. See Figures 17B and 17C for deeper horizons. Notice that the left column (1st Atoka limestone to top Wolfcamp) is the alloch- thonous slide block over in situ formations seen mainly in the right column (top 1st Wolfcamp downward).

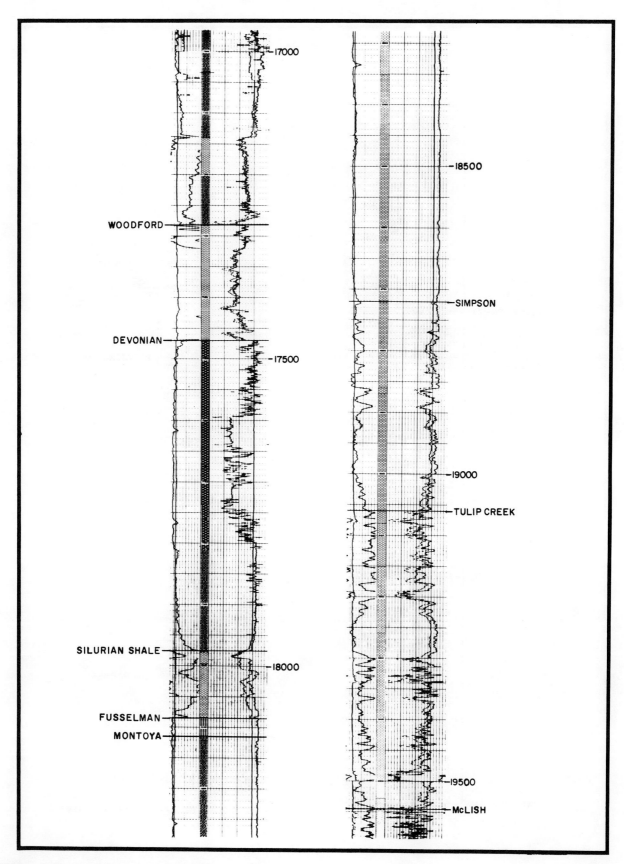

Figure 17B. Continuation of GR-density log from 2nd Mississippian limestone through the top of the Simpson McLish.

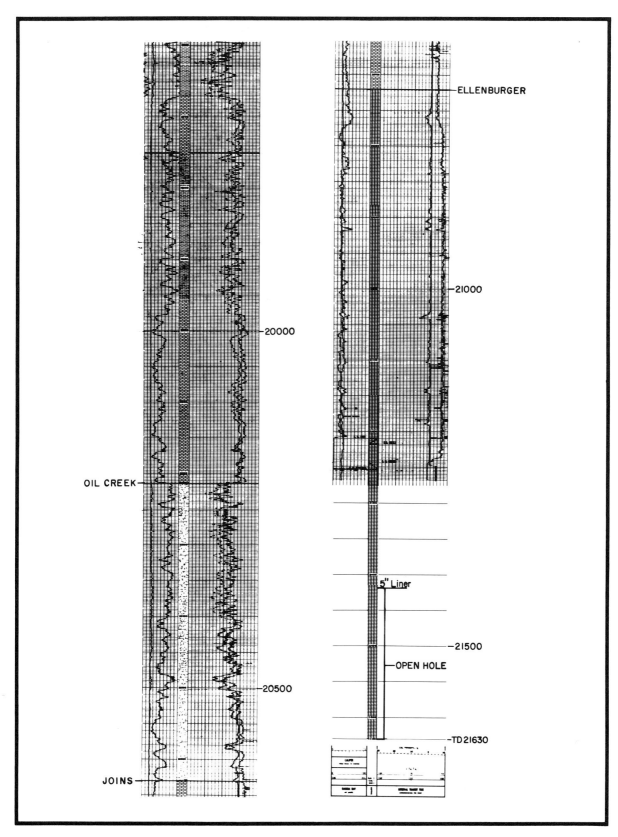

Figure 17C. Continuation of discovery well log from Simpson McLish to total depth of 21,630 ft (6489 m). Bottom 390 ft (117 m) were not logged.

of the fact that this rock is rich in organic content. The thickness of the lower and upper Mississippian sections combined averages 600 ft (180 m).

The Pennsylvanian Atoka section contains dark gray, firm shales at the upper and lower contacts. Shale also occurs throughout the section interbedded with the limestone. The limestone occurs in shades of tan and gray. It has a fine, siliceous, biomicrite texture. Fossils found within this section are foraminifera and crinoids. A very small percentage of basinal sand deposits are found. The sandstone is composed of subrounded grains with siliceous cement. It is gray in color and has a very fine to medium texture. The interbedded cherts are light blue to gray in color and occur as conglomerates. The environment of deposition of this section was that of a deeper marine embayment. The Pennsylvanian accumulations are thin in this portion of the Delaware basin deposited at a time when the environment was sediment starved. The Atoka section varies in thickness from 73 ft (22 m) along the thrust fault line to 450 ft (135 m) thick along the flank of the anticlinal structure.

The Delaware Mountain Group of Guadalupian age is the youngest of the productive horizons within the Rojo Caballos field. This section consists of three separate formations: the Brushy Canyon, the Cherry Canyon, and the Bell Canyon, all of which are basically siltstone interbedded with some beds of limestone and/or sandstone. The upper portion of the Delaware Mountain Group is predominantly a well-sorted, very fine grained sandstone interbedded with siltstones and organic-rich shales. These sediments were transported by saline density currents and deposited in broad anastomosing channels within the stagnant depths of the Delaware basin. The total thickness of the section is approximately 2800 ft (840 m) thick.

EXPLORATION AND DEVELOPMENT CONCEPTS

Subtle traps such as the Rojo Caballos, South field do not abound in the geologic literature, for to the author's knowledge, this field may be unique. However, a combination of detailed subsurface studies combined with new and improved seismic techniques tailored to the specific problem may unravel the most baffling geologic conundrums.

Once discovery has been made, development should proceed with close cooperation between development and exploration geologists and geophysicists to further define the original concept and to position wells to maximize results.

ACKNOWLEDGMENTS

The authors wish to thank Mr. Robert A. Manning at the Permian Basin Stratigraphic Lab for his sample work on the stratigraphy in the area of study and Mr. Robert J. Pervinsek, a consulting geophysicist, for his interpretation of the seismic sections. Thanks go to Mr. A. T. Carleton with Pogo Producing Company, Mr. Willard R. Green with Forrest Oil Company for the drafting, and Mr. George R. Gibson for reviewing the manuscript. Thanks to Ms. Celeste G. Dale with Hanson Corporation for her work on the stratigraphy sections. We are indebted to Mr. David Wright with Mobil Producing for some of the field characteristics and source rock data.

REFERENCES CITED

Galley, J. E., 1958, Oil and geology in the Permian Basin of Texas and New Mexico, in L. J. Weeks, ed., Habitat of oil; a symposium: American Association of Petroleum Geologists, p. 395–446.

Guinan, M. A., 1971a, Slide-block geology, Coyanosa and adjacent areas: Pecos & Reeves Counties, Texas (abstr.): American Association of Petroleum Geologists Bulletin, v. 55, pt. 1, p. 340.

Guinan, M. A., 1971b, More evidence of the slide-block event will follow Delaware basin drilling: Oil & Gas Journal, July 5, p. 120–127.

Hanson, B. M., and M. A. Guinan, 1975, Heart Mountain in west Texas (abstr.): American Association of Petroleum Geologists Bulletin, v. 59, n. 5, p. 911.

Hanson, B. M., et al., 1988, The Permian Basin, Economic Geology, U.S.: Boulder, Colorado, Geological Society of America, The Geology of North America, v. P-2.

Pierce, W. G., 1941, Heart Mountain & South Fork thrusts, Park County, Wyoming: American Association of Petroleum Geologists Bulletin, v. 25, p. 2021–2045.

Pierce, W. G., 1957, Heart Mountain and South Fork detachment thrusts of Wyoming: American Association of Petroleum Geologists Bulletin, v. 41, n. 4, p. 591–626.

Appendix 1. Field Description

Field name .... *Rojo Caballos, South field*

Ultimate recoverable reserves .... *Ellenburger, 125 bcf; Devonian, 105 bcf; Mississippian, 3.5 bcf*

Field location:

    Country .... *U.S.A.*

    State .... *Texas*

    Basin/Province .... *Delaware basin*

Field discovery:

    Year first pay discovered .... *Ellenburger 1973*

    Year second pay discovered .... *Devonian 1977*

    Year third pay discovered .... *Mississippian 1982*

Discovery well name and general location:

    First pay .... *Gulf Oil Corporation, Fred Schlosser Est. No. 1, Sec. 25, Blk. 49, T8, TPRR Co Survey, Pecos County, Texas, 10.5 mi south of Coyanosa (Ellenburger)*

    Second pay .... *Gulf Oil Corporation, Zauk Gas Unit #1, Sec. 35, Blk. 49, T8 TPRR Co. Survey, Pecos County, Texas (Devonian)*

    Third pay .... *Gulf Oil Corporation, Ivy B. Weatherby No. 3, Sec. 24, Blk. 49, T8, TPRR Co. Survey, Pecos County, Texas (Mississippian)*

Discovery well operator .... *Gulf Oil Corporation, Fred Schlosser Est. No. 1 (Ellenburger)*

    Second pay .... *Gulf Oil Corporation, Zauk Gas Unit No. 1 (Devonian)*

    Third pay .... *Gulf Oil Corporation, Ivy B. Weatherby No. 3 (Mississippian)*

IP:

    First pay .... *Ellenburger, 84 MMCFG/day*

    Second pay .... *Devonian, 148 MMCFG/day*

    Third pay .... *Mississippian, 17 MMCFG/day*

All other zones with shows of oil and gas in the field:

Age	Formation	Type of Show
Permian	*Delaware Sand*	*Oil and gas*
	Wolfcamp	*Gas*
Pennsylvanian	*Atoka-Morrow*	*Gas*
Mississippian	*Mississippian limestone*	*Gas*
Devonian	*Devonian*	*Gas*
Ellenburger	*Ellenburger*	*Gas*

Geologic concept leading to discovery and method or methods used to delineate prospect

Prior to the discovery of the Rojo Caballos, South field, Mobil Oil Company drilled the No. 1 K. J. Moore in 1960. This well was the discovery well for the Rojo Caballos field at a total depth of 15,300 ft (4590 m). It was completed in Pennsylvanian Atoka pay from perforation between 15,041 ft (4512 m) and 15,147 ft (4544 m). Development of the Atoka pay was initiated and two wells were drilled deeper that penetrated the Mississippian limestone and re-entered the Wolfcamp shale at about the same stratigraphic interval. One of these wells was drilled to the Ellenburger which was nonproductive. This was when a slide block was first suspected. Using this concept a seismic shooting option was taken over a 4 section block and it confirmed the theory of a slide block and the existence of an underlying structure.

Structure:

    Province/basin type .... *Bally 222; Klemme IIA*

    Tectonic history

    The Rojo Caballos, South field is located in the south-central portion of the deep Delaware subbasin, which is the western element of the Permian basin. The field has an east-west striking fault with 1000+

ROJO CABALLOS

105

ft (300 m) of throw on the south side. There is also a probable fault which has a down to the west displacement on the steep west flank, thereby giving an approximate 1000 ft (300 m) of effective closure at the Ellenburger horizon.

Regional structure
The field lies near the eastern margin of the Delaware basin.

Local structure
Beneath the allochthonous block is a folded and faulted anticlinal structure.

Trap:

Trap type(s)
The allochthonous block has Delaware and Pennsylvanian production on a structural high. Below the block is a faulted anticline where gas is accumulated in the apex of the fold.

Basin stratigraphy (major stratigraphic intervals from surface to deepest penetration in field):
Note that in this stratigraphic column "1st" after formation name indicates the formation in the allochthonous block and "2nd" indicates the formation in situ.

Chronostratigraphy	Formation	Depth to Top in ft (m)
Ochoan	Rustler	984 (300)
Guadalupian	Bell Canyon	5200 (1590)
	Cherry Canyon	5400 (1650)
	Brushy Canyon	7160 (2180)
Leonardian	Bone Spring	8030 (2450)
Wolfcamp	Wolfcamp 1st	10,200 (3110)
	Wolfcamp 2nd	15,870 (4840)
Pennsylvanian	Atoka 1st	14,880 (4540)
	Atoka 2nd	16,300 (4970)
Mississippian	Barnett Shale 1st	15,180 (4630)
	Barnett Shale 2nd	16,750 (5110)
	Mississippian limestone 1st	15,250 (4650)
	Mississippian limestone 2nd	16,940 (5170)
	Woodford	17,280 (5270)
Devonian	Devonian	17,470 (5330)
Silurian	Silurian	17,980 (5480)
	Fusselman	18,080 (5510)
Ordovician	Montoya	18,120 (5530)
	Simpson	18,720 (5710)
	Ellenburger	20,720 (6320)

Reservoir characteristics:
Number of reservoirs 5

Formations .... Bell Canyon formation of Delaware Mountain Group, Atoka-Morrow, Mississippian, Devonian, Ellenburger

Ages .... Permian, Pennsylvanian, Mississippian, Devonian, Ordovician

Depths to tops of reservoirs
Delaware sand, 5200 ft (1560 m)
Atoka-Morrow, 14,000 ft (4200 m)
Mississippian, 14,800 ft (4400 m)
Devonian, 17,800 ft (5340 m)
Ellenburger, 20,000 ft (6000 m) to 21,600 ft (6480 m)

Gross thickness (top to bottom of producing interval)
Delaware, 710 ft (213 m)
Atoka-Morrow, 700 ft (210 m)
Mississippian, 400 ft (120 m)

Devonian, 500 ft (150 m)
Ellenburger, 1100+ ft (330 m)

Net thickness—total thickness of producing zones

Average
Delaware, 80 ft (24 m)
Atoka-Morrow, 150 ft (45 m)
Mississippian, 160 ft (48 m)
Devonian, 120 ft (36 m)
Ellenburger, 900 ft (270 m)

Maximum
Delaware, 200 ft (60 m)
Atoka-Morrow, 250 ft (75 m)
Mississippian, 200 ft (60 m)
Devonian, 300 ft (90 m)
Ellenburger, 1800 ft (540 m)

Lithology
The Ellenburger is predominantly medium to fine-grained crystalline, gray to brown dolomite or biomicrite with fractures and traces of quartz veins and gilsonite filled fractures.
The Devonian consists of predominantly white, brown, mossy, to mottled chert with interstratified limestone and dolomite.
The Mississippian is composed of fine to very fine crystalline (mixtures) limestone, along with interstratified finely crystalline, gray to tan dolomite. Dark gray shale overlays and is interbedded with limestone.
The Pennsylvanian Atoka section contains fine crystalline biomicrite, dark gray to buff-colored limestone interbedded with medium gray to black shales.
Well-sorted very fine grained sandstone and shale constitute the Delaware Mountain Group.

Porosity type
Ellenburger dolomites consist of intercrystalline and fractured porosity. The Devonian consists of fractured and some vugular porosity. Generally, the Mississippian limestone displays only small amounts of vugular and fractured porosity. The Pennsylvanian limestone section contains vugular and secondary porosity. The Delaware Group has both primary and secondary porosity development within the sandstone.

Average porosity
Delaware, 23%
Pennsylvanian, 12%
Mississippian, 4%
Devonian, 7%
Ellenburger, 2%

Average permeability
Delaware, 100 md
Pennsylvanian, 0.1 md
Mississippian, unknown
Devonian, 0.14 md
Ellenburger, 0.02 md

Seals:

Upper

Formation, fault, or other feature	Lithology
Simpson Group	Shales with occasional limestone and sandstone
Woodford Shale	Shale
Pennsylvanian	Shale
Wolfcamp Series	Cyclic sequence of shale with limestone and some conglomerate
Bone Spring formation	Debris flow

107

Lateral

Formation, fault, or other feature	Lithology
Ellenburger fault blocks and anticlines	Dolomite
Devonian horsts and faulted anticlines	Dolomite with chert

Mississippian
  irregularly distributed porous beds
  with low permeability
	Limestones

Pennsylvanian anticlines	Limestones

Delaware
  pinch-outs, or porosity, or structural
  traps
	Sandstones with intermittent bands with shale

Source:

Formation and age	Lithology
Simpson Ordovician	Shales
Woodford Devonian	Shales
Pennsylvanian	Shales
Wolfcamp Permian	Shales
Bone Spring Permian	Debris flow deposit clastics with interbedded porous limestone and sandstone

Average total organic carbon (TOC)
100 ft (30 m) to 5000 ft (1500 m), mean 0.14%
5000 ft (1500 m) to 13,600 ft (4080 m), mean 2.16%
13,600 ft (4080 m) to 18,200 ft (5460 m), mean 2.20%
18,200 ft (6412 m), mean 0.26%

These hydrocarbon sources are from a well located 17 mi (27 km) west of the Rojo Caballos, South field

Maximum TOC 5.63%
Kerogen type (I, II, or III) .... Type II mixed with some type III
Vitrinite reflectance (maturation) .... R_o = mean 0.57% at 5000–13,600 ft (1500–4080 m);
mean 0.80% at 13,600–18,200 ft (4080–5460 m)

Time of hydrocarbon expulsion
The most rapid generation from lower Paleozoic source rocks was from Early Permian (Leonard) through the Triassic. Gas generation from Simpson rocks occurred in the Triassic and has continued to the present. Oil generation from the Middle Ordovician Simpson rocks occurred in the late Leonardian. Gas generation from the Woodford Shale occurred in the Late Triassic–Jurassic and has continued to the present.
Oil generation from Upper Pennsylvanian–Lower Permian shales began in Early Triassic and continued to the present (Ralph Horak, personal communication).

Present depth to top of source .... 13,000 ft (4000 m)
Thickness .... 10,000 ft (3000 m)
Potential yield .... NA

Appendix 2. Production Data

Field name .... Rojo Caballos, South field
Field size:

Proved acres .... 10,800 (4370 ha)
Number of wells all years ... 11 Delaware, 5 Pennsylvanian, 1 Mississippian, 10 Devonian, 5 Ellenburger

Well spacing .... *640 ac (259 ha) on Pennsylvanian, Mississippian, Devonian, and Ellenburger wells; 40 ac (16 ha) on Delaware Mountain Group wells*

Ultimate recoverable .... *Ellenburger, 125 bcf; Devonian, 105 bcf; Mississippian, 3.5 bcf (est.)*

Cumulative production
Ellenburger, 86.554 bcf gas
Devonian, 65.205 bcf gas
Mississippian, 2.229 bcf gas
Pennsylvanian, 38.789 bcf gas
Delaware Mountain Group, 667,000 bbl oil and 1 bcf gas

Annual production (1989)
Delaware Mountain Group, 44,567 bbl oil plus 48,000 mcf
Pennsylvanian, 393,483 mcf
Mississippian, 303,575 mcf
Devonian, 2,730,760 mcf
Ellenburger, 1,398,319 mcf

Present decline rate
Ellenburger, 12%
Devonian, 8%
Mississippian, 8%
Pennsylvanian, 15%
Delaware, 15%

Initial decline rate
Ellenburger, 8%
Devonian, 4%
Mississippian, 4%
Pennsylvanian, 6%

Overall decline rate
Same as presented above

Annual water production .... *Insignificant*

In place, total gas reserves .... *Ellenburger, 175 bcf; Devonian, 122 bcf; Mississippian, 5 bcf*

Primary gas recovery .... *Ellenburger, 125 bcf; Devonian, 105 bcf; Mississippian, 3.5 bcf*

Secondary recovery .... *None anticipated*

Enhanced recovery .... *None anticipated*

Drilling and casing practices:

Amount of surface casing set .... *5225 ft (1568 m)*

Casing program
13⅜-in. set at 5225 ft (1568 m); 10¾-in. set at 12,900 ft (3870 m); 7⅝-in. set at 17,034 ft (5114 m); 5-in. liner set from 16,850 ft (5055 m) to 21,429 ft (6429 m)

Drilling mud
Brine 9.4 lb/gal, 0-5225 ft (1568 m); fresh water mud 13.8 lb/gal, 5225-12,900 ft (1568-3870 m); salt water mud 10.1 lb/gal 12,900-17,045 ft (3870-5114 m); 17,045-21,630 ft (5114-6489 m), 10 lb/gal brine water

Bit program
17½-in. (44 cm) bit to 5225 ft (1568 m)
12½-in. (32 cm) bit to 12,900 ft (3870 m)
9½-in. (24 cm) bit to 17,034 ft (5114 m)
6½-in. (16 cm) bit to 21,400 ft (6420 m)
4¾-in. (12 cm) bit to 21,630 ft (6489 m)

High pressure zones
These wells started to have gas kicks below 13,000 ft (3900 m) which required numerous strings of pipe to be set in the well because of the pressure differentials in the various formations. This practice eliminated blowouts and loss of hole.

Completion practices:

Interval(s) perforated
Ellenburger, 20,500–21,600 ft (6150–6480 m)
Devonian, 17,800–18,300 ft (5340–5490 m)
Mississippian, 14,800–15,200 ft (4440–4560 m)
Pennsylvanian, 14,800–15,500 ft (4400–4650 m)
Delaware Mountain Group, 5200–6400 ft (1560–1620 m)

Well treatment
Average well was acidized with 15% HCl acid; some wells have fracture treatments

Formation evaluation:

Logging suites
Composite dual induction-laterolog and dual laterolog; compensated formation density log, borehole compensated sonic log, gamma ray-compensated neutron log; BHC and PC neutron, continuous dip meter

Testing practices
Because of the depth of these wells and the numerous pipe strings no successful drill-stem test was complete although some attempts were made

Mud logging techniques
Standard mud logging methods and units were used on these deep wells with gas recorders reading methane, ethane and propane, butane, and pentane

Gas characteristics (calculated at 14.650 PSIA and 60°F [approx. 1 bar at 15.5°C]):

Fractional Analysis

Pennsylvanian

	Mol%	GPM
Hydrogen sulfide	0.00	
Nitrogen	0.43	
Carbon dioxide	0.83	
Methane	91.30	
Ethane	4.53	1.205
Propane	1.33	0.364
Iso-butane	0.32	0.104
Nor-butane	0.32	0.100
Iso-pentane	0.19	0.069
Nor-pentane	0.14	0.050
Hexanes	0.24	0.098
Heptanes+	0.37	0.170
Total	100.0	2.160

Sulfur determination:
Grains/100 SCF

Hydrogen sulfide	2.640
Mercaptans	0.000
Sulfides	0.000
Residual sulfur	0.000
Total	2.640

Liquefiable hydrocarbons:

	GPM
Propane	0.364
Butanes	0.204
LPG	0.568
Gasoline	0.387
Subtotal	0.955

110

| Ethane | 1.205 |
| Total | 2.160 |

Fractional Analysis

Devonian

	Mol%	GPM
Hydrogen sulfide	0.00	
Nitrogen	0.51	
Carbon dioxide	3.72	
Methane	95.40	
Ethane	0.35	0.093
Propane	0.02	0.005
Iso-butane	0.00	0.000
Nor-butane	0.00	0.000
Iso-pentane	0.00	0.000
Nor-pentane	0.00	0.000
Hexanes	0.00	0.000
Heptanes+	0.00	0.000
Total	100.00	0.098
Sulfur determination	None	

Liquefiable hydrocarbons:

	GPM
Propane	0.005
Butanes	0.000
LPG	0.005
Gasoline	0.000
Subtotal	0.005
Ethane	0.093
Total	0.098

Ellenburger

Component	Mol%	GPM	GPM SUM
Nitrogen	0.567		
Methane	95.118		
Carbon dioxide	1.712		
Ethane	1.894	0.505	0.505
Propane	0.38	0.104	0.184
Iso-butane	0.089	0.029	0.184
Nor-butane	0.082	0.026	0.055
Iso-pentane	0.042	0.015	
Pentane	0.022	0.008	
Hexanes+	0.095	0.039	0.062
Total	100.00	0.726	0.726

Field characteristics:

Average elevation .... 2744 ft (832 m)

Initial pressure

Ellenburger, surface pressure 4900–6900 psi (338.1–476.1 bar); bottom hole pressure 6700–9100 psi (462.3–627.9 bar)

Devonian, surface pressure 4500–7400 psi (310.5–510.6 bar); bottom hole pressure 7000–9400 psi (483.0–648.6 bar)

Mississippian, surface pressure 5513 psi (380.4 bar); bottom hole pressure 7119 psi (491.2 bar)

ROJO CABALLOS

Present pressure

Ellenburger, surface pressure 1850–4000 psi (127.6–276.0 bar); bottom hole pressure 1850–3700 psi (127.6–255.3 bar)

Devonian, surface pressure 1700–3500 psi (117.3–241.5 bar); bottom hole pressure 3300–4200 psi (227.7–289.8 bar)

Mississippian, surface pressure 2000 psi (138 bar); bottom hole pressure 2730 psi (188.4 bar)

Pennsylvanian, no current readings

Pressure gradient

Ellenburger bottom hole pressure/z 2400–5100 psi/ft

Devonian bottom hole pressure/z 3600–4500 psi

Mississippian bottom hole pressure/z 2907 psi

Temperature .... *Bottom hole temperature 300°F (149°C)*

Geothermal gradient .... *1.2°F/100 ft (2.2°C/100 m)*

Drive .... *Gas solution in Ellenburger, Devonian, Mississippian, and Pennsylvanian*

Gas column thickness .... *Ellenburger, 900 ft (270 m); Devonian, 1250+ ft (375+ m)*

Gas-water contact .... *Ellenburger, 18,800 ft (5460 m); Devonian, 15,700 ft (4788 m)*

Water salinity, TDS

Ellenburger, 75,000 ppm

Devonian, 40,000 ppm

Mississippian, 135,000 ppm

Pennsylvanian, 150,000 ppm

Resistivity of water

Ellenburger, 0.025

Devonian, 0.04

Mississippian, 0.022

Pennsylvanian, 0.023

Bulk volume water (%) .... *Insignificant amount*

Transportation method and market for oil and gas:

Pipeline

Chicontepec Field—Mexico
Tampico-Misantla Basin

DANIEL A. BUSCH
Tulsa, Oklahoma

FIELD CLASSIFICATION

BASIN: Tampico
BASIN TYPE: Passive Margin
RESERVOIR ROCK TYPE: Sandstone
RESERVOIR ENVIRONMENT OF
    DEPOSITION: Submarine Canyon Fill
TRAP DESCRIPTION: Multiple lenticular sandstones that pinch out updip and onlap canyon
    walls laterally

RESERVOIR AGE: Eocene
PETROLEUM TYPE: Oil
TRAP TYPE: Multiple Sandstone
    Lens Pinch-Outs

LOCATION

The giant Chicontepec field, operated by the Mexican national oil company, Petroleos Mexicanos (Pemex), is located in contiguous portions of Veracruz, Hidalgo, Tlaxcala, and Puebla states of east-central Mexico (Figure 1). Geologically, it occurs in the Tampico-Misantla basin. Significant older fields in the immediate area include the Golden Lane, Remolino, San Andres, Presidente Alemán, Coatzintla, Corallilo, M.A. Camacho, and Coapechaca, the latter seven of which produce from the Chicontepec formation in the eastern one-third of the field (Figure 2). Newer fields discovered since a D. A. Busch and Associates subsurface study commissioned in 1975 (Busch and Govela, 1978) are the Tajin, Miguetla, and North Soledad, all of which have undergone extensive development drilling. The Chicontepec field is bordered on the west and southwest by the Sierra Madre Orientale, on the northeast by the Golden Lane oil field, and on the east by the Jalapa (or Tzuitlan) high.

As shown by Figure 1, the area of the Chicontepec field is very large. Reservoir sediments are turbidites deposited in a deep-water canyon that was eroded into the floor of the Chicontepec basin. The basin is estimated to be about 260 km in length and covers an area of 11,300 km² (Figures 1 and 2). Turbidite sediments accumulated in a canyon about 123 km in length, having an average width of 25 km.

The ultimate recoverable reserves are estimated to be 10.96 billion bbl of oil and 1.32 billion bbl of condensate. Chicontepec ranks as a giant oil field, one of the largest in the western hemisphere. Original oil in place is enormously larger than the estimated recoverable reserves, but the reservoir has a low recovery factor because of discontinuous, multiple sandstone reservoirs, reservoir heterogeneities, and low permeabilities.

HISTORY

The presence of hydrocarbons in the lenticular Chicontepec sandstones has been known for decades through the drilling over time of approximately 1200 wells. The prime objectives, however, in all of these wells were the Cretaceous Tamaulipas limestone of the Golden Lane and the Jurassic Pimiento and San Andres formations, all of which are prolific producers. It was during this intensive drilling that oil and gas in commercial quantities were noted in the lower Eocene and upper Paleocene sandstones of the Chicontepec formation. In fact, these lower Tertiary sandstones were producing from a scattering of fields and isolated wells, shown in Figure 2. Oil and gas shows had been noted in the Chicontepec sandstones in the great majority of the wells targeted for deeper formations.

In 1975 Busch (Busch and Govela, 1978) was commissioned by Pemex to undertake a detailed subsurface study of the area with the following objectives:

1. Develop an understanding of the trapping mechanisms of known accumulations of hydrocarbons.
2. Determine the distribution and variations in thickness of the sandstones.
3. Determine the depositional environment.
4. Map the subcrop distribution of the subjacent formations.
5. Map the structure of the Chicontepec.
6. Delineate prospect areas for commercial hydrocarbon occurrence.

The study was a team effort involving stratigraphers, a geophysicist, and several micropaleontologists. All of the objectives of the study were realized by the efforts of this interdisciplinary team:

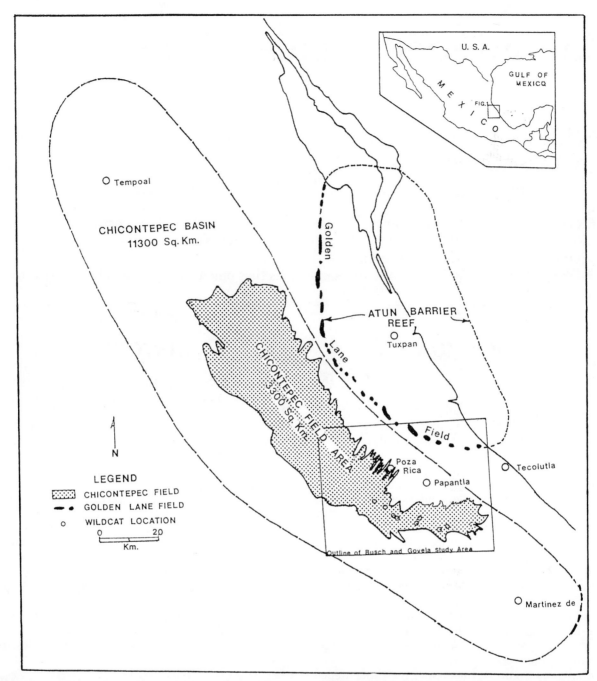

Figure 1. Chicontepec basin and field area, east-central Mexico. Inset shows area of Figure 1 (square). Rectangular outline in Chicontepec basin is the area of study. (Modified after Matheny, 1979.)

The environment of deposition of the Chicontepec sediments, the trapping mechanism, and the geographic extent and commercial significance of the field were determined. Extensions of the study to the northwest were made by Busch and his associates, and detailed reports were prepared for Pemex. The results of these latter studies have never been published, but it is from these that the northwest extension of the Chicontepec play is known.

On the basis of the first study, eight wildcat locations were recommended for drilling in the deeper part of the Chicontepec canyon. All eight locations (Figure 10) proved to be commercial wells, and dozens of commercial offsets were drilled soon afterward. In November 1978, Jorge Diaz Serrano (1978), Director General of Petroleos Mexicanos, announced at the API annual meeting in Chicago that, "The new field . . . is one of the largest in the Western

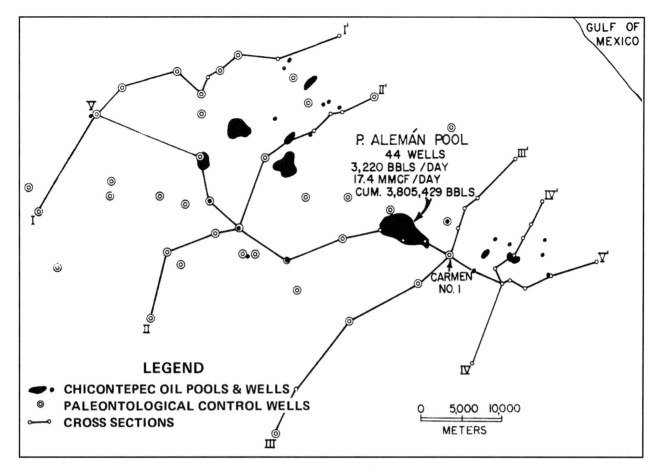

Figure 2. Map showing location of cross sections, paleontological control wells, and pools producing in 1977. The single-circle well symbols are for well control other than paleontological control wells. Presidente

Alemán pool had cumulative oil production of 3.8 MMBO (through 1975) from 44 wells. (Modified after Busch and Govela, 1978.)

Hemisphere, containing about 100 billion barrels of oil and 40 trillion cubic feet of natural gas in place." The new developments were followed by an extensive exploration and development drilling program in several parts of the basin.

Matheny (1979) pointed out that, "The Pantepec River geographically divides the basin so that roughly 20% of the reservoir volume lies to the north, and 80% to the south. Permeabilities and porosities are lower in the northern part. In the south they improve and so do reservoir pressures. . . . The southern part of the basin, with more solution gas and higher pressures, holds the most promise. Some of the wells are flowing, but many of them are on gas lift or rod pumps. Each new well placed on production averages 90 barrels/day initially. Pressure maintenance and/or secondary recovery will be required."

Serrano (1978) estimated that "16,000 wells will be required to fully develop Chicontepec and this will require about 13 years of steady drilling." The Pemex chief said the 13-year program is one of several alternative plans being studied. Under this plan Pemex would increase the number of rigs used for Chicontepec development by 30 each year for four

years, with a total of 120 rigs active there in the fourth year. Such a tentative program would have to be developed on a step-by-step basis and harmonized with Pemex's capabilities, price of crude oil and natural gas, and the needs of both Mexico and the purchasers abroad. At this writing the tentative 13-year development program has never been carried out by Pemex. This is due to the comparatively low initial Chicontepec well potentials, the drop in the price of crude oil, and more attractive payouts in the sound of Campeche and the Chiapus-Tabasco area to the southeast.

STRATIGRAPHY

Figure 3 illustrates diagramatically the relationship of the subsurface Chicontepec formation canyon fill, which includes the Chicontepec field reservoirs, to the eroded, underlying formations of the enclosing canyon walls. Surface observations of the Chicontepec formation west of Poza Rica, together with subsurface investigations, leave little doubt that this

115

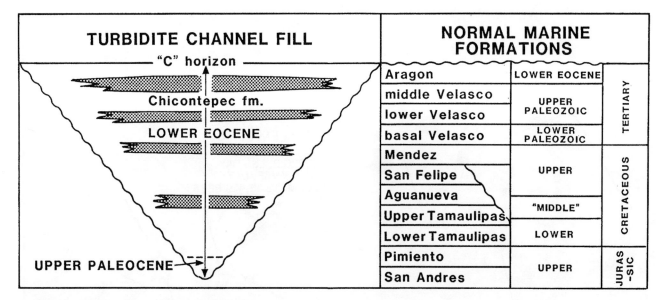

TURBIDITE CHANNEL FILL	NORMAL MARINE FORMATIONS		
"C" horizon Chicontepec fm. LOWER EOCENE UPPER PALEOCENE	Aragon	LOWER EOCENE	TERTIARY
	middle Velasco	UPPER PALEOZOIC	
	lower Velasco		
	basal Velasco	LOWER PALEOZOIC	
	Mendez	UPPER	CRETACEOUS
	San Felipe		
	Aguanueva	"MIDDLE"	
	Upper Tamaulipas		
	Lower Tamaulipas	LOWER	
	Pimiento	UPPER	JURAS-SIC
	San Andres		

Figure 3. Stratigraphic subdivisions of Upper Jurassic, Cretaceous, and lower Tertiary, showing relationship of unconformity at base of Chicontepec canyon fill. (From Busch and Govela, 1978.)

formation consists of a repetitive sequence of graded beds typical of most turbidites. The Chicontepec of the subsurface is confined to the deep-water (as determined from associated microfauna) canyon eroded into the floor of a pre-Tertiary basin (Figure 4). Multiple tributaries flow into it, especially on the northeast side.

Certain benthic Foraminifera were identified and used as a basis for determination of water depths. Benthos are generally scarce and exhibit little variation in species. *Uvigerina* sp. and *Bulimina* sp. are indicative of the shallowest water depths (135–200 m) whereas a water-depth range of 200–500 m is indicated by the presence of *Vulvulina advena*, *Chilostomella* sp., *Chilostomelloides* sp., *Heterolepa* sp., *Gyroidinoides* sp., and *Oridorsalis* sp.

Faunal zonation of planktonic Foraminifera does not occur within the sediments of the Chicontepec canyon fill, whereas distinct faunal-age determinations are readily made of the uneroded parts of the Jurassic, Cretaceous, and lower Tertiary strata. Distinctive plankton of early Eocene age were identified from the Chicontepec canyon fill and include *Globorotalia wilcoxensis-quertra*, *G. formosa formosa*, *G. formosa gracilis*, and *G. rex*. They are present in association with recycled Foraminifera derived from eroded Upper Jurassic and Cretaceous deposits.

Chicontepec canyon sediments thicken downward at the expense of the underlying stratigraphic units of early Eocene to Late Jurassic age (Figure 4). Most of the Chicontepec Formation is of early Eocene age, with only the lowermost part being late Paleocene (Figure 3).

Approximately half of the Chicontepec consists of shales or silty shales, with the rest of the formation made up of multiple, thin sandstone beds and zones of sandstone beds. Reservoir sediments consist of lenticular sandstones and clusters of sandstone beds interstratified with shale. The sandstones are generally fine to very fine grained and consist of mixtures of micritic limestone, quartz, plagioclase feldspar, volcanic rock fragments, chert, metamorphic rock fragments, and several accessory minerals. They are commonly argillaceous and calcareous.

The numerous submarine tributaries on the northeast side of the Chicontepec canyon fill originate along the detrital southwest margin of the Golden Lane reef trend (Figure 1). Thus, there are admixtures of micritic and pelitic reef-derived clastic materials "contaminating" the turbidites of the canyon fill. The contamination of the reservoir sandstones has much to do with their relatively low porosity and permeability. Although the sandstones are known to contain commercial oil and gas, the reservoir quality is less than ideal. For example, numerous wells produce oil and gas from several Chicontepec sandstone zones in the Presidente Alemán pool, as shown in Figure 4, but these zones have limited areal extent.

Nine stratigraphic cross sections were constructed within the Chicontepec area by Busch and his associates (Busch and Govela, 1978). The locations of five of the more generally important of these are shown on Figure 2; of these five, three were selected for illustration and description in this study (cross sections II, IV, and V, shown by Figures 5, 6, and 7).

Stratigraphic Cross Sections

Each of the three cross sections use for datum the "C" horizon, which coincides with the top of the Chicontepec canyon fill and for practical purposes was essentially parallel to sea level.

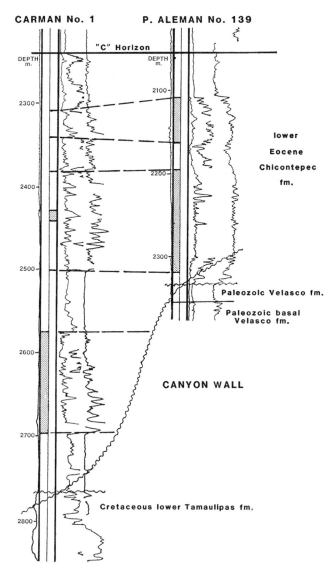

CARMAN No. 1   P. ALEMAN No. 139

"C" Horizon

DEPTH m.   DEPTH m.

2100

2300

lower
Eocene
Chicontepec
fm.

2200

2400

2300

2500

Paleozoic Velasco fm.

Paleozoic basal
Velasco fm.

2600

CANYON WALL

2700

Cretaceous lower Tamaulipas fm.

2800

Figure 4. Two typical electric logs of the Presidente Alemán pool (see Figure 2) showing the stratigraphic positions of the producing zones in the Chicontepec formation. The canyon wall is the surface of unconformity between the valley-fill Chicontepec on the left and the dissected normal marine sequences on the right. In the Presidente Alemán pool, 19 wells produced from the upper Chicontepec zone shown here, 24 from the middle zone, and two from the lower.

Cross Section II-II'

Cross section II-II', shown by Figure 5, trends generally northeast-southwest. Using the "C" horizon as datum, the cross section serves to illustrate a low-relief asymmetric anticline in the Jurassic-Cretaceous strata during Chicontepec deposition. A pronounced erosional unconformity separates the Chicontepec from the underlying Velasco (Tertiary) and Cretaceous deposits.

The maximum thickness of the Chicontepec formation along this profile is approximately 650 m.

The low rate of northeastward thinning of the canyon fill was influenced by the low angle of regional dip of the underlying Velasco Formation. The opposite (southwest) side of the canyon is considerably steeper because this was a scarp slope, rather than a dip slope.

The best development of the sandy zones in the Chicontepec occurs in the upper half of well 2. However, this development does not persist to the northeast. In well 3, the sandy zones are present only in the basal third of the Chicontepec. Still farther northeast, sandy zones are either absent or sparsely developed. The thin sandstones present in wells 6 and 8 occur only in the uppermost part of the Chicontepec.

Cross Section IV-IV'

Easternmost of the several cross sections whose locations are shown on Figure 2 is cross section IV-IV', trending northeast-southwest, shown on Figure 6. "Hanging" this stratigraphic profile on "C" horizon (top of Chicontepec canyon fill) shows that the canyon was eroded into the axial part of an asymmetric anticline of the Jurassic-Cretaceous strata (Figure 6). The steeper slope on the southwest side of the canyon is directly related to the scarp slope on this side of the underlying asymmetric anticline.

In Figure 6, well 28 exhibits the thickest (560 m) canyon fill. In all of the wells of this profile, the canyon fill consists primarily of a series of sandy zones with thin interbeds of shale. The high percentage of sandstone is attributed to the fact that this cross section occurs nearest the primary source of the canyon-fill sediments. Extreme lenticularity of the sandstone zones of the Chicontepec is the most conspicuous feature of the cross section.

Cross Section V-V'

The west-northwest trend of cross section V-V' (Figure 7) coincides generally with the long axis of the main Chicontepec canyon; hence, canyon fill is present in every well. Undulations of the unconformity at the base occur where the trend of the cross section fails to coincide with the long axis of the canyon. Thus, local thickening is due to the influence of tributaries, whereas local thinning of the Chicontepec occurs on the divides that separate the tributaries.

"Hanging" this cross section on the "C" horizon shows that the Jurassic, Cretaceous, and Velasco formations had a west component of dip during Chicontepec deposition. Although it is not apparent from this stratigraphic profile (because of the use of the "C" horizon datum), all of these formations (including the Chicontepec) later were tilted eastward.

The submarine escarpment that bounds the canyon fill on the south-southwest is on the steeper flank of an asymmetric Jurassic-Cretaceous anticline that had a westerly plunge. Thus, truncation of the subcropping formations was most pronounced

117

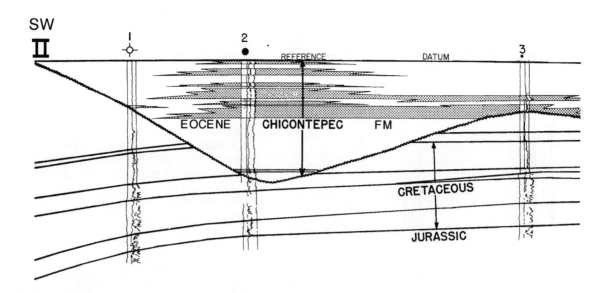

Figure 5. Stratigraphic cross section II–II'. For location see Figures 2, 8, and 9. (From Busch and Govela, 1978.)

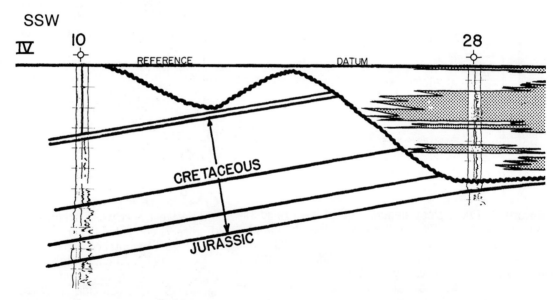

Figure 6. Stratigraphic cross section IV–IV'. For location see Figures 2, 8, and 9. (From Busch and Govela, 1978.)

on the east where Chicontepec lies on Jurassic rocks, whereas on the west the canyon fill directly overlies the Velasco. This relation is understood better by referring to Figure 8, which shows the subcrop distribution of the Jurassic, Cretaceous, and Paleocene formations of this part of the Tampico-Misantla basin.

This cross section (Figure 7) shows an abundance of lenticular sandy zones in the Chicontepec because its trend for the most part follows the axis of the canyon.

Isopach Map of Chicontepec Genetic Sequence of Strata

The Chicontepec formation consists of a genetic sequence of strata (GSS) and, as such, is defined at the top by a stratigraphic time marker ("C" horizon) and at the base by an erosional unconformity.

Figure 8 is an isopach map of this GSS drawn with a contour interval of 100 m. The overall picture is that of a deep-water canyon fill with numerous tributary canyon fills along the northern margin. The

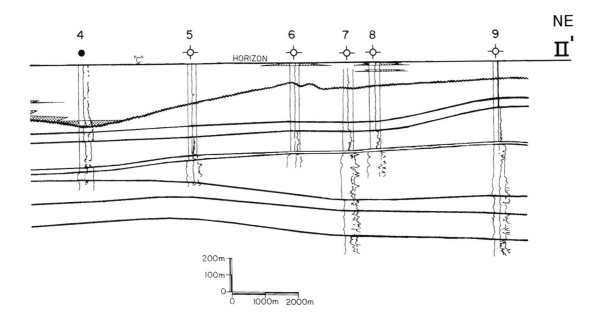

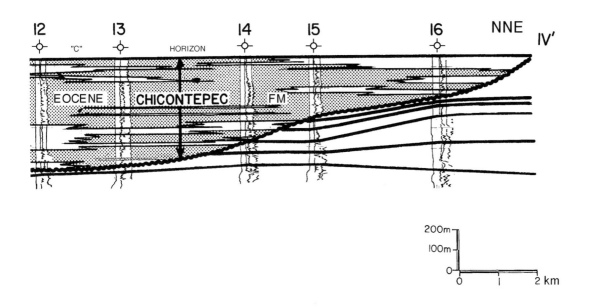

tributaries along the north side of the canyon flowed down a dip slope of the strata underlying the Chicontepec and thus are more numerous and longer than those along the southern margin. The southern margin of the canyon was a scarp slope; hence, it is steeper than the north slope. The relative scarcity of tributaries along the south margin of the canyon is in part only apparent, due to the paucity of subsurface data in this area.

The thickness of the Chicontepec along the main axis of the canyon ranges from approximately 500 m on the east to an estimated 900 m on the west within the original study area. The thickness of the axial sediments continues to increase to the northwest. The gradual east to west thickening along the canyon axis clearly indicates westerly submarine-current movement during erosion and deposition.

Most of the wells within the study area (Figure 2) were drilled through the Cretaceous and into the underlying Jurassic. Hence, it is easy to map the subcrop distribution of the Paleocene, Cretaceous, and Jurassic formations where they are in direct

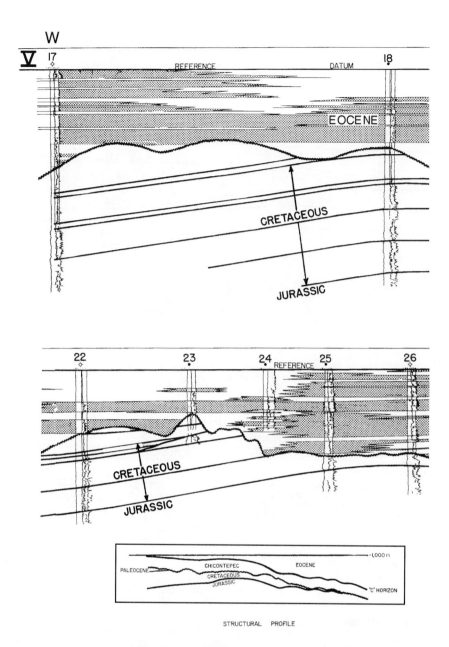

Figure 7. Longitudinal stratigraphic cross section V-V'. For location see Figures 2, 8, and 9. The west half of the section is at the top and is contiguous with the east half on the bottom. (From Busch and Govela, 1978.) Small inset at the bottom shows the location of the cross section within 50 m isopach lines.

contact with the overlying Chicontepec canyon fill. All of the units deposited before the canyon fill have been identified and correlated by a combination of electric-log and lithologic characteristics supplemented by paleontologic studies.

The Jurassic subcrop is confined to a triangular area in the easternmost part of the study area and underlies the upstream part of the canyon fill (Figure 8). Two narrow bands of lower Tamaulipas strata subcrop north and south of the Jurassic subcrop and converge westward to form a single subcrop band under the Chicontepec canyon axis. This band disappears toward the west (central part

of Figure 8), where it dips under the Agua Nueva formation. The Agua Nueva, in turn, dips under the Mendez formation midway between cross sections I–I' and II–II'. The Mendez is a subcrop under the Chicontepec canyon fill in two narrow bands north and south of the Tamaulipas and Agua Nueva formations. In the westernmost part of Figure 8 these bands converge to form a single subcrop that disappears just before it reaches the position of cross section I–I'. The thinner parts of the Chicontepec canyon fill are underlain by the Valasco (Paleocene) formation and are represented by the unshaded parts of Figure 8.

120

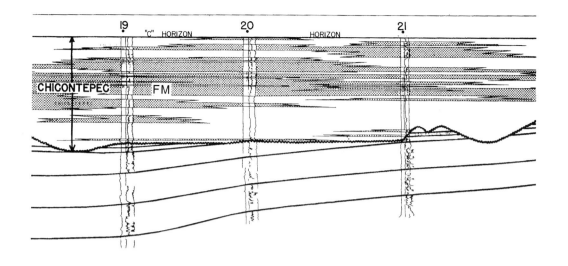

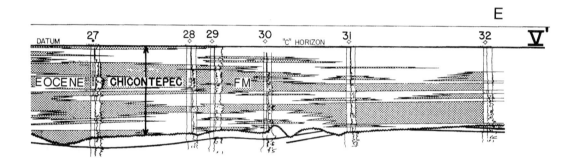

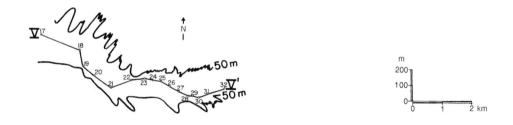

The successively younger pairs of subcrop bands of Cretaceous and Paleocene formations underlying the Chicontepec canyon fill, together with their convergence and systemmatic westward disappearance under the canyon axis, clearly confirm the westerly direction of flow of density currents that were responsible for the erosion of the Chicontepec canyon system. Furthermore, there was a west-northwest regional plunge of the asymmetric anticline into which the Chicontepec canyon was eroded.

Isopach and Net Sandstone Zones in Chicontepec Formation

The Chicontepec formation consists of individual beds and zones of argillaceous fine-grained sandstone alternating with shale and siltstone. Figure 9 illustrates the net amount of sandstone in the Chicontepec formation. The distinction between siltstone and sandstone is an arbitrary one involving a judgment factor applied to electric log differentiation. To eliminate personal differences in electric

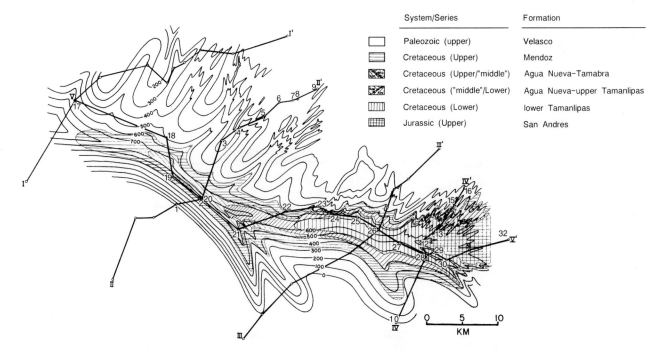

System/Series	Formation
Paleozoic (upper)	Velasco
Cretaceous (Upper)	Mendoz
Cretaceous (Upper/"middle")	Agua Nueva–Tamabra
Cretaceous ("middle"/Lower)	Agua Nueva–upper Tamanlipas
Cretaceous (Lower)	lower Tamanlipas
Jurassic (Upper)	San Andres

Figure 8. Isopach map of the Chicontepec formation, also showing subcrop of formations of the Upper Jurassic, Cretaceous, and Paleocene. Contour interval, 100 m. See Figure 2 for location. (From Busch and Govela, 1978.)

log determination, a single investigator distinguished the sandstones from the shales and siltstones.

The distribution of net Chicontepec sandstone (Figure 9) is restricted considerably more than that of the Chicontepec formation (with its shales and siltstones). As would be expected, the greatest thicknesses of net sandstone occur in the deepest part of the canyon. The estimated maximum thickness within the study area exceeds 600 m.

It is clear that the Presidente Alemán pool (Figure 2) is producing from a restricted area along the north flank of the canyon fill where the net sandstone ranges in thickness from 0 to 275 m. The northern margin of this pool is the erosional contact between the Chicontepec and the Cretaceous. The eastern and southern margins of the pool have not been defined by drilling and are not related to a possible oil-water contact.

STRUCTURE

A structural interpretation of the top of the Chicontepec ("C" horizon) canyon fill was made to determine the significance of structure in localizing hydrocarbon accumulation in the sandstones of this formation (Figure 10). In the northeastern half of the study area, an abundance of deep well data serves as the basis for the structural interpretation of "C" horizon. In the southwestern half of the area, however, it is not possible to draw a meaningful

structure map of "C" horizon because of the paucity of well data.

It was thought that seismic data in the southwestern area might be used in mapping "C" horizon. However, no reliable reflections are apparent within the lower Tertiary. Seismic reflections at the top of the Mendez formation (Upper Cretaceous), however, are good. Thus, the structural interpretation shown on Figure 10 is partly of the top of the Mendez and partly of the "C" horizon. It is a reasonable assumption that the structural configuration of the "C" horizon is similar to that of the top of the Mendez. The stratigraphic interval thickness between these two horizons is approximately 600 m. Gaps in contouring of the Mendez portion of the map are the result of deep-water erosion of the Mendez formation that preceded Chicontepec canyon fill. The seismic data were corrected for variable velocities before contouring.

Although a structural interpretation was made of the eastern part of the Tampico-Misantla canyon fill, only that part of the structure that coincides with the area of known Chicontepec sandstone development (Figure 9) is shown in Figure 10. The northern and southern boundaries of the mapped area are coincident with the 50 m net sandstone thickness contours. However, in the northwestern part of the mapped area, where the net sandstone is less than 50 m, the zero-sandstone thickness contour was used because of known Chicontepec oil production.

The most conspicuous features of the "C" horizon/ Mendez structure map (Figure 10) are the general

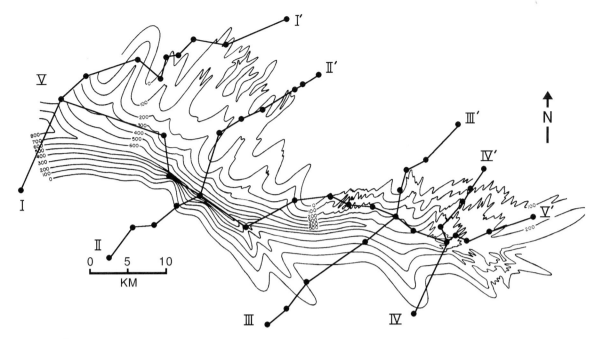

Figure 9. Isopach map of net sandstone in Chicontepec formation. (From Busch and Govela, 1978.) Contour interval, 100 m.

northeasterly tilt of the strata and the presence of numerous northwest–southeast-trending structural noses and a few closures. This structural grain is clearly normal to the northeast thrusting that occurred during post-early Eocene (Laramide) time. Thus, the high area on the west was the low area during Chicontepec deposition. The Jalapa high area, east of the mapped area, was a positive land mass in Chicontepec time and furnished much of the canyon fill sediment.

Bitter (1986) measured many dips of outcropping Chicontepec beds to the northwest of this study area. From these measurements, he observed two modes of dip; namely, northwest (N 52 W) and southeast (N 128 E). The preponderence of dips are southeast, and therefore he concluded that the paleocurrent direction was southeast. In this conclusion he failed to take into account that the Chicontepec sediments were regionally tilted to the southeast in post-Chicontepec time. Thus, these dip measurements in no way indicate the paleocurrent direction, which was to the northwest.

The extrapolated "C" horizon along the western portion of the map shown by Figure 10 is approximately 600 m above the Mendez, giving it a subsea elevation of about –1200 m. A cluster of Chicontepec oil wells is present in this area. The structurally lowest Chicontepec occurs far to the east at approximately –2575 m. All other production occurs between these two extremes of structural position. Thus, there is as much as 1400 m of structural difference between the highest and lowest Chicon-

tepec sandstone wells. The regional tilt averages 1.5° to the east-northeast.

Trapping Mechanism and Source

A review of the cumulative production from each of the Chicontepec wells shows that the range of cumulative production for the scattered wells is so great that productive trends are not apparent. Likewise, the structural position of a well appears to have no bearing on the cumulative production.

Practically all of the traps in the Chicontepec sandstones are of the stratigraphic type. They consist of clusters of sandstone bodies with thin, interbedded shales and isolated sandstone beds. Porosities and permeabilities are of low orders owing to a combination of fine to very fine grain texture and interstitial micrite and clay contamination.

Chemical analyses of the Jurassic and Chicontepec oils are strikingly similar. It appears, therefore, that much of the Chicontepec oil originally accumulated in the Jurassic Pimiento and San Andres formations and migrated updip to the west. In the easternmost part of the study area (Figure 8), the Chicontepec rests directly on the subcrop of the Jurassic, and this is the most likely area for the escape of the hydrocarbons into the lenticular sandstones of the Chicontepec. The linear trends of these sandstones are quite extensive along the Canyon axis (Figure 8), and all of them shale out at one place or another updip to the west.

123

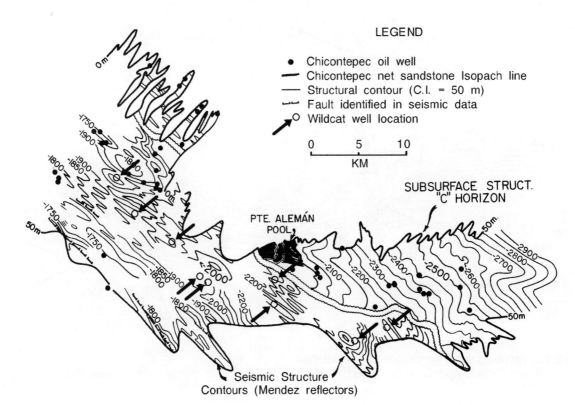

Figure 10. Combination structure map of tops of Mendez (Upper Cretaceous) and horizon "C" of Chicontepec formation within area of turbidite canyon fill, showing recommended wildcat locations. (Modified from Busch and Govela, 1978.)

Production and Economics

The Presidente Alemán pool (Figure 2) had a cumulative production through 1975 of 3,817,548 bbl of oil. The pool is on the updip part of a southeast-plunging structural nose. The northern margin of the pool coincides approximately with the trend of the 50 m net sandstone-thickness contour line (Figure 10). Here the sandstone becomes silty and shaly and the permeability is low. The southern, western, and eastern margins of the pool have not been determined by drilling.

In 1978, production from the Chicontepec sandstones was 30,000 bbl/day from approximately 300 wells. More up-to-date figures are not available at this writing. Oil averages 30° API. Most of the wells in the northern part of the basin are on artificial lift, mostly on rod pumps. Each new well placed on production averages 90 bbl/day initially. There are more solution gas and higher pressures in the southern part of the basin. Some wells flow naturally, but the majority are on gas lift or sucker rod pumps.

Matheny (1979) notes that, "Drilling has been fairly easy due to the type of section and shallow depths. Where the formations have more clay, there have been some fluid loss and swelling problems." The average depth of Chicontepec wells is 5850 ft. Thus, they are drilled rapidly and are relatively inexpensive. He re-states that, "One possible development plan has already been drawn. This plan would complete Chicontepec development with some 16,083 wells over the next 13 years, adding 30 drilling rigs during each of the first four years." Peak production of oil would be 740,000 bbl/day in year 12 and peak gas production about 1.2 bcfd in year 13. Average well production would peak at 46 bbl/day well with a GOR of 615:1 (mcfg/bbl).

"Cumulative production over the 13 development years is estimated at 2.6 billion bbl, with an approximate value at constant pricing of $31 billion." It has been previously noted that the estimated recoverable reserves from this giant field are 10.96 billion bbl of oil and 1.32 billion bbl of condensate. None of this prediction of a large number of wells, numerous drilling rigs, and peak production has been realized. Drilling activity has been suspended owing to more attractive initial potentials in the onshore and offshore areas far to the southeast, drop in the price of crude oil, and low permeabilities of the reservoir sandstones. Conceivably development activity will resume when other sources of Mexican oil decline and market prices of crude oil improve.

EXPLORATION CONCEPTS

Although the Chicontepec formation occurs in close proximity to the world-famous Golden Lane reef trend, its significance as a major source of hydrocarbons was not recognized until Busch and Govela (1978) completed the first of three studies of this turbidite canyon fill. Well to well correlations within the canyon sediments are extremely difficult to impossible because of the absence of conventional marker beds, i.e., limestone, bentonite, coal, evaporite, etc. Microfauna, although abundant, are predominantly Cretaceous in age and occur in intimate association with Upper Jurassic, Paleocene, and early Eocene microfauna. In other words, the entire canyon fill consists of recycled sediments and their contained fauna. The sandstone beds are extremely lenticular, occur abundantly throughout the canyon fill, and generally exhibit shows of hydrocarbons.

The key to evaluating the Chicontepec formation is to gain an early understanding of its environment of deposition. This was accomplished by the construction of a series of stratigraphic cross sections of not just the Chicontepec but the enclosing sediments as well (Figures 4, 5, 6, and 7). In so doing, the abrupt truncation of the Cretaceous formations on opposite sides of the canyon could be readily recognized and their respective subcrops mapped. In the eastern part of the study area it could be seen that the Chicontepec rests directly on the subcrop of the oil-bearing Upper Jurassic (Figure 8). The striking chemical similarity of the Jurassic and Chicontepec (Paleocene and early Eocene) oils is readily explained by leakage of Jurassic oil into the Chicontepec lenticular sandstones. Migration of the oil has been updip to the west-northwest within the lenticular sandstones of the Chicontepec. The trapping mechanism for the oil accumulations is the updip shaleout of all sandstone lenses along the axial trend of the Chicontepec canyon fill. Thus, these multiple reservoirs constitute a gigantic stratigraphic trap along the west-southwest side of the Golden Lane reef trend.

The canyon-fill depositional environment is not unique with Chicontepec. For example, similar studies of the Meganos canyon fill (maximum 3500 ft) by D. A. Busch (unpublished) in the Sacramento basin of California have been made. With the exception of the uppermost reaches of this canyon fill, the sediments consist of silty shale. Here, again, the construction of stratigraphic cross sections of both the fill and the enclosing massive Cretaceous sandstones is the key to understanding the environment of deposition. The only hydrocarbon

production in this canyon fill is in the lenticular sandstones occurring in the headwaters area. Several other pools, however, are related directly to this canyon fill. For example, the large Buena Vista gas pool and the Brentwood oil field occur on structural noses that plunge more or less at right angles to the axis of the shale-filled canyon.

The Yoakum gas pool similarly occurs along the west side of the Yoakum canyon fill of East Texas. Here, again, the canyon fill is almost entirely shale. The trapping mechanism for all three of these pools is a combination of structure and stratigraphy. The reservoir sandstones, in each instance, are overlain by impermeable shale and the updip limits of these reservoirs occur where the shale of the canyon fill rests directly against the truncated canyon wall.

REFERENCES CITED

Bitter, M. R., 1986, Sedimentology and petrology of the Chicontepec formation, Tampico-Misantla basin, eastern Mexico: Unpublished M. S. Thesis, University of Kansas, 174 p.

Busch, D. A., and S. A. Govela, 1978, Stratigraphy and structure of Chicontepec turbidites, southeastern Tampico-Misantla basin, Mexico: American Association of Petroleum Geologists Bulletin, v. 62, n. 2, p. 235-246.

Matheny, Jr., S. L., 1979, Giant Chicontepec given 42% of Mexican oil reserves: Oil and Gas Journal, v. 77, n. 34, p. 82-85.

Serrano, J. D., 1978, Pemex discloses big oil-field find at API meet: Oil and Gas Journal, v. 76, n. 47, p. 45, 46.

SUGGESTED READING

Barker, R. W., and W. A. Berggren, 1977, Paleocene and early Eocene of the Rio Grande and Tampico embayments: Foraminiferal biostratigraphy and paleoecology: Mar. Micropaleontology, v. 2, n. 1, p. 67-103.

Chapa, A. C., 1985, Is there a Chicontepec paleocanyon in the Paleocene of eastern Mexico?: Journal of Petroleum Geology, v. 8, n. 4, p. 423-434.

Gomez, A. H., 1979, Analysis and testing to improve the productivity of Chicontepec field: Ing. Petrol., v. 19, n. 2, p. 5-11.

Martinez, J. M., 1965, Geological study of the northern part of Chicontepec basin, State of San Luis Potosi: Geol. and Metal., v. 2, n. 12, p. 18-61.

Rodriguez, J. L. R., 1974, Possibilities of producing the Chicontepec formation in the southern district of the northern zone (Mexico): Ing. Petrol., v. 14, n. 9, p. 373-389.

Salaza, T., 1979, Chicontepec: 17.64 billion barrels: Pet. Int., v. 37, n. 11, p. 40, 55-56, 58.

Appendix 1. Field Description

Field name .... *Chicontepec field*

Ultimate recoverable reserves .... *10.9 billion bbl and 1.32 billion bbl of condensate*

Field location:

Country .... *Mexico*

State .... *Veracruz, Hidalgo, Tlaxcala, and Puebla*

Basin/Province .... *Tampico-Misantla*

Field discovery:

Year first pay discovered

An old producing area considered as noncommercial until 1978; confirmation was accomplished by drilling eight successful wildcats and working over older wells. Multiple lower Eocene Chicontepec formation sand lenses.

Discovery well operator .... *Petroleos Mexicanos (Pemex)*

IP:

First pay .... *Avg. 90 BOPD*

Geologic concept leading to discovery and method or methods used to delineate prospect:

A detailed subsurface study (Busch and Govela, 1978) served to identify the sediments as being turbidites in a deep-water canyon fill on the southwest side of the Golden Lane barrier reef field.

Structure:

Province/basin type

Deep-water canyon eroded between the Sierra Madre Oriental on the west and southwest, and the Golden lane barrier reef trend on the east.

Tectonic history

From the end of Cretaceous time through the Eocene there was active uplift and thrusting (Laramide orogeny) of the Sierra Madre Oriental along the west and southwest side of the Chicontepec canyon. Likewise, the Jalapa high to the southeast came into existence at this time. Both were source areas for Chicontepec sediments.

Regional structure

Irregular homoclinal slope to the southeast and northeast of 1500+ m.

Local structure

No structural closures.

Trap:

Trap type(s)

Traps consist of multiple lenticular sandstones that pinch out updip to the northwest and onlap the canyon walls on the northeast and southwest.

Basin stratigraphy (major stratigraphic intervals from surface to deepest penetration in field):

Chronostratigraphy	Formation	Depth to Top in m
Lower Eocene	*Chicontepec*	*Avg. depth 2155*

Reservoir characteristics:

Number of reservoirs .... *Dozens*

Formations .... *Chicontepec sandstones*

Ages .... *Lower Eocene*

Depths to tops of reservoirs

For 45 randomly picked wells, as follows:

2155 m—avg. depth to top of zone; depth range to top is 1300–3100 m

2450 m—avg. depth to bottom of zone; depth range to bottom is 1525–3425 m

126

CHICONTEPEC

There are three reasons for these great depth ranges, namely:
(1) Well elevations range from 17 m to 469 m above sea level
(2) Locations of well sites relative to canyon axis vs. canyon walls
(3) Regional (homoclinal) tilt is 2.3 (212 ft/mi)

Gross thickness (top to bottom of producing interval) .... *293 m (avg. thickness in 45 randomly selected wells)*

Net thickness—total thickness of producing zones
    Average .... *200 m*
    Maximum .... *500± m*
Lithology
Micritic limestone (over 59%), fine to very fine grained quartz (14–15%), plagioclase feldspar (8.4%), volcanic rock fragments (6.7%), chert (4%), metamorphic rock fragments and accessory minerals

Porosity type .... *Mostly intergranular porosity*
Average porosity .... *No data*
Average permeability .... *No data*

Seals:
  Upper
    Formation, fault, or other feature .... *Updip shale out of lenticular sandstones*
  Lateral
    Formation, fault, or other feature .... *Onlap of lenticular sandstones against canyon walls (e.g., Presidente Alemán pool)*

Source:
  Formation and age .... *Upper Jurassic and Cretaceous (reworked)*
  Lithology .... *Micritic reef detritus (Cretaceous) and Pimienta sandstone (Upper Jurassic)*
  Average total organic carbon (TOC) .... *No data*
  Maximum TOC .... *No data*
  Kerogen type (I, II, or III) .... *No data*
  Vitrinite reflectance (maturation) .... *No data*
  Time of hydrocarbon expulsion .... *Late Paleocene and early Eocene*
  Present depth to top of source .... *NA*
  Thickness .... *No data*
  Potential yield .... *10.96 billion bbl (1,742,448,300 m³) of oil; 1.32 billion bbl (209,855,900 m³) of condensate*

CHICONTEPEC

Appendix 2. Production Data

Field name .... *Chicontepec field*
Field size:
  Proved acres .... *597,760 ac (241,913 ha)*
  Number of wells all years .... *NA (plan for development to 16,000 wells awaits favorable markets and economies)*
  Current number of wells .... *Approx. 300 wells as of 1979*
  Well spacing .... *Approx. 1320 ft*
  Ultimate recoverable .... *10.96 billion bbl oil; 1.32 billion bbl condensate*
  Cumulative production .... *3.8 million bbl through 1975 from Presidente Alemán pool alone; total Chicontepec NA*
  Annual production .... *About 3.8 million bbl from all Chicontepec sandstone wells (approx. 300 wells) as of 1979*

Present decline rate .... *No data*
    Initial decline rate .... *No data*
    Overall decline rate .... *No data*
Annual water production .... *No data*
In place, total reserves .... *100 billion bbl and 40 tcf of gas*
In place, per acre foot .... *836.5 bbl*
Primary recovery .... *NA*
Secondary recovery .... *NA*
Enhanced recovery .... *NA*
Cumulative water production .... *NA*

Drilling and casing practices: .... *NA*

Completion practices: .... *NA*

Formation evaluation: .... *NA*

Oil characteristics:

    Type .... *NA*
    API gravity .... *30°*
    Base .... *No data (probably asphaltic)*
    Initial GOR .... *NA*
    Sulfur, wt% .... *NA*
    Viscosity, SUS .... *NA*
    Pour point .... *NA*
    Gas-oil distillate .... *NA*

Field characteristics:

    Average elevation .... *165 m (avg. of 45 wells)*
    Initial pressure .... *NA*
    Present pressure .... *NA*
    Pressure gradient .... *NA*
    Temperature .... *NA*
    Geothermal gradient .... *NA*
    Drive .... *NA*
    Oil column thickness .... *NA*
    Oil-water contact .... *NA*
    Connate water .... *NA*
    Water salinity, TDS .... *NA*
    Resistivity of water .... *NA*
    Bulk volume water (%) .... *NA*

Transportation method and market for oil and gas:
NA

Pecos Slope Field—U.S.A.
Permian Basin, New Mexico

LESLIE M. BENTZ
Yates Petroleum Corporation
Artesia, New Mexico

FIELD CLASSIFICATION

BASIN: Permian
BASIN TYPE: Foredeep
RESERVOIR ROCK TYPE: Sandstone
RESERVOIR ENVIRONMENT
  OF DEPOSITION: Fluvial

RESERVOIR AGE: Permian
PETROLEUM TYPE: Gas
TRAP TYPE: Regional Depositional
  Facies Change

TRAP DESCRIPTION: Lateral wedge-out of fluvial clastic facies coupled with tectonically induced fracture systems; updip seal unknown but probably coincides with change from meandering channel to braided channel facies

LOCATION

Pecos Slope field, located in Chaves County, New Mexico, is situated on the Northwestern shelf of the Delaware basin, the western portion of the U.S. Permian basin (Figure 1). The pool is the most northwesterly production in the Permian basin.

From 1981 through 1983, the Abo Formation in this field was the leading target for natural gas drilling in New Mexico (Figures 2 and 3). Today the Pecos Slope field covers an area of 731 mi² (1893 km²) and is geographically one of the largest gas fields in the northwestern section of the Permian basin; it ranks in the top ten fields in gas reserves in the state of New Mexico. Pecos Slope field is unique in that production occurs from a continental red bed sequence. Estimated ultimate recovery of gas from Pecos Slope and West Pecos Slope fields is 750 bcf.

HISTORY

Pre-Discovery

Prior to the discovery of gas in the Abo Formation, the Pecos slope was sparsely drilled. Less than a dozen wells had penetrated the Abo Formation in a 600 mi² (1554 km²) area. Most of these boreholes were unsuccessful Silurian–Devonian or Ordovician tests on structures and updip pinch-out prospects. Production in the area was limited to marginal oil production from the shallow San Andres Formation (Permian Guadalupian).

Leasing activity in the Pecos slope area was not highly competitive, and a large amount of acreage remained unleased. The majority of the minerals was owned by the state of New Mexico and the U.S. government; acreage could be leased inexpensively with costs averaging $2.00 an acre. Typically, state lands were leased for the minimum bonus of 50 cents per acre.

Discovery

Yates Petroleum Corporation of Artesia, New Mexico, successfully re-entered the No. 1 McConkey Estate well, hereafter referred to as the Yates Petroleum McConkey "HX" #1, located in Sec. 10, T9S, R26E in May 1977 (Figure 4; Figure 8 shows well location). The well had been drilled to a depth of 6371 ft (1942 m) and abandoned as a dry hole by the Honolulu Oil Corporation in 1951.

The objective of the re-entry was to test reported gas shows in the Silurian–Devonian and Ordovician intervals. The well had been logged with old "IES" (induction electric survey) logs; however, the decision was made to log the old hole again with modern porosity and resistivity logs to better plan for completion attempts. This decision was critical to the discovery of gas in the Abo Formation on the Pecos slope. After the well was logged with a modern compensated-neutron-formation density log and a dual lateral log with an R_{xo} curve (shallow-reading resistivity for flushed zone), a geologist detected an 18 ft (5 m) thick sandstone with "gas effect."

Yates Petroleum immediately began a detailed geologic study of the area and determined that the sandstone was within the Abo Formation (Permian Leonardian). With the limited data available, it was found that the Abo red bed facies contained sandstones over a large geographic area (Figure 7).

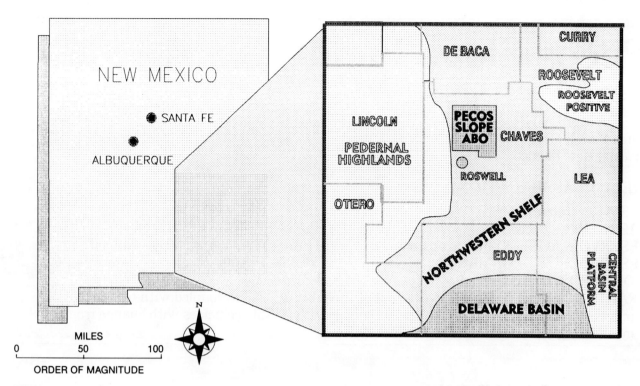

Figure 1. Location map showing major geological features in the New Mexico portion of the Permian basin. The Pecos Slope field, productive from the Permian Abo Formation, is located on the Northwest shelf of the Delaware basin.

The original deep targets (lower Paleozoic) were tested initially in the McConkey "HX" #1 but failed to yield commercial amounts of gas. The well was then plugged back to 5416 ft (1651 m). The Abo sandstone was perforated in an interval from 4764 to 4782 ft (1452–1458 m) to confirm the presence of natural gas on 27 June 1977. The well flowed 540 MCFG/day naturally.

Although concern was expressed that the gas might have a high nitrogen content because the producing formation was a "red bed" sequence, an analysis of the gas showed 1049 Btu/ft^3 (standard conditions) (Table 1). After extensive testing, the Abo zone was fracture-treated on 7 September 1977. The well was completed on 23 September 1977, at a rate of 2.55 MMCFG/day and 1 BCPD (51.3° API).

Post-Discovery

The completion of the McConkey "HX" #1 was a significant discovery, but uncertainty about reservoir performance slowed drilling activity for a few years. Because no pipeline connection was immediately accessible, no pressure draw-down could be made; hence no prediction could be made as to whether the reservoir was simply subnormally pressured (1126 psig) or whether it was a limited reservoir.

Only one more well, a confirmation test, was drilled in 1978; however, in 1979, Yates Petroleum and McClellan Oil of Roswell, New Mexico, made great strides in proving that production from the Abo sandstones covered a large area. Eleven wells were drilled and successfully completed as Abo gas producers (See Figure 8 for location of early wells).

In May 1979, the first Abo producer, the Yates Petroleum Federal "HY" #2, was placed on production and performed poorly. Subsequently, El Paso Natural Gas canceled plans to install a gathering system. Instead, Transwestern Pipeline finished construction of their pipeline and gathering system in the area in 1980. Twenty-eight Abo wells were put on production, and early Abo producers performed well, proving the Federal "HY" #2 to be an exception rather than the rule in Abo gas deliverability and reserves.

Pecos Slope Abo field attracted the attention of other oil operators in 1980. A total of 34 Abo wells were completed. Using data from these wells, Mesa Petroleum Corporation and Yates Petroleum Corporation applied jointly for a "tight gas" designation under Section 107 TF of the Natural Gas Policy Act. Section 107 TF of the NGPA made it possible to increase the maximum ceiling price for high-cost gas.

The Abo sandstones with their natural low permeability met all the criteria outlined by FERC

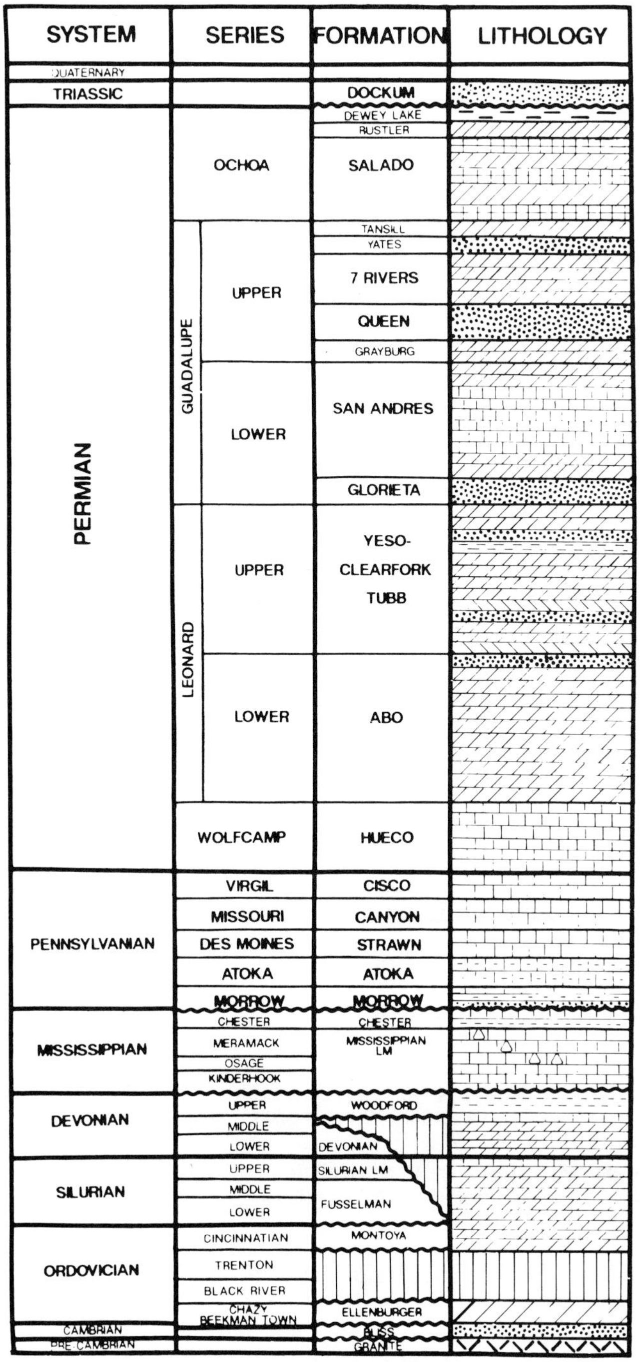
SYSTEM
SERIES
FORMATION
LITHOLOGY
QUATERNARY
TRIASSIC
DOCKUM
DEWEY LAKE
RUSTLER
PERMIAN
OCHOA
SALADO
TANSILL
YATES
GUADALUPE
UPPER
7 RIVERS
QUEEN
GRAYBURG
LOWER
SAN ANDRES
GLORIETA
LEONARD
UPPER
YESO-
CLEARFORK
TUBB
LOWER
ABO
WOLFCAMP
HUECO
PENNSYLVANIAN
VIRGIL
CISCO
MISSOURI
CANYON
DES MOINES
STRAWN
ATOKA
ATOKA
MORROW
MORROW
MISSISSIPPIAN
CHESTER
CHESTER
MERAMACK
MISSISSIPPIAN LM
OSAGE
KINDERHOOK
DEVONIAN
UPPER
MIDDLE
LOWER
WOODFORD
DEVONIAN
SILURIAN
UPPER
MIDDLE
LOWER
SILURIAN LM
FUSSELMAN
ORDOVICIAN
CINCINNATIAN
TRENTON
BLACK RIVER
CHAZY
BEEKMAN TOWN
MONTOYA
ELLENBURGER
CAMBRIAN
PRE CAMBRIAN
BLISS
GRANITE

Figure 2. Generalized stratigraphic section of Northwest shelf of the Permian basin. The Abo Formation is described as shelf evaporite dolomites and shelf margin carbonates over most of the Northwest shelf of the Delaware basin.

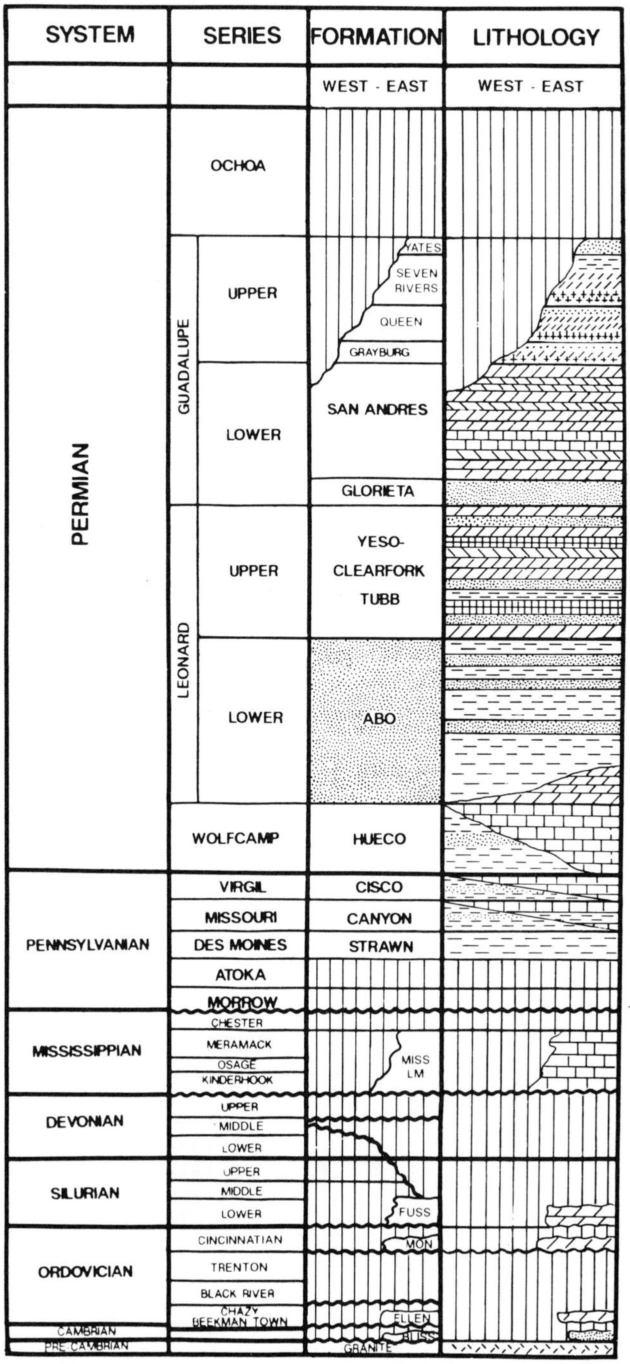
SYSTEM
SERIES
FORMATION
LITHOLOGY
WEST - EAST
WEST - EAST
PERMIAN
OCHOA
GUADALUPE
UPPER
YATES
SEVEN RIVERS
QUEEN
GRAYBURG
LOWER
SAN ANDRES
GLORIETA
LEONARD
UPPER
YESO-
CLEARFORK
TUBB
LOWER
ABO
WOLFCAMP
HUECO
PENNSYLVANIAN
VIRGIL
CISCO
MISSOURI
CANYON
DES MOINES
STRAWN
ATOKA
MORROW
MISSISSIPPIAN
CHESTER
MERAMACK
OSAGE
KINDERHOOK
MISS LM
DEVONIAN
UPPER
MIDDLE
LOWER
SILURIAN
UPPER
MIDDLE
LOWER
FUSS
ORDOVICIAN
CINCINNATIAN
MON
TRENTON
BLACK RIVER
CHAZY
BEEKMAN TOWN
ELLEN
BLISS
CAMBRIAN
PRE CAMBRIAN
GRANITE

Figure 3. Generalized stratigraphic section of the Pecos slope portion of the Northwest shelf. The stratigraphic section indicates that the Pecos slope is located on the westernmost limits of the basin. Much of the section represented on the remainder of the shelf area is absent or is represented by continental clastics or marginal marine sediments rather than marine carbonates.

Order 99, and in May 1981, the Abo Formation was designated a tight formation in an area that covered 1.536 million ac (621,600 ha) in Chaves and DeBaca Counties. This allowed the ceiling price for Abo gas to increase from the Section 102 gas price of $2.81/mcf to a Section 107 price of $4.92/mcf, the price in June 1981 (Figure 5).

Under this protected environment the Pecos slope Abo field flourished. In late 1981, the Abo Formation became the leading target for natural gas exploration development in New Mexico. The number of wells

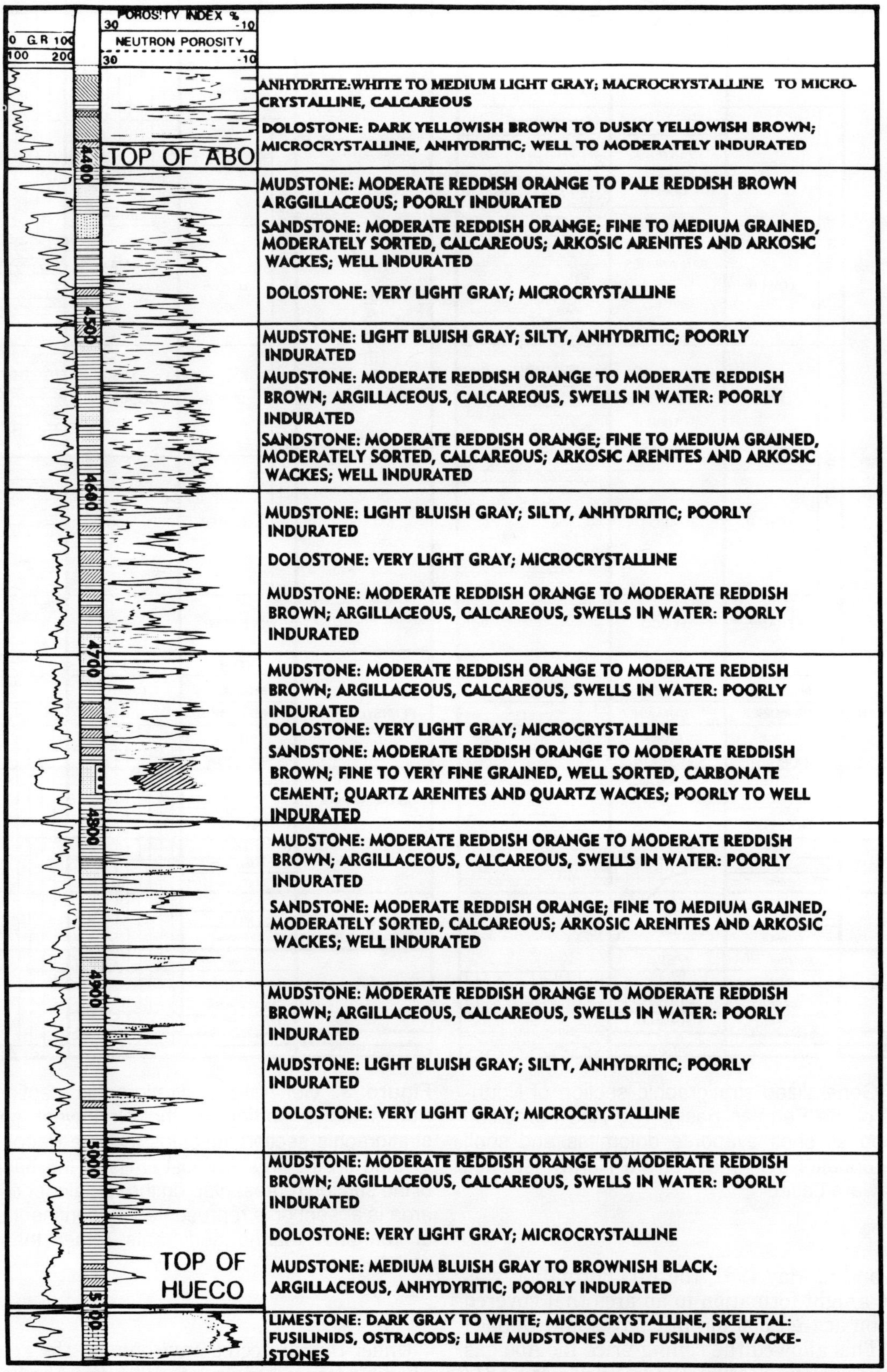

Figure 4. Type log of Abo sequence, Yates Petroleum Corp. #1 McConkey, Sec. 10, T9S, R26E, Chaves County, New Mexico. Sample descriptions, Broadhead, 1984.

Table 1. Gas quality test report, Yates Petroleum Corporation, Pecos Slope (South) Desert Rose Unit #2, Abo reservoir, 3/14/88.

Components	Specific Gravity	Mole Fraction	Liquefiable Hydrocarbons	Component GPM	GPM Content
Nitrogen	0.9672	0.0472	Propane	27.514	0.4677
Carbon dioxide	1.5195	0.0027	Isobutane	32.698	0.1014
Helium	0.1382		N-Butane	31.510	0.1859
Oxygen	1.1048	0.0000	LPG		0.7550
Hydrogen sulfide	1.1766	0.0000	Isopentane	36.582	0.0658
Water vapor	0.6220	0.0000	N-Pentane	36.213	0.0652
			Hexanes	41.111	0.0822
			Heptanes+	46.126	0.0323
Methane	0.5539	0.8710	Natural gasoline		0.2455
Ethane	1.0382	0.0468			
Propane	1.5225	0.0170	Total liquefiable GPM		1.0005
Isobutane	2.0068	0.0031			
N-Butane	2.0068	0.0059	Water vapor content:		
Isopentane	2.4911	0.0018	Gas mixture static PSIG		145.0
N-Pentane	2.4911	0.0018	Flowing gas temp (F)		53.0
Hexanes	2.9753	0.0020	Water vapor dew point (F)		52.0
Heptanes+	3.5807	0.0007	LBS water vapor / MMCF		61.0
			Dehy installed (TW)		NO
Composition		1.0000	Instrument type		RAN
			Mol fraction		0.0013
Mixture specific gravity					
Calc. from anal. (real)		0.643			
Determined by test inst.		0.643	Mixture heating value		
			(Btu/cf @ 14.73 PSIA, 60°F, Sat.)		
			Calculated from analysis		1049
Compressibility (Z)		0.9976	By Calorimetry		None
Sp. gr. deviation allowed for water vapor: 0.004					

drilled that year for Abo gas increased to 158 wells, of which 149 were successfully completed as producers.

The state and federal lease sales in 1981 served as the most accurate barometer of the excitement generated by the Pecos slope Abo immediately after the area received the "tight formation" designation. A state sale, held early in the year, saw an average per-acre bid of $325 for 30,000 ac (12,140 ha) northwest of the main play in Chaves and DeBaca Counties. The acreage drew $9.4 million in total bonuses for the state of New Mexico. Bonuses paid for leases in the Pecos slope continued to escalate through the year. New records were set in the December 1981 Bureau of Land Management sale, with Getty Oil Company successfully acquiring leases for $4,571.43 per acre and $3,571 per acre for small tracts in the main gas fairway (Anonymous, 1983, Petroleum Frontiers).

The rapid expansion continued and accelerated into 1982, when development of the Pecos Slope field reached its pinnacle with 325 new gas completions (Figure 5). Total annual production reached its highest level in 1984 with 44.6 bcf gas produced from 636 wells (Figure 17). From 1983 to the present, effects of the surplus of natural gas coupled with the deregulation of natural gas has greatly reduced developmental activity on the Pecos slope. An average of only 35 wells are now drilled each year.

Today, the Pecos slope Abo field, as developed on 160 ac spacing, covers over 700 mi^2 (1813 km^2). A total of 1030 wells have been drilled in the play, of which 906 have been completed as gas producers. Annual production from the field is 25 bcf gas, and total cumulative production through 1 January 1991 is 272.7 bcf.

DISCOVERY METHOD

The field was discovered, as described before, by relogging an old, abandoned hole with new logging techniques and then thoroughly examining the entire borehole in addition to the deeper Silurian, Devonian, and Ordovician main objectives. No statistics are readily available, but many fields have been discovered in the Permian basin while drilling for entirely different objectives. Therefore, it is always important to evaluate the entire sequence in multipay basins with adequate logging techniques.

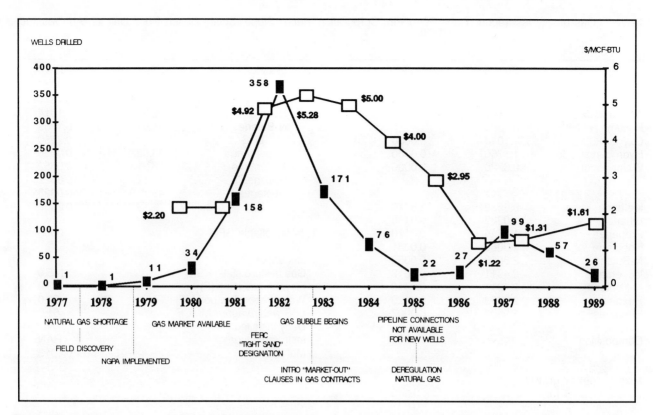

Figure 5. History of Pecos Slope field drilling activity as compared to the average price of natural gas per mcf adjusted for Btu content. The number of wells drilled per year in the Pecos Slope, in black, is plotted against the average price of gas, in white.

The discovery of the Pecos Slope field also resulted from testing the prospective interval through pipe even though there was no analogous production in the area. In summary, sound geological and engineering procedures combined with new logging technologies led to discovery of the Pecos Slope.

After the discovery, subsurface methods—log analysis, gross isoliths, and net sandstone maps—were employed in the exploration and the subsequent exploitation of the Abo Formation in the Pecos Slope field.

STRUCTURE

Tectonic History

The Permian basin structural framework took form in Proterozoic time (Hills, 1984). Located at the southern margin of what is now the North American craton, the Permian basin area was greatly affected by the late Precambrian–early Paleozoic break-up of North America. Structures formed at this time, such as the Pedernal massif (Figure 1), a Precambrian landmass, played a significant role in controlling the location of younger features, particularly those formed during the late Paleozoic (Keller, 1984; Galley, 1984).

As the region stabilized, an Atlantic-type, stable platform basin evolved. The Tabosa basin, a shallow depression lying between the Pedernal massif and the Concho arch, was characterized by the wide deposition of shelf carbonates (Galley, 1984; Hills, 1984; Horak, 1984) (Figures 6A and 6D). The region underwent only mild tectonism until Late Mississippian time (Hills, 1984). Tectonism increased as the African and South American plates approached the North American continent.

The Permian basin evolved into a basement-controlled deformed foreland basin during the late Paleozoic as the southern margin of North America collided with the South American–African plate (Horak, 1984) (Figures 6B, 6C, and 6E). Associated tectonism during the Pennsylvanian resulted in the emergence of the Pedernal highlands as a southern extension of the Ancestral Rockies (Broadhead, 1982). The precise outline and the tectonic nature of the Pedernal uplift is not understood; however, it is partly a broad upwarp and partly fault-bounded (Kelly, 1979). Coinciding with the ascent of the Pedernal highlands, the Central basin uplift arose in the center of the Tabosa basin, dividing it into two basins: the Midland basin and the deep Delaware basin (Galley, 1984; Hills, 1984).

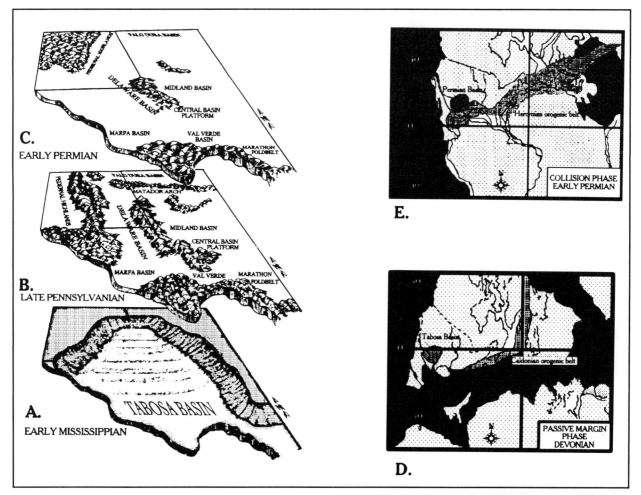

Figure 6. Paleogeography of the Permian basin. (A) The Tabosa basin, an Atlantic-type stable platform, was characterized by wide deposition of shelf carbonates. (B) A basement controlled deformed foreland basin, the Permian basin, formed during the Pennsylvanian. (C) The final thrusting of the Marathon fold belt in Early Permian signaled the end of strong tectonic movement in the Permian basin. Pennsylvanian and Permian tectonism played an important role in dictating the distribution of sedimentation. (D) The ancestral Permian basin was situated on a passive continental margin from late Precambrian through Late Mississippian (Horak, 1984). (E) Illustrates the Hercynian collisional orogeny. Suturing along the southern continental margin was progressive from east to west. Advancing through the Appalachians and the Ouachitas during the Pennsylvanian, culmination was in the Early Permian in West Texas (Horak, 1984).

Both features pulsed positively again during Wolfcampian time. These uplifts played an important role in dictating the distribution of Pennsylvanian and Permian depositional systems (Figures 6C and 6E).

The final thrusting of the Marathon fold belt in the Early Permian signaled the end of strong tectonic movement in the Permian basin area (Hills, 1984), and the remainder of the Permian was characterized by only mild tectonic activity. Cyclical changes in sedimentation in the Permian resulted from eustatic changes in mean sea level rather than from tectonism.

The Abo Formation (Permian Leonard) in "the Pecos country" (a general term for a broad area along the Pecos River of southeastern New Mexico) was deposited as a fluvial clastic wedge on the north-western limits of the stable Northwestern shelf, the transitional area between the Pedernal highlands to the west-northwest and the Delaware basin to the southeast. The siliciclastics, derived from the Pedernal uplift, were deposited downslope by fluvial processes during a sea level lowstand (Figure 7).

Regional Structure

The producing area is located on the north-central part of the Pecos slope, a term applied by Kelley and Thompson (1964) for the broad, very gentle eastward-

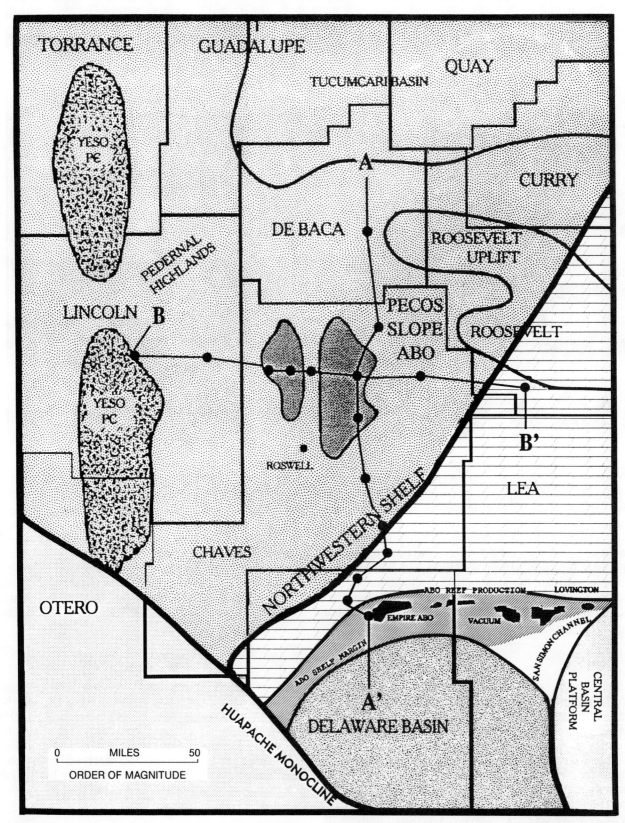

Figure 7. Paleogeography map of the Permian Abo Formation. (Modified from Kelley, 1971, and Scott et al., 1983.) The Abo was deposited as a fluvial silicilastic wedge on the northwestern limits of the stable Northwestern shelf. Derived from the Pedernal highlands, the clastics were deposited downslope during a sea level lowstand. Carbonate deposition (horizontal crosshatch) dominated the remainder of the shelf area and the shelf margin. Cross sections A–A' and B–B' are shown by Figures 10 and 11, respectively.

136

dipping homocline. Descending at a rate of 50 to 100 ft/mi (0.5° to 1°), the Pecos slope is the structural descent from the Mescalero arch and the crests of the Sacramento and Guadalupe uplifts into the Delaware basin (Kelley, 1971). The structure of the Pecos slope is attributed to the late Tertiary rise of the Sacramento and Guadalupe uplifts (Kelley, 1971).

Although the Pecos slope as seen today certainly reflects the effects of the Laramide orogeny (Kelley, 1971), it is probable that the structure was very similar during Early Permian on the northern part of the slope, with the exception of a slight variance in the dip direction from east to east-southeast. As the Mescalero arch corresponds vaguely with the ancient Pedernal uplift (Kelley, 1971), the Permian Pecos slope could be defined as the structural descent from the Pedernal highlands into the Delaware basin.

The most significant structural features on the Pecos slope are a series of long, narrow, northeast-wardly trending "buckles" paralleling each other 8 to 20 mi (13–32 km) apart (Kelley, 1971) (Figure 8). The buckles named by Merritt (1920) are from west to east: the Border, Six Mile, and Y-O. As described by Kelley (1971), the buckles are "right-wrench fold-faults which are undoubtedly Precambrian rooted and show evidence of activity at least as old as Permian" (Figure 9).

STRATIGRAPHY

Regional Stratigraphy

The Abo was first described by Lee (1909) as a ". . . coarse-grained sandstone, dark red to purple, usually conglomeratic at base; [sic] with subordinate amount of shale which attains prominence in some places." Since the Abo was described in Abo canyon at the southern end of the Manzano Mountains, Soccorro and Torrance Counties (Broadhead, 1984), the term has been applied to similiar facies that range in age from Pennsylvanian to Permian Leonardian in age. In addition to describing the diachronous red bed sequence, the term *Abo* has also been used to define a time-stratigraphic sequence between the marine Hueco Formation and the marine Yeso Formation in the Permian basin. Lower Leonardian shelf evaporite-dolomites and shelf margin dolomites have also been labeled Abo (Jones, 1953) (Figures 2 and 3).

At the type section, the Abo Formation is thought to be primarily Wolfcampian age (Kottlowski, 1963). In the Pecos slope country, as well as in most of the subsurface in southeastern New Mexico, the Abo appears to be early to middle Leonardian age. This is supported by physical stratigraphic correlations and biostratigraphic criteria. Leonardian fusulinids were described in Abo dolomites in Lea County (Lloyd, 1949). *Schubertella Malonica, Schwagerina crassitecotoria,* and *S. hawkinsi* are present in the carbonate just below the "Third Bone Spring

sandstone" (Silver and Todd, 1969, from personal communications with J. Skinner and G. Wilde). The Third Bone Spring sandstone is correlated to be partly coeval with the green and red quartzose claystone and siltstone above the Abo reef and above Abo shelf dolomites (Silver and Todd, 1969) (Figure 10). This shelf detritus section appears to be time equivalent to the fluvial clastic wedge on the Pecos slope. Silver and Todd (1969) recommend that the term *Abo* be ". . . restricted to the shelf clastic lithofacies and that a nomenclatural framework be proposed for the Leonardian that is similiar to the one developed for the Guadalupian series (King, 1948, p. 12) using the principle of arbitrary cutoff (Wheeler and Mallory, 1953, p. 2412) for designation of stratigraphic units." As the *Abo* is a term widely used and accepted in the subsurface in southeastern New Mexico and does appear to represent a rough time-stratigraphic unit on the Northwestern shelf and its adjacent margin, it is highly unlikely that the nomenclature will be modified.

Depositional Model

Two stratigraphic cross sections, a north-south segment (Figure 10) and a west-east section (Figure 11), were constructed in an attempt to define the regional time-stratigraphic framework as well as to describe various lithofacies associated with the Abo Formation. Both sections were generated by recognizing three main time lines: the top of the Tubb sandstone (upper Leonardian) that provides the stratigraphic datum for each section; the base of the shelf detritus representing a relative sea level fall and its subsequent lowstand; and the marine Hueco Formation (Wolfcampian). After the time-stratigraphic structure was in place, it was possible to envision the depositional model.

The Hueco Formation conformably underlies the Abo Formation. Consisting of alternating beds of thick limestones and thin mudstones, the Hueco sediments have been interpreted as having a shallow open marine origin (Broadhead, 1984). Inasmuch as the Hueco limestones are very extensive laterally, it is believed that sea level was at a relative highstand during the Wolfcampian (Figure 12A). This is consistent with Vail et al. (1977) who document a global highstand of sea level during Wolfcampian and earliest Leonardian. The exception to this is Wolfcampian-age sediments in close proximity to the buried Pedernal landmass. There marine limestones abruptly change laterally into coarse-grained clastics. It is evident that the Pedernal was actively uplifted during the Wolfcampian and the depositional relief was great (Broadhead, 1984). Active erosion and deposition during that period nearly inhumed the Pedernal in its own debris.

As sea level remained at a relative stillstand through earliest Leonardian, the deposition of carbonates on the shelf and the shelf margin continued at a maximum (Figure 12B). This is

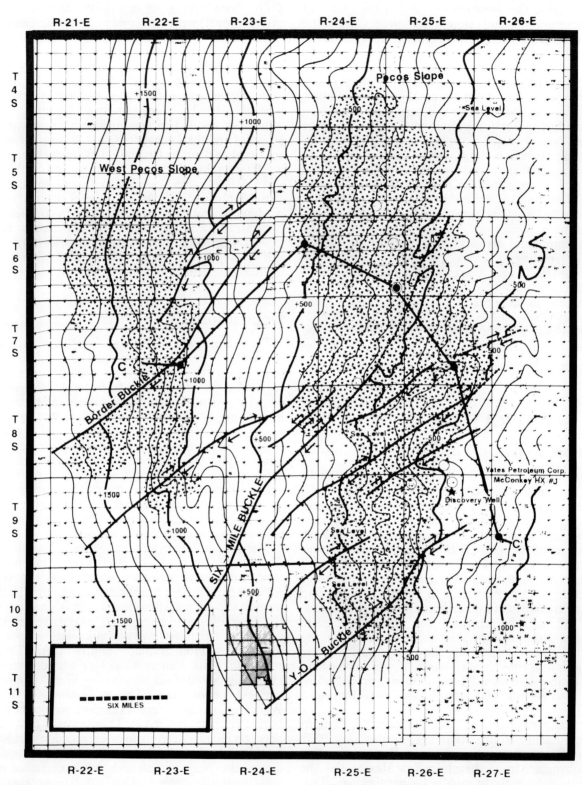

Figure 8. Structural field map of the Pecos Slope field contoured on top of the Abo Formation. The contour interval is 100 ft. Gas production is noted by the stippled area. The line of structural cross section C–C′ (Figure 9) is labeled. Field discovery well, Yates Petroleum, McConkey HX #1, Sec. 10, T9S, R26E is located by a star. Wells highlighted by a large circle indicate important wells drilled early in the play that proved Abo production over a large geographic area. In addition to the northeastward buckles—the Border Buckle, Six-Mile Buckle, Y.O. Buckle—there are numerous smaller parallel faults that also exhibit right lateral movement.

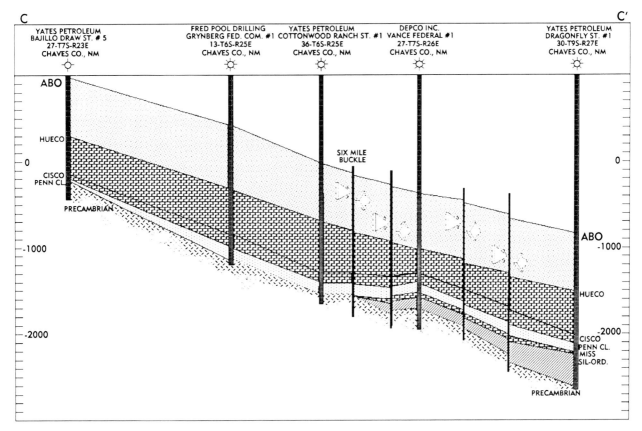

Figure 9. Structural relief on top of the Abo Formation in the field area is 2500 ft from west to east. The average dip rate is 66 ft/mi. Lateral displacement associated with both the large fold faults as well as the smaller features varies from several miles to less than 1320 ft. Vertical movement is relatively minor. Often the upthrown block changes sides along strike, but generally the blocks are displaced down to the southeast. Location of cross section C–C' is shown on Figure 8.

evidenced by the growth of a barrier reef complex along the basin rim and the deposition of a thick sequence of evaporitic dolomites on the shelf. The increase in Abo sedimentation to the south also suggests the continued subsidence of the basin. At the Empire Abo Reef field in Eddy County, New Mexico, the Abo Formation is over 1200 ft (366 m) thick (Figure 10). Northward, the shelf evaporite dolomites grade laterally into and intertongue with a mudstone lithofacies that prevails as the lowermost one-third of the Abo Formation in the Pecos country.

The sudden change from carbonate deposition to clastic deposition in the shelf area implies a drop in mean sea level during mid-Leonardian time (Figure 12C). Again this concurs with work done by Vail et al. (1977). The drop in sea level is thought to have been eustatically controlled by glaciation in the southern hemisphere (Jacka et al., 1968). With sea level at a relative lowstand, erosional processes were reactivated and detrital sediments were swept from the upper slopes of positive elements, to be transported and deposited downslope by fluvial processes. The main Pecos slope area appears to have been a fluvial depositional center. Channel facies occupies the middle one-third of the Abo Formation

in the main Pecos slope producing area. Further to the west, this facies has no representation, indicating nondeposition and/or erosion on the upper slopes during this time period. As the influx of clastics continued, land-derived detritus prograded south and east across the shelf. Shelf detritus was then able to enter the basin through submarine canyons and other re-entrants (Silver and Todd, 1969).

The remainder of the Abo Formation is characteristic of the effects of a gradual rise in sea level. As the sea began its encroachment, the main depositional center for the meandering channel facies moved laterally to the west (Figure 12D). Fluvial processes continued into early Yeso time as indicated by the facies climbing higher stratigraphically to the west. The Abo and lowermost Yeso beds almost completely buried the Pedernal.

The Pedernal was only mildly manifested during the balance of Yeso time. Anhydrite and dolomite beds in the Yeso immediately above the red bed section mark the return to a shallow marine environment. These sediments rest unconformably on the Precambrian Pedernal.

In summary, the fall and then rise of sea level in mid-Leonardian resulted in a fluvial clastic wedge

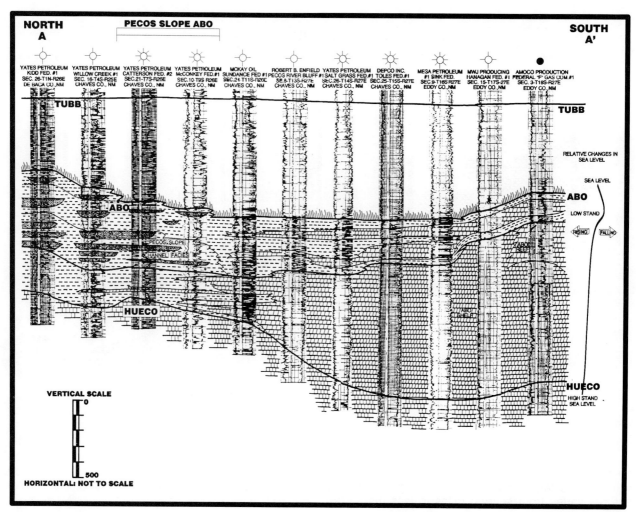

Figure 10. Three main time lines were used to define the time-stratigraphic framework: the top of the Tubb sandstone (upper Leonardian) that provides the stratigraphic datum for each section; the base of the shelf detritus representing a relative sea level fall and its subsequent lowstand; and the marine Hueco Formation (Wolfcampian). The Hueco Formation conformably underlies the Abo Formation. Consisting of alternating beds of thick limestones and thin mudstones, the Hueco sediments have been interpreted as having a shallow open-marine origin. Early Abo deposition is characterized by the growth of a barrier reef complex along the basin rim and the deposition of a thick sequence of evaporitic dolomites on the shelf.

The increase in Abo sedimentation to the south also suggests the continued subsidence of the basin. Northward, the shelf evaporite dolomites grade laterally into and intertongue with a mudstone lithofacies that represents the lowermost one-third of the Abo Formation in the Pecos country. The main Pecos slope area appears to have been a fluvial depositional center; as the influx of clastics continued, land derived detritus prograded south and east across the shelf. Shelf detritus was then able to enter the basin through submarine canyons and other re-entrants. The line of cross section is shown on Figures 7 and 13. (Sealevel curves after Vail, 1977.)

covering all but the highest Precambrian peaks of the Pedernal. Gas production from the Abo is limited to the distal end of the clastic wedge (Figure 13).

TRAP

The exact trapping mechanism is not well understood. However, trapping probably resulted, at least partly, from the tectonically induced fracturing of a stratigraphic wedge-out of the clastic facies, as will be described. Bottom hole pressures, averaging 1125 psig, are subnormal and constant throughout the Pecos Slope field. Similiar pressures are measured in the West Pecos Slope field, 5 mi (8 km) removed from the Pecos Slope field and 2000 ft (610 m) shallower. The uniformity of these data over a wide area strongly indicates that a regional trapping mechanism is responsible for the large accumulation of gas.

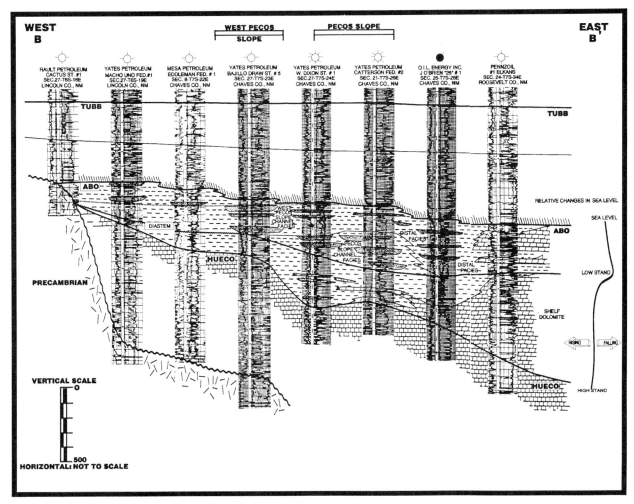

WEST
B

WEST PECOS
SLOPE

PECOS SLOPE

EAST
B'

Figure 11. Channel facies occupies the middle one-third of the Abo Formation in the main Pecos Slope producing area. Further to the west, this facies is not represented, indicating nondeposition and/or erosion on the upper slopes. As the sea encroached, the main depositional center for the meandering channel facies moved laterally to the west. Fluvial processes continued into early Yeso time (Figures 2 and 3) as indicated by the facies climbing higher stratigraphically to the west. The Pedernal uplift was only mildly manifested during the balance of Yeso time. Anhydrite and dolomite beds in the Yeso immediately above the red bed section mark the return to a shallow marine environment. The sediments rest unconformably on the Precambrian Pedernal. The location of cross section B-B' is shown on Figures 7 and 13. (Sealevel curves after Vail, 1977.)

Structure

The structure mapped on the top of the Abo facies over the field area is very similiar to the overall structure as previously described (Figure 8). It must be pointed out, however, that this map represents the top of the Abo facies, which is diachronous; so a true time line has not been mapped. The depth of the top of the Abo varies from 2550 ft (+1800 ft) (770 m; +549 m) on the west side of the field to 4700 ft (–700 ft) (1432; –213 m) on the eastern boundary. The average dip rate is 66 ft/mi (¾°) and the dip direction is E20°S.

In addition to the northeastward buckles mentioned previously, numerous smaller parallel faults also exhibit right-lateral movement. Lateral displacement associated with both the large fold faults as well as the smaller features varies from several miles to less than 1320 ft (402 m). Vertical movement is relatively minor, but often the upthrown block changes sides along strike (Broadhead, 1984).

It is not possible to determine if these buckles or any other structural features played a significant role in the deposition of the Abo or if they played any major part in the accumulation of gas. There are no adequate penetrations below the Abo to reconstruct the pre-existing topography that may or may not have influenced the sites of deposition.

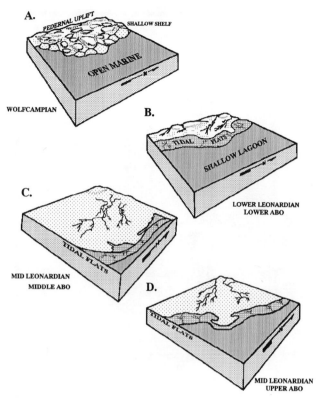

Figure 12. Schematics of depositional environments. (Modified after Speer, 1983.) (A) Sea level highstand; Wolfcampian sediments consist of laterally extensive, alternating beds of thick limestones and thin mudstones; marine limestones abruptly change laterally into coarse-grained clastics in close proximity to the Pedernal uplift. (B) Sea level stillstand; the deposition of carbonates on the shelf margin and shelf continued at a maximum. (C) The sudden change from carbonate deposition to clastic deposition in the shelf area implies a drop in mean sea level; fluvial processes dominated the shelf. (D) The remainder of Leonardian time was characterized by a gradual rise in sea level; facies shifted laterally to the west-northwest.

Depositional Mechanics

The productive interval (the upper two-thirds) of the Abo Formation in the Pecos slope country represents the distal end of a fluvial clastic wedge. Over time, changes can be seen in the channel patterns and sedimentation behavior resulting from outside influences such as changes in climate or changes in sea level (Figures 10 and 11).

The middle one-third of the Abo is believed to have been deposited in the lower reaches of a meandering channel system. Because there are few cores available in the Pecos slope area, this depositional facies has been predicated by the detailed mapping of individual sandstones, as well as by placing the entire sequence in its proper relationship to laterally adjacent environments. In places it appears that the meandering nature of the channels becomes more of a braided channel system, but perhaps this could better be described by the term "anastomosing" (Schumm, 1968) for channels of alluvial plains that branch and rejoin (Figure 13). Rust (1978) also recommends this term for highly sinuous multichannel patterns. This may happen when the channels carry only flood waters with a high suspended load and very little bed load.

Individual channel sandstones can be mapped in a longitudinal direction nearly the length of the field (Figure 13). The channels average less than a mile in width and show a high degree of sinuosity. In a cross-section view, the geometry of the sand body is concave downward and flat on top (Figures 10 and 11). There is an abrupt contact between the channel sands and adjacent mudstones. The major depositional feature produced by this type of channel is point bar deposits (Reineck and Singh, 1980). Point bar deposits are characterized by an upward-fining sequence, and this sequence can be observed in productive Abo sandstones from the gamma ray curve on geophysical logs (Figure 14).

In observing this package of sediments as a whole, several points are worth noting. Channel thickness can exceed 40 ft (12 m) but averages around 20 ft (6 m). The oldest channels are located on the eastern and southeastern edge of the meanderbelt. In a general way, the channels rise stratigraphically in the section to the north and west; however, the channels do stack in the heart of the main Pecos slope producing area. The typically water-bearing sandstones become more abundant to the north-northwest of the producing area and may be more of a braided type channel sequence. Other water-bearing sandstones can be found to the east of the area of gas production. Immediately to the south of the Pecos Slope field as well as to the west of current gas production, mudstone facies become predominant at the expense of sandstone, which decreases dramatically (Figure 13). Farther to the west, the entire facies wedges out. The most prolific production in the Pecos Slope occurs from channel point bar deposits in this facies that occupy the middle one-third of the Abo Formation (Figures 4, 10, and 11).

The deposits of the upper one-third of the Abo Formation in the main Pecos Slope field productive area are similiar to the meandering channel system as previously described, but there are also some notable differences. Channel deposits are common but do not reach the thickness of the lower channels and cannot be mapped over an extensive area. The sandstones often exhibit a geometry differing from the meandering channel, point bar deposits. This could be explained by the operation of any of several other types of fluvial processes in addition to those resulting in channel, point bar deposits: natural levee deposits, crevasse splay deposits, or possibly even flood plain deposits.

Regardless of the type of deposition, all of the deposits illustrate that flooding was important in the

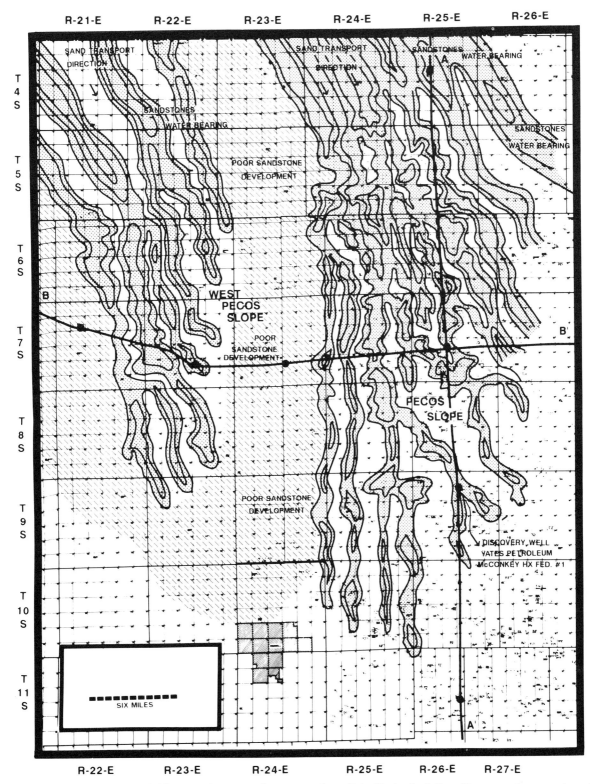

Figure 13. An isolith map of Abo sandstones shows that gas production is from lower reaches of a meandering channel system. Individual channel sandstones can be mapped in a longitudinal direction nearly the length of the field. Sandstones become more abundant to the north-northwest of the producing area and probably represent a braided type channel environment. They are typically water-bearing. There seems to be little evidence to support deltaic sedimen- tation. It is likely that the Abo-age rivers entered the lagoon as estuaries and there was no well-developed delta complex. As a transgressive sequence has been documented, it is likely that rising seas did not allow the formation of a delta as Abo river valleys were drowned by the rising marine lagoonal waters. Cross sections A–A′ and B–B′ are shown on Figures 10 and 11.

143

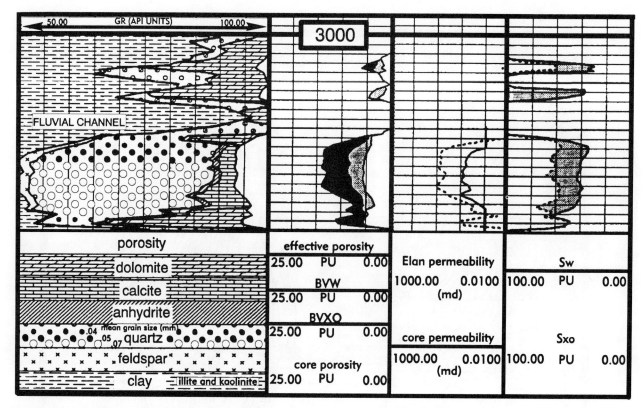

Figure 14. Comparison of geophysical log and core data in the Mitchell and Halbouty Energy No. 3 M & M Federal, SW/4 NW/4 NW/4 Sec. 31, T5S, R23E, Chaves County, New Mexico. The gamma ray curve (left) illustrates the correlation between gamma ray response and mean grain size. The upward fining sequence from 0.07 mm to 0.04 mm indicates the fluvial channel nature of the sandstone. Quartz is the dominant mineral, with other constituents being dolomite, calcite, anhydrite, feldspar, and clays. The clays are illite and kaolinite. This plot graphically defines the mineralogy in their relative percentages. Geophysical log and core porosity are described in porosity units (PU). The solid line indicates effective log porosity whereas core porosity is described by the dashed line. Porosity determined from both means correlated favorably although core porosity peaks higher at certain points. Bulk volume water (BVW) is shown in white, residual hydrocarbon saturation in gray, and movable hydrocarbons (BVXO) (gas) in black. Permeability is described by both methods in a logarithmic plot in md. Elan (log derived) permeabilities are consistently higher than core-derived permeabilities. The final plot illustrates core derived water saturations (SW or S_w) (solid line) versus hydrocarbon saturation (SXO or S_{xo}) (dashed line). Geophysical log plots were provided courtesy of Schlumberger and core data were provided courtesy of Mitchell Energy.

deposition of the upper Abo. Flooding could have resulted from changes in the following environmental factors: lower relief of the deposition slope, subtle changes in the climate, and rising sea level. Each could have contributed separately, but at least two of these factors can be documented: the lower relief of the depositional slope and the rise in sea level.

Speer (1983) details upper Abo ephemeral streams in outcrops in the north-central Sacramento Mountains. These streams were deposited on a broad, low-relief alluvial plain. He also notes that flashy discharge was an important process and states that the climate was seasonal, probably semi-arid. In brief, it seems that the processes described which resulted in the deposition of the upper Abo west of the Pedernal highlands are very similiar to the processes which led to the deposition of the upper one-third of the Abo Formation east of the Pedernals in the Pecos slope country.

The producing facies in the West Pecos slope area is time-equivalent to the upper one-third of the Abo in the main Pecos Slope field (Figure 11). However, this facies exhibits depositional characteristics similar to those of the meandering channel facies that occupies the middle two-thirds of the Abo Formation in the Pecos Slope field. Detailed mapping of individual sandstones implies some overbank-type deposits, but certainly not to the extent of those in the upper one-third of the Abo in the Pecos Slope field. This suggests that as the sea encroached from the south and east, facies shifted laterally to the north and west. The sandstones become more abundant to the north and again may represent more of a braided sequence as the depositional slope increased.

The sandstones become more water-bearing to the north and west of the West Pecos Slope field producing area. Water-bearing sandstones can also be found on the eastern perimeter of the field. The sandstones of the West Pecos Slope field channel facies decrease as the amount of mudstones increases to the west. Ultimately the entire interval wedges out against the buried Pedernal. Therefore, the depositional mechanics of the West Pecos Slope field are very similiar to those described in the Pecos Slope field. However, one notable difference is the frequency of the sandstones in a vertical sequence. In the Pecos Slope field, sandstones are very abundant in the upper two-thirds of the Abo. In the West Pecos Slope, the main sandstone deposition is nearly confined to two stratigraphic intervals.

To summarize, it appears that both the Pecos Slope field and the West Pecos Slope field were deposited by a fluvial system. Both were located on the lower reaches of that system, but not necessarily as a delta. There seems to be little evidence to support deltaic sedimentation. It has been observed that the sandstones are almost always upward-fining rather than upward-coarsening as characteristic of distributary mouth-bar deposits common to a delta (Figure 14). This is not to say that additional work to the south and east of the producing areas may not ultimately delineate an Abo delta complex or that additional core information from the producing area may not prove that the sands are partly deltaic sedimentation. However, the extant data do not support a deltaic complex at this time. One possibility is that the Abo-age rivers entered the lagoon as estuaries and that there was not a well-developed delta complex. Because a transgressive sequence has been noted in Abo sedimentation after the initial drop in sea level, it is possible that the rising seas did not allow the formation of a delta. It is also possible that an estuarine environment was developed as the Abo river valleys were drowned by the rising marine lagoonal waters.

Reservoir Characteristics

The gross thickness of the Abo Formation in the producing area varies from over 650 ft (198 m) in thickness in the Pecos Slope field to less than 400 ft (122 m) thick in the West Pecos Slope field (Figure 11). Production is limited to the upper two-thirds of the formation, with pay thicknesses averaging 30 ft (9 m). However, pay thickness can exceed 80 ft (24 m) with a minimum figure being 10 to 12 ft (3–4 m). Producing sandstones are described as red, fine-grained to silt, with the major constituents being quartz and plagioclase feldspar. Mica and heavy minerals can be found in trace amounts. Clays (illite and chlorite), calcite, dolomite, and anhydrite are the cementing agents (Figure 15). The natural permeability of the sandstones is very low, 0.03 to 0.05 md (Figure 14). The average porosity is 12–14%, but porosities can exceed 20%. The minimum producing

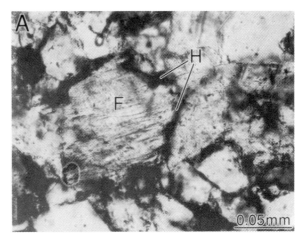

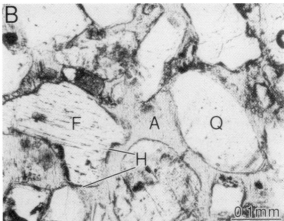

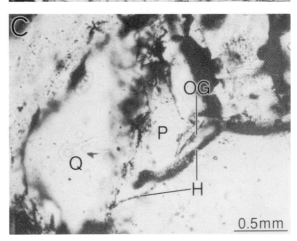

Figure 15. Thin section photomicrographs (Broadhead, New Mexico Bureau of Mines and Mineral Resources, 1984). (A) Abo sandstone, Yates Petroleum Corp. No. 2 Thorpe Federal, 3962.4 ft. Note intergranular clay hematite cement (H) and slightly altered potash feldspar (F). (B) Abo sandstone, Yates Petroleum Corp. No. 1 McConkey 4780–4790 ft. Note poikilotopic anhydrite (A) cementing loosely packed subangular to sub-rounded quartz (Q) and feldspar (F) clay hematite rims (H) separate anhydrite cement from framework grains. (C) Abo sandstone, Yates Petroleum Corp. No. 1 Willow Creek, 4190–4200 ft. Note relict intergranular porosity (P), quartz framework grains (Q), clay hematite rims (H), and authigenic quartz overgrowths (OG).

145

porosity is around 9%. As the average natural flow rate of a typical Abo well in the Pecos Slope is 70 MCFG/day, all of the producing wells have been artificially stimulated, "sand frac'd," to produce gas commercially. Fracture treatment effectively increases flow rates as much as tenfold. This type of treatment is believed to be so successful in that it opens and enhances existing, naturally occurring but partially healed fractures in the sandstones.

Water saturations in the field are highly variable, with the average being 38.5% (Figure 14). When determining if an Abo sandstone is gas productive or water-bearing, bulk volume water (BVW) calculations are often more beneficial. The average calculated bulk volume water for producing sandstone is 0.045%, and calculations above 0.065% generally indicate that the sandstone may produce gas with water. Calculations above 0.07% indicate that the sandstone is probably water-bearing.

Source

To understand the occurrence and distribution of natural gas in the Pecos Slope fields it is critical to determine the source. Broadhead (1984) has presented a good analysis which indicates that the gas is not derived from the local Abo red bed sequence. The red color of the beds results from oxidation during early diagenesis that would have also resulted in the rapid aerobic decay of organic material. A burial history plot also suggests that depth of burial was not sufficient for the generation of hydrocarbons locally (Figure 16). However, the possibility exists that the gas could have been generated in the marine shelf, shelf margin, and especially the basinal equivalents of the Abo (Bone Spring). Submarine canyons that were conduits for introduction of sediment to the basin could have been prime avenues of migration of hydrocarbons from the organic-rich basinal sediments back up to the shelf margin and shelf. The Abo marine shelf deposits also may have generated hydrocarbons.

In addition to a stratigraphically equivalent source, the Hueco marine limestones lying conformably below the Abo also may have been a source rock (Broadhead, 1984). Gas analyses from Hueco production in the vicinity of the Pecos Slope field are very comparable to the compositional analyses of Abo gas (Table 2).

Perhaps the best possibility for the source may be marine rocks in the Pennsylvanian system. Gas produced from Pennsylvanian sandstones and carbonates, as with Hueco Formation gas, is very similar in compositional analysis to Abo gas. The predicate for placing the Pennsylvanian as the prime candidate exists in the occurrence of gas in Ordovician dolomites and even in Precambrian arkoses on the Pecos slope. Again, the gas produced from these horizons is compositionally comparable to Abo gas, but these reservoirs historically produce only when overlain unconformably by the Pennsylvanian.

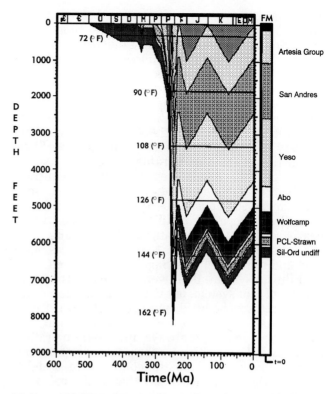

Figure 16. Burial history plot Pecos Slope Abo, Yates Petroleum Corp. McConkey "HX" Federal #1. Burial history indicates hydrocarbon generation did not occur locally. However, the thickness of sediments eroded during periods of uplift is not well documented. It is possible that hydrocarbon generation did, in fact, occur locally.

The enigma of the source of Abo gas continues and has been further complicated by discovering trace amounts of organic arsenic compounds in the gas. On 8 June 1988, the Pecos Slope field was shut in after Southern California Gas Company discovered a white, chalky precipitate in their transportation system. Upon investigation, the material was identified as an organic arsenic compound and the gas bearing this compound was traced to gas delivered via Transwestern pipeline. Transwestern targeted the gas from the Pecos Slope field. The arsenic levels, averaging roughly 500 $\mu g/m^3$, did not at any time constitute a health hazard since the exposure was no greater than from ambient air; however, the solid precipitate did pose operational problems downstream in the Socal system.

The source for the arsenic compounds has never been fully explained. Core samples from the Abo Formation in the Pecos slope area were examined by X-ray fluorescence and X-ray diffraction methods. Samples were also analyzed using ICP (inductively coupled plasma) mass spectrometer. No arsenic-bearing minerals were detected in any of the samples. Trace amounts of arsenic, from <1 ppm to 5 ppm, were noted in Abo shales and siltstones, but these values are well within the normal ranges for

Table 2. Compositional gas analyses. Analyses of gases from Hueco Formation, Pennsylvanian sandstones and carbonates, Ordovician dolomites, and even Precambrian arkoses in Pecos Slope are compositionally comparable to Abo gas. The exception is the occurrence of trace amounts of organic arsenic compounds in Abo Formation gas.

Producer, lease, well location, field, reservoir	Nitrogen	Carbon Dioxide	Methane	Ethane	Propane	iso-Butane	n-Butane	iso-Pentane	n-Pentane	Hexanes	Heptanes*	Measured Specific Gravity	BTU/ft3 14.73 psi 60°F
Yates Petroleum Corp. Redman "OY" St. #5 35-4S-24E Chaves Co. Pecos Slope Abo	0.0719	0.0004	0.8592	0.0424	0.0181	0.0031	0.0064	0.0020	0.0021	0.0018	0.0016	0.654	1031
Yates Petroleum Corp. China Draw St. #1 36-6S-22E Chaves Co. West Pecos Slope Abo	0.0537	0.0001	0.9030	0.0229	0.0100	0.0016	0.0042	0.0009	0.0015	0.0021		0.617	1021
Yates Petroleum Corp. Desert Rose Unit #2 11-9S-26E Chaves Co. South Pecos Slope Abo	0.0472	0.0027	0.8710	0.0468	0.0170	0.0031	0.0059	0.0018	0.0018	0.0020	0.0007	0.643	1049
Elk Oil Runyan St. #3 24-9S-26E Chaves Co. Bitter Lakes Hueco	0.0286	0.0004	0.8719	0.0568	0.0217	0.0035	0.0066	0.0019	0.0021	0.0029		0.65	1100
Yates Petroleum Corp. Desert Rose Unit #1 11-9S-26E Chaves Co. Foor Ranch Pre-Permia Penn	0.0296	0.0260	0.9138	0.0226	0.0030	0.0006	0.0015	0.0004	0.0006	0.0014	0.0005	0.616	978
Plains Radio Broadcasting Camel St. #1 6-9S-27E Chaves Co. Foor Ranch Pre-Permia Penn	0.0313	0.0013	0.9100	0.0365	0.0108	0.0018	0.0037	0.0011	0.0013	0.0009	0.0013	0.616	1036
Yates Petroleum Corp. Sandalwood "AEW" St. 31-8S-27e Chaves Co. Foor Ranch Pre-Perm Penn	0.0335	0.0122	0.8963	0.0376	0.0107	0.0017	0.0034	0.0010	0.0011	0.0015	0.0010	0.627	1023
Yates Petroleum Corp. Dragonfly St. Unit #1 30-9S-27E Chaves Co. Foor Ranch Pre-Perm Ordovician	0.0406	0.0108	0.8706	0.0475	0.0158	0.0026	0.0052	0.0017	0.0018	0.0025	0.0009	0.648	1046

sediments. It does not appear that the Abo Formation, itself, is the source of any arsenic that may be present in Abo gas; however, arsenic mineralization could be uneven and not present in the samples analyzed (Ron Broadhead, 1988, personal communication).

Organically occurring arsenic in natural gas is thought to be very rare. No other Chaves County gas tested has any levels of arsenic, and it is not known to exist anywhere else in the Permian basin. The Gas Research Institute is investigating the occurrence of organic arsenic in natural gas. This study may help unravel the mystery of the gas source in the Abo Formation in the Pecos Slope field.

On 15 December 1988, the Pecos Slope field was put back on production stream after a system was installed using a solid bed absorber to strip the arsenic compounds from the gas.

Reserves and Economics

The typical Abo well initially averages 600 MCFC/day, declining approximately 35% the first year and 19% per year thereafter, with a life expectancy of 15 years. The average Abo well will ultimately recover 600 mmcf of gas, with top producers cumulating over 2 bcf. Poor Abo producers may make less than 100,000 mcf of gas. The total field production through 1990 is 273 bcf. Primary gas recovery is expected to be 750 bcf (Figure 17).

Pecos slope Abo field is very sensitive economically to the natural gas market. Deterioration in the natural gas market and the deregulation of natural gas has dramatically changed the economics in the Pecos Slope (Figure 5). For efficient, economic development of the Pecos Slope, the price of gas per mcf/Btu should be $2.00 to $2.50 (Boneau, 1988, personal communication).

EXPLORATION AND DEVELOPMENT CONCEPTS

The Pecos Slope field is unusual in the fact that production occurs from a continental red bed sequence. Although unique in that respect, the Abo

147

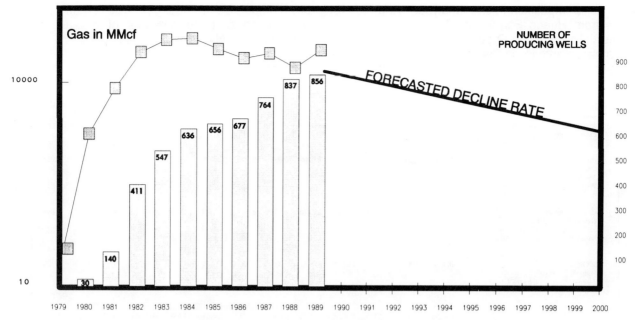

Figure 17. Pecos Slope Abo production illustrates number of wells producing (bars) and gas production in mmcf (squares) and showing projected decline rate.

The total field production through 1990 is 273 bcf. Primary gas recovery is expected to be 750 bcf.

fluvial regime is not uncommon. An early working model of the fluvial depositional environment led to an understanding of the preferred orientation of the channel systems. This resulted in the successful exploration and development as the field was developed entirely as a subsurface play.

The Pecos Slope field is also uncommon in that the bottom hole pressures are constant and subnormal throughout the entire field. This suggests a large regional trapping mechanism possibly tectonically controlled or hydrodynamically trapped. Investigations into other large gas accumulations with subnormal pressures, such as Hugoton, may be helpful in understanding the nature of the Pecos Slope accumulation.

Advances in technology in drilling and completion practices made the Pecos Slope economically successful. Early drilling programs were plagued with hole problems resulting from heaving and caving red shales, as well as lost circulation due to the natural fracturing in the Abo Formation. Improved drilling mud programs and drilling procedures made it possible to drill the wells much more efficiently and economically.

Because Abo sandstones have low permeability, they must be artificially stimulated to produce commercially, and all of the producing wells in the Pecos Slope area have been "sand frac'd." The methodology and materials of fracture treating wells have evolved with experience.

Finally, the Natural Gas Policy Act provided a positive economic environment to explore and develop gas reserves. The Pecos Slope field is representative of reserves that may not have been developed to the extent they are today without the help of a favorable domestic energy policy.

ACKNOWLEDGMENTS

Sincere thanks are extended to S. P. Yates, John A. Yates, and Peyton Yates for permission to publish this paper. Great appreciation is extended to the Yates Petroleum Corporation Geology Department staff for their assistance.

REFERENCES

Anonymous, 1987, Natural gas handbook: Federal Programs Advisory Service, Washington, D.C.

Anonymous, 1983, Pecos Slope Abo red beds shallow target for New Mexico gas: Petroleum Frontiers Premier Issue.

Boneau, D. F., et al., 1982, Completion practices and reserve estimates for Pecos Slope Abo gas field: SPE 11336.

Broadhead, R. F., 1982, Preliminary report on sedimentology and gas production of tight Abo sandstones, Chaves County, New Mexico: Annual Report New Mexico Bureau of Mines and Mineral Resources, Socorro.

Broadhead, R. F., 1984, Stratigraphically controlled gas production from Abo red beds (Permian) east-central New Mexico: New Mexico Bureau of Mines and Minerals Resources, Circular 183, Socorro.

Galley, J. E., 1984, Geologic evolution of the Permian basin of Texas and New Mexico, in S. J. Mazzullo, ed., The geological evolution of the Permian basin: SEPM, Permian Basin Sect., Midland, TX.

Hills, J. M., 1984, The structural evolution of the Permian basin of West Texas and New Mexico, in S. J. Mazzullo, ed., The geological evolution of the Permian basin: SEPM, Permian Basin Sect., Midland, TX.

Horak, R. L., 1984, Sequential tectonism and hydrocarbon distribution in the Permian Basin, *in* S. J. Mazzullo, ed., The geological evolution of the Permian basin: SEPM, Permian Basin Sect., Midland, TX.

Jacka, A. D., R. H. Beck, L. C. St. Germain, and S. C. Harrison, 1968, Permian deep-sea fans of the Delaware Mountain Group (Guadalupian), Delaware Basin, *in* B. A. Silver, ed., Guadalupian facies; Apache Mountains area: West Texas Society of Economic Paleontologists and Mineralogists Permian Basin Sec. Guidebook, Pub. 68-11.

Keller, G. R., 1984, Regional gravity and aeromagnetic anomalies in the Permian basin area, *in* S. J. Mazzullo, ed., The geological evolution of the Permian basin: SEPM, Permian Basin Sect., Midland, TX.

Kelley, V. C., 1971, Geology of the Pecos County: New Mexico Bureau of Mines and Mineral Resources, Memoir 24.

Mickey, V., 1987, High tech approach to Abo success: Southwest Oil World, vol. 36, n. 3.

Reineck, H. E., and I. B. Singh, 1980, Depositional sedimentary environments: Berlin-Heidelberg, Springer-Verlag.

Scott, G. L., et al., 1983, Pecos Slope Abo field of Chaves County, New Mexico: Guidebook for field trip to the Abo red beds (Permian), central and south-central New Mexico: The Roswell Geological Society, New Mexico Bureau of Mines and Mineral Resources, Socorro, New Mexico.

Silver, B. A., and R. G. Todd, 1969, Permian cyclic strata, northern Midland and Delaware basins, west Texas and southeastern New Mexico: The American Association of Petroleum Geologists Bulletin, v. 53, n. 11.

Speer, S. W., 1983, Abo Formation, north-central Sacramento Mountains: an onlapping fluvial clastic wedge: Guidebook for field trip to the Abo red beds (Permian), central and south-central New Mexico: The Roswell Geological Society and New Mexico Bureau of Mines and Mineral Resources, Socorro, New Mexico.

Vail, P. R., et al., 1977, Seismic stratigraphy and global cycles of relative changes of sea level, seismic stratigraphy applications to hydrocarbon exploration: American Association of Petroleum Geologists Memoir 26.

SUGGESTED READING

Boneau, D. F., et al., 1982, Completion practices and reserve estimates for Pecos Slope Abo gas field; SPE 11336.

Broadhead, R. F., 1984, Stratigraphically controlled gas production from Abo red beds (Permian) east-central New Mexico: New Mexico Bureau of Mines and Mineral Resources, Circular 183, Socorro.

Dickey, P. A., and W. C. Cox, 1977, Oil & gas in reservoirs with subnormal pressures: American Association of Petroleum Geologists Bulletin, v. 61, n. 12.

Kelly, V. C., 1971, Geology of the Pecos County: New Mexico Bureau of Mines and Mineral Resources Memoir 24.

Appendix 1. Field Description

Field name .... *Pecos Slope field*

Ultimate recoverable reserves .... *750 bcf of gas*

Field location:

    Country .... *U.S.A.*

    State .... *New Mexico*

    Basin/Province .... *Permian basin*

Field discovery:

    Year first pay discovered .... *Lower Leonardian Abo Sandstone   1977*

Discovery well name and general location:

    First pay .... *McConkey "HX" #1 Sec. 10, T9S, R26E, Chaves County, New Mexico*

    Discovery well operator .... *Yates Petroleum Corporation*

    IP .... *2550 MCFGPD + 1 BCPD*

All other zones with shows of oil and gas in the field:

Age	Formation	Type of Show
Permian lower Guadalupian	*San Andres*	*Oil*
Permian Wolfcamp	*Hueco*	*Gas*
Pennsylvanian Virgil	*Cisco*	*Gas*
Pennsylvanian Des Moines	*Strawn*	*Gas*
Silurian	*Undifferentiated*	*Gas*
Ordovician	*Undifferentiated*	*Gas*

Geologic concept leading to discovery and method or methods used to delineate prospect

This discovery resulted from the application of modern geophysical logging techniques to evaluate the re-entry of the Honolulu Oil Corp. McConkey Estate #1 well, plugged in 1951. Subsurface methods were employed after the initial discovery.

Structure:

    Province/basin type .... *Bally 222, Klemme IIA*

    Tectonic history

The tectonic history as applicable to the field area began with the rise of the Pedernal highlands during early Pennsylvanian time and the subsequent subsidence of nearby basinal areas. The renewed uplift of the Pedernal in Permian Wolfcampian and the continued subsidence of the Delaware basin coupled with a drop in sea level in mid-Leonardian resulted in the deposition of a clastic wedge on the slope area that continued through the Leonardian period.

    Regional structure

The field lies on the Pecos slope, the structural descent from the Mescalero arch and the Sacramento and Guadalupe uplifts into the Delaware basin.

    Local structure

Homoclinal east-southeast dip (E20° S) at an average rate of 66 ft/mi (¾°). The uniform dip is interrupted by a series of long, narrow, north-eastwardly trending fold faults that exhibit right-lateral wrenching.

Trap:

Trap type(s)

Unconfirmed, but trapping probably resulted from tectonically induced fracturing of the stratigraphic wedge-out of fluvial clastic facies.

Basin stratigraphy (major stratigraphic intervals from surface to deepest penetration in field):

Chronostratigraphy	Formation	Depth to Top in ft
Permian:		
Lower Guadalupian	*San Andres*	*1028*
Lower Guadalupian	*Glorieta*	*2156*
Upper Leonard	*Yeso*	*2218*
Lower Leonard	*Abo*	*4406*
Wolfcamp	*Hueco*	*5094*
Pennsylvanian:		
Virgil	*Cisco*	*5686*
Des Moines	*Strawn*	*5802*
Mississippian	*Mississippi ls*	*5982*
Silurian–Ordovician	*Undifferentiated*	*6050*
Precambrian	*Precambrian*	*6364*

Reservoir characteristics:

Number of reservoirs *1*

Formations .... *Abo*

Ages .... *Permian lower Leonard*

Depths to tops of reservoirs .... *2550 (+1800) ft west side, 4700 (−700) ft east side*

Gross thickness (top to bottom of producing interval) .... *250–450 ft*

Net thickness—total thickness of producing zones

Average .... *30 ft*

Maximum .... *80 ft*

Lithology

Sandstone, red, very fine to silty, subangular to subrounded; major constituents are quartz and plagioclase feldspar; cementing material may be clay (illite and chlorite), calcite, dolomite, or anhydrite.

Porosity type .... *Intergranular and fracture*

Average porosity *12–14%*

Average permeability .... *0.03–0.05 md*

Seals:

Upper

Formation, fault, or other feature .... *Yeso Formation*

Lithology .... *Anhydrite*

Lateral

Formation, fault, or other feature .... *Abo Formation; wedge out of fluvial facies*

Lithology .... *Shale, sandstone, and dolomite*

Source:

Formation and age .... *Unknown; probable Lower Permian or Pennsylvanian source*

Lithology .... *NA*

Average total organic carbon (TOC) .... *NA*

Kerogen type (I, II, or III) .... *NA*

Vitrinite reflectance (maturation) .... *NA*

Time of hydrocarbon expulsion .... *NA*

PECOS SLOPE

151

Appendix 2. Production Data

Field name .... *Pecos Slope field*

Field size:

    Proved acres .... *138,240 ac*
    Number of wells all years *864*
    Current number of wells .... *764 producing*
    Well spacing .... *160 ac*
    Ultimate recoverable .... *750 bcf*
    Cumulative production .... *206 bcf*
    Annual production .... *1979, 0.032 bcf; 1980, 1.7 bcf; 1981, 8.1 bcf; 1982, 27.9 bcf; 1983, 42.5 bcf; 1984, 44.5 bcf; 1985, 31.1 bcf; 1986, 22.7 bcf; 1987, 26.9 bcf; 1988, 16.5 bcf; 1989, 30.2 bcf*
    Present decline rate .... *16% est.*
    Initial decline rate *35%*
    Overall decline rate .... *19% est.*
    Annual water production .... *NA*
    In place, total reserves .... *1000 bcf*
    In place, per acre foot .... *560 mcf/ac-ft*
    Primary recovery .... *750 bcf*
    Cumulative water production .... *NA*

Drilling and casing practices:

    Amount of surface casing set .... *850 ft*
    Casing program
    Surface casing, 10¾-in. or 8⅝-in.; production string, 4½-in., 9.5#, J-55
    Drilling mud .... *Brine with salt gel and starch*
    Bit program .... *Surface 14¾-in. or 12½-in.; after surface 7⅞-in. Reed J-44, Hughes J-44*
    High pressure zones .... *None*

Completion practices:

    Interval(s) perforated ...... *All potential pays are perforated simultaneously; for limited entry the number of perforations is 0.5 to 0.7 per foot of pay*

    Well treatment
    The zones are acidized individually down tubing, but frac'd together down 4½-in. casing; the frac fluid is gelled 2% KCl water with 20 pounds of gel per 1000 gals and the proppant is 2 pounds/gal of 20/40 mesh sand.

Formation evaluation:

    Logging suites .... *Compensated-neutron-litho density and dual laterolog with micro-resistivity device*
    Testing practices .... *Production test*
    Mud logging techniques .... *None*

Oil characteristics: .... *Gas (see Table 1 in the text for analysis)*

Field characteristics:

    Average elevation .... *4075 ft*
    Initial pressure .... *1125 psi*
    Present pressure .... *600 psi*
    Pressure gradient .... *0.267 psi/ft*
    Temperature .... *102°F*
    Geothermal gradient .... *0.024°F/ft*
    Drive .... *Gas expansion*
    Gas column thickness .... *Indefinite (about 2900 ft)*
    Gas-water contact .... *Indefinite*

Connate water *38.5%*
Water salinity, TDS .... *104,000 ppm*
Resistivity of water .... *0.07 at 72°F*
Bulk volume water (%) *0.045%*

Transportation method and market for oil and gas:
Enron Pipeline to the West Coast market

Glenn Pool Field—U.S.A.
Northeast Oklahoma Platform, Oklahoma

MICHAEL D. KUYKENDALL
MASERA Corporation
Tulsa, Oklahoma

THOMAS E. MATSON
Gemini Oil Company
Tulsa, Oklahoma

FIELD CLASSIFICATION

BASIN: Arkoma
BASIN TYPE: Foredeep
RESERVOIR ROCK TYPE: Sandstone
RESERVOIR ENVIRONMENT OF DEPOSITION: Alluvial/Deltaic
TRAP DESCRIPTION: Updip pinch-out of thick, multistoried sandstone

RESERVOIR AGE: Pennsylvanian
PETROLEUM TYPE: Oil
TRAP TYPE: Pinch-Out

LOCATION

The Glenn Pool field, located in portions of Tulsa and Creek Counties, Oklahoma, U.S.A., was discovered in December 1905 and quickly became the first giant oil field in Oklahoma. It has produced an estimated 330 million barrels of oil (June 1990), primarily from the Middle Pennsylvanian (Desmoinesian) age Bartlesville ("Glenn") sandstone. The field is near the center of the Northeast Oklahoma platform, which is situated between the Ozark uplift to the east, the Nemaha ridge to the west, and the Arkoma basin to the south (Figure 1). Other significant fields producing from Middle Pennsylvanian sandstone reservoirs include the Avant, Bartlesville, Burbank, Cushing, Muskogee, Okmulgee, and Red Fork fields (Figure 1).

The Glenn Pool field covers approximately 43 mi^2 (27,440 ac; 11,113 ha) and was originally developed on a lease-by-lease basis by several operators. Initial production rates from wells completed open-hole, at an average reservoir depth of 1500 ft (460 m), ranged from 75–500 BOPD, up to 4000 BOPD. Rapid development of the field resulted in peak production of approximately 117,000 BOPD in June 1907. Field-wide reserves average 10,000 BO/ac, with some portions of the field having produced over 40,000 BO/ac. The field currently has approximately 750 producing wells, with cumulative yearly production over 1 MMBO. It is estimated that the field will ultimately produce over 400 MMBO.

HISTORY

Pre-Discovery

Natural oil seeps and springs were known in Indian Territory (Oklahoma) in the early 1820s, but the small amounts of petroleum collected were of little practical or economic worth. A few shallow, low production wells had been drilled in the area by the late 1890s. The most famous, the Cudahy Oil Company, Nellie Johnston No. 1, was discovered in 1897 near the townsite of Bartlesville, Oklahoma, and became the territory's (state's) first commercial oil well, producing approximately 100,000 BO from the "Bartlesville sandstone" until becoming uneconomic in 1946 (Weirich, 1968). The same productive interval in the territory's first commercial oil well would, eight years later and 60 mi (95 km) to the south, be locally known as the "Glenn sandstone," in what was to become the state's first giant oil field. Several other discoveries were made near Bartlesville; however, because of the uncertainty of Indian leases and lack of transportation facilities in Indian Territory, it was several years before there was any substantial production.

An increase in the price of oil from $.60 to $1.10/ bbl resulted in increased exploration and production by the early 1900s. However, with the discovery of the Glenn Pool in December 1905, oil prices dropped back to $.60/bbl and were even as low as $.25/bbl

155

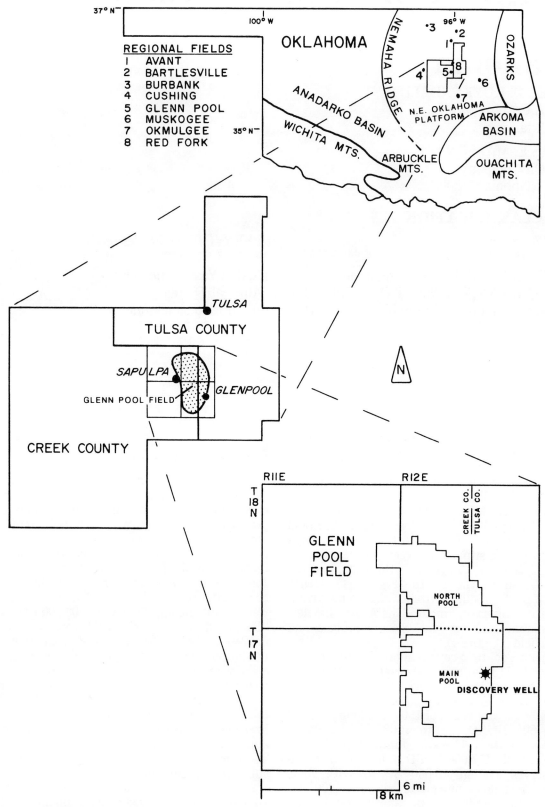

Figure 1. Index map showing location of Glenn Pool
field, tectonic features, nearby fields, Glenn Pool field
boundaries, and discovery well.

during peak production in 1907 (Weirich, 1968). It was during these early "boom" years that drillers and prospectors were attracted to the area. They followed the oil seeps from outcrops of Pennsylvanian sandstones and Mississippi limestones around the Ozark uplift, randomly drilling ("wildcatting") what were later determined to be entirely stratigraphic traps with no substantial structural expression. It was this surface prospecting or "creekology" and wildcat drilling that were the exploration methods of the early Oklahoma oil pioneers in the time before petroleum geology had advanced as a science.

Discovery

The discovery well of the Glenn Pool field was drilled by two early wildcatters, Robert Galbreath and Frank Chesley, in the fall of 1905. The well was located in the Creek Indian Nation on the Ida Glenn allotment near the center of the SE/4 of Sec. 10, T17N, R12E, in Tulsa County (Figure 1). It blew out at a depth of 1458 ft (444 m) and was later completed with a flowing rate of 75 BOPD. The productive interval was given the name "Glenn sandstone" and soon became the target of several offset wells. The Ida Glenn No. 2 (300 ft [91 m] south) produced 700 to 800 BOPD, and No. 3 (600 ft [182 m] north of No. 1) produced up to 1600 BOPD. These wells proved to be near the eastern edge of the field; a subsequent well 0.25 mi (400 m) east of the discovery well was a dry hole.

An important point to consider is that this field contained 240 ft (73 m) of productive oil column that was most unique compared to nearby fields. This, along with excellent reservoir conditions, resulted in the Glenn Pool field being a major accumulation of oil in the Mid-Continent. In 1907 the field produced 20 MMBO, or 45% of the state's annual production; and by 1911 had produced over 92 MMBO (Chenoweth, 1979).

The field could have been found early by means of the pronounced small anticlines in the mappable surface beds. Mr. Carl D. Smith, who examined the field in 1912 for the U.S. Geological Survey, did observe, "very favorable conditions exist in the Glenn Pool—a combination of a thick, porous sand with anticlinal structure" (Smith, 1914). However, it wasn't until the 1920s, when development was completed, that existence of a major large-scale sandstone pinch-out was recognized. Wilson's 1927 article, "Geology of Glenn Pool in Oklahoma," in *Structure of Typical American Oil Fields*, was the first published recognition of this pinch-out (Figure 2). Rich (1928) also published an article on the geology of the Glenn Pool, which aided in the early understanding of the field geometry.

Post-Discovery

Wells were drilled with cable-tool rigs. Surface casing (8⅝-in.) was set at approximately 275 ft (85 m)

and open-hole drilling (8-in. hole) continued to the top of the Bartlesville sandstone reservoir. The hole size was reduced to 6 in. through the productive interval. The productive interval was shot with 250 to 300 (235–285 L) quarts of nitroglycerin, casing set to the top of the sandstone, and the shot hole cleaned out.

By the summer of 1906, well completions were averaging three per day, with 50 to 100 wells drilling concurrently. Orderly spacing of wells was neglected in the rush to produce the oil; later development was on 10 ac patterns. Deeper drilling found isolated production in the Lower Pennsylvanian (Atokan), Mississippian, and Middle Ordovician (Simpson) formations. Flush production exceeded the storage and distribution facilities available to the field. Oil was shipped by railroad to the Texas Gulf Coast, and wooden and iron tank batteries were continually being constructed. Earthen "lakes" provided storage on many leases, but large quantities of oil were lost to fires, spills, and contamination (Figure 3). It was estimated that over 5000 BOPD were lost in the field as a result of evaporation and fires (Franks, 1984).

On 16 November 1907, Oklahoma and Indian Territories were combined as the 46th state. Under new regulations, pipelines entered the state and connected the Glenn Pool with the refineries of the Gulf Coast. At the end of that year, nearly 100 oil companies were operating in the field. In 1908, annual production peaked at 20.5 MMBO and by 1912 it is estimated several billion cubic feet of natural gas had been vented, flared, or used as fuel for lighting and drilling operations. During this time, practically every lease had installed a small natural gas gasoline plant. Although the field originally used a solution-gas drive, vacuum lifting was required to produce the oil by 1916. Pumping by central power was introduced and continued until increased fluid volumes from waterflooding operations required a combination of beam and submersible pumps. The field was fully defined by 1920, and a pipeline to Coffeyville, Kansas, connected the Glenn Pool with Chicago and the Great Lakes markets. By 1926, 22 major and independent refineries served the Glenn Pool area.

Secondary recovery by gas injection began in May 1940 on a 160 ac (65 ha) lease operated by the Sinclair Prairie Oil Company. Gas repressuring in five 5-spot patterns was successful in increasing oil recovery from 61 BOPD to 300 BOPD. The repressuring project expanded in three years to include nearly 2000 ac (810 ha) in the "South Glenn Pool," or "Main Pool," with pattern size and shape adjusted to accommodate existing wells and adjacent lease interests (Figure 4). Gas collected at production wells was recycled to the injection wells. Development continued and included new producing wells in addition to new gas input. The response was rapid and within a year oil production increased generally in the range of 100% to 300% (Barnes and Sage, 1943). The great increase in production resulted in the recovery of a large volume of light fraction as gas liquids—so

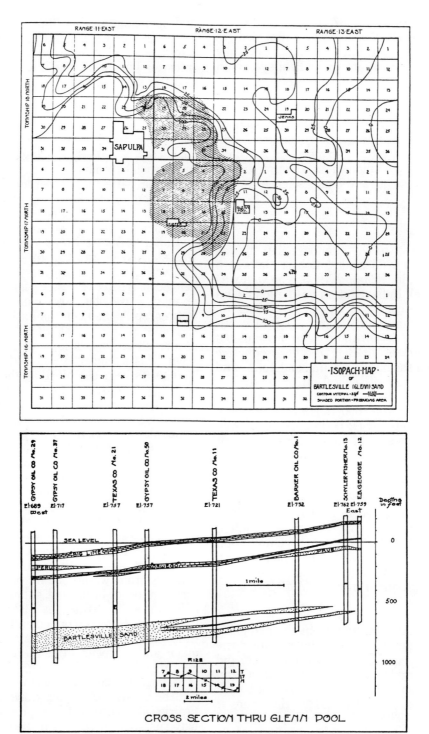

Figure 2. Wilson's (1927) isopach map of the Bartlesville (Glenn) sandstone and cross section through Glenn Pool field showing the large-scale sandstone pinch-out of the Bartlesville. (Each small square is 1 mi².)

much so that gravity of oil in "South Glenn Pool" is about 1° API unit less than in "North Glenn Pool."

Several single-well, unconfined waterflood pilots were conducted from 1944 to 1951 in "North Glenn Pool"; most were unsuccessful. The first successful waterflood was operated by Fair Oil Company (now Ramey) in North Glenn Sand Unit No. 1, Sec. 28,

T18N, R12E (Figure 4). It was unitized in October 1953 and required almost two years for significant response, but its success caused very rapid development of other waterfloods in "North Glenn Pool." The William Berryhill Unit (NE/4, Sec. 17, T17N, R12E) was the first multipattern pilot in "South Glenn Pool." It was initiated in 1955 and proved to

Figure 3. Early photograph of a portion of the Glenn Pool field showing earthen "lake of oil" temporarily used to store excess oil that resulted from early over-production (Franks, 1984).

be successful; it caused rapid development of "South Glenn Pool" waterfloods, including the largest, the Kiefer Unit (Figure 4), in 1959. The W. B. Self Unit (S/2, NE, and N/2, SE, Sec. 21, T17N, R12E) was another multipattern waterflood conducted in 1957 by Sinclair Oil Company (Figure 4). The flood was not as successful as the William Berryhill pilot but furnished valuable data about problems to be expected concerning waterflood operations in the Glenn Pool. Waterflood eventually was conducted field-wide resulting in substantial additional recoveries ranging from 5000 to over 8000 BO/ac (12,300 to 19,800 BO/ha).

Cumulative oil production records prior to field-wide waterflooding operation are somewhat incomplete. However, a complete history on one lease, the Thompson-Clayton Lease (SW/4, SW/4, Sec. 4, T17N, R12E), shows that this 40 ac (16.2 ha) produced a total of 1,791,930 BO, or 44,798 BO per ac (110,612 BO/ha), from 1908 to 1955. Recovery was both primary and by secondary gas injection. By 1943 it was estimated that the cumulative production from the field was between 222 and 236 MMBO (Barnes and Sage, 1943). Over 100 MMBO have been produced to date by secondary gas repressuring, waterflooding, and recent tertiary recovery methods, for a total of approximately 330 MMBO.

The Glenn Pool field has had a long history of primary and secondary oil recovery (Figure 5). The field is now nearing depletion under current waterflood operations in several large units, while a few smaller units such as the Chevron U.S.A. William Berryhill Unit (NE/4, Sec. 17, T17N, R12E) have undergone testing and implementation of micellar-polymer enhanced oil recovery (EOR) methods. Successful results have shown that significant volumes of residual oil are recoverable. The 160 ac (65 ha) William Berryhill Unit has produced approximately 2.3 MMBO, 1.1 MMBO during secondary waterflood operations from 1955

to 1977 (22 years), and an additional 1.2 MMBO during tertiary micellar-polymer flooding from 1977 to 1990 (13 years) (Figure 6). During EOR operations, the 160 ac (65 ha) unit's production increased from 50 to 60 BOPD up to 1200 to 1500 BOPD, which in turn substantially increased cumulative field production (Figure 6). As of June 1990, the unit was producing 250–350 BOPD.

STRUCTURE

The Northeast Oklahoma platform has been a relatively stable region since Cambrian–Ordovician time. Periods of transgressive marine inundation and deposition were interrupted by intervals of regional uplift, erosion, and deltaic progradation. The area is bounded by the Ozark uplift to the east, the buried Nemaha ridge to the west, and the Arkoma basin to the south (Figure 1).

Tectonic events that affected the region began with a widespread mid-Mississippian emergence. The Ozark and Nemaha features were structurally and topographically positive. The Wichita and Ouachita orogenies occurred in the Early to Middle Pennsylvanian Period, with the Arkoma basin subsidence in Atokan time. The platform dipped to the east and southeast until post-Cherokee time, when regional uplifting reversed the dip to the west and produced localized domes, noses, and anticlines. The Nemaha ridge remained topographically positive until this period. The Arbuckle orogeny occurred in the Late Pennsylvanian as determined by regional thickness patterns of lower Desmoinesian sediments. Continued regional uplift during the Jurassic and Cretaceous produced the present-day monocline, which dips at a rate of 35 to 50 ft/mi (6.6–9.5 m/km) to the west-southwest.

Structure does not appear to control the accumulation at Glenn Pool, although some structural features may be a result of basement structure and/or depositional irregularities causing differential compaction of sealing shales over thick (100–180 ft; 30–55 m) reservoir sandstones.

Detailed surface mapping by Bennison (1972) reveals a concentric zone of normal faulting on the east flank of the southwest-plunging structural nose associated with the Bartlesville sandstone. This down-to-the-east zone of faulting creates an eastward reversal of regional dip of surface beds which, according to Bennison (1972), produces structural closure that, interestingly, coincides closely with the eastern limits of oil production in the field as well as with the eastward pinch-out of the Bartlesville sandstone. However, subsurface mapping in the area does not substantiate this condition as a primary trapping mechanism.

Local structural conditions and reservoir distribution in the Glenn Pool field are illustrated by subsurface contour maps depicting structure on top of the Bartlesville sandstone (Figure 7) and thickness

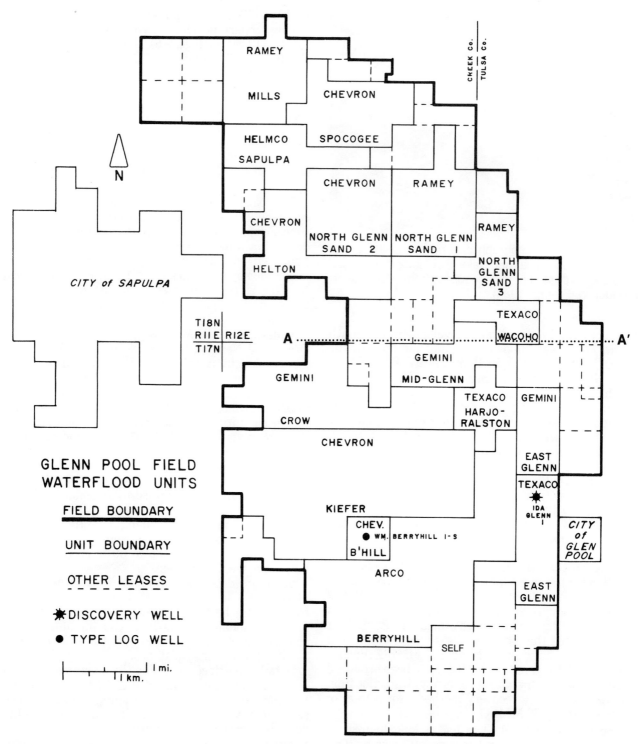

Figure 4. Location map of major waterflood units and leases within the Glenn Pool field. Dotted line A–A′ divides the field into the "North Glenn Pool" and the "South" or "Main Glenn Pool."

of the Bartlesville sandstone (Figure 8). The structural configuration on top of the Wilcox ("Mounds") sandstone (Figure 9) reflects deeper structure more or less independent of the structural features associated with the trapping of hydrocarbons in the Bartlesville sandstone reservoir.

STRATIGRAPHY

The geologic column in the area of the Glenn Pool field is composed of formations from Precambrian to Paleozoic (Upper Pennsylvanian) (Figure 10). Approximately 90% of the oil is obtained from the

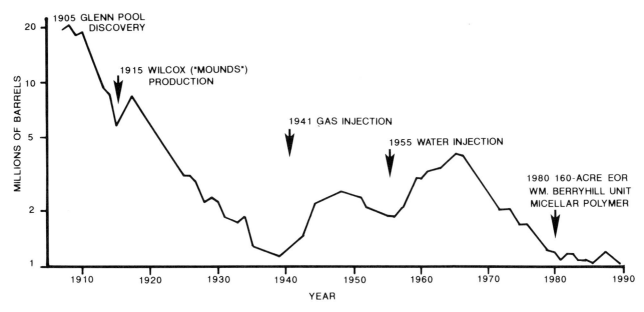

Figure 5. Glenn Pool oil field production history (1907–1990).

Middle Pennsylvanian Bartlesville sandstone, with the balance from other Pennsylvanian sandstones (Red Fork, Booch, Dutcher) and the Middle Ordovician Wilcox sandstone (Figure 10).

The eroded Precambrian Spavinaw Granite basement is reached at a depth of just over 3900 ft (1189m) and is unconformably overlain by the Cambrian–Ordovician Arbuckle Group. The Arbuckle Group is unconformably overlain by the Middle Ordovician Simpson Group, which is mainly silty and sandy shales and includes the Wilcox sandstone as the upper member. Production from the Wilcox sandstone is found only on small, isolated domes or anticlines (Figure 9). The sandstone is 5 to 15 ft (1.5–4.5 m) thick, and consists of nearly pure white, subangular to well-rounded quartz grains that often are cement-free or cemented with carbonate or silica. The sandstone is an excellent reservoir and is interpreted as a widespread shallow-marine deposit (Dickey and Rohn, 1955).

A pronounced unconformity is represented by the contact of the Late Devonian Chattanooga (Woodford) Shale and the Simpson formations. Absent due to erosion are the Upper Ordovician Viola and Sylvan formations and the Devonian Hunton Group (Figure 10).

Conformably overlying the Chattanooga Shale is the Mississippian, consisting of basal Kinderhookian shale and overlying Osagean, Meramecian, and Chesterian series limestones (Figure 10). The Mississippi limestones consists of interbedded fine- to coarse-grained argillaceous limestone, calcareous shale, and chert.

Unconformably overlying the Mississippian are the Middle Pennsylvanian Atokan, Desmoinesian, and Missourian series consisting of organic-rich shales, thin limestones, and shaly sandstones (Figure 10).

The Bartlesville, or "Glenn" as it is called locally, is equivalent to the Bluejacket Member of the surface in the Cherokee Group (rocks within the Krebs and Cabaniss groups of the Desmoinesian Series). The Cherokee Group (Figure 11) is characterized by lenticular sandstones, shales, coal beds, and thin but persistent limestones (Shelton, 1973). These thin limestones are transgressive regionally and enable one to define genetic increments of strata, useful for regional and local mapping. The discontinuous nature of the strata was not recognized when the original stratigraphic order was developed and only recently have difficulties of correlation of the Cherokee Group been emphasized (Ebanks, 1979; Hemish, 1989).

TRAP

The Glenn Pool field in the Bartlesville reservoir is a stratigraphic trap resulting from the updip (eastward) pinch-out of thick (80–185 ft [24–56 m]), porous (16–24%), multistoried, alluvial-deltaic/valley-fill sandstones into laterally sealing siltstones and shales and overlying black organic marine shales (Figure 12). The trapping mechanism of most of the other Pennsylvanian sandstone reservoirs within the field is also stratigraphic. Relatively small and minor structural traps are associated with the deeper Ordovician Wilcox sandstone within the field (Figure 9).

The Bartlesville reservoir contains up to 240 ft (73 m) of closed oil column and several small, isolated gas caps in structurally favorable areas. Reservoir

161

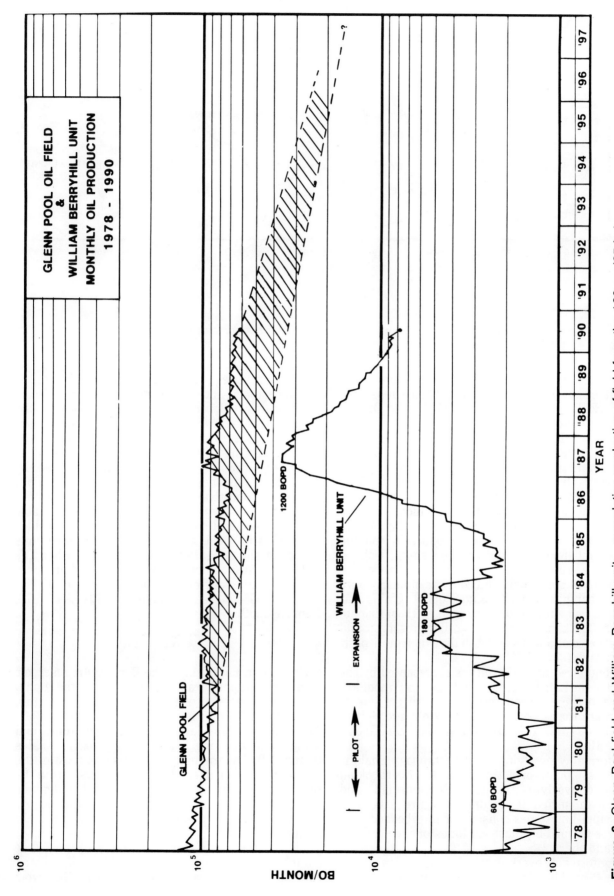

Figure 6. Glenn Pool field and William Berryhill unit cumulative production of field from the 160 ac (65 ha) monthly oil production history (1977–1989). Shaded William Berryhill micellar-polymer unit. area shows contribution of tertiary oil recovery to

162

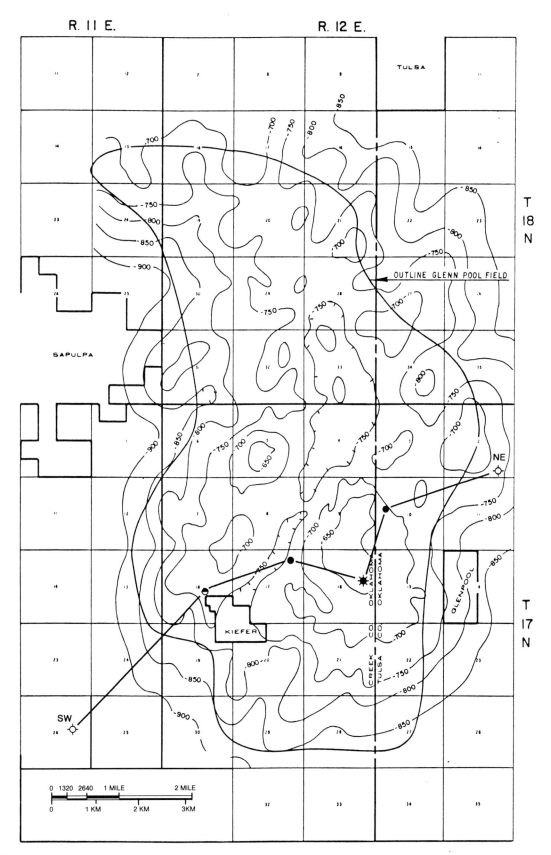

Figure 7. Structural contour map on the top of the
Bartlesville (Glenn) sandstone, Glenn Pool field.
Contour interval, 50 ft.

163

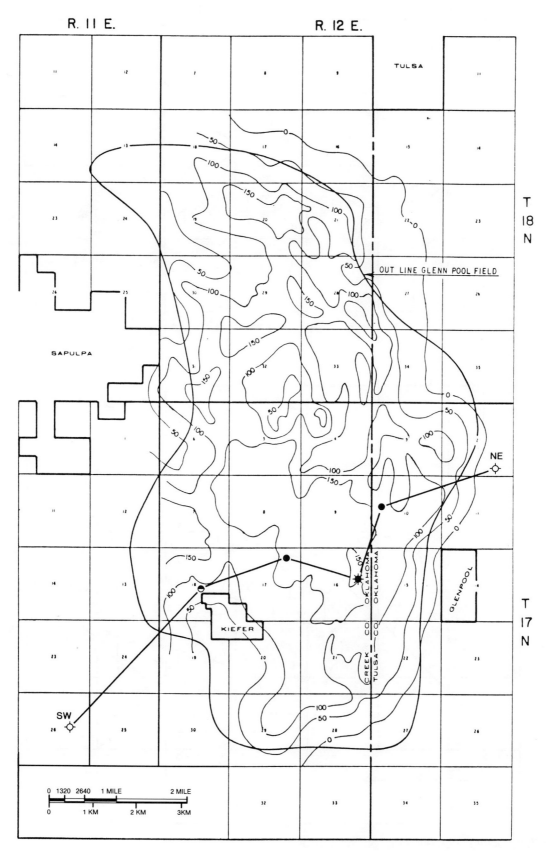

Figure 8. Isopach map of Bartlesville (Glenn) sandstone, Glenn Pool field. Contour interval, 50 ft.

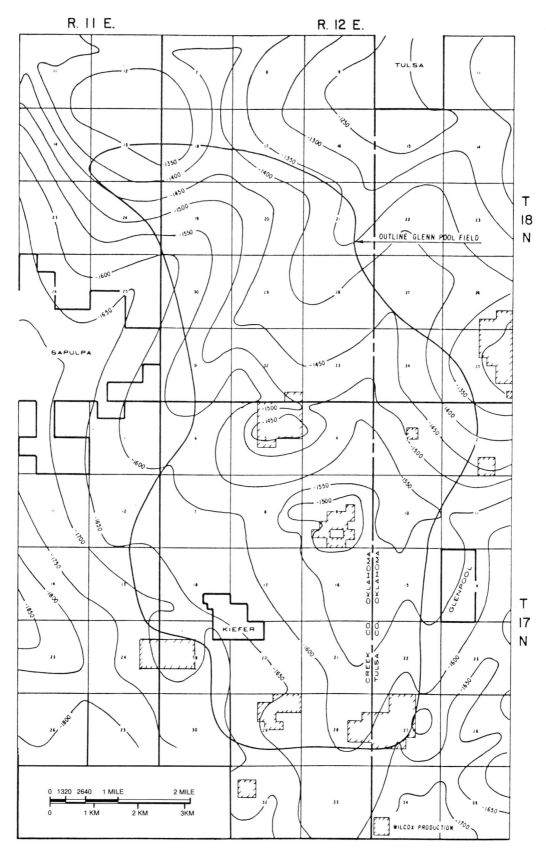

Figure 9. Structural contour map on the top of the
Wilcox ("Mounds") sandstone, Glenn Pool field. Contour
interval, 50 ft.

165

SYSTEM	SERIES	FORMATION	MEMBER
PENNSYLVANIAN	MISSOURIAN	SKIATOOK	COFFEYVILLE
PENNSYLVANIAN	DESMOINESIAN	MARMATON	
PENNSYLVANIAN	DESMOINESIAN	CABANISS / CHEROKEE	PRUE
PENNSYLVANIAN	DESMOINESIAN	CABANISS / CHEROKEE	SKINNER
PENNSYLVANIAN	DESMOINESIAN	KREBS / CHEROKEE	RED FORK
PENNSYLVANIAN	DESMOINESIAN	KREBS / CHEROKEE	BARTLESVILLE (GLENN)
PENNSYLVANIAN	DESMOINESIAN	KREBS / CHEROKEE	BOOCH (TANEHA)
PENNSYLVANIAN	ATOKAN	ATOKA	DUTCHER (GILCREASE)
MISSISSIPPIAN	CHESTERIAN	MISSISSIPPI LIME	
MISSISSIPPIAN	MERAMECIAN	MISSISSIPPI LIME	
MISSISSIPPIAN	OSAGEAN	MISSISSIPPI LIME	
MISSISSIPPIAN	KINDERHOOKIAN		
DEVON.		CHATTANOOGA	(WOODFORD)
MIDDLE-ORDO.		SIMPSON	MOUNDS (WILCOX)
€−ORDO.		ARBUCKLE	
PRE−€		SPAVINAW GRANITE	

Figure 10. Generalized stratigraphic column of the Glenn Pool field. (See the type log, Figure 11, for more detail.)

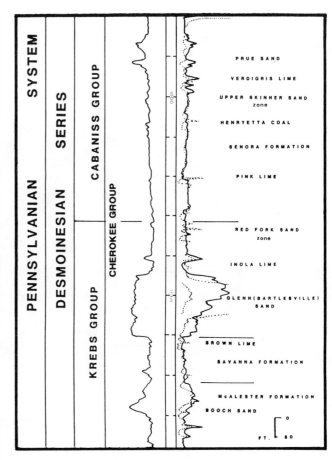

Figure 11. Stratigraphy and type log of the Desmoinesian Cherokee Group and Bartlesville (Glenn) sandstone in the Glenn Pool field. The log response curves show typical "signatures" of the lithologies and are not intended to show quantitative values. Log is Gulf Oil Corp., #1 Wm Berryhill, Sec. 17, T17N, R12E.

energy originally consisted of solution-gas drive with the presence of downdip edge water. Large volumes of gas were originally vented in those wells in the gas cap area until they would flow oil. Early depletion of the original gas caps resulted in water encroachment in those portions of the reservoir when waterflood operations began. By 1940 a depleted oil zone (−696 to −755 ft; −212 to −230 m) had developed and cooperative gas repressuring in portions of the field was initiated with very successful results; by 1955 the entire field was under waterflood.

The oil-water contact varies with depth in several areas in the field, ranging from −826 to −846 ft (−252 to −258 m). Overall the position of oil-water contacts has not changed since initial production. Variations in the oil-water contact are attributed to the compartmentalization and associated heterogeneities within the reservoir and subsequent capillary-pressure differences. Three distinct genetic units of sandstone ("upper," "middle," and "lower") are recognized, each separated by apparent permeability barriers consisting of interlaminated/interbedded siltstones and shales (Figure 12).

Bae and Petrick (1986) measured the wettability of the upper and middle sandstones in a portion of the field using the Amott test and obtained an index of −0.48 and 0.0, respectively, indicating oil-wet conditions. Typical relative permeability curves by the steady-state method for the sandstone unit show strong oil-wet behavior (Figure 13). However, portions of the sandstone unit have shown water-wet characteristics.

Reservoir

The general character of the Bartlesville sandstone reservoir in the Glenn Pool is more or less consistent, but locally stratigraphic variations are great among closely spaced wells. Thickness may vary substantially, and certain other sedimentary features present

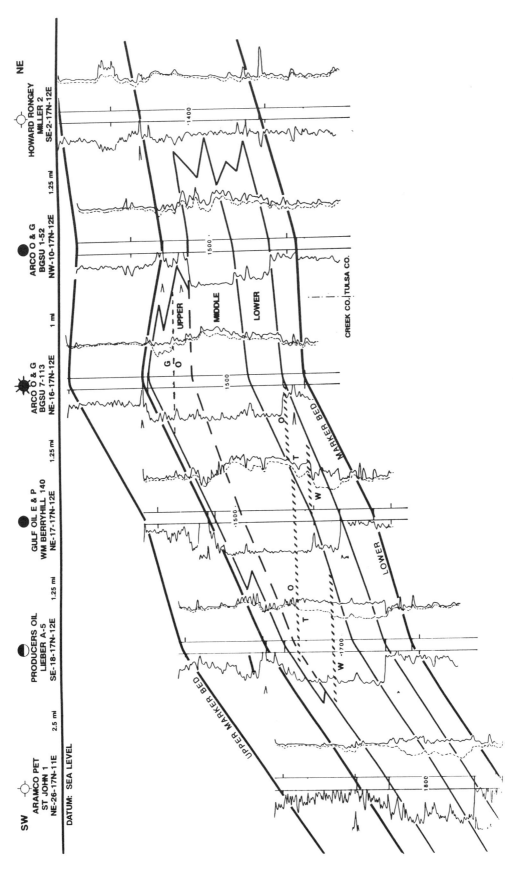

Figure 12. Structural cross section (SW-NE) across the Glenn Pool field showing the generalized updip pinch-out of the Bartlesville (Glenn) sandstone and basic trapping mechanism. (For each log, track 1 curve [left] is gamma ray and tracks 2 and 3 [right] are resistivity curves.) Relatively isolated gas (G) cap(s) and several distinct oil-water (O/W) contacts and associated transition (T) zones are common. (Line of section shown on Figures 7 and 8. Overall length of section is 7.25 mi or 11.7 km.)

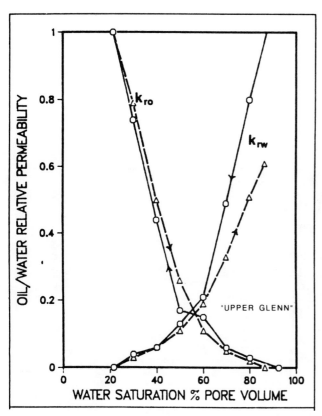

Figure 13. Relative permeability curves characteristic of the upper and portions of the middle Bartlesville (Glenn) sandstone, Glenn Pool field. (Modified from Bae and Petrick, 1986. Copyright 1986 Society of Petroleum Engineers. Bae, J. H. and Petrick, C. B.: "Glenn Pool Surfactant Flood Pilot Test: Comparison of Laboratory and Observation-Well Data," **SPE Reservoir Engineering** (November 1986) 593–603.)

Table 1. General reservoir characteristics of the Bartlesville (Glenn) sandstone, Glenn Pool field.

Depth		1400–1700 ft (427–518 m)
Thickness	Gross Sand	180 ft (55 m)
	Net Pay	25–110 ft (7.6–33 m)
Porosity	Average	16–20%
	Range	to 26%
Permeability	Upper and middle sand	120–200 md to 950 md
	Lower sand	30–43 md to 8 md
Oil saturation		30%
Water saturation	Upper and middle sand	53%
	Lower sand	65%
Formation temperature		95°F (35°C)
Oil viscosity		4 cp at 95°F
Oil gravity		35.8–41.3° API

in one core may be entirely different in a nearby core, although the distance between the two wells may be as little as 150 ft (50 m). Thus, internal stratigraphic correlation over relatively short distances may be quite difficult in some instances. Table 1 summarizes the general reservoir characteristics of the Bartlesville sandstone.

In the central portion of the field the Bartlesville sandstone is present at a depth of approximately 1500 ft (460 m) and ranges in thickness from 100 to 185 ft (30–55 m) (Figures 7 and 8). As mentioned, it is divided into three genetic sandstone units (upper, middle, and lower) separated by thin, laterally discontinuous units of interbedded sandstone and shale and/or shale rip-up clasts, known as the upper and lower nonporous breaks (Figure 14). The upper and middle sandstone units are the productive intervals in the central portion of the field, whereas the lower Glenn unit is below the oil-water contact to the west but produces updip a short distance to the east. The type log and average core-analysis data in Figure 14 indicates the general reservoir quality

and fluid saturation of each of the genetic sandstone units.

Depositional Environments

Lower Desmoinesian sediments were deposited during overall transgression onto the existing shelf, interrupted by episodes of regression that were marked by progradation of deltas. It is generally accepted that major deltaic systems of the Cherokee Group prograded from a northerly source area and resulted in deposits of thick sequences of silt, sand, and clay (Figure 15). Weirich (1953) demonstrated that during Atokan and Desmoinesian times a hinge-line (Boggy hinge line) developed that defined the northerly limit of the subsiding Arkoma basin (Figure 15). Basinward from the hinge line, strata thicken southward at a rate approximately six times greater than the rate at which sediments on the shelf thicken toward the hinge line.

The general character of the Bartlesville sandstone may change greatly within a relatively short distance. Numerous authors describe the Bartlesville sandstone as an erratic and lenticular sandstone that passes laterally within short distances into shales (Bass et al., 1937; Berg, 1963; Saitta and Visher, 1968; and Phares, 1969). In the area described by Saitta and Visher (1968) (Figure 16), the Bartlesville sandstone is distributed in lenses with an average thickness of 100 ft (30 m).

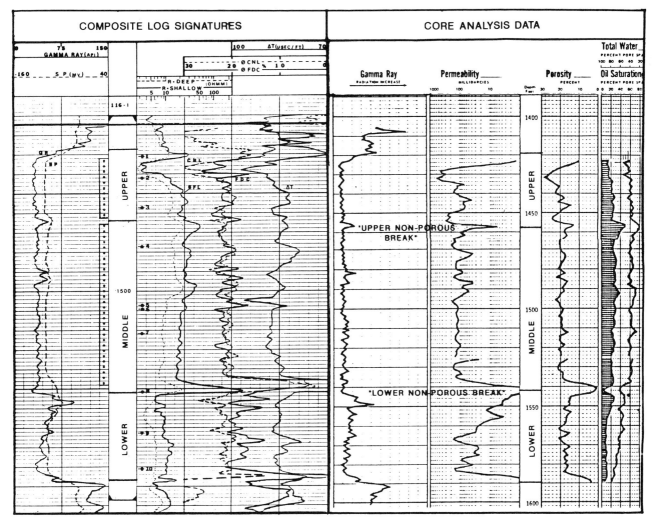

COMPOSITE LOG SIGNATURES	CORE ANALYSIS DATA

Figure 14. Type log/composite log-signature diagram of Bartlesville (Glenn) sandstone calibrated with permeability, porosity, and fluid saturation data from core analysis.

Regionally, the Bartlesville sandstone is composed of several genetic sandstone units believed to have been formed in several specific depositional environments within the proposed early Desmoinesian deltaic complex (Berry, 1963; Hawissa, 1965; Shulman, 1965; Dogan, 1969; Saitta, 1969; Visher et al., 1971; and others). According to Visher et al. (1971), six environmental units evolved during progradation: (1) lower alluvial valley, (2) upper deltaic plain, (3) lower deltaic plain, (4) distributary-mouth bar, (5) marginal basin, and (6) marginal depositional plain.

An alternative interpretation proposed by J. W. Shelton (personal communication, 1989) integrates accepted depositional processes and physiography with emerging and widely accepted concepts of cyclicity and sequence stratigraphy to explain the depositional setting/environment and distribution of the Bartlesville sandstone as well as other Pennsylvanian sandstones in the Mid-Continent (Figure 17). Shelton points out that many of the variations in

Pennsylvanian sandstone development have been related primarily to modern depositional settings and in turn to laterally shifting processes during stillstand sea level stages (Al-Shaieb et al., 1989). The thick, commonly multistoried, and laterally restricted channel sandstones of the Bartlesville have, in most cases, been interpreted as alluvial or deltaic distributaries within an overall progradational deltaic sequence (Visher et al., 1971). However, according to Shelton, a sea level drop during "Bartlesville time" to a point where the shelf edge was exposed would incise existing streams during extension, and deposition beyond their mouths would be on a somewhat steeper slope than the flat shelf to the north. As sea level began to rise, deposition would occur in the channels as valley-fill, with channel-filling phases largely responsible for the complex sand-body geometry along thick trends. During temporary stillstands, deltaic conditions would exist in the previously exposed part of the

169

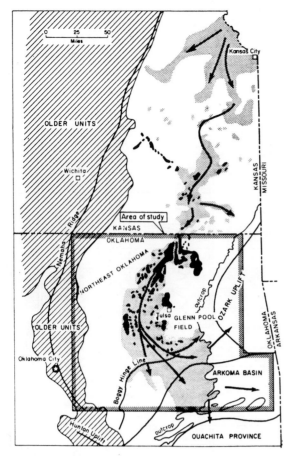

Figure 15. Generalized depositional framework of the Bartlesville-Bluejacket (Glenn) sandstone and location of producing fields (black). (Modified from Visher et al., 1971.) Area of study is about 140 × 140 mi (225 × 225 km).

stable shelf. Further rise of sea level would inundate the stream systems to form estuarine conditions, and then during the highest sea-level stand, widespread shallow-marine deposition would occur.

The alluvial-deltaic/alluvial valley-fill setting or variant thereof is regarded as being generally acceptable as the basic depositional environment of the Bartlesville sandstone in the Glenn Pool field area. This overall geologic setting is supported by integration of isopach patterns, log shapes, composition, texture, sedimentary structures, and other characteristic features associated with many of the Mid-Continent Pennsylvanian sandstone reservoirs (Figure 17).

Lithofacies

The lower sandstone unit is sublitharenite to litharenite, light gray to gray, fine to medium grained, subangular to subrounded, moderately sorted and silty, with abundant sand-sized rock fragments and thin beds of shale, siltstone, and siderite. The sandstone is primarily massively bedded, with portions medium crossbedded (Figure 18C). A thin conglomeratic sandstone or carbonate-cemented

sandstone lies at the base in abrupt contact with shale (Figure 19G). The lower unit typically has over 50% water saturation and is below the oil-water contact level across the field, except along the eastern edge.

The lower, nonporous break consists of interbedded, laminated silty sandstone and shale with localized thin beds of shale, shale rip-up clasts, and sideritic clay pebbles and with intervals of carbonate-cemented sandstone. Locally an effective permeability barrier to vertical fluid movement, it varies in thickness and is not laterally continuous throughout the field (Figure 19D, E, F).

The middle sandstone unit is light brown to brown where oil stained, fine to very fine grained, subangular to subrounded, and well sorted. It has abundant carbonaceous filaments, small sideritic pebbles and clay galls, and thin intervals of carbonate-cemented sandstone and shale rip-up clasts. It is primarily massively bedded, with portions medium crossbedded, and forms the major part of the reservoir (Figure 18B).

The upper "nonporous break" consists of thin silty shale or interbedded, laminated, silty sandstone and silty shale (Figure 19F). Locally this interval is an effective permeability barrier, but has limited lateral extent, which may result in localized contacts between the upper and middle sandstone units and subsequent hydraulic communication.

The upper sandstone is in part massively bedded and/or medium crossbedded sublitharenite to litharenite. It is gray to brown where oil stained, very fine to medium grained, angular to subangular, moderately sorted, and contains abundant carbonaceous filaments and a few sand-sized rock fragments. The upper portion of the unit is generally very fine to medium grained, poorly sorted with silty interlaminations, sparse carbonate or silica cement, and visible porosity (Figure 18A).

Petrography

Major detrital constituents of the Bartlesville sandstone are quartz (both monocrystalline and polycrystalline) and subordinate amounts of feldspar (both plagioclase and potassium) and sand-sized fragments of metamorphic and sedimentary rock (shale and chert) (Figures 20 and 21). Minor detrital constituents, ranging from trace amounts to 1–2%, include mica (muscovite and/or biotite), pyrite, hematite, hornblende, magnetite, rutile, zircon, tourmaline, collophane, and leucoxene. Glauconite, in the form of small (0.05–0.1 mm) rounded pellets or compacted pellets that compose a green pseudomatrix, occurs near the top and/or base of the sandstone. A trace to 5% of finely particulate plant debris and fine carbonaceous filaments also occurs throughout the sandstones as thin (0.5–3 mm) partings and dispersed filaments (Figure 19B, C).

In addition to the framework grains and minor detrital constituents, detrital matrix, cements (silica, calcite, dolomite, and siderite), pore-filling, pore-

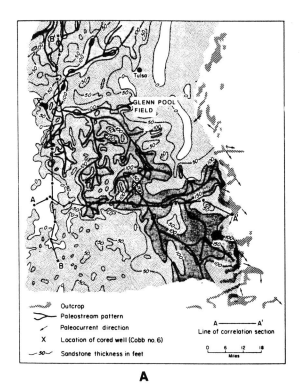

A

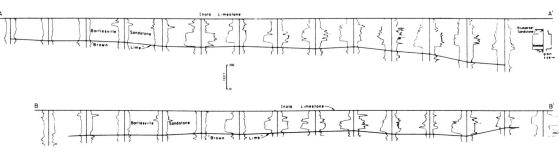

B

Figure 16. (A) Gross-thickness map of Bartlesville-Bluejacket sandstone in the area surrounding the Glenn Pool field, with delineation of thick sandstone trends and paleocurrent data from outcrop direction. (B) Correlation and stratigraphic position of the Bartlesville-Bluejacket sandstone within the genetic interval defined by the Inola (above) and Brown (below) limestones as shown by Visher et al. (1971). Lines of section are shown in (A). Log-response signatures are for correlation purposes and to illustrate facies variations only. (Modified from Visher et al., 1971.) Map rectangle is about 88 × 110 mi (142 × 177 km).

lining, and pore-bridging authigenic clay minerals (kaolinite, chlorite, and illite) (Figure 22), and other authigenic constituents (iron-oxides, pyrite) contribute to the subtle compositional differences observed in the Bartlesville. Table 2 lists the average mineralogic composition of each of the genetic sandstone bodies within the Bartlesville.

Constituents of the upper, middle, and lower sandstone units basically are similar in kind but moderately variable in amounts. These subtle differences influence the reservoir quality and log-response characteristics of each genetic sandstone unit. However, the major differences in reservoir quality and log-response characteristics primarily result from changes in texture, grain size, pore geometry, volume and distribution of clay minerals, and fluid content.

The Bartlesville sandstone reservoir is a sublitharenite to litharenite (Figure 23). Diagenesis has been a major factor in the development and composition of the reservoir, and originally the rock probably was more feldspathic; a significant percentage of the feldspar grains appear to have been dissolved or altered to clay. Compositional differences among the genetic sandstone units, in terms of major detrital constituents, seem to be related primarily to relative abundances of sedimentary rock fragments and detrital matrix (Figures 20, 21, and 23).

The lower sandstone unit ranges from sublitharenite to litharenite to a feldspathic litharenite. The

171

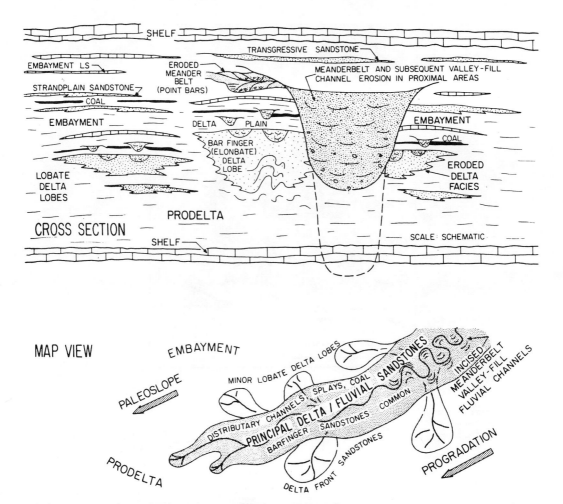

Figure 17. Summary of the characteristics of Mid-Continent fluvial and deltaic sandstone bodies based on the work of many Mid-Continent geologists (Brown, 1979).

middle unit is not as varied in composition as the upper unit and is a sublitharenite. The upper unit ranges from nearly quartz arenite to predominantly sublitharenite, approaching feldspathic litharenite to litharenite.

Porosity/Permeability

Intergranular porosity in the Bartlesville sandstone ranges from 10 to 20% in the lower unit, 16 to 25% in the middle unit, and 18 to 28% in the upper unit and includes both primary and secondary porosity as determined from thin section analysis and point counting estimates (Figures 20 and 21). Primary intergranular porosity is low, consistently 2–4% in all units. Secondary porosity averages 8–17% in the lower unit, 14–23% in the middle unit and upper unit, and as much as 25% in portions of the upper unit (e.g., lower unit 2% primary + 8% secondary = 10% total porosity).

All three of the genetic sandstone units in the Bartlesville show evidence of extensive secondary porosity. However, secondary porosity is best developed in the fine- to medium-grained lithofacies that are relatively free of detrital matrix (i.e., most portions of the upper and middle units, and the basal portions of the lower unit). Partial to complete dissolution of detrital grains (feldspars and sedimentary rock fragments) and small amounts of clayey matrix are the most common features related to the development of secondary porosity in the sandstone units (Figure 20).

Inhomogeneity of packing and "floating" grains are common in lithofacies that are very fine to medium grained, poorly sorted, and that contain irregularly distributed clayey matrix (detrital and/or pseudomatrix) (Figure 20A, B). Oversized pores result from connection of adjacent grain molds and/or dissolution of detrital matrix or cement. Oversized pores occur with inhomogeneous packing and form "channels" that may increase permeability significantly. Elongate pores also are common; generally they are associated with inhomogeneous packing. They tend to be along the boundaries of carbonate-cemented rock where calcite has been dissolved. Corroded grain boundaries are commonly associated with intergranular porosity, and they generally occur in conjunction with enlarged intergranular pores.

172

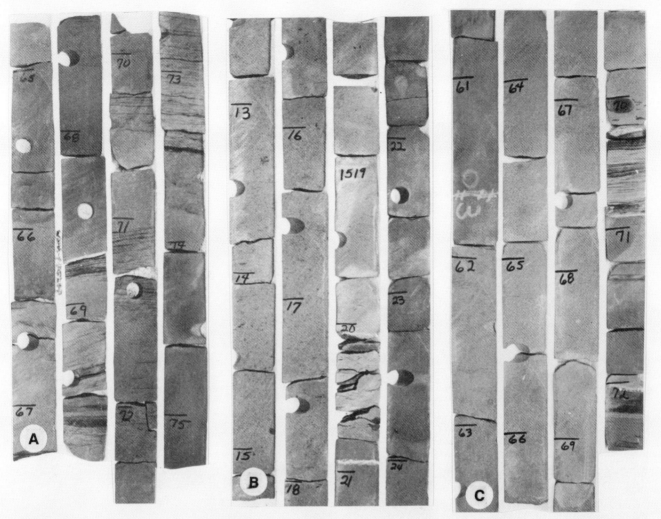

Figure 18. Core photographs of selected portions of the Bartlesville (Glenn) sandstone. (A) Upper sandstone with characteristic cross-bedding features (1467–1470 ft), silty laminations (1473 ft), and carbonaceous filaments (1473.6 ft). (B) Middle sandstone with characteristic massive bedding, abundant carbonaceous filaments, siderite pebbles and clay galls (1513–1518 ft), and thin intervals of shale rip-up clasts (1520–1521 ft). (C) Lower sandstone with oil/water contact (1561.7 ft) in massively bedded interval (1560.5–1570.0 ft), and pebble conglomerate/shale rip-up interval (1570.0 ft) and thinly interlaminated/interbedded sandstone, shale, and siltstone (1570.1–1572.2 ft).

Semilogarithmic plots of porosity and permeability from several conventional core analyses are shown in Figure 24 for each of the three genetic sandstone units. Summary statistics were estimated from sets of 50 random samples. The upper and middle unit plots are somewhat similar in that they both tend to show a close grouping of data points and a general straight-line relationship. However, among the three sandstone units there is notable difference in the amount of scatter of the data points. Larger scattering of data in the upper unit appears to be a result of more varied grain sizes and textures associated with particular lithofacies in addition to the relative abundance and influence of pore-filling clays. Significantly larger porosities and permeabilities are associated with the medium-grained lithofacies of the upper unit (Figure 20A, B), whereas the finer grained lithofacies tends to have somewhat less porosity and permeability. The clustering of data points in the middle is probably due in part to its "massive," more homogeneous nature and less varied grain size (Figure 20C, D). Bae and Petrick (1988) estimate the permeability variation in the Bartlesville, using the Dykstra-Parsons coefficient (V_{dp}), to be 0.55. This coefficient of permeability variation (V_{dp}) is a good descriptor of reservoir heterogeneity, where a homogeneous reservoir has a V_{dp} that approaches zero while an extremely heterogeneous reservoir has a V_{dp} that approaches 1.0.

In the upper and middle units, data points that indicate relatively large porosities (18–24%) and relatively small permeabilities (10–50 md) are

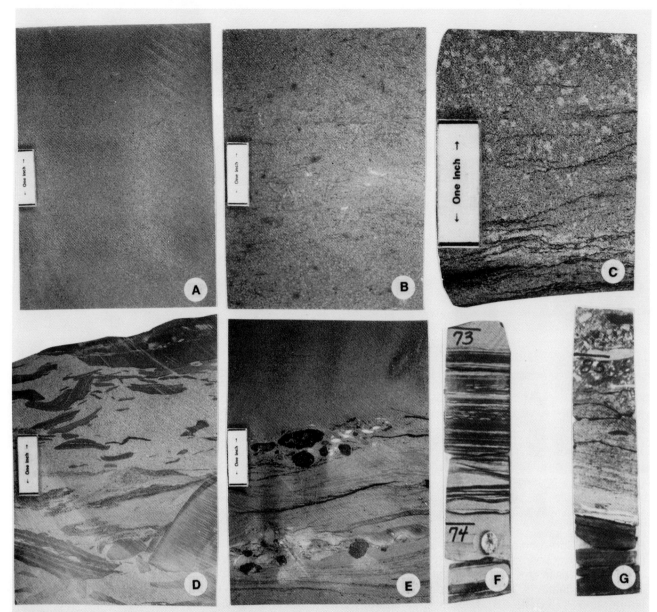

Figure 19. Core photographs of selected lithofacies of the Bartlesville (Glenn) sandstone. (A) Massively bedded sandstone with few carbonaceous filaments, siderite pebbles, and clay galls. (B) Abundant flat-elongate shale rip-up clasts and siderite pebbles in massively bedded sandstone. (C) Fine carbonaceous laminations/stylolites and patchy carbonate-cement (light areas). (D) Interval of flat-elongate shale rip-up clasts and subrounded sideritic shale clasts. (E) Thin intervals of shale pebble conglomerate and finely laminated siltstone and shale. (F) Interlaminated/interbedded black shale and sandstone. (G) Basal pebble conglomerate and carbonate-cemented sandstone above sharp, slightly inclined contact with underlying black marine (prodelta?) shale.

indicative of lithofacies that contain abundant clay minerals and/or shale rip-up clasts or variations in the extent of secondary grain molds. Comparison of porosities and permeabilities from the lower unit with those from the upper and middle units shows a distinct difference in this relationship (Figure 24). Average porosities and permeabilities of the lower unit are less, and variation in porosity is greater owing in part to the type and distribution of secondary porosity in the sandstone. The lower unit contains more interlaminated shale, as well as detrital matrix, sedimentary rock fragments, and feldspar than the upper or middle unit (Table 2). Dissolution of these unstable constituents creates enlarged, isolated pores that result in increased porosity but lack of permeability.

Figure 25 shows mercury-injection capillary pressure tests of three selected samples representative of the three sandstone units. Relative displacement of the curves for samples with similar porosities

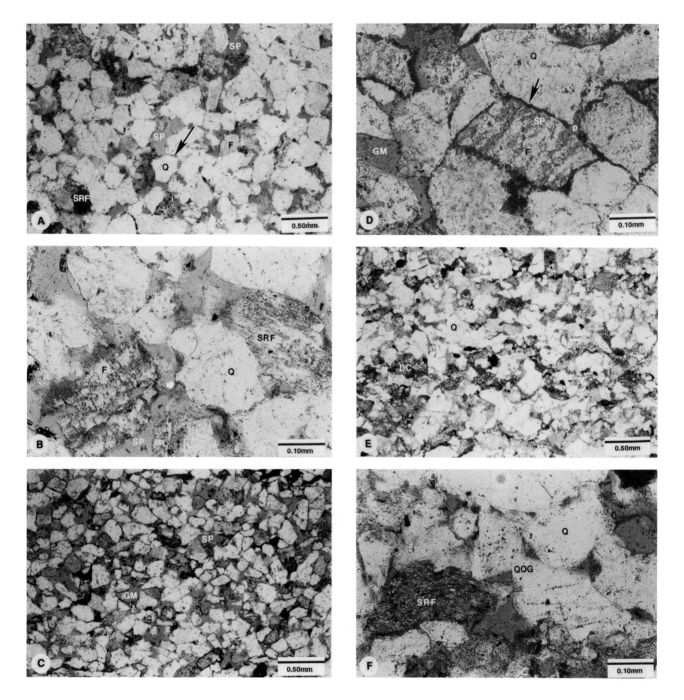

Figure 20. Thin section photomicrographs of selected samples of the Bartlesville (Glenn) sandstone showing characteristic constituents and general texture. (A, B) Upper Glenn; very fine- to medium-grained, poorly sorted, subangular to subrounded sublitharenite to litharenite showing major detrital constituents such as quartz (Q), feldspar (F), and sand-sized sedimentary rock fragments (SRF) and abundant quartz overgrowths (arrow) and secondary porosity (SP). (C, D) Middle Glenn; very fine to fine-grained, moderate- to well-sorted, subrounded-subangular sublitharenite with abundant siderite (arrow) which coats grains and grain molds (GM). Abundant porosity (20–23%) is both primary (P) and secondary (SP) resulting in relatively high permeabilities (200–500 md). (E, F) Lower Glenn; very fine to medium-grained, moderate to poorly sorted, subangular to subrounded litharenite to sublitharenite with abundant detrital clay (DC) and sand-sized sedimentary rock fragments (SRF) and quartz overgrowths (QOG); porosity (12–17%) is mostly secondary and generally not well connected, which results in relatively lower permeabilities (15–30 md).

175

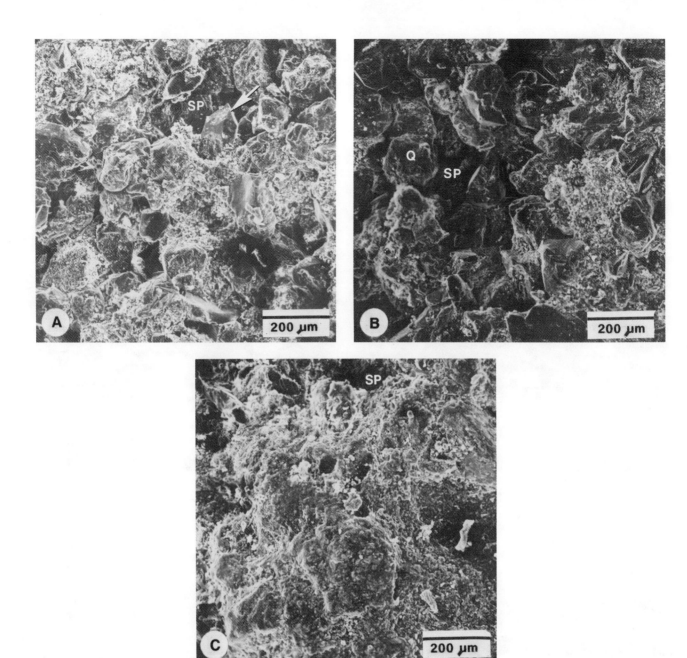

Figure 21. SEM photomicrographs of selected samples of the Bartlesville (Glenn) sandstone showing characteristic framework grains, authigenic clays, and general textures. (A) Upper sandstone with characteristic quartz overgrowths (arrow), authigenic clays, and secondary pores (SP). (B) Middle sandstone with characteristic interconnected primary and secondary pore spaces (SP) among quartz (Q) framework grains and authigenic clays. (C) Lower sandstone with characteristic clayey texture and isolated secondary pore spaces (SP).

(i.e., upper and middle) suggest differences in matrix and/or clay content, pore size, or pore-throat radii as noted in thin section and SEM analysis (Figures 20 and 21).

Production records of wells completed within the lower unit on the east side of the field reflect these reservoir differences by showing lower production rates and less recovery per acre-foot.

Pore Geometry

Diagenetic processes also have influenced the pore system in terms of amounts and directions of permeability in the Bartlesville sandstone. As demonstrated, secondary porosity is controlled by the size, shape, and distribution of relatively unstable or soluble rock components. SEM examination of relief pore casts of sandstone samples allow further study of the pore geometry and porosity types (Figure 26). Irregularity and inhomogeneity of porosity is evident in the pore casts. However, good interconnected porosity in some samples is apparent from continuity of the solid parts of casts that represent pore space. Smaller voids within the solid material (epoxy) represent authigenic clays (Figure 26).

176

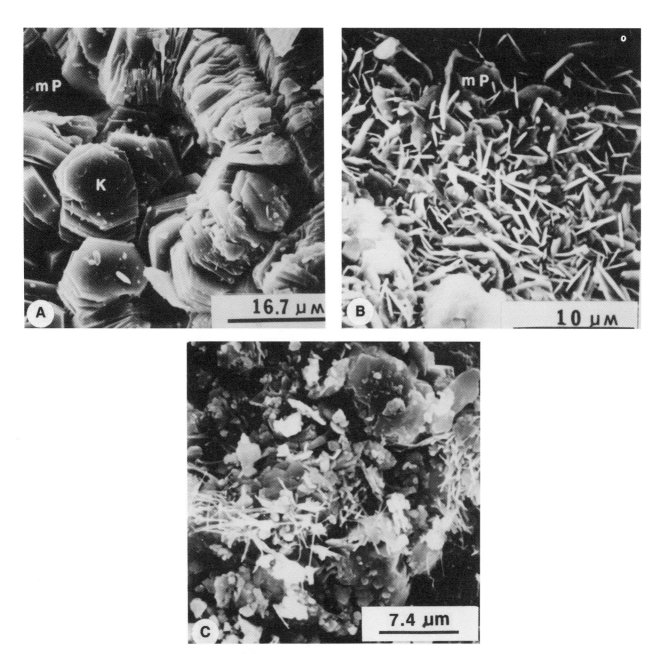

Figure 22. SEM photomicrographs of characteristic authigenic clay minerals within the Bartlesville (Glenn) sandstone. (A) Pore-filling kaolinite and associated microporosity (MP). (B) Pore-lining chlorite and associated microporosity (MP). (C) Pore-bridging illite.

Variations in recovery efficiency within the Bartlesville reservoir are a function of the subtle compositional differences among the three genetic sandstone units, as well as the geometric aspects or microheterogeneity of each respective unit's pore system. According to Wardlaw and Cassan (1979), increased heterogeneity and the common increase in ratio of pore size to aperture size associated with secondary porosity are likely to decrease recovery efficiency. Obviously spatial arrangement of secondary pores can affect recovery efficiency, because connected secondary pores can increase permeability. In the Bartlesville sandstone secondary pores tend to be well connected, particularly in the upper and middle units (Figure 26). The lower unit has less interconnected secondary porosity, thus generally lower permeability and, consequently, lower recovery efficiency.

Source and Burial History

The source for the Glenn Pool hydrocarbons is thought to be primarily the Pennsylvanian Cherokee sediments, which are an assemblage of coal-cyclothem lithologies. The total organic carbon content of the marine, dark-gray to gray-black shales

Table 2. Average mineralogic composition of the Bartlesville (Glenn) sandstone, Glenn Pool field.

	Percentage (%)		
	Upper Glenn	Middle Glenn	Lower Glenn
Detrital Constituents			
Quartz			
Monocrystalline	70	68	61
Polycrystalline	5	2	3
Feldspar			
Undifferentiated	1	1	2
Plagioclase	2	3	3
Microcline	1	1	1
Rock Fragments			
Low Rank Metamorphic	4	3	5
Sedimentary	3	2	4
Chert	1	–1	1+
Other Detrital Constituents			
Mica	1	1	1+
Glauconite	TR-1	TR	TR-1
Zircon	TR	TR	TR
Tourmaline	TR	TR	TR
Hornblende	TR	TR	TR
Opaque Minerals	TR	TR	TR
Detrital Matrix	2	1	4+
Diagenetic Constituents			
Cement			
Quartz Overgrowths	3	2	1
Calcite	1	3+	2+
Dolomite	TR	1	–1
Siderite	–1	3+	2
Authigenic Clay			
Kaolinite	3	3	2
Illite	–1	1	3
Chlorite	1+	1	2
Other			
Iron Oxides	–1	–1	1
Pyrite	–1	1	1
Pseudomatrix	1+	1	3+

TR, trace; TR-1, trace to 1%; –1, less than 1%; 2+, greater than 2%.

of the Cherokee Group ranges from 1 to 8%, and of the laminated, phosphatic black shales from 4 to 28% (Hatch and Leventhal, 1982). The black phosphatic shales contain extractable organic matter that is most similar to Cherokee crude oils from northeast Oklahoma and southeast Kansas (Hatch and Leventhal, 1982). Maximum depth of burial of the Bartlesville at Glenn Pool is estimated to be between 5000 and 5500 ft (1528–1675 m). This depth is not enough to generate significant amounts of hydrocarbons. However, it is believed that the Cherokee sediments to the west and south (Arkoma basin) were buried more deeply and underwent a greater degree of thermal alteration required to generate large amounts of hydrocarbons.

The significance of this, in terms of reservoir development, is that early migrating Cherokee pore fluids become more acidic in the presence of CO_2, one of the by-products of the hydrocarbon generation process (Al-Shaieb and Shelton, 1981). The CO_2 gas reacted with pore waters to form carbonic acid that in turn lowered the pH of the pore fluid. As a result, the early migration of these enriched pore fluids dissolved the more unstable constituents (sedimentary rock fragments, feldspars, etc.) of the Bartlesville sandstone and other Cherokee sandstone reservoirs, creating the secondary porosity that constitutes the principal porosity type in the Bartlesville sandstone in the Glenn Pool. Migration and trapping of hydrocarbons in the reservoir essentially halted any

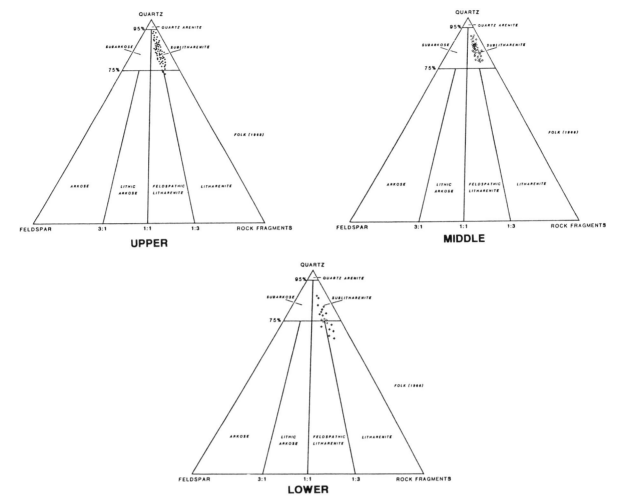

Figure 23. Ternary diagrams depicting composition and sandstone classification of the upper, middle, and lower Bartlesville (Glenn) sandstone in the Glenn Pool field (Kuykendall, 1985).

further diagenesis of the sandstones by impeding water circulation in the reservoir.

Oil Chemistry and Field Conditions

Oil from the Bartlesville reservoir in the Glenn Pool field is 35.8° to 41.3° API, contains 3.12 to 11.46% paraffin (Smith, 1914), and has a sulfur content of 0.19% (Engel, 1988).

Original formation pressure in the Bartlesville interval has been estimated at 600 to 700 psi (4137–4826 kPa). Current waterflood injection pressures range from 100 to over 1100 psi (690–7584 kPa).

Typical dissolved solids content of the Bartlesville formation water in northeast Oklahoma average 168,427 mg/L (R_w = 0.04–0.05 ohm-m at 85°F or 29.4°C) (Case, 1934), but has been diluted to a level of approximately 81,200 mg/L in the portions of the Glenn Pool field by the Arkansas River water used for waterflood programs (Bae and Petrick, 1986). This dilution of the field water substantially increased the regional R_w values and must be considered in the

evaluation and interpretation of electric logs within the field.

The oil produced from the Wilcox sandstone reservoir is green, 32.4° API, and contains 8.44% paraffin. Formation pressure reported from a productive well in the SE/4 of Sec. 18, T17N, R12E is 1098 psi (76.6 kg/cm^2).

EXPLORATION AND DEVELOPMENT CONCEPTS

Potential for New Discoveries

According to Rascoe and Adler (1983), an estimated 8.8 BBO and 31.9 tcf of gas have been produced from Pennsylvanian reservoirs in the Mid-Continent region as of 1978, primarily from stratigraphic traps associated with lenticular alluvial, deltaic, and shallow-marine sandstones. The area is also consid-

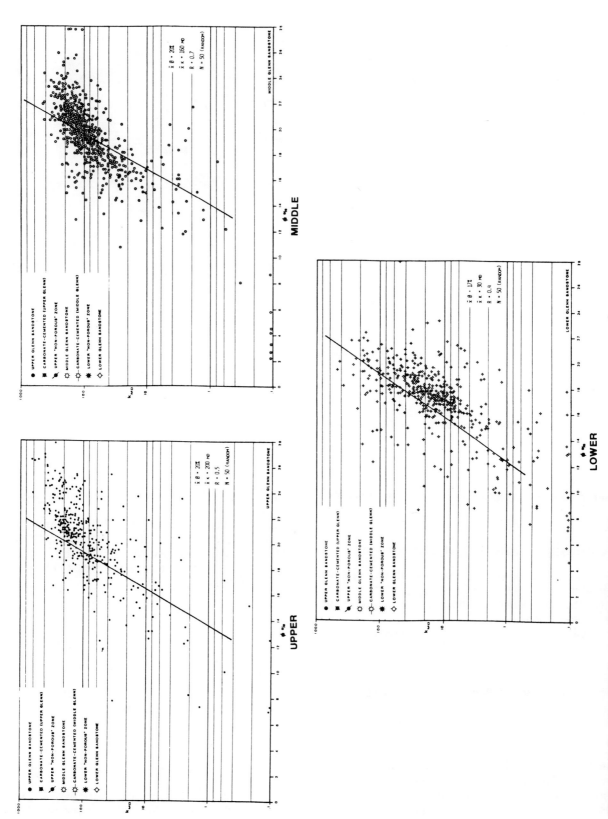

Figure 24. Semilogrithmic plots of porosity compared to permeability of the upper, middle, and lower Bartlesville (Glenn) sandstone in the Glenn Pool field (Kuykendall, 1985).

180

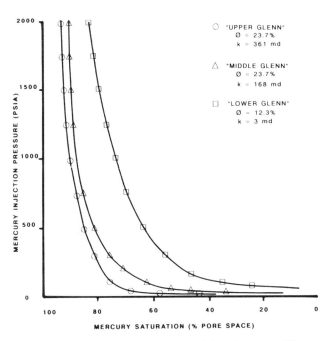

Figure 25. Typical mercury-injection capillary-pressure curves of representative samples from the upper, middle, and lower Bartlesville (Glenn) sandstone in the Glenn Pool field (Kuykendall, 1985).

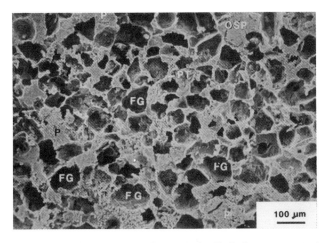

Figure 26. SEM photomicrograph. Relief pore cast of sandstone characteristic of portions of the upper and/or middle Bartlesville (Glenn). Note the relatively large size of pores (P) (lighter areas) and oversized pores (OSP), and interconnection of pore throats (PT). Preserved molds of framework grains (FG) show characteristic subangular-subrounded shape.

ered to be in a late-mature stage of exploration with only those deeper areas (Anadarko and Arkoma basin, and southern Oklahoma) offering large field (oil and/or gas) potential. Although future discovery of giant oil field(s) in the Mid-Continent area within the Middle Pennsylvanian Cherokee sandstones seems unlikely, the potential exists for discoveries of much smaller, yet similar style traps.

Unlike the early wildcatters who, by random drilling, discovered many of the first giant stratigraphic type fields in Oklahoma, today Mid-Continent explorationists are given the task of discovering smaller stratigraphic traps utilizing and integrating many new concepts, tools, and techniques. Detailed mapping of genetic intervals within alluvial-deltaic and alluvial valley-fill systems containing sandstone reservoirs such as the Bartlesville, and an understanding and application of petrography, diagenesis, log analysis, and environments of sandstone deposition—all are required to delineate areas for exploration and discovery of stratigraphic traps within similar thick, multistoried, multilateral sandstones. Exploration in such systems should be concentrated along the updip edge of the sandstone trend and/or within those areas of the system displaying potential structural enhancement. Careful interpretation of the types and quality of hydrocarbon shows in exploration test wells would aid in recognition of potential transition zone reservoir conditions and proximity updip to the possible oil/gas reservoir.

Enhanced Recovery

Enhanced oil recovery from prolific sandstone reservoirs such as the Bartlesville sandstone in the Chevron U.S.A., William Berryhill Unit (Figures 4 and 6) has been shown to be a very successful process (Crawford and Crawford, 1985). A detailed understanding of the reservoir characteristics and heterogeneities is required in order to maximize the efficiency needed in EOR operations. Development of these secondary, depleted-type reservoirs could add significant reserves to the ever-declining domestic oil reserves.

Careful study and calibration of cores and well logs from the Bartlesville sandstone reservoir in the Glenn Pool field provide data sufficient for the formation and testing of working hypotheses concerning prediction of reservoir geometry and continuity, directions of permeability, and extents of possible fluid-flow barriers (Kuykendall, 1985). Recognition of the principal levels or scales of heterogeneity (Figure 27) in the Bartlesville reservoir and other similar sandstone reservoirs is important in order to determine the degree of hydraulic interconnection and, in turn, to maximize recoveries.

A gamma-ray/lithofacies correlation section across the 160 ac (65 ha) William Berryhill unit (NE/4 Sec. 17, T17N, R12E) shows the moderately complex, short-distance changes in the geometry of the Bartlesville sandstone and attendant reservoir heterogeneity that makes extensive correlation of individual lithofacies difficult (Figure 28). Correlation on the basis of well-log signatures alone may be complicated by changes in depositional trend of the rock units, as well as by lithic variation. Axial trends of "channel" units and thin interbedded shales of the Bartlesville in the field influence the directional

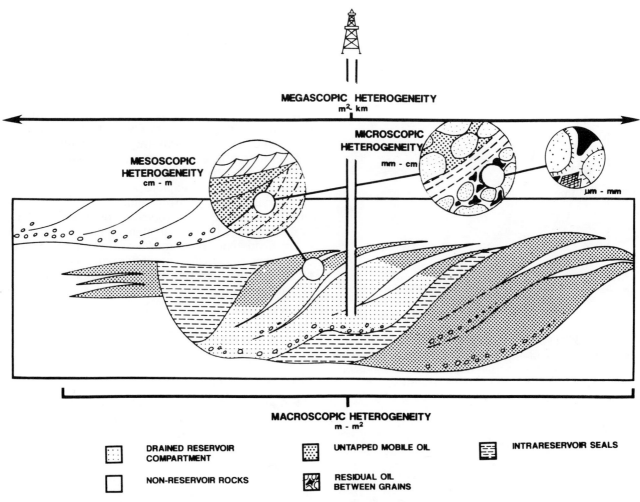

MEGASCOPIC HETEROGENEITY
m² km

MICROSCOPIC HETEROGENEITY
mm - cm

MESOSCOPIC HETEROGENEITY
cm - m

µm - mm

MACROSCOPIC HETEROGENEITY
m - m²

☐ DRAINED RESERVOIR COMPARTMENT

☐ NON-RESERVOIR ROCKS

▦ UNTAPPED MOBILE OIL

▦ RESIDUAL OIL BETWEEN GRAINS

▦ INTRARESERVOIR SEALS

Figure 27. Principal scales of reservoir heterogeneity recognized in sandstone reservoirs such as the Bartlesville (Glenn) sandstone in the Glenn Pool field. (Modified after Tyler, 1988.)

permeability and preferential flow of fluids within the reservoir. A log-signature map of the 160 ac (65 ha) unit (Figure 29) shows gamma-ray and/or spontaneous potential curves of the Bartlesville sandstone that aid in visualizing the three genetic sandstone units and general changes in gross thickness of each across the unit.

Petrographic information and calibration of logs in sandstone reservoirs similar to the Bartlesville in the giant Glenn Pool field should lead to improved interpretation of logs and correlation of lithofacies, which in turn should contribute to improved delineation and discovery of subtle stratigraphic traps and to implementation and prediction of secondary or enhanced oil recovery operations.

particular, the Cherokee Group sandstone reservoirs of the Mid-Continent.

Special thanks to those who contributed directly to the development and interpretation of the data within the Glenn Pool field and/or this paper, either as an operator, co-worker, advisor, editor, or friend. They include Robert F. Lindsay and Michael E. Crawford and others of Chevron U.S.A.; Gary F. Stewart and Zuhair Al-Shaieb of Oklahoma State University; John W. Shelton of MASERA Corporation; J. Glenn Cole, Gail G. Gibbon, and Bill Brownfield, independent geologists; and Mary Livingston of MASERA Corporation, who graciously typed and processed the manuscript.

ACKNOWLEDGMENTS

We greatly acknowledge the many geologists who have contributed their experiences and knowledge over the years of Pennsylvanian sandstones, and in

REFERENCES CITED

Al-Shaieb, Z., and J. W. Shelton, 1981, Migration of hydrocarbons and secondary porosity in sandstones: American Association of Petroleum Geologists Bulletin, v. 65, n. 11, p. 2433–2436.
Al-Shaieb, Z., J. W. Shelton, and J. O. Puckette, 1989, Sandstone reservoirs of the Mid-Continent: Oklahoma City Geological

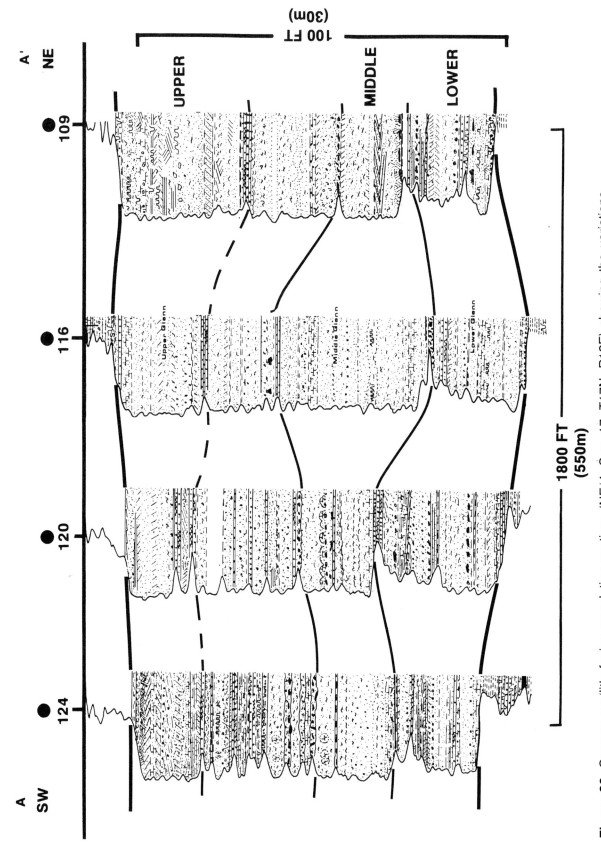

Figure 28. Gamma-ray/lithofacies correlation section (NE/4, Sec. 17, T17N, R12E) showing the variations (A–A') of the Bartlesville (Glenn) sandstone across the of lithology and sedimentary features in cores from 160 ac (65 ha) William Berryhill micellar-polymer unit closely spaced wells (Kuykendall, 1989).

183

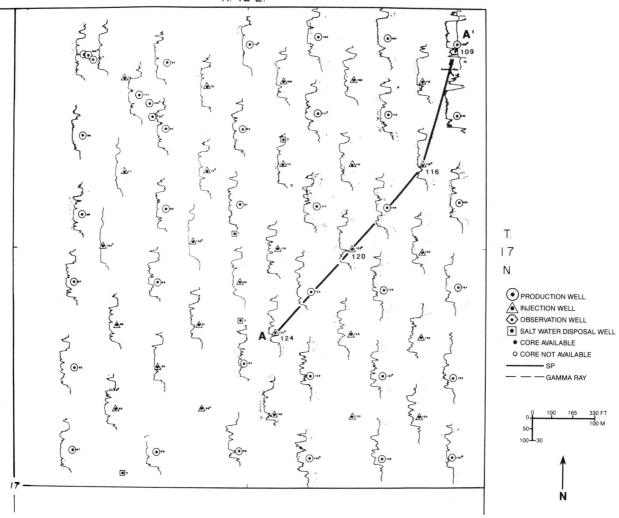

R. 12 E.

A'
109
116
120
A
124

T.
17
N

PRODUCTION WELL
INJECTION WELL
OBSERVATION WELL
SALT WATER DISPOSAL WELL
CORE AVAILABLE
CORE NOT AVAILABLE
SP
GAMMA RAY

0   100 165   330 FT
100 M

N

Figure 29. Log-signature (gamma-ray and/or spontaneous potential) map of the Bartlesville (Glenn) sandstone within the 160 ac (65 ha) William Berryhill micellar-polymer unit (NE/4, Sec. 17, T17N, R12E) illustrating the moderately complex, short distance changes in the geometry of individual lithofacies (Kuykendall, 1985).

Society Syllabus for short course, AAPG mid-continent section meeting, Oklahoma City, 125 p.

Bae, J. H., and C. B. Petrick, 1986, Glenn Pool surfactant flood pilot test: comparison of laboratory and observation well data: Paper SPE 12694 presented at the SPE/DOE Fourth Symposium on Enhanced Oil Recovery, Tulsa, OK, April 15-18, 14 p.

Bae, J. H., and C. B. Petrick, 1988, Glenn Pool surfactant flood pilot test: Part 2—field operations: Paper SPE 15551 presented at the 1986 SPE Technical Conference and Exhibition held in New Orleans, October 5-8.

Barnes, K. B., and J. F. Sage, 1943, Gas repressuring at Glenn Pool: Oil and Gas Journal, v. 42, n. 3, p. 45-48, 65, 67.

Bass, N. W., C. Leatherock, W. R. Dillard, and L. E. Kennedy, 1937, Origin and distribution of Bartlesville and Burbank shoestring oil sands in parts of Oklahoma and Kansas: American Association of Petroleum Geologists Bulletin, v. 21, p. 30-66.

Bennison, A. P., 1972, Structural framework of Tulsa County, in A. P. Bennison, ed., Tulsa's physical environment: Tulsa Geol. Soc. Digest, v. 37, p. 113-117.

Berg, O. R., 1963, The depositional environment of a portion of the Bluejacket Sandstone: M. S. Thesis, University of Tulsa, 84 p.

Berry, C. G., 1963, Stratigraphy of the Cherokee Group, eastern Osage County, Oklahoma: M. S. Thesis, University of Tulsa, 76 p.

Brown, L. F., Jr., 1979, Deltaic sandstone facies of the Mid-Continent, in N. J. Hyne, ed., Pennsylvanian sandstones of the Mid-Continent: Tulsa Geological Society Special Publication 1, p. 35-65.

Case, L. C., 1934, Subsurface water characteristics in Oklahoma and Kansas, in W. E. Wrather and F. H. Lahee, eds., Problems of petroleum geology: American Association of Petroleum Geologists Publ., p. 855-868.

Chenoweth, P. A., 1979, Geological prospecting for Mid-Continent sandstones, in N. J. Hyne, ed., Pennsylvanian sandstones of the Mid-Continent: Tulsa Geological Society Special Publication 1, p. 13-33.

Crawford, C. C., and M. E. Crawford, 1985, William Berryhill micellar polymer project: a case history: Paper SPE 14444 presented at the 1985 SPE Annual Technical Conference and Exhibition, Las Vegas, September 22-25.

Dickey, P. A., and R. E. Rohn, 1955, Facies control of oil occurrence: American Association of Petroleum Geologists Bulletin, v. 39, n. 11, p. 2306-2320.

Dogan, N., 1969, A subsurface study of Middle Pennsylvanian rocks (from the Brown limestone to the Checkerboard

Limestone) in east-central Oklahoma: M. S. Thesis, University of Tulsa, 64 p.

Ebanks, W. J., 1979, Correlation of Cherokee (Desmoinesian) sandstones of the Missouri-Kansas-Oklahoma tri-state area, *in* N. J. Hyne, ed., Pennsylvanian sandstones of the Mid-Continent: Tulsa Geological Society Special Publication 1, p. 295-313.

Engel, M. H., et al., 1988, Organic geochemical correlation of Oklahoma crude oils using R and Q-mode factor analysis: Organic Geochemistry, v. 12, n. 2, p. 157-170.

Franks, K. A., 1984, The rush begins: A history of the Red Fork, Cleveland, and Glenn Pool oil fields: Oklahoma Heritage Association, 163 p.

Hatch, J. R., and Leventhal, 1982, Comparative organic geochemistry of shales and coals from Cherokee Group and lower part of Marmaton Group of Middle Pennsylvanian age, Oklahoma, Kansas, Missouri, and Iowa (abs.): American Association of Petroleum Geologists Bulletin, v. 66, n. 5, p. 579.

Hawissa, I., 1965, Depositional environment of the Bartlesville, the Red Fork, and the lower Skinner sandstones in portions of Lincoln, Logan, and Payne counties, Oklahoma: M.S. Thesis, University of Tulsa, 31 p.

Hemish, L. A., 1989, Bluejacket (Bartlesville) Sandstone member of the Boggy Formation (Pennsylvanian) in its type area: Oklahoma Geology Notes, Oklahoma Geological Survey, v. 49, n. 3, June 1989, p. 72-89.

Kuykendall, M. D., 1985, The petrography, diagenesis, and depositional setting of the Glenn (Bartlesville) sandstone, William Berryhill Unit, Glenn Pool oil field, Creek County, Oklahoma: Unpublished M. S. Thesis, Oklahoma State University, 383 p.

Kuykendall, M. D., 1989, Reservoir heterogeneity within Bartlesville sandstone, Glenn Pool oil field, Creek County, Oklahoma: American Association of Petroleum Geologists Bulletin, v. 73, n. 8, p. 1048.

Phares, R. S., 1969, Depositional framework of the Bartlesville sandstone in northeastern Oklahoma: M. S. Thesis, University of Tulsa, 56 pp.

Rascoe, B., Jr., and F. J. Adler, 1983, Permo-Carboniferous hydrocarbon accumulations, mid-continent, U.S.A.: American Association of Petroleum Geologists Bulletin, v. 67, n. 6, p. 979-1001.

Rich, J. L., 1928, Geology of Glenn Pool of Oklahoma: American Association of Petroleum Geologists Bulletin, v. 12, n. 2, p. 213-215.

Saitta, S., 1969, Bluejacket Formation—a subsurface study in northeastern Oklahoma: M. S. Thesis, University of Tulsa, 142 p.

Saitta, S., and G. S. Visher, 1968, Subsurface study of the southern portion of the Bluejacket delta, *in* A guidebook to the geology of the Bluejacket-Bartlesville sandstone, Oklahoma: Oklahoma City Geological Society, p. 52-65.

Shelton, J. W., 1973, Models of sand and sandstone deposits: a methodology for determining sand genesis and trend: Oklahoma Geological Survey Bulletin, v. 118, 122 p.

Shulman, C., 1965, Stratigraphic analysis of the Cherokee Group in adjacent portions of Lincoln, Logan, and Oklahoma counties, Oklahoma: M.S. Thesis, University of Tulsa, 28 p.

Smith, C. D., 1914, The Glenn oil and gas pool vicinity: U.S. Geological Survey Bulletin, v. 541, p. 34-39.

Tyler, N., 1988, New oil from oil fields: Geotimes, July, p. 8-12.

Visher, G. S., 1968, Depositional framework of the Bluejacket-Bartlesville sandstone, *in* G. S. Visher, ed., A guidebook to the geology of the Bluejacket-Bartlesville sandstone, Oklahoma: Oklahoma City Geological Society, p. 32-42.

Visher, G. S., B. S. Saitta, and R. S. Phares, 1971, Pennsylvanian delta patterns and petroleum occurrences in eastern Oklahoma: American Association of Petroleum Geologists Bulletin, v. 55, p. 1206-1230.

Wardlaw, N. C., and J. P. Cassan, 1979, Estimation of recovery efficiency by visual observation of pore systems in reservoir rocks: Canadian Society of Petroleum Geology Bulletin, v. 26, n. 4, p. 572-585.

Weirich, T. E., 1953, Shelf principle of oil origin, migration and accumulation: American Association of Petroleum Geologists Bulletin, v. 37, n. 8, p. 2027-2045.

Weirich, T. E., 1968, History of the Bartlesville oil sand, *in* G. S. Visher, ed., A guidebook to the geology of the Bluejacket-Bartlesville sandstone, Oklahoma: Oklahoma City Geological Society, p. 69-72.

Wilson, W. B., 1927, Geology of Glenn Pool in Oklahoma, *in* Structure of typical American oil fields: Vol. I, Symposium, American Association of Petroleum Geologists, p. 230-242.

SUGGESTED READING

Bae, J. H., and C. B. Petrick, 1986, Glenn Pool surfactant flood pilot test: comparison of laboratory and observation well data: Paper SPE 12694 presented at the SPE/DOE Fourth Symposium on Enhanced Oil Recovery, Tulsa, OK, April 15-18, 14 p. Details of experimental procedures and process performance—Chevron U.S.A., William Berryhill Unit.

Bae, J. H., and C. B. Petrick, 1988, Glenn Pool surfactant flood pilot test: Part 2—field operations: Paper SPE 15551 presented at the 1986 SPE Technical Conference and Exhibition held in New Orleans, October 5-8. Details of facilities, injection and production operations—Chevron U.S.A., William Berryhill Unit.

Barnes, K. B., and J. F. Sage, 1943, Gas repressuring at Glenn Pool: Oil and Gas Journal, v. 42, n. 3, p. 45-48, 65, 67. Details of implementation and initial response of early (1943) gas repressuring in the field.

Crawford, C. C., and M. E Crawford, 1985, William Berryhill micellar polymer project: a case history: Paper SPE 14444 presented at the 1985 SPE Annual Technical Conference and Exhibition, Las Vegas, September 22-25. Describes implementation of expansion phase—Chevron U.S.A., William Berryhill Unit.

Franks, K. A., 1984, The rush begins: a history of the Red Fork, Cleveland, and Glenn Pool oil fields: Oklahoma Heritage Association, 163 p.

Kuykendall, M. D., 1985, The petrography, diagenesis, and depositional setting of the Glenn (Bartlesville) sandstone, William Berryhill Unit, Glenn Pool oil field, Creek County, Oklahoma: Unpublished M. S. Thesis, Oklahoma State University, 383 p. Detailed description of Bartlesville ("Glenn") sandstone in 160 ac lease utilizing information from over 70 modern logs and 18 cores.

Rich, J. L., 1928, Geology of Glenn Pool of Oklahoma: American Association of Petroleum Geologists Bulletin, v. 12, n. 2, p. 213-215. Brief geologic assessment of Glenn Pool field.

Smith, C. D., 1914, The Glenn oil and gas pool vicinity: U.S. Geological Survey Bulletin, v. 541, p. 34-39. Early description of stratigraphy and structure of the Glenn Pool field.

Weirich, T. E., 1968, History of the Bartlesville oil sand, *in* A guidebook to the geology of the Bluejacket-Bartlesville sandstone, Oklahoma: Oklahoma City Geological Society, p. 69-72. Brief history of the development of several early oil fields in the Bartlesville sandstone.

Wilson, W. B., 1927, Geology of Glenn Pool in Oklahoma, *in* Structure of typical American oil fields, v. I, Symposium: American Association of Petroleum Geologists, p. 230-242. Early paper with excellent overview of Glenn Pool field and proposed trapping mechanism.

Appendix 1. Field Description

Field name .... *Glenn Pool (includes "North Glenn" and "South Glenn") field*

Ultimate recoverable reserves .... *Approx. 400,000,000+ BO; 330,000,000 BO as of 6/90*

Field location:

    Country .... *U.S.A.*

    State .... *Oklahoma*

    Basin/Province .... *Northeast Oklahoma platform*

Field discovery:

    Year first pay discovered .... *Bartlesville ("Glenn") sandstone 1905*

    Year second pay discovered .... *Wilcox ("Mounds") sandstone 1908*

Discovery well name and general location:

    First pay .... *Ida Glenn No. 1, C SE/4 Sec. 10, T17N, R12E*

    Second pay .... *J. Berryhill Lease, SW SW NE, Sec. 29, T17N, R12E*

Discovery well operator .... *Galbreath & Chesley*

    Second pay .... *Eastern Oil Co.*

IP:

    First pay .... *75 BOPD at 1458 ft (445 m), Bartlesville ("Glenn")*

    Second pay .... *120 BOPD at 2331 ft (711 m), Wilcox ("Mounds")*

All other zones with shows of oil and gas in the field:

Age	Formation	Type of Show
Pennsylvanian	*Oswego*	*Minor gas*
	Red Fork	*Minor oil and gas*
	Booch (Taneha)	*Minor oil and gas*
	Dutcher	*Gas*
Mississippian	*Mississippi*	*Minor oil and gas*
Ordovician	*Wilcox ("Mounds")*	*Oil/gas, isolated structure*

Geologic concept leading to discovery and method or methods used to delineate prospect
Early wildcat drilling based on reported nearby oil seeps, recent discoveries 30 mi north, and "creekology"

Structure:

    Province/basin type .... *Klemme IIA craton margin, composite (for Anadarko); Bally 221 foredeep with ramp (for Anadarko)*

Tectonic history
Stable platform area since Cambrian–Ordovician time. Extensive uplift and erosion occurred in Late Devonian and post-Mississippian. Widespread epeirogeny with gentle tilting of the Central Oklahoma platform to the west-southwest in post-Permian.

Regional structure
Gently undulating homoclinal dip to the west-southwest at approximately 40 ft/mi (7.6 m/km). Situated west of the Ozark uplift, east of the Nemaha ridge and Anadarko basin, and north of the Arkoma basin.

Trap:

    Trap type(s) .... *Stratigraphic; abrupt facies change updip*

Basin stratigraphy (major stratigraphic intervals from surface to deepest penetration in field):

Chronostratigraphy	Formation	Depth to Top in ft (m)
Pennsylvanian (Missourian)	*Coffeyville*	*Surface*
Pennsylvanian (Desmoinesian)	*Bartlesville "Glenn"*	*1450 (440)*
Mississippian	*Mississippi*	*2000 ft (610)*

| Ordovician/Cambrian | Simpson/Arbuckle | 2300 (700 m) |
| Pre-Cambrian | Granite | 3900 (1190) |

Reservoir characteristics:

Number of reservoirs ..... *1 major with 5 minor pays contributing less than 10% of recoverable reserves*

Formations .... *Locally known as the Glenn sandstone, regionally referred to as the Bartlesville (Bluejacket) sandstone of the Boggy Formation*

Ages .... *Pennsylvanian, Desmoinesian Series, Krebs Group*

Depths to tops of reservoirs .... *Bartlesville (Glenn), 1450 ft (440 m)*

Gross thickness (top to bottom of producing interval) .... *200 ft (61 m)*

Net thickness—total thickness of producing zones

    Average .... *100 ft (30 m)*

    Maximum .... *180 ft (55 m)*

Lithology

Very fine to medium-grained, subangular-subrounded, moderately well sorted, sublitharenite-litharenite with abundant authigenic clay minerals (kaolinite, chlorite, and illite) and interbedded/interlaminated siltstones and shales.

Porosity type ...... *Secondary: intergranular and moldic due to dissolution of unstable framework grains*

Average porosity *17–24%*

Average permeability .... *Variable, 0–450 md*

Seals:

Upper

    Formation, fault, or other feature .... *Sonora Formation*

    Lithology .... *Transgressive marine shales*

Lateral

    Formation, fault, or other feature .... *Boggy Formation*

    Lithology .... *Interdistributary bay silts and shales*

Source:

Formation and age .... *Pennsylvanian Cherokee Group shales*

Lithology .... *Shale*

Average total organic carbon (TOC) *1–8%*

Maximum TOC *10%*

Kerogen type (I, II, or III) .... *II, III*

Vitrinite reflectance (maturation) .... $R_o = 0.60–0.65$

Time of hydrocarbon expulsion .... *Middle Permian to post-Cretaceous*

Present depth to top of source .... *800–2000 ft (240–610 m)*

Thickness .... *1200–3000 ft (365–915 m)*

Potential yield .... *Unknown*

Appendix 2. Production Data

Field name .... *Glenn Pool (including "North Glenn" and "South Glenn") field*

Field size:

    Proved acres .... *27,440 ac (11,113 ha)*

    Number of wells all years .... *4000+*

    Current number of wells *750*

    Well spacing .... *10 ac (4 ha)*

    Ultimate recoverable .... *400 MMBO*

    Cumulative production (6/90) .... *330 MMBO*

Annual production .... *1 MMBO*
Present decline rate *10-15%*
    Initial decline rate *20-30%*
    Overall decline rate *25%*
Annual water production .... *Unknown*
In place, total reserves .... *1 billion bbl (est.)*
Primary recovery .... *222-236 MMBO (est. 1943)*
Secondary recovery .... *100+ MMBO*
Enhanced recovery .... *1+ MMBO (1979-1990)*
Cumulative water production .... *Unknown*

Drilling and casing practices:

Amount of surface casing set .... *275 ft (85 m); 10-in.*
Casing program
Cable tool holes; multiple strings set to depth immediately above Bartlesville "Glenn," with open-hole completion of the sandstone
Drilling mud .... *Natural*
Bit program .... *Cable tool chisel bit*
High pressure zones .... *None*

Completion practices:

Interval(s) perforated .... *Open-hole completion*
Well treatment .... *Natural or 200-250 quarts of nitroglycerine, flow or pump*

Formation evaluation:

Logging suites .... *Drillers logs, cores*
Testing practices .... *Open hole and completion production tests*
Mud logging techniques .... *Core/sample examination*

Oil characteristics:

Type .... *NA*
API gravity .... *35-40°*
Base .... *Paraffin*
Initial GOR .... *350 ft³ gas/bbl oil*
Sulfur, wt% *0.19%*
Viscosity, SUS .... *5 cp*
Pour point .... *NA*
Gas-oil distillate .... *NA*

Field characteristics:

Average elevation .... *650-850 ft (198-259 m)*
Initial pressure .... *600 psi (4137 kPa)*
Present pressure .... *100-1100+ psi (waterflood pressures)*
Pressure gradient .... *0.45 psi/ft (10.2 kPa/m)*
Temperature .... *85-100°F (47-55°C)*
Geothermal gradient .... *1.14°F/100 ft (0.63°C/305 m)*
Drive .... *Solution gas drive*
Oil column thickness .... *80-180 ft (24-55 m), max. 240 ft (73 m)*
Oil-water contact .... *Variable; -826 ft (-252 m) "Upper" and "Middle" Bartlesville*
Connate water *70%*
Water salinity, TDS .... *Original, 168.427 mg/L; present, 81.181 mg/L*
Resistivity of water .... *1-3 ohms (field); 0.035-0.05 ohms (regional)*
Bulk volume water (%) *5.4%*

Transportation method and market for oil and gas:
Pipeline

Mene Grande Field—Venezuela
Maracaibo Basin, Western Venezuela

LUISA ALCALÁ
Maraven S. A.
Caracas, Venezuela

FIELD CLASSIFICATION

BASIN: Maracaibo
BASIN TYPE: Foredeep
RESERVOIR ROCK TYPE: Sandstone
RESERVOIR ENVIRONMENT OF
   DEPOSITION: Fluvial-Deltaic

RESERVOIR AGE: Eocene and Miocene
PETROLEUM TYPE: Oil
TRAP TYPE: Faulted Plunging Anticline
   and Porosity Pinch-Outs

TRAP DESCRIPTION: Porosity pinch-outs in channel and crevasse splay sandstones of
   Miocene; plunging anticlinal traps in Eocene

LOCATION

Mene Grande field is located some 120 km southeast of the city of Maracaibo in Zulia State in western Venezuela (Figure 1). It lies in the foothills of the Misoa mountain range and along the Misoa anticline. The field is bordered by the Misoa river to the north, the Raya river to the east, and the Barua river to the south. The town of Mene Grande, located within the field itself, grew during the boom of the 1920s and 1930s and still is today the center of activities in the area. On the Lake Maracaibo shore, 15 km to the west, a refinery and tank farm were built at the town of San Lorenzo to handle the production from this field and nearby fields (Figure 2).

The more important fields in the vicinity are the Bachaquero field to the northwest and the Barua–Motatan fields to the south and southeast (Figure 1). The Bachaquero field together with Cabimas, Tia Juana, and Lagunillas fields are collectively known as the Bolivar Coastal fields and contain the bulk of the Miocene heavy oil reservoirs in the Lake Maracaibo basin. These have been producing for over 70 years. On the other hand, the Barua–Motatan fields have produced heavy and medium gravity oil from Eocene reservoirs since 1940.

Mene Grande field consists of 10,378 proven acres (4203 ha) wherein 759 wells have been drilled. Of these, 270 wells still produce today. Ultimate recoverable reserves are estimated at 707 million barrels and cumulative production since 1914 has been 639 million barrels or 90%.

HISTORY

Pre-Discovery

The presence of oil around Lake Maracaibo that emanated from large seeps had been known for several centuries. It was not until the first few years of the twentieth century that an attempt was made to exploit an asphalt deposit 72 km west of Maracaibo. Between 1912 and 1914 a few geologists began regional surface geological and topographical surveys of the major seepages around Lake Maracaibo. It was during this time that Mene Grande hill with its extraordinary oil seepages was discovered. The surface evidence of petroleum was so impressive that the first well to be drilled using cable tool was located among the seepages on the outcrop of the oil sands at 250 ft (76 m) above sea level.

Discovery

Perhaps the one person most responsible for the discovery and description of the initial work on the Mene Grande field is Ralph Arnold. His company reports, written between 1912 and 1916 while working for the Caribbean Petroleum Company, contain a detailed description of the Mene Grande seepage and precise information regarding the Zumaque No. 1 well. Spudded on 12 January 1914 and finished on 15 April 1914, it was the first commercial well drilled in Venezuela. Located on Mene Grande hill, it was drilled to a depth of 443 ft

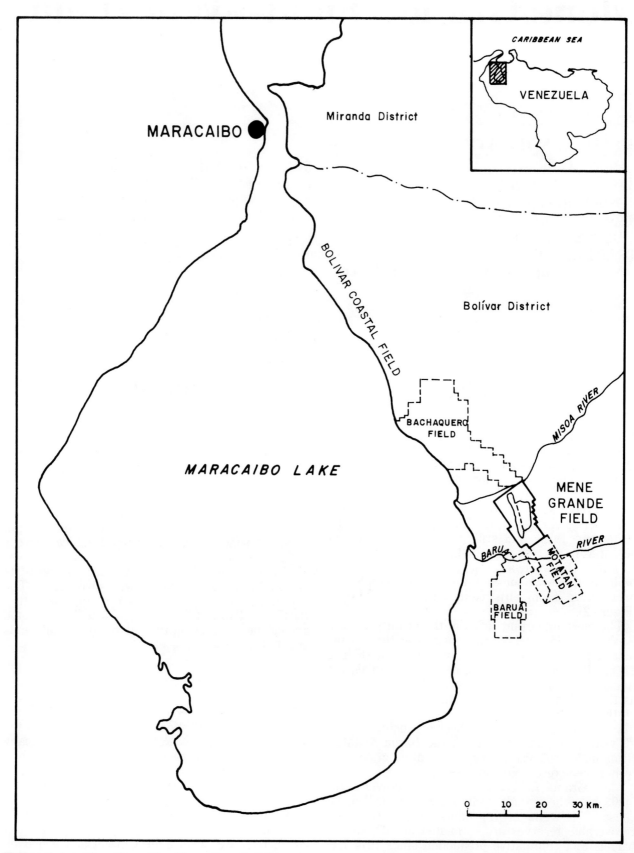

Figure 1. Location map of the Mene Grande field.

190

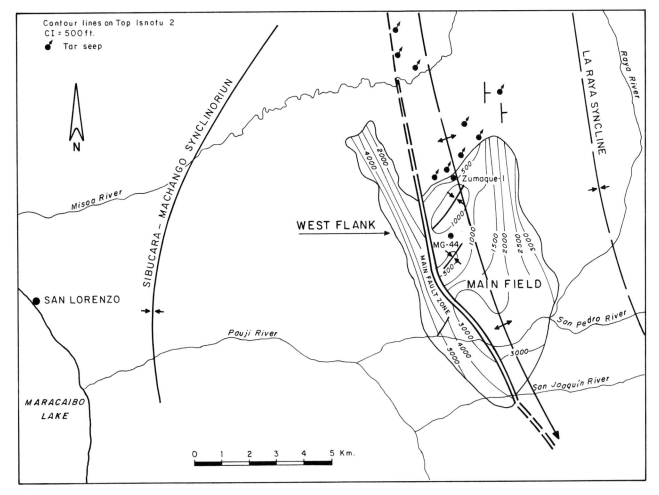

Figure 2. Regional structure map of the Mene Grande field. The Main field is astraddle the south-plunging Misoa anticline.

(135 m) and produced 15° API oil with an initial production of 264 bbl/d. The producing interval, which contains sands of Miocene age, was called then the Maracaibo Series but is known today as the Isnotú Formation.

Post-Discovery

Based on information from the Caribbean Petroleum Company Staff's publication (1948), only 50 wells had been completed by the end of 1925. At this time rotary drilling was introduced and old wells were deepened into the Eocene, Pauji, and Misoa formations. The discovery well, of the deeper reservoirs MG-44, produced 24° API oil with an initial production of 1130 bbl/d. A geological review of the Eocene main crestal high (Goddard, 1985) indicates that the existing Eocene wells were drilled between 1925 and 1941. By 1988 these produced 53.5 million barrels of the 58 million barrels of recoverable reserves of the Eocene reservoirs. In the early stages

of production the wells began producing abundant water, up to 30% in some cases (Clark, 1932). In 1988, only three wells produced from the Eocene Misoa Formation with a 98% water cut. Today almost the total production of 15° to 18° API oil is obtained from the Miocene Isnotú Formation from the two operational areas known as the West Flank and the Main field. These cover areas of 13 km² and 25 km², respectively (Figure 2).

DISCOVERY METHOD

The field was discovered from the surface evidence of petroleum where abundant oil seepages existed on Mene Grande hill. Later, surface geology led to the recognition of a plunging anticline, and the field was extended primarily in a southerly direction. It was not until 1940 that a seismic survey was used to locate drilling areas that eventually expanded the deeper Eocene accumulation. If a similar prospect were found today, the original concepts for developing the field would probably be used. Since the Miocene accumulations are at such shallow depths and since the main structure can be mapped from surface geology, seismic methods would be unnecessary and initial drilling on a grid system would again be the way to proceed.

The following two paragraphs taken from Ralph Arnold's 1914 report are not only the first but probably the most accurate description made of the Mene Grande seepages:

> The surface evidence of petroleum in the Mene Grande District is probably as impressive as in any other oil region in the world. This statement applies particularly to Mene Grande hill, which in itself is practically one great oil seepage, two miles long by one-half to one mile in width. In addition to this, there are large seepages at Menito and Ultimo Menito, on the west side of the Rio Misoa in the Aranguren concession, and a large seepage at Pauji, adjoining properties of The Caribbean Petroleum Company. Minor seepages are found near the edge of the Sierra Trujillo on the Rio Raya and Quebrada Casadora, and also some near the Rio San Pedro. Most of these seepages are believed to be emanations from outcropping oil sands although in some instances the actual sands themselves are covered with alluvium or swamp material.

> Mene Grande hill consists of a scimitar-shaped ridge which strikes nearly east and west at its southern end and north and south at its northern end. The area of active seepages extends from the southwestern edge of the hill around its eastern and western face, and northward to just east of the highest point on the main part of the northward striking ridge. The area covered by active seepages includes about two square miles. Within this area occur thousands of individual seepages, pitch cones, and asphalt deposits. Standing in the cirque-like basin north of the west end of the hill, the eye can follow down the inside of the ridge for two miles, noting a surface practically entirely covered with asphalt and fresh oil seepages for the entire distance. This scimitar-shaped hill marks the outcrop of the lower part of the Maracaibo series, which is the source of the major portion of the oil in this field. As described above, these sands vary from white to pink and green and are interbedded with even more brilliant clays. The seepages take the form of exudations from cracks in the sand or exude directly from the sand itself. Again, the oil may break up through the more or less incoherent surface material. Certain areas seem to show more activity than others, and the activity of the seepages varies from time to time over different portions of the seepage area.

STRUCTURE

Tectonic History

The Mene Grande field lies within the Lake Maracaibo basin, one of the most prolific petroleum provinces in the world. Its geologic evolution includes numerous marine transgressions and regressions responsible for the deposition of source and reservoir rocks. Accompanying orogenesis and epeirogenesis produced the structural traps that have held the petroleum in place until the present. The principle structural boundaries of the basin are the Perijá fault to the west, the Oca fault to the north, and the Bocono fault to the east. These three strike-slip faults are the result of transcurrent movement along the Caribbean–South American plate boundary.

The Permian–Triassic igneous-metamorphic rocks form the basement in the Maracaibo basin. The beginning of an Early Cretaceous transgressive period was responsible for the coarse-grained clastic deposits of the Rio Negro Formation resting on the basement. Throughout middle and Late Cretaceous, a thick carbonate sequence interbedded with shales was deposited in a marine shelf environment. These rocks include the Cogollo Group limestones and the Luna Formation limestones and calcareous shales, considered to be the source rock in the basin. Also some local clastic deposits are present (González de Juana et al., 1980).

Tectonic movements that occurred at the end of the Cretaceous converted areas near the Perijá and Andes into positive areas. Also, gravity faulting along north-south alignments began in the center of the basin. Later, Paleocene sedimentation became prevalent in three distinct provinces: one in the southwest corner where the Perijá and the Andean alignments meet; the second, a marine shelf province that covered the entire present-day lake up to a "hinge line" located near the present-day Coastal Bolivar fields; and the third, a Paleocene geosynclinal province northeast of the "hinge line."

Complex fluvio-deltaic sedimentation accompanied by slight epeirogenic uplifts characterizes the early and middle Eocene. The Mirador and Misoa formations were deposited on top of shelf carbonates at this time within the basin. Later, deep marine shales of the Pauji Formation covered the fluvio-deltaic sequence. Late Eocene uplift throughout the basin, extensive faulting, and a long period of deep erosion were followed by down-tilting of the Eocene basin to the southwest. In parts of the basin the period of erosion continued through the Oligocene and the lower Miocene.

On the eroded Eocene surface, middle and late Miocene fluvio-deltaic sedimentation resulted in the excellent reservoirs that are the channel sands of the Coastal Bolivar and Mene Grande fields. The later southwest tilt favored updip migration of deeper Cretaceous and Eocene oil through faults and along major unconformities such as the Eocene unconformity. Evidence for this are the numerous oil seeps found where the Eocene unconformity outcrops along the eastern coast of Lake Maracaibo from as far south as Mene Grande field to Cabimas to the north (Dickey and Hunt, 1972).

The end of the Miocene marked the end of the Andean uplift. The Andes and the proto-Misoa range were the major source areas of sediment to the Maracaibo basin, including the Mene Grande area (Figure 3). Eventually these sediments were folded during the Andean orogeny resulting in the Misoa anticline and the Raya syncline.

Regional Structure

The Mene Grande field is situated on the south-plunging asymmetric Misoa anticline that is the continuation of the Misoa mountain range located to the north. The Raya syncline borders the field on the east; on the west and northwest, the Sibucara-Machango synclinorium separates the Mene Grande field from the Bachaquero field (Figure 2).

Local Structure

Locally, the structure is an anticline that is separated by a major north-south fault zone into two structural units named the West Flank and the Main fields (Figures 4 and 5). The West Flank is characterized by its steep dip (40°-60°) perpendicular to the main fault. East of the fault zone, the Main field plunges gently (5°-10°) in a southerly direction, almost parallel to the fault zone (Figure 5). Two small domal structures exist in the northwest corner of the main field. The larger dome (main uplift) is bounded by high angle faults (Figures 4 and 5) and is represented on the surface by the Mene Grande hill where the numerous seepages are found. In the subsurface, the uplifted Eocene (Figure 4) contains the reservoirs that have produced considerable hydrocarbon at this level for many years (Schenk and Kao, 1980).

STRATIGRAPHY

The stratigraphic column in the Mene Grande field consists of Eocene and Miocene formations, both time units being separated by a major unconformity. The post-Eocene comprises a 3000 ft (914 m) thick succession of unconsolidated clastic sediments that unconformably overlie the Eocene shaly marine Pauji Formation and the Misoa Formation. In the field, the two formations that have been recognized above the unconformity are the middle Miocene Isnotú Formation and the Miocene–Pliocene Betijoque Formation. Both are basin marginal equivalents of the La Puerta Formation and can be correlated to the outcrop as far as the Trujillo foothills to the southwest (Figure 6).

The Isnotú Formation comprises a 1200–1500 ft (366–457 m) thick succession of 60–80% mottled clays and discontinuous sand stringers that are channel sands deposited in a fluvial-deltaic environment (Figure 7). Unconformably overlying the Isnotú Formation is the Betijoque Formation, which consists of massive beds of red conglomerates (25%), sand, silt, and clays, all deposited in a terrestrial environment.

In the Mene Grande field, the Eocene unconformity cuts deep into the Pauji Formation reaching the lowermost part (Figure 4). This formation is rather uniform in lithology, consisting of brittle, dark gray to black shales, and in places, fine sand, specifically in the lower 400 ft (122 m) (Alcalá et al., 1985).

Nutall (1932) subdivided the formation into three parts on the basis of foraminifera and of the evidence of the surface and well sections. Stratigraphic thicknesses are approximately 1100 ft (335 m) each for the upper and middle subdivisions and 350–400 ft (91–122 m) for the lower Pauji. A sandstone layer within the Pauji Formation is reported to have produced small amounts of oil; however, the lithological characteristics at this level are unfavorable for the production of oil in commercial quantities.

The underlying Misoa Formation of lower to middle Eocene age consists of hard quartzitic sandstones interbedded with more or less hard, dark, sandy shale and shale comprising a thick group of strata that was extensively fractured during the process of folding. The Misoa intervals penetrated by the wells are divided into three zones on the basis of lithology (Nutall and Dufour, 1932). The uppermost transitional zone, just below the Pauji shale, contains very few sandstone bodies interbedded with mostly shale and is 200 to 350 ft (61–107 m) thick. The middle unit, called the main sandstone zone, contains interbedded sandstone and shale with a predominance of sandstone beds. This unit averages 550 ft (168 m) in thickness and is the most prolific oil reservoir in the Eocene. The lowermost unit was named the lower sandstone and shale zone after its predominant lithology. The total thickness is unknown since it was never completely penetrated in the Mene Grande field, but it can be estimated to be over 2000 ft (610 m) (Goddard, 1985).

TRAP

Trap Type

At the Eocene level, the three upper sandstone units of the Misoa Formation form the main reservoirs. According to the staff of the Caribbean Petroleum Company (1948), which produced the field for 34 years, trapping conditions in these Eocene

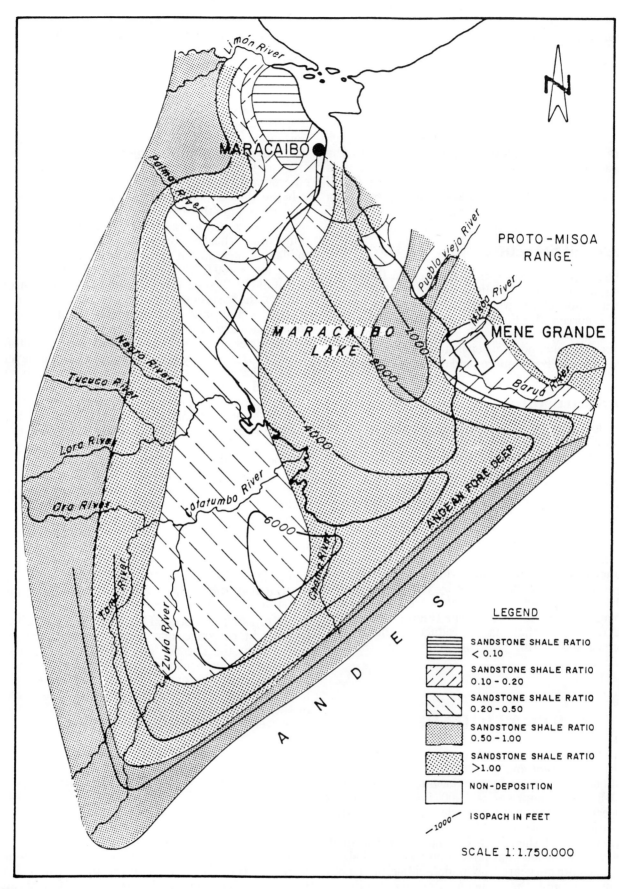

Figure 3. Lithofacies map of the middle Miocene in the Maracaibo basin (Pooley, 1956).

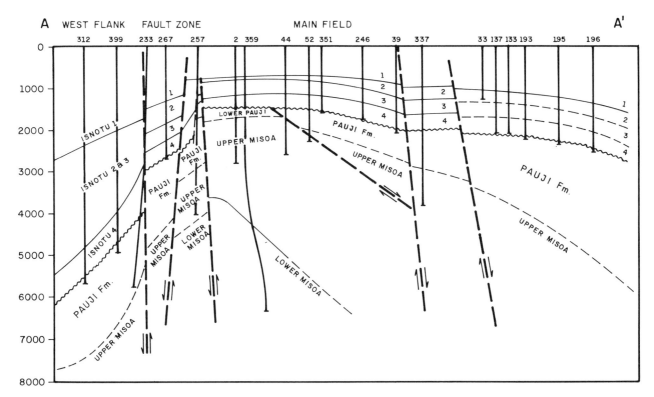

Figure 4. Cross section through Mene Grande field. Vertical and horizontal scales are equal. (Updated from staff of Caribbean Petroleum Company, 1948.)

reservoirs are partly tectonic and partly stratigraphic. The main uplift is a faulted dome. The dome and the faulted plunging anticline of the Main field are responsible for the accumulations at this level (Figure 4). The trapping is also stratigraphic since the sandstones are mostly distributary channels of a fluvial-deltaic environment.

Fracture porosity has been influential in the oil accumulation and drainage and is considered important in providing vertical connection between the various sandstone horizons. Initially, production results indicated an oil-water contact at 3000 ft (914 m) below lake level. Today the entire Eocene reservoirs are watered-out (Goddard, 1985).

Trapping conditions in the Miocene reservoirs, the remaining producing reservoirs of today, are mostly stratigraphic.

Reservoir

The Isnotú Formation, which includes all of the Miocene reservoirs, comprises a 1200 to 1500 ft (366–457 m) thick succession of 60 to 80% mottled clays and discontinuous sandstone stringers. It was originally subdivided (Clark, 1932; Richardson, 1951; Pooley, 1956) on the basis of oil gravity into four units, which were from top to base:

1. Tar sandstone
2. K sandstone/upper heavy oil zone

3. Main oil zone
4. Lower sandy clay

In a more recent study, Fiorillo, (1976) renamed the units numerically; i.e., Isnotú 1, 2, 3, and 4 (Figures 6 and 7) and this subdivision is adhered to in this paper. Within these units, the net oil sand occupies 10% to 20% of the reservoir rock and consists of a large number of individual sandstone stringers. The isopach map (Figure 8) illustrates the sandstone development in the reservoir.

The paleogeographic and depositional setting for the Miocene reservoirs can be considered as beginning somewhere between the Oligocene and lower Miocene. During this time, the area of the Mene Grande field underwent erosion. With a strong uplift of the Andes some 50 km to the south (Pooley, 1956), the marine-brackish influence in the Maracaibo basin was forced to retreat, while to the north of the rising mountain chain, a thick, extensive belt of mottled clay molasse built up. Deposition in the area of the Mene Grande field began during the middle Miocene. A general trend of increasing sand content (Isnotú 4 to 2) culminated in braided river or piedmont plain conglomerates and sandstones in the late Miocene and Pliocene (Isnotú and Betijoque formations) time.

Contemporaneously, the center of deposition in the Andean foredeep shifted to the northeast closer to the Mene Grande area. It appears that sedimentary characteristics in surrounding fields differ consid-

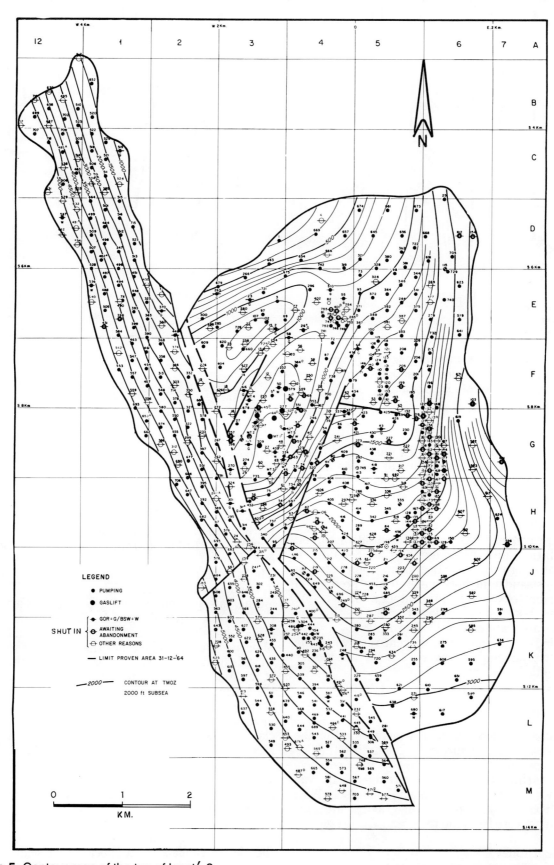

Figure 5. Contour map of the top of Isnotú 3.

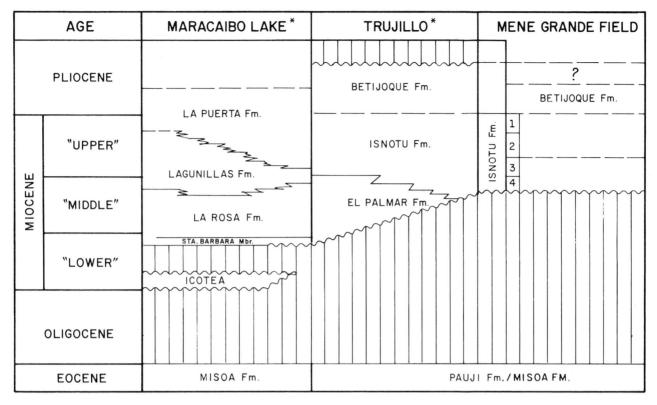

AGE		MARACAIBO LAKE*	TRUJILLO*	MENE GRANDE FIELD
PLIOCENE			BETIJOQUE Fm.	?
		LA PUERTA Fm.		BETIJOQUE Fm.
MIOCENE	"UPPER"		ISNOTU Fm.	ISNOTU Fm. 1 2 3 4
		LAGUNILLAS Fm.		
	"MIDDLE"		EL PALMAR Fm.	
		LA ROSA Fm.		
	"LOWER"	STA. BARBARA Mbr.		
		ICOTEA		
OLIGOCENE				
EOCENE		MISOA Fm.	PAUJI Fm. / MISOA FM.	

Figure 6. Tertiary correlation table. (* Geologia de Venezuela, C. González de Juana.)

erably and that the Mene Grande field was located in a somewhat restricted area. The restriction was possibly caused by synsedimentary tectonic movements that created small, independently subsiding basins dominated by fluviatile deposition (Pooley, 1956).

The sands are primarily fluvial channel fills of small size with average widths of 75 m and average thicknesses of 3 m. Their porosities average 30% and permeabilities 280 md. Of the six channel types distinguished, three show clear evidence of lateral migration and three belong to the group of nonmigrating channels. However, migration of oil into its present position from the Cretaceous La Luna Formation occurred through faults in the Eocene and up along the Eocene unconformity. Once in the Miocene reservoirs, the oil moved laterally via the channel sands in contact with one another (Figure 9) (Delgado et al., 1985).

Core plug measurements in active channel fill deposits showed an average porosity of 30% and permeabilities between 100 and 6900 md in irregular distribution within channel profiles. Abandoned channel fills and other heterolithic beds are of poorer quality, with average porosity of 26% and permeability of 23 md. The factors controlling reservoir properties seem to be complex; a major influence is clay content (Ward, 1985).

Studies from core analyses indicate that most syn- to post-depositional changes in the Isnotú Formation are related to soil-forming processes that mainly affect overbank clays and sands. In the Mene Grande field two major alterations were observed: (1) Kaolinite and to a lesser degree, illite, crystallized at the expense of feldspar and lithics. (2) Iron dissolved from primary detrital compounds and redistributed.

Potential problem-causing minerals for future enhanced oil recovery projects are the iron-bearing minerals, pyrite and chlorite (Delgado et al., 1985).

With regard to the hydrocarbon characteristics, the West Flank and Main field crudes have similar properties: gravity of 18° API, equivalent density 0.95 g cm^{-3}, and viscosities at reservoir temperature ranging from 30 to 50 cp. Since no initial gas caps were discovered in the West Flank and the Main field, the crudes in each part of the reservoir must have been initially undersaturated. For the West Flank crude, this was confirmed by a flash liberation experiment that gave a bubble-point pressure of 935 psig, well below the static reservoir pressure in the area around well 494. For the Main field crude, however, a bubble-point pressure of 1250 psig was measured that even exceeded the initial reservoir pressure in the area around well 585. This indicates that at the time of sampling, free gas was already

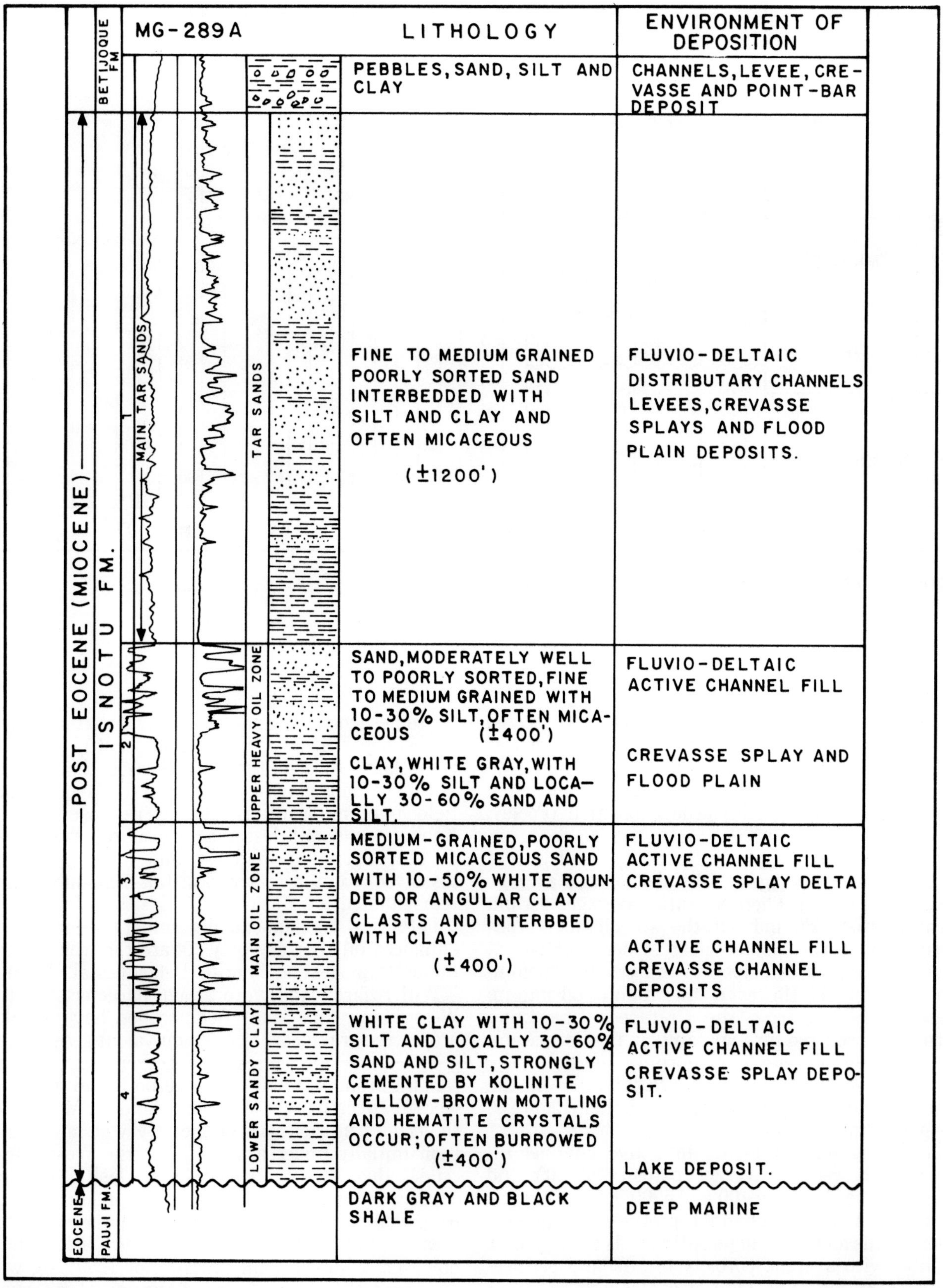

		MG-289A				LITHOLOGY	ENVIRONMENT OF DEPOSITION
POST EOCENE (MIOCENE)	BETIJOQUE FM.					PEBBLES, SAND, SILT AND CLAY	CHANNELS, LEVEE, CREVASSE AND POINT-BAR DEPOSIT
	ISNOTU FM.	MAIN TAR SANDS			TAR SANDS	FINE TO MEDIUM GRAINED POORLY SORTED SAND INTERBEDDED WITH SILT AND CLAY AND OFTEN MICACEOUS (±1200')	FLUVIO-DELTAIC DISTRIBUTARY CHANNELS LEVEES, CREVASSE SPLAYS AND FLOOD PLAIN DEPOSITS.
		2			UPPER HEAVY OIL ZONE	SAND, MODERATELY WELL TO POORLY SORTED, FINE TO MEDIUM GRAINED WITH 10-30% SILT, OFTEN MICACEOUS (±400')	FLUVIO-DELTAIC ACTIVE CHANNEL FILL
						CLAY, WHITE GRAY, WITH 10-30% SILT AND LOCALLY 30-60% SAND AND SILT.	CREVASSE SPLAY AND FLOOD PLAIN
		3			MAIN OIL ZONE	MEDIUM-GRAINED, POORLY SORTED MICACEOUS SAND WITH 10-50% WHITE ROUNDED OR ANGULAR CLAY CLASTS AND INTERBBED WITH CLAY (±400')	FLUVIO-DELTAIC ACTIVE CHANNEL FILL CREVASSE SPLAY DELTA ACTIVE CHANNEL FILL CREVASSE CHANNEL DEPOSITS
		4			LOWER SANDY CLAY	WHITE CLAY WITH 10-30% SILT AND LOCALLY 30-60% SAND AND SILT, STRONGLY CEMENTED BY KOLINITE YELLOW-BROWN MOTTLING AND HEMATITE CRYSTALS OCCUR; OFTEN BURROWED (±400')	FLUVIO-DELTAIC ACTIVE CHANNEL FILL CREVASSE SPLAY DEPOSIT. LAKE DEPOSIT.
EOCENE	PAUJI FM.					DARK GRAY AND BLACK SHALE	DEEP MARINE

Figure 7. Post-Eocene type log and stratigraphic column of the Mene Grande field.

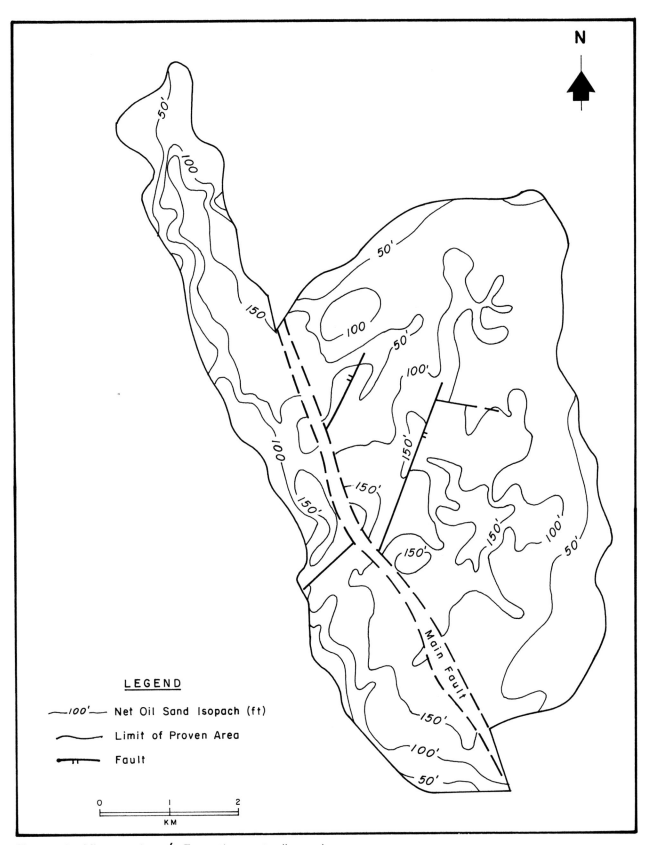

Figure 8. Miocene Isnotú Formation net oil sand
isopach map. Contour interval = 50 ft.

199

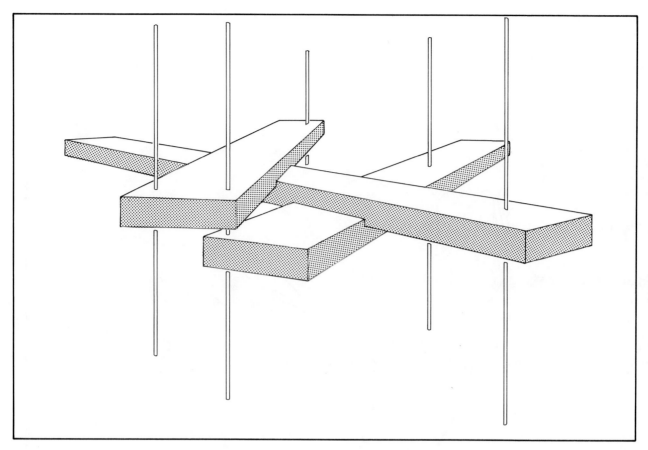

Figure 9. Schematic representation of possible intricate communication between wells via sands deposited in channels that have scoured downward into earlier channel sands. (After Van de Graaff and Ealey, 1989.)

present in this part of the Main field and therefore no information on the original bubble-point conditions can be determined from this sample. Nevertheless, for this medium crude, the trends of the PVT parameters with pressure can still be used as valid approximations (Drent and Heemskerk, 1985).

Gas production from the reservoir has only been recorded from 1960 onwards. The majority of wells with high GORs (600 SCF/STB) were found in the updip parts of both the West Flank and the Main field. In addition to these wells, others were found scattered in the Main field, mainly along the main fault and the downdip parts. During the period between 1973 and 1977, the number of wells producing with high GORs did not increase significantly, but a marked increase in the number of wells with moderate GORs (200–400 SCF/STB) was found. The concentration of high GOR wells in the updip part of the West Flank indicates strong gravity segregation. The spread of a large number of wells with moderate to high GORs over most of the Main field indicates that gravity segregation had also occurred there. Segregation has been greater in the West Flank field because of a much steeper dip than the Main field (Schenk and Kao, 1980).

The spacing between the Mene Grande wells, as with the wells in the Coastal Bolivar fields, is 230 m. This spacing is based on reservoir engineering considerations for viscous crudes, taking into account the effective drainage area around each well.

Faults

The faults within the main fault zone, as well as the minor faults in the Main field, were determined from well data (Figure 4). The faults become more obvious while constructing the structure contour map of the top of Isnotú 3 (Figure 5). Pressure data from wells on both sides of the main fault zone and water production across the faults indicate that they are nonsealing. The faults in the Mene Grande fields have also been routes of escape to the surface for the hydrocarbons as evidenced by the numerous seepages associated with the fault zone.

Source

The La Luna Formation, of Cretaceous age, is considered the primary source rock for most of the hydrocarbons found in the Maracaibo basin, which include the Mene Grande field. It consists of approximately 300 ft (91 m) of limestone, calcareous shale, and chert and has an average total organic carbon content of 3.8% and a maximum of 9.6%. From burial history plots, the time of hydrocarbon expulsion is estimated to have occurred in the Eocene and Miocene. The depth to the top of the La Luna Formation in the Mene Grande field is close to 15,000 ft (4572 m). The potential yield in barrels is estimated to be 10 kg of hydrocarbon per ton of rock from this type II kerogen source. The maturation level (R_o) from vitrinite reflectance is approximately 1.2.

EXPLORATION CONCEPTS

Regional Play

The Mene Grande field forms the southernmost extension of the enormous Miocene play that includes all of the Coastal Bolivar fields from as far north as the Cabimas field. The play includes the unconsolidated sand reservoirs that consist primarily of distributary channel sands, crevasse splays, and stream-mouth bar deposits of a widespread fluvio-deltaic environment. Similar plays, also of Miocene age, exist in the eastern Venezuela basin. These are the sediments of the Oficina Formation that are extensive to the south of and also within the region called the Orinoco Heavy Oil Belt in eastern Venezuela.

Lessons

This field, as well as others in the Coastal Bolivar region on the east coast of Lake Maracaibo, were discovered by the means of surface geology and by drilling on and around oil seeps. For the shallower Miocene reservoirs, similar techniques would probably be used today. However, for the deeper Eocene play, seismic reflection techniques would be most helpful, as later used in the 1940s in the Mene Grande field.

The most unique feature of this field is the amount of oil seepages, which were first described in 1914. Even today these seeps are still active on the Mene Grande hill after 74 years of production from as many as 759 wells in the area. Another interesting aspect is the rapid rate with which the Eocene reservoirs began to produce large quantities of water. As early as 1932, Clark's detailed water analysis showed that they were meteoric in origin. This is understandable since the Eocene Misoa Formation outcrops some 10 km to the north and northeast of Mene Grande field and today water cuts of the remaining three Eocene producers is 98%.

ACKNOWLEDGMENTS

The author wishes to thank Donald Goddard and Gordon Young for their help and suggestions in writing the manuscript and the AAPG staff and reviewers for their constructive comments and suggestions. She also wishes to thank the management of Maraven S.A. and Petróleos de Venezuela S.A. for permission to publish this paper.

REFERENCES

Alcalá, L., 1982, Revisión de La Geologia de Mene Grande: MARAVEN S.A., EPC-7596.

Alcalá, L., P. J. Ealey, C. Hocker, and F. Wonink, 1985, Reservoir geology of the preselected area in the Mene Grande Main Field, Venezuela: MARAVEN, S.A. EPC-6380.73.

Arnold, R., 1915, Report on the Mene Grande Oil Field Zulia, Western Venezuela: MARAVEN, S. A. EPC-31.

Caribbean Petroleum Company, 1948, Oil fields of Royal Dutch-Shell Group in Western Venezuela: American Association of Petroleum Geologists Bulletin, v. 32, n. 4.

Clark, E., 1932, The stratigraphical, structural and accumulation conditions of the Mene Grande heavy oil field, with special reference to water problems: MARAVEN, S.A., EPC-7385.

Delgado, J., C. Hocker, and P. J. Ealey, 1985, Geological investigations of cores from well MG-289A, Mene Grande Field, W. Venezuela: MARAVEN, S.A. EPC-6380-74.

Dickey, P. A., and P. J. Hunt, 1972, Geochemical and hydrogeologic methods of prospecting for stratigraphic traps, in Stratigraphic oil and gas fields. Classification, exploration methods and case histories: American Association of Petroleum Geologists Memoir 16, p. 136–167.

Drent, A. J., and J. Heemskerk, 1985, Options for improving the recovery efficiency in the Mene Grande Field, Venezuela: MARAVEN, S.A. EPC-6380.

Fiorillo, G., 1976, Revision geologica del Post-Eoceno Costa Bolivar, Campo Mene Grande: MARAVEN, S. A. EPC-5674.

Goddard, D., 1985, Revision de la geologia Eocena del levantamiento Crestal, Campo Mene Grande: MARAVEN, S.A., Rs-221.

González, C., J. Iturralde, and X. P. Cadillat, 1980, Geologia de Venezuela y sus Cuencas Petroliferas: Foninves, Caracas.

Nutall, W. L. F., 1932, Preliminary results of a revision of the smaller foraminifera of the Pauji Series of Mene Grande and parts of Bolivar District: MARAVEN, S.A., EPC-8096.

Nutall, W. L. F., and J. Dufour, 1932, Status correlation of the Eocene of the Bolivar District and Mene Grande: MARAVEN, S.A. EPC-8105.

Pooley, R. W., 1956, Post-Eocene of the Maracaibo Basin, Venezuela: MARAVEN, S.A. EPC-28467.

Richardson, J. A., 1951, Mene Grande Field, Subsurface studies: MARAVEN, S.A., EPC-1008.

Richardson, J. A., 1955, Note on the Eocene appraisal south-east Mene Grande: MARAVEN, S.A., EPC-2421.

Ritter, E. A., 1929, Brief summary on the geology of the Mene Grande Field: MARAVEN, S.A., EPC-3407.

Schenk, L., and J. Kao, 1980, Mene Grande Post-Eocene reservoir: MARAVEN, S.A., EPC-51575.

Van de Graaff, W. J. E., and P. J. Ealey, 1989, Geological modeling for simulation studies: American Association of Petroleum Geologists Bulletin, v. 73, n. 11, p. 1436.

Ward, R. C., 1985, Petrophysical study, of the area pre-selected for an EOR project in the Mene Grande Main Field, Venezuela: MARAVEN, S.A., EPC-6380.67.

Appendix 1. Field Description

Field name .... *Mene Grande field*

Ultimate recoverable reserves .... *707 million bbl (1989)*

Field location:

    Country .... *Venezuela*

    State .... *Zulia*

    Basin/Province .... *Maracaibo basin*

Field discovery:

    Year first pay discovered .... *Lower Miocene Isnotú Formation 1914*

    Year second pay discovered .... *Eocene Misoa Formation 1924*

Discovery well name and general location:

    First pay .... *Zumaque I, 120 km SE of Maracaibo*

    Second pay .... *MG-44 120 km SE of Maracaibo*

Discovery well operator .... *Caribbean Petroleum Company*

    Second pay .... *Caribbean Petroleum Company*

IP in barrels per day and/or cubic feet or cubic meters per day:

    First pay .... *264 bbl/d*

    Second pay .... *1.130 bbl/d*

All other zones with shows of oil and gas in the field:

Age	Formation	Type of Show
None		

Geologic concept leading to discovery and method or methods used to delineate prospect, e.g., surface geology, subsurface geology, seeps, magnetic data, gravity data, seismic data, seismic refraction, nontechnical:

The discovery of this field was based on field surface geology and oil seeps.

Structure:

    Province/basin type .... *Maracaibo basin (Continental Wrench)*

    Tectonic history

Mene Grande field is located within the unstable zone bounded by the Oca, Perija, and Bocono transcurrent fault systems in northwestern Venezuela. These systems are related to right-lateral strike-slip movement along the Caribbean–South American plate boundary. Major periods of tectonic activity occurred in the Tertiary including the late Miocene Andean uplift.

    Regional structure

South-plunging asymmetric Misoa anticline which is bordered on the east by the Raya syncline and on the west by the alluvial plain covering the wide Machango-Sibaragua synclinorium, which separates Mene Grande from Bachaquero.

    Local structure

Two structural units, the West Flank (WF) and the Main field (MF), separated by a main fault trending in a northwesterly direction. The West Flank is characterized by its steep dip perpendicular to the main fault (dip angles of 40° to 60°) while the Main field dips gently almost parallel to the main fault (at angles ranging from 7° to 10°).

Trap:

    Trap type(s)

Plunging anticlinal trap at the Eocene level; stratigraphic pinch-out traps, channel sands, and crevasse splay deposits in the Miocene.

Basin stratigraphy (major stratigraphic intervals from surface to deepest penetration in field):

Chronostratigraphy	Formation	Depth to Top in ft
Pliocene	Betijoque	±300
Miocene	Isnotú	3590
Eocene	Misoa	9630

Reservoir characteristics:

Number of reservoirs 2

Formations .... Isnotú and Misoa

Ages .... Lower Miocene, Eocene

Depths to tops of reservoirs .... 3590 ft, 9630 ft

Gross thickness (top to bottom of producing interval) .... ±1200 to ±1600 Miocene;
±3600 to 5000 ft (Eocene)

Net thickness—total thickness of producing zones

    Average .... 100 ft Miocene and 1000 ft Eocene

    Maximum .... 200 ft Miocene and 1500 ft Eocene

Lithology

Miocene: fine to medium sands interbedded with fine-grained, shaly sands, mudstones, and dark-gray shales

Eocene: fine- to medium-grained sandstone interbedded with dark, sandy shale and shale

Porosity type .... Miocene, primary; Eocene, primary

Average porosity .... Miocene, 30%; Eocene, 12%

Average permeability .... Miocene, ±1000 md; Eocene, ±1 md

Seals:

Upper

    Formation, fault, or other feature .... Betijoque Formation

    Lithology .... Shales and siltstone

Lateral

    Formation, fault, or other feature .... Fault/lithology

    Lithology .... Shales

Source:

Formation and age .... La Luna Formation, Cretaceous

Lithology .... Limestones, calcareous black shales, cherts

Average total organic carbon (TOC) 3.5%

Maximum TOC 9.6%

Kerogen type (I, II, or III) II

Vitrinite reflectance (maturation) .... $R_o = >1.2$

Time of hydrocarbon expulsion .... Eocene, Miocene

Present depth to top of source .... ±15,000 ft

Thickness .... ±300 ft

Potential yield .... 10 Kg hydrocarbon per ton of rock

Appendix 2. Production Data

Field name .... Mene Grande field

Field size:

Proved acres .... 10.378 ac

Number of wells all years 759

Current number of wells 270
Well spacing .... ±400 m
Ultimate recoverable .... 707 million bbl
Cumulative production .... 639 million bbl
Annual production .... 2.6 million bbl
Present decline rate 6%
    Initial decline rate 12%
    Overall decline rate 9%
Annual water production .... 1.7 million bbl
In place, total reserves .... 2633.3 million bbl
In place, per acre-foot .... 1691.6 bbl
Primary recovery .... 707 million bbl
Secondary recovery
Enhanced recovery
Cumulative water production .... 149.3 million bbl

Drilling and casing practices (1950–1983):

Amount of surface casing set .... 1100 ft
Casing program .... 10¾-in. from surface to ±1100 ft; 7-in. from surface to 2500 ft
Drilling mud .... Clay-based mud (CBM) and Benex
Bit program .... NA
High pressure zones .... None

Completion practices:

Interval(s) perforated .... Isnotú Formation and Misoa Formation
Well treatment .... None

Formation evaluation (Old wells prior to 1930 no logs available):

Logging suites .... More recent wells have the following suites: DLL, MSFL, SP, GR, FDC, LS
Testing practices .... Standard production test
Mud logging techniques .... Standard ditch sample analysis

Oil characteristics:

Type
API gravity .... 17.8°
Base .... Asphalt
Initial GOR .... 180 ft³/bbl
Sulfur, wt% .... NA
Viscosity, SUS .... 32 to 50 cp
Pour point .... NA
Gas-oil distillate .... NA

Field characteristics:

Average elevation .... 254 ft
Initial pressure .... 1050 psi
Present pressure .... 510 psi
Pressure gradient .... 0.3 psi/ft
Temperature .... 130°F
Geothermal gradient .... 0.065°F/ft
Drive .... Solution gas and water drive
Oil column thickness .... 26.16 ft
Oil-water contact .... Not determined
Connate water 20%
Water salinity, TDS .... 500 ppm (NaCl)

Resistivity of water .... *10 ohm/m² m*
Bulk volume water (%)

Transportation method and market for oil and gas:
Pipeline from Mene Grande field to Bachaquero and then to Puerto Miranda, Zulia State.

Elk-Poca Field—U.S.A.
Appalachian Basin, West Virginia

DOUGLAS G. PATCHEN
West Virginia Geological Survey
Morgantown, West Virginia

KATHERINE R. BRUNER
MILTON T. HEALD
West Virginia University
Morgantown, West Virginia

FIELD CLASSIFICATION

BASIN: Appalachian
BASIN TYPE: Foredeep
RESERVOIR ROCK TYPE: Sandstone
RESERVOIR ENVIRONMENT OF DEPOSITION: Shallow Water, High Energy Marine Shelf
TRAP DESCRIPTION: Most of trap is an updip sandstone pinch-out; however, southern end is broadened by presence of an anticline

RESERVOIR AGE: Devonian
PETROLEUM TYPE: Gas
TRAP TYPE: Updip Pinch-Out

LOCATION

The large Elk-Poca (Sissonville) gas field is located in Kanawha, Jackson, and Putnam Counties, West Virginia (Figure 1), on the western side of the Appalachian basin. The field is "L" shaped and 38 mi (61 km) long from north to south, with an average width of 8 mi (13 km) (east to west) in Jackson County and a maximum width of 17 mi (27 km) in Kanawha County. The field is located on the western side of the Appalachian structural basin in an area characterized by minor, low-amplitude folds. Regional dip in this area is down to the east, and although minor structural features controlled early drilling trends, for the most part production was controlled by an updip loss of permeability as the Oriskany Sandstone (Lower Devonian) thins westward and by the presence of salt water in the permeable Oriskany beds downdip to the east.

The productive area of the field covers approximately 165,000 ac (66,773 ha) (Cardwell, 1977). A larger figure of 193,000 ac (78,105 ha) (McLain, 1949) includes several nearby areas with production from the Oriskany (Figure 2). Although the thinner Oriskany is much tighter updip, effectively limiting the westward extension of the field during the 1940s, with the advent of hydraulic fracturing smaller, less-productive fields were developed in the Oriskany in that area. During the late 1960s two small but prolific gas fields were developed updip in the Newburg sandstone (Upper Silurian) as well (Figure 2).

More gas has been produced from the Elk-Poca field than from any other field in West Virginia. Although most of the field has been either abandoned or converted to storage, nearly 1 tcf of gas has been produced, and a few wells are still in production. By 1973, a total of 962,207 MMcf of gas had been produced and an estimated 91,793 MMcf of cushion gas was left in the wells when they were converted to storage. Thus, the field originally held at least 1,054,000 MMcf that could have been produced.

FIELD HISTORY

Pre-Discovery

The first deep well that penetrated the Oriskany Sandstone in Kanawha County was the Slaughter Creek Coal and Land Company #1 completed in 1912 by the William Seymour Edwards Oil Company. The well was drilled low on the eastern flank of the Warfield anticline, updip from the axis of the Handley syncline that controlled the prolific oil production from the Berea Sandstone (Lower Mississippian) in the Cabin Creek field. The total depth in this first deep test was 5595 ft (1705 m), 560 ft (170 m) below the top of the Oriskany. Drilling stopped in the lower Salina beds (Upper Silurian), approximately 100–110 ft (30–33 m) above the not-yet-discovered Newburg sandstone, when salt water, entering the well bore 3 ft (1 m) above total depth, rose 4000 ft (1219 m) in the well. Shows of oil and gas were observed when drilling through the Oriskany Sandstone.

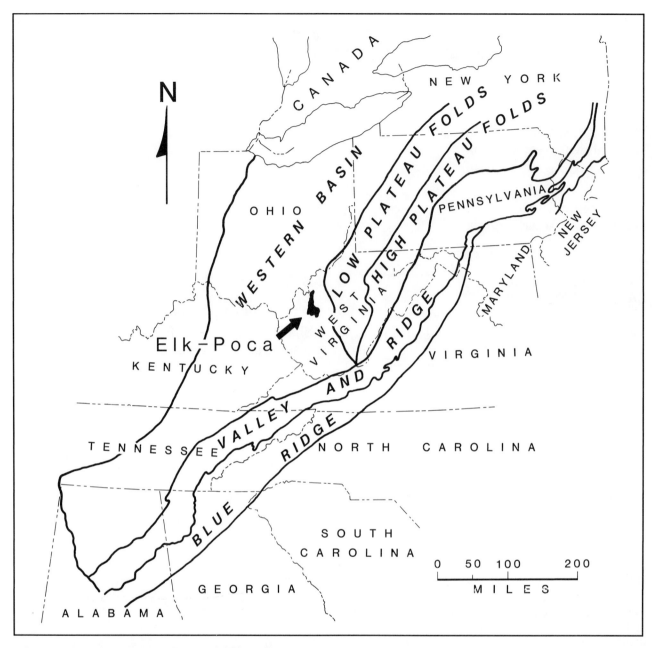

Figure 1. Appalachian basin structural provinces and location of Elk-Poca field in West Virginia.

Seventeen years later United Fuel Gas Company drilled another deep test to the Salina, 8 mi (13 km) updip to the northwest, near the axis of the Warfield anticline. Total depth was 5225 ft (1593 m) in the Black Band Coal and Coke #1954 well (Figure 2), which was 544 ft (166 m) below the top of the Oriskany. Again, drilling stopped when salt water from the same zone in the Salina entered the well. However, gas was present throughout the thin (8 ft) Oriskany, and the entire Oriskany was shot. ("Shooting" is a technique in which the open well bore is loaded with explosives that are detonated, creating a cavity at the bottom of the well. This older completion technique eventually was replaced by perforating through casing and then hydrofracturing the wells.) Gas flow decreased to 29 Mcfg/d after shot, and the well was abandoned.

On 25 September of the following year United Fuel completed the first Oriskany gas well in the county, the Black Band Coal and Coke #4067 (state permit number Kanawha 43), drilled 3.5 mi (5.6 km) to the west, but closer to the crest of the Warfield structure. Drilling stopped at 4610 ft (1405 m), 25 ft (8 m) below the top of the Oriskany. Gas was present in two zones, from 4610 to 4614 and 4622 to 4630 ft (1405–1406 and 1409–1411 m). The final open flow was 467 Mcfg/d, with 1250 psi rock pressure, figures not high enough to encourage much future drilling in the area.

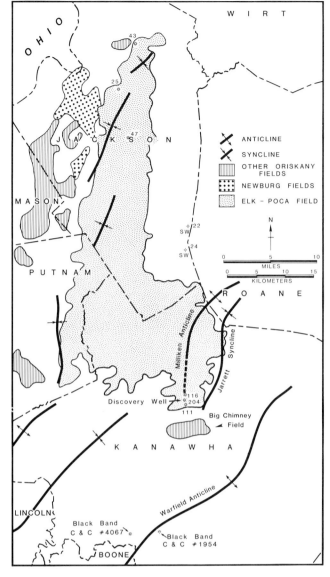

Figure 2. Location of Elk-Poca and adjacent Oriskany and Newburg fields. Structural axes from surface features. Early Oriskany wildcats to the south also are shown, as is the Big Chimney field immediately south of Elk-Poca.

The following year, 1931, operators moved northward, and two unsuccessful deep tests were drilled. The Virgil C. Tate #1 by B. F. Bess and Company (Kanawha 110) was abandoned at a total depth of only 3 ft (1 m) into the Oriskany, which was logged by the drillers as very hard and tight with no porosity. An oil show was noted 60 ft (18 m) above the Oriskany in the Huntersville Chert. The second well, the S. M. Burdette #1 by Estes Drilling (Kanawha 111), was abandoned when the tools were lost in a sandy, cherty, glauconitic zone in the lower Huntersville, from which 45 Mcfg/d were tested. This well was drilled on the southern end of the north–south-trending Milliken anticline on the waters of

Cooper Creek. Approximately half a mile to the north, the Cooper Creek Oil and Gas Company had drilled a Big Injun sandstone (Lower Mississippian) gas well in 1925 on the P. H. Frankenberger lease. When N. N. Grosscup and others purchased this old Big Injun well for the purpose of deepening it to test the Milliken structure at the level of the Oriskany, the discovery of the Elk-Poca Field was imminent.

Discovery Well

On 4 October 1933, Grosscup et al. completed deepening the P. H. Frankenberger #2 to a total depth of 4950 ft (1509 m), 18 ft (5 m) below the top of the Oriskany Sandstone (4932 ft). Gas was noted in a thin zone between 4942 and 4946 ft (1506–1507 m) during drilling, and consequently the entire Oriskany open to the well bore was shot with explosives. Although the final open flow after shooting (AS) was only 134 Mcfg/d, this was the discovery well for the Elk-Poca field (Figure 2), preceding completion of another shallow well deepened by Grosscup, the Grant Copenhaver #4, by just 19 days. The Grant Copenhaver #4, located less than a mile to the north and also on the Milliken anticline, was deepened to 4812 ft (1467 m), and after a 10 ft (3 m) zone near the top of the Oriskany was shot, the final open flow (FOF) was 143 Mcfg/d. Soon afterward, Grosscup et al. deepened the unsuccessful S. M. Burdette well from the Huntersville to the Oriskany and tested 147 Mcfg/d natural from a 2 ft zone in the top of the Oriskany, of which only 4 ft (1.2 m) were penetrated.

It is unlikely that flows of this range, 134 to 147 Mcfg/d, would have encouraged the rapid development of the Elk-Poca field that occurred during the next few years. It was not until Grosscup et al. completed a 200 bbl per day Oriskany oil well on the W. L. Burdette farm (Kanawha 131) on 11 November 1934 that interest in the Oriskany in this area again increased. It was indeed fortuitous that this well, the only one that ever produced much oil, was drilled when it was, at a time when interest in the Oriskany was declining. The prospect of drilling large oil wells encouraged rapid development of acreage along the crest of the Milliken anticline.

Within the next two years, 1935–1936, six wells were drilled around the W. L. Burdette oil discovery, resulting in three dry holes and three low-volume gas wells. All of these wells, including the oil discovery, are south of Elk-Poca proper, in the Big Chimney field (Figure 2). However, to the north, active drilling to the Oriskany Sandstone on the Milliken anticline continued, with increasing success. Following completion of the discovery well, nine additional wells were completed within three years, resulting in eight gas wells, some of which tested large flows. Two of the four wells drilled by Columbian Carbon on the W. F. Copenhaver Heirs lease tested 8125 Mcfg/d natural and 9979 Mcfg/d AS. Other wells were in the 1000 to 5000 Mcfg/d range, encouraging rapid development of the field.

Post-Discovery

The initial Oriskany wells in the Cooper Creek area usually did not penetrate the entire Oriskany thickness. The first pay in the Oriskany was usually encountered within 10 to 15 ft (3–5 m) of the top of the sandstone, and drilling stopped either because of high gas flows or because limestone was encountered (Figure 3). This limestone, however, often proved to be only 8 to 10 ft (2–3 m) thick with more sandstone (20–25 ft; 6–8 m) between it and the thick Helderberg carbonates below. Thus, it came to be a common practice to re-enter a well that had been producing for two or three years and deepen the well to those lower sandstone beds. This practice resulted in the discovery of additional pay sections in both the upper and lower sandstones of the Oriskany.

These older wells that were later deepened were wells with high initial open flows (IPs) that had been completed as natural producers. Other wells, with somewhat lower IPs, were usually shot, although in a few wells the sandstone was perforated with no further stimulation. A common casing program was to run 8¼ in. through the "Big Lime" and Big Injun and cement the lower 300–500 ft (91–152 m) to keep salt water from shallow units out of the hole during drilling. The lowest string of casing was usually 6⅝ in. that was set in the upper part of the Onondaga Limestone or Huntersville Chert, leaving the entire Oriskany open to the well bore to produce naturally or to be shot (Figure 3).

Prior to 1940, every Oriskany gas well in the field had been drilled in Elk and Poca Districts, Kanawha County, or in Jackson County within 2 mi (3 km) of the Kanawha County line, with three exceptions. These three were the first field wells to be drilled in the large north-south Jackson County portion of the field, although it would be nearly five years before drilling outlined the entire length of the productive area. The first two Oriskany wells to be drilled anywhere in Jackson County (permit nos. 22 and 24, Figure 2) were completed in November and December 1937. Unfortunately, both were drilled downdip to the east, nearly in Roane County, in an attempt to extend production northward on the Milliken anticline. Because that structure swings to the northeast and plunges out in Roane County, both wells penetrated a well-developed upper Oriskany sandstone full of salt water. In 1938, however, an Oriskany well (permit Jac-25, Figure 2) was drilled 17 mi (27 km) west and north, on the updip edge of what would become the Jackson County portion of the Elk-Poca field. The well experienced problems owing to stuck tools that required a fishing job lasting several months, but eventually tested 50 Mcfg/d from the Oriskany. The following year two additional successful Oriskany wells were completed, one in the middle of the trend (Jac-47, Figure 2) and one at the northern edge that tested 2534 Mcfg/d AS.

From 1940 to 1944 the majority of the productive acreage was drilled (Figure 4), beginning with the western half of Poca District and then moving northward into Jackson County. It is interesting to note that what began as a structural play soon became a search for thick sandstone (a stratigraphic play) in the Oriskany. Drilling moved northward from Poca District into Jackson County until an area of thinner sandstone was reached (Figures 4 and 5). Then drillers moved eastward, encountered thicker sandstones downdip, and followed this thick trend northward, keeping between salt water downdip to the east and thinner sandstones with lower permeability updip to the west (Figures 4, 5, and 6). During this same time period (1940–1944), many of the better upper Oriskany natural producers in Poca District (Figure 4) were deepened in search of a lower sandstone pay, especially in one particular area of high IPs in the 10,000 to 15,000 Mcfg/d range.

By the end of the Second World War, most of the more productive areas of the field had been drilled, its entire north-south length had been defined, and many of the earliest wells had been deepened or abandoned. With most of the areas of thick sandstone drilled up, operators were forced to move updip into tighter, thinner sandstone. Three areas were developed, two in Jackson County and one in Putnam County (Figure 4). During the 1950s, a second area in Putnam County was developed. The thickness of the Oriskany ranged between 30 and 50 ft (9–15 m) in the two areas in Jackson County, but was usually less than 30 ft (9 m) in the two Putnam County areas. Although a few wells with high natural IPs were completed in one of the Jackson County updip areas, most of the wells were relatively poor producers even after stimulation, reflecting the tighter nature of the sandstone.

Hydraulic fracturing of wells began in the mid-1950s and was common during the 1960s in this area. Thus, during the 1960s companies drilled small infill areas in Jackson and Putnam Counties updip from the best production (Figure 4). Relatively few wells were drilled during the 1970s. By that time large areas of the field had been abandoned or converted to storage, and companies were more interested in developing the deeper Newburg sandstone (Upper Silurian) in the Ripley fields west of Elk-Poca in Jackson County, and in the Rocky Fork deeper pool in Poca District, Kanawha County. Additional drilling in the early 1980s filled in areas that had been passed over during the 1940s, completing the field as we know it today.

DISCOVERY METHOD

Most of the Oriskany wells drilled in Kanawha County prior to discovering the Elk-Poca field were structural tests drilled on axes (or occasionally on the flanks) of anticlinal features delineated by surface mapping. Shallow structural maps of this area were constructed on the top of the Pittsburgh coal (Upper Pennsylvanian), and shallow wells to the Big Injun sandstone (Lower Mississippian), in addition to the

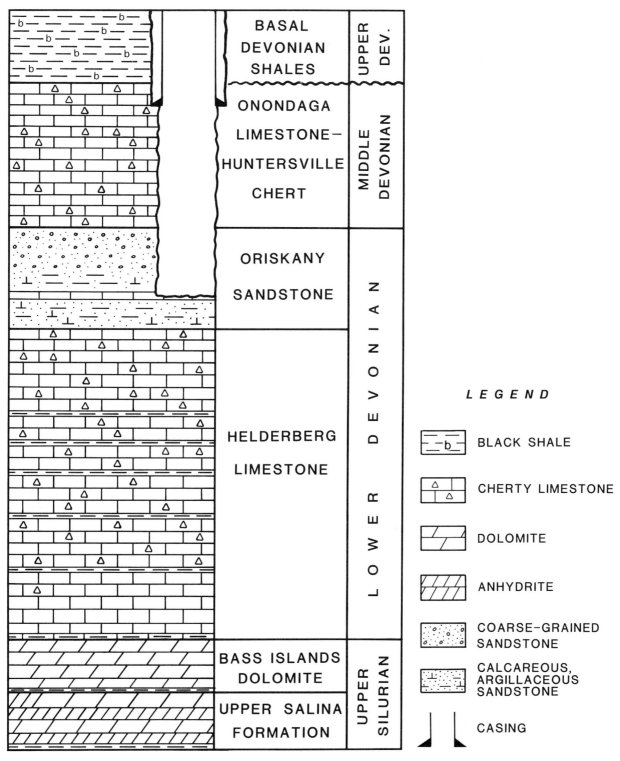

Figure 3. Generalized Middle and Lower Devonian stratigraphic section in Elk-Poca field and typical drilling and completion practices. Casing usually was set in the upper Onondaga and wells were drilled only through the upper sandstone in the Oriskany. The wells were then completed in the open-hole section below the casing by shooting the well with explosives.

211

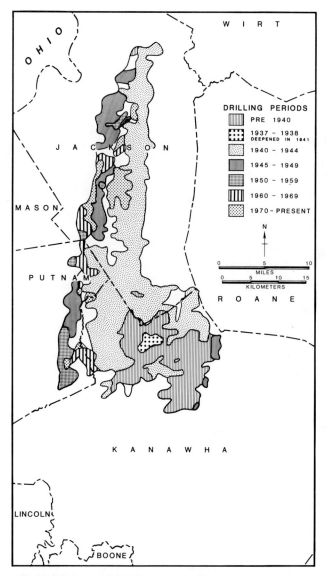

Figure 4. Map depicting the historical drilling pattern that developed Elk-Poca field.

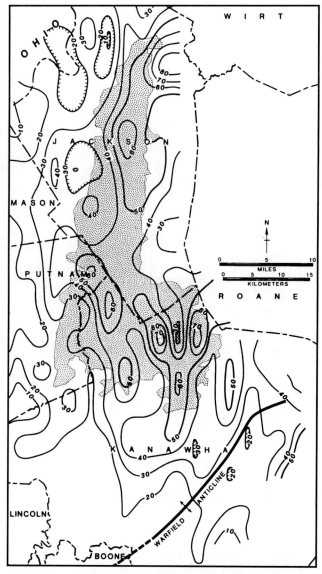

Figure 5. Isopach map of the Oriskany Sandstone in Elk-Poca (stippled area) and adjacent areas. Data from both geophysical and drillers' logs. Contour interval, 10 ft.

deeper Oriskany wells, were drilled to test the anticlinal features. The discovery well of Elk-Poca was originally drilled to the Big Injun in 1925 and deepened to the Oriskany in 1933 to test the Milliken structure at a greater depth. Once gas was discovered in the Oriskany on the Milliken anticline, operators extended the play northward along the axis of the structure and began to develop an exploration technique to locate other deep structural plays.

Although initial gas wells (1933–1936) that followed the discovery of the Elk-Poca field were drilled along the north–south-trending Milliken anticline in the Cooper Creek area, operators also attempted to develop the Big Chimney area immediately to the south. However, these early wells

confirmed that the Oriskany Sandstone thinned to the south toward the Warfield anticline, so operators moved northward from Elk District into Poca District, and then westward (along the Sissonville high) toward Putnam County. By 1936, nearly 100 Oriskany tests had been drilled in Kanawha County, enabling Tucker (1936) to construct an isopach map of the Devonian shales, that interval of fine-grained clastics between the base of the Lower Mississippian Berea Sandstone and the top of the Middle Devonian Onondaga Limestone approximately 100 ft (30 m) above the Oriskany. Tucker used this isopach map, surface structures, and the elevation of the Berea Sandstone from numerous shallow wells drilled during the previous 30 years, to formulate an

212

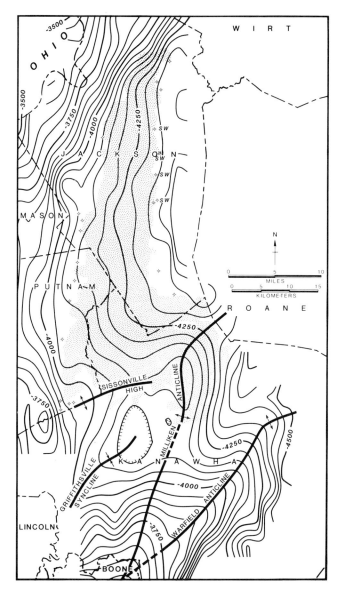

Figure 6. Structural map of the Oriskany Sandstone in Elk-Poca (stippled area) and adjacent areas. Contour interval, 50 ft.

STRUCTURE

Regional structural deformation exerts significant control on the location of Oriskany gas fields across the state of West Virginia. Four structural provinces can be delineated across the state. These are the Valley and Ridge, High Plateau, Low Plateau, and western basin provinces (Figure 1). These decrease in structural complexity, respectively, from east to west (Diecchio, 1985).

Fractured Oriskany reservoirs have been discovered on narrow, high-amplitude, detached folds in the Valley and Ridge and High Plateau provinces, but relatively few Oriskany fields have been developed in the Low Plateau area of the state. The area to the west beyond the Low Plateau, the western basin, is an area with more Oriskany fields, controlled by both local structure and regional sandstone thickness patterns. Thus, whereas fracture porosity is more important in Oriskany structural fields to the east, both fracture and intergranular porosity are important in western fields.

Jackson, Putnam, and Kanawha Counties are located on the western side of the Appalachian structural basin, in an area of relatively low-amplitude anticlines and synclines that are developed on the regional slope, which is down to the east. The major anticline in the area is the Warfield (Figure 6), which is asymmetric, being steeper on the east. The Griffithsville syncline flanks the Warfield on the northwest, and the Jarrett syncline separates the Warfield from the Milliken anticline to the northeast. The Sissonville high extends east-west from the Milliken anticline to Putnam County. The Sissonville and Milliken structural highs are responsible for the broader productive area of Elk-Poca field in the south. In Jackson County, only minor structural noses can be observed on Figure 6, but the dip on the Oriskany can be observed to decrease to the east, with a gradual flattening toward Roane County.

STRATIGRAPHY

The only important gas production in the Elk-Poca field comes from the Lower Devonian Oriskany Sandstone. The Oriskany is a white to light gray, fine- to medium-grained, subrounded to rounded, calcareous sandstone. The major cement, however, is quartz, with calcite being a minor cement in the upper pay section, but increasing in amount with depth. The upper contact with the Huntersville Chert is usually abrupt both in samples and on wireline logs, but in some areas a siltstone or poorly developed cherty sandstone is present at the base of the Huntersville.

The contact between the Oriskany and the underlying Helderberg Limestone is gradational and placed at various depths by different geologists. Usually two sandstones are developed in the

exploration tool to use in the search for Oriskany gas. The thickness of the shales was shown to increase at a nearly constant rate from west to east across the county from 2100 ft to 3350 ft (640–1021 m) (Tucker, 1936). Where the rise on the Berea exceeded this rate of eastward thickening, the Oriskany top would rise as well; where the rate of rise of the Berea was less than the rate of thickening of the shales, and where the Berea surface descended, the top of the Oriskany would drop into synclinal areas. Thus, the early drillers in Kanawha County had a technique that they could use to predict the location of structural highs on the Oriskany and to concentrate their drilling programs in those areas.

Oriskany separated by a thin limestone (Figures 3 and 7). The upper sandstone is more variable in thickness, less calcareous, and contains coarser, more rounded grains. Porosity and permeability are higher and the upper sandstone is interpreted from logs as a clean sandstone with good reservoir qualities. Thus, many geologists place the base of the Oriskany beneath this clean, upper sandstone. Other geologists, however, place the contact beneath the lower sandstone, defining the Oriskany as a calcareous, noncherty sandstone between two chert-bearing carbonate units.

The lower sandstone underlies a thin (8–10 ft; 2–3 m) limestone and in general is darker in color, finer grained, and more calcareous. In cuttings from many wells it appears that the basal Oriskany changes from a calcareous sandstone downward into a sandy limestone and then grades into the Helderberg by a decrease in quartz grains accompanied by the appearance of chert in the Helderberg.

The basal Devonian Helderberg Limestone consists of beds of gray, cherty, sandy limestone, sandy calcareous chert, and cherty calcareous sandstone (Martens, 1939). Thin, shaly zones also are present, particularly in the middle portion. Martens (1939) noted that the lower Helderberg beds were principally limestone with less chert and sandstone than above. On wireline logs the lower Helderberg appears cleaner and more uniform in lithology. A well-defined dolomite unit, the Bass Islands Dolomite, separates the clean, lower Helderberg from the Upper Silurian Salina Formation.

The Oriskany is overlain by a cherty carbonate sequence, the Huntersville Chert, which includes a thin limestone cap equivalent to the Onondaga Limestone. The thick (2000–3000 ft; 609–914 m) interval of fine-grained clastics between the top of the Onondaga Limestone and the base of the Mississippian includes several gray shale–black shale cycles, particularly in the lower half of the sequence (Figure 8). The black, organic-rich shales include the Marcellus, Geneseo, Middlesex, Rhinestreet, and Huron. These black shales were the source rocks for much of the oil and gas found in shallower reservoirs as well as for the gas in the deeper Oriskany Sandstone.

The Oriskany ranges in thickness from less than 10 ft (3 m) in westernmost Jackson and Putnam Counties, to more than 80 ft (24 m) in northeastern Jackson County (Figure 5). In addition to thinning from east to west, the Oriskany also thins from north to south toward the Warfield anticline (Figure 5). On the crest of this structure, just across the Boone County line, the Oriskany is less than 10 ft (3 m) thick. Changes in thickness are usually due more to changes in the amount of clean sandstone developed in the upper Oriskany than to changes in thickness of the lower, darker, more calcareous sandstones overlying the Helderberg.

Within the limits of Elk-Poca field, areas of thicker Oriskany trend north-south (Figure 5). One interpretation of these trends is that the clean, upper sandstone in the Oriskany was deposited as a series of offshore bars in a shallow shelf, high-energy environment.

TRAP

Although the Elk-Poca field was discovered as a structural play on the Milliken anticline, the field as a whole is not structurally controlled. Instead, gas production in the Elk-Poca field has been controlled by both stratigraphy and structure. Updip to the west (Figure 8), production has been limited by decreasing permeability; perhaps the more permeable, upper sandstones pinched out or were eroded prior to deposition of the overlying Onondaga-Huntersville section. Downdip to the east, salt water is present in the reservoir below the –4350 ft (–1326 m) elevation. In the southern end of the field, structural highs (the Sissonville high and the Milliken anticline) are responsible for broadening the productive area to the east, creating the L-shaped configuration of the field. By the late 1930s, enough wells had been drilled so that the westward pinch-out of the Oriskany Sandstone into carbonates that sealed the updip edge of the trap could be documented.

The thick (200 ft; 61 m) Onondaga-Huntersville carbonate section immediately above the Oriskany sealed the top of the trap, preventing subsequent migration of gas from the Oriskany into fractured Devonian shale above the carbonate section. This combination of factors caused Martens (1939) to predict that conditions existed for the accumulation of gas in areas that would be more important than those on the anticlinal structures on which the earliest wells had been drilled. Such indeed proved to be the case. Production throughout most of the field was controlled by sandstone thickness, even on the updip edge where good production was developed in areas with more than 40 ft (12 m) of sandstone. Updip areas with thinner sandstone, however, are tighter and yielded less productive wells even with more advanced stimulation techniques. Downdip to the east, where the upper sandstone is well developed, production was good right up to the gas–saltwater contact. One Jackson County well less than a mile from the saltwater contact has produced nearly 4 bcf of gas. In general, wells in which the Oriskany is above –4350 ft (–1326 m) subsea were productive.

Reservoir

The gas reservoir is developed in the upper part of the Lower Devonian Oriskany Sandstone where incomplete cementation by quartz and carbonate has resulted in high permeabilities and consistent, but low, porosities. The Oriskany thins from east to west, accompanied by a loss of the highly permeable upper section to the west. Tighter areas on the western edge of the field in Jackson County have been developed (with lower production) by using fractur-

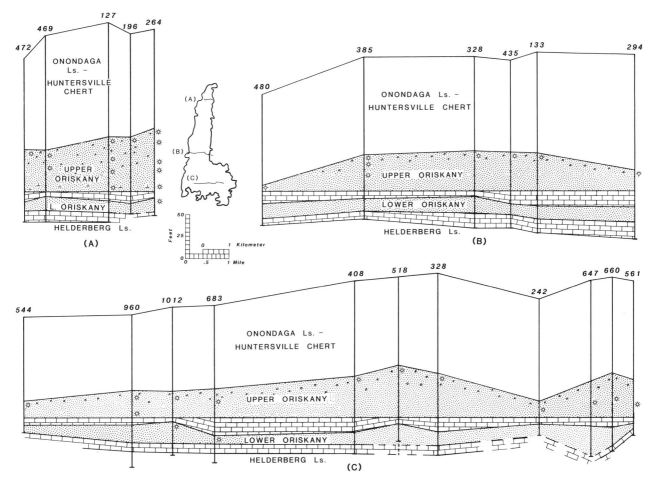

Figure 7. Schematic east-west stratigraphic cross sections, based on cable-tool drillers' logs, illustrating the upper and lower sandstones (dot pattern) and middle limestone (rectangular pattern) in the Oriskany: (A) northern end of field; (B) through Ripley District; (C) southern section from near Putnam County line east to Cooper Creek area. Well symbols indicate stratigraphic position of gas pays (☼), gas shows (☼), and dry holes (◇). Datum is base of upper Oriskany.

ing techniques not available when most of the better areas of the field were drilled.

Lithology

In the Elk-Poca field a middle 5 to 10 ft (1.5-3 m) limestone, shaly limestone, or carbonate-cemented sandstone separates the Oriskany into two distinct sandstone units (McClain, 1949). This change in the lithologic nature of the Oriskany is common throughout the basin and has been observed elsewhere by Bierderman (1986) and Bruner (1986). Lafferty (1938) and Bierderman (1986) suggested that the variations in lithology and grain size reflect deposition in a shallow environment affected by currents of widely varying intensities.

In the Cooper Creek area of Kanawha County, where the first Oriskany wells were drilled on the Milliken anticline, the uppermost Oriskany beds are light gray to white, fine- to medium-grained sandstone. The grains are nearly all quartz, which are subround to round. (It should be noted that roundness estimated from well cuttings is less than roundness estimated from thin sections, probably because quartz overgrowths adhering to grains give a false impression of angularity.) Coarse sand-sized grains and granules are common. Below this upper sandstone, the Oriskany beds become finer grained, with very fine to fine sand size predominant, but still subround and fairly well sorted. In general, the lower beds are darker in color and more calcareous than the uppermost beds. A thin (8-10 ft; 2-3 m) limestone is commonly described from samples and on older cable tool drillers' logs (Figure 7). Below this, the lowest sandstone beds are light gray to brownish gray, fine to very fine grained, subrounded, with fair sorting, and are more calcareous. Intergranular porosity occurs in samples throughout the entire interval but is better in the upper half of the formation. The main gas pay usually begins within 10 ft (3 m) of the top of the Oriskany and is 10 to 12 ft (3-4 m) thick. Stimulated zones average 30 ft (9 m) thick, usually from the top of the pay to total depth.

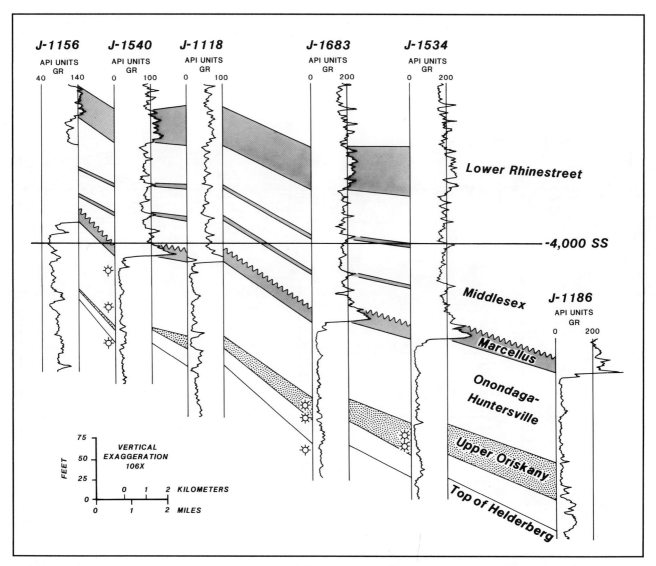

Figure 8. Structural cross section, west to east, illustrating the trap in the Oriskany Sandstone. The Oriskany thins updip to the west owing to an unconformity in that area. Carbonate rocks seal the trap to the west and over the top. Salt water defines the downdip edge of the reservoir.

In Ripley District, in the middle of the Jackson County trend, the pay section in the Oriskany is within a light gray, fine-grained sandstone that contains scattered medium to coarse grains of quartz. Most grains are subround to round, with fair sorting and intergranular porosity throughout. The pay in this central area is thicker than to the south, often 40 to 50 ft (12–15 m), and usually occurs at the very top of the Oriskany (Figure 7). The Oriskany has a more blocky shape on a gamma ray log in this area, versus the inverted Christmas tree shape typical of coarsening upward sequences in the Cooper Creek area to the south (Figures 9 and 10).

At the extreme northern end of the trend, downdip wells produce from a fine-grained sandstone that is present below a thin, fine- to coarse-grained sandstone that caps the Oriskany. In this northern area, thinning updip to the west is rapid, with no well-developed reservoir sandstone present just 5 mi (8 km) west of the easternmost well in the field (Figure 11). Farther west, the Oriskany again thickens.

The east-west cross sections, both those based on cable tool drillers' records (Figure 7) and gamma-ray logs (Figures 9–11), also illustrate variations in thickness of the upper sandstone that result in north-south thickness trends. To the south (Figure 7C), the lower sandstone in the Oriskany also thickens and thins from west to east across the field. In a few wells, cable tool drillers recorded gas flows from

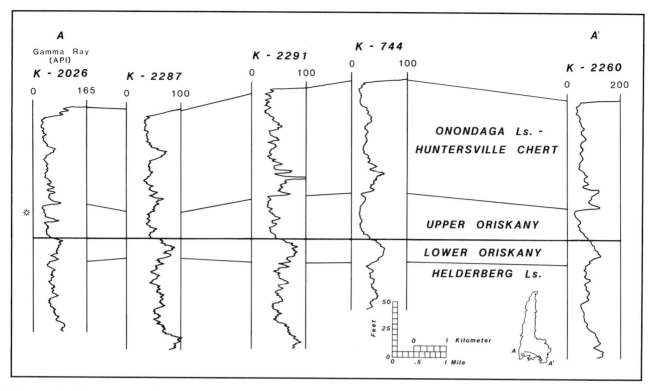

Figure 9. Gamma-ray log cross section through southern end of Elk-Poca field, illustrating clean, upper sandstone with calcareous, more argillaceous sandstone and limestone below.

the lower sandstone. However, in most wells, all reported pays are in the upper sandstone, usually beginning near the top of the unit (Figure 7).

Petrography and Pore Types

The petrographic nature of the Oriskany Sandstone is highly variable across the Appalachian basin in terms of lithology, grain size, and cement. Examination of well cuttings (Lafferty, 1938) and thin sections (present study) from the Elk-Poca field shows the Oriskany in this region to be no exception. Gas production in the field is confined to the more quartzose units of the Oriskany. The mineralogy and porosity data presented below were collected from Oriskany samples expelled from wells by high, natural open flow, blown out by shot or bailed out during cleaning operations (Headlee and Joseph, 1945), and, therefore, apply only to the productive quartzose facies of the Oriskany.

Well-rounded monocrystalline quartz is the predominant clastic component, forming more than 95% of the grain volume of the rock. Quartz grain size ranges from coarse to fine sand. Other detrital grains include polycrystalline quartz, feldspar (commonly showing overgrowths), phosphatic grains, chert, glauconite, and a heavy mineral assemblage of tourmaline, zircon, and rutile. The detrital carbonate fraction comprises less than 2% of the grain volume and is composed of brachiopod, trilobite, bryozoan, and ostracode fragments. Some recrystallization of fossil fragments has occurred. In

all wells, alternating coarse- and fine-grained sandstones occur without any definite pattern, although the unit displays an overall coarsening-upward sequence (Lafferty, 1938; Wilcox, 1957).

Silica, in the form of quartz overgrowths, and carbonate, in the form of spar and microspar, commonly cement the Oriskany Sandstone. Many quartz grains appear subangular in thin section because of syntaxial overgrowths, and euhedral prismatic overgrowths commonly extend into pores. The amount of secondary silica is difficult to determine because dust rings on detrital grains are poorly developed. However, Wilcox (1957) and Heald et al. (1962) observed between 2% and 16% quartz cement in the Oriskany. Secondary quartz is the primary cementing agent in producing zones.

Lafferty (1938) identified carbonate as the main Oriskany cement and stated that siliceous cement increases westward as the sandstone pinches out. However, the present study shows that the unit becomes increasingly more calcareous in that direction. Wilcox (1957) and Heald et al. (1962) observed 5% or less total carbonate in the productive sandstones, and recent observations support this lower amount. Carbonate cement occurs most commonly as sparry calcite, syntaxial overgrowths, and coarse to fine dolomite. Cement fillings within large brachiopod shells consist of a first-generation dogtooth cement followed by coarse calcite spar and saddle dolomite. Elsewhere, calcite and dolomite are present as coarse, intergranular, pore-filling cement,

217

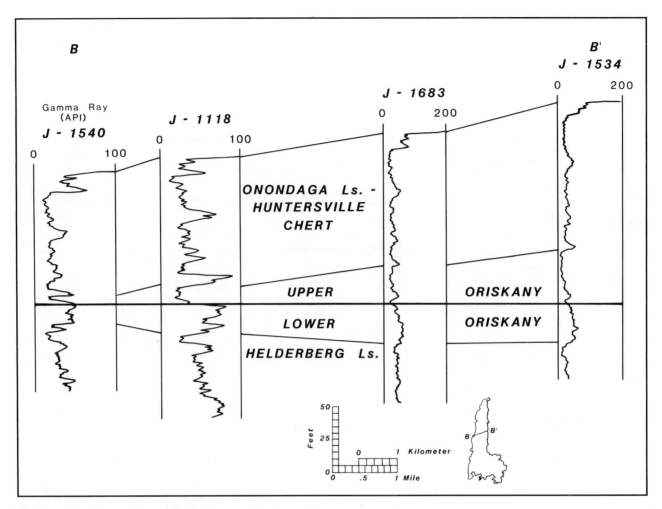

Figure 10. Gamma-ray log cross section through Ripley District, Jackson County, illustrating westward thinning of clean, upper sandstone.

as small isolated rhombs intergrown with secondary quartz, and as fine, granular crystals in pores.

Porosity in the Oriskany varies widely. Finn (1949) recorded very low porosities throughout much of the Oriskany, except in productive zones where porosity averages 9%. Measured porosities by Headlee and Joseph (1945) range from 1.5% to 13%. Thin section porosities averaged 12% in samples examined in the present study.

In recent years, the origin of sandstone porosity has been widely discussed, and secondary porosity resulting from the dissolution of framework grains and cements has gained wide acceptance. Early studies on Oriskany porosity by Krynine (1941) concluded that leaching of carbonate following cementation resulted in porous zones. The etching of quartz, the presence of calcite as dust rings and inclusions within secondary quartz, and oversized pores have generally been cited as evidence to support leaching of carbonate in the Oriskany. Wilcox (1957) and Heald et al. (1962) disagreed, citing the euhedral character of quartz overgrowths, the presence of

undissolved carbonate fossils, and the absence of oversize pores as evidence for primary porosity.

To gain a better understanding of the nature of Oriskany porosity, 300 pores per thin section were examined to determine their origin. The criteria set forth by Heald et al. (1962) and Choquette and Pray (1970) were used for the recognition of original porosity, and the work of Schmidt and McDonald (1979) and Shanmugam (1985) was applied to determine secondary pores.

The most common primary pore type is one in which euhedral, often prismatic quartz overgrowths define or delineate the pore margins (Figure 12A). Fifty-five percent of all pores fall into this group. The pores commonly display more than one euhedral face or prism along their perimeter and are invariably free of carbonate. The shape of the pores varies from triangular to irregular, reflecting the inverse of negative grain shape slightly modified by overgrowths. Size of the pores is smaller than surrounding grains, and pore distribution is fairly uniform throughout the rock. Euhedral overgrowths indicate

218

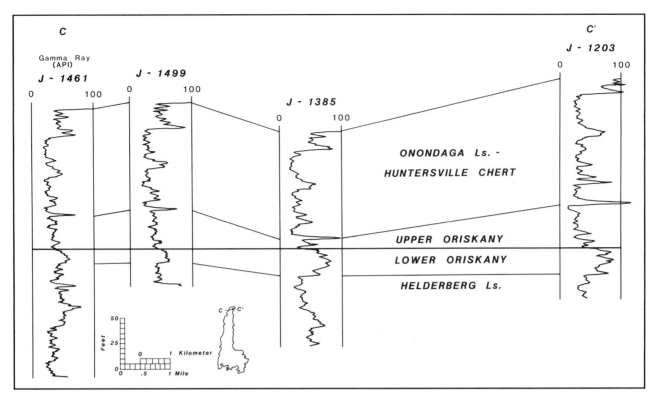

Figure 11. Gamma-ray log cross section through northern edge of Elk-Poca field illustrating clean, well-developed sandstone to east (well 1203) that thins rapidly to west (well 1385 on edge of field). Farther west upper sandstone does thicken but is not as clean as the Elk-Poca reservoir sandstone.

that voids were present at the time of quartz growth. The existence of undissolved fossil fragments and the absence of molds or corroded grain margins indicate that these pores were not formed by secondary processes.

Secondary porosity in the Oriskany is clearly documented in two broad categories of pore types: intragranular secondary pores and framework grain dissolution pores. The most common intragranular pore type appears as corroded porous channels within detrital monocrystalline and polycrystalline quartz grains (Figure 12B). In some grains, the channels have developed along Boehm lamellae or bubble-train inclusions, whereas other grains experienced dissolution of inclusions. Partial to complete dissolution of framework grains, typically feldspar and phosphate, also has created porosity (Figure 12C). Partial dissolution of feldspar occurred along twin planes, and in some cases detrital grains were completely dissolved, leaving remnant overgrowths. Phosphate grains also exhibit partial to complete dissolution, and in some areas phosphate-lined pores remain. Eleven percent of the pores are attributed to secondary processes, with intragranular quartz porosity responsible for approximately 8%. Other secondary porosity types, though minor, include elongate and oversize pores, pores exhibiting corroded grains along their margins, and pores within miscellaneous carbonate material.

Combination pores account for an additional 13% of the pore types. These pores appear to be primary pores enhanced by secondary processes resulting in an enlargement of the pore. Typical types include pores enlarged by an adjacent partially dissolved framework grain and, although minor, pores that contain small amounts of calcite microspar. The remaining 21% of the pores observed in thin section have no distinct features by which they could be classified.

Variations in cement types and porosity have played a significant role in gas accumulation in the Elk-Poca field. Unconformities, both at the top and bottom of the Oriskany, have been alluded to in the past (Woodward, 1943; Dennison, 1961), and secondary porosity in carbonates is often associated with subaerial exposure. However, the effect of an unconformity, if one exists, does not appear to have played a significant role in Oriskany porosity development. Production is entirely from the quartzose facies where porosity has been preserved by incomplete cementation and enhanced by the formation of secondary pores.

Porosity, Permeability, Pressures, and Production

The Elk-Poca field is the largest Oriskany field in the Appalachian basin, covering approximately 165,000 ac (66,773 ha). In a field of this size, well

219

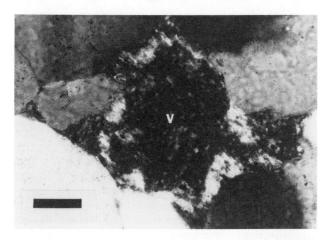

Figure 12. Photomicrographs of the Oriskany Sandstone, Elk-Poca field, West Virginia. (A) Primary porosity showing (1) euhedral overgrowths on detrital quartz grains bordering and extending into pores, (2) triangular shape and typical size of pores. Dark areas are pores. Plain light. Bar equals 0.1 mm. (B) Intragranular porosity, V, within channelized and corroded quartz. Bar equals 0.1 mm. Crossed polarizers. (C) Secondary porosity, V, resulting from the dissolution of framework feldspar. Remnant of feldspar overgrowth remains as evidence. Bar equals 0.1 mm.

depths should be expected to range considerably, and they do, from 4600 to 5300 ft (1402–1615 m), averaging 4900 ft (1493 m). The thickness of the Oriskany ranges from less than 30 to more than 80 ft (9–24 m) in the productive area, and averages 40 ft (12 m) (Diecchio, 1982), whereas net pay thickness ranges from 10 to 20 ft (3–6 m) in a typical well.

The average reservoir temperature in the field was 125°F (51.6°C), and rock pressure averaged 1940 psi (Diecchio, 1982). Porosity is primarily intergranular and ranges from 4 to 13%, with an average of 8%. Permeability ranges from 0.1 to 93.4 md and averages 27.5 md, as measured on individual pieces (Headlee and Joseph, 1945).

Headlee and Joseph (1945) collected fragments of Oriskany sandstone blown out of gas wells in the Cooper Creek area by high volume gas flows and pressure and by shooting and the recovery of fragments during cleaning out operations. The porosity and mineral specific gravity measured from these samples are uniform, but the porosity (8% average) is low. Permeabilities, however, also are uniform, but high (27.5 md average). Therefore, gas wells in this area were characterized by high flow rates, rapid decrease in pressure, and rapid decline in production (Headlee and Joseph, 1945). Headlee and Joseph observed a relationship between permeability and original open flows when these parameters were plotted one versus the other and when both were mapped (Figure 13). Permeabilities for samples blown out of wells by high flows were greater than for samples that were blown out by shooting. Each piece tested contained both oil and brine in pore spaces. Headlee and Joseph also observed that gas in the less permeable sections above and below the main pay may eventually flow into the pay section, increasing the ultimate recovery. In updip wells to the west where the main, highly permeable pay is thinner or absent, low-volume but commercial wells have been completed in these tighter sandstones.

Although production was predominantly gas, a small amount of oil was produced from several wells, and the gas was wet throughout the field, containing rather high percentages of distillate (Haught, 1960). However, no records of the amount of distillate produced are available. During the 1980s at least one operator attempted to remove the fluid—a mixture of distillate and salt water—from old nonproducing Oriskany gas wells to put them back into gas production.

The oil and gas database at the West Virginia Geological Survey contains data for 1170 Oriskany penetrations in this field, of which 1103 were productive, a success rate of 94%. The average well spacing on the 165,000 productive acres is 150 ac (60 ha) per well.

Thermal gradient values range from 1.2 to 1.7°F per 100 ft in the field.

During the 40 year period from 1933, when Grosscup et al. completed the Frankenberger #2 gas discovery in the Cooper Creek area, until 1973, the

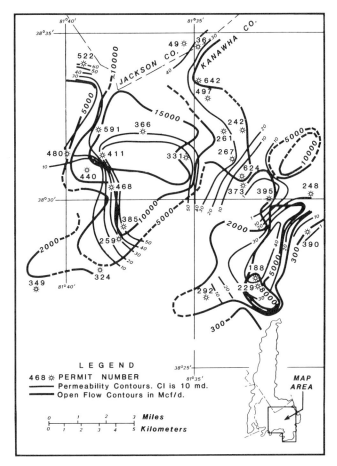

Figure 13. Isometric permeability and open-flow contours. Map compares initial potentials (IPs) and measured permeabilities in the Cooper Creek area (after Headlee and Joseph, 1945).

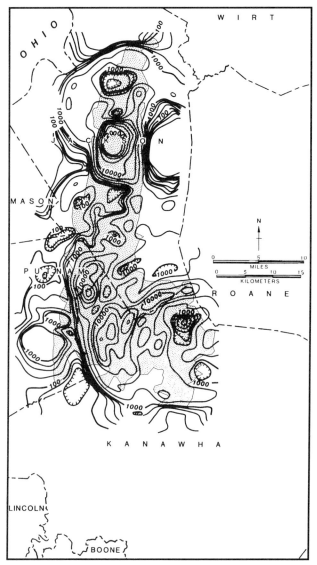

Figure 14. Computer-generated map of natural initial open flows of gas in Elk-Poca field and adjacent areas. Contoured values are in Mcf/d; contour interval varies.

1100 gas wells in Elk-Poca field produced nearly 1 tcf (962,207 MMcf) of gas. Production since 1973 in isolated wells still not converted to storage or abandoned, and in wells drilled in tighter areas during the past 15 years, has pushed production to the 1 tcf mark. Gas production ranged from a few million cubic feet from wells that were abandoned shortly after going on line to more than 4 bcf from wells that produced more than 40 years. Most wells, however, were relatively short-lived and were plugged before producing for as long as ten years.

Two productive trends, separated by an area with sparse drilling, both aligned north-south, are apparent in the field (Figure 4). The lack of drilling in the central area, especially in Jackson County, is due to the poor performance of the few wells drilled there. Of the two productive trends, the eastern, downdip trend in the thick upper sandstone above the salt water contact is the more productive, with the updip trend drilled since the end of World War II less productive. In Kanawha County, the eastern trend is much wider, with the narrow, updip trend developed in Putnam County. The 1000 Mcf isopotential line for natural wells (Figure 14) essentially

separates the two trends in the southern part of the field. For wells that were stimulated, the 2500 Mcf isopotential line (Figure 15) approximates this same division.

Natural IPs for Oriskany wells in Elk-Poca and nearby fields range from less than 50 Mcfg/d to more than 20,000 Mcfg/d (Figure 14). Three areas with high natural flows (7500 Mcfg/d) are obvious from the isopotential map, two in Poca District, Kanawha County, and the third in Ripley District, Jackson County. The two high natural IP areas in Poca District correlate closely with areas where the Oriskany is greater than 50 ft (15 m) thick. The high IP area in Ripley District also coincides with thick sandstone areas, especially the northeastern spur where the Oriskany is 60 to 70 ft (18-21 m) thick (see Figures 5 and 14).

221

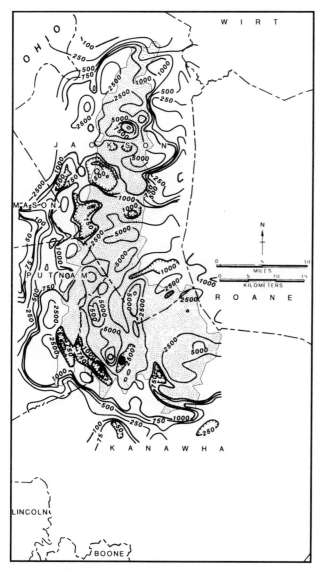

Figure 15. Computer-generated map of open flows of gas following stimulation of wells in Elk-Poca field and adjacent areas. Contoured values are in Mcf/d; contour interval varies.

The southernmost high, natural, IP bull's-eye in Poca District bifurcates to the north, and a long, linear trend extends to the northeast and then nearly eastward, through southern Jackson County (Figure 14), cutting across the north-south sandstone thickness trends (Figure 5). This linear trend correlates with the change in structural strike from north-south in most of Jackson County to nearly east-west as the axis of the Milliken anticline bends northeastward (Figure 6).

The isopotential map of Oriskany wells that were stimulated by either shooting or fracturing (Figure 15) indicates that high IPs (7500 Mcfg/d) are found only in a few small areas. However, these small areas correlate closely with the high IP areas for natural wells. There also is a high correlation between the two maps in the south where the 1000 Mcfg/d lines

nearly match and effectively outline the southern edge of the field. A close correlation also exists between the two maps on the northern edge of the field. On the western, updip edge of the field and in adjacent areas, IPs after stimulation generally are low in areas when the Oriskany thins to 20 ft (6 m) or less (see Figures 5 and 15).

One of the areas with high post-stimulation IPs is an updip area in Putnam County that was drilled relatively late in the life of the field when wells were treated using more modern completion techniques. This area contains wells that tested in excess of 2500 Mcfg/d following treatment (Figure 15) although natural IPs were less than 1000 Mcfg (Figure 14). The Oriskany ranges in thickness from only 30 to 40 ft (9–12 m) in this area. However, net sandstone is even thinner immediately to the south (Figure 5) of this "sweet spot," so sandstone thickness may have exercised some control on production. The area does not show up on the map of five-year production (Figure 16), but eventually some wells produced more than 2 Bcfg (Figure 17).

A production decline curve for a representative set of wells in Elk-Poca field can be seen in Figure 18A. The wells are characterized by high first-year production (1.6 MMcfg/d) followed by a rapid decline over the next four years. Rock pressure (Figure 18B) shows a similar drop over the same period of time. This is characteristic of highly permeable reservoirs with low porosity: Deliverability is high, but reserves are low. The average recovery of gas per acre was 6 MMcf in the Elk-Poca field where the average porosity was 8%. In the tighter areas updip to the west, beyond the field limits, lower porosity and reserves/acre are expected. From the plot of porosity versus permeability prepared by Headlee and Joseph (1945), permeabilities below 1 md will have about 6% porosity at best. Fracturing of these tighter, thinner, updip sandstones could yield 2 MMcf/ac. On 140 ac spacing, this would be 280 MMcf/well reserve. Good correlations have been demonstrated between porosity and permeability and between measured permeability and open flows in the field (Headlee and Joseph, 1945). It could be expected, therefore, that there would be a good correlation between actual production and initial open flows. The relationship between IPs and cumulative production for all wells for which we were able to obtain production data is illustrated in Figure 18D. Although there is some scatter in the data, a direct relationship between IPs and production can be observed.

The aerial distribution of five-year production (Figure 16) shows two areas of good production. The northern area matches an area of high IP values after treatment (Figure 15), whereas the southern area matches an area of high natural flow (Figure 14). These highly productive areas correlate with areas of thick (50–70 ft; 15–21 m) sandstone (Figure 5) but show a lower correlation with structure (Figure 6).

A better correlation between production and geology is observed by using ultimate production. Ultimate recovery of Oriskany wells prior to

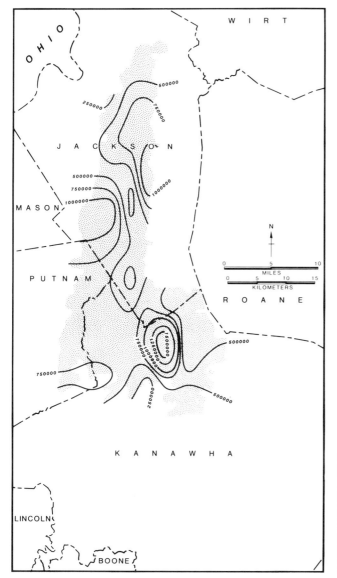

Figure 16. Computer-generated map of cumulative production after the fifth year, based on nearly 300 wells in Elk-Poca field. Dry holes were not used in the contouring program. Contour interval, 250,000 Mcf.

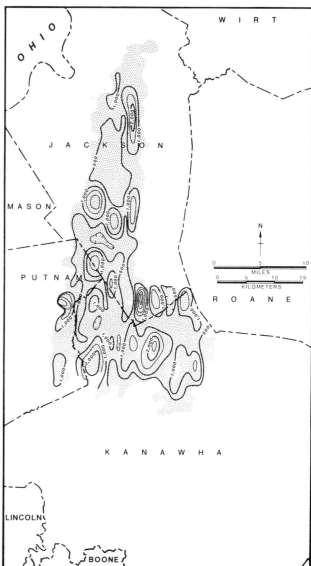

Figure 17. Computer-generated map of cumulative production (ultimate recovery) for wells prior to abandonment or conversion to storage. Dry holes were not used in the contouring program. A few wells are still producing but at rates too low to affect contours. Contour interval, 500 MMcf.

abandonment or conversion to storage is shown in Figure 17. Ultimate recovery is tied closely to more permeable and porous zones developed in thicker sandstones. Six separate areas in which cumulative production ranged from 1 to 2.5 bcf of gas per well all correlate with areas of thick Oriskany (40–70 ft; 12–21 m), including the updip area in Putnam County. A narrow area with less than 0.5 bcf of gas per well matches a corresponding narrow zone of thin Oriskany (30 ft; 9 m) in north-central Kanawha County. Two of these areas of high ultimate recovery also correlate with two structural features, the Sissonville high and the Milliken anticline.

Following primary production, the Elk-Poca field was considered to be a good candidate for gas storage because of the updip permeability barrier, downdip saltwater barrier, and confining carbonate units above and below, as well as favorable porosity and permeability.

Source

Sandstones of the Oriskany were deposited following a long time interval when thick carbonates from the Middle Silurian Lockport Dolomite through

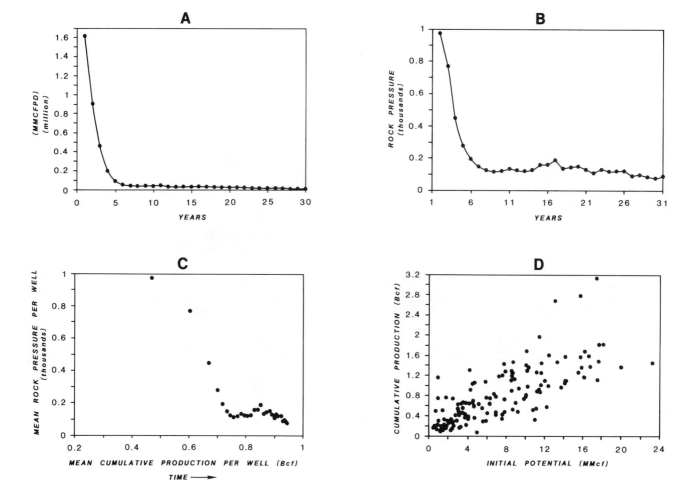

Figure 18. Production and rock pressure data from a representative set of nearly 200 wells in Elk-Poca field. (A) Production decline curve, plotting mean production per day, all wells, versus years of production up to the 30th year; (B) rock pressure decline curve, plotting mean rock pressure for all wells versus years of production; (C) decline in mean rock pressure, all wells, per year plotted versus mean annual cumulative production, all wells, calculated for 27 years; (D) relationship between initial potential and cumulative production, all wells in data set.

the Helderberg Limestone were laid down. The higher carbonate content of the lower sandstones in the Oriskany reflects the transition from carbonate to clastic deposition. Thus, the carbonate is related to original depositional factors and is not a relic of post-depositional leaching followed by reprecipitation. Within the Oriskany, the main difference between permeable beds and tighter beds in the Elk-Poca field is the amount of carbonate cement present. Because the amount of carbonate interbeds and cement decreases upward, the gas reservoir was located in the upper sandstones of the Oriskany.

Following deposition of the Oriskany, erosion may have removed some of the uppermost beds to the west, thinning the sandstones. Thus, instead of enhancing permeability by leaching out carbonate grains, post-Oriskany erosion may have created the updip permeability barrier 10 to 15 mi (16–24 km) east of the sandstone pinch-out.

Although the Huntersville Chert overlies the Oriskany in this area, it is predominantly a limestone over the entire field, whereas to the east a predominantly cherty facies of the Huntersville is present (Diecchio, 1982). The implication is that the dense limestones would provide better gas seals than a chert that is more readily fractured over structural highs. Gas produced from the Huntersville to the east probably migrated into those fractured zones from the Oriskany.

Following deposition of the Onesquethaw (the Huntersville Chert and Onondaga Limestone), the thick sequence of Devonian shales was deposited. This sequence thickens from 2300 to nearly 2900 ft (700–880 m) over the 17 mi (27 km) width of Elk-Poca field in Kanawha County. This increase in thickness is due to basin subsidence to the east.

As the Devonian shales were deposited, the basin continued to subside more to the east, with evidence of uplift and erosion of Middle and lowermost Upper Devonian shale to the west. At the end of the Devonian, this increase in total shale thickness to the east would have created a dip of at least 40 ft/

mi on the top of the Oriskany, placing black, organic-rich source beds in the east at the same subsea elevation as Oriskany reservoir beds to the west. Once this critical dip was reached, gas under low permeable conditions in the lower shale section could have migrated laterally into the Oriskany. Neither compaction of the Oriskany, which would tend to dissolve silica and lead to quartz overgrowths, nor cementation by carbonate had proceeded to the point where permeability was significantly impeded, although porosity had been reduced. Further cementation probably was inhibited by the presence of gas in the pores.

During deposition of Pocono clastics following the end of the Devonian, subsidence continued to be greater in the east than in the west. Restoring the Middle Mississippian Greenbrier Limestone to a flat surface would add an additional dip to the Oriskany. Thus, by the end of Greenbrier deposition, there was a dip of 60 ft/mi, or 1020 ft (310 m) over the 17 mi (27 km) distance across the southern edge of the field on the Oriskany (Figure 19). This created a situation above and just east of the field where black shales of the Marcellus, Geneseo, Middlesex, and Rhinestreet were structurally lower than the Oriskany reservoir. As these sediments matured, gas migrated into the Oriskany up to the permeability barrier to the west, collecting above the saltwater downdip to the east in the classic stratigraphic-structural trap that resulted in this giant gas field.

Biofacies indicators collected from Devonian shale cores in West Virginia indicate that organic matter (i.e., kerogen) in the oldest black shales are dominated by algae forms in the west and terrestrial forms to the east. In the vicinity of Elk-Poca field, shale cores yielded *Tasmanites*, a green algae deposited in a marine environment, and assorted normal marine forms that make up a second major facies, a "marine facies." With time, a third facies, a "terrestrial" facies derived from the east, became more important in the younger shales (Zielinski and McIver, 1982). The amount of this organic matter increases from west to east across the state and ranges from 4 to 5% in black shales above the Elk-Poca field (Tetra Tech, 1979).

The hydrocarbon-producing potential of these shales depends not only on the type and amount of organic matter present, but also on the degree of conversion of organic matter to hydrocarbons. Factors 1 and 2 (type and amount) depend on the original deposition of the shale, whereas factor 3 (degree of conversion) depends on the post-depositional burial and heating history of the sediments. Claypool et al. (1978) calculated 40%

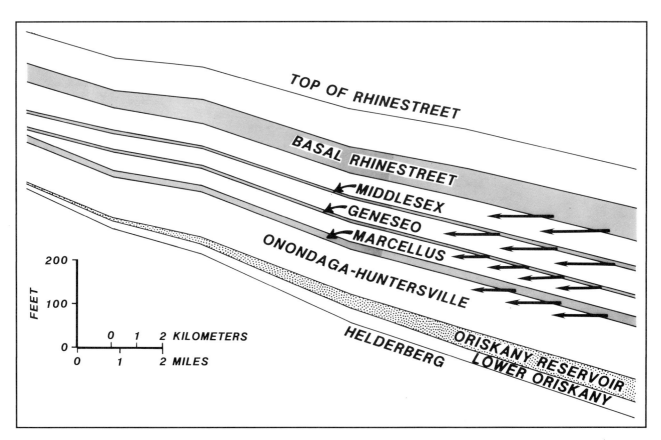

Figure 19. Schematic cross section illustrating regional dip down to the east on the Oriskany reservoir following deposition of Devonian and Pocono clastics and the Middle Mississippian Greenbrier Limestone. Adjusted "Big Lime" to flat surface; 60 ft/mi dip on the Oriskany. Lateral migration of gas from black shale source beds to the Oriskany is illustrated by horizontal arrows.

225

conversion in shales from a core taken in Lincoln County, 25 mi (40 km) southwest of Elk-Poca field, and 13% conversion of organics to hydrocarbons in shales from a core from Mason County, 15 mi (24 km) west of the northern end of Elk-Poca field. These calculations were based on an estimate of the original gas-generating capacity (3.1 SCF/ft^3 shale) and remaining gas potential from pyrolysis (Claypool et al., 1978).

Vitrinite reflectance values, as mapped by Tetra Tech, range from 1.0 to 1.5 over the field. Thermal maturity, based on the composition of natural gas collected from the shales, wet gas in the west to dry gas in the east, also varies across the state (Claypool et al., 1978). Carbon isotope ratios of methane and carbonization of solid organic matter show similar trends, reflecting deeper burial history, higher temperatures, and increased metamorphism of organic matter in the east, less to the west. Thus, the potential source beds in the lower part of the Devonian shale sequence range from just mature to mature on the west side of the basin in the vicinity of Elk-Poca field.

EXPLORATION CONCEPTS

The Elk-Poca field was discovered as a structural play on the Milliken anticline, and drilling then moved westward along the Sissonville high. As drillers moved northward, however, exploration became stratigraphic in nature as drilling activity closely followed thickness trends in the Oriskany and the good production that correlated closely with areas of thick sandstone. Ultimately, nearly 1200 wells were drilled in the field, of which the 1100 productive wells yielded approximately 1 tcf of gas. Gas recovery averaged 6000 Mcf/ac and nearly 0.9 bcf/well. The average well was completed in the 1930s or 1940s at an average cost of $15,000 per well, or $18 million for the field. If gas sold for $0.20/Mcf at the well head, then approximately $200 million of gas were produced, a return on investment for the field of 11 to 1 (prior to paying for the gathering system, field overhead, and taxes).

It was hoped, following the discovery of this field, that by gaining an understanding of the geologic factors that controlled gas accumulation in this large area, further giant Oriskany fields would be discovered in areas where similar stratigraphic and structural conditions existed. However, following the development of the field, only one small Oriskany field was developed along this same structural trend to the north in Wood County, and two small fields were developed on the Warfield anticline to the south. Other small fields were developed west of Elk-Poca field in areas of thinner, tighter sandstone that were stimulated by fracturing. It now appears that Elk-Poca is located in a place where a certain combination of geologic factors exist that are not repeated elsewhere in West Virginia. The structural strike is north-south, except in the southern end where the strike swings eastward because the Sissonville high and Milliken anticline. South of the field, however, the strike changes abruptly to the northeast owing to the presence of the major structural feature in the area, the Warfield anticline. North of the field, the structure also swings northeastward.

This north-south structural trend coincides with two other trends: a progressive east to west thinning of the Oriskany and a west to east thickening of the Devonian shales. Also, within the Devonian shale section, abrupt facies changes from predominantly black, organic-rich shales to gray, silty, less organic shales occur in both the lower Huron Member of the Ohio Shale and the Rhinestreet Shale Member of the West Falls Formation. However, black source beds were located above the Elk-Poca field, with gray shales downdip to the east. If this facies change had occurred 10 mi (16 m) to the west, no source beds would have been available for this reservoir.

Thus the Elk-Poca field came to be located where critical geologic factors coincided. Clean, marine sands were dispersed westward in relatively high-energy, shallow-water environments on a carbonate platform such that thickness trends of the sandstone paralleled later structural slope. Post-Oriskany erosion updip to the west eliminated uppermost permeable beds, creating a permeability barrier parallel to structure and thickness trends. Finally, following deposition of an appropriate seal, a thick sequence of marine shales, which included several black, organic-rich intervals, was deposited as the basin subsided to the east. Again, black shale thickness trends and black shale to gray shale facies changes were parallel to structural strike and depositional strike of the sandstone and reservoir, and the facies change was located fortuitously above the eastern edge of the field, not farther west. This increase in dip on the Oriskany, created by deposition of thicker shales to the east, was followed by gas migration updip to the western permeability barrier, accumulating above a saltwater barrier to the east, effectively creating the Elk-Poca field in this unique geologic area.

ACKNOWLEDGMENTS

Robert F. Kleinschmidt created various data files and ran the procedures to produce the computer-generated maps of sandstone thickness, structure on the Oriskany, historical drilling trends, and production. Michael E. Hohn produced maps of initial open flows, the production and rock pressure decline curves, and the correlation between rock pressure and production, and IPs and production. Production data contributed by Columbia Natural Resources, Occidental USA, and Cabot Oil and Gas were collected by Renee LaValle and Bascombe Mitch Blake. Katharine Lee Avary, assisted by Marie Patchen, used these data to create a production file within our database from which the production maps and graphs were generated. Renee LaValle and Ray Strawser drafted the maps and illustrations in this report, and Janice Bloniarz entered and produced the text. Sample descriptions by Glasco Rector, of Geolog, Inc., were utilized in the section on reservoir lithology.

REFERENCES CITED

Bierderman, Jr., E. W., 1986, Thornwood Gas Field, Oriskany Sandstone, Pocahontas County, West Virginia, *in* E. W. Bierderman, Jr., Atlas of oil and gas reservoir rocks from North America: New York, John Wiley and Sons, p. 41-49.

Bruner, K. R., 1986, Fair-weather and storm sedimentation of the Devonian Oriskany Sandstone (abs.): Geological Society of America, Abstracts with Programs, v. 18, p. 281.

Cardwell, D. H., 1977, Oil and gas fields of West Virginia: West Virginia Geological Survey, Mineral Resources Series MRS-7, 171 p.

Choquette, P. W., and L. C. Pray, 1970, Geologic nomenclature and class of porosity in sedimentary carbonates: American Association of Petroleum Geologists Bulletin, v. 54, p. 207-250.

Claypool, G. E., C. N. Threlkeld, and N. H. Bostick, 1978, Natural gas occurrence related to regional thermal rank of organic matter (maturity) in Devonian rocks of the Appalachian basin, *in* Preprints, 2nd Eastern Gas Shales Symposium: U.S. Department of Energy, Publication METC/SP-78/6, v. 1, p. 54-65.

Dennison, J. M., 1961, Stratigraphy of Onesquethaw Stage of Devonian in West Virginia and bordering states: West Virginia Geological Survey Bulletin 22, 87 p.

Diecchio, R. J., 1982, Compilation of regional stratigraphic and production trends, Oriskany Sandstone, Appalachian basin: West Virginia Geological Survey, Open File Report, 41 p.

Diecchio, R. J., 1985, Regional controls of gas accumulation in Oriskany Sandstone, Central Appalachian basin: American Association of Petroleum Geologists Bulletin, v. 69, p. 722-732.

Finn, F. H., 1949, Geology and occurrence of natural gas in the Oriskany Sandstone in Pennsylvania and New York:
American Association of Petroleum Geologists Bulletin, v. 33, p. 305-335.

Haught, O. L., 1960, Oil and gas report on Kanawha County, West Virginia: West Virginia Geological Survey Bulletin 19, 24 p.

Headlee, A. J. W., and J. S. Joseph, 1945, Permeability, porosity, oil, and water content of natural gas reservoirs, Kanawha-Jackson and Campbells Creek Oriskany fields: West Virginia Geological Survey Bulletin 8, 16 p.

Heald, M. T., A. Thomson, and F. B. Wilcox, 1962, Origin of interstitial porosity in the Oriskany Sandstone of Kanawha County, West Virginia: Journal of Sedimentary Petrology, v. 32, p. 291-298.

Krynine, P. D., 1941, Petrographic studies of variations in cementing material in the Oriskany sand: Proceedings of 10th Pennsylvania Mineral Industries Conference, Pennsylvania State College, Bulletin 33, p. 108-116.

Lafferty, R. C., 1938, The Oriskany in West Virginia: American Association of Petroleum Geologists Bulletin, v. 22, p. 175-188.

Martens, J. H. C., 1939, Petrography and correlation of deep-well sections in West Virginia and adjacent states: West Virginia Geological Survey, v. XI, 255 p.

McClain, A. H., 1949, Stratigraphic accumulation in Jackson-Kanawha Counties area of West Virginia: American Association of Petroleum Geologists Bulletin, v. 33, p. 336-345.

Schmidt, V., and D. A. McDonald, 1979, Texture and recognition of secondary porosity in sandstones, *in* Aspects of diagenesis: SEPM Special Publication 26, p. 209-225.

Shanmugam, G., 1985, Significance of secondary porosity in interpreting sandstone composition: American Association of Petroleum Geologists Bulletin, v. 69, p. 378-384.

Tetra Tech, 1979, Evaluation of Devonian shale potential in West Virginia: U.S. Department of Energy, Publication DOE/METC-120, 51 p. with appendices.

Tucker, R. C., 1936, Deep-well records: West Virginia Geological Survey, v. VII, 560 p.

Wilcox, F. B., 1957, Origin of interstitial porosity in the Oriskany Sandstone: Unpublished Masters thesis, West Virginia University, 57 p.

Woodward, H. P., 1943, The Devonian System of West Virginia: West Virginia Geological Survey, v. XV, 655 p.

Zielinski, R. E., and R. D. McIver, 1982, Resource and exploration assessment of the oil and gas potential in the Devonian gas shales of the Appalachian basin: U.S. Department of Energy, Publication DOE/DP/ 0053-1125, 325 p.

Appendix 1. Field Description

Field name .... *Elk-Poca (Sissonville) field*

Ultimate recoverable reserves .... *1 tcf of gas*

Field location:

    Country .... *U.S.A.*

    State .... *West Virginia*

    Basin/Province .... *Appalachian basin*

Field discovery:

    Year first pay discovered .... *Lower Devonian Oriskany Sandstone   1933*

Discovery well name and general location:

    First pay .... *N. N. Grosscup #2 P. H. Frankenberger (old well deepened);*
    extreme southeastern end of the field, northern Kanawha County, West Virginia, U.S.A.

Discovery well operator .... *N. N. Grosscup*

IP in barrels per day and/or cubic feet or cubic meters per day:

    First pay .... *134 Mcfg/day after shot*

All other zones with shows of oil and gas in the field:

Age	Formation	Type of Show
Middle Mississippian	*"Big Lime"*	*Gas*
Lower Mississippian	*Big Injun sandstone*	*Gas*
Upper Devonian	*Huron*	*Gas*

Geologic concept leading to discovery and method or methods used to delineate prospect, e.g., surface geology, subsurface geology, seeps, magnetic data, gravity data, seismic data, seismic refraction, nontechnical:

Initial wells were structural tests on the Milliken anticline, a feature mapped following extensive shallow drilling to Mississippian targets. One early method of predicting structural highs at the Oriskany level was to calculate the eastward "rise" of the basal Mississippian Berea as versus eastward thickening of the Devonian shales between the Berea and Oriskany. Where the Berea rise exceeded the increase in shale thickness, the Oriskany would be on a structural high and would be drilled.

Structure:

    Province/basin type .... *Bally 221, Klemme IIA*

    Tectonic history

    The field lies on the western side of the Appalachian basin in an area known as "low amplitude fold province." The field lies above the "Rome trough," a Cambrian-age graben. Reactivation of the trough and other basement features affected Paleozoic sedimentation patterns. At the end of the Paleozoic, the Alleghenian orogeny deformed rocks in the foreland to the east. Low amplitude folds were created west of the foreland by either detached deformation or movement of basement blocks.

    Regional structure

    Lies on the west side of the Appalachian basin, with regional dip to the east. Lies above the "Rome trough," west of the New York–Alabama lineament.

    Local structure

    Southern end of the field is on a broad, low-amplitude anticline that plunges eastward; northern end developed on regional dip.

Trap:

    Trap type(s)

    Stratigraphic trap with permeability barrier updip to the west. Southern end primarily a stratigraphic trap developed on a broad, low-amplitude anticline.

Basin stratigraphy (major stratigraphic intervals from surface to deepest penetration in field):

Chronostratigraphy	Formation	Depth to Top in ft
Upper Mississippian	Mauch Chunk	1250
Middle Mississippian	Greenbrier Limestone	1350
Lower Mississippian	Pocono Group	1550
Upper Devonian	Devonian shale formations	2000
Middle Devonian	Onondaga Limestone	4650
Lower Devonian	Oriskany Sandstone	4750

Reservoir characteristics:

Number of reservoirs 1
Formations .... Oriskany Sandstone
Ages .... Early Devonian
Depths to tops of reservoirs .... 4750 ft (range from west to east 4600–4900 ft)
Gross thickness (top to bottom of producing interval) .... 30–80 ft; avg. 40 ft
Net thickness—total thickness of producing zones
  Average .... 10 ft
  Maximum .... 22 ft
Lithology .... Sandstone, white to light gray, medium to fine grained, calcareous; larger quartz grains well-rounded
Porosity type .... Intergranular
Average porosity 8%
Average permeability .... 27.5 md

Seals:

Upper
  Formation, fault, or other feature .... Huntersville Chert
  Lithology .... Chert, cherty limestone
Lateral
  Formation, fault, or other feature .... Sandstone thins updip, loss of permeability
  Lithology .... Calcareous sandstone, carbonate

Source:

Formation and age .... Huron and Rhinestreet, Late Devonian
Lithology .... Black shale
Average total organic carbon (TOC) 4–5%
Maximum TOC .... NA
Kerogen type (I, II, or III) .... NA
Vitrinite reflectance (maturation) .... $R_o = 1.0–1.5$ over the field
Time of hydrocarbon expulsion .... NA
Present depth to top of source .... 3500 ft
Thickness .... 400 ft
Potential yield .... NA

Appendix 2. Production Data

Field name .... Elk-Poca (Sissonville) field
Field size:
  Proved acres 165,000
  Number of wells all years 1280

Current number of wells .... <100 (many gas storage areas)
Well spacing .... 150 ac
Ultimate recoverable .... 1 tcf of gas
Cumulative production .... 1 tcf of gas
Annual production .... Nil (gas storage)
Present decline rate .... NA
    Initial decline rate .... Rapid decline of about 95% in first 5 years
    Overall decline rate .... NA
Annual water production .... NA
In place, total reserves .... 1 tcf of gas (recoverable)
In place, per acre-foot .... 6000 Mcfg
Primary recovery .... 1 tcf of gas
Cumulative water production .... NA

Drilling and casing practices:

Amount of surface casing set .... 13 in., 30–50 ft
Casing program .... 10 in., 350–400 ft; 8¼ in., 1500–1900 ft; 6⅝ in., 4600–4900 ft
Drilling mud .... Cable tool drilling (no mud)
Bit program .... Cable tool drilling
High pressure zones .... None

Completion practices:

Interval(s) perforated .... Not applicable; produced "natural" from open hole
Well treatment .... Shot entire Oriskany pay sand (nitroglycerine, etc.)

Formation evaluation:

Logging suites .... None available
Testing practices .... Production tests from cased hole
Mud logging techniques .... None

Oil characteristics:

Type .... NA
API gravity .... 42.1°
Base .... NA
Initial GOR .... Mostly gas production
Sulfur, wt% 0.19
Viscosity, SUS .... NA
Pour point .... NA
Gas-oil distillate .... NA

Field characteristics:

Average elevation .... Reservoir 4100–4300 ft subsea
Initial pressure .... 1940 psi
Present pressure .... Not applicable (storage reservoirs)
Pressure gradient .... NA
Temperature .... 125°F
Geothermal gradient .... 1.2–1.7°F
Drive .... Water drive and gas expansion
Oil column thickness .... NA
Oil-water contact .... Unknown

Transportation method and market for oil and gas:
Exploitation essentially complete; various parts of field are used for gas storage.

Red Wash Field—U.S.A.
Uinta Basin, Utah

J. M. KELLY
Chevron U.S.A. Inc.
Denver, Colorado

J. W. CASTLE
Cabot Oil and Gas Corporation
Pittsburgh, Pennsylvania

FIELD CLASSIFICATION

BASIN: Uinta
BASIN TYPE: Continental Multicycle Basin on the Craton
RESERVOIR ROCK TYPE: Sandstone
RESERVOIR ENVIRONMENT OF DEPOSITION: Lacustrine Deltas and Nearshore Facies
TRAP DESCRIPTION: Multiple pinch-outs of sandstone intervals across a broad anticlinal nose

RESERVOIR AGE: Tertiary
PETROLEUM TYPE: Oil and Gas
TRAP TYPE: Pinch-Out across Anticlinal Nose

LOCATION

Red Wash field is in Uintah County in northeastern Utah, 130 mi (210 km) southeast of Salt Lake City (Figure 1). In this paper Red Wash field includes the Chevron-operated Red Wash unit and the Exxon-operated Walker Hollow unit (Figure 2).

The field is on the eastern side of the Uinta basin, immediately to the south of the present basinal synclinal axis and to the west of the north-plunging Douglas Creek arch. The structural basin is also a topographic depression that is bordered on the west by the Wasatch plateau and mountains, on the south by the Book cliffs, and on the north by the Uinta Mountains (Figure 1).

Cumulative production from the Red Wash field, which consists of an 84 mi² (215 km²) area, is 87 million barrels of oil and 277 bcf of gas. Current production is 3200 BOPD and 6 MMCFGPD. For the year 1987, 1.45 million barrels of oil and 1.9 bcf of gas were produced (Figure 3). Estimated ultimate recovery is 106 million barrels of oil and 302 bcf of gas.

In the Uinta basin, hydrocarbons are produced from reservoirs of Tertiary and Cretaceous age. Major accumulations include oil and gas in the Tertiary Green River and Wasatch formations. In addition, significant amounts of gas have been produced from the Cretaceous Mesaverde Formation and minor volumes of oil and gas have been produced from the Eocene Uinta Formation (Figure 4).

Tertiary rocks in the Uinta basin contain one of the world's largest nonmarine petroleum accumulations. Conventional oil reserves of over 1 billion

barrels are listed by Fouch (1975, p. 164). An additional 7 billion barrels of oil are in bituminous or tar sands, 20 billion barrels in oil shale, and 30 million tons are present as solid bitumens (Reed and Henderson, 1972, p. 499).

Important oil and gas fields near Red Wash include Bluebell-Altamont, 25 mi (40 km) to the northwest; Wonsits Valley, adjoining Red Wash to the southwest; Natural Buttes, 5 mi (8 km) to the south; and the giant Rangely, 20 mi (32 km) to the east (Figure 5).

HISTORY

Pre-Discovery

Significant hydrocarbon production was not established in Utah until 1925 when natural gas was produced from Jurassic and Cretaceous rocks at Ashley Valley field, to the north of the Uinta basin, and 10 mi (16 km) north of Red Wash (Figure 5). Permian–Pennsylvanian Weber production was found in the field later, in 1948.

The magnitude of Tertiary-age oil potential of the Uinta basin was recognized early by the presence of potential source rocks, oil shale, oil seeps, and tar-sand deposits. Although exploratory drilling began as early as 1900, the first commercial success in Tertiary rocks did not occur until 1949, with the discovery of the Roosevelt field, 30 mi (48 km) to the northwest of the future Red Wash field (Figure 5). Roosevelt field produces from fractured shales,

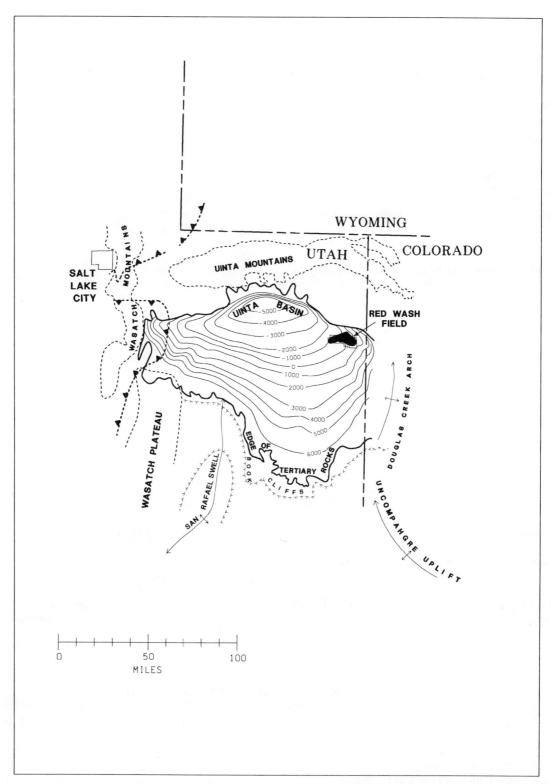

Figure 1. Map of the Uinta basin and adjacent geological and geographic features showing location of Red Wash field. Structural contours are on the base of the Green River Formation, on a sea level datum. (After Osmund, 1968.)

232

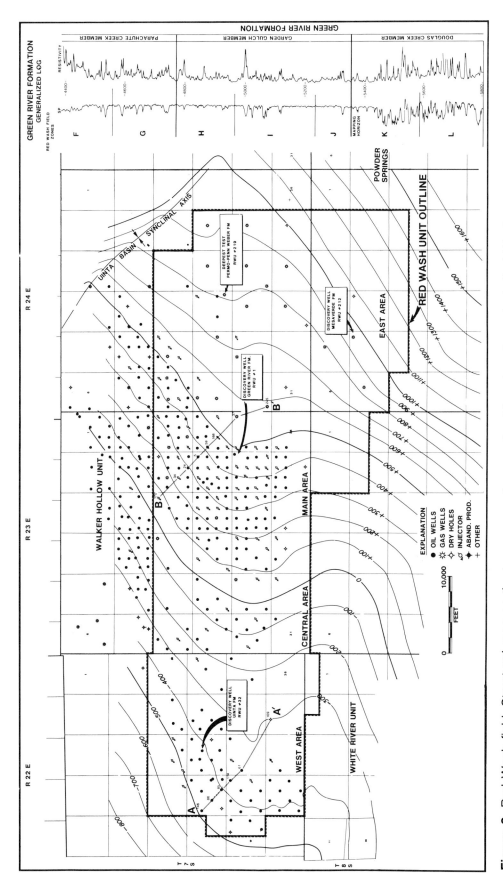

Figure 2. Red Wash field. Structural map on the top of the Douglas Creek Member of the Green River Formation and field "K" marker on a sea level datum. Lines of cross sections A–A′ and B–B′ are shown. Red Wash field includes the West, Central, Main, and East areas. A generalized type log shows both Red Wash field and Uinta basin subdivisions of the Green River Formation. Uinta basin subdivisions are those of Bradley (1931) and correlated to the Red Wash field area by Picard (1957).

233

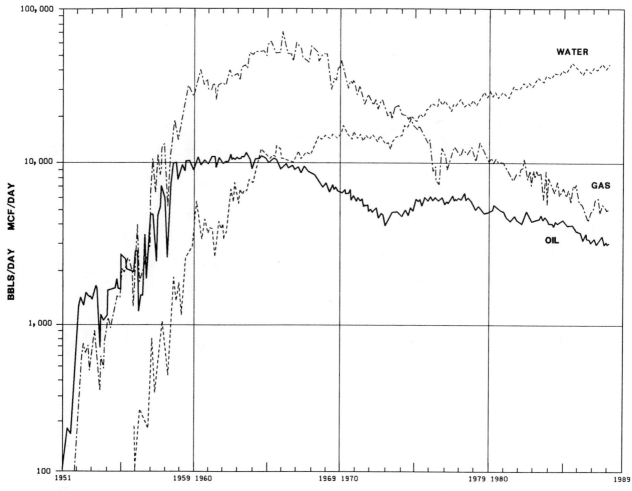

Figure 3. Production history curves for the Red Wash unit.

siltstones, tight, very fine grained sandstones, and limestones in the basal Douglas Creek Member of the Eocene Green River Formation. Production is from a depth of 9300 ft (2840 m) on a northwest-plunging structural nose. The discovery well flowed initially at a rate of 1500 BOPD and then declined to about 100 BOPD. The oil is 30° API with a 90°F (32°C) pour point.

Discovery

The discovery history of Red Wash field was discussed in detail by Chatfield (1972) and is summarized here, with additions.

Standard Oil Company of California (Chevron) explored the Uinta basin in the 1920s. Reconnaissance surface geological work and studies of hydrocarbon potential were conducted initially in 1920 and 1921. Following this early work interest ebbed until 1945, when Standard reentered the basin with renewed interest and began a detailed exploratory program.

Standard's program included a sequence of photogeological mapping, reconnaissance structural and stratigraphic surface work, and reconnaissance gravity and seismic surveys. Photogeologic mapping identified several surface leads, including a west-plunging nose at Red Wash, that became the targets of surface geological mapping. A surface structure map on the Uinta Formation by C. T. Shelley in 1949 (unpublished Chevron map) showed a northwest-plunging structural nose in surface rocks (Figure 6). Gravity interpretation indicated the possibility of a low-relief westward-plunging nose. A seismic survey shot between August and December 1949 confirmed the existence of a west-plunging anticlinal nose without structural closure (Figure 7; compare with Figure 2).

Surface stratigraphic work focused on stratigraphic equivalents of the anticipated Red Wash objective section. The rocks studied crop out at Raven ridge, 6 mi (9.5 km) to the east of the field. Detailed mapping identified rocks and facies relationships that would later prove to be similar to those in the subsurface at Red Wash: a succession of alluvial,

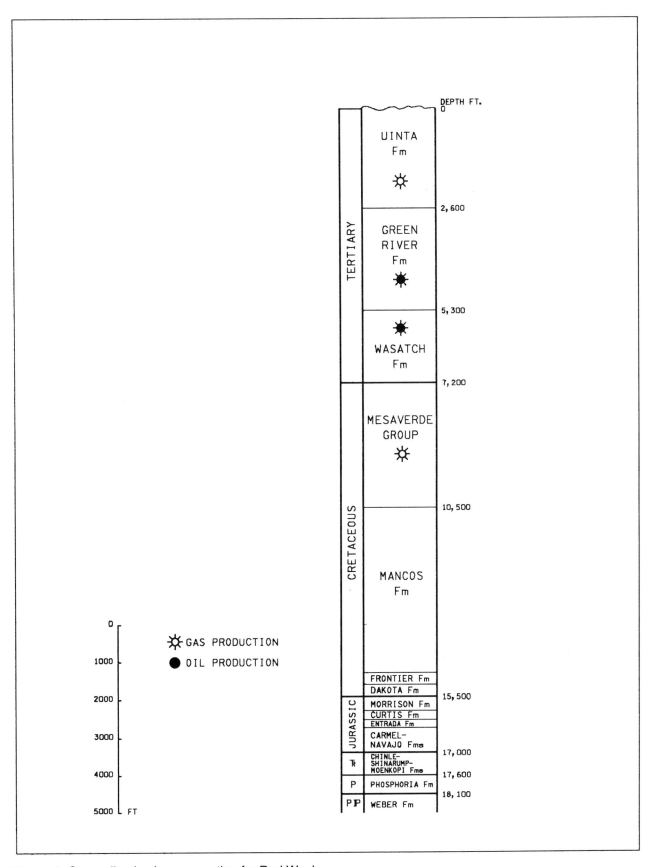

Figure 4. Generalized columnar section for Red Wash
field, East area.

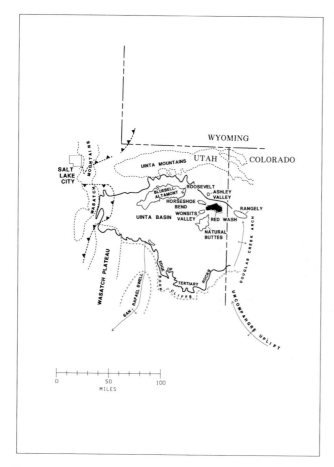

Figure 5. Map of the Uinta basin and nearby areas, showing significant oil and gas fields. (Modified from Brown and Ritzma, 1982.)

marginal lacustrine, and lacustrine rocks, including sandstones, pinching out basinward to the south. The presence of oil staining and tar deposits in the sandstone outcrop was especially encouraging.

The Red Wash prospect matured and was recommended in June 1950 by J. H. (Jim) Kinser and R. B. (Bob) Austin as a potential stratigraphic trap for porous Green River and Wasatch sandstones pinching out updip on a seismically defined structural nose, with an additional objective of fractured Green River shales similar to Roosevelt field.

All the ingredients for a prospect were present: structure, favorable stratigraphy, and direct indications of hydrocarbons. Standard Oil of California Red Wash Unit #1 (Sec. 26, T7S, R23E) was spudded on 13 November 1950. In late November, oil shows were described in Green River sandstones at a depth of 2685 ft (819 m) by geologist Bill Reid. Shows continued with depth, increasing in quality. Gas was recovered on a drill-stem test (DST) of the lower part of the Parachute Creek Member of the Green River Formation on 12 December 1950. DSTs of two additional deeper zones in the Parachute Creek Member gauged gas flows of 4.9 and 8.1 MMCFPD. Drilling continued with shows. Several more DSTs

were run in deeper Parachute Creek intervals but with no significant hydrocarbon recovery. High-quality oil shows were penetrated in a 100 ft (30.5 m) thick zone in the uppermost part of the Douglas Creek Member of the Green River Formation. A DST of the show interval unloaded mud, water, and oil and recovered 480 ft (146 m) of free oil plus 4000 ft (1220 m) of a mixture of oil, gas, and mud. The well was completed in open hole between 5160 ft and 5270 ft (1579 m and 1607 m) in porous sandstones for 339 BOPD with a 2060 GOR in January 1951. By 1963 production from the well had declined to 24 BOPD and 600 MCFGPD. The well was subsequently deepened to 5450 ft (1662 m) in middle and lower Douglas Creek sandstones in April 1963 and recompleted for 239 BOPD and 1.3 MMCFGPD.

Post-Discovery

Red Wash Field

Development drilling followed on a step-out basis. Four separate accumulations were defined, including the West, Central, Main, and East areas (Figure 2). Eocene Uinta Formation gas production was established from RWU 32 (Sec. 32, T7S, R22E) in 1955 at a rate of 1.65 MMCFGPD. A deep test, RWU 212 (Sec. 8, T8S, R24E), established Cretaceous Mesaverde Formation production at a rate of 1.4 MMCFGPD and 20 BCPD in 1966. To date 358 wells have been drilled in the field, of which 254 are currently active.

The field was produced by solution gas drive until 1957. Produced gas was reinjected into gas caps of individual reservoirs from 1957 to 1960 in an attempt to maintain reservoir pressure and to prevent oil migration into the associated gas caps. This program was later discontinued because of severe gas cycling problems.

Several waterflood projects followed. Peripheral waterflooding was initiated in 1960 on a pilot basis in the West area and expanded between 1964 and 1970. Peripheral waterflooding began in the Main area in 1962 and was expanded between 1965 and 1967. Pattern waterflooding started on an irregular spacing in 1971. A 5-spot pilot pattern was initiated in 1979 in the Main area and expanded in 1982.

Present well spacing is on 20 and 40 ac (8.1 and 16.2 ha) in the Main area, 80 ac (32.4 ha) in the Central and West areas, and 320 or 640 ac (129.6 or 259.2 ha) in the East, which is a gas-producing area. In the Main area a 40 ac (16.2 ha) infill program began in 1970 and continued into 1986. Drilling on a pilot 20 ac (8.1 ha) well spacing for future conversion to a 4-spot waterflood commenced in 1984 but was soon discontinued because of a decline in oil prices.

Current reservoir management efforts concentrate on increasing the efficiency of the present waterflood. Detailed geological and engineering mapping of individual reservoirs provides a basis for the selection of effective injector-producer well combinations, for determination of the effectiveness of profile and areal

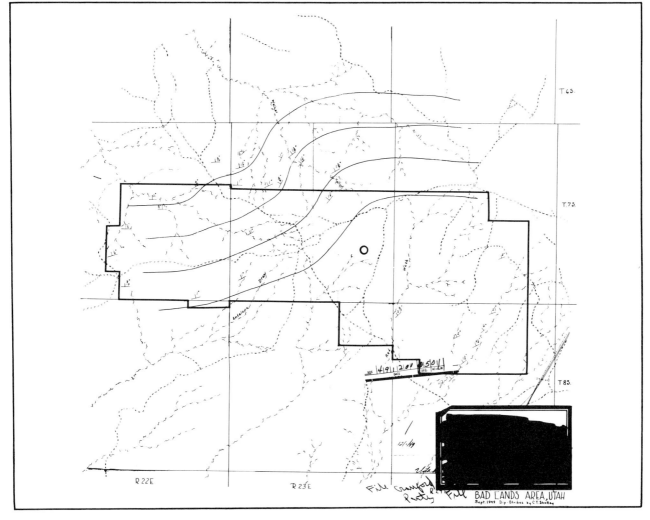

Figure 6. Surface structure map of Bad Lands area, Utah, by C. T. Shelley, unpublished map, The California Company (Chevron), September 1949. The Red Wash unit outline and emphasis on the form lines were added later. The location of the Red Wash discovery well is marked by "o." The map shows a low relief, northwest-plunging structural nose in the Uinta Formation (Eocene) surface rocks in T7S, R23E, which was the prospect lead for more detailed exploratory work.

control of floods, and for identification and solution of problems of reservoir communication in this extremely complex field. An evaluation of CO_2 EOR systems is under way.

Uinta Basin

Following the success of Red Wash field, exploration activity moved westward and resulted in the discovery of many smaller accumulations, including Greater Natural Buttes in 1952 and Wonsits Valley in 1962 (Figure 5). Several periods of renewed activity alternating with industry quiescence followed, but significant discoveries were elusive.

By 1969 Uinta basin discovery activity had shifted to the central and western part of the basin. Several wells were drilled into deeper rocks below shallow accumulations, delineating the giant Bluebell-Altamont trend, which is nearly 50 mi (80 km) in length (Figure 5). Production in that trend is from fractured Green River and Wasatch siltstones and shales in an overpressured regime. More than 200 MMBO and 270 bcf of gas have been produced from over 470 wells on 320 and 640 ac (129.6 and 259.2 ha) spacing.

Activity in the basin since the late 1970s has consisted mostly of infilling and expansion of old fields. No significant discoveries were made during this time.

DISCOVERY METHOD

A review of events leading up to the discovery of Red Wash field emphasizes two points: the success of an exploration program consisting of an integrated and sequential application of basic exploration

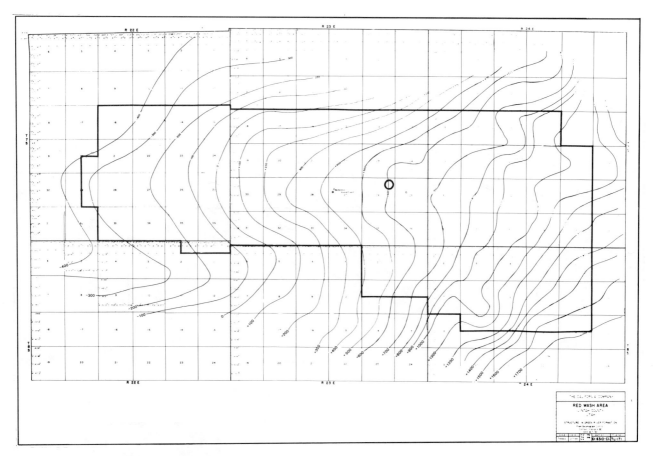

Figure 7. Structure on a marker in Green River Formation from seismograph control, 7 December 1949. The location of the Red Wash discovery well is shown by "o." The map accompanied the recommendation to drill the Red Wash unit and shows the structure interpreted in 1949. Compare this prospect interpretation with the field subsurface structure map shown in Figure 2, which was produced by the addition of over 350 control wells drilled later.

methods, followed by more sophisticated techniques; and the confirmation of the original exploration model by subsequent drilling. The discovery was the result of a lead developed by initial reconnaissance photogeology and surface geology in a relatively unexplored hydrocarbon-rich basin, followed by surface stratigraphic work and geophysical surveys. The original exploration concept of porous sandstones pinching out into lacustrine shales across a structural nose, with no structural closure, has survived 40 years and over 350 wells! In the case of Red Wash, it is doubtful that today's more sophisticated exploration methods could improve on the original discovery technique.

An additional important concept is that of perseverance in prospecting for stratigraphic traps. Several areas in the field have dry holes between local accumulations, updip beyond the pinch-out of a structurally lower but stratigraphically equivalent hydrocarbon zone and downdip in the water leg of a structurally higher hydrocarbon zone. An example is in the vicinity of RWU 169 (cross section A–A', Figure 8). An exploration program for a stratigraphic trap dependent on a single exploratory well at the location of RWU 169 would have produced a dry hole and an overlooked field if not followed up by additional drilling. Failure to recognize the possibility of separate and unique fluid contacts in individual reservoirs in stratigraphic traps could lead to premature abandonment of a well in wet sands above major oil accumulations such as in the Garden Gulch and Parachute Creek intervals of RWU 59 (cross section B–B', Figure 9). Complete penetration of the Green River section is necessary in exploratory (and development) wells in the Red Wash area because of the occurrence of stacked stratigraphic traps in multiple reservoir zones.

STRUCTURE

The Uinta basin is a structural, depositional, and topographic basin, asymmetric in form, with a gentle southern flank and a steeply dipping northern flank, which is probably related to movement along a deep high-angle reverse fault on the flank of the Uinta uplift to the north. The boundary between the basin

238

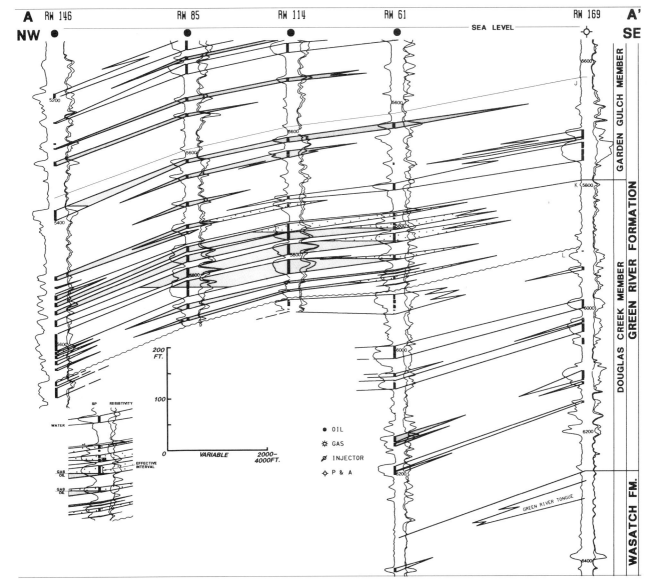

Figure 8. Northwest-southeast dip section across the Red Wash West area. The line of section is shown in Figure 2. The cross section shows stratigraphic traps formed by updip pinch-outs of individual sandstone reservoirs and downdip hydrocarbon-water contacts. Note the vertical noncoincidence of fluid contacts and interlayering of sands with different fluid contents in the stacked reservoirs.

and Uinta Mountains follows the approximate location of the east-trending Archean continental margin and is related to later structural events in Paleozoic and Mesozoic times (Bryant, 1984). Other structural elements bordering the basin include the Wasatch Mountains and Wasatch plateau to the west, the San Rafael swell to the southwest, the Uncompahgre uplift to the southeast, and the Douglas Creek arch to the east (Figure 1).

The Uinta basin is classified as a IIA type basin by Klemme, a "Continental Multicycle Basin on the Craton Margin" (St. John et al., 1984). The depositional and structural history of the basin and its present configuration are a result of basin subsidence concurrent with uplift of the Uinta Mountains to the north. Movements began in Late Cretaceous time and

extended into Late Oligocene time. Over 16,000 ft (4880 m) of Paleocene–Eocene sediments were deposited in the basin (Ritzma, 1972).

Red Wash field is localized on a simple, low-relief anticlinal nose with no mapped structural closure. The anticline plunges to the west into the Uinta basin at 1° to 2° and has 75 ft (23 m) of transverse arching. This very subtle structure is important in localizing the oil accumulation in a significant stratigraphic trap.

Faults have not been positively identified in Red Wash field, although pronounced northwest-southeast local porosity variations suggest some structural grain. Fractures have been described in cores, but their effects on reservoir performance have not been established.

239

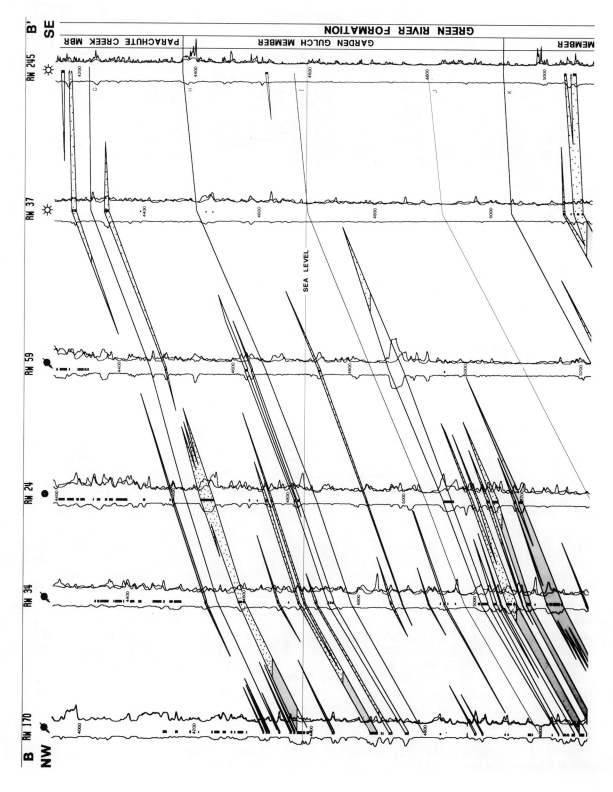

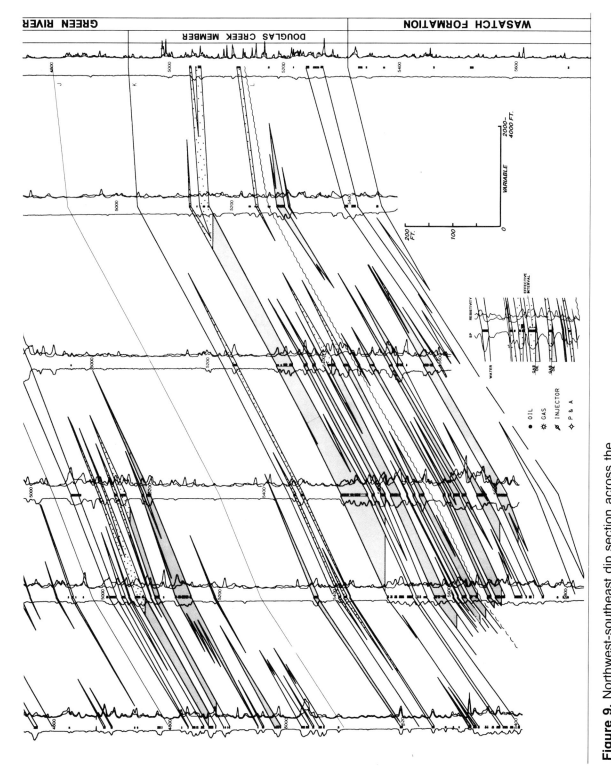

Figure 9. Northwest-southeast dip section across the Red Wash Main area. The line of section is shown in Figure 2.

Structural development of the Red Wash nose occurred after Green River Formation deposition and was associated probably with the rejuvenation of the Douglas Creek arch to the east (Porter, 1963). Chatfield (1972, p. 351) postulates a post-Duchesne River Formation age (Oligocene) for the development of the structure. However, divergence between Uinta Formation surface structure (Figure 6) and Green River Formation subsurface structure (Figure 2) suggests that some movement occurred prior to the Late Eocene deposition of the Uinta. Minor unconformities within the Green River Formation at Red Wash also indicate earlier Eocene movements. Porter (1963, p. 195) suggests that the minor folding which formed the Red Wash nose was produced by compressional forces related to subsidence and deposition in the basin.

STRATIGRAPHY

The most important Uinta basin reservoirs are in rocks of Eocene age. These rocks were deposited in a closed lacustrine system and were subdivided into three major lithofacies by Fouch (1975) (Figure 10). The open lacustrine facies occupies the central or axial portion of the depositional basin and consists of oil shale, marl, dense fine-grained mud-supported limestone, and dark-colored shale. A marginal lacustrine facies encloses the open lacustrine facies and includes sandstone, claystone, shale, micrite, and grain-supported carbonate rocks that represent deposition in fluvial, deltaic, beach, bar, carbonate flat, clastic mudflat, and lagoonal environments. An alluvial facies rims the depositional basin and consists of lenticular beds of conglomerate, sandstone, and varicolored siltstone and shale representing deposition in channel, overbank, deltaic plain, mudflat, and paludal environments. The major facies of the Uinta basin Tertiary are complexly interbedded and intertongue, with abrupt facies changes both laterally and vertically.

Nearly all Red Wash reservoirs are in normally pressured, stratigraphic-structural traps where porous deltaic and bar sandstones of marginal lacustrine origin pinch out into open lacustrine shales across an anticlinal nose. The stratigraphic framework of the field is unique to the basin in that flanking Mesozoic and Paleozoic siliciclastic rocks of the Uinta uplift provided a large volume of mineralogically mature clastic sediments that were deposited in an area of relatively high energy to produce the high quality Green River Formation reservoir sandstones of Red Wash field.

Eocene hydrocarbon accumulations in the Uinta basin have strong overprints of facies control. Marginal and open lacustrine rocks contain more than 1 billion barrels of liquid hydrocarbons. Additional billions of barrels of oil occur in bituminous (tar) sands and oil shales (Fouch, 1975, p. 164, 172).

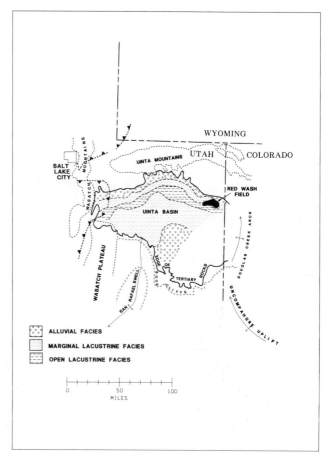

Figure 10. Generalized Uinta basin facies map of a zone near the boundary of the Parachute Creek and Garden Gulch members of the Green River Formation. (After Fouch, 1975, p. 171.)

Additional reservoirs are present in Cretaceous rocks and in the Eocene Uinta Formation. Cretaceous gas is produced in the East area of Red Wash and to the south, at Southman Canyon. Production is obtained from littoral marine sandstones in updip permeability traps across structural noses. Minor amounts of gas have been produced from channelform sandstones of the Uinta Formation at Red Wash and from other fields in the Uinta basin. Those reservoirs will be only briefly treated in this paper.

TRAP

Hydrocarbons in Red Wash field occur in a combination stratigraphic-structural trap. The structural feature localizing the accumulation is an anticlinal nose that plunges to the west at 1° to 2° and has 75 ft (23 m) of north-south arching and no structural closure (Figure 2). Depths to the top of the Douglas Creek Member of the Green River Formation, which is the top of the main producing zone, range from 4400 ft (1340 m) at the eastern end

242

of the field to 5800 ft (1770 m) at the western margin of the field.

The stratigraphic trap is present in multiple stacked sandstones within a vertical interval of over 1500 ft (460 m). The sandstone reservoirs pinch out to the southeast and east across the nose into shales, forming the updip seal. The downdip limits are defined by hydrocarbon-water contacts parallel to structural contours (cross section A-A', Figure 8; cross section B-B', Figure 9 and Figure 11). As many as 78 individual reservoirs are present, each a unique lateral and vertical accumulation. Oil reservoirs occur stratigraphically and vertically below and above water and gas sands. Nonassociated gas/water, associated gas/oil, and oil/water systems are present in individual reservoirs. Vertical seals consist of tight shales and siltstones. Minor unconformities are present within the field but have only minor effects on production. The field is normally pressured.

Precise timing of trap formation is difficult to establish. Chatfield (1972, p. 352) proposed an initial early hydrocarbon accumulation to the north of Red Wash, which took place prior to the formation of the Red Wash nose and prior to development of the present structural configuration of the basin. This early accumulation was in a stratigraphic trap formed in porous sandstones and localized by a northerly decrease in the reservoir capacity of the

rocks as a result of a facies change to the north into floodplain deposits. Following the formation of the Red Wash nose in post-Duchesne River (Oligocene) time, hydrocarbons remigrated to the south into their present position on the structure. An alternate interpretation is that hydrocarbon migration into the sandstone reservoirs on the Red Wash nose took place after the formation of the structure. These concepts are not provable with presently available data.

RESERVOIR

Lithologies and Depositional Environments

The most common Red Wash lithologies are sandstone, siltstone, shale, carbonate mudstone, and carbonate grainstone. Minor lithologies include conglomerate and carbonate packstone. Sandstones, which form nearly all reservoirs, consist of quartz grains with minor amounts of sedimentary rock fragments, ooids, ostracode fragments, and feldspar grains. Mean grain size in the sandstones ranges from very fine to very coarse. The sandstones are generally well sorted but range from poor to very well sorted.

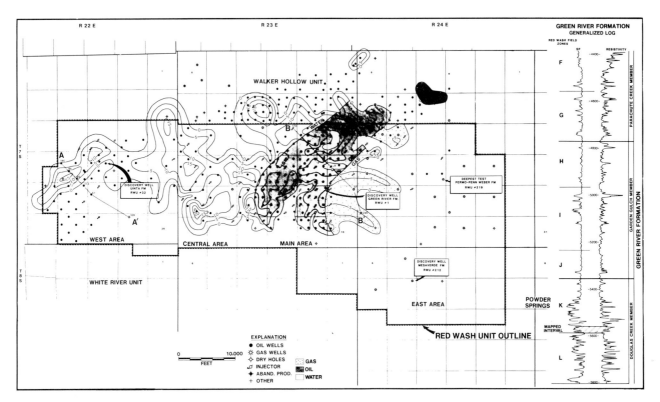

Figure 11. Typical producing interval, upper Douglas Creek Member of the Green River Formation. Net effective sandstone isolith shows the thickness of porous gas, oil, and water effective reservoir. This map is one example of the numerous individual traps at Red Wash that are formed by the updip (southeast and east) pinch-out of effective sandstone and downdip fluvial contacts parallel to structural contours.

243

Carbonate grainstone is secondary in importance to quartz sandstone as a reservoir facies and consists of variable proportions of ooids, ostracodes, carbonate-coated quartz grains, and minor amounts of uncoated quartz grains.

Porosity and permeability in Red Wash reservoir rocks are controlled primarily by the energy level in the depositional environment and to a lesser degree by diagenetic processes. The highest porosity and permeability values occur in the clastic rocks that represent deposition from high-energy unidirectional channel flow or from wave processes localized at the lake shoreline. Porosity and permeability are reduced locally by growth of diagenetic cements in the sandstones. Ferroan calcite is the most pervasive cement, with ferroan dolomite and quartz overgrowths also reducing porosity but to a lesser degree. Petrographic observations indicate that diagenetic clays, which include illite and mixed layer illite/smectite, are rare in reservoir sandstones, but moderately abundant in nonreservoir sandstones (P. E. Flynn, Chevron unpublished report, 1988). Secondary dissolution of grains and cements is locally important, accounting for as much as 25% of the porosity in some reservoir sandstones.

Stratigraphy and Facies

Two depositional facies (after Fouch, 1975, and Ryder et al., 1976) are represented by the lower Green River Formation in Red Wash field: marginal lacustrine and open lacustrine. Interpretations of depositional environment are based on recent Chevron studies of cores from Red Wash and the surrounding area (Castle, 1988, in press; Thompson, 1988). Earlier studies of Red Wash cores were conducted by Koesoemadinata (1970) and by Webb (1978).

Marginal Lacustrine Facies

Reservoir sandstones and minor reservoir carbonates occur in the marginal lacustrine facies and represent deposition in fluvial-deltaic, mudflat-lagoon, and barrier-beach environments (Figure 12).

The fluvial-deltaic system includes siliciclastic sediments that were transported from the north toward the Red Wash area through a network of channels in floodplain clays and silts. In the Red Wash area, channels were predominantly small, possibly braided or of low-sinuosity and meandering in form and may have been ephemeral. Fluvial deposits are most common in the northern part of the Red Wash Main area, and become less abundant to the west, south, and east. Channel sandstones observed in cores typically fine upward from medium to very coarse grained sandstone at the base to very fine grained sandstone interbedded with channel-fill or overbank siltstones and shales at the top of the sequence (Figures 13A and 14A). The channel sandstones are usually less than 10 ft (3 m) in thickness and the basal contact is generally very sharp and locally scoured. Reservoir quality is highly variable both vertically and laterally because of channel geometry and very localized carbonate cementation. Porosity values to 21% and permeability as high as 500 md have been measured in the channel sandstones.

Along the shoreline of Lake Uinta in the Red Wash area, small delta lobes prograded into the lacustrine shallows at the mouths of fluvial channels. The resulting depositional sequence in the Main area coarsens upward from silty shale into very fine to medium-grained sandstone and is commonly overlain by fluvial-channel deposits (Figure 13A). Porosity ranges between 10% and 15% with permeability from less than 1 md to 45 md.

Some of the coarsening-upward sequences are capped by 5 to 10 ft (1.5 to 3 m) thick carbonate grainstone beds rather than channel sandstones in the Main area of Red Wash. The carbonate grainstones, which consist of mostly ooids and ostracode fragments, represent deposition during a period of wave reworking of the shoreline, probably during a lacustrine transgression. Minor carbonate shoals and minor clastic bars and beaches that developed along the shoreline between channel mouths are represented by thin carbonate grainstones and quartz sandstones in the Main area of Red Wash.

Carbonate flats and clastic mudflats developed in lake-margin areas that were protected from waves and isolated from coarse-grained clastic input (Figure 13B). Those environments are represented, respectively, by tight calcareous and dolomitic mudstones and by silty shales, which commonly show mudcracks and root traces.

Laterally continuous, lacustrine barrier-beach sandstone complexes were deposited in the upper part of the Douglas Creek Member in the West area (Castle, 1988, in press). Although the complexes are a product of an overall lower energy than is represented by shallow marine barrier beaches, the deposits show similarities in vertical sequence related to upward increase in wave energy. The lacustrine barrier-beach sequences, which range in thickness from a few feet to 35 ft (11 m), coarsen upward from shallow lacustrine shale, to crossbedded, very fine to fine-grained sandstone (Figure 13C). The sequence of sedimentary structures and variation in grain size are a product of an upward increase in energy level. Ooids and carbonate-coated quartz grains are common in the upper part of the sequence. Effective reservoir occurs in the upper shoreface and swash/backwash zones of the barrier-beach sequence, with porosity values typically between 10% and 15% and permeability from 10 md to 150 md (Figure 14B). Patchy carbonate cement locally reduces porosity and permeability in the sandstones. The upper foot of the sandstones is commonly oolitic and extensively cemented by carbonate. The lower shoreface sandstones form, at best, only marginal reservoirs. Although porosity may be as high as 13%, permeability is low, generally less than 4 md, due to abundant interlaminations

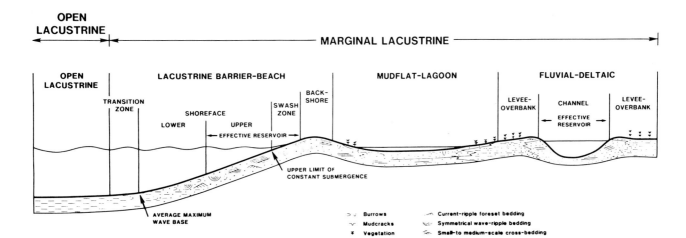

OPEN
LACUSTRINE

MARGINAL LACUSTRINE

Figure 12. Schematic diagram of a shoreline profile interpreted from core studies of the lower Green River Formation, Red Wash field. In general, the offshore direction is to the southwest in the area of Red Wash field. Alluvial facies occur to the north of Red Wash.

Other depositional environments interpreted from cores but not illustrated on the profile include shallow water carbonate shoals, carbonate flats, and prograding delta lobes. The diagram is not to scale. (Simplified from Castle, in press.)

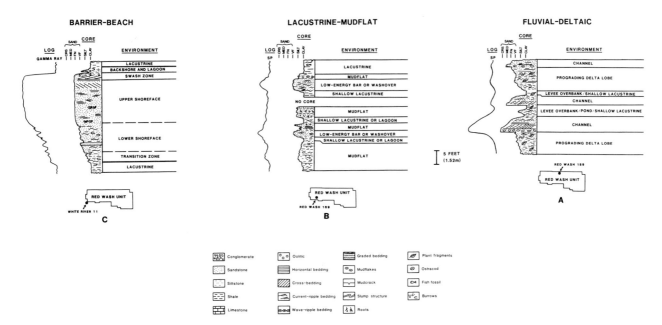

Figure 13. Typical sequences, marginal lacustrine facies, described and interpreted from cores of the lower Green River Formation, Red Wash field. Depositional environments are interpreted from grain size, primary structures, and vertical facies sequences. Effective reservoir occurs most commonly in the upper

shoreface-swash zone of barrier-beach deposits and in fluvial-deltaic channels. The three sequences shown are considered part of the marginal lacustrine facies of Fouch (1975) and Ryder et al. (1976). Sequences based on core descriptions from J. W. Castle, Chevron unpublished reports.

of siltstone and shale (Figure 14C, D). The sands deposited in the Red Wash barrier-beach complexes were probably transported southward by longshore currents and subsequently reworked by wave activity. A coarsening-upward sequence was produced as the shoreline prograded (Figure 12).

Open Lacustrine Facies

The open lacustrine facies contains rocks deposited in both shallow-nearshore and offshore lacustrine environments. Offshore lacustrine rocks include evenly laminated, organic-rich, medium- to dark-gray shales that are interpreted as representing very quiet

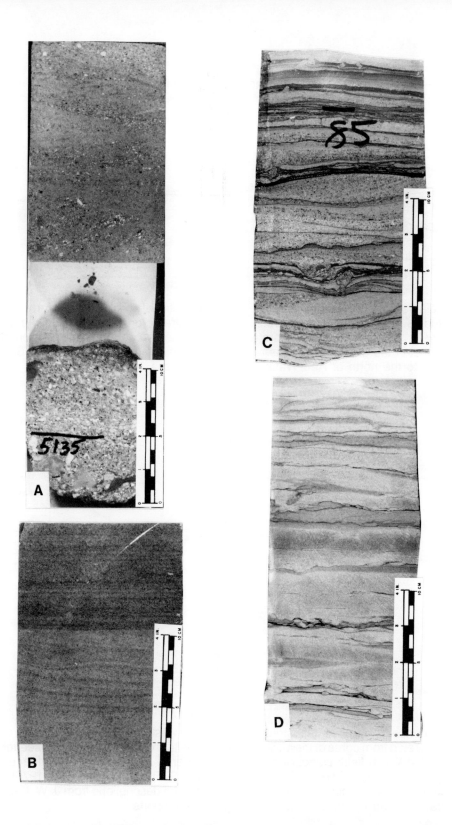

Figure 14. Core photographs of Red Wash sandstones. (A) Channel. Thin channel sandstone with basal granule-pebble conglomerate. 16% to 17% ϕ, 550 md to 660 md k. RWU 301, 5134 to 5136 ft (1565.8 to 1566.5 m) (middle Garden Gulch Member). (B) Upper shoreface/swash zone sandstone. Sandstone, very fine grained, calcareous, spotty oil stain and yellow fluorescence. 12% ϕ, 72 md k. RWU 216, 5802 ft (1769.6 m) (upper Douglas Creek Member). (C) Lower shoreface sandstone. Sandstone, very fine grained, with laminations of fine sandstone, siltstone, and gray shale, locally bioturbated, spotty oil stain. 5% ϕ, 0 md k. RWU 216, 5785 ft (1764.4 m) (upper Douglas Creek Member). (D) Lower shoreface sandstone. Sandstone, very fine grained, with irregular laminations of sandstone and shale. No stain nor fluorescence. 9% ϕ, 3 md k. RWU 218, 5770.5 ft (1760.0 m) (upper Douglas Creek Member).

246

water deposition. The offshore lacustrine shales are potential source rocks and become thicker and more abundant to the west, south, and east of Red Wash field in the basinward direction. Shallow and nearshore lacustrine rocks include light- to medium-gray and brown shales containing common siltstone laminae and lenses that are gradational with very fine grained sandstone. Deposition associated with algal activity is marked by thin, brown, dolomitic shale laminae in some lacustrine shales. Rocks of the open lacustrine facies form poor reservoirs.

Reservoir Geometry

The Main area of Red Wash field is typified by very heterogeneous and laterally discontinuous reservoir sandstones deposited in fluvial-deltaic and lacustrine-shoreline environments. Multiple, interbedded, thin sandstone and limestone reservoirs are typical of this area. The fluvial-channel sandstones are thin, relatively narrow, and poorly connected. Lacustrine shoreline rocks form laterally discontinuous but high quality reservoirs and are a product of lateral variations in clastic input to the lake margin and lateral variability in wave and current energy along the lake shoreline. Abrupt vertical lithologic changes were probably produced in part by fluctuations of lake level along a low-relief shoreline.

In contrast to the very heterogeneous deposits of the Main area, reservoirs in the West area of Red Wash are thicker (up to 35 ft or 10.6 m) and more laterally continuous but of slightly poorer quality. Deposition in barrier-beach complexes produced continuous sand bodies that are 10 mi (16 km) long and 3 mi (5 km) wide and extend from the West area of Red Wash into Wonsits Valley field to the southwest (Castle, 1988, in press). Organic-rich, potential source-rock shales were deposited in juxtaposition with reservoir sandstones as a result of the proximity of the open-lacustrine environment to the barrier-beach environment. Organic-geochemical analysis indicates that the shales are rich in type I kerogen (alginite). Subsequent lacustrine transgression over the barrier-beach sands provided a hydrocarbon seal.

Fluid Flow and Pressure Communication

Pressure communication and fluid-flow characteristics differ between the barrier-beach sandstones in West Red Wash and the fluvial-deltaic-shoreline sandstones in the Main area. Main area sandstones typically have very complex fluid drainage patterns because of reservoir discontinuity and poor pressure communication. Fluid movement through fluvial channels in the Main area follows very tortuous pathways that are difficult to predict. Diagenetic barriers, in addition to stratigraphic variability, may have a major effect on fluid movement in channel sandstones.

In the West area, fluid movement through the barrier-beach sandstone bodies is generally more even and continuous, with appropriate production and injection patterns and rates. Laterally discontinuous permeability barriers, such as thin shales and cemented zones within the major barrier-beach deposits, probably affect fluid movement only locally. Pressure communication between wells is generally good in the barrier-beach sandstones. Because efficient well spacing is a function of the reservoir continuity, wells in the West area of Red Wash have been drilled at a wider spacing (80 ac or 32.4 ha) than wells in the Main area (40 ac or 16.2 ha). In general, the stratigraphic differences between the two areas result in a lower estimated recovery factor in the Main area than in the West area.

Reservoir and Fluid Characteristics

Red Wash oil is an asphaltic, intermediate-paraffinic crude with typically 10.5% paraffin and consequently a high pour point of between 80°F (27°C) and 95°F (35°C) (Figure 15). The oil is sweet, with 0.13% sulfur and a gravity between 28° and 32° API. Initial solution GOR was approximately 292 SCF/STB. The oil had an original viscosity of 6 to 8 cp and contained 17% gas oil distillate.

Average initial pressure in Red Wash field was 1925 psi (13,270 kPa), with a pressure gradient of 0.4 psi/ft (9.04 kPa/m), and has declined to 1200 psi (8274 kPa). Reservoir temperature is 149°F at 5260 ft (65°C at 1600 m). Formation volume factor at original reservoir pressure was 1.1 RB/STB.

The composition of Red Wash formation waters is highly variable because of initial variations and injection of combinations of river and produced water. The resistivities of original Wasatch and lower Douglas Creek water were between 0.5 and 2.0 ohm-m, increasing to the north and east. The resistivities of upper Douglas Creek and lower Garden Gulch waters were between 0.5 and 3.0 ohm-m, increasing to the north, east, and west. Upper Garden Gulch water resistivity ranged from 1.0 to 2.5 ohm-m, also increasing to the north, east, and west. All resistivities were measured at 68°F (20°C) and are generally at a minimum on the crest of the Red Wash nose. Original connate and bulk volume water saturation averaged 25%.

Formation Evaluation

Formation evaluation at Red Wash spans over 37 years and consequently has been subjected to several generations of approaches. Formation evaluation techniques attempt to determine basic reservoir characteristics including definition of effective reservoir, fluid content, and deliverability. Parameters for defining effective reservoir are listed in Table 1.

Drill-stem testing in Red Wash is one of the more effective evaluation tools when used in conjunction

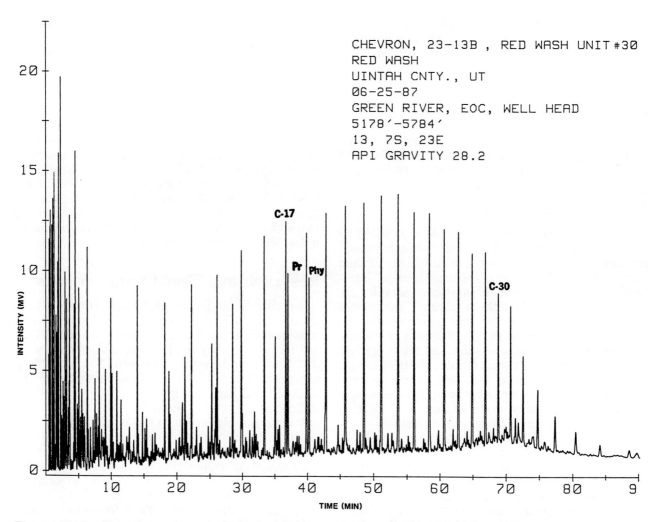

CHEVRON, 23-13B , RED WASH UNIT #30
RED WASH
UINTAH CNTY., UT
06-25-87
GREEN RIVER, EOC, WELL HEAD
5178'-5784'
13, 7S, 23E
API GRAVITY 28.2

Figure 15. Capillary chromatogram of a typical oil from the Garden Gulch and Douglas Creek members of the Green River Formation in the Main area of the Red Wash unit. Note the high paraffin content of this crude oil from lacustrine source beds. API gravity 28.2°, pour point 95°F (35°C).

with nitrate tracer techniques for qualifying and quantifying mud filtrate in fluid recoveries. Methods used include bottom-hole and straddle tests, both with conventional and inflatable packers, and either drill pipe-collar or sidewall anchors, and conventional or multiflow test periods. These techniques have proved successful in identifying fluid content, reservoir volume and limits, amount of previous drainage, and deliverability of individual reservoirs.

The development of an adequate rock database early in field development is critical in complex reservoirs such as Red Wash. The solution to a number of Red Wash reservoir problems has been based to a great extent on the ability to retrieve rock samples from core archives when needed. Cores have been used for calibration of wireline logs, reservoir characterization, quantification of reservoir parameters, show evaluation, environmental interpretation, evaluation of secondary and tertiary recovery techniques, and determination of directional permeability. Coring programs have included conventional

full diameter, sidewall percussion, sidewall slicing, and sidewall rotary techniques.

Evaluation after drilling in Red Wash consists of the analysis of open-hole wireline-log suites and through-casing testing supplemented with cased hole wireline-logs. Open-hole wireline-log suites currently run include spontaneous potential (SP)-resistivity, micrologs, and gamma ray-neutron-LDT combinations. The SP log is valuable for definition and correlation of effective section if produced water is not used as a drilling mud make-up water. Micrologs have proved useful in the definition of effective section, especially in thin beds, but are unreliable in quantitative determination of porosity values. Gamma ray-neutron-LDT logs are used to derive lithology, interpret rock cement type, and provide accurate porosity values, especially when calibrated by core analysis data.

The derivation of precise water-saturation values from resistivity-porosity log combinations is a problem in Red Wash for a number of reasons.

Table 1. Parameters for effective reservoirs.

Core	$\phi > 10\%$	Oil/water: k > 10 md (air) (West Area)
	$\phi > 10\%$	Oil/water: k > 40 md (air) (Main Area)
		Gas: k > 1 md (air)
Acoustic log	$\phi > 12\%$	Vm = 19,500
Microlog	Positive microlog separation and mud cake; Quantitative ϕ is unreliable; net effective = gross X (0.87 to 1.0)	
Neutron-Density	$\phi > 10\%$	
SP	"2/3" rule	

Quantitative porosity values are difficult to obtain from older wireline logs. Accurate Rt values are difficult to derive because of thin beds and the presence of shale both in laminations and in thin beds. Variations in lithology, and consequently basic log parameters such as formation factor and a, m, and n, create saturation exponent difficulties in calculating valid Archie-type water-saturation values. Adding to all of these problems are uncertainties of obtaining valid formation water resistivities.

Wireline formation testers, especially when used in combination with modern high-precision pressure sensors, have proved valuable in obtaining the current pressure of individual reservoirs and in determining their relative status, such as at original (undrained) pressure, overpressured (needing a take point), or depleted (needing pressure support). Plots of pressure gradients aid in distinguishing fluid content and contacts. Results of testing for fluids have met with little success owing to generally low permeability resulting in the recovery of only small volumes of problematical mixtures of fluids.

Formation evaluation through casing involves cased-hole logging programs combined with well testing. Of the multitude of cased-hole logging tools evaluated over the years, only the gamma spectrometry log shows promise in distinguishing fluid content in oil-water reservoir systems. The determination of accurate quantitative saturation values is typically very difficult in gas reservoirs. Discrete well tests of individual reservoirs are vital to establish fluid content and reservoir continuity but, owing to high costs, are increasingly difficult to obtain. Problems with cement-bond quality are common and greatly complicate interpretation of reservoir fluid content. Extensive mud filtrate invasion is pervasive, necessitating long period swab tests and nitrate monitoring.

One of the more basic and valuable techniques for predicting and defining fluid content in Red Wash is the precise correlation and geological mapping of individual reservoirs, integrated with documentation of offset production and testing data and relative structural position.

Development Considerations

Well spacing is controlled by individual well, pattern, and field economics, configuration and size of drainage area, potential EOR support, and individual reservoir heterogeneity. Decisions on locating take points and injectors must consider the necessity of running dual completion-injector strings because optimum take wells for one reservoir are optimum injection wells for other reservoirs. Oil migration into associated gas caps can be a problem if sand continuity is not accurately mapped and pressure maintained in the gas cap to offset produced oil voidage. Although dispersed clays are generally not a significant problem, some formation damage may be induced by injecting untreated exotic waters during waterflooding operations.

Recovery efficiency is variable, depending on the method used and area of the field for which calculated. Average primary recovery of Green River Formation oil is estimated to be 7% of OOIP. Average secondary recovery is estimated to also average 7% of OOIP.

HYDROCARBON SOURCE

Organic geochemical studies (Tissot et al., 1978; Chevron unpublished data) indicate that the source for most hydrocarbons in Red Wash was open lacustrine shales of the lower Green River Formation. That interpretation is consistent with concepts of sources for Uinta basin oils dating back to Felts (1954) and even earlier, unpublished Chevron reports. Microscopic and Rock Eval analyses indicate that the source material for most of the hydrocarbons is type I kerogen (S. Nelson and S. R. Jacobson, Chevron unpublished reports, 1987, 1988).

Microscopically, the composition of the organic material is related to lithofacies and depositional environments as interpreted from core studies (Castle, in press). In general, shales interpreted as offshore lacustrine contain a large proportion of alginite relative to vitrinite and inertinite. In contrast, floodplain shales, which are common in northeastern Red Wash field, contain a larger proportion of vitrinite and inertinite relative to alginite. Alginite is derived from algal material produced primarily within the lacustrine depositional environment. The vitrinite and inertinite were derived from terrestrial sources, probably within and near the site of deposition.

In the Red Wash area Chevron studies show that potential source beds containing type I kerogen are richer and more abundant to the west and southwest, toward the lake depocenter. The ratio of alginite to vitrinite within individual continuous shale beds increases gradually in that direction. An increase in total organic carbon (TOC) content that generally parallels the increasing alginite proportion suggests that the change in alginite content is caused by increased algal production to the west and southwest or, conversely, by increased oxidation of algal material to the northeast. TOC values range between 1% and 6.5%, averaging 2.5%.

The maximum burial depth of the lower Green River Formation in Red Wash field may have been a few thousand feet deeper than the present depth of 4000 to 6000 ft (1220 to 1830 m), according to previous studies (Tissot et al., 1978; Sweeney et al., 1987). Results of recent organic geochemical analyses by Chevron indicate that the lower Green River shales in Red Wash field have been subjected to paleotemperatures almost high enough to reach the onset of oil generation, which is consistent with results reported by Tissot et al. (1978). This conclusion is supported by maturation data including T_{max} from Rock Eval, thermal alteration index (TAI), and vitrinite reflectance (S. R. Jacobson, S. N. Nelson, and R. C. Haack, Chevron unpublished data and reports, 1987, 1988). Average T_{max} values from Rock Eval analyses of samples from 28 wells at depths between 5200 and 5900 ft (1586 and 1800 m) in the general area of Red Wash field range from approximately 425°F to 450°F (218°C to 232°C), and average 435°F (224°C). TAI and vitrinite reflectance values from eight samples at depths of between 5240 and 5480 ft (1598 and 1671 m) in the Red Wash main area average 2.5 and 0.47, respectively, indicating paleotemperatures almost high enough to reach the onset of oil generation.

In summary, results from the recent Chevron geochemical and sedimentological studies indicate that source rocks for most of the oil in Red Wash field are probably open lacustrine shales stratigraphically equivalent to similar shales in Red Wash field. The source beds were probably buried somewhat deeper than the maximum burial depth of their stratigraphic equivalents in Red Wash field. Following oil generation, the oil migrated updip to the east and northeast from the more deeply buried, open lacustrine rocks.

EXPLORATION CONCEPTS

Large Tertiary age fields in the Uinta basin fall into two categories: fracture accumulations (Bluebell-Altamont and Roosevelt) and stratigraphic-structural traps (Red Wash–Walker Hollow). All are in stratigraphic fairways in marginal lacustrine facies and are between and interbedded with alluvial and open lacustrine facies.

Classical concepts of regional plays are absent. Neither significant intergranular porosity nor structural closure is necessary for major accumulations. Fracture reservoirs are prolific producers because of occurrence in an overpressured regime, with pressure gradients of over 0.8 psi/ft (18.1 kPa/m) and of the natural propping of fractures by crystal growth that prevent collapse with production. Stratigraphic traps are in sandstone porosity pinchouts on low-relief structural features without structural closure.

Exploration activity was stimulated by extensive hydrocarbon occurrences in surface exposures that overwhelmed the conventional negative view of nonmarine reservoir and source rocks and of traps lacking structural closure. Oil shales, gilsonite and other solid hydrocarbons, oil seeps, tar sands, and "fossil" oil fields abound in the basin. The secrets to success, as always, are optimism and a sequential application of basic geological concepts, followed by, most important, drilling and reservoir evaluation.

As stated earlier, it is difficult to imagine that modern geological techniques would be more successful in finding a Red Wash field today. An effective utilization of basic photogeologic and surface structural mapping, integrated with surface stratigraphic studies, and supported by geophysical information, produced a drillable prospect and a discovery.

The importance of perseverance in exploring for stratigraphic traps is graphically illustrated at Red Wash. As detailed earlier in this paper, dry holes with porous wet sandstones are present between and both updip and downdip from hydrocarbon accumulations. Failure to adequately explore potential stratigraphic traps could lead to the abandonment of a significant potential accumulation on the basis of a single, unfortunately located dry hole.

ACKNOWLEDGMENTS

Chevron U.S.A. Inc. permitted and aided the publication of this paper. Numerous unpublished Chevron reports and geologic data formed the framework of this publication. Exxon furnished Walker Hollow engineering and geologic data. V. A.

Baginski of Chevron provided the engineering and reservoir information from Red Wash Unit. D. M. Thompson of Chevron furnished geological information from work in progress. Core photographs and petrographic descriptions of reservoir rocks were provided by P. E. Flynn of Chevron. Source rock and geochemical data were obtained from S. N. Nelson and S. R. Jacobson of Chevron.

REFERENCES

Brown, K. W., and H. R. Ritzma, 1982, Oil and gas fields and pipelines of Utah: Utah Department of Natural Resources and Energy, Utah Geological and Mineralogical Survey, Map 61.

Bradley, W. H., 1931, Origin and microfossils of the oil shale of the Green River Formation of Colorado and Utah: USGS Professional Paper 168, 58 p.

Bryant, B. F., 1984, Structural ancestry of the Uinta Mountains, *in* A. E. Aigen, ed., Uinta basin geologic resources: Utah Geological Association, Publication 11, p. 115–120.

Castle, J. W., 1988, Sedimentological model for lacustrine shoreline deposition, lower Green River Formation (Eocene), northeastern Uinta basin, Utah (abs.): American Association of Petroleum Geologists Bulletin, v. 72, p. 170.

Castle, J. W., in press, Sedimentation in Eocene Lake Uinta (lower part of Green River Formation), northeastern Uinta basin, Utah, *in* B. J. Katz, ed., Lacustrine basin exploration: case studies and modern analogues: American Association of Petroleum Geologists Memoir.

Chatfield, J., 1965, Petroleum geology of the greater Red Wash area, Uintah County, Utah: Mountain Geologist, v. 2, n. 3, p. 115–121.

Chatfield, J., 1972, Case history of Red Wash field, Uintah County, Utah, *in* R. E. King, ed., Stratigraphic oil and gas fields: classification, exploration methods, and case histories: American Association of Petroleum Geologists Memoir 16, p. 342–353.

Felts, W. M., 1954, Occurrence of oil and gas and its relation to possible source beds in continental Tertiary of Intermountain region: American Association of Petroleum Geologists Bulletin, v. 38, p. 1661–1670.

Fouch, T. D., 1975, Lithofacies and related hydrocarbon accumulations in Tertiary strata of the western and central Uinta basin, Utah, *in* D. W. Bolyard, ed., Symposium on deep drilling frontiers in the central Rocky Mountains: Rocky Mountain Association of Geologists Special Publication, p. 163–173.

Koesoemadinata, R. P., 1970, Stratigraphy and petroleum occurrence, Green River Formation, Red Wash field, Utah: Colorado School of Mines Quarterly, v. 65, p. 1–77.

Osmund, J. C., 1968, Natural gas in Uinta basin, Utah: American Association of Petroleum Geologists Memoir 9, v. 1, pt. 1, p. 174–198.

Picard, M. D., 1957, Red Wash-Walker Hollow field, stratigraphic trap, eastern Uinta basin, Utah: American Association of Petroleum Geologists Bulletin, v. 41, n. 5, p. 923–936.

Porter, L., Jr., 1963, Stratigraphy and oil possibilities of the Green River Formation in the Uinta basin, Utah, *in* Oil and gas possibilities of Utah, reevaluated: Utah Geological and Mineralogical Survey Bulletin, v. 54, p. 193–198.

Reed, W. E., and W. Henderson, 1972, Proposed stratigraphic controls on the composition of crude oils reservoired in the Green River Formation, Uinta basin, Utah, *in* Advances in geochemistry: Oxford, Pergamon Press, p. 499–515.

Ritzma, H. R., 1972, The Uinta basin, *in* W. W. Mallory, ed., Geologic atlas of the Rocky Mountain region: Rocky Mountain Association of Geologists, p. 276–278.

Ryder, R. T., T. D. Fouch, and J. H. Elison, 1976, Early Tertiary sedimentation in the western Uinta basin, Utah: Geological Society of America Bulletin, v. 87, p. 496–512.

St. John, B., A. W. Bally, and H. D. Klemme, 1984, Sedimentary provinces of the world-hydrocarbon productive and nonproductive: American Association of Petroleum Geologists Map Series, 35 p.

Sweeney, J. J., A. K. Burnham, and R. L. Braun, 1987, A model of hydrocarbon generation from type I kerogen: application to Uinta basin, Utah: American Association of Petroleum Geologists Bulletin, v. 71, p. 967–985.

Thompson, D. M., 1988, Determining reservoir quality, distribution, and continuity in complex lacustrine margin sandstones, Red Wash field (Main Area), Uintah County, Utah (abs.): American Association of Petroleum Geologists Bulletin, v. 72, p. 253.

Tissot, B., G. Deroo, and A. Hood, 1978, Geochemical study of the Uinta basin: formation of petroleum from the Green River Formation: Geochemica et Cosmochimica Acta, v. 42, p. 1469–1485.

Webb, M. G., 1978, Reservoir description, K_f sandstone, Red Wash field, Utah: Society of Petroleum Engineers, Paper 7046, p. 97–101.

SUGGESTED READING

Chatfield, J., 1972, Case history of Red Wash field, Uintah County, Utah, *in* R. E. King, ed., Stratigraphic oil and gas fields: classification, exploration methods, and case histories: American Association of Petroleum Geologists Memoir 16, p. 342–353. Excellent summary of the discovery of Red Wash Field.

Clem, K., 1985, Oil and gas production summary of the Uinta basin, *in* M. D. Picard, ed., Geology and energy resources, Uinta basin of Utah: Utah Geological Association Publication, p. 159–167.

Fouch, T. D., 1975, Lithofacies and related hydrocarbon accumulations in Tertiary strata of the western and central Uinta basin, Utah, *in* D. W. Bolyard, ed., Symposium on deep drilling frontiers in the central Rocky Mountains: Rocky Mountain Association of Geologists Special Publication, p. 163–173. Good summary of Uinta Basin tertiary stratigraphy.

Ryder, R. T., T. D. Fouch, and J. H. Elison, 1976, Early Tertiary sedimentation in the western Uinta basin, Utah: Geological Society of America Bulletin, v. 87, p. 496–512. Benchmark paper on Uinta basin Tertiary stratigraphy.

Sweeney, J. J., A. K. Burnham, and R. L. Braun, 1987, A model of hydrocarbon generation from type I kerogen: application to Uinta basin, Utah: American Association of Petroleum Geologists Bulletin, v. 71, n. 8, p. 967–985. Most recent paper on Uinta basin hydrocarbon generation.

Appendix 1. Field Description

Field name .... *Red Wash field (Red Wash and Walker Hollow units)*

Ultimate recoverable reserves .... *106 MMBO; 302 BCFG*

Field location:

    Country .... *U.S.A.*

    State .... *Utah*

    Basin/Province .... *Uinta basin*

Field discovery:

    Year first pay discovered .... *Eocene Green River Formation 1951*

    Year second pay discovered .... *Eocene Uinta Formation 1955*

    Third pay .... *Cretaceous Mesaverde Formation 1966*

Discovery well name and general location:

    First pay .... *Red Wash Unit #1 NE NE Sec. 26, T7S, R23E, Uintah County, Utah*

    Second pay .... *Red Wash Unit #32 SW NE Sec. 22, T7S, R22E, Uintah County, Utah*

    Third pay .... *Red Wash Unit #212 NE NE Sec. 8, T8S, R24E, Uintah County, Utah*

Discovery well operator .... *California Oil Co. (Chevron)*

    Second pay .... *California Oil Co. (Chevron)*

    Third pay .... *CalOil (Chevron)*

IP in barrels per day and/or cubic feet or cubic meters per day:

    First pay .... *F 339 BOPD, 0.1% water, ⅛–¼″ ck, GOR 2060, FTP 600 psi (4137 kPa), 32° API*

    Second pay .... *F 1.65 MMCFGPD*

    Third pay .... *F 1.4 MMCFGPD, 20 BCPD, 21 BWPD*

All other zones with shows of oil and gas in the field:

Age	Formation	Type of Show
Cretaceous	*Mancos*	*Oil on pits, mud gas show*
Cretaceous	*Frontier*	*Perfs tested with 2–3 ft flare*
Permian–Pennsylvanian	*Weber*	*Oil stain, mud gas show*

Geologic concept leading to discovery and method or methods used to delineate prospect, e.g., surface geology, subsurface geology, seeps, magnetic data, gravity data, seismic data, seismic refraction, nontechnical:

Sequential and integrated photogeology, surface structure, and stratigraphic work, and gravity and seismic surveys.

Structure:

    Province/basin type .... *Bally 22, Klemme IIA*

    Tectonic history

Formation of the Uinta basin commenced in Late Cretaceous time with a shift from earlier north-south tectonic and sedimentary patterns to an east-west orientation, dominated by the Uinta uplift to the north. Subsidence and deposition through Eocene time produced a strongly asymmetric basin with a highly complex, faulted north flank and a gentle south flank. Precise dating of movements forming the Red Wash nose is difficult but is of possibly post-Eocene Tertiary age.

    Regional structure

Red Wash is on the northeast flank of the Uinta basin, an asymmetric structural, depositional, and topographic basin with a steep north flank and gentle south flank, between the Wasatch uplift on the west, San Rafael swell and Uncompahgre uplift to the south, Douglas Creek arch to the east, and Uinta Mountain uplift to the north.

    Local structure

Structural nose, plunging to the west at 1° to 2° with 75 ft (23 m) of arching in a north-south direction. No apparent structural closure.

RED WASH

Trap:

Trap type(s)

Stratigraphic-structural trap formed by multiple sandstone pinch-outs updip and hydrocarbon-water contacts parallel to structural contours downdip.

Basin stratigraphy (major stratigraphic intervals from surface to deepest penetration in field):

Chronostratigraphy	Formation	Depth to Top in ft (m)
Tertiary	Uinta	Surface
	Green River	2600 (795)
	Wasatch	5300 (1615)
Cretaceous	Mesaverde	7200 (2195)
	Mancos	10,500 (3200)
	Frontier	14,900 (4545)
	Dakota	15,200 (4635)
Jurassic	Morrison	15,500 (4725)
	Curtis	15,900 (4850)
	Entrada	16,100 (4910)
	Carmel	16,300 (4970)
	Navajo	16,400 (5000)
Triassic	Chinle	17,000 (5185)
	Shinarump	17,100 (5215)
	Moenkopi	17,150 (5230)
Permian	Phosphoria	17,600 (5370)
Permian-Pennsylvanian	Weber	18,100 (5520)

Reservoir characteristics:

Number of reservoirs 3

Formations .... Uinta, Green River, Mesaverde

Ages .... Uinta and Green River, Eocene; Mesaverde, Cretaceous

Depths to tops of reservoirs .... Uinta, surface; Green River, 2600 ft (795 m); Mesaverde, 7200 ft (2195 m)

Gross thickness (top to bottom of producing interval) .... Uinta, 9 ft (2.7 m); Green River, 1500 ft (455 m); Mesaverde, 1300 ft (395 m)

Net effective thickness .... Uinta, 7–9 ft (2.1–2.7 m); Green River, 170 ft (52 m) max; Mesaverde, 320 ft (95 m)

Lithology

Uinta: sandstone, very fine to siltstone, fair sorting, subrounded, well indurated calcareous
Green River: variable; sandstone from clean quartzose to clayey, conglomerates and ostracodal limestone; better reservoirs are in cleaner quartz sandstones
Mesaverde: sandstone, very fine to clayey, salt and pepper

Porosity type .... Uinta, Green River, and Mesaverde, intergranular

Average porosity .... Uinta, 20%; Green River, 13%; Mesaverde, 15%

Average permeability .... Uinta, no data; Green River, 50–125 md; Mesaverde, 0.01–12 md

Seals:

Upper

Formation, fault, or other feature .... Associated shales and siltstones

Lateral

Formation, fault, or other feature .... Porosity and permeability loss due to facies change to lacustrine shale and siltstone or cementation of sandstones

Source:

Formation and age .... Lower Eocene Green River Formation

Lithology .... Shale

Average total organic carbon (TOC) 2.5%

RED WASH

Maximum TOC .... *Normally 6.5%; a few samples from 17% to 20%*
Kerogen type (I, II, or III) .... *Type I, minor type II and III*
Vitrinite reflectance (maturation) .... *R_o = 0.4-0.8 (Chevron; other values reported to 1.2)*
Time of hydrocarbon expulsion .... *Approx. 10-40 m.y. B.P. (Miocene-Oligocene)*
Present depth to top of source .... *2000-7000 ft (610-2135 m);*
outside of Red Wash, 7000-10,000 ft (2135-3050 m)

Thickness .... *4500 ft (1370 m)*
Potential yield .... *NA*
Formation and age .... *Cretaceous Mesaverde Formation*
Lithology .... *Coaly shales*
Average total organic carbon (TOC) .... *Unknown*
Maximum TOC .... *Unknown*
Kerogen type (I, II, or III) .... *Type II, III*
Vitrinite reflectance (maturation) .... *R_o = 0.72*
Time of hydrocarbon expulsion .... *Unknown*
Present depth to top of source .... *7000-9000 ft (2745 m)*
Thickness .... *1500 ft (458 m)*
Potential yield .... *Unknown*

Appendix 2. Production Data

Field name .... *Red Wash field*

Green River-Wasatch formations

Field size:

Proved acres .... *31,000 ac (12,555 ha)*
Number of wells all years *358*
Current number of wells *254*
Well spacing .... *40 ac and 80 ac (16.2 ha and 32.4 ha)*
Ultimate recoverable .... *106 MMBO, 300 BCFG*
Cumulative production .... *87 MMBO, 275 BCFG*
Annual production .... *1.1 MMBO, 1.9 BCFG*
Present decline rate .... *3% to 8%*
    Initial decline rate *30%*
    Overall decline rate *15%*
Annual water production .... *18 MMBW*
In place, total reserves .... *747 MMBO, 688 BCFG*
In place, per acre-foot .... *500-700 bbl/ac-ft*
Primary recovery .... *53 MMBO*
Secondary recovery .... *53 MMBO*
Enhanced recovery .... *NA*
Cumulative water production .... *211+ MMBW*

Mesaverde Formation

Field size:

Proved acres .... *1280 ac (518 ha)*
Number of wells all years .... *4 drilled, 2 completed*
Current number of wells *1*
Well spacing .... *640 ac (259 ha)*
Ultimate recoverable .... *2.3 BCFG*

Cumulative production	2.1 BCFG
Daily production	138 MCFGPD, 10 BCPD
Present decline rate	
Initial decline rate	30%
Overall decline rate	15%
Annual water production	NA
In place, total reserves	64 BCFG
In place, per acre-foot	NA
Primary recovery	2.1 BCFG
Secondary recovery	NA
Enhanced recovery	NA
Cumulative water production	6.6 MBW

Uinta Formation
Several wells have tested and produced minor amounts of gas from channel sandstones of the Uinta Formation. Documentation and delineation of reservoirs are poor and few data are available.

Drilling and casing practices (Green River Formation development well):

Amount of surface casing set	400–500 ft (122–153 m)
Casing program	9⅝-in. surface casing; 5½ to 7-in. completion string
Drilling mud	Freshwater gel of polymer; water loss below 10 cc
Bit program	8¾-in.
High pressure zones	Generally none; may occur locally in reservoirs overpressured by injection

Completion practices:

Interval(s) perforated	Multiple potential reservoir zones; perforate with 4-in. guns, casing jets, 4 SPF, 90° phasing
Well treatment	Selective acid stimulation with 15% HCl and/or frac

Formation evaluation:

Logging suites	GR-CNL-LDT, Microlog, SP-DIL-MSFL
Testing practices	RFT (pressure only) and open hole DSTs (bottom hole and straddle); completion testing through perforations
Mud logging techniques	Conventional 2-man unit with chromatograph and FID from 2000 ft (610 m) to TD

Oil characteristics:

Type	Asphaltic, paraffinic
API gravity	28°–32°
Base	Intermediate-paraffinic
Initial GOR	292
Sulfur, wt%	0.13
Viscosity, SUS	6–8 cp
Pour point	80°–95°F (26°–35°C) (10.5% paraffin)
Gas-oil distillate	17%

Field characteristics:

Average elevation	5500 ft (1680 m)
Initial pressure	1925 psi (13,270 kPa)
Present pressure	1200 psi (8275 kPa)
Pressure gradient	0.4 psi/ft (9.0 kPa/m)
Temperature	149°F @ 5260 ft (65°C @ 1604 m)
Geothermal gradient	1.3°F/100 ft (2.4°C/100 m)
Drive	Solution gas with water drive
Oil column thickness	2–30 ft (0.6–9.2 m); average 10 ft (3 m)
Oil-water contact	Multiple contacts

Connate water .... Ave. 25%
Water salinity, TDS .... 200 to 10,000 ppm
Resistivity of water .... Original, 0.5 to 3.0 ohm-m @ 68°F (20°C)
Bulk volume water (%) .... Ave. 25%

Transportation method and market for oil and gas:
Oil via pipeline to refinery at Salt Lake City, Utah. Gas to Northwest Pipeline and field use.

RED WASH

Kuparuk River Field—U.S.A.
North Slope, Alaska

W. D. MASTERSON
J. T. EGGERT
ARCO Alaska, Inc.
Anchorage, Alaska

FIELD CLASSIFICATION

BASIN: North Slope
BASIN TYPE: Foredeep
RESERVOIR ROCK TYPE: Sandstone
RESERVOIR ENVIRONMENT OF
 DEPOSITION: Shallow Marine
TRAP DESCRIPTION: One anticline, two unconformity truncations, one unconformity onlap, and one pinchout

RESERVOIR AGE: Cretaceous
PETROLEUM TYPE: Oil
TRAP TYPE: Anticline and Various
 Stratigraphic Traps

LOCATION

The Kuparuk River field covers an area of 210 mi^2 (544 km^2) on the northern coast of Alaska between the Arctic National Wildlife Refuge (ANWR) and the National Petroleum Reserve in Alaska (NPRA; Figure 1). The Atlantic Richfield Company (ARCO) is the sole operator of the Kuparuk River Unit, which includes the entire producing area. Among currently producing oil fields in the United States, Kuparuk is second only to the Prudhoe Bay field in production rate and remaining reserves. The Prudhoe Bay and Kuparuk River fields are located in the North Slope sedimentary basin, which stretches from the ANWR to the Chukchi Sea and is bounded on the south by the Brooks Range. Kuparuk oil production in 1988 averaged 302,000 barrels per day from Lower Cretaceous sandstones in the Kuparuk River Formation (1988 Atlantic Richfield Company Annual Report).

Recoverable reserves are estimated to be 1.6 billion barrels of oil, which ranks Kuparuk as number 146 in total hydrocarbon reserves among the giant fields of the world (Carmalt and St. John, 1986). Solution gas is not included in the reserve estimate. Low-gravity oil accumulations with more than 18 billion barrels of oil in place are also trapped above the Kuparuk River Formation in the West Sak and Ugnu sandstones (Werner, 1987). If a significant proportion of this low-gravity oil is eventually recovered, total reserves within the Kuparuk River Unit may someday surpass those of the East Texas field, which would make Kuparuk the second-largest oil field in the United States.

The Prudhoe Bay and Endicott fields are located 10 to 40 mi (16–64 km) east of the Kuparuk field and produce from reservoirs that are stratigraphically below the Kuparuk River Formation (Figure 1). Several other North Slope oil accumulations have been discovered in Lower Cretaceous reservoirs outside of the Kuparuk field, but to date the only other production from the Kuparuk River Formation has come from the Milne Point Unit to the northeast of the Kuparuk River field. Other Kuparuk oil accumulations in the Niakuk and Point McIntyre areas north of Prudhoe Bay are also being considered for development (Harris, 1988; 1989 Atlantic Richfield Company First Quarter Report; Figure 1).

HISTORY

Pre-Discovery

The discovery of the Kuparuk River field was preceded by ten years of field parties, seismic shooting, and exploratory drilling on the Alaskan North Slope (Jamison et al., 1980). The discovery of surface oil seeps in the western North Slope led to the formation of the Naval Petroleum Reserve (now NPRA) in 1923. During the period 1943 to 1953, 37 deep exploratory wells were drilled in NPRA, and an uneconomic oil field was discovered at Umiat (Jamison et al., 1980; Figure 1). Sinclair Oil and Gas Company and the British Petroleum Company were both impressed by the results of the Navy wells and agreed to form a joint exploratory venture in 1959 (Bowsher, 1987). Their venture began inauspiciously when the first five wells failed to find any oil in Cretaceous rocks near Umiat. Sinclair and British

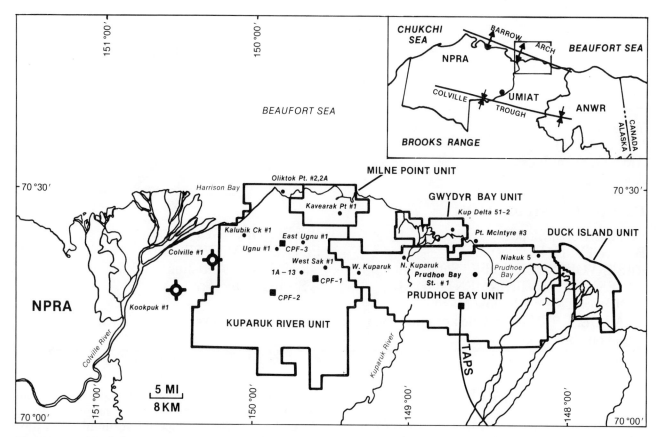

Figure 1. Location of study area on Alaskan North Slope. Oil from the Kuparuk River field is processed at three Central Production Facilities (CPF-1, -2, -3) before transport to the Trans-Alaskan Pipeline (TAPS). The Lisburne pool is located within the Prudhoe Bay Unit, and the Endicott field is located within the Duck Island Unit.

Petroleum then became interested in the coastal area to the north of Umiat, where it would be easier to assemble large blocks of acreage in competitive lease sales (Morgridge and Smith, 1972). It was difficult to assemble large acreage blocks under the noncompetitive, simultaneous filing system in effect near Umiat (Bowsher, 1987).

The coastal acreage was also attractive from a geologic standpoint. Pre-Cretaceous rocks were deeply buried near Umiat, but field studies in the ANWR and exploratory drilling in the NPRA indicated that pre-Cretaceous reservoirs would be at drillable depths along the coast. Former Sinclair geologist Allan Bennison recalls that a photogeology study also indicated the presence of a structural anomaly in the area east of the Colville River delta (Bennison, 1986 and oral communication, 1987).

In 1963, Sinclair and British Petroleum moved a Western Geophysical Company crew north to the Arctic coast to make a 17 mi by 17 mi (27 by 27 km) seismic grid survey. According to G. L. Scott, former Sinclair geophysicist, large structures beneath the Colville River delta and Prudhoe Bay were first identified and mapped from these seismic lines (oral communication, 1987). The Colville prospect was considered to be larger and structurally simpler than the Prudhoe Bay prospect (Kent, 1970). Former BP Alaska executive Alwyne Thomas recalls that seismic interpretations were shared between Sinclair and British Petroleum, which led to a high level of confidence in the final maps (written communication, 1988). The encouraging results of the initial seismic surveys led British Petroleum to approach the State of Alaska and request that state lands in the area be put up for competitive bidding (Cooper, 1973).

The acreage over the Colville prospect was the first area selected for leasing, and Sinclair Exploration Manager Loren Ware advocated strong bidding (Bowsher, 1987). The Colville acreage was offered at the 13th Competitive Lease Sale on 9 December 1964, at which time essentially all of the leases that make up the present-day Kuparuk River Unit were acquired (Figure 2). Sinclair Oil and Gas Company and the British Petroleum Company were high bidders on a total of 317,934 ac (128,664 ha) in a 50–50 partnership at the sale (British Petroleum Company Limited, 1977). Smaller acreage positions were acquired by the Atlantic Refining Company, Standard Oil Company of California, and a partnership between Richfield Oil Company and Humble Refining Company.

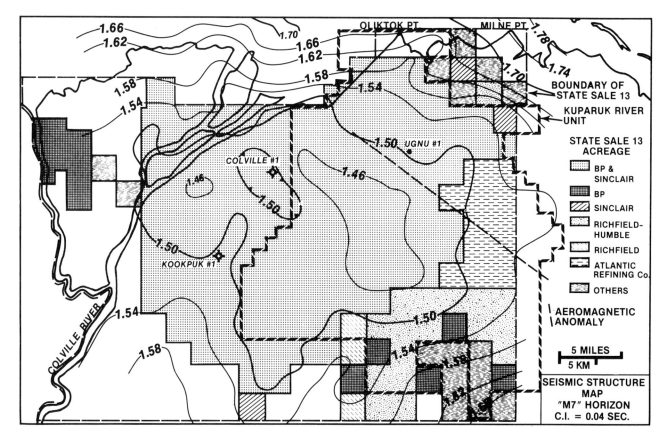

Figure 2. Seismic structure map constructed by British Petroleum geophysicist J. S. Buchanan in 1965. The "M7" horizon is a reflector near the Lower Cretaceous unconformity, which separates the lower and upper members of the Kuparuk River Formation.

The first test of the Colville acreage was the Sinclair Colville #1, which began drilling in 1965. The Colville #1 was the first well in the vicinity of both the Kuparuk River and Prudhoe Bay fields. According to E. R. Bush, former Sinclair district geologist, and P. W. Marsh, geologist, the primary objectives of the well were Paleozoic carbonates that crop out in the ANWR some 100 mi (160 km) to the east (oral communication, 1987). Cretaceous rocks were not considered to be a viable target because their reservoir thickness was thought to be insufficient to support the billion barrel field size that was required for commercial development on the North Slope.

As it turned out, excellent oil shows were encountered in a few feet of Kuparuk upper member sandstone in the Colville #1. Charlie Davis, Sinclair wellsite geologist, then attempted to core the sandstone, but recovered only shale below the base of the Kuparuk River Formation (oral communication, 1988). Gas and oil were recovered from a drill-stem test of Triassic Shublik limestone. Executives from the Atlantic Refining Company visited the rig site shortly after the Shublik flow test, and the evidence of oil recovery may have encouraged Atlantic Richfield to drill the discovery well at Prudhoe Bay (E. R. Bush, written communication,

1988). After the Colville #1 was plugged and abandoned in 1966, Union Oil Company used the rig for another test of the Colville acreage on a farm-out from British Petroleum. The Union Kookpuk #1 tested a small structural closure 7 mi (11 km) southwest of the Colville #1 (Figure 3) and also failed to find commercial quantities of oil.

After the disappointment of the Colville well, Sinclair had participated in a total of seven wells on the North Slope without a commercial discovery, and corporate management was unwilling to continue exploration in the area. Former ARCO Oil and Gas Company President Glenn Simpson recalls that one manager even offered to "drink all the oil that would ever be found on the North Slope" (oral communication, 1988). Sinclair's weakening commitment to the North Slope was also reflected in their earlier reluctance to join partner British Petroleum in bidding for the Prudhoe Bay structure in 1965, despite Sinclair Exploration Manager Loren Ware's pleas to participate (Bowsher, 1987). Ironically, Sinclair's seismic map of Prudhoe Bay was more accurate than the maps prepared by its competitors (Specht et al., 1986). After leasing part of the structure at the sale, British Petroleum contacted Sinclair Alaska District Manager Alan Mabra and offered to let Sinclair buy into the Prudhoe Bay

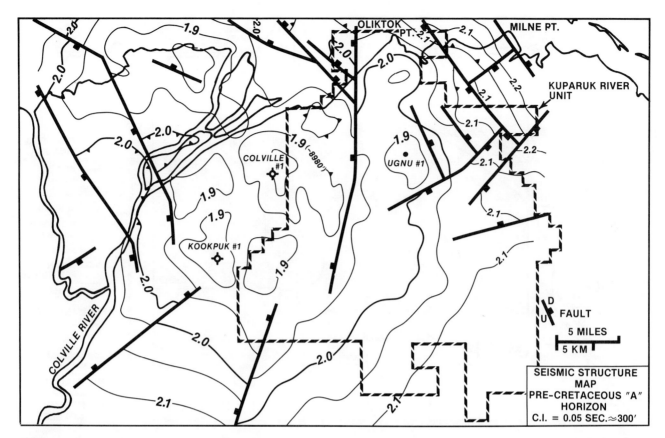

Figure 3. Seismic structure map of pre-Cretaceous "A" horizon constructed by Sinclair geophysicist G. L. Scott in 1965 and modified in 1967. The pre-Cretaceous "A" horizon corresponds to the top of the Triassic Sag River Formation. This map was used to locate several of the first wells on the Colville structure, including the Ugnu #1 discovery well.

acreage for their acquisition cost (Brown, 1986; D. A. Mabra, oral communication, 1988). Sinclair management refused to accept the offer.

The remainder of the Prudhoe Bay structure was leased by Richfield and Humble (now Exxon). In 1966, Richfield and Atlantic merged to form the Atlantic Richfield Company. By the time that the Prudhoe Bay State #1 well was spudded by Atlantic Richfield and Humble in late 1967, most of Sinclair's original Alaskan staff had been transferred into other districts, and the new exploration team was instructed not to spend time on any North Slope projects (F. D. Raffalovich, Sinclair geophysicist, oral communication, 1987). British Petroleum also cut their Alaskan staff to a bare minimum and awaited the results of the Prudhoe Bay test well (British Petroleum Company Limited, 1977).

Discovery

Two events in 1968 combined to change Sinclair's attitude toward the North Slope: Atlantic Richfield's announcement in March that the Prudhoe Bay State #1 well tested 1152 barrels of oil per day, and the hostile tender offer by Gulf+Western Industries for Sinclair stock in late October. Francis Raffalovich, Sinclair geophysicist, was sent on a quixotic mission in March 1968 to inquire if British Petroleum was still willing to sell half of its Prudhoe Bay acreage. Sinclair's request was politely turned down by British Petroleum staff (F. D. Raffalovich, oral communication, 1987). In July, Atlantic Richfield announced that the results of a second well at Prudhoe Bay indicated reserves of 5 to 10 billion barrels of oil.

On the takeover front, Sinclair found itself under attack by Charles Bluhdorn, the head of Gulf+Western Industries, Inc. Sinclair Vice President Joe Downer was present at the first meeting between Sinclair and Gulf+Western. At the meeting Bluhdorn warned that he had already swallowed six or seven companies, and that if Sinclair managers refused to support the takeover they would find themselves "out in the gutter" (J. P. Downer, oral communication, 1988). Sinclair management felt that Bluhdorn's offer for the company was inadequate, and when Atlantic Richfield Chairman R. O. Anderson called with a higher offer, management agreed to Anderson's terms after only two meetings (J. P. Downer, oral communication, 1988). Less than a week after the announcement of Gulf+Western's hostile takeover offer, Sinclair and Atlantic Richfield sought shareholder approval for a friendly merger that was the largest oil merger in history up to that time. Against the backdrop of the battle for control of Sinclair and the frenzied exploration boom that was beginning on the North Slope, a search was begun for the best location to spud a well on Sinclair North Slope acreage. A successful well, if completed before consummation of the merger, could have substantially increased Sinclair's reserves and stock price, and might have allowed the company to remain independent.

Sinclair Alaska Exploration Supervisor R. C. Heiny, Chief Geophysicist P. L. Lyons, and geophysicist F. D. Raffalovich met with British Petroleum's Peter Kent and geophysicist H. D. G. Piggott in November 1968 at Sinclair's corporate headquarters in New York to select a well location (P. L. Lyons, written communication, 1968; R. C. Heiny, oral communication, 1987). Paul Lyons named the proposed well the Ugnu #1, after the Ugnuravik River. The primary objectives of the Ugnu #1 were the Permian–Triassic Sadlerochit sandstones and Carboniferous Lisburne limestones that produced oil at the Prudhoe Bay State #1 well. Because the location was selected very quickly, there was little time to prepare new maps, and N. A. Bassett, former Sinclair geophysicist, recalls that Sinclair geophysicist G. L. Scott's 1967 structure map was used to help locate the well (oral communication, 1987; Figure 3). The Ugnu location was structurally lower than the Colville well, but was separated from it by faulting and dip reversal. It was also thought that prior to Tertiary eastward tilting of the area, the Ugnu location was structurally higher than the Colville well and could have been the highest trap in the area during Cretaceous time. A Tertiary tilting event was inferred from eastward thickening of Tertiary rocks (G. L. Scott, oral communication, 1987).

A secondary objective of the Ugnu well was a Cretaceous structural closure that appeared on a seismic structure map constructed by a British Petroleum geophysicist, J. S. Buchanan (Figure 2). On the British Petroleum map, the highest point on the closure was located about 6 mi (10 km) south of the proposed Ugnu location, and Sinclair staff debated the merits of moving the location south for a better test of the Cretaceous closure. Ultimately it was decided not to change the location, because it was felt that moving the location to the south would result in a less than optimum test of the deeper formations that were the primary objectives of the well (Figure 3). The tract that was finally selected for the well location had been purchased for an average cost of $6.27 per acre at the 1964 lease sale.

Management's approval to drill the Ugnu #1 was given in mid-November on the first day that the sun failed to rise above the Arctic Circle (former ARCO President O. G. Simpson, oral communication, 1988). C. J. Lewis, Sinclair geologist, staked the location in the winter twilight while arrangements were being made to transport the Parker Drilling Company National 100M rig from Oklahoma City to Fairbanks, Alaska, via train and barge. Once in Fairbanks, the rig and supplies were flown to the North Slope in a total of 162 round trips on a Hercules C-130 cargo aircraft. The movement of the Ugnu rig to the North Slope in late 1968 was part of the greatest civilian airlift in history, as oil companies rushed to evaluate their acreage prior to the upcoming State of Alaska lease sale in September 1969.

The Ugnu #1 was spudded in February, and on March 4 the merger between Atlantic Richfield and Sinclair was consummated. It was decided to continue to operate the two companies in tandem for a period of time, and the Sinclair Ugnu crew was not replaced by Atlantic Richfield personnel. After drilling 6000 ft without significant shows, core no. 2 (6178 ft to 6227 ft; 1883–1898 m) recovered oil-stained porous sandstone from the lower member of the Kuparuk River Formation. While waiting for a replacement sub for the core barrel, geologist C. J. Lewis requested that an open-hole drill-stem test be run, and 5585 ft (1702 m) of oil flowed into the drill pipe during a one-hour flow period. The discovery zone was later retested through perforations from 6160 to 6182 ft (1877–1884) at a rate of 1056 barrels of oil per day. The deeper horizons that were the primary objectives of the well did not produce oil, and the well was suspended on 9 May 1969. Although it was not clear at the time, the 20 ft (6 m) of Cretaceous oil reservoir penetrated by Sinclair's last well would one day be recognized as the largest discovery in the history of Sinclair.

Post-Discovery

The Ugnu #1 discovery was announced shortly after the 23rd Competitive Lease Sale held by the State of Alaska in September 1969. At testimony presented to the Alaska Oil and Gas Conservation Committee in November, it was disclosed that three additional wells had discovered oil in Kuparuk River sandstones in the Prudhoe Bay area: Socal Kavearak Point #1 (the discovery well for the Milne Point field), Mobil North Kuparuk State, and Mobil West Kuparuk State (Basye, 1969; Figure 1). In 1970, the Hamilton Brothers Kuparuk Delta #51-2 was completed as another Kuparuk discovery, and oil was encountered in the British Petroleum East Ugnu #1 and the Union Kalubik Creek #1 (Figure 1). The Kalubik well was drilled on farm-out acreage and earned Union a partial interest in several tracts along the western margin of the present-day Kuparuk River Unit. Even though the East Ugnu and Kalubik wells penetrated more than 15 ft (5 m) of oil-saturated Kuparuk lower member sandstone, both British Petroleum and Atlantic Richfield were preoccupied with the development of Prudhoe Bay at the time, and it was not until the ARCO West Sak #1 was drilled in 1971 that the significance of the Ugnu discovery began to be realized. The West Sak #1 was the first well in the field area to penetrate a significant thickness of the Kuparuk upper member sandstones.

In September 1971, an internal Atlantic Richfield engineering study concluded that primary and waterflood reserves in the Ugnu #1–West Sak #1–West Kuparuk area totaled 1808 million barrels of recoverable oil and that these reserves could be economically developed under certain conditions. The 1808 MMbbl figure included reserves penetrated by the Mobil West Kuparuk well, which is not part of the present-day Kuparuk River Unit (Figure 1). Despite this early recognition of a potential super-giant field, former ARCO Exploration Company President H. C. Jamison recalls that it was a constant struggle to sustain interest in potential Kuparuk development during the early 1970s because of the relatively thin Kuparuk reservoir and the political problems that caused delays in the construction of the Trans-Alaska Pipeline (written communication, 1987). Another factor that slowed delineation of the field was the lack of an operating agreement between ARCO and BP, which meant that ARCO was faced with bearing the full risk and cost of continued exploration on jointly held acreage (C. J. Lewis, written communication, 1988).

The first Arab oil embargo in 1973 and resulting oil price hike provided an important stimulus to evaluate Kuparuk reserves, and the first well drilled expressly for Kuparuk delineation was spudded in 1974 (Jamison et al., 1980). Eleven additional wells were drilled prior to Atlantic Richfield's commitment in 1979 to begin production from 20 sections of wholly owned acreage that had been leased by the Atlantic Refining Company in 1964 (Figure 2). Several of the delineation wells were marginal producers, and former ARCO Geological Manager Les Brockett recalls that the productivity of the Kuparuk reservoir was a continuing cause for concern prior to unitization (written communication, 1988). The first correlations of the thin Kuparuk sandstones by ARCO geologist David Hite (written communication, 1977) and BP geologists Carman and Hardwick (1983) recognized the presence of an unconformity within the Kuparuk River Formation along the margins of the field. Concerns about lenticularity of the sandstones prompted debate about the relative merits of primary and secondary recovery plans. The records of former BP Alaska President Peter Hardwick indicate that British Petroleum began proposing waterflood tests in early 1978 and persuaded ARCO that secondary recovery was essential to economical development of the field (written communication, 1988). In December 1981, the field was unitized and began producing oil from Central Production Facility 1 (CPF-1) (Figure 1) at an initial rate of 80,000 BOPD.

The completion of CPF-2 and replacement of the original 16-in. Kuparuk pipeline with a 24-in. pipeline increased the field production rate to 200,000 BOPD in late 1984. A pilot waterflood that began in 1983 was expanded into a full-field waterflood in 1985 when a seawater treatment plant with capacity of 300,000 barrels of water per day became operational. The successful completion of Oliktok Point wells 2 and 2A provided the basis for a 1985 expansion of the Kuparuk River Unit into offshore tracts that ARCO had acquired at State Sale 39 in 1983 (Figure 1). Since the completion of the third and final Central Production Facility in 1986, field production has attained an average rate of 300,000 BOPD and reached a record level of 328,261 BOPD in January 1989. ARCO Alaska operates the field and has an interim working interest of approximately 56%, compared to 39% for BP Exploration, 4% for Unocal, and 1% divided between Mobil, Exxon, and Chevron. A final re-determination of working interests is scheduled for 1990.

DISCOVERY METHOD

The initial impetus for seismic exploration at the Kuparuk River field was provided by a combination of geological and political circumstances: Surface oil seeps and exploratory drilling had confirmed the existence of small fields in the Naval Petroleum Reserve to the south and west, the state and federal governments were considering whether to hold competitive lease sales on coastal acreage, field work in the ANWR had identified prospective reservoir rocks, and a geomorphic anomaly was recognized east of the Colville River delta. Seismic data obtained in 1963 clearly identified the presence of an areally extensive Cretaceous structural closure that was considered a secondary objective of the Ugnu discovery well (Figure 2). Atlantic geophysicists Larry Pipes and Howard Cobb noticed that aeromagnetic data also supported the seismic evidence of the existence of the structural closure, and the Atlantic Refining Company acquired acreage along the trend of the aeromagnetic anomaly at the 1964 State Sale (Figure 2; L. A. Pipes and H. Cobb, written communication, 1987).

At the time of the selection of the location for the Ugnu well, the geologic concept that eastward tilting had occurred during Tertiary time provided some hope that prior to Tertiary time the Ugnu well location had been updip from those of the two dry holes that had already been drilled to the west. Eastward tilting of pre-Tertiary strata is now widely accepted and has been cited as a cause of the tilted tar mat at the Prudhoe Bay field (Jones and Speers, 1976; Bird, 1987). The authors believe that the absence of oil in the Paleozoic formations beneath the Colville delta has nothing to do with tilting but is caused by lack of structural closure north of the coastline. Thinning of the permafrost layer from 2000 ft (610 m) onshore to zero feet offshore causes a velocity change that affects the northern part of the closure on the pre-Kuparuk horizons (Specht et al., 1986). When this velocity change is taken into account in converting seismic travel times to depth, the structure no longer closes off to the north (Jamison et al., 1980, their figure 11). Even with today's seismic technology it is difficult to correct for velocity changes in the permafrost transition zone, and ARCO's Oliktok Point #2 and #2A wells had to be drilled to confirm the offshore extension of oil in the Kuparuk River field (Figure 1).

Seismic identification of the large Cretaceous structural closure was possible in the 1960s, but since that time data quality has improved substantially and has allowed greater resolution of small faults and thin Cretaceous stratigraphic intervals. However, even with recent improvements in technology, it is sometimes not possible to identify the base of the Kuparuk River Formation on seismic data, and the unconformity between the Kuparuk upper and lower members often cannot be distinguished.

STRUCTURE

Tectonic History

Economic basement in the Prudhoe–Kuparuk area is argillite of Ordovician and Silurian age that was metamorphosed during the Middle Devonian to Early Mississippian Ellesmerian orogeny (Lerand, 1973; Carter and Laufeld, 1975). From Carboniferous to Early Cretaceous time, the Ellesmerian stratigraphic sequence was deposited during repeated transgressions and gradual onlap of a source terrain to the north. In Early Cretaceous time, the North Slope was tectonically separated from its northern source terrain, and the Kuparuk River Formation was deposited during a period of tectonism characterized by uplift and development of northwest-striking faults in the field area. From Early Cretaceous time until the present, the Brookian sequence filled the Colville trough with a northeastward-prograding wedge of sediment that was shed from the Brooks Range and the Herald arch (Mull, 1985).

Regional Structure

The dominant structural feature in the subsurface of the Arctic coast is the Barrow arch, which parallels the coastline from Point Barrow to Prudhoe Bay (Figure 1). The Barrow arch is not a true structural arch, but can be thought of as a remnant of the northern Ellesmerian source terrain that remained structurally elevated relative to the subsided Colville trough. The Kuparuk River field is located along the south flank of the Barrow arch.

Local Structure

Oil is trapped in the Kuparuk River Formation along an anticline that plunges 0.8° to the southeast (Figure 4). Geohistory analysis indicates that the anticline probably did not form until eastward tilting began during the Eocene epoch. The mechanism that created the anticline is uncertain. As tilting progressed, the anticlinal closure may have formed when the northeastern flank of the field subsided

more than the western flank. Differential subsidence could have been caused by a zone of weakness in the pre-Mississippian basement along the heavily faulted northeastern flank of the field (Figures 4 and 5). All of the faults in the Kuparuk River field area are normal faults, most of which strike either north-northeast or northwest. Fault throws typically range from 30 to 80 ft and can be up to 300 ft (91 m).

STRATIGRAPHY

The Kuparuk River Formation was deposited during Early Cretaceous (Neocomian) time and is divided into two members that are separated by a regional Lower Cretaceous unconformity (Tabbert and Bennett, 1976; Figure 6). The lower member consists of interbedded marine sandstones, siltstones, and mudstones that contain abundant terrestrial palynomorphs of Berriasian (?) to Valanginian age (Bennett, written communication, 1984). The lower member is divided into units A and B, and reservoir sandstones within unit A are further subdivided into intervals A-1 through A-6.

The Kuparuk upper member overlies the Lower Cretaceous unconformity and contains more glauconite and siderite than the lower member. The upper member is divided into units C and D, which are composed of a sequence of bioturbated marine sandstones, siltstones, and mudstones deposited during Hauterivian to Barremian time (Bennett, written communication, 1984). Reservoir sandstones within unit C are subdivided into intervals C-1 through C-4.

Several other potential reservoir intervals are found both above and below the Kuparuk River Formation in the area surrounding the Kuparuk field. Major oil accumulations have been discovered in the Carboniferous Endicott Group sandstones and Lisburne carbonates, Permian–Triassic Sadlerochit Group sandstones, Triassic Sag River sandstone, and Late Cretaceous/Tertiary West Sak and Ugnu sandstones. Excellent source rocks for oil exist within Triassic Shublik carbonate and shale, Jurassic Kingak shale, and Cretaceous HRZ shale.

TRAP

Both structural and stratigraphic traps are present within the field area. The western and southern limits of the field are controlled by stratigraphy rather than by structure. To the west, the unit A sandstones are truncated by the unconformity at the base of the upper member and the unit C sandstones pinch out. This western truncation is the primary trapping mechanism for sandstones in intervals A-1 and A-2 and forms the western boundary for the anticlinal traps in intervals A-3 and A-4. To the south, the C-1 sandstone pinches out as it onlaps the

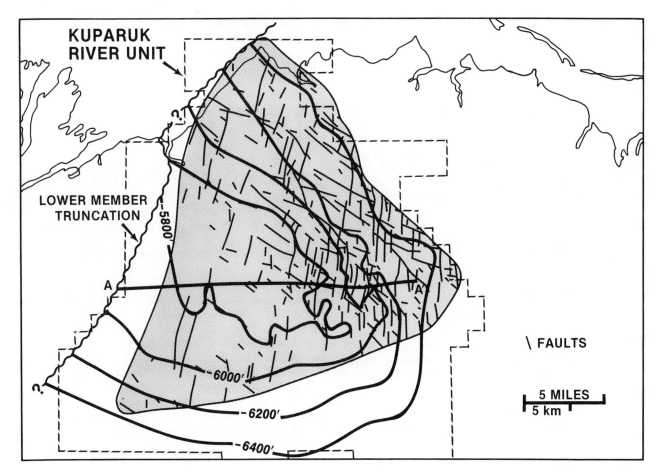

KUPARUK
RIVER UNIT

LOWER MEMBER
TRUNCATION

5800'

A ——————————— A'

6000'

6200'

6400'

\ FAULTS

5 MILES
5 km

Figure 4. Structure map (feet subsea) on the top of the Kuparuk River Formation. The field outline (shaded) was established by the Kuparuk River Unit Second Interim Equity Redetermination in 1984. Faults are mapped from seismic data. Structural cross section A–A' is shown on Figure 5. (Modified from Masterson and Paris, 1987.)

unconformity surface, and the A-5 sandstone grades into mudstone. The other reservoir sandstones in the field (intervals A-3, A-4, and C-3/C-4) all have structural closure and would therefore be classified as part of the anticlinal trap.

Along the northeastern flank of the anticline, the field is bounded by oil-water contacts within A and C sandstones that range in depth from 6530 ft (1990 m) subsea to at least 6650 ft (2027 m) subsea. Oil has been encountered as deep as 6870 ft (2094 m) subsea along the northeastern flank of the field, but because of sparse well control and the possibility of isolated, fault-block closures, the downdip limit of the field is uncertain. Structural relief from the crest of the structure to the oil-water contact totals 1000 ft (305 m). The upper seal for the Kuparuk oil accumulation is provided by mudstones of the Kalubik and HRZ formations, which are several hundred feet thick in the field area (Carman and Hardwick, 1983).

Paleostructural reconstructions in the Prudhoe–Kuparuk area indicate that the present Kuparuk field anticlinal closure began to form during the Eocene epoch. Prior to the Eocene epoch, a large structural closure existed east of the Kuparuk field in the area between the Milne Point and Prudhoe Bay fields. All of the Kuparuk River Formation cores that we have examined from the area east of the Kuparuk field have been uniformly oil-stained a light brown color and have average oil saturations that are on the order of 10% in water-productive zones. The fact that oil staining occurs uniformly throughout the Kuparuk interval, in both highly permeable and less permeable facies, suggests that a substantial oil column once existed in the paleostructural closure east of the Kuparuk field. Free gas has also been tested from several wells to the east of the Kuparuk River Unit.

When the eastern paleostructural closure was partially destroyed by eastward tilting of the area during early Tertiary time, oil in the eastern trap may have migrated west into the present-day Kuparuk field structure. This model explains the occurrence of gas to the east of the Kuparuk field and the lack of a natural gas cap in the field itself. It has previously been suggested that the Kuparuk oil accumulation spilled from the deeper pool at Prudhoe during Tertiary eastward tilting (Carman and Hardwick, 1983), and it is possible that Prudhoe

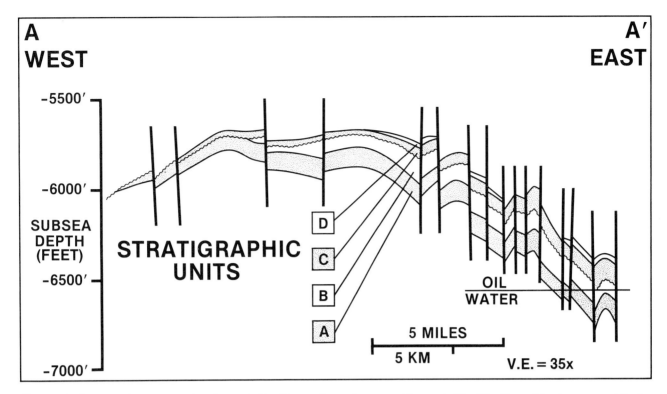

Figure 5. Structural cross section through the Kuparuk River field showing the stratigraphic units of the Kuparuk River Formation. The location of the cross section is shown on Figure 4. (Modified from Masterson and Paris, 1987.)

oil mixed with oil that was already trapped in the Kuparuk River Formation.

Reservoirs

Lower Member of the Kuparuk River Formation

Units A and B are a cyclic sequence of interbedded sandstone, siltstone, and mudstone. The six cycles within unit A (intervals A-1 through A-6) are separated by mudstones that can be identified by their high gamma ray and low resistivity log readings (Figures 6 and 7). Reservoir sandstone, which is present in intervals A-1 through A-5, consists of very fine- to fine-grained, well-sorted quartz arenite with only a trace amount of glauconite (Figure 8A, B; Eggert, 1985). Sandstone beds are thicker and more numerous in the upper part of each interval (Figure 7, interval A-4).

Isopachs of net sandstone within each unit A interval trend northeast-southwest (Figure 9). The sandstones are truncated to the west by the unconformity at the base of the upper member. Within each interval the sandstone beds gradually thin in the northwest direction and abruptly grade into mudstone to the southeast. Each interval can be up to 80 ft (24 m) thick, 40 mi (64 km) long, and 15 mi (24 km) wide and can contain up to 30 ft (9 m) of reservoir sandstone. Southeastward prograda-

tion of intervals A-1 through A-5 created an imbricate stack of stratigraphically separated sandstone bodies with an aggregate reservoir thickness of up to 70 ft (21 m) (Figure 10).

The unit A sandstones were deposited in graded, ripple-laminated, parallel-laminated, and massive sandstone beds that vary in abundance vertically and laterally within each interval (Figure 11A, B). Lithofacies within unit A have been described by Gaynor and Scheihing (1988). Graded and ripple-laminated beds predominate at the base and along the southeastern flank of each interval, and parallel-laminated and massive sandstone beds become increasingly abundant toward the interval top and along the thin northwestern flank of each interval. The uppermost few feet of each interval in unit A is a transgressive sequence consisting of bioturbated sandstone that fines upward into mudstone. A bioturbated mudstone also overlies the transgressive surface at the base of unit B.

Unit B resembles unit A in physical appearance and sedimentary structures but differs in grain size, grain composition, and distribution of reservoir sandstone. Medium to coarse sand and glauconite grains are more abundant in unit B than unit A (Masterson and Paris, 1987). Reservoir sandstones comparable in thickness to intervals A-1 through A-4 are not developed within unit B in the Kuparuk River Unit. A 20 ft (6 m) sandstone within unit B produces oil in the Milne Point Unit to the northeast of the Kuparuk field (Figure 1).

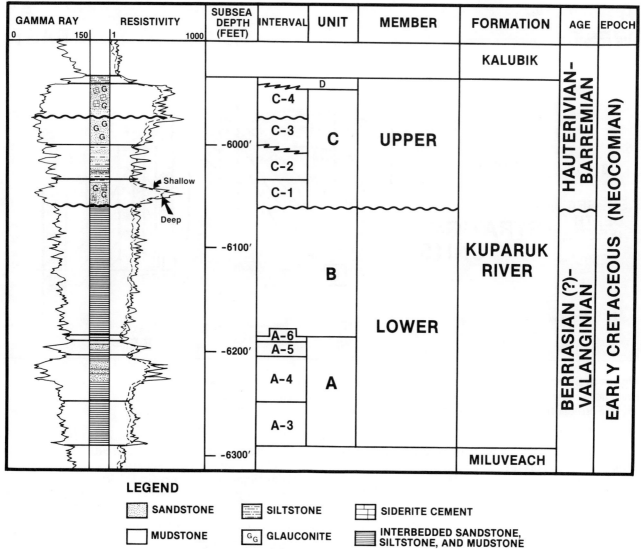

Figure 6. Stratigraphy of the Kuparuk River Formation in well 1A-13. Intervals A-1 and A-2 are not present in this well. The location of well 1A-13 is shown on Figure 1. (Modified from Masterson and Paris, 1987.)

The lower member sandstones are interpreted to have been deposited during storms on a shallow marine shelf. Graded beds within the lower member were deposited from suspension by storm-generated currents. The absence of wave reworking in the graded beds indicates deposition below storm wave base. The ripple-laminated and parallel-laminated sandstone beds exhibit characteristics of hummocky cross-stratification and are interpreted to have been deposited above storm wave base as sand settled out of suspension and was reworked by wave-generated motion on the shelf bottom. The massive sandstone beds are interpreted to have formed during the highest energy storm conditions when sand was rapidly dumped onto the shelf bottom and waves were unable to work the sand into hummocks.

The transgression and abrupt decrease in depositional energy indicated by the presence of mudstone at the top of each interval in unit A reflects either a decrease in the frequency and intensity of storms, a rise in sea level, or a shift in the source of sand at the shoreline. When progradation resumed, the thickest part of each interval was deposited seaward (southeast) of the previous interval (Figure 10). Cyclical progradation of intervals A-1 through A-6 created a regressive shelf sequence composed of individual coarsening-upward cycles. The intervals were detached from the shoreline, and the shelf topography played an important role in localizing the sand accumulations (Gaynor and Scheihing, 1988; Masterson and Paris, 1987).

Diagenesis of unit A sandstone resulted in a pore network characterized by preserved primary intergranular porosity (Figure 8), reduced slightly by quartz overgrowths, kaolinite, and illite-smectite cements (Figure 12). In addition, ankerite cement

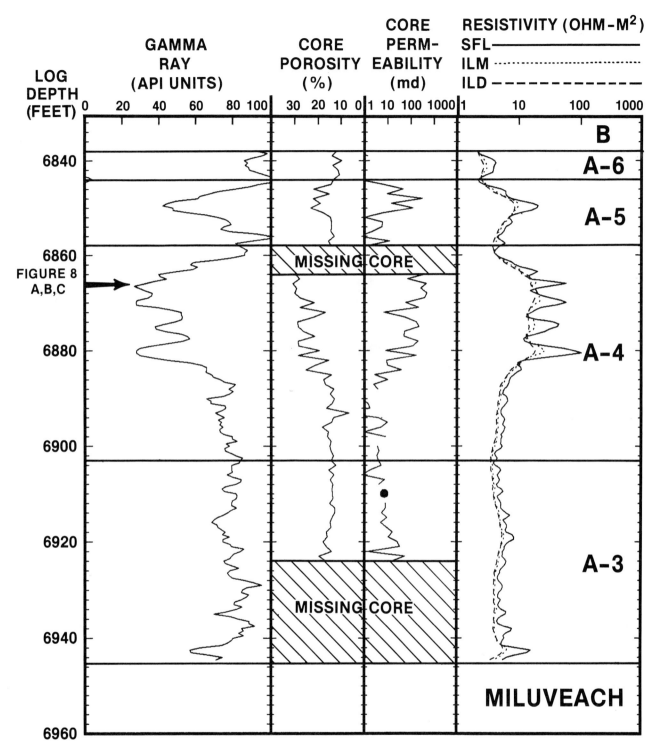

Figure 7. Depth-shifted core data and wireline log response from unit A in Kuparuk River Unit well 1A-13. Porosity, permeability, and log response vary with the number and thickness of interbedded mudstones within the producing horizons.

eliminates porosity in some areas of the field. Ankerite-cemented sandstones (Figures 8C and 11A) can be up to 15 ft (5 m) thick. Petrographic and pore cast measurements indicate that pores range in size from 0.02 to 0.15 mm, with an average size of about 0.05 mm (Figure 8D).

Porosity and permeability within unit A sandstones are controlled more by lithofacies than by

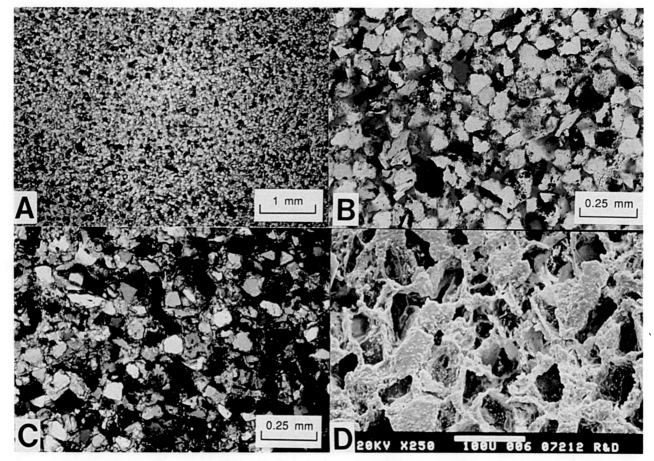

Figure 8. Photomicrographs and SEM photograph of unit A sandstones. (A) Very fine to fine-grained, well-sorted quartzose sandstone with excellent intergranular porosity. (B) Close-up showing intergranular porosity (blue). Note moldic pores where feldspar grains have undergone dissolution. (C) Sandstone with ankerite cement filling all intergranular pore space. View with polarizers crossed. (D) SEM photograph of pore cast. Note regularity of both pore and pore throat size distribution. Scale bars: 0.67 mm (A), 0.18 mm (B–C), 162 microns (D).

diagenesis (Gaynor and Scheihing, 1988). The arithmetic average of reservoir porosity is 23% and ranges up to 33%. Horizontal permeability in unit A reservoir sandstone has an arithmetic average value of 113 md and a maximum value of 1828 md. The presence of mudstone laminae causes scatter in the porosity/permeability cross plot (Figure 13) and reduces vertical permeability in the reservoir. Table 1 summarizes the reservoir characteristics of unit A.

Upper Member of the Kuparuk River Formation

The Kuparuk upper member consists of a basal transgressive sandstone (interval C-1), a regressive, coarsening-upward sequence of sandstone and silty mudstone (intervals C-2 and C-3), and an upper transgressive sandstone (interval C-4) that grades into mudstone (unit D; Figure 6). All of the sandstones within the upper member are intensely bioturbated

and were deposited during a period of tectonism characterized by northwest-striking normal faults that caused syndepositional thickening of units C and D (Figures 14 and 15). The base of unit C is a regional Lower Cretaceous unconformity that locally represents erosion down to basement along the Barrow arch and removal of at least 300 ft (91 m) of underlying sediments in the field area. The unconformity surface at the base of unit C is easily distinguishable by glauconite-filled borings that extend several inches into the underlying Kuparuk lower member (Figure 11C).

Intervals C-1 and C-4 have similar textures, mineralogies, and diagenetic histories. Quartz and glauconite are the most abundant framework grains, and siderite cement replaces mud matrix and fills pores (Figures 11C, D and 16A, D). Rounded pebbles and occasional rounded cobble-sized chert, quartzite, and sedimentary rock fragments are often concentrated at the unconformable base of interval C-1 and, in some areas, at the base of interval C-4. Grain size

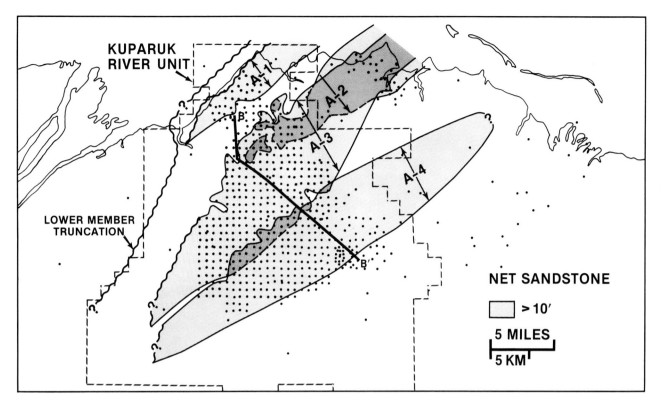

Figure 9. Isopach map showing areas with at least 10 ft of net sandstone in intervals A-1 through A-4. Darker shading indicates area where the sandstones overlap. Stratigraphic cross section B-B' is shown on Figure 10. (Modified from Masterson and Paris, 1987.)

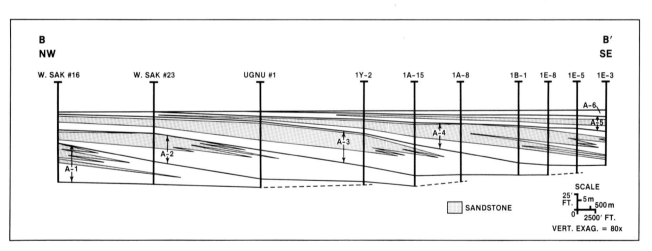

Figure 10. Stratigraphic cross section of unit A. The datum is the top of unit A, and the location of the cross section is shown on Figure 9. (Modified from Masterson and Paris, 1987.)

varies from very fine to coarse sand, and sorting is poor to moderate.

The distribution of reservoir sandstone within unit C was controlled by the topography of the marine shelf and by the availability of sandy sediment from the source areas. Interval C-1 sandstone was deposited in structural depressions as the area between the Colville and Prudhoe highs was differentially uplifted and eroded during Early Cretaceous time. Reservoir sandstone in interval C-1 averages 6 ft (2 m) thickness where present and reaches a maximum thickness of 30 ft (9 m). Grain size within interval C-1 decreases upward into mudstone, causing decreasing resistivity and

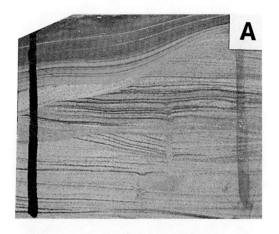

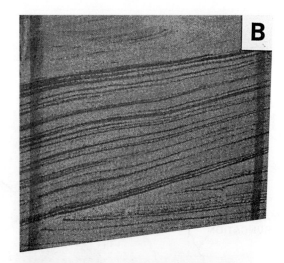

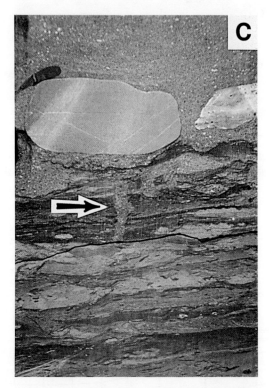

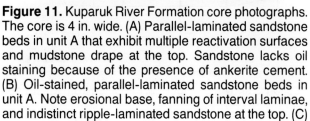

Figure 11. Kuparuk River Formation core photographs. The core is 4 in. wide. (A) Parallel-laminated sandstone beds in unit A that exhibit multiple reactivation surfaces and mudstone drape at the top. Sandstone lacks oil staining because of the presence of ankerite cement. (B) Oil-stained, parallel-laminated sandstone beds in unit A. Note erosional base, fanning of interval laminae, and indistinct ripple-laminated sandstone at the top. (C) Lower Cretaceous unconformity at the base of interval C-1. Note cobble on unconformity surface and abundant glauconite (green) in interval C-1. Glauconite also fills borings (arrow) that penetrate into unit B of the underlying Kuparuk lower member. (D) Oil-stained sandstone (brown) and siderite cement (light gray) in interval C-4. Note presence of open fractures in siderite-cemented layer.

increasing gamma ray log response toward the top of the interval (Figure 17). The upward-decreasing grain size is interpreted to reflect an environment of decreasing wave and current energy coupled with gradual drowning of the sediment source area during a marine transgression.

Interval C-1 is usually overlain conformably by intervals C-2 and C-3 which prograded from southwest to northeast across the field area (Figure 15). Grain size in interval C-3 is predominantly fine sand, and concentrations of glauconite and siderite are reduced relative to those in intervals C-1 and

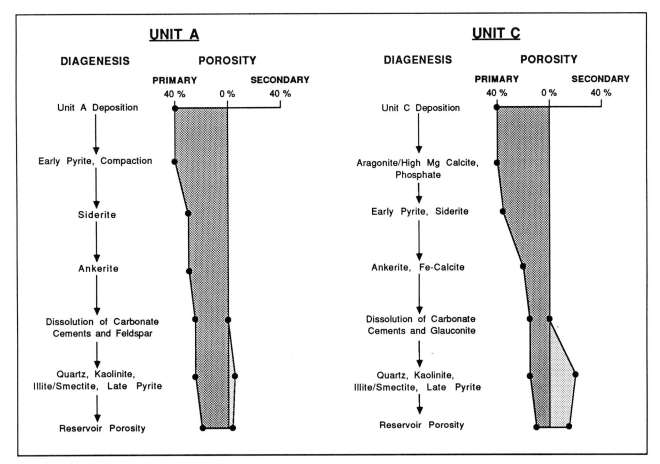

Figure 12. Schematic comparison of diagenetic history, porosity evolution, and resultant proportions of primary and secondary porosity in Kuparuk reservoir sandstones. Reservoir porosity in unit A sandstone is predominantly preserved primary porosity, whereas porosity in unit C sandstone is both primary and secondary. Although the sequence of events is shown to occur in discrete steps, it is possible that some of the diagenetic events may have occurred simultaneously.

C-4. The reduced glauconite content of interval C-3 reflects increased clastic input of the regressive C-2/C-3 package within the predominantly transgressive environment of unit C. Interval C-3 sandstone grades northward into the silty sandstones and mudstones of interval C-2. Up to 40 ft (12 m) of reservoir sandstone can be present within interval C-3, and pay thickness averages 8 ft (2 m) in wells in which the interval is present. Poorly developed reservoir sandstones are also sometimes found within interval C-2.

The unconformable contact between intervals C-3 and C-4 is usually marked by a grain-size change from fine or, rarely, medium sand grains in interval C-3 to medium-, coarse-, and pebble-sized grains in interval C-4. The upward increase in grain size is accompanied by an increased proportion of glauconite and collophane to as much as 40% of C-4 framework grains. The unconformity at the base of interval C-4 is abrupt in the southwestern part of the field and becomes more transitional toward the northeast as interval C-4 grades into unit D mudstone (Figure 15). The thickness of underlying section removed and represented by the C-4 unconformity is uncertain but appears to be less than the section eroded at the base of unit C. Reservoir sandstone averages 10 ft (3 m) in wells in which interval C-4 is present and reaches a maximum thickness of 40 ft (12 m).

The presence of dinoflagellates and glauconite in the Kuparuk upper member indicates an open marine environment. Water depths during upper member deposition are uncertain, but glauconite is thought to form in water depths of at least 100 ft (30 m) (Odin and Letolle, 1980). The marine processes responsible for deposition of unit C are difficult to decipher because of pervasive bioturbation that has destroyed almost all sedimentary structures. The extreme winnowing and coarse grain size in intervals C-1 and C-4 argue for deposition in water shallow enough to be subjected to tide or storm currents.

Reservoir quality in unit C is heterogeneous compared with that of unit A. The variability is greatest within intervals C-1 and C-4, whereas interval C-3 has more uniform reservoir characteristics (Figures 13 and 17). Diagenesis produced a pore system characterized by secondary porosity in

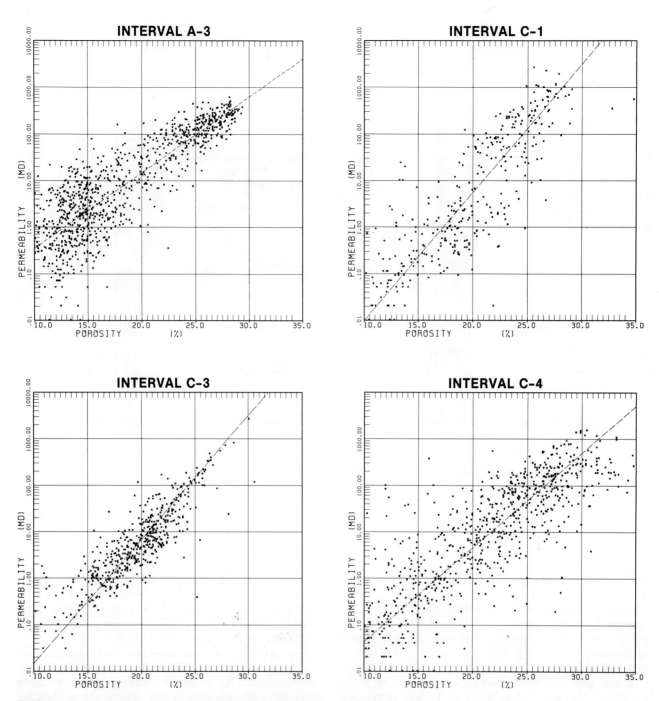

Figure 13. Correlation between helium porosity and horizontal air permeability in intervals A-3, C-1, C-3, and C-4. Fractured samples are not included.

intervals C-1 and C-4 (Figure 16A, D, E). Extensive dissolution of siderite and, to a lesser degree, glauconite, produced intergranular and moldic macroporosity. Both intragrain and microporosity occur where glauconite grains are partially dissolved (Figure 16E). Some secondary porosity is also present in C-2 and C-3 sandstone, but most of interval C-3 is characterized by preserved primary intergranular porosity that has been partially reduced by quartz overgrowths, kaolinite, and illite-smectite cements (Figure 16B,C). The good correlation between porosity and permeability in C-3 sandstone reflects the lack of siderite cementation (Figure 13). Interval C-4 exhibits the worst correlation between porosity and permeability, due to variable siderite cementation and dissolution (Figure 13).

Pores in unit C reservoir sandstones range in size from 0.02 mm to 2.0 mm, with an average of 0.07

Table 1. Comparison of unit A and unit C reservoir characteristics. Helium porosity and air permeability values are arithmetic averages of horizontal plug data from 50 cored wells. Nonreservoir and fractured samples are not included. Pore size values are based on petrographic and SEM pore cast measurements.

	Unit A	Unit C
Porosity Type	Homogeneous, preserved primary intergranular porosity	Heterogeneous, secondary and preserved primary porosity, fractures
Average Porosity	23%	24%
Average Permeability	113 md	138 md
Average Pore Size	0.05 mm (0.02–0.15)	0.07 mm (0.02–2.0)
Minerals Exposed to Pore System	Kaolinite Quartz Illite-smectite (minor) Ankerite	Siderite Glauconite Kaolinite Illite-smectite (minor) Quartz Chert
Mobile Fines	Kaolinite Illite-smectite (minor)	Kaolinite Illite-smectite (minor) Siderite Glauconite Unconsolidated Sand Grains

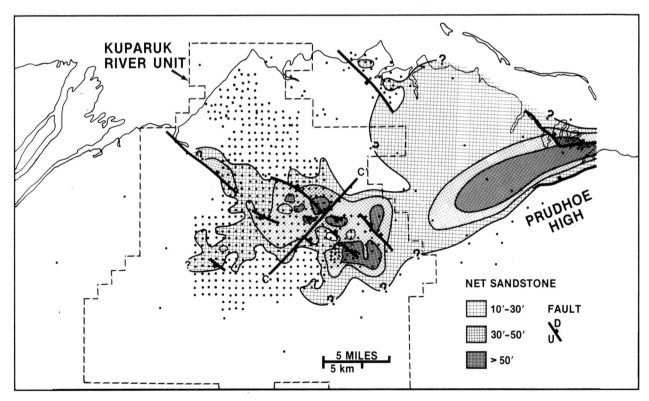

Figure 14. Isopach map showing net sandstone within unit C and the location of selected northwest-striking faults that affect sandstone thickness. Stratigraphic cross section C–C′ is shown on Figure 15. (Modified from Masterson and Paris, 1987.)

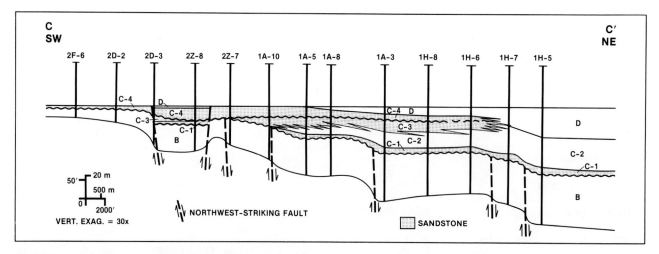

Figure 15. Stratigraphic cross section of units B, C, and D. The datum is the top of the Kuparuk River Formation, and the location of the cross section is shown on Figure 14. (Modified from Masterson and Paris, 1987.)

mm, based on petrographic and pore cast measurements (Figure 16F). Average porosity is 24% and ranges up to 37%. Permeability is effective in both horizontal and vertical directions, averages 138 md in horizontal core plugs, and reaches a maximum value of 2644 md. The highest porosities and permeabilities typically are found along the unconformable surfaces at the base of intervals C-1 and C-4 (Figure 17). Unit C reservoir characteristics are summarized and compared with those of unit A in Table 1.

Field Performance

The textural and diagenetic differences between the Kuparuk lower and upper members are reflected in field performance during both primary production and waterflooding. The upper member sandstones are capable of producing at rates of up to 5000 barrels of oil per day, compared with maximum lower member sandstone rates of 1300 BOPD. Hydraulic fracture stimulation raises lower member sandstone production up to a maximum of 2600 BOPD.

To minimize environmental impact on the North Slope tundra, production and injection wells are directionally drilled from gravel drillsites that typically drain a 4 mi^2 (10 km^2) area with 16 wells. Recoverable oil reserves are expected to total 33% or 1.6 billion bbl of the estimated 4.8 billion bbl of oil in place. Because waterflooding began early in the development of the field, it is difficult to allocate production between primary and secondary recovery. It is thought that primary production by solution gas drive would recover only 11% of the original oil in place. Enhanced oil recovery began in 1988 with a small-scale project in which miscible natural gas liquids are injected into the reservoir.

Faults

The complex fault patterns in the Kuparuk field area were not mappable from the early reconnaissance seismic grids. ARCO Alaska Geophysical Technology Manager Don Gerwin recalls that widespread faulting was not recognized until a grid of swath seismic lines was shot in 1980 (oral communication, 1988). Each swath line consisted of three seismic lines spaced 660 ft (201 m) from each other, with 0.5 mi between swaths. Early development wells confirmed the existence of faults seen on swath lines, and many wells have intersected small faults that are either between swath lines or are too small to be resolved. In 1988, acquisition of a 3D (three-dimensional) seismic grid began to allow better correlation and identification of these small faults.

Stratigraphic and seismic evidence indicates that the northwest- and north–northeast-striking faults formed at different times. The northwest-striking faults were active during deposition of the Kuparuk upper member in Early Cretaceous time. The upper member thickens along the downthrown sides of the northwest-striking faults, and the lower member is thinned by post-depositional erosion on the upthrown sides (Figures 14 and 15). On seismic lines, some of the northwest-striking faults cut the base of the Kuparuk River Formation but display no measurable displacement at the top, indicating that fault movement ceased at the end of upper member deposition (Figure 18). Some faults remained active until Late Cretaceous time. Seismic data indicate that northeast- and southwest-dipping fault planes are equally abundant among northwest-striking faults.

Most of the north–northeast-striking faults formed after deposition of the Kuparuk River Formation and do not affect its thickness. Apparent thickening across north–northeast-striking faults is sometimes

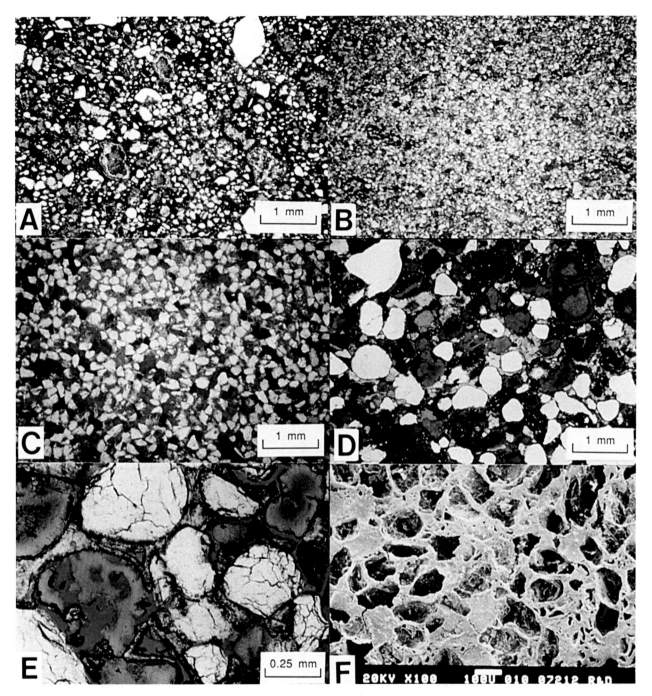

Figure 16. Photomicrographs and SEM photograph of unit C sandstone. (A) Interval C-1 sandstone. Very fine to coarse-grained, poorly to moderately sorted glauconitic sandstone with chert grains. (B) Interval C-2 sandstone. Very fine grained, well-sorted, slightly glauconitic quartzose sandstone. (C) Interval C-3 sandstone. Very fine to fine-grained, occasionally medium-grained, moderately well-sorted quartzose sandstone. Intervals C-2 and C-3 have less siderite cement and glauconite than intervals C-1 and C-4. (D) Interval C-4 sandstone. Very fine to coarse-grained, poorly to moderately sorted, glauconitic, sideritic, phosphatic, quartzose sandstone with chert grains. (E) Secondary porosity (blue) produced by dissolution of siderite cement and glauconite grains. (F) SEM photograph of unit C pore cast. Note combination of well-connected intergranular and moldic pores and pore throats. Scale bars: 0.67 mm (A–D), 0.18 mm (E), 185 microns (F).

275

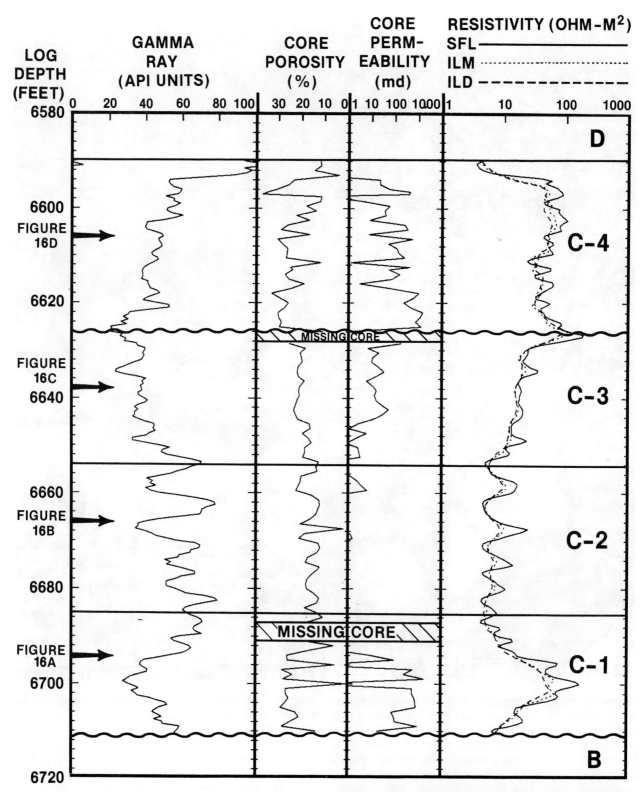

Figure 17. Depth-shifted core data and wireline log response from unit C in Kuparuk River Unit well 1A-13. Porosity and permeability are best developed in intervals C-1 and C-4. Interval C-3 is also a producing horizon, and producible sandstones are sometimes encountered in interval C-2.

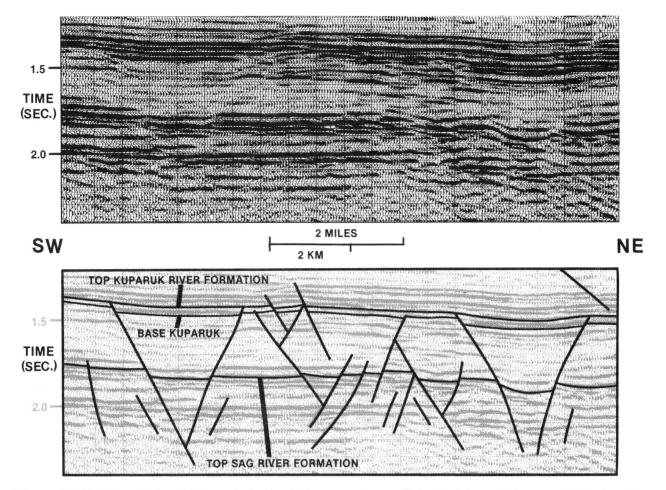

Figure 18. Uninterpreted and interpreted seismic line located in the northwest corner of the Kuparuk River field. Note thickened Kuparuk River Formation in grabens. Seismic interpretation provided by Don Brizzolara and Mike Wiley.

observed, but it is possible that this thickening is caused by northwest-striking faults that are not mappable from current seismic data. North–northeast-striking faults that dip to the east outnumber those that dip to the west by a ratio of 5 to 1 in the field area. The predominance of east-dipping faults suggests that most of them formed during Tertiary eastward tilting of the area.

Because they appear to act as both conduits and seals for reservoir fluids, identification of faults is critical to primary development, waterflood management, and infill drilling. North-south directional permeability in the field is attributed to north–northeast-striking faults that caused fracturing of the brittle, siderite-cemented unit C sandstones (Figure 11D; Williams et al., 1984). North-south directional permeability has also been seen in unit A sandstones but is of a lesser magnitude than seen in unit C. Pressure declines during production have also indicated the existence of fault barriers to fluid flow, and available data indicate that both northwest- and north–northeast-striking faults can act as seals. The recognition of north-south directional permeability in the field has led to the implementation of a line drive waterflood pattern in which north-south rows of producing wells alternate with rows of injection wells.

Sources

The oils in the Prudhoe, Kuparuk, Endicott, and Lisburne reservoirs all appear to be genetically related and are thought to be a mixture from sources in the Triassic Shublik carbonates and shale, Jurassic Kingak shale, and possibly the Cretaceous HRZ shale (Seifert et al., 1979; Sedivy et al., 1987). Kuparuk oil gravity ranges from 21 to 27° API, with an average value of 24° at 60°F (Carman and Hardwick, 1983). The gas-oil ratio varies from 350 to 575 SCF/STB (Clutterbuck and Dance, 1982). The oil is rich in aromatic and naphthenic components and has a relatively low paraffin content, with a pour point of –55°F. A gas chromatogram of the saturate fraction of Kuparuk oil is shown on Figure 19.

The source rocks for Kuparuk oil are not mature in the Prudhoe-Kuparuk area but mature rapidly to the south in the Colville trough, where vitrinite

277

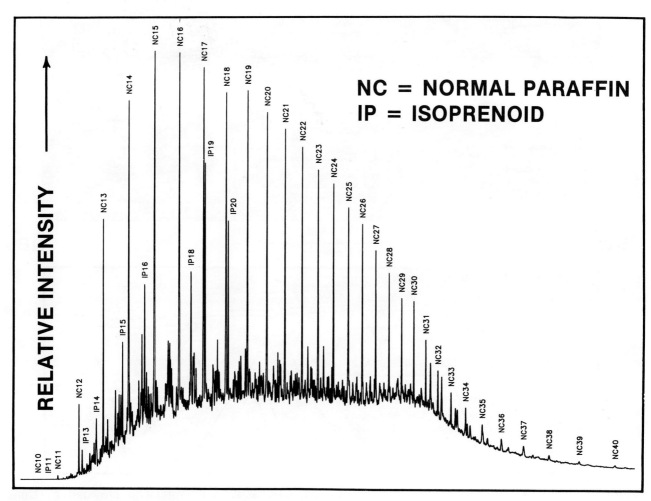

NC = NORMAL PARAFFIN
IP = ISOPRENOID

Figure 19. Saturate fraction gas chromatogram of oil from the Kuparuk River field. Relative intensities are plotted against retention time.

reflectance values increase to more than 2% (Magoon and Bird, 1987). All three of the potential source rocks have average organic carbon contents in excess of 1.5%. Organic matter in the Shublik Formation is predominantly type I kerogen, but type II or type III kerogen predominates in the Kingak and HRZ formations (Magoon and Bird, 1987). Generation and expulsion of oil is believed to have begun during Late Cretaceous and early Tertiary time when the source intervals in the Colville trough were buried by sediments shed from the Brooks Range orogeny (Bird, 1987). Assuming an arbitrary area of 5,000,000 ac (approximately 7800 mi^2; 20,202 km^2) for oil generation in the Colville Trough, the three formations are capable of generating more than 250 billion barrels of oil.

EXPLORATION CONCEPTS

Regional Play

Regional uplift and erosion in Early Cretaceous time resulted in deposition of Kuparuk and age-equivalent sandstones over much of the Barrow arch. When source rocks to the south were deeply buried and reached maturity from Late Cretaceous through Eocene time, the Prudhoe-Kuparuk area was the highest point along the arch and became the focal point for hydrocarbons migrating updip from the Brooks Range foredeep (Hubbard et al., 1987). Widespread Cretaceous faulting and syndepositional thickening of the Kuparuk River Formation has resulted in many structural and stratigraphic traps in the area between the Colville and Prudhoe highs. Thus far the Milne Point field has provided the only Cretaceous production outside of the Kuparuk River Unit, but several other accumulations have been discovered and will eventually be developed.

The anticlinal closure at the Kuparuk River field extends beyond the western boundary of the field. Any paleotopographic lows with preserved Kuparuk sediments are likely to be oil-productive within the area of closure. Beyond the Prudhoe-Kuparuk area, oil staining in Kuparuk-age Kemik Sandstone has been reported as far east as the ANWR (Knock, 1987), and a gas field of unknown areal extent has been discovered on the western coast of the NPRA in the Walakpa #1 and #2 wells (Schindler, 1983).

The position of the Kuparuk River field on an arch updip from an orogenic foredeep is duplicated in many other petroleum provinces of the world, including the supergiant Athabasca tar accumulations in Canada and the oil fields of the Middle East Arabian platform (Bally and Snelson, 1980). The shallow marine regressive and transgressive sandstone facies in the Kuparuk field also have counterparts in many other reservoirs, such as the Cretaceous Cardium, Viking, Gallup, and Tocito sandstones (Bergman and Walker, 1987).

Lessons

The discovery of the Kuparuk River field demonstrates the roles of intuition and luck in the exploration process. Sinclair's early recognition of the petroleum potential of the North Slope led to the first private industry field party in 1958 and the first seismic crew in 1962 with partner British Petroleum (Jamison et al., 1980). Despite the technical expertise of the Sinclair and British Petroleum staffs, discovery of the Kuparuk River field came down to luck. If the Prudhoe Bay State #1 had not discovered 10 billion barrels of oil reserves at Prudhoe Bay, the Kuparuk discovery well would not have been drilled in 1969. Even today the Kuparuk River field would be uneconomic to develop without the pipeline and infrastructure constructed as a result of the Prudhoe Bay discovery.

The first exploratory wells in the Prudhoe-Kuparuk area were targeted for the Colville and Prudhoe basement uplifts where the Kuparuk interval is thin or absent. Today we know that it is best to explore for Kuparuk sandstones along the downthrown sides of Cretaceous faults along the flanks of structural uplifts. Modern seismic techniques allow better definition of thin intervals such as the Kuparuk, but it is still often difficult to reliably predict thickness and lithology of intervals that are less than 30 ft (9 m) thick. Development of the field has demonstrated that thin, siderite-cemented lithologies such as the Kuparuk unit C sandstones can be excellent producers because of the presence of secondary porosity and fractures.

The recognition of differences in reservoir quality between the Kuparuk upper and lower members has led to different completion techniques in units A and C. In a pilot waterflood project, it was found that if both members were open to a single completion, almost all the injected water entered the high-permeability, fractured upper member sandstones (Williams et al., 1984). Selective single completions are used to combat the imbalance in productivity between the two members, and the lower member sandstones are hydraulically fractured to increase their productivity.

Widespread faulting in the field was not recognized until swath seismic lines became available just prior

to unitization, and the presence of many faults in the early development wells confirmed the seismic data. The influence of faults and associated fractures upon directional permeability in the reservoir was recognized in the pilot waterflood project and was confirmed with pressure interference tests in other areas of the field. A line drive waterflood pattern is used to combat north-south directional permeability caused by faults and fractures.

A final lesson to be drawn from Kuparuk history is the value of persistence in an exploration program. Even though the Kuparuk trap covers 210 mi^2 (544 km^2) and was easily seen on early seismic surveys, it nevertheless took three wells to find the field and 17 wells to delineate it. If Sinclair had not become discouraged by its lack of early exploration success, it would have owned a large part of the Prudhoe Bay field in addition to its interest in Kuparuk. Instead, the discovery well at Kuparuk turned out to be the final, and largest, discovery in Sinclair's history.

ACKNOWLEDGMENTS

Publication of this paper was permitted by ARCO, BP Exploration, and Unocal Corporation. Construction of the figures and tables would not have been possible without the generous assistance of the Kuparuk Geology and Engineering groups, especially Dan Fortier, Don Brizzolara, Dean Gingrich, and Mike Wiley. The paper was reviewed by Naresh Kumar and Mason Hill. Special thanks are also due to the unending patience of Myrtle Osterhaus and the drafting department.

REFERENCES

Atlantic Richfield Co., 1987 Annual Report.
Atlantic Richfield Co., 1988 Annual Report.
Atlantic Richfield Co., 1989 First Quarter Report.
Bally, A. W., and S. Snelson, 1980, Realms of subsidence: Bulletin of Canadian Petroleum Geology, v. 28, p. 9–75.
Basye, D., 1969, Secrecy shroud lifts on giant Prudhoe Bay field: Oil & Gas Journal, November 24, p. 49–54.
Bennison, A. P., 1986, Readers' forum: AAPG Explorer, September, p. 28.
Bergman, K. M., and R. G. Walker, 1987, The importance of sea-level fluctuations in the formation of linear conglomerate bodies; Carrot Creek Member of Cardium Formation, Cretaceous Western Interior Seaway, Alberta, Canada: Journal of Sedimentary Petrology, v. 57, p. 651–665.
Bird, K. J., 1987, The framework geology of the North Slope of Alaska as related to oil-source rock correlations, in L. B. Magoon and G. E. Claypool, eds., Alaska North Slope oil-rock correlation study: American Association of Petroleum Geologists Studies in Geology 20, p. 3–29.
Bowsher, A. L., 1987, Sinclair Oil and Gas Company on the Alaskan North Slope, 1957–69, in I. Tailleur and P. Weimer, eds., Alaskan North Slope geology: Pacific Section SEPM, Bakersfield, California, v. 1, p. 13–18.
British Petroleum Company Limited, 1977, Our industry, petroleum: p. 158–161.
Brown, D., 1986, Prudhoe Bay had its doubters: AAPG Explorer, June, p. 17.

Carmalt, S. W., and B. St. John, 1986, Giant oil and gas fields, *in* M. T. Halbouty, ed., Future petroleum provinces of the world: American Association of Petroleum Geologists Memoir 40, p. 11-54.

Carman, G. J., and P. Hardwick, 1983, Geology and regional setting of Kuparuk oil field, Alaska: American Association of Petroleum Geologists Bulletin, v. 67, p. 1014-1031.

Carter, C., and S. Laufeld, 1975, Ordovician and Silurian fossils in well cores from the North Slope of Alaska: American Association of Petroleum Geologists Bulletin, v. 59, p. 457-464.

Clutterbuck, P. R., and S. E. Dance, 1982, The use of simulation in decision-making for the Kuparuk River field development: Society of Petroleum Engineers paper 10762 presented at the California Regional Meeting, San Francisco, California.

Cooper, B., 1973, Alaska, the last frontier: William Morrow and Company, Inc., New York, p. 127.

Eggert, J. T., 1985, Petrology, diagenesis, and reservoir quality of Lower Cretaceous Kuparuk River Formation sandstone, Kuparuk River field, North Slope, Alaska [abs.]: American Association of Petroleum Geologists Bulletin, v. 69, p. 664.

Gaynor, G. C., and M. H. Scheihing, 1988, Shelf depositional environments and reservoir characteristics of the Kuparuk River Formation (Lower Cretaceous), Kuparuk field, North Slope, Alaska, *in* A. J. Lomando and P. M. Harris, eds., Giant oil and gas fields: SEPM Core Workshop No. 12, v. 1, p. 333-389.

Harris, M., 1988, Beaufort causeways: Alaska Construction and Oil, December, p. 12-16.

Hubbard, R. J., S. P. Edrich, and R. P. Rattey, 1987, The geologic evolution and hydrocarbon habitat of the 'Arctic Alaska Microplate': Marine and Petroleum Geology, v. 4, p. 2-34.

Jamison, H. C., L. D. Brockett, and R. A. McIntosh, 1980, Prudhoe Bay—a ten-year perspective, *in* M. T. Halbouty, ed., Giant oil fields of the decade, 1968-1978: American Association of Petroleum Geologists Memoir 30, p. 289-314.

Jones, H. P., and R. G. Speers, 1976, Permo-Triassic reservoirs of Prudhoe Bay field, North Slope, Alaska, *in* J. Braunstein, ed., North American oil and gas fields: American Association of Petroleum Geologists Memoir 24, p. 23-50.

Kent, P. E., 1970, Entry into Alaska: BP Shield, The British Petroleum Company Limited, p. 5-9.

Knock, D. G., 1987, Lithofacies, depositional setting, and petrography of the Kemik sandstone, Arctic National Wildlife Refuge (ANWR), northeastern Alaska: M. S. Thesis, University of Alaska, Fairbanks, Alaska, 135 p.

Lerand, M., 1973, Beaufort Sea, *in* R. G. McCrossan, ed., Future petroleum provinces of Canada—their geology and potential: Canadian Society of Petroleum Geologists, Memoir 1, p. 315-386.

Magoon, L. E., and K. J. Bird, 1985, Alaskan North Slope petroleum geochemistry for the Shublik Formation, Kingak Shale, pebble shale unit, and Torok Formation, *in* L. B. Magoon and G. E. Claypool, eds., Alaska North Slope oil-rock correlation study: American Association of Petroleum Geologists Studies in Geology 20, p. 31-48.

Masterson, W. D., and C. E. Paris, 1987, Depositional history and reservoir description of the Kuparuk River Formation, North Slope, Alaska, *in* I. Tailleur and P. Weimer, eds., Alaskan North Slope geology: Pacific Section SEPM, Bakersfield, California, v. 1, p. 95-107.

Morgridge, D. L., and W. B. Smith, Jr., 1972, Geology and discovery of Prudhoe Bay field, eastern Arctic Slope, Alaska, *in* R. E. King, ed., Stratigraphic oil and gas fields—classification, exploration methods, and case histories: American Association of Petroleum Geologists Memoir 16, p. 489-501.

Mull, C. G., 1985, Cretaceous tectonics, depositional cycles, and the Nanushuk Group, Brooks Range and Arctic Slope, Alaska, *in* A. C. Huffman, ed., Geology of the Nanushuk Group and related rocks: U. S. Geological Survey Bulletin 1614, p. 7-36.

Odin, G. S., and Letolle, R., 1980, Glauconitization and phosphatization environments: A tentative comparison, *in* Y. K. Benton, ed., Marine phosphorites—geochemistry, occurrence, genesis: Society of Economic Paleontologists and Mineralogists Special Publication 29, p. 227-237.

Schindler, J. F., 1983, National Petroleum Reserve in Alaska history of the second exploration 1975 to 1982: U.S. Geological Survey Office of the National Petroleum Reserve in Alaska, p. 78.

Sedivy, R. A., I. E. Penfield, H. I. Halpern, R. J. Drozd, G. A. Cole, and R. Burwood, 1987, Investigation of source rock-crude oil relationships in the northern Alaska hydrocarbon habitat, *in* I. Tailleur and P. Weimer, eds., Alaskan North Slope geology: Pacific Section SEPM, Bakersfield, California, v. 1, p. 169-179.

Seifert, W. K., J. M. Moldowan, and R. W. Jones, 1979, Application of biological marker chemistry to petroleum exploration: Proceedings of the 10th World Petroleum Congress in Bucharest, Heyden and Son, London, p. 425-440.

Specht, R. N., A. E. Brown, J. H. Carlisle, and C. H. Selman, 1986, Geophysical case history, Prudhoe Bay field: Geophysics, v. 51, p. 1039-1049.

Tabbert, R. L., and J. E. Bennett, 1976, Lower Cretaceous microplankton from the subsurface of northern Alaska [abs]: Geoscience and Man, v. 15, p. 146.

Werner, M. R., 1987, West Sak and Ugnu sands: low-gravity oil zones of the Kuparuk River area, Alaskan North Slope, *in* I. Tailleur and P. Weimer, eds., Alaskan North Slope geology: Pacific Section SEPM, Bakersfield, California, v. 1, p. 109-118.

Williams, S. M., S. Suellentrop, W. D. Masterson, L. Blacker, R. May, and J. Brandstetter, 1984, Kuparuk River field fullfield waterflood project—testimony for application for additional recovery: Alaska Oil and Gas Conservation Commission, May 23, Anchorage, Alaska.

SUGGESTED READING

Adams, B. H., 1983, Stress-sensitive permeability in a high-permeability sandstone reservoir—the Kuparuk field: Society of Petroleum Engineers paper 11718 presented at the California Regional Meeting, Ventura, California. Presents evidence that fractures in some wells close during drawdown tests and open during buildup tests. Although not stated in the paper, most wells with high buildup permeabilities are also faulted.

Bihn, G. C., and S. A. Brown, 1985, Perforation performance in the Kuparuk River field: Society of Petroleum Engineers paper 14323 presented at the 60th Annual Technical Conference and Exhibition, Las Vegas, Nevada. Evaluates field performance of different perforating techniques.

Boyer, R. C., and C. Wu, 1983, The role of reservoir lithology in design of an acidization program: Kuparuk River Formation, North Slope, Alaska: Society of Petroleum Engineers paper 11722 presented at the Regional Meeting, Ventura, California. Assesses the effects of different acid treatments upon two Kuparuk lithologies.

Griffin, K. W., 1985, Induced fracture orientation determination in the Kuparuk reservoir: Society of Petroleum Engineers paper 14261 presented at the 60th Annual Technical Conference and Exhibition, Las Vegas, Nevada. Reports results of several techniques used to determine the in-situ stress regime at the Kuparuk field.

Halgedahl, S. L., and R. D. Jarrard, 1987, Paleomagnetism of the Kuparuk River Formation from oriented drill core: evidence for rotation of the Arctic Alaska plate, *in* I. Tailleur and P. Weimer, eds., Alaskan North Slope geology: Pacific Section SEPM, Bakersfield, California, v. 2, p. 581-617. Presents evidence that the Canada Basin opened by counter-clockwise separation of Arctic Alaska from the Canadian Arctic islands.

Paris, C. E., 1981, Petrography, lithofacies, and depositional setting of the Kuparuk River Formation, North Slope, Alaska: M. S. Thesis, University of Alaska, Fairbanks, Alaska, 95 p. The seminal research that led to our present-day understanding of Kuparuk depositional history.

Appendix 1. Field Description

Field name .... *Kuparuk River field*

Ultimate recoverable reserves .... *1.6 billion bbl*

Field location:

    Country .... *U. S. A.*

    State .... *Alaska*

    Basin/Province .... *North Slope*

Field discovery:

    Year first pay discovered *1969*

    Year second pay discovered .... *1971 (West Sak sandstones; no production at present)*

    Third pay

Discovery well name and general location:

    First pay .... *Ugnu State No. 1, Sec. 22, T12N, R9E*

    Second pay .... *West Sak State No. 1, Sec. 2, T11N, R10E*

    Third pay

Discovery well operator .... *Sinclair (now ARCO)*

    Second pay

    Third pay

IP in barrels per day and/or cubic feet or cubic meters per day:

    First pay .... *1056 bbl/day*

    Second pay

    Third pay

All other zones with shows of oil and gas in the field:

Age	Formation	Type of Show
Maastrichtian–Paleocene	*Ugnu*	*Bitumen*
Maastrichtian	*West Sak*	*Low-gravity oil*

Geologic concept leading to discovery and method or methods used to delineate prospect, e.g., surface geology, subsurface geology, seeps, magnetic data, gravity data, seismic data, seismic refraction, nontechnical:

The Kuparuk River field area was considered prospective because potential reservoir rocks outcropped in the Arctic National Wildlife Refuge (ANWR) to the east, and indications of source rocks were provided by oil seeps and exploratory drilling in the Naval Petroleum Reserve to the south and west. When land in the area became available for leasing, the Kuparuk structural closure was clearly delineated by seismic surveys. Aeromagnetic and geomorphic anomalies provided additional supporting evidence for the seismic interpretation.

Structure:

    Province/basin type .... *Bally 221; Klemme II Cc*

    Tectonic history

Late Devonian orogeny created metamorphic basement on the Alaskan North Slope. From Carboniferous to Neocomian time, sediments on the North Slope were derived from tectonic highlands along the Barrow arch to the north of the Kuparuk River field. After deposition of the Kuparuk lower member, regional Neocomian extension caused by a rifting event produced an unconformity surface. The Kuparuk upper member was deposited on the unconformity surface. The field area was then buried by northeastward prograding sediments of Late Cretaceous to Tertiary age that were shed during the Brookian orogeny. During early Tertiary time, the area was tilted to the east.

    Regional structure

South flank of Barrow arch.

KUPARUK

Local structure
Northwest-trending anticline that plunges 0.8° to the southeast.

Trap:

Trap type(s)
One anticlinal trap (intervals A-3, A-4, and C-3/C-4), 2 truncation unconformity traps (intervals A-1 and A-2), 1 pinchout trap (interval A-5), and 1 onlap trap (interval C-1).

Basin stratigraphy (major stratigraphic intervals from surface to deepest penetration in field):

Chronostratigraphy	Formation	Depth to Top in ft
Tertiary	Sagavanirktok	50
Late Cretaceous	Colville Group	2500
Early Cretaceous	Ugnuravik Group (includes Kuparuk River Fm.)	5500
Jurassic	Kingak	7000
Permian/Triassic	Sadlerochit Group	8000
Carboniferous	Lisburne Group	9000
Pre-Mississippian	Basement complex	10,000

Location of well in field

Reservoir characteristics:

Number of reservoirs 1

Formations .... Kuparuk River (units A and C)

Ages .... Unit A: Early Cretaceous (Berriasian [?] to Valanginian)
Unit C: Early Cretaceous (Hauterivian to Barremian)

Depths to tops of reservoirs .... 6000 ft

Gross thickness (top to bottom of producing interval) .... 30–400 ft

Net thickness—total thickness of producing zones

	Unit A	Unit C	Total Kuparuk
Average	20	15	35
Maximum	70	74	105

Lithology
Unit A: very fine to fine-grained, well-sorted, quartzose sandstone
Unit C: very fine to coarse-grained, poorly sorted, quartzose, glauconitic and sideritic sandstone

Porosity type .... Unit A: intergranular porosity with minor secondary porosity
Unit C: secondary porosity with minor intergranular porosity

Average porosity .... Unit A, 23%; Unit C, 24%

Average permeability .... Unit A, 113 md; Unit C, 138 md

Seals:

Upper
Formation, fault, or other feature .... Kalubik Formation
Lithology .... Mudstone

Lateral
Formation, fault, or other feature .... Pinchout and truncation of A and C sandstones
Lithology .... Mudstone

Source:

Formation and age .... Shublik, Triassic; Kingak, Jurassic; HRZ, Cretaceous

Lithology .... Shublik, mudstone, siltstone, limestone; Kingak, mudstone, siltstone; HRZ, mudstone

Average total organic carbon (TOC) .... Shublik, 1.7%; Kingak, 1.5%; HRZ, 2.4%

Maximum TOC .... Shublik, 5.6%, Kingak, 3.6%; HRZ, 5.1%

Kerogen type (I, II, or III) .... Shublik, I; Kingak, II/III; HRZ, II/III

Vitrinite reflectance (maturation) .... $R_o = 0.5$–1.3 (Shublik and Kingak), 0.4–1.0 (HRZ)

282

Time of hydrocarbon expulsion .... *Late Cretaceous–Eocene*
Present depth to top of source .... *Shublik, 8000–15,000 ft; Kingak, 7000–13,000 ft;*
HRZ, 5000–12,000 ft
Thickness .... *Shublik, 150 ft; Kingak, 1500 ft; HRZ, 200 ft*
Potential yield .... *Shublik, 20 billion bbl; Kingak, 200 billion; HRZ, 40 billion*

Appendix 2. Production Data

Field name .... *Kuparuk River*

Field size (All figures as of 9/1989):

Proved acres .... *135,000 ac*
Number of wells all years *610*
Current number of wells *590*
Well spacing .... *160 ac*
Ultimate recoverable .... *1600 million bbl*
Cumulative production .... *560 million bbl*
Annual production .... *110 million bbl*
Present decline rate .... *NA*
Initial decline rate .... *NA*
Overall decline rate .... *NA*
Annual water production .... *62 million bbl*
In place, total reserves .... *4800 million bbl*
In place, per acre-foot .... *375 bbl*
Primary recovery .... *533 million bbl*
Secondary recovery .... *1067 million bbl*
Enhanced recovery
Cumulative water production .... *67 million bbl*

Drilling and casing practices:

Amount of surface casing set .... *3500 ft*
Casing program .... *9.625 in. to 3500 ft, 7 in. to TD*
Drilling mud .... *Nondispersed, lignosulfate*
Bit program .... *12.25 in. to 3500 ft; 8.5 in. to TD*
High pressure zones

Completion practices:

Interval(s) perforated .... *A-1 through A-5; C-1, C-3, C-4*
Well treatment .... *Unit A, hydraulic fracture stimulation; Unit C, none*

Formation evaluation:

Logging suites .... *GR/SP/DIL/SFL/CAL/FDC/CNL all wells;*
BHCS/GR, SHDT 1 well per pad (each pad has 16 wells)
Testing practices
Mud logging techniques .... *Basic mudlogging on one well per pad*

Oil characteristics:

Type .... *Aromatic-naphthenic*
API gravity .... *20–27° (average 24°)*
Base .... *Naphthene-intermediate*
Initial GOR .... *350–575 SCF/STB*

KUPARUK

Sulfur, wt% *1.4–2.0*
Viscosity, SUS .... *370 at 60°F*
Pour point .... *–55°F*
Gas-oil distillate .... *19% over range 650–840°F*

Field characteristics:

Average elevation .... *–6000 ft subsea*
Initial pressure .... *3135 psi @ 6000 ft*
Present pressure .... *2500 psi*
Pressure gradient .... *0.52 psi/ft*
Temperature .... *155°F @ 6000 ft*
Geothermal gradient .... *0.023°F/ft*
Drive .... *Solution gas*
Oil column thickness .... *1000 ft*
Oil-water contact .... *–6530 to –6650 ft subsea*
Connate water *25%*
Water salinity, TDS .... *25,000 ppm*
Resistivity of water .... *0.12 ohm-m*
Bulk volume water (%) *6%*

Transportation method and market for oil and gas:

Oil is transported to the Trans-Alaska Pipeline via the Kuparuk Pipeline. Produced gas is either injected back in the reservoir, used for gas lift, or used for fuel.

KUPARUK

284

Dauletabad-Donmez Field— Commonwealth of Independent States (Former USSR)
Amu-Dar'ya Basin, Turkmenistan/Uzbekistan

JAMES W. CLARKE
U. S. Geological Survey
Reston, Virginia

KONSTANTIN KLESHCHEV
USSR Ministry of Geology
VNIGNI
Moscow, Russia

FIELD CLASSIFICATION

BASIN: Amu-Dar'ya
BASIN TYPE: Cratonic Sag
RESERVOIR ROCK TYPE: Sandstone
RESERVOIR ENVIRONMENT OF
   DEPOSITION: Fluvial

RESERVOIR AGE: Cretaceous
PETROLEUM TYPE: Gas
TRAP TYPE: Combination of Faults,
   Pinch-Outs, and Hydrodynamics

LOCATION

The Dauletabad-Donmez gas field is located in the southern part of the Amu-Dar'ya gas-oil province, which has an area of 360,000 km². This province extends across central and eastern Turkmenistan and western Uzbekistan in southern Central Asia (Figure 1). The province lies within the Turan platform, where a basement that was consolidated during the Hercynian orogeny is overlain by marine and continental Mesozoic and Cenozoic platform sedimentary rocks 1–7 km thick.

The province is bounded on the northeast by shallow occurrence of basement in the Kyzyl Kum desert and on the southwest by the Kopet Dag (Range). The northwestern boundary is drawn along a structurally high terrane. The southeastern boundary at the Afghan border is artificial because the gas-oil basin extends into Afghanistan, where it covers an additional area of 45,000 km².

The region is within the desert zone of Central Asia. The surface is covered by unconsolidated Tertiary and Quaternary deposits, and barkhan dunes and playas are common. Dust storms are frequent. Precipitation is scant, occurring mostly in the spring. The Amu-Dar'ya River, which flows across the region, is supplied by precipitation that falls to the east in the Pamir Range. The climate is hot and well suited for growing cotton, grapes, and melons (Berg, 1950).

The province is gas prone; significant oil is present only in the eastern part (Semenovich, 1976). Gas production in the province during 1980 was 3.6 trillion cubic feet (tcf) (0.103 trillion m³), and total production until the beginning of 1981 was 35 tcf (1 trillion m³). This gas is piped to the Urals and central European Commonwealth. Older fields, such as Gazli, are approaching depletion, whereas new fields, such as the giant Dauletabad-Donmez, have just come onstream.

Recoverable reserves in Dauletabad-Donmez field are estimated at 48.7 tcf. This field ranks fortieth in the world in recoverable hydrocarbons (Carmalt and St. John, 1986). The Dauletabad-Donmez field

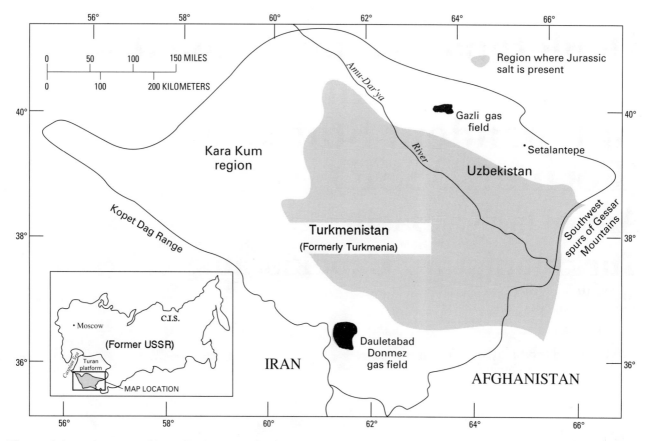

Figure 1. Location map of Amu-Dar'ya gas-oil province.

is so large that it extends across the greater part of the 1° quadrangle bounded by latitudes 36–37°N and longitudes 61–62°E (Figure 1).

The field is named for the settlement Dowlatabad, which is just across the border in Iran. The main center of habitation in the area is Sarakhs, a town that is largely in Turkmenistan with a suburb in Iran. The name Sarakhs has been given to a gas field in Iran just west of the town of Sarakhs. These two fields are thus named for localities across the border in the opposite country. The field has also gone under the name Sovetabad.

The Amu-Dar'ya gas-oil province is described in English by Clarke (1988).

HISTORY

Pre-Discovery

Exploration for oil and gas began in the region in 1929. Geological studies were made along with gravity and magnetic surveys. The first discovery was the Setalantepe gas field in 1953. Coordinated regional and detailed geological and geophysical studies of the entire region began in 1957 after discovery of the giant Gazli gas field (Aliyev et al., 1983) (Figure 1).

Discovery

The Dauletabad structural feature was first detected by small-scale geological surveys on the Neogene sediments during the years 1957–1960 (Mirzakhanov et al., 1975). Seismic surveying by the Geological Association of the Turkmen SSR was begun in 1968 and confirmed the large Dauletabad arch. This arch extends 60 km east-west and contains three highs, the westernmost of which is the Dauletabad high. The first exploration well was spudded in 1972 on this Dauletabad high and bottomed at 3542 m in 1973. Hauterivian Age (Early Cretaceous) sandstone was tested in 1974, yielding a strong flow of gas (Semenovich et al., 1983, p. 33).

Post-Discovery

The Dauletabad-Donmez gas field is now onstream. The gas enters the pipeline system of the Amu-Dar'ya oil-gas province through which it is transported to the European Commonwealth market.

STRUCTURE

Regional Structure

The Amu-Dar'ya oil-gas province lies within the Turan platform. A Mesozoic and Cenozoic sedimentary cover as much as 7 km thick rests on Paleozoic

286

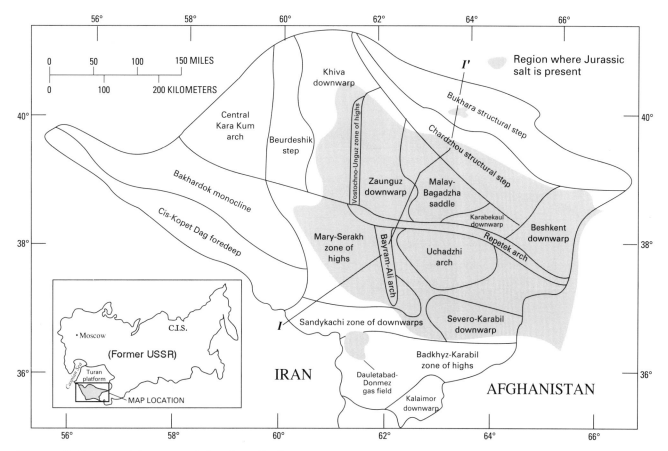

Figure 2. Structural features of the Amu-Dar'ya gas-oil province. I–I' shows the location of the structure section shown on Figure 3.

geosynclinal sedimentary rocks that were folded and mildly metamorphosed during the late Paleozoic Hercynian orogeny. Evaporites of the Upper Jurassic Kimmeridgian Gaurdak Formation divide the sedimentary section into sub-salt and supra-salt parts (Figures 2 and 3).

On the west the Turan platform extends offshore into the Caspian Sea and continues farther westward as the Scythian platform. On the north the platform joins the West Siberian platform to become part of the single epi-Paleozoic Ural-Siberian craton. On the south is the Alpine Kopet Dag foldbelt, and on the east are the southwest spurs of the Gissar Mountains, where folding took place during Neogene time. On the southeast the platform extends into Afghanistan (Figure 1).

The structure of the sedimentary cover of the Amu-Dar'ya oil-gas province formed as a response to vertical tectonic movements during the Mesozoic and Cenozoic (Yanena and Mamedov, 1982). The Amu-Dar'ya regional low extends over the eastern three-quarters of the province. On the west are the Central Kara Kum arch, Bakhardok monocline, and Cis-Kopet Dag foredeep. Some workers (e.g., Bakirov et al., 1979) divide the Amu-Dar'ya regional low by the

Repetek-Yerbent basement fault (Repetek arch of Figure 2) into the Amu-Dar'ya depression on the north and the Murgab depression on the south.

The *Central Kara Kum arch* is 250 km long in a north-south direction and 150 km wide east-west (Figure 2). Depth to basement is 1600–2200 m at the crest and 3000-3500 m on the flanks. This structural feature may coincide with a microplate caught up in the Hercynian orogenic belt.

The *Bakhardok monocline* is on the south of the Central Kara Kum arch. It is the cratonal border and is transitional to the Cis-Kopet Dag foredeep to the south. Depth to basement is 3–5 km.

The *Cis-Kopet Dag foredeep* began to form at the end of the Paleogene simultaneously with intensive folding, northward thrusting, and general uplift of the Kopet Dag foldbelt on the south. It is filled by 2 km of Neogene clastic deposits. Maximum total sedimentary thickness (Jurassic and younger) here is 6–7 km.

The *Beurdeshik step* is the northwest monoclinal flank of the Amu-Dar'ya regional low. The sedimentary cover is about 3 km thick here.

The *Khiva downwarp* contains 4–5 km of Mesozoic and Cenozoic deposits. Beneath these rocks is a

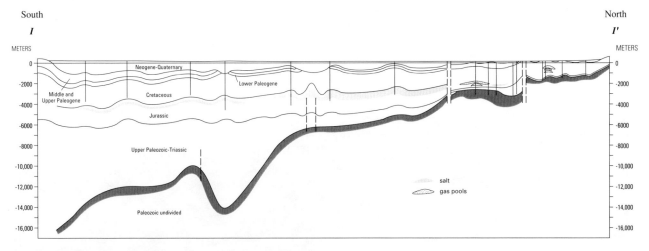

South

I

North

I'

METERS

METERS

Neogene-Quaternary

Lower Paleogene

Middle and Upper Paleogene

Cretaceous

Jurassic

Upper Paleozoic-Triassic

Paleozoic undivided

salt

gas pools

Figure 3. Structure section along line I–I' of Figure 2. (From Maksimov et al., 1987.) Length of the cross section is about 650 km (~400 mi).

graben filled by 3 km of Permian and Triassic deposits, below which is the Hercynian basement at a depth of 8–10 km.

The *Vostochno-Unguz zone of highs* is narrow and about 150 km long and has three highs along its axis.

The *Zaunguz downwarp* is a relatively flat feature where depth to pre-Jurassic basement is more than 4 km. Within it are several structural highs.

The *Malay-Bagadzha saddle* is structurally higher than downwarps on the east and west and structurally lower than linear zones on the north and south. Depth to pre-Jurassic basement here is about 4 km.

The *Karabekaul downwarp* is filled by 5–6 km of largely Jurassic and Cretaceous sedimentary rocks. Several large anticlines are present within this structural feature.

The *Beshkent downwarp* has a sedimentary thickness of 4–5 km. Within it are narrow anticlinal zones of southwest trend.

The *Chardzhou structural step* is characterized by block structure due to the intersection of northwest-trending Hercynian structure in the basement and northeast-trending Alpine structure. Depth to basement is 2.8–4 km.

The *Bukhara structural step* also consists of block structures reflecting the older northwest Hercynian trends and the younger Alpine trends. Sedimentary thickness is 1–2 km.

The *Repetek arch* is associated with the Repetek-Yerbent basement fault, which extends across the Amu-Dar'ya regional low. This arch is 450 km long and 12–15 km wide. The Jurassic salt occurs here as domes, which are 2000–3000 m high, even reaching the surface in places. A chain of anticlines extends along the arch, and most of these are salt-assist structural features. Depth to basement here ranges from 6 to 14 km.

To the south of the Repetek arch are the *Mary-Serakh zone of highs* and the *Uchadzhi arch*, which

are separated by the *Bayram-Ali arch*. These three structural features are combined by some authors (Luppov et al., 1972) into the Mary-Uchadzhi monocline, which dips southward as the northern flank of the Murgab depression. In the Mary-Serakh zone of highs, the base of the Jurassic is at depths of 5–6 km, and beneath this is another 4–5 km of upper Paleozoic and Triassic sedimentary rocks.

The *Severo-Karabil downwarp* is a structural low between the Uchadzhin arch on the north and the Badkhyz-Karabil zone of highs on the south. The base of the Jurassic here is at a depth of 6–7 km.

The *Badkhuz-Karabil zone of highs* is a system of raised basement blocks. Depth to the base of the Jurassic is as much as 3 km. Dauletabad-Donmez field is located in the northwest part of this zone.

The *Kalaimor downwarp* on the extreme south is largely in Afghanistan.

Structure of the Field

Dauletabad-Donmez field extends into two tectonic features, the Badkhyz-Karabil zone of highs on the south and the Sandykachi zone of downwarps on the north. Major north–south-trending faults are present on the east and west sides of the field (Figure 4).

Within the field, erosion surfaces are present at the base of the Cretaceous System and of the Neogene Subsystem. The Lower Cretaceous Hauterivian Shatlyk horizon, which is host to the gas pool, dips monoclinally to the north across the area of the field from an elevation of –2400 m on the south to –3450 m on the north. East–west-trending high-angle normal faults are present in the central part of the field (Figure 5). These east-west faults divide the field into south, central, and north blocks (Nepesov et al., 1984). Two gas pools compose the field, one in the north block and one in the south block (Figure 6). The reservoirs in the central block are water-bearing.

288

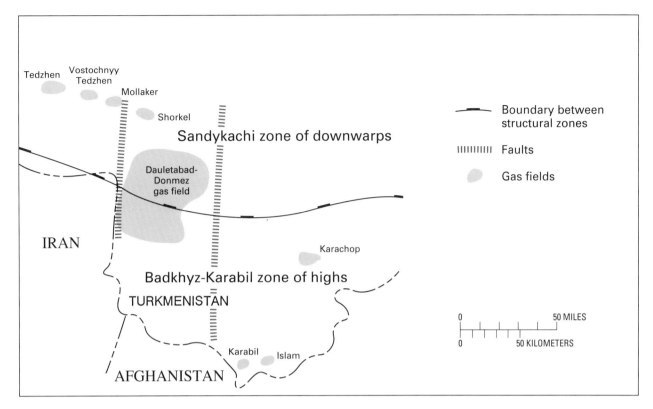

Figure 4. Structural features of the region of Dauletabad-Donmez and other fields of the southern part of the Amu-Dar'ya gas-oil province. (From Zhabrev et al., 1983.)

Satellite photographs show widely distributed fractures within the field, particularly in the central and eastern parts where these fractures appear to be only tens of meters apart (Amurskiy et al., 1984). Where high concentration of fracturing is indicated, drill cores commonly have slickensides. Wells close to fracture zones are significantly more productive than those at a greater distance.

The thickness of the Valanginian and lower Hauterivian rocks, which separate the overlying Shatlyk reservoir from the underlying Jurassic rocks, decreases from 180 m on the north to 30 m on the south. On the north this pre-Shatlyk Lower Cretaceous sequence consists of clastic and carbonate rocks that contain a large number of impermeable beds, whereas on the south, they are largely silt and sand, containing only thin, sporadic impermeable beds. Therefore, in the area south of the line A–A' in Figure 6 the Jurassic and Lower Cretaceous rocks could have been hydrodynamically connected during stages of tectonic activity.

Although the overall structure of the field is monoclinal, the southern half is a broad high, the Dauletabad arch; and the northern half spreads northward as a lobe, the Donmez nose (Figure 5). Ring features on satellite photographs coincide with the crest of the Dauletabad arch. A group of lineaments in the northeastern part of the field strike northwestward toward the Donmez nose (Figure 6) (Amurskiy and Solov'yev, 1982).

STRATIGRAPHY

Introduction

The stratigraphic section of the Amu-Dar'ya region is divided into two parts: pre-Jurassic and Jurassic to Holocene. The pre-Jurassic stratigraphy is synthesized on the basis of outcrops along the margins of the province and from geophysical surveys. The rocks of Jurassic to Holocene age are known from drilling and geophysical surveys.

Pre-Jurassic Rocks

During the Silurian and Devonian a marine basin was present just north of the study area. This basin was part of a seaway that extended eastward into northern China, northward as the Uralian miogeocline, and westward through the Caucasus into Central Europe and thence along eastern North America as the Appalachian miogeocline. Marine invasion into the study area itself took place only in Early Carboniferous time when coarse clastic and carbonate sediments were deposited (Table 1). Some volcanic rocks are also present in this section. Orogenic activity late in the Carboniferous resulted in folding, uplift, and erosion but not strong metamorphism of the Paleozoic sedimentary rocks. Granites were intruded during this orogenic activity.

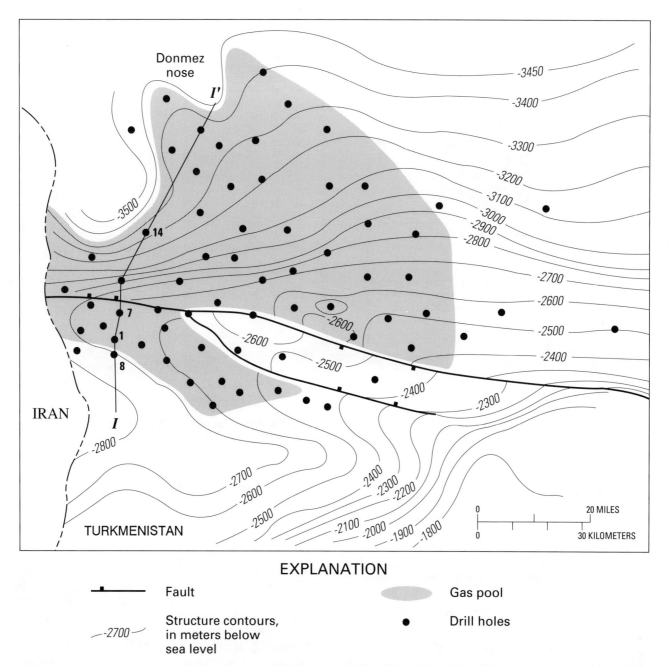

Fault

Gas pool

Structure contours,
in meters below
sea level

Drill holes

Figure 5. Structure map of Dauletabad-Donmez gas field on the top of the Lower Cretaceous Shatlyk horizon. (From Maksimov et al., 1987.) I–I' is the location of the cross section shown on Figure 7.

Following the Hercynian orogeny, some sectors subsided as narrow grabens where coarse Permian and Triassic redbeds were deposited. The pre-Jurassic rocks are the economic basement of the region.

Jurassic to Holocene Rocks

With the Jurassic, the Amu-Dar'ya region entered the sag stage of its development. Jurassic and younger rocks are covered everywhere by thick unconsolidated Neogene deposits; however, they are very well documented by the extensive drilling in the region.

The Lower Jurassic Series consists of clastic continental deposits; conglomerate, sandstone, siltstone, and coal-bearing shale are present.

The Middle Jurassic Series is an upward continuation of the clastic rocks of the Lower Jurassic. Thickness of the Lower and Middle Jurassic section in the central part of the region is as much as 1000 m. Toward the borders, however, it thins to less than 200 m or is not present at all.

The Upper Jurassic Series is represented in the Amu-Dar'ya area by the Callovian, Oxfordian, Kimmeridgian, and Tithonian Stages (Luppov et al., 1972). Limestones of Callovian and principally

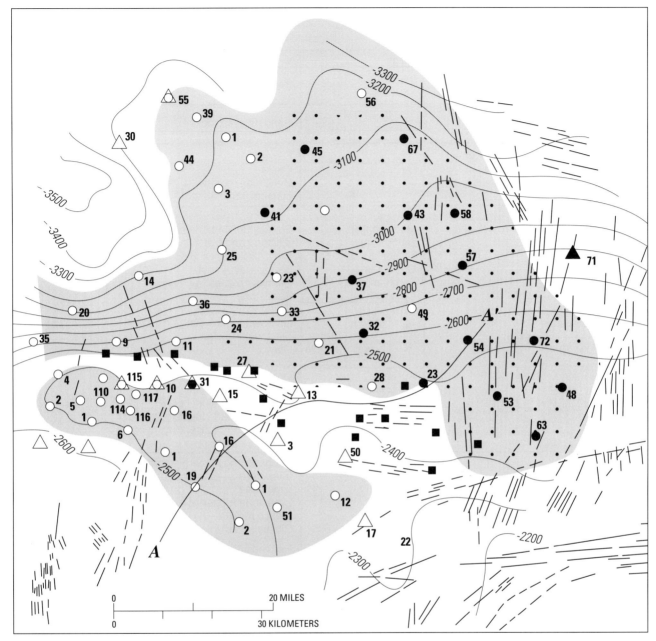

Structure contours on seismic
horizon close to top of Barremian
rocks, in meters. ■ Sectors where
wave picture is complex

Fractures recognized from
satellite photographs

Gas pools

Hydrogen sulfide present in gas

Wells yielding:
○ gas
△ water
△ gas and water

Hydrogen sulfide
present in:
● gas
▲ water

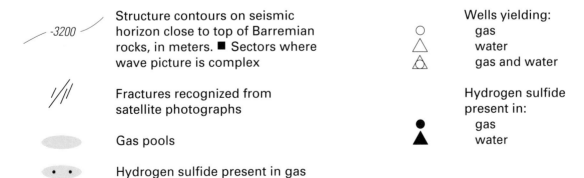

Figure 6. Distribution of hydrogen sulfide dissolved in gases, and also fractures in Dauletabad-Donmez gas field. (From Amurskiy et al., 1984.) Jurassic and Lower Cretaceous rocks could have been hydrodynamically connected south of line A-A' during stages of tectonic activity. (See text, *Structure of the Field.*)

291

Table 1. Generalized stratigraphic section of Amu-Dar'ya gas-oil province.

	System	Series	Stage	Lithology
Cenozoic	Quaternary	Holocene Pleistocene		Fluvial and eolian deposits
	Neogene	Pliocene Miocene		Sandy-clayey rocks
	Paleogene	Oligocene Eocene Paleocene		Clays Clays Clay, marl (northwest), limestone (central), dolomite, gypsum (southeast)
Mesozoic	Cretaceous	Upper	Danian Maastrichtian Campanian Santonian Coniacian Turonian Cenomanian	Sandstone, carbonate rocks Siltstone and clay Clay, siltstone, sandstone, limestone Sandy-clayey rocks Sandstone and clay Sandstone
		Lower	Albian — Upper / Middle	Siltstone and clay Limestone, marl, clay, siltstone
			Albian — Lower: Upper / Middle / Lower	Siltstone and clay Clay Clay, siltstone, limestone
			Aptian Barremian	Limestone, siltstone, marl, clay Limestone, marl, clay
			Neocomian — Hauterivian Valanginian Berriasian	Siltstone, sandstone, clay, limestone, marl, dolomite, gypsum Limestone, dolomite, clay, gypsum
	Jurassic	Upper	Tithonian Kimmeridgian Oxfordian Callovian*	Redbeds and some evaporites Evaporites Limestone Limestone (upper), clastics (lower)
		Middle Lower		Clastic rocks Clastic rocks
Paleozoic	Triassic Permian			Redbeds (local occurrence)
	Carboniferous			Coarse clastic and carbonate rocks, some volcanics

*The Callovian is placed in the Upper Jurassic by the Soviets.

Oxfordian Ages are the main gas and oil reservoir rocks of the region, and evaporites of Kimmeridgian Age are the main seals.

The lower Callovian consists of clastic rocks where present. The upper Callovian is limestone in places, a precursor of the overlying Oxfordian limestones. For example, in the area of Dauletabad-Donmez field, which is on the southern margin of the basin, Callovian limestones and dolomites 300–350 m thick rest on mildly metamorphosed Permian to Triassic shales (Mirzakhanov et al., 1975; Yanena and Mamedov, 1982). The absence of Lower and Middle Jurassic rocks here is due to either erosion or nondeposition.

The Oxfordian Stage consists of a thick blanket of limestone, which along with the underlying Callovian limestones is 500–600 m thick. These limestones are generally interpreted as reef deposits (Ryzhkov et al., 1983).

Resting unconformably on the Callovian and Oxfordian limestones is an evaporite unit as much as 650 m thick. This is the Gaurdak Formation of Kimmeridgian Age; it extends over an area of 300,000 km² (Figure 2). These evaporites generally consist of a lower anhydrite, lower salt, middle anhydrite, upper salt, and upper anhydrite. They have been variously interpreted as lagoonal deposits and as deep-water marine deposits. Overlying the evaporites are Tithonian redbeds, which contain some evaporites.

Total thickness of the Upper Jurassic section ranges from 1500 m in the southeastern part of the Amu-Dar'ya region to less than 100 m on the Central Kara Kum arch.

The Cretaceous System, as with the Jurassic System, is known in the Amu-Dar'ya region only from drilling. The base of the Cretaceous is generally placed at a change from continental redbeds of Jurassic affinities to overlying marine deposits.

The Lower Cretaceous section in the Amu-Dar'ya region consists of as much as 1200 m of marine and lagoonal-continental clastic and carbonate rocks. The Berriasian, Valanginian, Hauterivian, Barremian, Aptian, and Albian Stages are represented.

The Berriasian to Valanginian section consists of silty-clayey, organoclastic, dolomitic limestone, which is interbedded with dolomite, clay, and gypsum. This section is 105–155 m thick.

The Hauterivian rocks are subdivided into a lower, largely redbed siltstone and sandstone unit as much as 140 m thick and an upper siltstone, clay, limestone, marl, dolomite, and gypsum unit as much as 70 m thick. The Dauletabad-Donmez gas deposit is in this lower Hauterivian redbed unit.

The Barremian Stage consists of three parts. The lower is an oolitic limestone 70 m thick; the middle is limestone, marl, and clay 80 m thick; and the upper is largely dark-gray clay about 40 m thick. Total thickness of the Barremian is 163–180 m.

The Aptian rocks are alternating oolitic and silty limestones, siltstones, marls, and clays having a total thickness of 70–100 m.

The Albian Stage is subdivided into five parts, the lower three being lower Albian, the fourth middle Albian, and the fifth upper Albian. The lowest unit in this section is dark-gray clay, siltstone, and limestone as much as 50 m thick. The second unit is dark-gray clay as much as 240 m thick. The topmost part of the lower Albian is 80 m of siltstone and clay. The middle Albian is limestone, marl, clay, and siltstone 100–120 m thick, and the upper Albian consists of alternating siltstone and clay. Total thickness of the Albian is as much as 580 m.

Maximum thickness of the Lower Cretaceous Series in the Amu-Dar'ya region is 1300 m.

The Upper Cretaceous rocks of the Amu-Dar'ya region rest disconformably on the upper Albian clastic rocks. All stages of the Upper Cretaceous are represented.

The Cenomanian Stage consists largely of gray quartzo-feldspathic sandstone 170–300 m thick.

The Turonian Stage is mostly gray clay in the lower part and sandstone in the upper. Its total thickness is up to 247 m.

The Coniacian Stage is composed of sandy-clayey rocks and a few beds of limestone. Thickness ranges from 20 m in the south to 164 m in the north.

The Santonian Stage consists of clays, siltstone, sandstone, and limestone. Thickness is 58–160 m.

The Campanian Stage in the south is largely siltstone and clay; some limestone is present. Thickness is 260 m. In the north it consists of a lower siltstone and clay unit as much as 95 m thick and an upper clay unit 120 m thick.

The Maastrichtian Stage consists mostly of sandstone in the lower part and carbonate rocks in the upper. Thickness is 10–25 m.

Total thickness of the Upper Cretaceous is 1500 m in the eastern part of the Amu-Dar'ya region, 1300 m in the southern part, and only 400 m on the Central Kara Kum arch on the west.

Paleogene rocks crop out in several places in the valley of the Amu-Dar'ya River; however, these rocks are known largely from drilling. The Paleocene section consists of limy clay and marl on the northwest, limestone in the central area, and dolomite and gypsum on the southeast. Thickness is 25–110 m. The Eocene sediments are largely clays and may be more than 400 m thick. The Oligocene sediments are also largely clays, and their thickness is 0–82 m.

The Neogene sequence is composed mostly of continental sandy-clayey rocks. Red colors predominate in the lower part and gray in the upper part. Thickness ranges from 100 to 1500 m. There is a gradual transition from the upper part of the Oligocene to the Neogene Subsystem, but within the Neogene are several erosional breaks where Miocene and Pliocene rocks rest directly on Mesozoic and Paleogene rocks.

Pleistocene and Holocene sediments are fluvial and eolian deposits. They are less than 100 m thick.

Stratigraphy of the Field

At the base of the sedimentary cover in Dauletabad-Donmez field are Upper Jurassic (Callovian) limestones and dolomites 300–350 m thick. In the northern half of the field is a wedge of Kimmeridgian and Tithonian rocks 300 m thick that pinches out to the south at about the middle of the field (Figure 7).

The Cretaceous rocks rest on an erosion surface that truncates the Upper Jurassic rocks. At its base are Valanginian limestones, and these are overlain by Hauterivian sandstones and shales. The Hauterivian section is divided into lower, middle, and upper parts. The lower and upper parts are characterized by an east–west-trending zonation. The north zone consists of marl and silty clay; the central zone of sandstone, siltstone, and clay; and the south zone of sandstone and subordinate siltstone and gravel (Valkuliyev et al., 1983; Nepesov and Gendler, 1986.) The middle part of the Hauterivian section is generally called the Shatlyk horizon and is the reservoir of Dauletabad-Donmez field (Figure 8). Above the Hauterivian Stage are Barremian limestones, Aptian clayey carbonate rocks, Albian clayey-silty rocks, and Upper Cretaceous carbonate and various clastic rocks. Total thickness of the Cretaceous section is 1765 m.

Overlying the Cretaceous rocks are a 300 m section of Paleocene carbonate beds and a 500 m section of

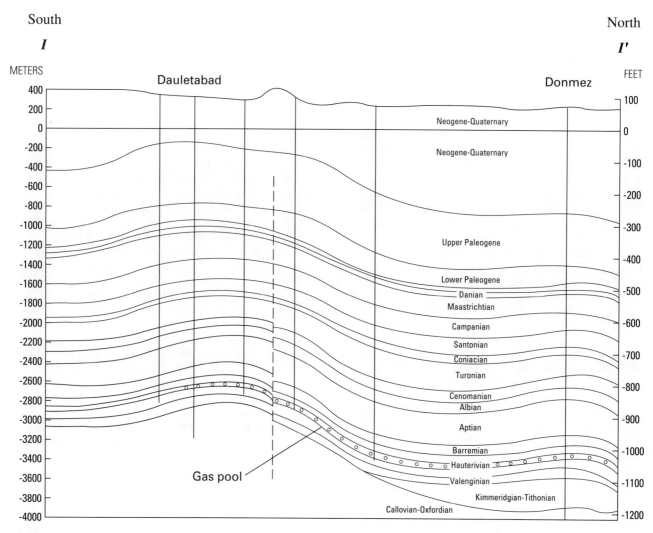

South I

North I'

METERS

FEET

Dauletabad

Donmez

Neogene-Quaternary

Neogene-Quaternary

Upper Paleogene

Lower Paleogene

Danian

Maastrichtian

Campanian

Santonian

Coniacian

Turonian

Cenomanian

Albian

Aptian

Barremian

Hauterivian

Valenginian

Gas pool

Kimmeridgian-Tithonian

Callovian-Oxfordian

Figure 7. South to north profile along line I–I' of Figure 5. (From Maksimov et al., 1987.) The cross section length is about 93 km (~58 mi).

Eocene clays. At the top of the section are about 500 m of Neogene and Quaternary continental clastic deposits.

TRAPS

Plays

Five plays are recognized in the sedimentary cover of the Amu-Dar'ya oil-gas province.

The *Lower and Middle Jurassic play* consists of 100–400 m of alternating clay, sandstone, and siltstone. Gas has been found in this part of the section in the northwestern part of the Amu-Dar'ya gas-oil provinces.

The *Upper Jurassic play* consists of Callovian to Oxfordian reef carbonate deposits up to 500 m thick.

It extends throughout the province. The seal is the thick Kimmeridgian to Tithonian evaporite. Along the margins of the province where this seal is not present (Figure 2), the gas has migrated into the overlying Cretaceous plays.

The *Lower Cretaceous play* is composed largely of alternating sandstone, siltstone, and clays. The seal is an Aptian–Albian clay unit, which separates this play from the overlying Albian–Cenomanian play. This Lower Cretaceous play is gas-bearing in most of the fields along the northern and southern margins of the Amu-Dar'ya province, including the Dauletabad-Donmez field.

The *Albian-Cenomanian play* is gas-bearing along the northeastern, northern, and northwestern margins of the province. The reservoirs are sandstone and siltstone, and the seal is a Turonian clay.

The *Paleogene play* is favorable in the northeastern part of the province. Several pools have been found in clastic reservoirs.

294

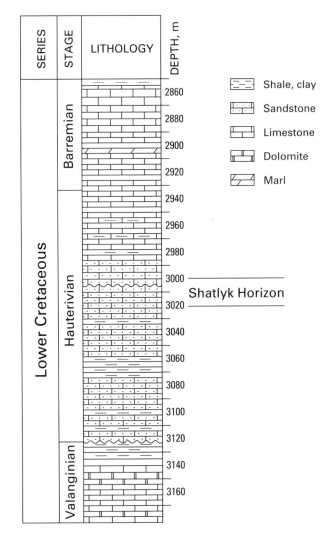

SERIES	STAGE	LITHOLOGY	DEPTH, m

Shale, clay

Sandstone

Limestone

Dolomite

Marl

Lower Cretaceous

Barremian

Hauterivian

Valanginian

Shatlyk Horizon

2860
2880
2900
2920
2940
2960
2980
3000
3020
3040
3060
3080
3100
3120
3140
3160

Figure 8. Typical lithologic log in Dauletabad-Donmez field. (From Maksimov et al., 1987.)

Reservoirs

Dauletabad-Donmez is one of several fields in the Amu-Dar'ya oil-gas province in which the gas occurs in red sandstone reservoirs of the Shatlyk horizon of Lower Cretaceous Hauterivian Stage (Amurskiy et al., 1984). This is a dry-gas play, which extends westward into Iran where the pools are in Upper Jurassic carbonate rocks.

The reservoir rock is fine- to medium-grained, reddish-brown sandstone, which contains thin beds of argillaceous siltstone (Mirzakhanov et al., 1975). In zones where the gas is sour, the sandstone is gray and pyrite is present. The sandstones consist of angular grains of quartz and feldspar cemented by calcite and clay (Nepesov et al., 1984). Overgrowth on quartz grains has lowered porosity and permeability, whereas leaching of cement has increased these parameters (Mavyyev and Nepesov, 1985).

The sandstone reservoirs thin toward the south and commonly pass into conglomerates (Figure 9).

These conglomerates are reddish brown, and the pebbles consist of silicic rocks, quartz, and, rarely, extrusive and carbonate rocks. The matrix is sand, silt, and clay. In calculating reserves, the sandstone and conglomerate facies cannot be combined; rather, each must be treated separately (Makarova and Bakun, 1987).

Effective thickness of the reservoir is 17.7 m on the north block and 10 m on the south and east. Porosity is 18–21%, and permeability is 200–700 md. Initial formation temperature was 133°C on the north block and 120°C on the south. Initial formation pressure was 39 MPa on the north block, 38 MPa on the south, and 34 MPa on the east (Zhabrev et al., 1983). The position of the water-gas contact is at –3438 m on the north and –2586 m on the south. The total drop to the north is more than 850 m, and the inclination is at 18 m per km (Kravchenko, 1983). In spite of this great inclination to the north, the formation pressure within the field has a narrow range (34–39 MPa). Initial gas yields were 830–920 thousand cubic meters per day (Maksimov et al., 1987).

The seal for the gas at Dauletabad-Donmez is carbonate rock of the Barremian Stage (Figure 8). Beneath the gas pool is dense, argillaceous carbonate rock of the lower part of the Hauterivian Stage (Mirzakhanov et al., 1975). The pool is contained structurally on the north and northwest by structural noses. On the east and southeast the pool is contained hydrodynamically and is compared with Hugoton field of the U.S. Mid-Continent (Kravchenko, 1983). The deposit must be young—indeed in progress of formation at the present time, because the seals are not effective enough to have held such a large accumulation for a long period of time.

Composition of the Gas

The composition of the gas of the north and south blocks is the same except for sulfur content. Hydrocarbons compose 97–98% of the gas and this in turn is 96–97% methane, 1.1–1.5% ethane, 0.10–0.23% propane, 0.04–0.13% butane, and 0.01–0.07% pentane. The carbon dioxide content is 0.8–1.7%. As much as 1% hydrogen sulfide is present in the gas of the north block, increasing in concentration from north to south. Hydrogen sulfide is absent on the south block (Kul'dzhayev and Sergiyenko, 1986).

Two aquifer systems are present in the region of Dauletabad-Donmez field: Upper Jurassic and Lower Cretaceous (Neocomian Series to Aptian Stage). Water in both these systems is saturated with hydrocarbon gases (Bayramov and Karryyev, 1982).

A surface mercury-methane survey was made along a north-south profile across the north, central, and south blocks of Dauletabad-Donmez field. This survey showed anomalously high mercury and methane above the south block but no anomaly above the water-flooded central block or the gas pool of the north block (Antsiforov et al., 1983).

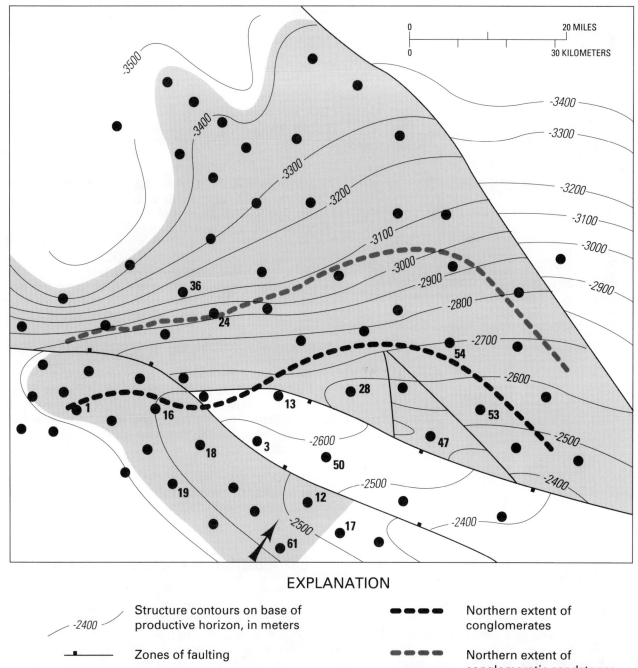

EXPLANATION

_-2400_ ⟋	Structure contours on base of productive horizon, in meters
■—■	Zones of faulting
(shaded ellipse)	Gas field
●	Drill holes

Northern extent of conglomerates

Northern extent of conglomeratic sandstones

Direction from which clastic material was derived

Figure 9. Distribution of gravel-bearing rocks of Hauterivian age of Dauletabad-Donmez gas field. (From Makarova and Bakun, 1987.)

Sources

According to Amurskiy et al. (1984), the gas of the Dauletabad-Donmez field had two sources: the Cis-Kopet-Dag foredeep on the west where sulfur-free gas was derived from source beds above the Upper Jurassic salt, and the southern Dauletabad area where hydrogen sulfide–bearing gas migrated vertically from source beds below the stratigraphic position where the Upper Jurassic salt would be if it were present. The trap was filled in late Pliocene to middle Pleistocene time as a result of a regional uplift of 300–400 m and degassing of the ground water as part of the Alpine orogenic activity.

Gavrilov et al. (1985) suggest, on a basis of a narrow range of carbon isotopic compositions, that the gas is derived entirely from source beds in the section between the Upper Jurassic salt and the top of the Lower Cretaceous (Hauterivian) Shatlyk horizon and that sufficient sulfates are present in this part of the section to supply the hydrogen sulfide found in the gas. Pankina et al. (1986) contend that the heavy isotopic composition (7.5 to 22.9 ‰) of the sulfur is indicative of a source in a zone of high temperature at great depths due to reaction of sulfates dissolved in water with organic matter.

An oil pool has been found on the central block. Two wells yielded commercial oil from rocks beneath the Shatlyk horizon (Maksimov et al., 1984). More oil is expected in the south block because thermal conditions have been less severe there, allowing formation of some oil rather than only condensate as on the north block where temperature and pressure are higher (Yermolkin et al., 1985).

EXPLORATION CONCEPTS

The largest fields of a petroleum basin are generally discovered early in the exploration of the basin. Dauletabad-Donmez, however, was found in 1974, which is 45 years after the beginning of exploration in 1929. How did this elephant of a field escape detection so long? It is in a subtle trap, held in along much of its margin by hydrodynamic pressure. The province contains scores of traps associated with fault blocks, reefs, and salt domes. These obvious structures were explored first. Only then did attention turn to the southern area, which had appeared to be less favorable. The lesson here is that exploration of a petroleum basin is not complete until the entire basin has been tested, including all those areas where subtle traps may be present. It is not over until it is over.

REFERENCES CITED

Aliyev, S. N., et al., 1983, Oil-gas provinces of the USSR [in Russian]: Nedra, 272 p.

Amurskiy, G. I., and N. N. Solov'yev, 1982, Ring photo-anomalies-predecessors of anticlinal structures [in Russian]: Sovetskaya Geologiya, n. 9, p. 36–43 (English translation in International Geology Review, v. 25, n. 2, p. 217–224).

Amurskiy, G. I., I. P. Zhabrev, N. N. Solov'yev, and Z. B. Khusnutdinov, 1984, Formation of Dauletabad-Donmez gas field [in Russian]: Sovetskaya Geologiya, n. 3, p. 11–21.

Antsiforov, A. I., A. V. Petukhov, M. W. Trofimov, V. Z. Furson, and D. Y. Shpagin, 1983, Scope of gas-mercury prospecting in the search for oil and gas [in Russian]: Sovetskaya Geologiya, n. 8, p. 108–113 (English translation in International Geology Review, v. 26, n. 6, p. 713–718).

Bakirov, A. A., et al., 1979, Oil-gas provinces and regions of the USSR [in Russian]: Moscow, Nedra, 456 p.

Bayramov, A., and A. C. Karryyev, 1982, Results of hydrogeological investigations of wells of the Dauletabad-Donmez gas-condensate field [in Russian]: Izv. Akad. Nauk Turkmen. SSR, Ser. fiz., tekh., khim., geol. nauk, n. 1, p. 71–81.

Berg, L. S., 1950, Natural regions of the U.S.S.R.: New York, Macmillan Company, 436 p.

Carmalt, S. W., and W. St. John, 1986, Giant oil and gas fields, in Future petroleum provinces of the world: American Association of Petroleum Geologists Memoir 40, p. 11–53.

Clarke, J. W., 1988, Petroleum geology of the Amu-Dar'ya gas-oil province of Soviet Central Asia: U.S. Geological Survey Open-File Report 88-272, 59 p.

Gavrilov, Y. Y., V. S. Goncharov, and G. I. Tellinskiy, 1985, Genesis of gases of Dauletabad-Donmez gas-condensate field [in Russian]: Geologiya Nefti i Gaza, n. 9, p. 35–39.

Kravchenko, K. N., 1983, Genetic features of the Dauletabad-Donmez and Hougoton fields [in Russian]: Sovetskaya Geologiya, n. 9, p. 24–29.

Kul'dzhayev, B. A., and S. R. Sergiyenko, 1986, Composition and properties of the natural gases of Dauletabad-Donmez field [in Russian]: Izv. Akad. Nauk Turkmen. SSR, Ser. fiz., tekh., khim., geol. nauk, n. 3, p. 95–98.

Luppov, N. P., et al., 1972, Geology of the USSR [in Russian], v. 22, Turkmen SSR: Moscow, Nedra, 768 p.

Makarova, Z. I., and N. N. Bakun, 1987, Characteristics and classification of gravel-bearing rocks of Dauletabad-Donmez field [in Russian]: Geologiya Nefti i Gaza, n. 2, p. 49–53.

Maksimov, S. P., V. D. Il'in, K. A. Kleshchev, A. M. Moksyakova, V. S. Shein, M. K. Mirzakhanov, A. A. Karryyev, and Y. A. Khodzhakuliyev, 1984, Prospects for geological exploration in Turkmen SSR [in Russian]: Geologiya Nefti i Gaza, n. 1, p. 1–9.

Maksimov, S. P., et al., 1987, Oil and gas fields of the USSR [in Russian]: Moscow, Nedra, v. 2, 304 p.

Mavyyev, N. C., and S. G. Nepesov, 1985, Post-sedimentation alteration of clastic rocks of the productive Hauterivian of Dauletabad [in Russian]: Izv. Akad. Nauk Turkmen, SSR, Ser. Fiz., tekh., khim., geol. nauk, n. 4, p. 64–69.

Mirzakhanov, M. K., L. M. Kuvasov, and S. P. Khalliyev, 1975, Dauletabad—a new gas field in Badkhyze [in Russian]: Geologiya Nefti i Gaza, n. 8, p. 76–77 (summary in Petroleum Geology, v. 13, n. 8).

Nepesov, S. G., and M. S. Gendler, 1986, New type of reservoir of Hauterivian sediments of Dauletabad-Donmez gas region [in Russian]: Izv. Akad. Nauk Turkmen SSR, Ser. fiz., tekh., khim., geol. nauk, n. 1, p. 76–81.

Nepesov, S. G., V. G. Dratsov, and K. M. Mamedov, 1984, Physical-lithologic characteristics of main producing member of Dauletabad-Donmez gas-condensate field [in Russian]: Izv. Akad. Nauk Turkmen. SSR, Ser. fiz., tekh., khim., geol. nauk, n. 5, p. 84–86.

Pankina, R. G., V. L. Mekhtiyeva, N. N. Bakun, and S. M. Guriyeva, 1986, Isotopic composition of forms of sulfur of Dauletabad-Donmez gas field with respect to genesis of hydrogen sulfide [in Russian]: Geologiya Nefti i Gaza, n. 12, p. 51–55.

Ryzhkov, O. A., I. Z. Maksudov, and A. M. Abdukakharov, 1983, Paleotectonic conditions of reef zones in Upper Jurassic carbonates of West Uzbekistan [in Russian]: Dokl. Akad. Nauk UzSSR, n. 1, p. 41–43 (summary in Petroleum Geology, v. 20, n. 3).

Semenovich, V. V., ed., 1976, Oil and gas map of the USSR, scale 1:2,500,000: Moscow, Ministry of Geology, 16 sheets.

Semenovich, V. V., S. P. Maksimov, R. G. Pankina, V. L. Mekhtiyeva, and S. M. Guriyeva, 1983, Genesis of hydrogen sulfide of Dauletabad-Donmez gas field [in Russian]: Geologiya Nefti i Gaza, n. 6, p. 32–37.

Valkuliyev, C. K., K. M. Mamedov, S. G. Nepesov, K. Kabulov, and G. K. Ovezberdyyev, 1983, Lithology and conditions of formation of Hauterivian sediments of the Dauletabad-Donmez gas region [in Russian]: Izv. Akad. Nauk Turkmen SSR, Ser. Fiz. -tekh, khim, geol, nauk, n. 3, p. 83–92.

Yanena, R. I., and K. M. Mamedov, 1982, History of tectonic development of Southeast Turkmenia [in Russian]: Izv. Akad. Nauk Turkmen SSR, Ser. fiz'-tekh., khim., geol. nauk, n. 5, p. 80–88 (summary in Petroleum Geology, v. 20, n. 1).

Yermolkin, V.I.,Y. I. Sorokova, A. S. Filin, and A. A. Bobyleva, 1985, Oil, gas, and condensate zoning in a petroleum province [in Russian]: Sovetskaya Geologiya, n. 9, p. 21–32 (English translation in International Geology Review, v. 27, n. 11, p. 1304–1314).

Zhabrev, I. P., et al., 1983, Gas and gas-condensate fields [in Russian]: Moscow, Nauka, 376 p.

Appendix 1. Field Description

Field name .... *Dauletabad-Donmez field*

Ultimate recoverable reserves .... *48.7 tcf (1.364 trillion m³) of gas*

Field location:

    Country .... *Commonwealth of Independent States*

    State .... *Turkmenistan*

    Basin/Province .... *Amu-Dar'ya*

Field discovery:

    Year first pay discovered .... *Lower Cretaceous Hauterivian sandstone 1974*

Discovery well name and general location:

    First pay .... *Dauletabad No. 1 located 28 km south-southeast of Serakhs, Ashkhabad Region*

Discovery well operator .... *USSR Ministry of Geology*

IP .... *28–32 MMcfgd (830–920 thousand m³/day)*

All other zones with shows of oil and gas in the field .... *NA*

Geologic concept leading to discovery and method or methods used to delineate prospect
The Lower Cretaceous productive Shatlyk horizon was played outward from discoveries on the northeast. Drilling was based on seismic surveys and core holes.

Structure:

    Province/basin type .... *Intracrational rift-sag basin*

    Tectonic history
Following the Hercynian orogeny in late Paleozoic time, the region subsided and became the site of platformal deposition. Block fault movements in the basement during Cenozoic time led to formation of gentle anticlinal traps.

    Regional structure
The field is in the Badkhyz-Karabil zone of highs.

    Local structure
A monocline that dips to the north and northwest at 1–7°. On the south the monocline is cut by a fault.

Trap:

    Trap type(s)
The trap is sealed hydrodynamically and also perhaps by faults and lithologic change.

Basin stratigraphy (major stratigraphic intervals from surface to deepest penetration in field):

Chronostratigraphy	Formation	Depth to Top in m
Neogene		*0*
Paleogene		*200*
Cretaceous		*1100*
Hauterivian	*Shatlyk horizon*	*3000*
Jurassic		*3200*

Reservoir characteristics:

    Number of reservoirs *1*

    Formations .... *Shatlyk horizon*

    Ages .... *Hauterivian–Early Cretaceous*

    Depths to tops of reservoirs .... *2400 m on south to 3400 m on north*

    Gross thickness (top to bottom of producing interval) .... *7–35 m, avg 20 m*

    Net thickness—total thickness of producing zones

        Average .... *10–17 m*

        Maximum .... *24 m*

Lithology
Fine- to medium-grained, poorly sorted red sandstone containing beds of clayey siltstone; also conglomerate and pebbly sandstone
Porosity type .... *Intergranular pore space*
Average porosity *18.3–20.2%*
Average permeability .... *350 md*

Seals:
Upper
    Formation, fault, or other feature .... *Barremian, Aptian*
    Lithology .... *Limestones, clays*
Lateral
    Formation, fault, or other feature .... *Hydrodynamically sealed on east; perhaps by faults and lithologic change on south*

Source:
Formation and age .... *Early and Middle Jurassic*
Lithology .... *Clays, siltstones, and sandstones*
Average total organic carbon (TOC) *0.5–0.9%*
Maximum TOC .... *NA*
Kerogen type (I, II, or III) .... *III*
Vitrinite reflectance (maturation) .... *NA*
Time of hydrocarbon expulsion .... *Paleogene*
Present depth to top of source .... *5000 m*
Thickness .... *500 m*
Potential yield .... *720 m³ of gas per m³ of rock*

Appendix 2. Production Data

Field name .... *Dauletabad-Donmez field*
Field size:
Proved acres .... *618,500 ac (250,300 ha)*
Number of wells all years *108*
Current number of wells .... *NA*
Well spacing .... *NA*
Ultimate recoverable .... *1.364 trillion m³ (48.7 tcf) of gas*
Cumulative production .... *97.8 billion m³ (3.42 tcf) of gas*
Annual production .... *31.7 billion m³ (1.11 tcf) of gas*
Present decline rate .... *NA*
    Initial decline rate .... *NA*
Annual water production .... *NA*
In place, total reserves .... *NA*
Cumulative water production .... *NA*

Drilling and casing practices .... *NA*

Completion practices .... *NA*

Formation evaluation .... *NA*

Oil characteristics .... *NA (gas)*

Field characteristics:

Average elevation .... *450 m (1480 ft)*
Initial pressure .... *39.5 mPa (35–41.5 mPa)*
Present pressure .... *NA*
Pressure gradient .... *NA (overpressure ranges from 1.04–1.32 [x hydrostatic], highest in south)*
Temperature .... *133°C*
Geothermal gradient .... *2.76–4.2°C/100 m*
Drive .... *NA*
Gas column thickness .... *NA*
Gas-water contact .... *–3437.8 to –2586.5 m*
Connate water .... *NA*
Water salinity, TDS .... *90–115 mg/L*
Resistivity of water .... *NA*
Bulk volume water (%) .... *NA*

Transportation method and market for oil and gas:

Gas moves by pipeline northward into the system that carries the gas of this province into the European Commonwealth gas distribution system.

Caçāo Field—Brazil
Espirito Santo Basin, Southeastern Brazil

VALÉRIO Q. LIMA
NESTOR AURICH
Petrobrás/Depex
Rio de Janeiro, Brazil

FIELD CLASSIFICATION

BASIN: Espirito Santo
BASIN TYPE: Passive Margin
RESERVOIR ROCK TYPE: Sandstone
RESERVOIR ENVIRONMENT OF
  DEPOSITION: Coastal Alluvial Fan
TRAP DESCRIPTION: Paleogeomorphic high adjacent to submarine canyon

RESERVOIR AGE: Cretaceous
PETROLEUM TYPE: Oil
TRAP TYPE: Paleogeomorphic
  Erosional High

LOCATION

The Caçāo field was discovered offshore Espirito Santo State along the eastern coast of Brazil, 47 km southeast of Sāo Mateus City, 7 km from the coastline, in a water depth of 19 m (Figure 1). The field is in the Espirito Santo basin that comprises an area of about 3000 km² onshore and 10,000 km² offshore within the 200 m bathymetric contour but extends beyond into deeper waters of the South Atlantic Ocean.

The onshore oil fields of the basin are in four geologic provinces (Figure 1): The Sāo Mateus platform, in the northern part of the basin, comprises an area of 1500 km²; the Fazenda Cedro paleocanyon has an area of 480 km²; the Regência platform comprises an area of about 900 km²; and the Regência paleocanyon has an area of approximately 200 km² in the southernmost part of the basin. Two onshore fields of the Espirito Santo basin are discussed in other papers of the *Atlas of Oil and Gas Fields*: the Rio Itaúnas field of the northern part of the Sāo Mateus platform, and the Lagoa Parda field of the Regência paleocanyon (Figure 1).

The exploration of the basin was initiated in the mid-1950s. Since then, 825 wells have been drilled onshore (283 exploratory and 542 development and infill wells) and 91 wells offshore (81 exploratory and 10 development wells). It should be noticed that all the services, seismic, drilling and interpretation have been sponsored by Petrobrás. Until now, 33 hydrocarbon accumulations have been found in the onshore area and one offshore, the Caçāo field.

The offshore Caçāo field is located in the central part of the basin where the Upper Cretaceous Fazenda Cedro paleocanyon is the most outstanding geological feature (Figure 2). The field is interpreted to be in a typical paleogeomorphic trap formed by an erosion-sculptured paleohigh in the eastern edge (offshore) of the paleocanyon (Figure 3).

In the onshore portion of the Fazenda Cedro paleocanyon, four other oil fields and one gas field have been discovered in turbidite sandstones interbedded with shale that fill up this paleocanyon. One oil field (Fazenda Cedro) is related to the paleotopography, similar to the Caçāo field.

Up to December 1988, the onshore fields have ultimate recoverable reserves of 72.4 million barrels (MMbbl) of oil and 106 bcf of gas; the cumulative productions are 57.8 MMbbl of oil and 37 bcf of gas. The offshore Caçāo field accounts for 12.6 MMbbl of oil and 21.6 bcf of gas of recoverable reserve and cumulative production of 10.4 MMbbl of oil and 11.3 bcf of gas.

HISTORY

Pre-Discovery

Exploration in the Espirito Santo basin effectively began onshore in the early 1950s with seismic, gravimetric, and magnetometric surveys. A stratigraphic test was drilled in 1959, and the first

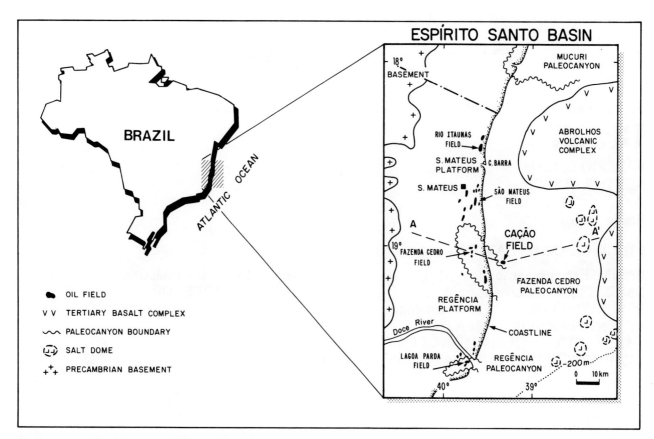

Figure 1. Location map of Espirito Santo basin and Cacão field. A-A′ is the location of the cross section shown on Figure 2.

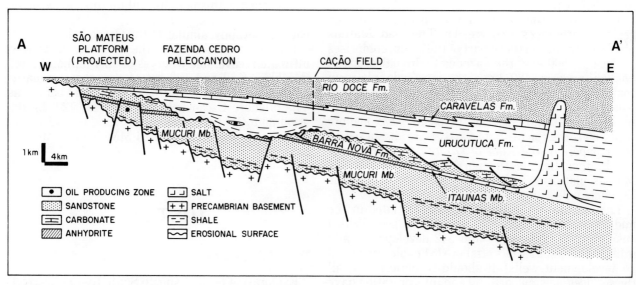

Figure 2. Schematic regional dip cross section of Espirito Santo basin through Cacão field. See Figure 1 for location of the cross section.

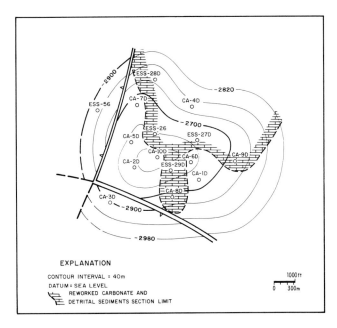

Figure 3. Structure contour map of the unconformity surface at top of Barra Nova Formation, Cacão field, showing reworked carbonates section limit.

CHRONOSTRATIGRAPHY		GROUP	FORMATION	MEMBER	LITHOLOGY W E	PRODUCTIVE BEDS SOURCE ROCKS
QUATERNARY			BARREIRAS			SANDSTONE
TERTIARY	PLIOCENE	ESPÍRITO SANTO	RIO DOCE			SANDSTONE
	MIOCENE					CARBONATES
	OLIGOCENE		CARAVELAS			
	EOCENE					SHALES
	PALEOCENE		URUCUTUCA			PRODUCTIVE BEDS (TURBIDITES)
	MAASTRICHT.					SANDSTONE
	CAMPANIAN					
	SANTONIAN TURONIAN					
CRETACEOUS	CENOMANIAN	NATIVO	BARRA NOVA			SANDSTONE CARBONATE	PRODUCTIVE BEDS
	ALBIAN			SÃO MATEUS REGÊNCIA		
	APTIAN		MARIRICU	ITAÚNAS		EVAPORITES
				MUCURI		SANDSTONE SHALE	PRODUCTIVE BEDS SOURCE ROCKS
	NEOCOMIAN					
PRE-CAMBRIAN			BASEMENT		+ + + + + + + +	

PETROBRAS – DEPEX

Figure 4. Espirito Santo basin stratigraphic column.

discovery onshore was made in 1969 in the São Mateus platform (São Mateus field). The first offshore exploratory drilling in Brazil was in 1968 in the Espirito Santo basin. Up to 1977, 25 exploratory offshore wells had been drilled in this basin for prospects in the Albian carbonate and sandstone reservoirs of the Barra Nova Formation and for Upper Cretaceous and Tertiary turbidite reservoirs of the Urucutuca Formation (Figure 4).

Discovery

The Cacão field was discovered in 1977 by the wildcat well 1-ESS-26 (Espirito Santo Submarine number 26), drilled by Petrobrás. The prospect was based on seismic mapping of the unconformable Fazenda Cedro paleocanyon basal surface. A paleohigh of the underlying Albian Barra Nova Formation, sealed by shales of the Urucutuca Formation that fills the canyon, was interpreted, as shown in Figures 2 and 3. The Barra Nova sandstone reservoirs were found at 2691 m (–2666 m), 36 m below the unconformity surface, with 51 m of oil pay zone. In this wildcat area, a section of reworked Albian sediments occurs, dominantly carbonates, between the reservoirs and the Urucutuca Formation. Completion of the well was made in September 1978, and it was put onstream with an initial flow rate of 3000 bbl of oil per day (37.5° API, GOR of 674 ft³/bbl).

An additional reflection seismic program in the area was shot in 1978 (387 km of seismic lines) to improve the definition of the field limits and for exploratory purposes. Three more wildcats were drilled without success on similar, seismically mapped structures.

Three directional step-out wells were drilled in the Cacão structure to prove economically exploitable volumes of oil in the field. The 3-ESS-28D well to the north was abandoned as subcommercial because most of the reservoir has been eroded away. The top of the reservoir was reached at 2778 (–2753) m, with an oil pay zone of 4 m beneath 97 m of tight, reworked Albian sediments. The wells 3-ESS-27D to the east and 3-ESS-29D to the south found oil pay zones of 55 m and 36 m, respectively, and proved an area of about 2 km² in Barra Nova sandstone reservoirs.

The western limit of the accumulation is controlled by the erosional surface of the canyon, probably related to a north-south fault system, as demonstrated by the dry well 3-ESS-56, drilled in 1983 (Figure 5).

Post-Discovery

Three exploratory wells, 1-ESS-26, 3-ESS-27D, and 3-ESS-29D, have been producing oil since 1978, using a tripod platform with an attached production facility platform. The initial production of 7600 barrels of oil per day (BOPD) flowing from these three wells decreased to 4300 BOPD after six months as a result of the low GOR of two of the wells, 3-ESS-26 and 3-ESS-29. The problem of a too rapid decline in production was solved in 1981 by installation of a gas lift production system, the gas coming from the Fazenda Cedro field (onshore) through a gas pipeline.

In 1984, four development wells were drilled: The 7-CA-2D is an oil producer (pay zone of 74 m); the

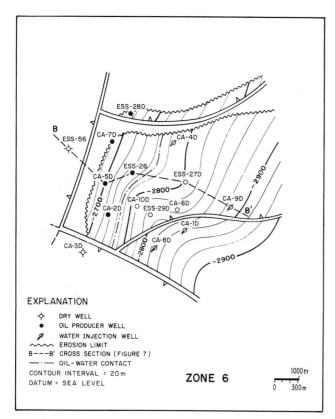

Figure 5. Structural map on the top of the zone 6 sandstone reservoir, Barra Nova Formation, Cacão field. B–B′ is the location of the structural cross section shown by Figure 7.

7-CA-3D was dry (lack of reservoir related to the paleocanyon erosion surface controlled by an east-west fault); and two of them, 7-CA-1D and 7-CA-4D, were subcommercial (Figures 3 and 5). The latter two were saved as water injection wells.

Accurate pressure and production data of the Albian Barra Nova reservoir rocks suggested water injection as the most efficient and profitable production strategy. Six more wells were drilled from a template, two of them for water injection and four for oil production, in order to complete the scheduled development system.

Near the base of the Urucutuca Formation the occurrence of turbidite reservoirs was confirmed by the 7-CA-5D and the 7-CA-7D wells. This turbiditic sandstone zone has an average net pay thickness of 10 m (38° API oil and GOR of 730 ft³/bbl). This bed formerly had been detected in the 1-ESS-26 with 5 m of net pay thickness. The turbidites produced only 30,000 bbl of oil in well 7-CA-5D with rapid pressure depletion, indicating a restricted reservoir.

Discovery Method

The main exploration method in the Espirito Santo basin is reflection seismic surveying, supported by gravimetric and magnetometric mapping. The geological information acquired from the offshore wells and from reinterpretation of the seismic lines pointed to the best targets in the basin—paleohighs or structural traps with potential reservoirs in Lower Cretaceous Mariricu Formation sandstones, in the Albian–Cenomanian Barra Nova Formation, and in Tertiary/Upper Cretaceous Urucutuca Formation turbidites.

STRUCTURE

Tectonic History

The Espirito Santo basin is one of the eastern Brazilian passive margin basins. Its tectonic history is related to South Atlantic Ocean opening resulting in African and South American plate separation and in drift and extensional events on a continental scale. The basement has a rift structural pattern controlled by a north-northeast to south-southwest tensional fault trend. The faults are dominantly down-to-the-basin step-like faults that result in a horst and graben tectonic style, dipping to the southeast (basinward) (Figure 2).

After the deposition of the Lower Cretaceous synrift continental terrigenous section, in Aptian time the basin was covered by evaporites as a result of the early proto-ocean stage, and it evolved to a coastal-sandstone and carbonate platform during Albian and Cenomanian times. At this stage a continuous shelf subsidence began, and the tilting has triggered salt movement, resulting in halokinetic listric faults affecting the overlying platform section.

In middle and Upper Cretaceous and Paleocene/Eocene times, a regional transgression with an open-marine environment took place, and pelitic deep-water sediments were deposited during a relatively quiescent tectonic period. After Santonian time several submarine excavation and deposition events occurred in the western part of the basin, forming the huge Fazenda Cedro and the Regência canyons. In the deeper part of the basin eastward, salt diapirism and intense igneous activity were the main episodes.

In late Tertiary, under relatively stable conditions, an open-marine carbonate platform, synchronous to a fan-delta sandstone system, was deposited.

Regional Structure

The Cacão field is located on the eastern border of the Fazenda Cedro paleocanyon between the São Mateus and Barra Nova platforms. During Santonian–Turonian time, these areas were subjected to several erosional/depositional events. The main depositional trough of this paleocanyon plunges to the south-southeast (Figure 1). The regional structural framework of the Barra Nova Formation (post-evaporitic sequence), which includes the Cacão reservoirs, is dominated by rollover structures related to listric or detached growth faults developed by gravity sliding and salt flowage.

Local Structure

As defined by reflection seismic and subsurface well data interpretation, the Cacão field is related to the local structure that is the eastern flank of a rollover (dipping 6° to 15° southeastward) whose western flank was faulted and further eroded by the Fazenda Cedro paleocanyon.

The structural pattern of the Barra Nova Formation is defined by major down-to-the-basin normal faults with associated antithetic faults. Sediments overlying the unconformity surface fill the paleocanyon.

STRATIGRAPHY

The stratigraphic columnar section of the Espirito Santo basin was initially based on biostratigraphic standards and later (Asmus, 1971) on lithostratigraphic sequences. Several modifications have been made subsequently as new data have been gathered, evolving to the present-day formal column (Barbosa, 1987), based upon litho- and chronostratigraphic concepts. The columnar section shown by Figure 4 is simplified and adapted to the Cacão field area. The pre-Quaternary sedimentary rocks are divided into two groups: the Nativo Group and the Espirito Santo Group.

The Nativo Group overlies unconformably the Precambrian basement rocks and comprises the Mariricu and the Barra Nova formation sediments, deposited from Early Cretaceous through Cenomanian times.

The Mariricu Formation Mucuri Member, related to the synrift phase of the basin, is represented by alluvial sandstones and conglomerates associated with normal fault scarps, fluvio-deltaic-lacustrine sandstones, and organic-rich shales deposited in the deeper parts, filling a series of half-grabens. The Mariricu Formation Itaúnas Member is represented by soluble salts and anhydrite deposits covering the lacustrine section, representing initial marine transgression. Toward the distal part of the basin to the east, the thickness of the Mariricu Formation is over 1600 m.

After the evaporitic stage, with the opening of the South Atlantic Ocean, an extensive Albian carbonate platform was deposited; this grades laterally into fan-delta sandstones in the shallower part of the basin. The section is named the Barra Nova Formation; the carbonates represent the Regência Member and the clastic sediments belong to the São Mateus Member. The Barra Nova Formation section thickens eastward to more than 1200 m.

The Espirito Santo Group includes the Urucutuca, Caravelas, and Rio Doce formations. In the open-marine stage, during the middle and Late Cretaceous and Tertiary, Urucutuca Formation pelitic deep-water sediments were deposited with occasional turbidite sands. Above the Urucutuca Formation the synchronous carbonate platform of the Caravelas Formation and fan-delta sandstones of the Rio Doce Formation complete the sequence (Figure 4). During this stage, submarine erosional events cut part of the predeposited section, creating huge submarine canyons filled with the Urucutuca sediments. In the Cacão area, the Urucutuca Formation is a thick shale sequence of about 800 m that fills the canyon and provides a seal for reservoir lithologies beneath.

TRAP

The Cacão field entrapment conditions were established in the Late Cretaceous time when the Fazenda Cedro canyon began to be filled by pelitic deep-water sediments of the Urucutuca Formation. In the field area, erosion, probably fault controlled (north, south, and westward), shaped a mound on the interbedded sandstone and carbonate sediments of the Barra Nova Formation, which dip to the southeast. In the northern area of the field, the Albian reworked carbonates section is the limit of hydrocarbon accumulation in Barra Nova clastics (Figure 3). The structural closure is about 180 m and the field has multiple oil-water contacts, varying from zone to zone.

RESERVOIR

The Barra Nova Formation reservoirs consist of submature fine- to coarse-grained feldspathic sandstones with some calcite cement and silt-sized, kaolinitic matrix; minor carbonate grains and skeletal fragments are present. These reservoirs are at depths ranging from –2600 to –2800 m. The maximum net oil-producing sandstone thickness is 74 m (7-CA-2D well) in a total oil column of 164 m (Figure 6).

Porosity values derived from well logs range from 8% to 23% (average of 16.6%). Permeability values measured by drill-stem test vary over a wide range, but in the central part of the field these values are from 500 to 600 md. The oil-water contact varies from –2740 to –2767 m depending on the zone. The original pressure of the reservoir was 3980 psi at –2600 m depth.

The reservoir rocks of the field are subdivided into seven productive zones on the basis of log responses and correlations (Figure 7). The zones are separated mainly by calcilutites, tight calcarenites and sandstones, and interbedded shales.

The Albian reworked carbonate and detrital sediments that partially overlie the Barra Nova Formation reservoirs in the field area are oil-bearing

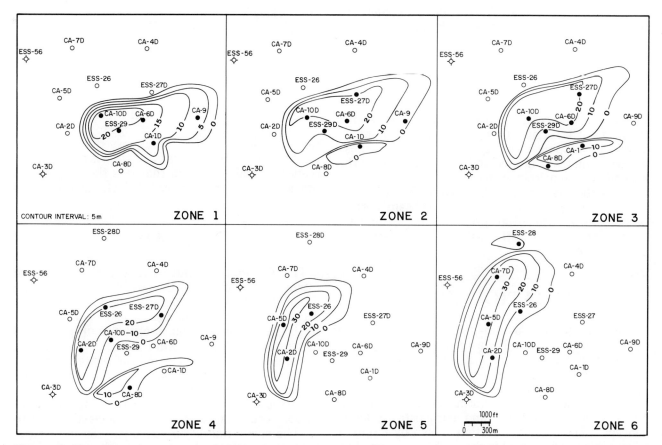

Figure 6. Net oil sandstone map of productive zones, Barra Nova Formation, Cacão field. The cross section on Figure 7 shows the Barra Nova Formation zones 1 through 7. The east-west isopachous "thin" north of CA-1D in zones 2, 3, and 4 results from the fault seen in Figure 5. Similarly the "thin" south of ESS-28 in zone 6 results from another fault and also erosion seen in the same figure.

(carbonate microporosity), and although they do not produce in the wells, they may feed into and contribute to the recoverable oil accumulation in the Barra Nova clastics (Figure 3).

During the first year of production, wells ESS-26, ESS-27, and ESS-29, producing from undersaturated reservoir conditions, showed a remarkable pressure and production decline (Figure 8). This was interpreted to result from a depletion drive production mechanism. Gas lift was initiated in 1981. After producing around 1.1 MMbbl of oil, the reservoir pressure reached the bubble-point and a secondary gas cap started to form, which was hastened by the relatively steep dip of the layers (ranging from 6° to 15°).

The first development well (CA-1D) was drilled in 1983 when the cumulative oil production was 5.4 MMbbl. Pressure data obtained from this well for oil-producing zones 1, 2, and 3 pointed to a rapid depletion (measured 1820 psi, a pressure decrease of 2160 psi). In water-bearing zones, a large pressure differential was observed in measured open-hole pressures between zone 4 (2276 psi) and zone 5 (3407 psi); after completion, these two zones were put in communication through the well casing in order to promote auto-injection; i.e., the water coming from zone 5 was injected into zone 4 to pressurize it. The process succeeded, and significant increases in pressure in nearby wells were observed. Although the natural water drive mechanism is not very important, the auto-injection experiment results and reservoir simulation studies indicated water injection to be the more profitable method for enhanced recovery.

Proved original oil in place in the Cacão field is estimated to be 50.4 MMbbl and ultimate recovery of 12.6 MMbbl (25%) is expected. In November 1988, the scheduled development system was completed and oil production was increased to 4000 bbl/day.

SOURCE ROCK AND BURIAL HISTORY

The geochemical analyses of the Espirito Santo basin indicate upper Neocomian and Aptian shales of the Mucuri Member of the Mariricu Formation is an excellent source rock for hydrocarbons, with a dominance of type II organic matter and an average

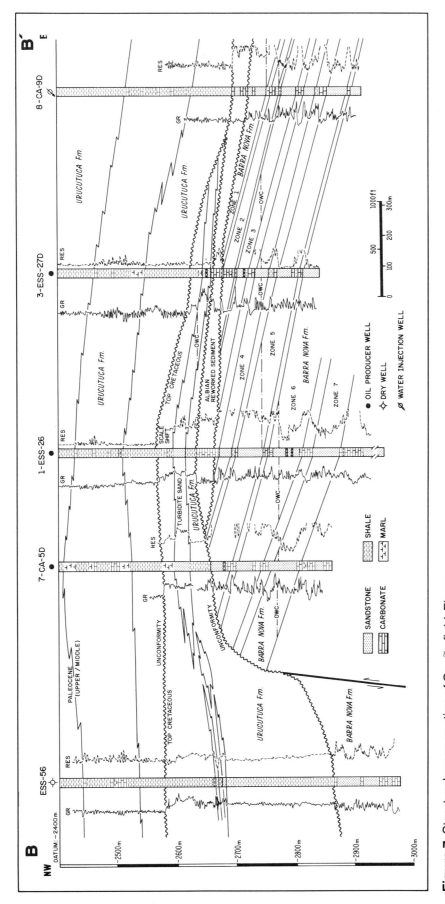

Figure 7. Structural cross section of Cacão field. Figure 5 shows the location of this cross section.

307

OIL PRODUCTION – History and Forecast
(CAÇÃO FIELD)

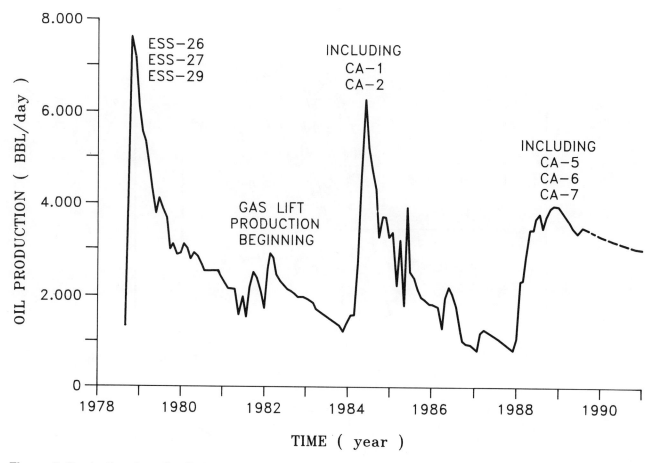

Figure 8. Production data, Cacão field.

total organic carbon (TOC) of 2%. The hydrogen index is high and the hydrocarbon source rock potential is higher than 5 kg HC/ton.

The source rocks attained thermal maturation only on the offshore area of the basin where the oil window is placed between the depths of 3000 m and 5000 m (Figure 9). Hydrocarbon migration process occurs through the faults connecting the pre-evaporitic source rocks to the post-evaporitic Barra Nova and Urucutuca reservoirs.

EXPLORATION CONCEPTS

The proved oil volume of the Albian fields in the Espirito Santo basin is about 85 MMbbl, and Cacão field contributes with 59% of that. The rest comes from carbonate reservoirs (oolitic and pisolitic calcarenites) in the Regência platform, always sealed by shales of the Urucutuca Formation.

The Albian reservoirs of the Barra Nova Formation in the Espirito Santo basin may be geologically correlated with the Macaé Formation carbonate section that occurs in the Campos basin, 230 km southward, which has six producing oil fields with a proved oil volume of 3.4 billion barrels.

Cacão field is a paleogeomorphic model of oil accumulation. Exploration for similar prospects throughout the basin is very attractive at any stratigraphic level when a paleotopographic surface generated by an erosional event is sealed by pelitic sediments. A similar geological setting for hydrocarbon entrapment occurs onshore, approximately 18 km northwest from the Cacão field, where the Fazenda Cedro field was found earlier, in 1972. In that case, the paleogeomorphic mound was sculptured at the bottom of the Fazenda Cedro paleocanyon on the Mucuri Member of the Mariricu Formation sediments, the entrapment sealed laterally and above by the Urucutuca Formation shales.

A scheduled Cacão delimitation program using directional step-out wells proved to be suitable for small oil accumulations. Modern techniques in seismic processing and data acquisition, such as 3D surveys, complex trace analyses, amplitude analyses

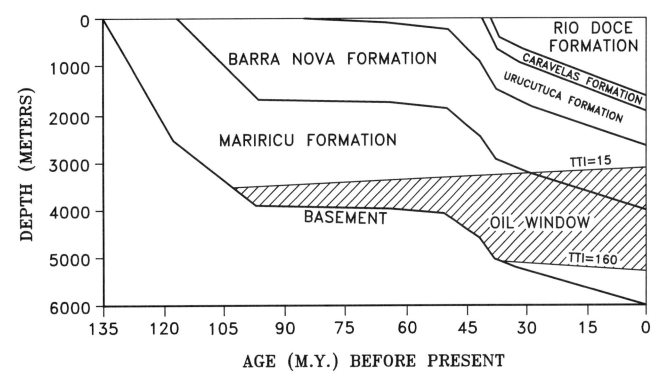

Figure 9. Burial history diagram, Cacão field.

and VSP data processing, and also seismic interpretation using work station facilities, may be implemented to get more accurate information about reservoir characteristics and delineation. These tools will be very helpful in geological mapping of reservoir quality and fundamental to planning delimitation strategy in the future.

ACKNOWLEDGMENTS

To Petróleo Brasileiro S.A. (Petrobrás) for permission to publish the paper. For unpublished Petrobrás studies by R. S. Carvalho, F. R. T. Lima, J. B. Gomes, E. T. C. Abdalla, L. Arantes, and L. A. F. Trindade and for conversations with M. A. Barbosa and R. Sousa. Also for review by G. A. V. Rosa and general coordination by A. M. F. Figueiredo.

REFERENCES

Asmus, H. E., J. B. Gomes, and A. C. B. Pereira, 1971, Integracão geológica regional da Bacia do Espirito Santo (Regional geological integration of the Espirito Santo Basin): XXV Congresso Brasileiro de Geologia (25th Brazilian Geological Congress, Proceedings), v. 2, p. 235–252.

Dauzacker, M. V., 1981, Basin analysis of evaporitic and post-evaporitic depositional systems, Espirito Santo Basin, Brazil, South America: Austin, University of Texas, Ph.D. thesis.

Estrella, G. O., et al., 1984, The Espirito Santo Basin (Brazil) source rock characterization and petroleum habitat, *in* G. Demaison and R. J. Murris, eds., Petroleum geochemistry and basin evolution: American Association of Petroleum Geologists Memoir 35, p. 253–271.

Rangel, H. D., 1984, Geologic evolution of Fazenda Cedro paleosubmarine canyon, Espirito Santo Basin, Brazil: Austin, University of Texas, Ph.D. thesis.

Appendix 1. Field Description

Field name .... *Cacão field*

Ultimate recoverable reserves .... *12.6 MMbbl of oil and 21.6 bcf of gas*

Field location:

    Country .... *Brazil*

    State .... *Offshore of Espirito Santo State*

    Basin/Province .... *Espirito Santo basin*

Field discovery:

    Year first pay discovered .... *Albian Barra Nova sandstones 1977*

    Year second pay discovered .... *Upper Cretaceous Urucutuca Fm. sandstones 1977*

Discovery well name and general location:

    First pay .... *#1-ESS-26-ES (Espirito Santo Submarine No. 26)*
                                         location 19°05'52"S, 39°39'19"W

    Second pay .... *#1-ESS-26-ES*

Discovery well operator .... *Petróleo Brasileiro S. A. (Petrobrás)*

    Second pay .... *Petróleo Brasileiro S. A. (Petrobrás)*

IP in barrels per day and/or cubic feet or cubic meters per day:

    First pay .... *3000 BOPD (Barra Nova Formation)*

    Second pay .... *500 BOPD (Urucutuca Formation)*

All other zones with shows of oil and gas in the field:

Age	Formation	Type of Show

None

Geologic concept leading to discovery and method or methods used to delineate prospect, e.g., surface geology, subsurface geology, seeps, magnetic data, gravity data, seismic data, seismic refraction, nontechnical:

The wildcat was drilled to test a paleogeomorphic trap delineated by seismic data that indicated a structural high mapped at the Barra Nova shallow-water sandstone reservoir level, sealed by deep-water Urucutuca shales.

Structure:

    Province/basin type .... *Bally 114; Klemme III C*

    Tectonic history

    The Espirito Santo basin is a Brazilian Coastal basin related to the South Atlantic evolution. Tectonic history involves a rift phase with a general tilt to east associated with some normal faults and gentle structures affecting the Upper Cretaceous and Tertiary sediments. The reservoirs of this field are associated with the mixed clastic-carbonate platform development that preceded the post-rift evaporitic sequence. The trap is mostly controlled by erosion associated with the excavation of the canyon developed during the open-marine phase.

    Regional structure

    Paleogeomorphic high caused by submarine erosion of the Upper Cretaceous of the Fazenda Cedro canyon.

    Local structure

    The structure is a 6° to 15° homoclinal dip to the southeast associated with an erosional event.

Trap:

    Trap type(s) .... *The trap is paleogeomorphic and the reservoirs are sealed by overlying shales*

Basin stratigraphy (major stratigraphic intervals from surface to deepest penetration in field):

Chronostratigraphy	Formation	Depth to Top in m
Tertiary	*Rio Doce Formation*	*-19 (ocean floor)*
Tertiary	*Caravelas Formation*	*-1230*
Eocene to Maestrichtian	*Urucutuca Formation*	*-1897*
Albian	*Barra Nova Formation*	*-2630*

Reservoir characteristics:

Number of reservoirs *2*

Formations .... *Barra Nova Formation and Urucutuca Formation*

Ages .... *Albian and Upper Cretaceous*

Depths to tops of reservoirs .... *Barra Nova Formation, -2666 m; Urucutuca Formation, -2599 m*

Gross thickness (top to bottom of producing interval) .... *164 m*

> **Net thickness—total thickness of producing zones**
> **Average** .... *46 m*
> **Maximum** .... *74 m*

Lithology .... *Fine- to coarse-grained feldspathic sandstones*

Porosity type .... *Intergranular porosity*

Average porosity *16.6%*

Average permeability .... *500 md*

Seals:

Upper

> **Formation, fault, or other feature** .... *Shales overlying unconformity*
> **Lithology** .... *Shale*

Lateral

> **Formation, fault, or other feature** .... *Shales overlying unconformity*
> **Lithology** .... *Shale*

Source:

Formation and age .... *Mucuri Member of Mariricu Formation*

Lithology .... *Shale*

Average total organic carbon (TOC) *2.0%*

Maximum TOC *3.5*

Kerogen type (I, II, or III) .... *I, II*

Vitrinite reflectance (maturation) .... $R_o = 1.0\%$

Time of hydrocarbon expulsion .... *Albian to the present*

Present depth to top of source .... *Not reached*

Thickness .... *NA*

Potential yield .... *5 kg HC/ton*

Appendix 2. Production Data

Field name .... *Cacão field*

Field size:

Proved acres .... *200 ha*

Number of wells all years *15*

Current number of wells *13*

Well spacing .... *500 m*

Ultimate recoverable .... *12.6 MMbbl of oil and 21.6 bcf of gas*

Cumulative production (through 1988) .... *10.4 MMbbl of oil and 11.3 bcf of gas*

311

Annual production (1988) .... *1.21 MMbbl of oil and 1.05 bcf of gas*
Present decline rate *26%*
    Initial decline rate *18%*
    Overall decline rate *26%*
Annual water production .... *21,000 bbl*
In place, total reserves .... *50.4 MMbbl*
In place, per acre-foot .... *772.62 bbl*
Primary recovery .... *9.0 MMbbl*
Secondary recovery .... *3.6 MMbbl*
Enhanced recovery .... *Not known*
Cumulative water production .... *377,500 bbl*

Drilling and casing practices:

Amount of surface casing set .... *540 m*
Casing program .... *30-in. (140 m); 20-in. (540 m); 13⅜-in. (1850 m);*
                                                  9⅝-in. or 7-in. (2750 m) liner; 7-in. (between 2600 and 3000 m)
Drilling mud .... *Oil base*
Bit program .... *26-in./36-in. with hole opener 26-in., 17½-in., 12¼-in., 8½-in.*
High pressure zones .... *None*

Completion practices:

Interval(s) perforated .... *Several zones completed with only one packer*
Well treatment .... *Acidizing*

Formation evaluation:

Logging suites .... *Induction, SP, GR, density, neutron, sonic, and dipmeter logs*
Testing practices .... *Drill-stem test, wireline test, and production tests*
Mud logging techniques .... *Not used*

Oil characteristics:

Type
API gravity .... *37.5°*
Base .... *Paraffinic (characterization factor UOPK = 12)*
Initial GOR .... *674 ft³/bbl*
Sulfur, wt% *20*
Viscosity, SUS .... *40 SUS (48.9°C), 37.4 SUS (60°C), 34.6 SUS (79.4°C)*
Pour point .... *Not available*
Gas-oil distillate .... *Not available*

Field characteristics:

Average elevation .... *-19 m*
Initial pressure .... *3980 psi*
Present pressure .... *1210 psi*
Pressure gradient .... *0.3093 psi/ft*
Temperature .... *109°C*
Geothermal gradient .... *0.0405°C/m*
Drive .... *Gravity segregation depletion drive*
Oil column thickness .... *164 m*
Oil-water contact .... *Varies around -2767 m*
Connate water *0.213%*
Water salinity, TDS .... *89,000 mg/L*
Resistivity of water .... *0.102 ohm-m (-25°C)*
Bulk volume water (%) *22.5%*

Transportation method and market for oil and gas:

Through marine pipeline from field to the onshore collecting station. Internal refining and distribution.

Quiriquire Field—Venezuela
Eastern Venezuela (Maturin) Basin

AMOS SALVADOR
University of Texas at Austin
Austin, Texas

HERNAN J. LEON
Lagoven, S.A.
Caracas, Venezuela

FIELD CLASSIFICATION

BASIN: Eastern Venezuela
BASIN TYPE: Foredeep
RESERVOIR ROCK TYPE: Sandstone and
  Conglomerate
RESERVOIR ENVIRONMENT OF DEPOSITION: Alluvial Fan
TRAP DESCRIPTION: Updip loss of porosity due to asphalt plugging in an alluvial fan

RESERVOIR AGE: Pliocene
PETROLEUM TYPE: Oil
TRAP TYPE: Diagenetic (Tar Seal)

LOCATION

The Quiriquire field is located in the northern part of the State of Monagas in eastern Venezuela in the southern foothills of the Serrania del Interior (Interior Range), 28 km (17 mi) north of the city of Maturin, the capital of the state (Figure 1).

The Quiriquire field was the first oil field discovered in what would become the rich eastern Venezuela petroleum province. With an estimated ultimate recovery of about 800 million bbl of oil, and perhaps as much as 4 or 5 billion bbl of oil in place, the Quiriquire field is also the largest oil field in eastern Venezuela and a giant oil field by world-wide standards. Carmalt and St. John (1986) list the Quiriquire field in 226th place in their table of 509 giant oil and gas fields of the world and assign to it recoverable oil reserves of 1 billion bbl. For earlier discussions of the Quiriquire field, see Regan (1938), Wallis (1953), Renz et al. (1963, p. 179–182), and particularly the very complete description by Borger (1952).

HISTORY

The Quiriquire field was discovered on 1 June 1928 by well Moneb-1, later named Quiriquire-1 (Figure 4). But the search for oil in the area had started almost 30 years before. Oil explorers had long been attracted to northeastern Venezuela by the hundreds of prolific surface oil seeps that stretch in an east-west belt parallel to the southern foothills of the Serrania del

Interior (Interior Range). As early as 1890, the Graham Company of Trinidad drilled several shallow wells near Pedernales, 100 km (62 mi) east of Quiriquire, but they encountered only small shows of asphalt and gas. In 1910, the New York and Bermudez Company, a subsidiary of the General Asphalt Company of Philadelphia, began to exploit the so-called Guanoco "asphalt lake," a particularly large cluster of oil seeps about 40 km (25 mi) northeast of Quiriquire (Figure 1). Twenty-seven wells were drilled in this area, some of which produced low-gravity oil (10°API), but the venture proved to be unprofitable and operations ceased in 1928. Other companies carried out exploratory drilling in the vicinity of the eastern Venezuela oil-seep belt during the 1910s and 1920s, but even though they frequently encountered oil shows, they failed to develop commercial production. Drilling, for the most part, was downdip from the seeps, based on the belief that they were the product of the updip migration of the oil to the surface from deeper accumulations (Borger, 1952).

Persistence, however, was eventually rewarded with success. The Standard Oil of Venezuela (later Creole Petroleum Corporation, a subsidiary of the Standard Oil Company of New Jersey, later Exxon Corporation), after drilling seven unsuccessful wildcats between 1922 and 1927 in the Quiriquire-Guanoco area, finally completed a well, the Moneb-1 (Quiriquire-1), as a commercial oil producer in 1928. It was drilled in the neighborhood of oil and gas seeps near the town of Quiriquire on the south flank of what was believed to be a surface anticline in the Cretaceous rocks of the southern foothills of the Serrania del Interior.

313

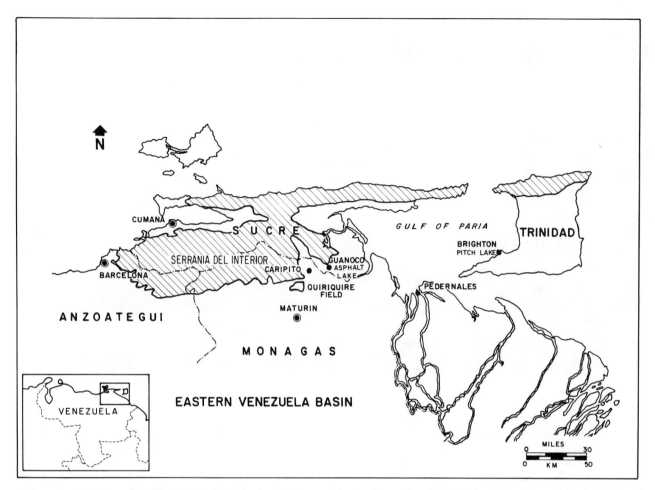

Figure 1. Location of the Quiriquire field on the northern margin of the Eastern Venezuela (Maturin) Basin. Cross-hatched areas are mountainous, including the Serrania del Interior. The Precambrian Guayana shield is just south of and all along the map area. Basin sediments thin to the south to the Orinoco River along the edge of the Guayana shield. The Orinoco Delta complex is seen in the southeastern quadrant.

As recounted by Borger (1952, p. 2292–2293),

Quiriquire-1 was spudded on February 10,1925, and suspended on October 6 of the same year at a depth of 1,849 feet after establishing production of 10.6° gravity oil which was not considered to be of commercial value. The recovery of small amounts of 16.0° API gravity oil from Pliocene beds penetrated in Monef-2, which is located near the same seep area, directed attention to the basal part of the Quiriquire formation in Quiriquire-1. Quiriquire-1 was then drilled 394 feet deeper [to a total depth of 2,243 feet] and successfully completed in Pliocene sands for an initial of 438 barrels of 16.3° API gravity oil per day on June 1, 1928. This date is considered to be the discovery date of the field.

The Quiriquire field was rapidly developed after its discovery. By 1931, 40 wells were producing 11,000 barrels of oil daily (BOPD), and by 1939, 294 development wells had been drilled in the field and its limits were thought to have been established. Drilling operations were resumed in 1942 when several wells were deepened, and by 1950 the number of wells had reached 533. To date, including deeper-pool tests drilled in search of deeper reservoirs, 676 wells have been drilled in the Quiriquire field and immediately surrounding areas.

All except the first few wells were drilled with rotary rigs. The early wells were extensively cored to establish the top and bottom of the commercial oil column. Electric logs were first used in 1932, and side-wall coring soon replaced the more expensive and slower conventional-coring procedure.

In the early years of development, wells were completed by setting casing above the oil-bearing interval and then running a preperforated liner opposite the section to be produced. Later casing was set through the productive section and perforations opened at the desired oil sands. Early wells produced by natural flow, but since 1943, all wells have had to be pumped because reservoir pressures declined and new wells would not flow.

The discovery of the thick oil-sand section in the central part of the field led to the drilling of twin wells at each location, one producing from the upper part of the section and the other from the lower part. This procedure minimized the production difficulties inherent in producing the entire section. The drilling and completion practices and production history of the Quiriquire field to 1951 have been discussed in detail by Borger (1952).

Recognizing that only a small percentage of the oil in place was being recovered by primary production, attempts at secondary recovery of additional oil were made for a number of years. The heavy nature of the oil, and probably even more likely, the strong lenticularity of the reservoir sands of the productive interval, caused all attempts to fail. No new tries have been made for a number of years.

The Quiriquire giant oil accumulation in Pliocene reservoirs is a "one-of-a-kind" oil field. Efforts to discover "another Quiriquire" in the area have failed. The Quiriquire field apparently represents the fortunate coincidence of favorable geological ingredients both in space and in time—a prolific source of oil and, unlike other areas along the northern flank of the Eastern Venezuela Basin, an effective reservoir ready to soak the oil as it was expelled from the source.

The Quiriquire reservoir is nearly depleted. Production from the Quiriquire Formation ceased in mid-1985, at which time water production reached almost 80%. The field has produced close to 800 million bbl of oil. Production in the Quiriquire field increased rapidly after its discovery, and by 1937 it was producing at a rate of 70 to 75 MBOPD (Figure 2). Production decreased to about 8 to 18 MBOPD during the World War II years but increased again after the end of the war and by 1952 reached 70 to 78 MBOPD. Production began to decline progressively in 1955, and by 1985 it was only about 6000 BOPD.

Deeper drilling in the Quiriquire field area has resulted in the discovery of deeper reservoirs in a large anticlinal structure that underlies the field: Gas and condensate have been tested in the Los Jabillos, Caratas, Vidoño, and San Antonio formations of Oligocene to Late Cretaceous age (Figure 6). None of these reservoirs, however, has yet been placed in production, and little is known about the dimensions and properties of the reservoirs, their reserves, or their producing characteristics.

DISCOVERY METHOD

As discussed above, the Quiriquire field was discovered as a result of reconnaissance surface geological work that located the prolific oil seeps in the neighborhood of the field. This, of course, was

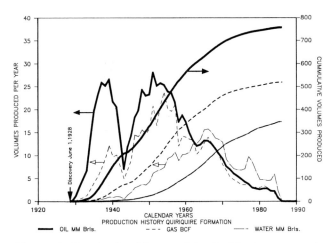

Figure 2. Production history of the Quiriquire reservoir showing cumulative production and production per year (oil, gas, and water).

the most common approach in the search for oil in the early part of the century, before the advent of geophysical exploration methods. Today, however, the presence of surface indications of oil updip from the field probably would still be the most important lead to its discovery. The Quiriquire field is a structureless, purely stratigraphic accumulation, and it is doubtful that geophysical methods would have been able to detect it. Exploratory drilling in the area was, and probably would still have to be, directed by geological reasoning, suggesting that oil accumulations may be present downdip from the oil-seep area.

Modern seismic surveys undoubtedly would have been able to map the large faulted anticlinal structure that underlies the Quiriquire field, and the field would have been discovered while drilling to test the structure. In that event, the discovery of a major oil field would have had to be attributed, once again, to serendipity.

STRUCTURE

Tectonic History

During most of the Cretaceous, eastern Venezuela was a northward-deepening marine shelf bordering to the north the Precambrian Guayana shield. Uplifted lands (island arcs?) began to emerge north of the present coast of eastern Venezuela (Figure 1) late in the Cretaceous, marking the initial stages of the formation of the Eastern Venezuela Basin to the south of these lands. The uplift propagated spasmodically and progressively southward (thrusting?) during the early Tertiary and culminated in the late Oligocene or early Miocene with the formation of the present Serrania del Interior (Interior Range) of northeastern Venezuela. Meanwhile, south of this orogenic front, the Eastern Venezuela Basin subsided persistently at the same time that the major depocenters shifted progressively eastward. Erosion of northern and northwestern uplifted landmasses provided most of the materials deposited south of them along the northern flank of the Eastern Venezuela Basin. The Pliocene Quiriquire Formation, the main reservoir of the Quiriquire field, represents an alluvial fan complex deposited by south-flowing streams coming out of the Serrania del Interior (Figures 6 and 8). For a more complete description of the Eastern Venezuela Basin, see Hedberg (1950), Young et al. (1956), Renz et al. (1958, 1963), and Gonzalez de Juana et al. (1980).

Regional Structure

The Quiriquire field is located in the steep, structurally complex north flank of the Eastern Venezuela Basin. The pre-Pliocene sediments along this north flank are thrusted and deformed into tight, locally overturned folds. The Pliocene sequences, on the other hand, form a gentle, south-dipping homocline that overlies unconformably the older deformed rocks (Figure 3).

Local Structure

The Quiriquire Formation in the Quiriquire field area forms a homocline with a general N55-60°E

strike and a gentle dip of 5–6° to the southeast (Figure 4). The older rocks below the Quiriquire Formation are folded into a sharp anticlinal structure trending N60°E and with dips of as much as 20–30° in the flanks. The northern flank of the syncline to the north of this anticline is overturned and complexly thrusted (Figures 3 and 5).

STRATIGRAPHY

In the Quiriquire field area and neighboring parts of the Eastern Venezuela Basin and the Serrania del Interior, the stratigraphic section includes rocks ranging in age from late Early Cretaceous (Barremian) to Holocene (Figure 6). The pre-Cretaceous "basement" has not been reached by wells in the Quiriquire field area and does not crop out in the Serrania del Interior north of the field. Its depth under the northern part of the Eastern Venezuela Basin and the Serrania del Interior has not been estimated.

Following is a brief description of the stratigraphic section of the Quiriquire area and nearby parts of northern Monagas. For more regional stratigraphic descriptions, see Hedberg (1950) and Gonzalez de Juana et al. (1980).

Cretaceous

No important unconformities have been recognized in the Cretaceous section of the area. From older

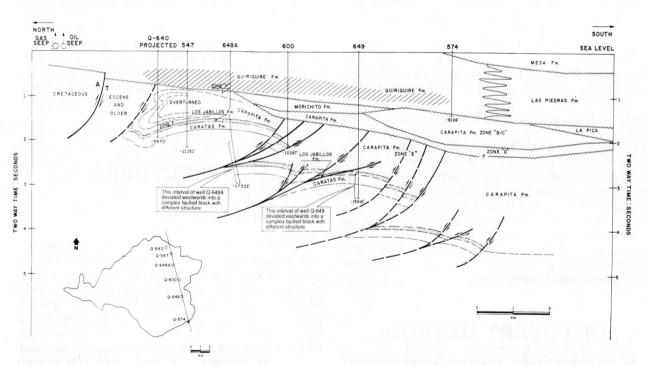

Figure 3. Regional cross section through the Quiriquire field. Cross-hatching indicates oil accumulation. The composite log, Figure 12, shows the stratigraphic positions of Carapita Formation foraminiferal zones "A" through "F."

316

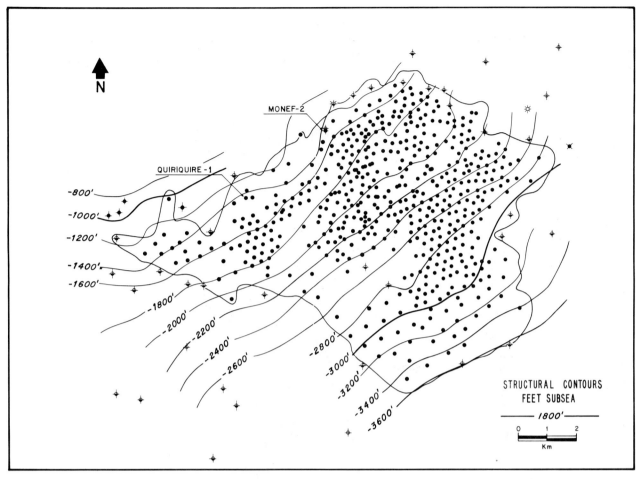

Figure 4. Structural map of the top of the "laminated marker" (top of Zeta member of Quiriquire Formation).

to younger, the Cretaceous section of the Quiriquire area has been subdivided into the following units.

Barranquin Formation

The Barranquin Formation is dominantly composed of medium- to coarse-grained, often cross-bedded sandstones with lesser amounts of siltstones, sandy shales, and carbonaceous shales. The base has not been observed at the surface or penetrated in the subsurface. Incomplete surface sections attain thicknesses of up to 1500 m (5000 ft). The Barranquin Formation probably represents the initial deposits of the Cretaceous marine transgression over eastern Venezuela. The lower part is mostly composed of sediments of fluvial origin that grade upward into a marine section.

El Cantil Formation

The El Cantil Formation consists of interbedded thick-bedded to massive limestones and calcareous shales. In northern Monagas, the El Cantil Formation ranges in thickness between 650 and 915 m (2130-

3000 ft). Neither the Barranquin Formation nor the El Cantil, which together form the Sucre Group, have been penetrated in the Quiriquire field area.

Querecual Formation

The Querecual Formation is a very distinctive unit composed of dark gray to black, thin-bedded, carbonaceous and bituminous shaly limestones and calcareous shales. Discoidal and ellipsoidal limestone concretions from a few centimeters to a meter in diameter are common in the formation. The Querecual limestones and calcareous shales emit a strong petroliferous odor when broken. They are considered to be excellent potential source rocks of petroleum.

San Antonio Formation

The San Antonio Formation is similar in lithology to the underlying Querecual Formation; this unit can, however, be differentiated by its content of cherty intervals and fine- to medium-grained, generally calcareous sandstones in beds a few centimeters to 10 m (33 ft) in thickness. The more shaly sections of the San Antonio Formation can also be considered as potential sources of petroleum.

317

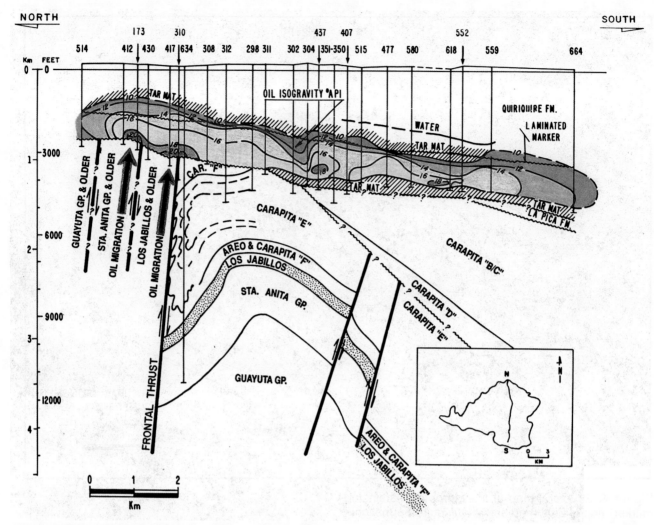

Figure 5. North-south cross section through the Quiriquire field showing distribution of API gravities of oil in the reservoir. Contour interval, 2° API. Heavy oils are dark green, successively lighter to yellow and red for higher gravities.

Because of their similar lithologic composition, the Querecual and San Antonio formations are often mapped jointly as the Guayuta Group, which in northern Monagas ranges in thickness between 780 and 1500 m (2550-4920 ft), most commonly about 1100-1200 m (3610-3930 ft). The Querecual Formation makes up roughly one-third of the Guayuta Group and the San Antonio Formation the other two-thirds.

San Juan Formation

The San Juan Formation is predominantly composed of thick-bedded, fine- to medium-grained, well-sorted quartz sandstones, locally calcareous. In northern Monagas, the San Juan Formation ranges in thickness between 100 and 215 m (330-700 ft) and is about 130 m (425 ft) thick in the Quiriquire field area, where it has been penetrated by several wells. When not cemented, the San Juan sandstones can provide excellent reservoirs for the accumulation of oil and gas.

Uppermost Cretaceous-Paleocene-Eocene

An ostensibly continuous section ranging in age from latest Cretaceous to middle Eocene overlies the previously described Cretaceous sequence in northern Monagas. It comprises two formations, the Vidoño and Caratas formations.

Vidoño Formation

The older formation is composed of a monotonous section of dark gray, generally glauconitic shale, rich in foraminifers. It includes local arenaceous zones and occasional thin beds of glauconitic sandstone. The thickness of the Vidoño Formation ranges between 125 and 300 m (410-985 ft) in northern Monagas and between 150 and 200 m (500-655 ft) in the Quiriquire field area. It includes beds of latest Cretaceous, Paleocene, and early Eocene age.

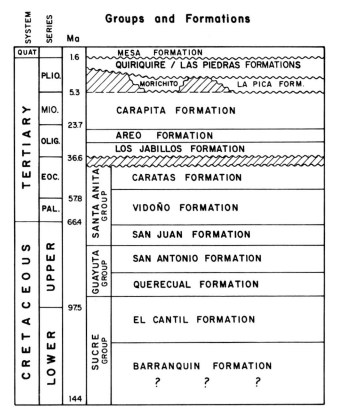

Figure 6. Generalized stratigraphic column of northern Monagas.

Caratas Formation

The Caratas Formation includes a section of gray to greenish-gray, calcareous, generally glauconitic siltstones, fine-grained calcareous sandstones, and occasional dolomitic limestones. It has a thickness of 250 to 400 m (820–1300 ft) in northern Monagas and from 300 to 350 m (985–1150 ft) in the Quiriquire area. The Caratas Formation is considered to be of early to middle Eocene age.

The San Juan, Vidoño, and Caratas formations have been mapped as the Santa Anita Group.

Oligocene and Miocene

An unconformity of regional extent has been postulated at the top of the Caratas Formation by some authors (Gonzalez de Juana et al., 1980), based on the absence of beds of recognized late Eocene age in eastern Venezuela and local evidence of a sedimentary hiatus in the section. In the Quiriquire field area, electric-log correlations show evidence of truncation of beds at the top of the Caratas Formation below overlying sediments, supporting the presence of the unconformity also in this area. The Oligocene-Miocene section is composed of three formations, from bottom to top, the Los Jabillos, Areo, and Carapita formations.

Los Jabillos Formation

The Los Jabillos Formation is a sequence predominantly composed of thick-bedded fine- to medium-grained quartz sandstones, locally pebbly. It has a fairly uniform thickness of 50 to 70 m (165–230 ft) in northern Monagas. The Los Jabillos sandstones are potential reservoirs of petroleum.

Areo and Carapita Formations

Overlying the Los Jabillos sandstone section in the Quiriquire field area is a very thick sequence of Oligocene and Miocene shales. The lower, thinner part, composed of 30 to 60 m (100–200 ft) of dark gray, often glauconitic and foraminiferal shales, has been called the Areo Formation, while the upper, much thicker section, composed of dark gray foraminiferal shales, has been included in the Carapita Formation. In outcrop, along the foothills of the Serrania del Interior, this combined shaly section has a thickness of 1000 to 2000 m (3300–6600 ft). In the Quiriquire field area the Carapita Formation ranges in thickness between 610 and 1525 m (2000–5000 ft), but further south, closer to its depositional center the thickness of the Areo-Carapita shale sequence has been estimated to reach 4500 to 6000 m (14,750–20,000 ft). Along the northern flank of the Eastern Venezuela Basin, the Carapita Formation contains a number of sandstone intervals, probably of turbiditic origin. On the basis of its contained foraminiferal fauna, the Carapita Formation has been subdivided in northern Monagas into six zones named, from top to bottom, "A" to "F" (Figure 12). An unconformity has been postulated between zones "E" and "D" in the Quiriquire area (Figures 5 and 12). The Carapita thick marine shale section has been considered by some as a possible source rock of petroleum in the Eastern Venezuela Basin.

Uppermost Miocene and Pliocene

Overlying unconformably older, structurally deformed, truncated, and eroded rocks along the northern flank of the Eastern Venezuela Basin is a sequence of gently dipping terrigenous clastics that have generally been mapped as four distinct upper Miocene and Pliocene units.

Morichito Formation

The Morichito is a conglomeratic unit composed predominantly of gravel and boulders derived from older units. It has been recognized in the subsurface of northern Monagas along a narrow belt, 10 to 15 km (6–9 mi) wide, just south of the foothills of the Serrania del Interior (Lamb and De Sisto, 1963), attaining local thicknesses of up to 1800 m (6000 ft). It overlies with strong unconformity formations ranging in age from Cretaceous to early Miocene and underlies also unconformably the Las Piedras or Quiriquire formations (Figure 3). The Morichito Formation probably represents alluvial fans depos-

319

ited over a deeply eroded and unstable area along a tectonically active mountain front.

La Pica Formation

Further basinward, the less deformed upper Tertiary section includes at the base a unit of interbedded shales and very fine to fine-grained sandstones, the La Pica Formation, which attains thicknesses of over 2500 m (8200 ft) near the axis of the Eastern Venezuela Basin. In the Quiriquire area, it pinches out a short distance south of the field (Figures 3 and 5).

Las Piedras and Quiriquire Formations

Over most of the eastern part of the Eastern Venezuela Basin, the Las Piedras Formation makes up the upper part of the upper Tertiary section. It is differentiated from the underlying La Pica Formation by containing more and coarser-grained sandstones. In the Quiriquire field area, the Las Piedras Formation grades northward into a yet coarser-grained section of terrigenous clastics predominantly composed of medium- to coarse-grained sandstones and conglomerates but which includes also lesser amounts of finer-grained sandstones and siltstones. Grain size decreases from north to south. This local development of the Las Piedras Formation has been called the Quiriquire Formation and is the main reservoir of the Quiriquire field (Figure 3). It reaches a maximum thickness of about 1600 m (5250 ft) and represents the deposits of overlapping, interfingering alluvial fans formed at the mouth of a stream or streams that drained the highlands to the north and dumped their poorly sorted load upon reaching the edge of the coastal area of the Pliocene littoral/marine embayment in eastern Venezuela.

Quaternary Mesa Formation

South of the Quiriquire field and extending over most of the eastern part of the Eastern Venezuela Basin, the flat-lying, poorly consolidated sands and gravels of the Quaternary Mesa Formation cover unconformably the Las Piedras and equivalent formations. The Mesa Formation is usually less than 75 m (250 ft) thick and forms distinctive savanna-covered mesas and cliffs.

TRAP

The oil accumulation in the Quiriquire Formation is purely stratigraphic. The laterally discontinuous, lenticular sandstones and conglomerates that provide the reservoirs of the Quiriquire field are only gently tilted homoclinally to the southeast (Figures 3 and 4), and the oil is trapped updip at the pinch-out of the coarse clastic lenses and by the formation of a tar mat or asphalt seal (Figures 3, 4, 5, and 7). This heavy oil seal resulted from the exposure of the oil to fresh meteoric water and its ensuing alteration caused by water washing, inorganic oxidation, and biodegradation. The source of the oil in the Quiriquire Formation and the path of its migration into the present accumulation has been the subject of considerable speculation. These subjects will be covered later under the discussion of the source.

In contrast to the stratigraphic oil accumulation in the Quiriquire Formation, the gas and condensate accumulations in older reservoirs—Cretaceous and lower Tertiary—have been trapped in faulted anticlinal structures.

In contrast to the stratigraphic oil accumulation in the Quiriquire Formation, the gas and condensate accumulations in older reservoirs—Cretaceous and lower Tertiary—have been trapped in faulted anticlinal structures.

RESERVOIRS

Quiriquire Formation

Stratigraphy and Sedimentology

The Quiriquire Formation is composed of irregularly interbedded, unconsolidated to poorly consolidated, poorly sorted, medium- to coarse-grained sandstones and conglomerates with lesser amounts of sandy claystones and occasional lignite beds. Individual beds show extreme lenticularity, and very rapid lateral lithologic variation is common. As a result, subsurface sand-by-sand correlation between wells is difficult, if not impossible. Groups of sands can only be correlated over short distances. The size of the clastic fragments decreases from the north, where conglomerates and even boulder beds form an important part of the formation. To the south, the Quiriquire Formation grades laterally to the finer-grained Las Piedras Formation (Salvador, 1961). The percentage of coarse clastics (conglomerates and sandstones) in the formation ranges from over 50% in the northern part of the field to less than 20% in its western, southern, and eastern periphery (Figure 8).

On the basis of the most workable electric-log correlations, the Quiriquire Formation has been subdivided for practical oil-field work into eight units, called "members"; from top to bottom, they are Alpha, Beta, Gamma, Delta, Epsilon, Zeta, Eta, and Theta (Figure 9). The lower six members, and particularly the lower three, are productive. The top of the Zeta member is placed at the top of a prominent, positive self-potential peak on the electric logs, the so-called "laminated marker," which is the most distinctive and widespread correlation key-bed in the entire field. It is characterized by thin laminae of interbedded shale and fine-grained sandstone; it averages 7.5 m (25 ft) in thickness, and has been interpreted to be associated with an unconformity within the Quiriquire Formation.

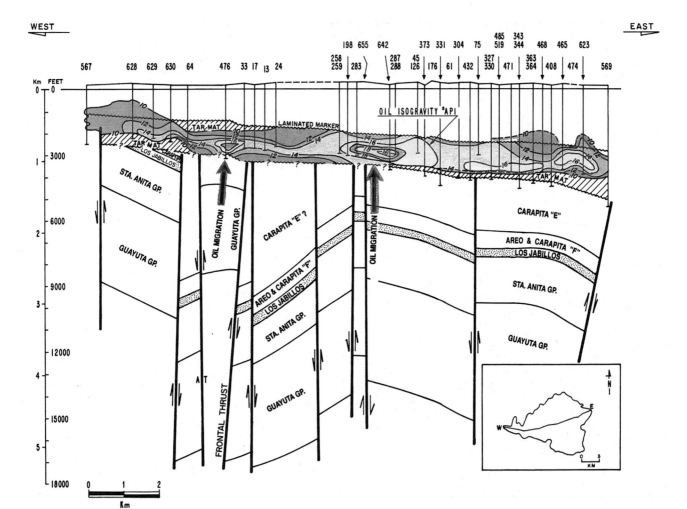

Figure 7. East-west cross section through the Quiriquire field showing distribution of API gravities of oil. Contour interval, 2° API. Heaviest oil, dark green; lightest oil, orange.

The Quiriquire Formation thickens from its northern pinch-out against the outcrop of the Cretaceous sequence to about 1600 m (5250 ft) at its downdip lateral transition to the Las Piedras Formation.

Porosity and Permeability

The porosity of the reservoir sandstones and conglomerates of the Quiriquire Formation is of the intergranular type. It averages about 20% but ranges considerably throughout the field. Average permeability is about 400 to 500 md but can range between 100 md and 11 darcys. The reservoir properties of the unconsolidated or poorly consolidated sandstones and conglomerates of the Quiriquire Formation do not appear to have been appreciably modified by either diagenetic processes or by fracturing.

Reservoir Size and Thickness

The oil accumulation in the Quiriquire Formation is an oval-shaped lens approximately 14 km (8.5 mi) in a southwest-northeast direction and 9 km (5.5 mi) in a northwest-southeast direction. It covers an area of 8267 ha (20,429 ac).

The wide range in the API gravity of the oils in the Quiriquire field and their irregular distribution within the reservoir make it difficult to determine the amount of gross thickness and net thickness of the reservoir in any particular well because the estimation of these quantities depends on the establishment of a lower limit for the specific gravity of the oil to be produced. For example, the amount of oil sand will be smaller if only sandstone beds containing oil lighter than 20° API are to be produced than if all sands containing oil lighter than 15° API are to be completed. Nevertheless, net reservoir thickness (from the top to the bottom of the productive interval) has been estimated to reach 250 m (820 ft) in the center of the field, and to average 70 m (230 ft). Figure 10 is a generalized isopach map of the estimated net oil reservoir thickness of the Quiriquire reservoir.

Even though the sandstone and conglomerate beds of the Quiriquire Formation are laterally discontin-

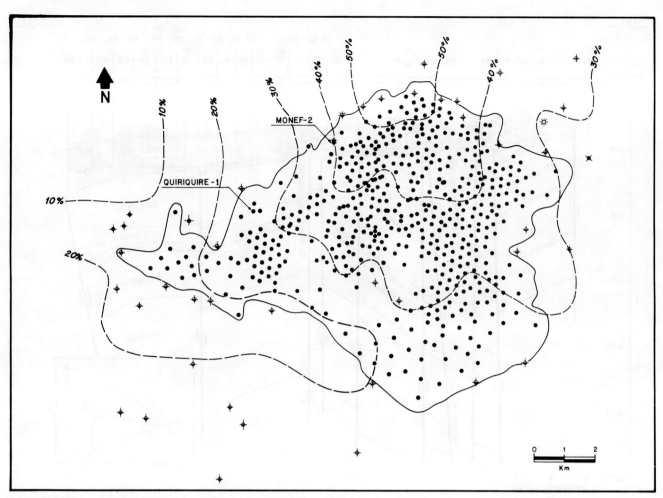

Figure 8. Coarse clastics (conglomerates and sandstones) percentages in the Quiriquire reservoir. Contour interval, 10%.

uous and each well penetrates numerous separate saturated sandstone and conglomerate beds, there apparently is a certain amount of intercommunication between these individual discontinuous beds. The Quiriquire field, therefore, has been treated as a single reservoir.

Reservoir Fluids

The API gravity of the oil in the Quiriquire Formation varies from heavier-than-water (HTW), semi-solid tar to 28° API. The oil accumulation has the shape of a large oval lens. In the northern part of the field, the lighter oils are generally at or near the base of the Quiriquire Formation, directly above the pre-Quiriquire unconformity; over most of the rest of the field, they are more commonly found in the middle part of the oil lens, underlain and overlain by increasingly heavier crudes (Figures 5 and 7). The outer upper and lower boundaries of the lenticular oil accumulation, therefore, contain the heaviest oils—semi-solid, viscous, heavier-than-water oil and tar (the so-called "tar mat") that forms a sheath around the lighter oils.

Figure 11 shows the distribution of the gravity of the oil produced in the Quiriquire field.

The oils produced from the Quiriquire Formation are dark brown and asphaltic. The average sulfur content is 1.2% by weight and the average pour point is –4° C (25° F).

No gas cap is believed to have been originally present in the Quiriquire field. Some isolated gas accumulations in lenticular sands, however, have been found in the northern part of the field.

Water occurs throughout the Quiriquire reservoir, but it is more prevalent around the edges of the field. From the surface to about 300 m (1000 ft), the water is fresh. Below this depth, the water becomes brackish. Salinities of over 35,000 ppm have been reported from the lower part of the Quiriquire Formation in the north-central part of the field, corresponding quite closely with the areas from where the lightest oils have been produced.

Reservoir Energy

The principal source of the reservoir energy is believed to be a dissolved-gas drive, but some water

322

AGE FM.	MEMB.	ELECTRIC LOG	REMARKS
PLIOCENE QUIRIQUIRE FORMATION	ALPHA 250'-1600'	Q-315 LOG	Interbedded boulders, cobbles, gravelly sands and clay. Some saturation of water and HTW oil.
	BETA 500'-600'		Lithology as above, shows of gas and HTW oil.
	GAMMA 310'		Lithology as above, saturated with HTW oil. Gas shows.
	DELTA 220'		Basal sands produce 16.5° API oil.
	EPSILON 280'		Lithology as above, oil producer
			~~ Laminated marker ~~~~~
	ZETA 380'-475'		Produces 15° to 21° API oil.
	ETA 0'-625'	Q-228 LOG / PRODUCTIVE SECTION	Main productive horizon of field 13° to 21° API oil. Pinches out against unconformity north of field limits.
	THETA 0'-750'		Lithology as in other members. upper and middle portions produce 13° to 17.5° API oil. Lower sands HTW oil saturation. Pinches out against unconformity.
MIOCENE TO CRETACEOUS			See Pre-Quiriquire composite log. (Fig. 12)

Figure 9. Composite type log of the Quiriquire Formation. HTW, heavier than water. (After Borger, 1952.)

drive may be locally active. The early wells in the Quiriquire field flowed naturally, but after about 10 years of production, pressures began to decline, and by 1943, 15 years after the discovery of the field, nearly all wells needed to be pumped.

Los Jabillos Formation

Of the pre-Quiriquire productive intervals, the Los Jabillos reservoir is the better known because 24 wells have been drilled into and have tested this formation. The reservoir is a fine- to medium-grained quartz sandstone, 50 to 70 m (165–230 ft) thick. The porosity is predominantly intergranular and averages 10.6% with a maximum of 18.3%. Permeability averages 69 md; maximum permeabilities of 112 to 120 md have been reported. Fractures are believed to contribute substantially to the reservoir characteristics. The Los Jabillos reservoir lies at depths of 2100 to 3140 m (6900 to 10,300 ft) and contains gas and condensate (55–56° API); it has not yet been placed on commercial production. A composite log of the Los Jabillos and other pre-Quiriquire formations is shown in Figure 12.

FAULTS

No faults are known to cut the Quiriquire Formation or to have contributed to the localization,

shape, or dimensions of the Quiriquire oil accumulation. However, as discussed later, faults may have played an important role in the migration of oil into the Quiriquire reservoir rocks.

The pre-Quiriquire section, on the other hand, is broken by the complex compressive system of thrusts and strike-slip faults that characterizes the mountain front of the Serrania del Interior. Part of the pre-Quiriquire section under the northern part of the Quiriquire field is overturned (Figures 3 and 5). The anticlinal structure that underlies the Quiriquire field is known to be cut by a number of faults that seem to separate the Los Jabillos gas and condensate accumulation into several separate reservoirs (Figure 13). Not enough is known about these reservoirs, however, to determine if faulting has contributed to the migration into and accumulation of the gas and condensate in the Los Jabillos Formation.

Source

Since it must be accepted that the nonmarine coarse clastics of the Quiriquire Formation cannot be regarded as the source of the oil it contains, an outside source and an avenue of migration have to be postulated. Two main possibilities have been considered: The first is that the oil was generated in a source-rock sequence laterally equivalent to the Quiriquire Formation deeper in the basin and that it migrated updip from there and accumulated in the porous Quiriquire Formation clastics (Borger, 1952; Wallis, 1953). The second possibility is that the oil had its origin in the underlying older rocks and that it migrated into the Quiriquire Formation reservoirs from below, probably along faults or fracture zones (Regan, 1938; Borger, 1952; Wallis, 1953). In either case, the migration and accumulation of the oil must have taken place toward the end of or after the deposition of the Quiriquire Formation, during the late Pliocene and/or the Pleistocene.

The second alternative seems more plausible because it is better supported by geological and geochemical evidence. Stratigraphic intervals known to underlie the Quiriquire field, particularly the Cretaceous Querecual and San Antonio formations (Guayuta Group), have been identified by geochemical analyses as the most likely source for the oil in the Quiriquire field. The average total organic carbon (TOC) content of the Querecual and San Antonio formations is about 2.35 to 2.4% with maximum measurements of 6.6% for the Querecual and 4.52% for the San Antonio. The kerogen contained by these units is predominantly of the amorphous marine type (type I), with vitrinite reflectances (R_o) of 0.59 to 0.97%, indicative of very favorable type and degree of maturation for the generation of oil. The potential yield of the source rocks of the Querecual and San Antonio formations has been estimated to range between 60 and 158 million bbl/km^3. Because of the high degree of oil degradation,

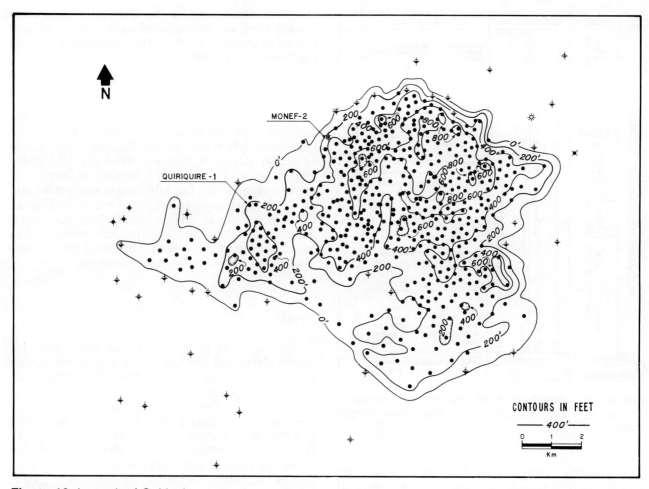

Figure 10. Isopach of Quiriquire reservoir net oil pay.
Contour interval, 200 ft (61 m).

it has not been possible, however, to attempt a correlation between the potential source rocks of the Querecual and San Antonio formations and the crude oil reservoired in the Quiriquire Formation.

The burial history diagram for the Quiriquire field area (Figure 14) supports the assumption that the oil in the Quiriquire field was generated in the Cretaceous Querecual and San Antonio formations. Stratigraphic and structural information clearly indicates that the oil must have migrated into the Quiriquire Formation toward the end of its time of deposition or shortly thereafter. This time corresponds to the time when the source rocks of the Querecual and San Antonio formations had reached the proper degree of maturity for the generation of oil.

The distribution of the API gravities of the oil accumulated in the Quiriquire Formation also favors a source of the oil in the underlying rocks and migration from underneath into the Quiriquire Formation. As shown in Figures 5 and 7, the lighter

oils are found at or just above the unconformity at the base of the Quiriquire Formation along the northern part of the field, particularly where the Cretaceous rocks are at the unconformity or a short distance below. Just on the basis of this evidence, it has been postulated that the oil must have migrated upward, most probably along faults or fractured zones, and that it permeated up through the porous and permeable sandstones and conglomerates of the Quiriquire Formation. After entering the Quiriquire Formation, part of the oil migrated updip and part was pushed downdip by the flow of meteoric water entering the formation at the surface. The oil exposed to the fresh meteoric water in the Quiriquire Formation was degraded by water-washing, oxidation, and perhaps by microbial alteration (biodegradation) so that it became progressively heavier away from the input areas. This resulted in the development of a roughly concentric distribution of gravity layers of the oil in the lens-shaped Quiriquire

324

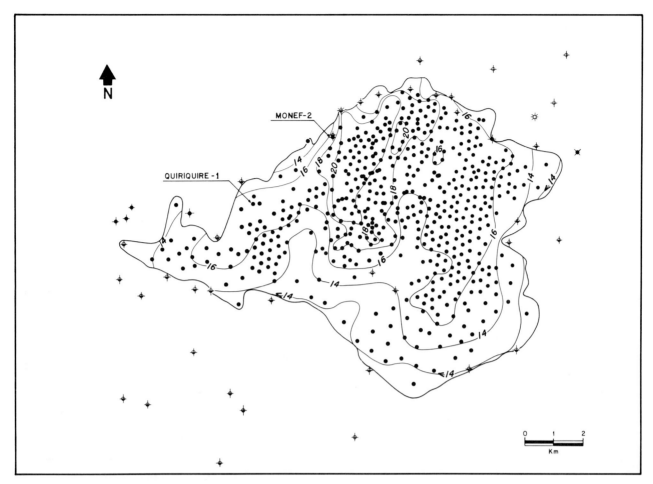

Figure 11. Distribution of API gravity of oil produced from Quiriquire reservoir. Contour interval, 2° API.

accumulation with an outer "tar mat" both updip and downdip from the areas of entry of the oil into the Quiriquire Formation.

The occurrence of formation waters with the highest salinity in close association with the lighter oils just above the pre-Quiriquire unconformity in the north-central part of the Quiriquire field supports this interpretation.

The Carapita Formation, directly underlying the Quiriquire Formation over most of the Quiriquire field, has also been considered as a possible source of the oil in the field, because it is composed of a very thick sequence of dark-colored marine shales (Regan, 1938; Borger, 1952; Wallis, 1953). However, the distribution of the oil gravities in the Quiriquire reservoir lends more support to a source in the older Cretaceous rocks.

Even though no geochemical studies of the section laterally equivalent to the Quiriquire Formation basinward have been yet undertaken, this section is not believed to have a high enough content of organic carbon or to have reached a high enough degree of maturation to have been able to generate the large volume of oil known to have accumulated in the Quiriquire Formation. In addition, an updip migration of oil from the center toward the northern margin of the basin would make it difficult to explain the distribution of the oil gravities in the Quiriquire reservoir as well as the concentration of the oil in the Quiriquire field and its much lesser abundance along other parts of the northern margin of the basin.

EXPLORATION AND PRODUCTION CONCEPTS

The Quiriquire field was discovered, like so many others during the early years of exploration for oil, by drilling downdip from a prolific belt of oil seeps.

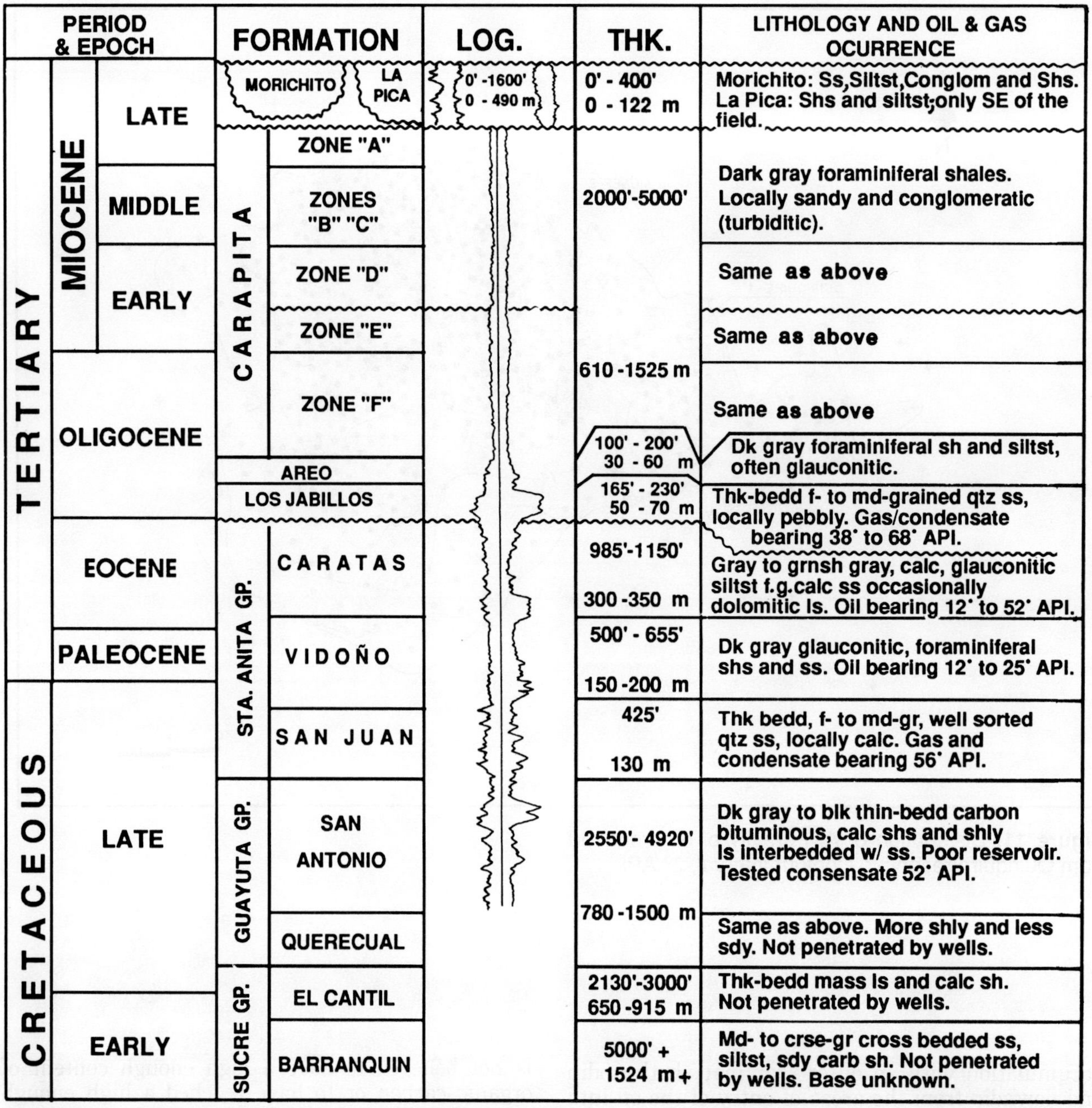

PERIOD & EPOCH			FORMATION		LOG.	THK.	LITHOLOGY AND OIL & GAS OCCURRENCE
TERTIARY	MIOCENE	LATE		MORICHITO / LA PICA	0'-1600' / 0-490 m	0'-400' / 0-122 m	Morichito: Ss,Siltst,Conglom and Shs. La Pica: Shs and siltst; only SE of the field.
				ZONE "A"		2000'-5000'	Dark gray foraminiferal shales. Locally sandy and conglomeratic (turbiditic).
		MIDDLE	C A R A P I T A	ZONES "B" "C"			
		EARLY		ZONE "D"			Same as above
				ZONE "E"			Same as above
				ZONE "F"		610-1525 m	Same as above
	OLIGOCENE			AREO		100'-200' / 30-60 m	Dk gray foraminiferal sh and siltst, often glauconitic.
				LOS JABILLOS		165'-230' / 50-70 m	Thk-bedd f- to md-grained qtz ss, locally pebbly. Gas/condensate bearing 38° to 68° API.
	EOCENE		STA. ANITA GP.	C A R A T A S		985'-1150' / 300-350 m	Gray to grnsh gray, calc, glauconitic siltst f.g.calc ss occasionally dolomitic ls. Oil bearing 12° to 52° API.
	PALEOCENE			V I D O Ñ O		500'-655' / 150-200 m	Dk gray glauconitic, foraminiferal shs and ss. Oil bearing 12° to 25° API.
CRETACEOUS	LATE			SAN JUAN		425' / 130 m	Thk bedd, f- to md-gr, well sorted qtz ss, locally calc. Gas and condensate bearing 56° API.
			GUAYUTA GP.	SAN ANTONIO		2550'-4920' / 780-1500 m	Dk gray to blk thin-bedd carbon bituminous, calc shs and shly ls interbedded w/ ss. Poor reservoir. Tested consensate 52° API.
				QUERECUAL			Same as above. More shly and less sdy. Not penetrated by wells.
	EARLY		SUCRE GP.	EL CANTIL		2130'-3000' / 650-915 m	Thk-bedd mass ls and calc sh. Not penetrated by wells.
				BARRANQUIN		5000'+ / 1524 m+	Md- to crse-gr cross bedded ss, siltst, sdy carb sh. Not penetrated by wells. Base unknown.

Figure 12. Composite log, pre-Quiriquire formations. Carapita Formation zones "A" to "F" are foraminiferal zones.

The Quiriquire field can, in fact, be viewed as a giant oil seep not unlike the equally large Guanoco "asphalt lake" 40 km (25 mi) northeast of Quiriquire and the renowned Brighton Pitch Lake of Trinidad (Figure 1). The only difference is that, while at Guanoco and at the Brighton Pitch Lake the oil was able to seep all the way to the surface, at Quiriquire, an extensive alluvial fan complex, the Quiriquire Formation, covered the seep area and soaked up and stored the oil like a sponge to form a giant oil accumulation. This fortuitous correspondence of a major source of oil (the oil seep area) and an excellent reservoir (the porous and permeable alluvial-fan sandstones and conglomerates of the Quiriquire Formation), combined with the propitious timing for the migration of the oil, is what makes the Quiriquire field a "one-of-a-kind" oil field. It also explains why, in spite of the persistent efforts that have been made over the

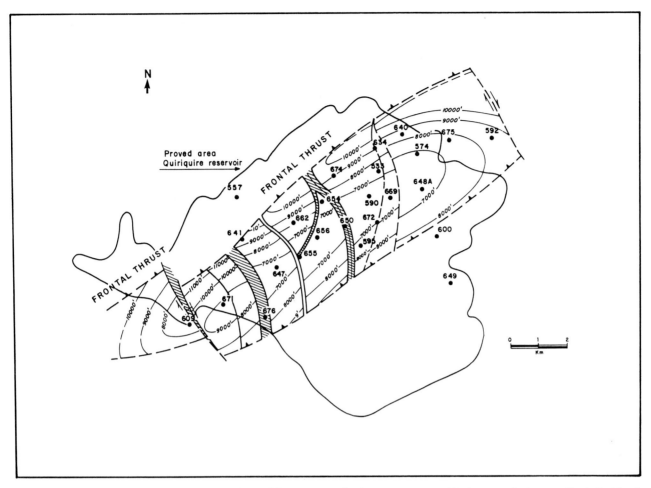

Figure 13. Structural map of the top of the Oligocene Los Jabillos Formation. This deeper gas and condensate reservoir, strongly folded by thrusting and cut by faults, contrasts with the gentle homoclinal Quiriquire Formation (Pliocene) above it. Contour interval, 1000 ft (305 m) (subsea values).

years to find "another Quiriquire" along the mountain front of northern Monagas, these efforts have failed.

What kind of exploration approach would be used today to explore for an oil accumulation similar to the Quiriquire field? It is doubtful that surface or geophysical methods would be able to direct attention to the Quiriquire area as the location of an important oil accumulation in the younger, gently tilted sediments of the Quiriquire Formation. Only the prolific oil seeps along the foothills of the Serrania del Interior indicated, as they would today, that the area was promising oil-hunting territory.

As mentioned earlier, seismic surveys in the Quiriquire area would have detected, sooner or later, the presence in the area of a large anticlinal structure in the older formations below the unstructured Quiriquire beds. Wildcats drilled to test this structure would have discovered, also sooner or later, the oil accumulation in the Quiriquire Formation. If this had been the case, the discovery would have been attributed to serendipity rather than to drilling downdip from oil seeps.

From the point of view of production, the Quiriquire field has presented, and still presents, the usual problems associated with the recovery of the greatest possible amount of the oil-in-place from a heavy-oil accumulation reservoired in discontinuous and lenticular sandstones and conglomerates. As already discussed, all attempts to increase the recovery of oil in the Quiriquire field have been unsuccessful. Under present economic conditions and with present technology, the expectations for better results with other methods are not bright. But in the more distant future, when oil becomes scarcer and demands a higher price, oil men may be attracted again to the several billion barrels of oil that will still remain in the Quiriquire reservoir.

ACKNOWLEDGMENTS

The authors are grateful to Lagoven, S.A., for furnishing much of the data used in this paper and for permission to publish it.

327

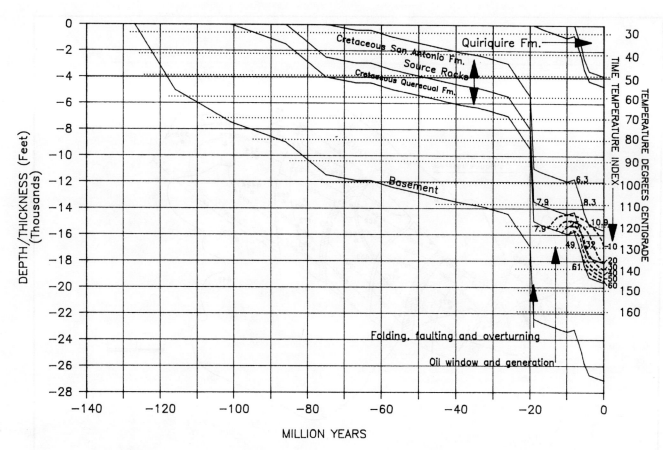

Figure 14. Burial history (diagenetic Lopatin) diagram of the Quiriquire field area.

REFERENCES CITED

Borger, H. D., 1952, Case history of Quiriquire field, Venezuela: AAPG Bulletin, v. 36, p. 2291-2330.

Carmalt, S. W., and B. St. John, 1986, Giant oil and gas fields *in* M. T. Halbouty, ed., Future petroleum provinces of the world: AAPG Memoir 40, p. 11-53.

Gonzalez de Juana, C., J. M. Iturralde de Arozena, and X. Picard Cadillat, 1980, Geologia de Venezuela y de sus cuencas petroliferas: Ediciones FONINVES, Caracas, 2 vol., 1031 p.

Hedberg, H. D., 1950, Geology of the Eastern Venezuela Basin (Anzoategui-Monagas-Sucre-eastern Guarico portion): GSA Bulletin, v. 61, p. 1173-1216.

Lamb, J. L., and J. De Sisto, 1963, The Morichito Formation of northern Monagas: Asociación Venezolana de Geologia, Mineria y Petróleo, Boletin Informativo, v. 6, p. 269-276.

Regan, J. H., 1938, Notes on the Quiriquire oil field, District of Piar, State of Monagas: Boletin de Geologia y Mineria (Venezuela), (English edition), Tomo II, Nos. 2, 3, 4, p. 187-201.

Renz, H. H., H. Alberding, K. F. Dallmus, J. M. Patterson, R. H. Robie, N. E. Weisbord, and J. MasVall, 1958, The Eastern Venezuela Basin *in* L G. Weeks, ed., Habitat of oil: AAPG Symposium, p. 551-600.

Renz, H. H., H. Alberding, K. F. Dallmus, J. M. Patterson, R. H, Robie, N. E. Weisbord, and J. MasVall, 1963, La Cuenca Oriental de Venezuela, *in* Aspectos de la industria petrolera en Venezuela: Primer Congreso Venezolano de Petróleo, p. 100-189.

Salvador, A., 1961, Nomenclature of the Las Piedras and related formations in eastern Venezuela: Asociación Venezolana de Geologia, Mineria y Petróleo, Boletin Informativo, v. 4, p. 295-327.

Wallis, W. E., 1953, Quiriquire field, *in* E. Mencher, H. J. Fichter, H. H. Renz, W. E. Wallis, J. M. Patterson, and R. H. Robie, Geology of Venezuela and its oil fields: AAPG Bulletin, v. 37, p. 744-746.

Young, G. A., A. Bellizzia, H. H. Renz, F. W. Johnson, R. H. Robie, and J. MasVall, 1956, Geologia de las cuencas sedimentarias de Venezuela y de sus campos petroliferos: Boletin de Geologia (Venezuela), Publicación Especial No. 2, 140 p.

Appendix 1. Field Description

Field name .... *Quiriquire field*

Ultimate recoverable reserves .... *812 million bbl of oil and 545 bcf of associated gas*

Field location:

    Country .... *Venezuela*

    State .... *Monagas*

    Basin/Province .... *Eastern Venezuela Basin*

Field discovery:

    Year first pay discovered .... *Pliocene Quiriquire Formation 1928*

Discovery well name and general location:

    First pay .... *Moneb-1, later renamed Quiriquire-1*

Discovery well operator *Standard Oil Company of Venezuela (later renamed Creole Petroleum Corporation)*

IP .... *438 BOPD of 16.3 API gravity on ½-in. choke*

All other zones with shows of oil and gas in the field:

Age	Formation	Type of Show
Oligocene	*Los Jabillos*	*Tested gas and 68° API condensate*
Eocene	*Caratas*	*Tested 34° API oil and gas*
Cretaceous–Eocene	*Vidoño*	*Tested gas and 52° API condensate*
Late Cretaceous	*San Antonio*	*Tested 47° API oil and gas*

None of these productive zones have been produced commercially

Geologic concept leading to discovery and method or methods used to delineate prospect

Reconnaissance surface mapping in the vicinity of prolific surface oil seeps. Location of discovery well chosen downdip from these seeps.

Structure:

    Province/basin type .... *Bally 221; Klemme IICa*

    Tectonic history

During most of the Cretaceous, eastern Venezuela was a northward-deepening marine shelf bordering to the north the Guayana shield. Uplifted lands began to emerge north of the present coast of Venezuela in Late Cretaceous, marking the initial stages of the formation of the Eastern Venezuela Basin. The uplift propagated progressively southward during the early Tertiary and culminated in the late Oligocene or early Miocene with the formation of the present Serrania del Interior (Interior Range) of northeastern Venezuela. Erosion of the uplifted landmass provided most of the materials deposited south of it along the northern flank of the Eastern Venezuela Basin. The upper Miocene–Pliocene Quiriquire Formation, the reservoir of the Quiriquire field, represents an alluvial fan deposited by a south-flowing river coming out of the Serrania del Interior.

    Regional structure

The Quiriquire field is located in the steep, structurally complex north flank of the Eastern Venezuela Basin. The pre-upper Miocene sediments along this north flank are thrusted and deformed into tight, locally overturned folds. The unconformable upper Miocene–Pliocene sequences form a gentle, south-dipping homocline.

    Local structure

The Quiriquire Formation, the main reservoir of the Quiriquire field, forms a homocline with a general N55–60° E strike and a dip of 5–6° SE. The older rocks below the Quiriquire Formation are folded into a sharp anticlinal structure, trending N60° E, with flank dips of as much as 20–30°. The syncline north of this anticline is overturned and complexly thrusted.

Trap:

Trap type(s)

The oil accumulation in the Quiriquire Formation is stratigraphic. The oil is trapped in all directions by a heavy-oil "tar" seal.

Basin stratigraphy (major stratigraphic intervals from surface to deepest penetration in field):

Chronostratigraphy	Formation	Subsea Depth in ft (m)
Pliocene	*Las Piedras/Quiriquire*	*400 (120)*
Upper Miocene	*La Pica/Morichito*	*2500–5200 (760–1580)*
Oligocene–Miocene	*Carapita*	*2500–5600 (760–1710)*
Oligocene	*Areo*	*6100–10,800 (1860–3290)*
	Los Jabillos	*6200–11,000 (1890–3350)*
Eocene	*Caratas*	*6350–11,250 (1940–3430)*
Upper Cretaceous–Eocene	*Vidoño*	*7350–12,400 (2240–3780)*
Upper Cretaceous	*San Juan*	*7850–13,050 (2390–3980)*
	Guayuta Group	*8250–13,450 (2510–4100)*

Reservoir characteristics:

Number of reservoirs *1*
Formations .... *Quiriquire*
Ages .... *Pliocene*
Depths to tops of reservoirs .... *1240 to 4350 ft (378–1325 m)*
Gross thickness (top to bottom of producing interval) .... *Up to 1600 ft (490 m)*
Net thickness—total thickness of producing zones
    Average .... *Very variable and difficult to estimate (about 230 ft; 70 m)*
    Maximum .... *820 ft (250 m) in central part of field*
Lithology

Irregularly interbedded sandy claystones and lenticular beds of poorly sorted silty sandstones, sandstones, and conglomerates; occasional lignite beds

Porosity type .... *Intergranular*
Average porosity *20%*
Average permeability .... *400–500 md*

Seals:

Upper
    Formation, fault, or other feature .... *Heavy-oil seal*
Lateral
    Formation, fault, or other feature .... *Heavy-oil seal*

Source (Probable):

Formation and age .... *Guayuta Group*
Lithology .... *Dark gray to black, bituminous shaly limestones and calcareous shales; sandstone and chert beds more common in upper part*
Average total organic carbon (TOC) *2.35–2.4%*
Maximum TOC *4.5–6.6%*
Kerogen type (I, II, or III) .... *I*
Vitrinite reflectance (maturation) .... $R_o = 0.59–0.97$
Time of hydrocarbon expulsion .... *Late Pliocene to Pleistocene*
Present depth to top of source .... *About 14,000 ft (4270 m)*
Thickness .... *3600–3900 ft (1100–1200 m)*
Potential yield .... *60 to 158 million bbl/km³*

Appendix 2. Production Data

Field name .... *Quiriquire field*

Field size:

    Proved acres .... *20,429 ac (8267 ha)*

    Number of wells all years *676*

    Current number of wells .... *282 capable of producing*

    Well spacing .... *300 m (985 ft)*

    Ultimate recoverable .... *812 million bbl of oil; 545 bcf of gas*

    Cumulative production .... *756.6 million bbl of oil; 519 bcf of gas*

    Annual production .... *Currently not under production*

    Present decline rate .... *NA*

        Initial decline rate .... *NA*

        Overall decline rate .... *2.8% per year during recent years*

    Annual water production .... *Almost 80% (18,000 bbl/day) during recent years*

    In place, total .... *About 4.0 billion bbl of oil*

    In place, per acre foot .... *NA*

    Primary recovery .... *812 million bbl of oil; 545 bcf of gas*

    Secondary recovery .... *Not feasible with current technology and oil prices*

    Enhanced recovery .... *Not considered*

    Cumulative water production .... *347 million bbl*

Drilling and casing practices:

    Amount of surface casing set .... *Variable*

    Casing program

    13⅜-in. surface casing; in early wells a second string of casing was set above producing interval and a preperforated liner run through the productive interval; in later wells the second string of casing was set and selectively perforated opposite oil-saturated sands

    Drilling mud .... *Lightweight mud (9.5–11.5 lb/gal or 1.14–1.37 kg/L)*

    Bit program .... *Drag bits in upper part, rock bits below about 2000 ft (610 m)*

    High pressure zones .... *None*

Completion practices:

    Interval(s) perforated .... *Multiple sands containing oil lighter than a predetermined gravity; variable from well to well*

    Well treatment .... *Oil pumped into formation when producing rates declined*

Formation evaluation:

    Logging suites .... *Older wells: electric, microlog, and dipmeter; more recent wells: induction, electric, formation density compensated, compensated neutron, sonic, and electromagnetic propagation tool*

    Testing practices .... *Common production tests*

    Mud logging techniques .... *Tested in some wells but found of limited usefulness*

Oil characteristics:

    Type .... *Naphthenic-asphaltic*

    API gravity .... *Heavier than water to 28°API (average 18°API)*

    Base .... *Naphthenic*

    Initial GOR .... *About 200 ft³/bbl, increasing with production*

    Sulfur, wt% *1.2*

Viscosity, SUS .... *230 cp at 100°F (37.7°C)*
Pour point .... *25°F (-4°C)*
Gas-oil distillate .... *40.8% 400-700°FVT*

Field characteristics:

Average elevation .... *75-200 ft (avg. 140 ft) (25-60 m, avg. 40 m)*
Initial pressure .... *1000 psi at 2600 ft (6.9 MPa at 792 m)*
Present pressure .... *Most sands depleted*
Pressure gradient .... *0.39 psi/ft (8.8 kPa/m)*
Temperature .... *90-120°F (32-49°C)*
Geothermal gradient .... *About 1°F/ft (1.8°C/m)*
Drive .... *Mostly solution gas, some local water drive*
Oil column height .... *Variable (about 2500 ft or 760 m from lowest to highest with average net thickness of about 400 ft or 120 m)*
Oil-water contact .... *No defined oil-water contact*
Connate water .... *Average $S_W = 51.4\%$*
Water salinity, TDS .... *7000 to 36,000 ppm*
Resistivity of water .... *NA*
Bulk volume water (%) .... *NA*

Transportation method and market for oil and gas:

Oil pumped 17 km (10 mi) through a 16-20-in. pipeline to Caripito, where part was refined and part was exported in tankers

QUIRIQUIRE

Burbank Field—U.S.A.
Anadarko Basin, Oklahoma

CHRISTOPHER L. JOHNSON
MASERA Corporation
Tulsa, Oklahoma

FIELD CLASSIFICATION

BASIN: Anadarko

BASIN TYPE: Foredeep

RESERVOIR ROCK TYPE: Sandstone

RESERVOIR ENVIRONMENT OF DEPOSITION: Fluvial/Deltaic

RESERVOIR AGE: Pennsylvanian

PETROLEUM TYPE: Oil

TRAP TYPE: Pinch-out

TRAP DESCRIPTION: Updip pinch-out of multistoried sands deposited in channels eroded into underlying marine shales

INTRODUCTION

Burbank field is located in northeastern Oklahoma (Figure 1), 60 mi (96 km) northwest of Tulsa in Osage and Kay Counties, with the majority of production from Osage County (Figure 2). Estimated ultimate recoverable reserves are expected to be approximately 600 million barrels of oil (MMBO) from approximately 50,000 ac (20,235 ha). The Burbank field consists of Burbank (or Burbank North), South Burbank, Stanley Stringer, East Little Chief, and West Little Chief pools. The last was found 34 years after the main part of the field, in 1954.

The field is located on the northeastern Oklahoma platform, west of the Ozark uplift and east of the Nemaha ridge at depths of 2800 to 3200 ft (850–975 m) (Figure 3).

Figure 1. Map of the United States showing the general location of the Burbank field in northeastern Oklahoma. 1, Appalachian Mountains; 2, Ouachita-Marathon trend; 3, Rocky Mountains.

HISTORY

As early as October 1897, the first producing oil wells in the Osage Nation, now Osage County, Oklahoma, were completed in the Middle Pennsylvanian Bartlesville sandstone. This zone continued as the main producing unit in Osage County through 1920. The western edge of the Bartlesville sandstone extends through the center of Osage County in a northeast to southwest direction. Because of this delineation, exploration was discouraged in western Osage County where the Burbank field is located.

The U.S. Geological Survey in 1915 began a study of the surface geology of western Osage County with the express purpose of assisting in the discovery of oil and gas; the U.S. government had begun management of the mineral leases in Osage County. This project eventually resulted in the mapping of the entire county (White et al., 1922). Foraker Quadrangle was the first area mapped in northwestern Osage County (Heald, 1916). Based on surface geology, 15 anticlines were mapped at the level of the Permian Foraker Limestone, a limestone that crops out along the east edge of the quadrangle. Heald (1916) predicted that oil would be found in the quadrangle because oil had been discovered previously in counties on three sides of Osage County, as well as in the east half of the county, and because of the presence of numerous potential reservoir sands in test wells nearby.

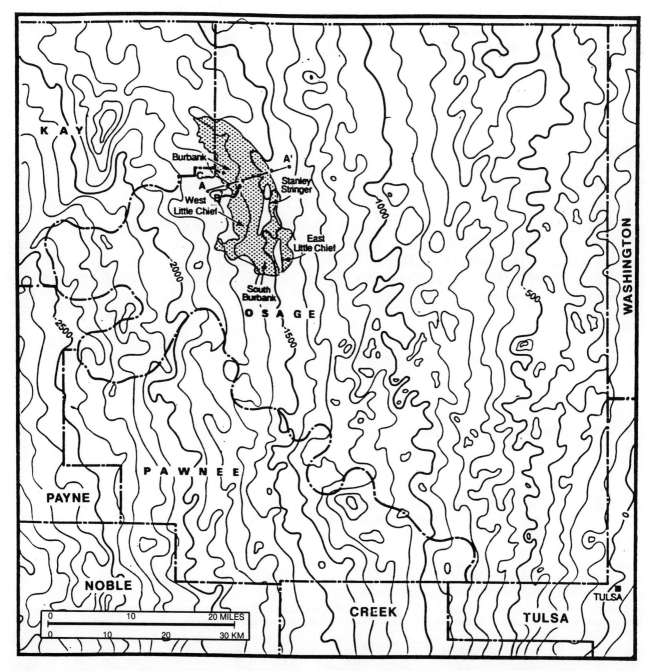

Figure 2. Index map of Burbank field: structural horizon-Oswego Limestone, showing the various pools and generalized structure. Contour interval, 100 ft (30 m). A-A', line of cross section, shown by Figure 8. B, location of type log (Figure 4). C, location of discovery well on Hay Creek anticline. Stippled pattern shows producing area. (A wider geographic area is shown by Figure 3 and all of the state of Oklahoma except the western "panhandle" is shown by Figure 5.)

By the end of 1919, several dry holes had been drilled in northwestern Osage County. In the spring of 1920, the Marland Oil Company drilled the No. 1 Tribal in the southeast/northeast Sec. 36, T27N, R5E on the small Hay Creek anticline (C in Figure 2; shown on larger scale maps by Figures 6, 7, and 9). This well proved to be the discovery well for the Burbank field. Initial potential of the well was 760 BOPD from the Burbank sandstone at 2950 ft (900

m). In September of that year Carter Oil Company drilled two wells on another small anticline 2 mi (3 km) to the southeast, in Sec. 9, T26N, R6E. Development drilling proceeded rapidly, and by 1924, 75% of the wells in the main part of the field had been drilled.

The initial potential of wells in the Burbank sandstone varied from 10 to 12,000 BOPD. Most of the wells flowed oil with associated gas at an original

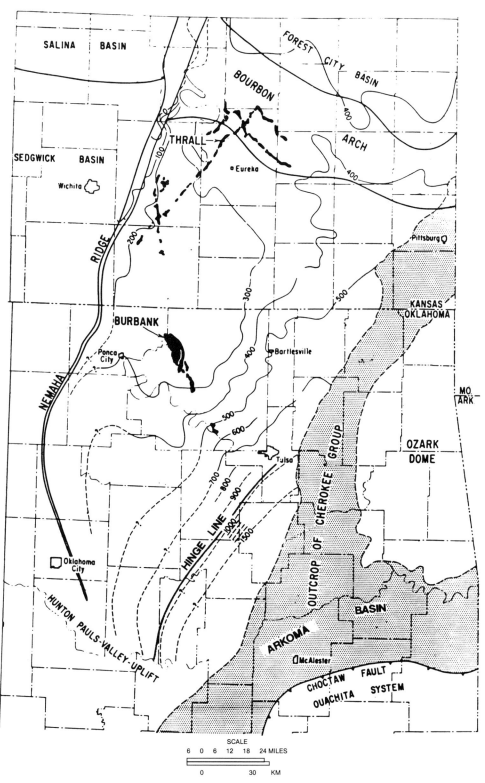

Figure 3. Generalized map of the Cherokee Group in northeastern Oklahoma and southeastern Kansas, showing outcrop area, Cherokee Group thickness, and major contemporaneous tectonic features (after Baker, 1962, and Weirich, 1953). The northeast Oklahoma platform is that area northwest of the hinge line.

335

pressure of 800 psi (55 bar). Little or no water was produced in the main part of the field until waterflooding began. The oil-water contact varied within the field owing to various horizontal permeability barriers and small variations in capillary pressure caused by facies changes.

The Stanley Stringer (Figure 2), which was not included as part of the main field, was discovered in 1926 by Kewanee Oil and Gas Company with a well in the northwest Sec. 34, T27N, R6E. Subsequent drilling proved this pool to be connected to the main field.

Peak production came in July 1923, when the average daily production was 122,000 BO from 1020 producing wells. Produced gas injection began in 1926 by various operators in the field. Approximately 220,000,000 BO had been produced under primary and gas injection processes by 1951 when what was then the world's largest waterflood project began operation. From 40,000 to 50,000 barrels of water from the nearby Arkansas River were pumped to the field for injection (Riggs, 1954). Approximately 250 to 300 MMBO have been produced by this secondary recovery phase. Ninety percent of the current production now comes from various units and operators who are still waterflooding and involved in tertiary flooding (EOR).

DISCOVERY METHOD

The initial discovery wells drilled in the Burbank field were based on surface geology, as mapped on the U.S.G.S. Foraker Quadrangle map. The anticlines that were drilled proved to be unimportant in localizing the accumulation because of the larger stratigraphic field underlying these smaller anticlines. Stratigraphic traps, such as this field, generally have been difficult to recognize and are generally found early in a productive basin by serendipity.

The Burbank field is located almost entirely on the Osage Indian Nation, therefore placing the minerals under federal administration. Oil leases on quarter-section (160 ac; 65 ha) tracts were awarded to highest bidders in regular public auctions. "The color and drama of these sales rivaled and surpassed fictitious situations found in novels or stories, as some of these tracts sold for nearly $2 million and on the succeeding day were the site of frantic activity as the preparation for the drilling of 16 wells simultaneously on the tract got under way. The Osage Indians receive a royalty payment of 1/6; as a result, the boom days in the Burbank field established the stereotype of the oil-rich Indian wrapped in a blanket with a Cadillac parked outside his shack or tepee" (Largent, 1968; all references to Largent are taken from the text and figures of his presentation).

STRUCTURE

The Burbank field is located on the northeastern Oklahoma platform (Figure 3), which has undergone a long period of regional stability since Cambrian–Ordovician time. The platform is marked by several tectonic events that have caused the following major unconformities: (1) the Middle Devonian emergence contributing to the Ozark uplift and the incipient Nemaha ridge in Oklahoma; (2) the Wichita and Ouachita orogenies occurring in Early to Middle Pennsylvanian time, the latter contributing to the formation of the Arkoma basin to the south of the field and the Nemaha ridge to the west; and (3) the Arbuckle orogeny occurring in Late Pennsylvanian (Adler et al., 1988). One of the most important structural features that contributed to the sand deposition which subsequently formed the Burbank field was the continental rift and the Nemaha ridge, which together trend from Iowa through Kansas. These features probably controlled the river systems that fed the Desmoinesian deltaic systems of the Mid-Continent.

Minor regional uplift and tilting continued until the present time. Local structure is a gently undulating homocline with dip to the west at about 35 ft/mi (6.5 m/km) (Figure 2). Several small anticlines with 20 to 40 ft (6 to 12 m) of closure are present within the productive area.

A vertical fracture system, which is probably part of a regional pattern, consists of two sets, trending N70°E and N30°W, respectively (Hagen, 1972). This fracture pattern, which is present on the surface, was not known to affect the producing interval until extensive waterflooding began in the 1950s.

STRATIGRAPHY

The stratigraphy in northeastern Oklahoma generally may be divided into two intervals: (1) pre-Pennsylvanian, consisting mostly of carbonates, and (2) Pennsylvanian–Permian, predominantly clastics and thin limestones deposited in cyclic sequences (Figure 4). The oldest Pennsylvanian strata are Desmoinesian (Middle Pennsylvanian). The pre-Pennsylvanian section has undergone extensive erosion. The Pennsylvanian onlaps older rocks from southeast to northwest with younger rocks resting on Mississippian and older rocks. Morrow and Atoka rocks were probably not deposited as far north as Osage County.

"Burbank sandstone" is the local informal name for the Red Fork sandstone. The Red Fork sandstone is part of the Desmoinesian Cherokee Group, a sequence of sandstones, shales, and thin limestones. Cherokee sandstones include, in ascending order, the Bartlesville, Red Fork, Skinner, and Prue; they are prolific producers in northeastern and central Oklahoma. These sandstones were deposited as fluvial-deltaic systems.

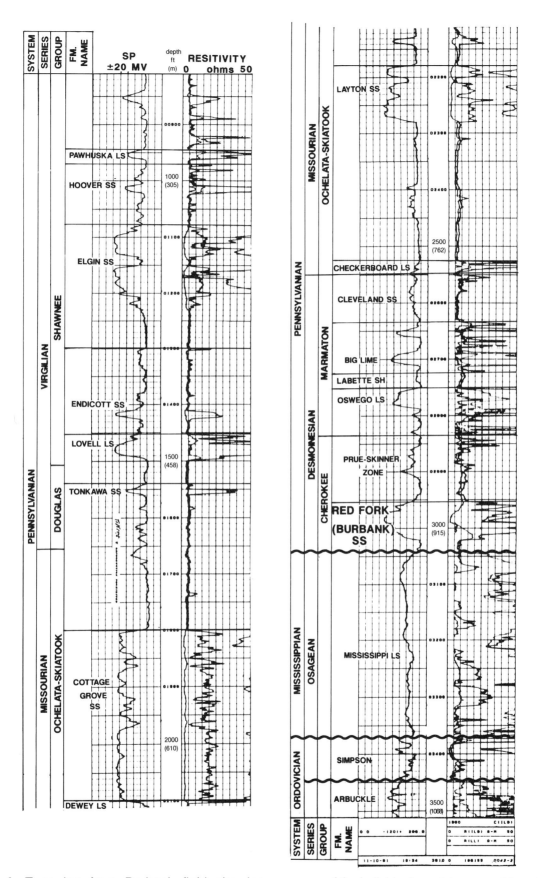

Figure 4. Type log from Burbank field showing relationship of Burbank (Red Fork) sandstone to zones above and below. Location B shown on Figure 2. The names of the individual sandstones and limestones are mostly informal stratigraphic nomenclature.

The depositional environment of the Burbank sandstone was originally interpreted to be either a fluvial or a marine bar system, with the early interpretation favoring marine bars (Sands, 1924, 1927, 1929; Bass et al., 1937, 1942). Further study, along with development drilling and coring, indicated that the area is fluvial, with probable deltaic to estuarine influences within the upper units of the sand (Hudson, 1970; Trantham et al., 1980). Evidence of fluvial origin includes sharp basal and lateral contacts, cross-bedding, ripple bedding (with climbing ripples), and fining-upward textural sequence. An individual channelized unit is estimated to be 1000 ft (300 m) wide, and multiple bodies indicate a multistoried section with lateral overlapping. Evidence for estuarine origin consists of black shale interlaminated with burrowed and contorted fine-grained sand (Trantham et al., 1980). Figure 5 shows the Red Fork deltaic complex in Oklahoma and the approximate location of the Burbank field.

TRAP TYPE

Burbank field is a stratigraphic trap. The productive portion of the field is about 24 mi (39 km) long and 2 to 4.5 mi (3 to 7 km) wide (Figures 6 and 7). The reservoir is bounded by overlying, underlying, and lateral shales that encase the Burbank (Red Fork) sandstone (Figure 8). The sandstone is multistoried, and individual sandstone units can be isolated reservoirs with internal oil-water contacts in some areas. The field, as a whole, has approximately 300 ft (92 m) of relief on the oil-water contact. This is illustrated in Figure 7, showing how the oil-water contact apparently does not follow the structural contours because of the numerous sand lenses.

The trap resulted from an abrupt updip change in depositional facies (Figure 6) that involved channel sandstones cutting down into marine shales. The sand was deposited in arcuate trends that are convex to the east (updip) (Figure 6), forming the trap. This

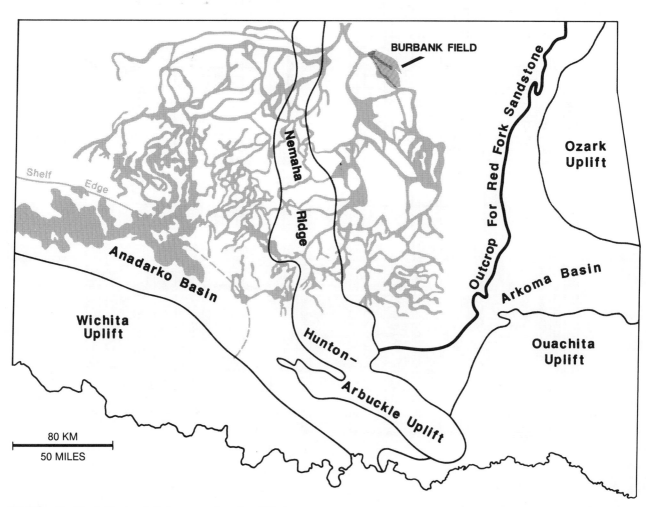

Figure 5. Red Fork deltaic complex in Oklahoma showing position of Burbank field (used by permission of MASERA Corp.).

338

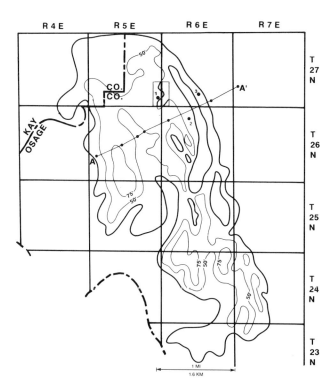

Figure 6. Isopach map of net Burbank sand showing production outlines as of 1968 (after Largent, 1968). Cross section A–A′ shown by Figure 8. Shaded area represents area of Figure 10. 1 is discovery well, 2 is Carter Oil Company's wells, and 3 is Kewanee Oil and Gas Company's Stanley Stringer well. Contour interval, 25 ft (7.6 m).

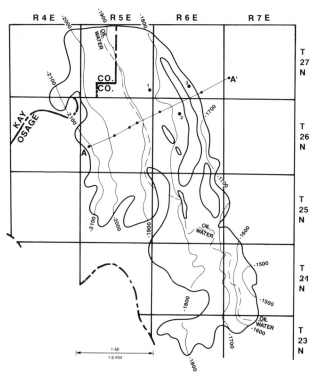

Figure 7. Structure contour map of the top of the Burbank sandstone. Approximate line of oil-water contact is indicated (after Largent, 1968). Numbers 1, 2, and 3 same as Figure 6. Contour interval, 25 ft (7.6 m).

geometry was the primary reason for the early marine bar interpretation (Bass et al., 1942). These arcuate sand trends are now interpreted as the axis of distributary channels. The sandstone extends west of the field limit—notice the oil-water contact in Figure 7—and gradually pinches out to the west.

Reservoir

The Cherokee Burbank sandstone is the main reservoir of the field, having produced more than 90% of the oil and minor gas from depths of 2800 ft (850 m) (in the east) to 3200 ft (980 m) (in the west). Minor oil and gas have been produced from younger Pennsylvanian sandstones, Mississippian "Chat," and Ordovician sandstones.

The Burbank is a fining-upward sequence of very fine to medium-grained sublitharenite. Quartz dominates, with metamorphic rock fragments, feldspar, chert, and mica. Typically, secondary porosity is more common than primary porosity (Hufford and Tieh, 1984). Porosity ranges from 10% to 33% and averages 17%. The overall highest porosities are present in the northeastern portion of the field. Chamosite (iron-rich chlorite) covers about 70% of quartz grains, which constitute 50% of the

sandstone, and is reportedly responsible for the oil-wet character of the reservoir (Trantham and Clampitt, 1977).

Initial production maps show a north-by-northwest trend and an east-west trend (Figure 9). These are considered to reflect depositional trends of distributary channels. The role of fracturing was not considered in the early development of the Burbank field. Initial production from the waterflood was promising, but water that had apparently flowed through open joints appeared in wells both east and west of the pilot area (Hagen, 1972). Further investigation revealed that an extensive fracture pattern was present throughout most of the field. The waterflood was switched to a line drive to offset the fracture effects and has been extremely successful (Hagen, 1972). Figure 10 shows a portion of the northern part of the field where the north-by-northwest (N25°W) fracture trend is diminished and the dominant east-by-northeast (N70°E) trend is diminished or absent (Hagen, 1972). Within this area, the waterflood injection pattern was modified from the unsuccessful line drive to one that successfully took advantage of both the primary sand trend (Figure 9) and the fractures.

Permeability ranges from 1 md to 2 darcys and averages 50 to 150 md (Largent, 1968) within the

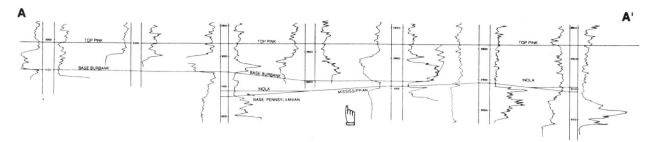

Figure 8. West to east cross section A–A′ in the Burbank field showing relationship of fluvial channel sand to enclosing shale units. The location of the cross section is shown on Figures 2, 6, and 7. Characteristic log responses illustrate correlations only. The length of the cross section is about 12 mi (19 km). The pointer indicates the downdip, western limit of the oil reservoir at the oil-water contact.

Burbank sandstone. However, permeability and therefore production are dramatically increased directionally by the dominant east-by-northeast fracture set (Figure 10). Reservoir engineering studies have shown that fractures open and close in response to injection pressure (Trantham et al., 1980). These studies involved tracer tests between water injectors and the producing wells and showed that water channeling between the wells was highly sensitive to the injector pressure.

Oil of the Burbank field had an original gas-oil ratio of 375 ft³/bbl (10.6 m³/bbl) and an API gravity of 38–42° (Largent, 1968). The oil is paraffin-based, low (0.21%) sulfur crude, and the reservoir exhibits a 150 ft (49 m) oil column. Minor gas production has occurred along the eastern updip margin, but it has not been significant in comparison to the oil production. Early wells flowed considerable oil by gas expansion drive. However, prudent injection of produced gas from the early 1930s to the late 1940s was a significant element in maintaining the reservoir pressure above the bubble point. Water-flooding of the field began in the late 1940s and at the present time the pressure within the waterflood units is above the original reservoir pressure. The oil is undersaturated, and there is probably no free gas saturation in the reservoir (Trantham et al., 1980). Initially, average reservoir pressure was approximately 800 psi (55 bar) and water saturation was 28–35%. Primary recovery was poor owing to oil-wet pores caused by chamosite-coated grains.

Several oil-water contacts have been identified ranging in depth from –1600 ft (480 m) to –1900 ft (580 m). These indicate isolated reservoirs; in fact, at least three main sand reservoirs are identified field-wide. The lower sandstone is always water wet (Largent, 1968). Individual shales that isolate sand lenses and the varying capillary-pressure differences within the sand contribute to the different oil-water contacts within the reservoir.

Presently, selected portions of the field are under tertiary flooding, but economic conditions will determine the extent of enhanced (polymer/surfactant) flooding that will take place field-wide.

SOURCE

Baker (1962) presented a classic study on the source rocks for the Cherokee Group reservoirs, with one of the cores examined being from the Burbank field. His results indicated that the primary, if not only, source for the Burbank field is the encasing marine shales. Local sourcing was indicated by typing of the oils to the organic content of the shales. Total organic content of the surrounding nonreservoir rocks averaged 2.1%, with values as high as 14%. This study did not indicate kerogen type, potential yield, or timing of migration.

EXPLORATION AND DEVELOPMENT CONCEPTS

Burbank field is part of the extensive Red Fork fluvial/deltaic system. Many fields produce from the "Cherokee" fluvial sandstones in Kansas and Oklahoma. The Red Fork in the Burbank area, occurring as channelized sand bodies, is a heterogeneous and anisotropic reservoir.

In general, a large amount of control within an area is needed for predicting locations of stratigraphic traps of this type. However, the recent development of sequence stratigraphy concepts could predict general areas where traps of this type could form. This would involve a regional understanding of sequence and parasequence concepts that would provide a framework for analyzing reservoir, source, and seal distribution on a regional scale (Van Wagoner et al., 1990).

Two factors influenced the efficient development of the Burbank field: (1) the Osage Indian Nation managed their minerals well by requiring a 160 ac tract to be evenly drilled up before the adjacent tracts could be leased, and (2) early in the field's development, operators realized the benefit of maintaining reservoir pressure. In the early 1950s when the field was waterflooded, it was one of the largest water-

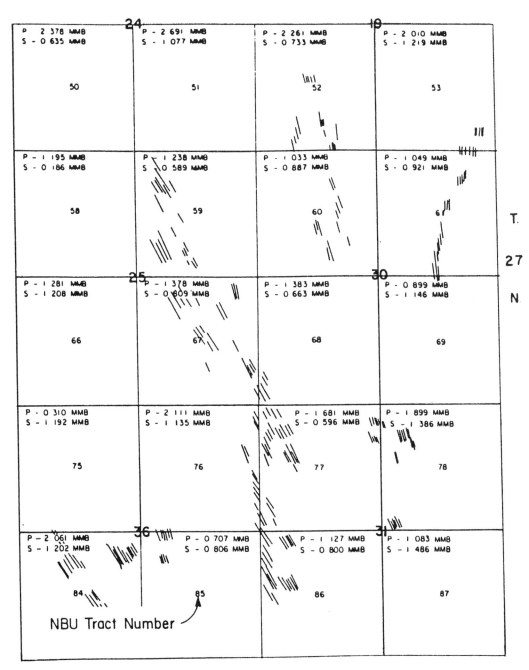

Figure 10. Plat of certain North Burbank unit tracts (NBU Tract Number), shaded on Figure 6, showing the relationship of north- to northwest-trending joints to those tracts having very poor secondary recovery. Symbol (S) is for secondary recovery, (P) is for primary recovery in millions of barrels of oil. Northeast-trending joints have been omitted. (After Hagen, 1972.) Compare joint orientation to isopotential map, Figure 9.

floods in the world (Barnes, 1952). The West Little Chief extension was not developed until 1954 owing to reservoir heterogeneities that made it difficult to predict viable extensions (Clinton, 1957). Extension development benefited from new technology, notably hydraulic fracturing techniques using propants.

The development history of the Burbank field was erratic, driven by both economic changes and technological advances. Other stratigraphic trap fields thought to be completely developed also should be examined to see if economic or technological factors such as horizontal drilling or cross-well

341

geophysical surveys (Greaves et al., 1991) could expand them also.

ACKNOWLEDGMENTS

Sincere appreciation is given to Dr. John Shelton for recommending me for this study and to Bailey Rascoe, Jr., for his invaluable insights into the details of the field and his excellent review. Also appreciation is given to Dr. Glenn Cole for his editing of all the small details. All errors or oversights, however, are the sole responsibility of the author.

REFERENCES CITED

Adler, F. J., W. M. Caplan, M. P. Carlson, E. D. Goebel, H. T. Henslee, I. C. Hicks, T. G. Larson, M. H. McCracken, M. C. Parker, B. Rascoe, Jr., M. W. Schramm, and J. S. Wells, 1971, Future petroleum provinces of the Mid-Continent, *in* Future petroleum provinces of the United States—their geology and potential: AAPG Memoir 15, v. 2, p. 985-1120.

Baker, D. R., 1962, Organic geochemistry of Cherokee Group in southeastern Kansas and northeastern Oklahoma: AAPG Bulletin, v. 46, p. 1621-1642.

Barnes, K. B., 1952, Community water pipe serves four producing areas: Oil and Gas Journal, v. 51, n. 23, p. 189-191.

Bass, N. W., C. Leatherock, W. R. Dillard, and L. R. Kennedy, 1937, Origin and distribution of Bartlesville and Burbank Shoestring Oil Sands in parts of Oklahoma and Kansas: AAPG Bulletin, v. 21, p. 30-66.

Bass, N. W., H. B. Goodrich, and W. R. Dillard, 1942, Subsurface geology and oil and gas resources of Osage County, Oklahoma: pt. 10. Burbank and South Burbank Oil Fields, Townships 26 and 27 North, Range 5 East and Townships 25 to 27 North, Range 6 East: U.S. Geological Survey Bulletin 900-J, p. 321-342.

Clinton, R. P., 1957, The geology of the Osage country: Shale Shaker, v. 8, n. Z., p. 8-16.

Greaves, R. J., W. B. Beydoun, and B. R. Spies, 1991, New dimensions in geophysics for reservoir monitoring: SPE Formation Evaluation, June, v. 6, n. 2.

Hagen, K. B., 1972, Mapping of surface joints on air photos can help understand waterflood performance problems North Burbank Unit: Master's Thesis, University of Tulsa, Tulsa, Oklahoma.

Heald, K. C. 1916, The oil and gas geology of the Foraker quadrangle, Osage County, Oklahoma, *in* Contributions to economic geology: U.S. Geological Survey Bulletin, 641, p. 17-47.

Hudson, A. S., 1970, Depositional environment of the Red Fork and equivalent sandstones east of the Nemaha Ridge, Kansas and Oklahoma: Shale Shaker Digest, Oklahoma City Geological Society v. 21, p. 128-143.

Hufford, W. R., and T. T. Tieh, 1984, Diagenesis of Burbank Sandstone, North Burbank Field, Osage County, Oklahoma (abs.): AAPG Bulletin, v. 68, p. 489.

Largent, B. C., 1968, Burbank field, Oklahoma—a giant grows (abs.): AAPG Bulletin, v. 52, p. 537-538.

Riggs, C. H., 1954, Burbank floods promise 180 million barrels of oil: Oil and Gas Journal, November 1, 1954, p. 88-92.

Sands, J. M., 1924, Burbank field, Osage County, Oklahoma: AAPG Bulletin, v. 8, p. 584-592.

Sands, J. M., 1927, Burbank field, Osage County, Oklahoma: AAPG Bulletin, v. 11, p. 1045-1054.

Sands, J. M., 1929, Burbank field, Osage County, Oklahoma, *in* Structure of typical American oil fields, a symposium: AAPG v. 1, p. 220-229.

Trantham, J. C., and R. L. Clampitt, 1977, Determination of oil saturation after waterflooding in an oil-wet reservoir—the North Burbank Unit, Tract 97 Project: Journal of Petroleum Technology, v. 29, p. 491-500.

Trantham, J. C., C. B. Threlkeld, and H. L. Patterson, Jr., 1980, Reservoir description for a surfactant/polymer pilot in a fractured, oil-wet reservoir—North Burbank Unit Tract 97: Journal of Petroleum Technology, v. 32, p. 1647-1656.

Van Wagoner, J. C., R. M. Mitchum, K. M. Campion, and V. D. Rahmamian, 1990, Siliciclastic sequence stratigraphy in well logs, cores, and outcrops: concepts for high-resolution correlation of time and facies: AAPG Methods in Exploration Series, No. 7.

Weirich, T. E., 1953, Shelf principal of oil origin, migration and accumulation: AAPG Bulletin, v. 37, p. 2027-2045.

White, D., et al., 1922, Structure and oil and gas resources of the Osage Reservation, Oklahoma: U.S. Geological Survey Bulletin 686, p. 1-427.

SUGGESTED READING

Hudson, A. S., 1970, Depositional environment of the Red Fork and equivalent sandstones east of the Nemaha Ridge, Kansas and Oklahoma: Shale Shaker Digest, Oklahoma City Geological Society, v. 21, p. 1288-143. Summary of several Cherokee fields and depositional environments.

Szpakiewicz, M. J., K. McGee, and B. Sharma, 1986, Geological problems related to characterization of clastic reservoirs for enhanced oil recovery: Society of Petroleum Engineers Paper 14888, 20 p. Discusses fracture problems discovered when waterflooding.

Trantham, J. C., C. B. Threlkeld, and H. L. Patterson, Jr., 1980, Reservoir description for a surfactant/polymer pilot in a fractured, oil-wet reservoir—North Burbank Unit Tract 97: Journal of Petroleum Technology, v. 32, p. 1647-1656. Good general reservoir description.

Appendix 1. Field Description

Field name .... *Burbank field, including South Burbank, Stanley Stringer,*
West Little Chief and East Little Chief pools

Ultimate recoverable reserves .... *Approx. 600+ million bbl of oil*

Field location:

    Country .... *U.S.A.*

    State .... *Oklahoma*

    Basin/Province .... *Anadarko*

Field discovery:

    Year first pay discovered .... *Desmoinesian Burbank (Red Fork) sandstone 1920*

Discovery well name and general location:

    First pay .... *No. 1 Tribal SE/4 NE/4 Sec. 36 T27N, R5E*

Discovery well operator .... *Marland Oil Co. (now Conoco)*

IP:

    First pay .... *760 BOPD at 2950 ft (900 m)*

All other zones with shows of oil and gas in the field:

Age	Formation	Type of Show
Ordovician	*Simpson*	*Minor oil and gas on structure*
Mississippian	*Detrital*	*Minor stratigraphic*
Upper Pennsylvanian	*Okesa, Torpedo, and*	
	Clem Creek sandstones	*Minor oil and gas on structure*
	Revard and Bigheart sandstones	*Minor gas, 2 wells*

Geologic concept leading to discovery and method or methods used to delineate prospect

Surface geology from 1916 U.S.G.S. Survey Bulletin 641. Small surface structure was assumed to reflect subsurface structure. However, Burbank sand was and could not be mapped because of lack of sufficient subsurface data.

Structure:

    Province/basin type .... *Klemme IIA craton margin, composite (for Anadarko);*
Bally 221 foredeep with ramp (for Anadarko)

    Tectonic history

Stable area since Cambrian–Ordovician time. The Nemaha ridge to the west was active during post-Mississippian–pre-Desmoinesian, when extensive erosion occurred.

    Regional structure

Gently undulating homocline with dip to the west at about 35 ft/mi. Several small anticlines are present within the production area. Vertical fracture system, probably part of a regmatic regional pattern, consists of two sets (N70°E amd N30°W, respectively).

Trap:

    Trap type(s)

Stratigraphic: updip abrupt facies change related to fluvial channels downcutting into marine shales

    Basin stratigraphy (major stratigraphic intervals from surface to deepest penetration in field):

Chronostratigraphy	Formation	Depth to Top in ft (m)
Pennsylvanian		*0–2900 (0–885)*
	Burbank (Red Fork)	*2900 (885)*
Mississippian	*"Mississippian"*	*3000 (915)*

343

Ordovician	Simpson	3300 (1005)
Cambrian–Ordovician	Arbuckle	3800 (1160)
Precambrian	Granite	4300 (1310)

Reservoir characteristics:

Number of reservoirs .... *1 major with 5 minor pays contributing less than 10% of field total*

Formations .... *Locally known as the Burbank sandstone, regionally referred to as the Red Fork sandstone*

Ages .... *Pennsylvanian, Desmoinesian*

Depths to tops of reservoirs .... *2900 ft (885 m)*

Gross thickness (top to bottom of producing interval) .... *2850–2950 ft (870–900 m)*

Net thickness—total thickness of producing zones

    Average .... *50 ft (15 m)*

    Maximum .... *100 ft (30.5 m)*

Lithology .... *Fining-upward, very fine to medium-grained sandstone with some carbonate silica and clay cement*

Porosity type .... *Intergranular and moldic due to dissolution of framework grains*

Average porosity *17%*

Average permeability .... *Variable: 0–420 md*

Seals:

    Upper

        Formation, fault, or other feature .... *Hard siltstone at top grading into Cherokee shale*

        Lithology .... *Shale*

    Lateral

        Formation, fault, or other feature .... *Basal Pennsylvanian Cherokee shale*

        Lithology .... *Shale*

Source:

Formation and age .... *Pennsylvanian Cherokee shales or Devonian–Mississippian, Woodford Shale*

Lithology .... *Shale*

Average total organic carbon (TOC) .... *Avg. 2.1%*

Maximum TOC *14%*

Kerogen type (I, II, or III) .... *Probably I*

Vitrinite reflectance (maturation) .... *NA*

Time of hydrocarbon expulsion ... *Thought to be middle Permian but could have been post-Cretaceous*

Present depth to top of source .... *2800–2900 ft (850–880 m)*

Thickness .... *150–200 ft (45–60 m)*

Potential yield .... *NA*

Appendix 2. Production Data

Field name .... *Burbank field, including South Burbank, Stanley Stringer, West Little Chief and East Little Chief pools*

Field size:

    Proved acres .... *36,905 (14,946 ha)*

    Number of wells all years *1289*

    Current number of wells *1073*

    Well spacing .... *10 ac*

    Ultimate recoverable .... *600 million bbl*

    Cumulative production (June 1988) .... *537 million bbl*

    Annual production .... *1.120 million bbl*

Present decline rate *10–15%*
    Initial decline rate *20–30%*
    Overall decline rate *25%*
Annual water production .... *Currently most of field is under tertiary recovery*
In place, total reserves .... *1200 million bbl*
In place, per acre foot .... *587 bbl*
Primary recovery .... *220 million bbl*
Secondary recovery .... *280 million bbl*
Enhanced recovery .... *40+ million bbl*
Cumulative water production .... *5270 million bbl*

Drilling and casing practices:

Amount of surface casing set .... *Almost all wells were drilled before 1930*
Casing program

With cable tool holes multiple strings were set to depth immediately above the Burbank sand, with open-hole completion of the sandstone

Drilling mud .... *NA*
Bit program .... *NA*
High pressure zones .... *NA*

Completion practices:

Interval(s) perforated .... *Open-hole completion*
Well treatment .... *Fracturing and acidizing was initiated in later and EOR infill wells*

Formation evaluation:

Logging suites .... *Drillers logs originally*
Testing practices .... *NA*
Mud logging techniques .... *NA*

Oil characteristics:

API gravity .... *38–40°*
Base .... *Paraffin*
Initial GOR .... *380 MCFG/bbl*
Sulfur, wt% *0.21*
Viscosity, SUS .... *48 sec at 100°F*
Pour point .... *NA*
Gas-oil distillate .... *NA*

Field characteristics:

Average elevation .... *2700–3000 ft (825–915 m)*
Initial pressure .... *1200 psi (8.268 MPa)*
Present pressure .... *NA*
Present gradient .... *NA*
Temperature .... *105°F (40.5°C)*
Geothermal gradient .... *11°F/1000 ft (2°C/100 m)*
Drive .... *Gas expansion*
Oil column thickness .... *150 ft (46 m)*
Oil-water contact .... *1650 to 1700 ft (505–520 m) (not active)*
Connate water *30–35%*
Water salinity, TDS .... *200,179 mg/L*
Resistivity of water .... *1–3 ohm*
Bulk volume water (%) *5.4%*

Transportation method and market for oil and gas:

Pipeline

345

Lima-Indiana Trend—U.S.A.
Cincinnati and Findlay Arches, Ohio and Indiana

BRIAN D. KEITH
Indiana Geological Survey and
Department of Geological Sciences, Indiana University
Bloomington, Indiana

LAWRENCE H. WICKSTROM
Ohio Geological Survey
Columbus, Ohio

FIELD CLASSIFICATION

BASIN: Cincinnati and Findlay Arches
BASIN TYPE: Cratonic Arch
RESERVOIR ROCK TYPE: Dolomite
RESERVOIR ENVIRONMENT
  OF DEPOSITION: Platform
TRAP DESCRIPTION: Complex combination of updip porosity pinch-out, regional anticline, faulting, and fractured reservoir

RESERVOIR AGE: Ordovician
PETROLEUM TYPE: Oil and Gas
TRAP TYPE: Combination Pinch-Out and
  Regional Anticline

LOCATION AND GENERAL INFORMATION

The Lima-Indiana trend describes a 260 mi (420 km) long arcuate oil- and gas-producing area (Figure 1) that extends from Toledo, Ohio (T in Figure 1), to near Indianapolis, Indiana (I in Figure 1), where it swings due south into southeastern Indiana. The trend varies considerably in width from less than 1 mi (1.6 km) in portions of Ohio to greater than 50 mi (80 km) in central Indiana. The Ohio portion of the trend consists of more than 60 individually named fields, but few distinct breaks exist between fields. In Indiana, the name Trenton field is applied only to the main producing area, although several isolated small fields north of the Trenton field are considered for the purposes of this paper as part of the trend. The position of the trend is controlled in part by the Findlay and Cincinnati arches, which are broad positive areas separating the Appalachian from the Michigan and Illinois basins (Figure 2). The trend is discussed as a single entity owing to certain similarities of the reservoir and in the setting throughout its extent.

The Lima-Indiana trend was the first giant oil and gas field discovered in North America and has a recovery in excess of 485 million bbl of oil, including more than 380 million bbl from Ohio and more than 105 million bbl from Indiana (Figure 3). Exact production figures are unknown owing to the lack of accurate production records. The trend is listed by Halbouty et al. (1970) as the 172d largest giant field out of 187 in the world. Moody et al. (1970) listed the trend as having a cumulative recovery of 482 million bbl and a projected ultimate recovery of 512 million bbl. Carmalt and St. John (1986) do not rank the trend, because they used a cut-off of 500 million bbl of ultimately recoverable oil, but mention the trend as having an estimated recoverable figure of slightly less than 500 million bbl. Because of the uncertainty of the production figures for the trend, and the wasteful production practices, all reported or estimated recoverable figures have a higher degree of uncertainty than usual for such numbers.

HISTORY

Pre-Discovery

A concise presentation of the pre-discovery, discovery, and post-discovery history of the Ohio part of the trend was made by Wickstrom et al. (in preparation). This history is based primarily on Ohio Geological Survey reports from the late 1880s. Information for this time in Indiana was summarized by Rarick (1980). The discussions for the following

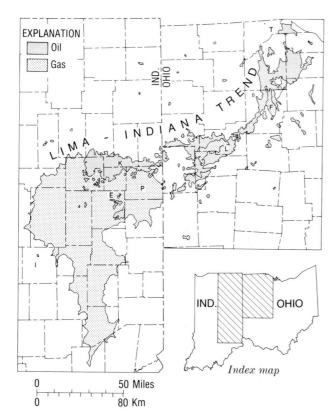

Figure 1. Map showing location of the Lima-Indiana trend and the distribution of oil- and gas-producing areas within the trend. (Modified from Debrosse and Vohwinkle, 1974, and Keith, 1985.) The letters are locations mentioned in text and are: T, Toledo; I, Indianapolis; F, Findlay; E, Eaton; P, Portland; L, Lima; and K, Keystone.

historical sections are drawn largely from these two sources.

Indications of natural gas seepages in Ohio date to early Indian legends telling of torches being used to ignite flames in rock crevices; the fires were then read by medicine men to foretell the future. The first white settlers in the area of Findlay, Ohio (F in Figure 1), in the 1830s provide more direct evidence of seepage because they were constantly plagued by the presence of gas and high levels of sulfur in their water wells. In October 1836, a farmer encountered gas at 10 ft in a dug water well. When accidentally ignited, the gas caused an explosion, and the well burned for three months before it was put out by rain and snow.

The first reported practical use for the gas was in 1838 when Daniel Foster struck gas at a depth of 8 ft in Findlay (F in Figure 1). He ran the gas from an inverted sugar kettle, which served as the well head, through a wooden conductor pipe to the fireplace in his house. The conductor pipe was connected in the fireplace to a perforated gun barrel that was plugged with a cork in one end. The

resulting gas burner provided light and heat and was used for some cooking. This plumbing arrangement was apparently used for the next 50 years until the house was connected to a commercial gas line. Foster's demonstration of the usefulness of natural gas apparently never caught on in all those years; it was the boom fever of the 1880s that truly ignited interest in this natural resource.

In 1876, a 2-in. hole was drilled near Eaton (E in Figure 1) in Delaware County, Indiana, to explore for coal. At a depth of 600 ft (180 m), natural gas was encountered in sufficient quantity to produce a 2 ft flame. The flare reportedly burned for 10 years as a curiosity, but no one thought of using the gas as a resource.

Discovery

Responsibility for commercial discovery of the Lima-Indiana trend rests primarily with the persistence of one individual, Charles Oesterlin, a German-educated physician and amateur geologist living in Findlay. Through years of study and observation, Oesterlin became convinced that the many gas seepages in the area emanated from an immense deposit of natural gas trapped beneath Findlay (F in Figure 1). In 1884, the Findlay Natural Gas Company was formed by selling stock to local citizens. The first well was drilled that year on Oesterlin's farm by a professional driller imported from Bradford, Pennsylvania. Several gas zones were encountered in the Ordovician shales before the Trenton Limestone was penetrated at a depth of 1092 ft (330 m). Drilling was stopped at 1648 ft (500 m) when salt water was encountered. The well was then shot with 30 quarts of nitroglycerine. The ignited flame could be seen 15 mi (24 km) away, and the well produced at an estimated rate of 250 mcf of gas/day. Following the discovery, drilling for gas continued despite lack of a market or transportation system.

The first commercial gas well in Indiana was probably drilled in 1886 near Portland (P in Figure 1) in Jay County, although in that same year the well at Eaton was deepened to 922 ft (280 m) and completed as a Trenton gas well.

Oil drilling followed closely behind the gas exploration frenzy, and the first commercial oil well in the trend was completed in Lima, Ohio (L in Figure 1), in 1885 on the Faurot farm. It was financed by local investors wishing to garner some of the publicity surrounding the gas boom at Findlay, but only a show of oil was found in the Trenton. Nevertheless, the well was shot with nitroglycerine, and to everyone's amazement it initially flowed 200 BOPD before settling down to a rate of about 25 BOPD.

The first commercial oil well in the Indiana part of the trend was drilled and completed in 1889 by Northern Indiana Oil Company on the Bryson farm near the town of Keystone (K in Figure 1) in southern Wells County. Its initial potential is unknown.

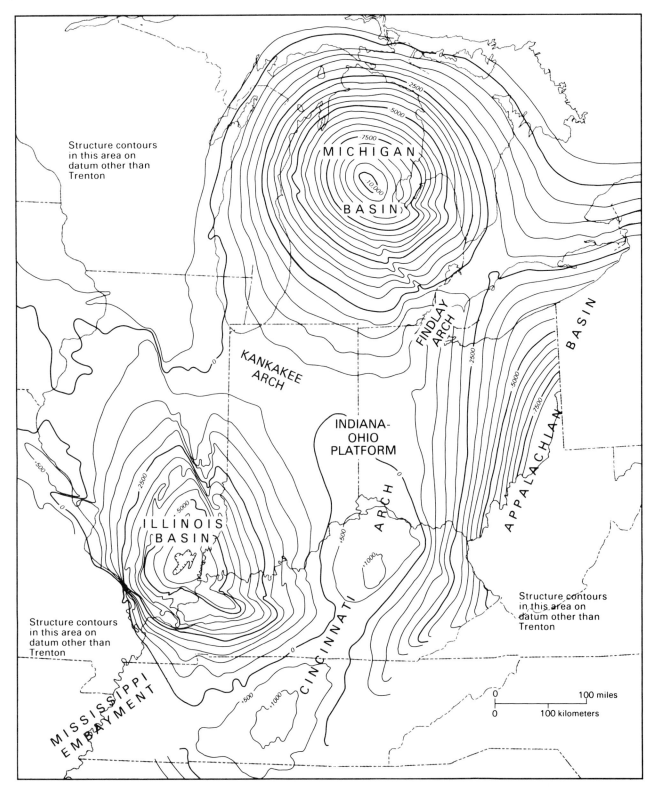

Figure 2. Map showing generalized structure on top of the Trenton Limestone and equivalent units. Regional structural features are also shown. Contour interval, 500 ft. (From Wickstrom, 1990.)

Post-Discovery

The discovery of natural gas, closely followed by the discovery of oil, kicked off a boom frenzy of gigantic proportions in Ohio and Indiana. In Ohio, a series of gas wells followed the discovery well, each increasingly more spectacular than the last. The most famous, however, was the well drilled in Findlay on the lot of the Karg Slaughter House in January 1886. At a depth of 1146 ft (350 m), the well roared

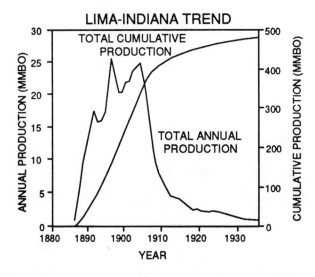

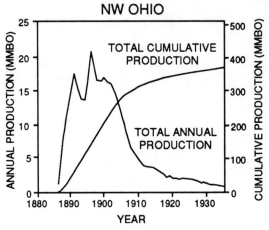

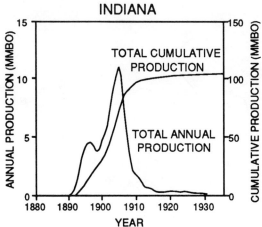

Figure 3. Plots of cumulative and annual oil-production figures for the Lima-Indiana trend, northwestern Ohio, and Trenton field in Indiana.

to life and blew at an estimated rate of 20,000 to 50,000 mcf of natural gas/day. The natural gas boom resulted in two phenomena that went hand in hand: (1) tremendous growth of industry in the area to utilize this abundant and cheap resource, and (2) rampant promotion and flagrant waste of this same resource. Within three years, gas pressure dropped precipitously, causing factories to close, and by 1891 the boom was over. The gas boom lasted longer in Indiana, into the early 1900s, before it also tapered off there for the same reasons.

The oil boom was not as large a promotional success as was natural gas, but it had a greater lasting impact on the petroleum industry. By 1887, gushers began to flow in the area between Findlay and Bowling Green. One well flowed at a rate of 500 BOPD, followed by one at 2000 BOPD, another at 5000, and then three at the same time each flowing more than 10,000 BOPD. Over the next two years, high-volume wells continued to come in, some with reported rates as high as 50,000 BOPD.

These high flow rates produced serious problems for the Standard Oil Trust, which had a monopoly on crude oil refining and transportation in Pennsylvania. The high sulfur content of the Trenton crude prevented its use until a refining process could be worked out to remove the sulfur, yet Standard was afraid that if they did not buy up all the crude they would lose their monopoly. Buckeye Pipeline Company was set up by Standard to buy up (at $0.40/bbl) and store the crude, which was literally gushing forth at an ever-increasing volume. The price rapidly dropped to $0.15/bbl, but wells were still being drilled at a total cost of $1,200 that could return as much as $1,500/day even at this depressed price because of the enormous flow rates. A group of producers who could not compete at this low price formed a combine named the Ohio Oil Company to pull their production off the market in an effort to get Standard to pay at least $0.40/bbl.

Several events then took place to quickly change the whole economic situation. Standard decided to

350

change its corporate policy and become involved in the production part of the business to attempt to control the flow, even if it meant shutting down production along the whole trend when necessary. It bought the Ohio Oil Company and other producers and soon owned 75% of the field. In the meantime, two of Standard's refining specialists, Van Dyke and Frasch, perfected the sweetening still, a process to remove the sulfur from the crude. On the legal front, the Pennsylvania Supreme Court ruled that the "law of capture" rather than the "law of mineral rights" applied to crude oil. This meant that a property owner did not own the oil under his property until it was produced or "captured." Thus, an individual could capture the oil on his own property, claim it, and pump the oil from under a neighbor's property in addition. The bottom line for Standard was that even though it controlled 75% of the production from the trend, the company could not prevent the field from being pumped dry by other operators. So Standard, and everyone else, began pumping the crude as fast as they could. The very rapid peak and decline in oil production (Figure 3) is not surprising in hindsight.

Since the boom time, drilling activity has been sporadic but generally low throughout the trend. During the 1920s in Indiana, a spurt of increased drilling activity in the areas of Jay and Adams Counties was carried out by local operators. It apparently met with scant success, although very little documentation exists for this period of drilling. The boom of the 1980s also brought about an increase in activity along the trend but with little success.

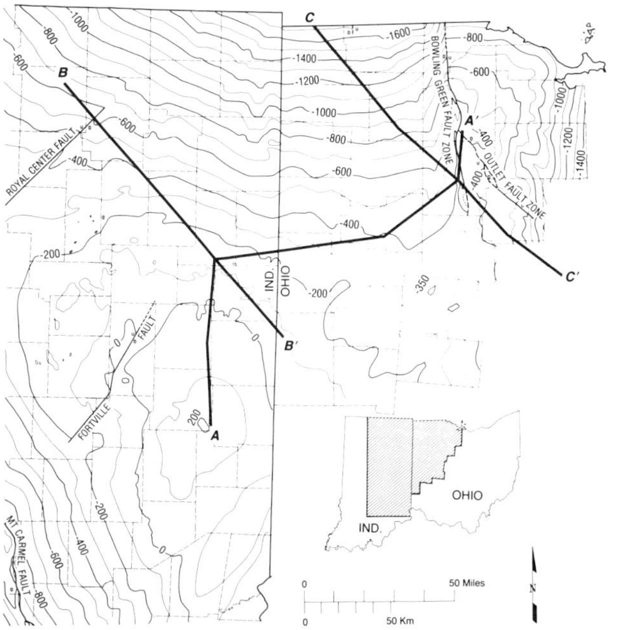

Figure 4. Map showing the structure on top of the Trenton Limestone and the major faults in the vicinity of the Lima-Indiana trend. Contour interval, 100 ft with 50 ft dashed contours in part of Ohio. Lines of section for Figures 9 (A-A'), 10 (B-B'), and 11 (C-C') are also shown.

it is hard to imagine what other possible development strategy could have been used in the trend.

DISCOVERY METHOD

The first location drilled in the trend was serendipitous, and drilling continued as it was encouraged by the presence of hydrocarbons over a very large area. As a result, development was guided by a boom mentality that led to drilling of every available location until a dry hole was drilled. Then drilling was continued in another direction or location. The geologic control over the production was not realized until Orton (1889) and Phinney (1891) were able to make amazingly accurate geologic interpretations of the tremendous volume of drilling data. Both men made structure maps on the top of the Trenton, which when combined (see Owen, 1975, figure 5-3) show the general structural configuration of the trend that is quite close to present mapping (Figure 4). Orton (1889) also had an understanding of the role of dolomitization in reservoir development. The heterogeneity of porosity development in the trend was a problem whose solution has eluded drillers even to this day. Aside from certain areas, such as along the Bowling Green fault zone, a well-defined pattern of porosity development is not evident. Without the driving force of a boom fever,

STRUCTURE

The Lima-Indiana trend is located on the Indiana-Ohio platform along the Cincinnati and Findlay arches between the Appalachian, Michigan, and Illinois basins (Figure 2). This area was not an uplifted arch but rather a relatively stable area that became positive as the adjacent basins subsided. These basins appear to have had their origins during Precambrian time and were reactivated at various times during the Paleozoic Era, but did not assume their present general configurations until the Silurian Period (Droste and Shaver, 1983).

Along the Findlay arch in northwestern Ohio, the most prominent structural feature is the Bowling Green fault zone (Figure 4). Wickstrom and Gray (1988) noted that this feature has been interpreted variously, including as a high-angle normal fault, a high-angle reverse fault, and a monocline. Wickstrom and Gray (1988) interpreted the structure as a fault zone up to 5 mi (8 km) wide. The zone is upthrown on the east side and has an associated anticline on the west (Figures 4 and 5). The zone is approximately 45 mi (72 km) long in Ohio (Figure 4), extending from Hancock County to Lucas County and then into

351

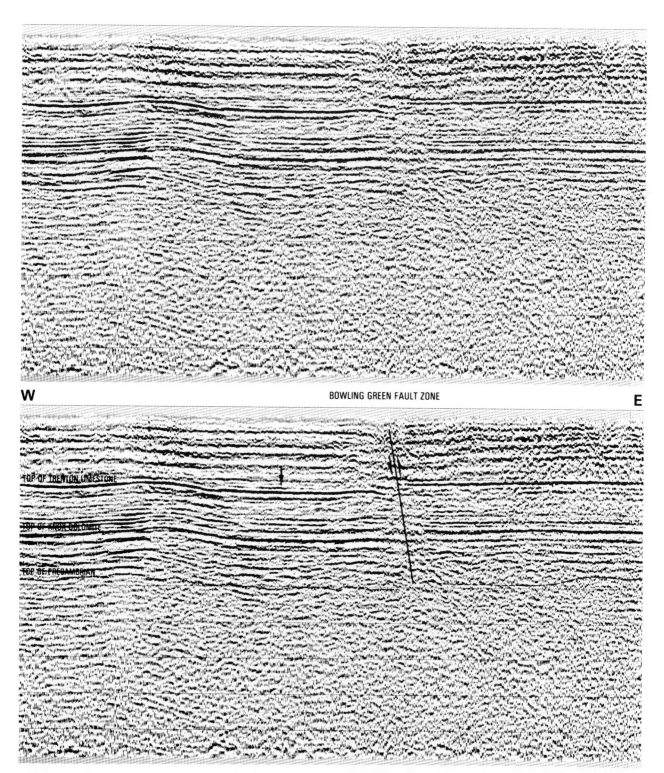

W   BOWLING GREEN FAULT ZONE   E

TOP OF TRENTON LIMESTONE

TOP OF KNOX DOLOMITE

TOP OF PRECAMBRIAN

Figure 5. East-west seismic profile across the Bowling Green fault zone in Wood County, Ohio. The upper profile is uninterpreted, and the lower profile shows fault interpretation and key stratigraphic horizons. An Ordovician episode of faulting is suggested by a reflection horizon (arrow) that terminates into the anticlinal structure (on downthrown side) west of the fault zone. The profile shown is about 4.5 mi (7.2 km) long and extends to a depth of 1.0 second. (The original nonexclusive seismic line is the property of CGG American Services, Inc., and is used here with permission.)

Michigan for a short distance along a general but somewhat sinuous north-south trend (Wickstrom and Gray, 1988). This structural trend coincides with the proposed position of the Grenville front in Ohio, which separates the Precambrian Grenville province to the east from the Central Granitic province to the west. It is unclear from existing data how much of the 500 ft (150 m) of vertical displacement along the fault zone is related to folding versus faulting. There are indications of episodes of Precambrian, Ordovician (Figure 5), and Silurian movement on the Bowling Green fault zone (Kahle and Floyd, 1968; Wickstrom, 1990).

Smaller scale faults have been mapped in Ohio (Wickstrom and Gray, 1988) and Indiana (Keith, unpublished). Actual displacements are often hard to document because of the scarcity of well control, but they are generally on the order of tens of feet. Small-scale anticlines, generally less than 10 mi long and 1 to 2 mi wide, and having less than 10 to a few tens of feet of closure, are found in places along the Lima-Indiana trend.

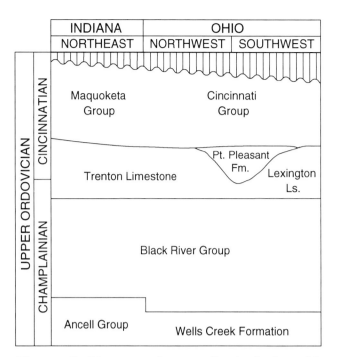

Figure 6. Diagram of generalized stratigraphic relationships for Upper Ordovician units in parts of Indiana and Ohio. This diagram is somewhat simplified in terms of the relationship of the Lower Maquoketa to both the Trenton and Point Pleasant rocks. See section on *Facies and Depositional Environment* for a more detailed discussion.

STRATIGRAPHY

The reservoirs in the Lima-Indiana trend are found in the Ordovician Black River Group (Limestone) and Trenton Limestones. These rocks are late Champlainian to early Cincinnatian in age (Figure 6). They are underlain by the Wells Creek Formation in Ohio and the Ancell Group in Indiana. In southwestern Ohio, the Point Pleasant Formation is for the most part the same age as the Trenton. Overlying units make up parts of the Cincinnati Group in Ohio and the Maquoketa Group in Indiana. Wells drilled in the trend encounter the Pleistocene cover first and then pass into Lower Silurian rocks. In some places, where pre-Pleistocene erosion has cut entirely through the Silurian rocks, Upper Ordovician rocks are encountered immediately below the cover. The total thickness of the Trenton along the trend ranges from nearly 100 to 300 ft (30 to 90 m) (Figure 7).

TRAP

As one might expect for a trend as long as the Lima-Indiana trend and for one that is not itself the whole of a large-scale structural feature, the trapping conditions vary considerably from one end to the other (Figure 8). In addition, no primary limestone porosity in the Trenton Limestone exists anywhere along the trend. All porosity development is related to dolomitization and possibly to fracturing as well. The general nature of the trap being related to a lateral facies change from nonporous limestone to porous dolomite (resulting from dolomitization of the limestone) was first proposed by Orton (1889).

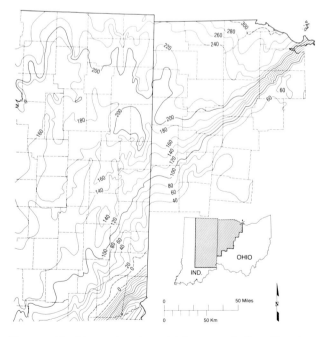

Figure 7. Map showing thickness of the Trenton Limestone in the vicinity of the Lima-Indiana trend. Contour interval, 20 ft. (Indiana portion modified from Keith, 1985.)

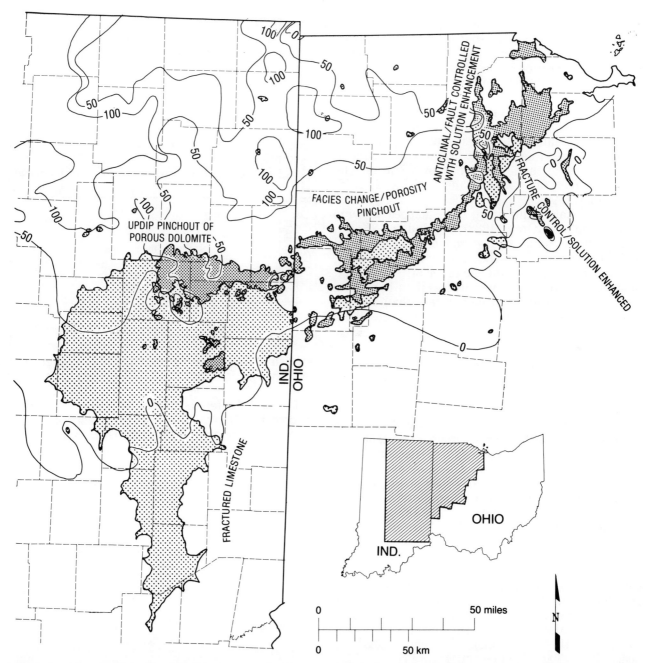

Figure 8. Map showing the following: (1) Percentage of the Trenton Limestone interval that is dolomite in the vicinity of the Lima-Indiana trend. The variation in thickness of dolomite in the Trenton is highly variable and complex. The percentage map is used to convey the regional pattern of this thickness distribution. (2) Distribution of oil- and gas-producing areas of the Lima-Indiana trend (same symbols as Figure 1). (3) Nature of trapping conditions in different areas of the trend. Estimated recoveries for the different areas are fractured limestone, below commercial gas volumes; updip pinch-out of porous dolomite, 500 bbl of oil/acre; facies change/porosity pinch-out, 100–500 bbl of oil/acre; anticlinal/fault controlled with solution enhancement, 4000–12,000 bbl of oil/acre; and fracture control/solution enhanced, no information available.

A number of different trapping situations are evident in Ohio. The most prolific petroleum-producing part of the Lima-Indiana trend is along the Bowling Green fault zone, where an estimated 60% of the total oil from the trend was produced (Wickstrom et al., in preparation). On the upthrown side of the fault zone, porous dolomitic reservoirs in the upper part of the Trenton are juxtaposed with the shales of the Cincinnati Group, and on the downthrown side the reservoir rocks are juxtaposed to the impermeable limestones of the lower part of the Trenton (Figures 9 and 11). Thus, a trap is provided on either side of the fault zone. Reservoirs on the downthrown side are further enhanced by

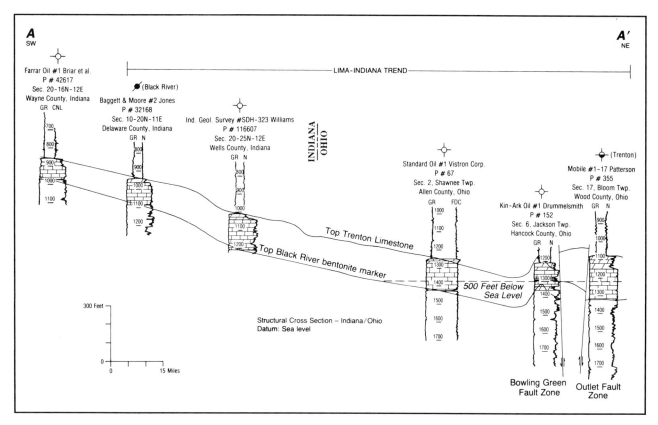

Figure 9. Structural cross section A-A' along the Lima-Indiana trend from Indiana to Ohio (see Figure 4 for location) showing vertical and horizontal distribution of limestone and dolomite in the Trenton Limestone. The southern end of the section is on the crest of the Cincinnati arch. The line then drops structurally down to follow along the north flank of the Findlay arch to the Bowling Green fault zone. In the Briar well at the southwest end of the section, the Trenton is all limestone. The cap dolomite appears in the next well to the north (Jones), whereas both the cap dolomite and a few feet of regional dolomite appear in the Williams well, which is in the Trenton field. Only the cap dolomite is again present in the Vistron well. Several zones of saddle dolomite are present near the Bowling Green and Outlet fault zones.

dolomitized solution zones associated with fractures. In other areas of the trend in Ohio, hydrocarbons are trapped on structural highs associated with the fault zone and along the crest of the Findlay arch itself. Reservoirs are also found in minor fractured or faulted anticlines and synclines. A facies change southward, from porous dolomite to nonporous shale and limestone of the Point Pleasant Formation (Figure 11), forms the probable trapping conditions along the middle part of the trend in western Ohio (Wickstrom et al., in preparation).

In Indiana, structure appears to have played a relatively minor role in trapping hydrocarbons. The trap for the oil-yielding part of the trend is an updip pinch-out of porous dolomite facies into nonporous dolomite on the northern flank of the Cincinnati arch (Figure 10). A more detailed discussion of the dolomite types in the Trenton Limestone is presented in the section on *Facies and Depositional Environment,* below.

The trapping mechanism for the gas part of the trend in Indiana is not clear. Gas production came from a very large area south of the oil-yielding part of the trend (Figure 8). Examination of the relatively few logs and samples from modern wells in the gas area indicates that the reservoir is limestone that has no apparent porosity. This suggests that the gas is flowing from fractures in the limestone. The gas-yielding area occurs on the north and west flanks of the Cincinnati arch but does not extend to the crest of the arch. The Trenton thins to the south and east over the Cincinnati arch as the overlying shale of the Maquoketa Group thickens. This thickness transition may have contributed to the trapping conditions in some manner that is not presently understood.

RESERVOIR

Depth

The depth to the top of the Trenton along the trend ranges from 1000 to 1320 ft (305–400 m). The

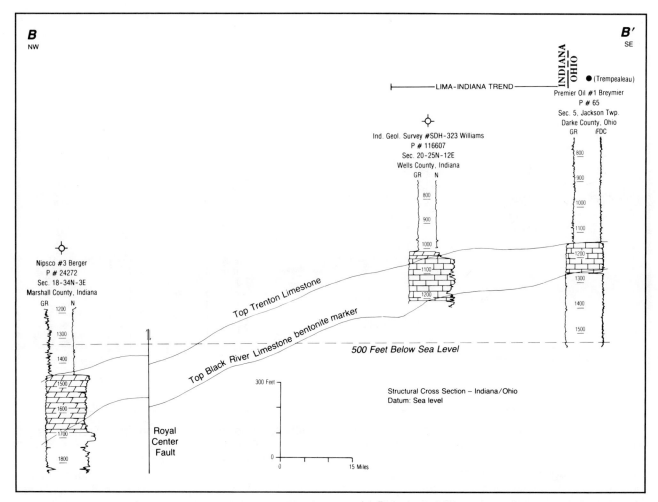

Figure 10. Structural cross section B–B' across the Lima-Indiana trend from northern Indiana to western Ohio (see Figure 4 for location). The northern end of the section is in the Michigan basin, and then it rises structurally onto the Cincinnati arch. The updip pinch-out of porous regional dolomite from the Berger well in the north to the Williams well in the Trenton field can be seen. The cap dolomite then disappears between the Williams well and the Breymier south of the trend.

production intervals generally occur within the top 100 ft (30 m) of the formation. In the area of the Bowling Green fault zone, reservoirs are found throughout the Trenton and Black River section and extend to depths in excess of 1900 ft (580 m).

Facies and Depositional Environment

The facies sequence and distribution within the Trenton Limestone is quite complex, being composed of a mosaic of skeletal mudstones, wackestones, packstones, and grainstones. The skeletal grains are dominated by crinoid and bryozoan fragments. Understanding of this sequence is incomplete because of the scarcity of cores through the Trenton section. A generalized facies model (Figure 12), however, is presented by using Fara and Keith (1988), Keith (1988a), and Wickstrom and Gray (1988). Deposition of this facies mosaic occurred during the development of a broad carbonate platform across most of Indiana, southern Michigan, and northern Ohio. Initially, open marine shelf conditions covered most of this area, and skeletal mudstones to wackestones were deposited in a generally low-energy subtidal environment in which the grainstones represent storm deposits and possibly local shoaling. In Indiana, energy conditions appear to have been higher to the northwest, where skeletal packstones are dominant in the lower part of the Trenton. To the southeast, in south-central Ohio, this marine shelf then became differentiated into a restricted marine shelf that was separated by a marine trough from a higher energy platform to the northwest. The interbedded argillaceous limestones and shales of the Point Pleasant Formation were deposited on the restricted shelf while shales and some thin limestones were deposited in the trough. Platform-margin mudstones and grainstones accumulated adjacent to the trough on the north. Bryozoan-dominated packstones and wackestones, possibly accumulating as an organic mound

356

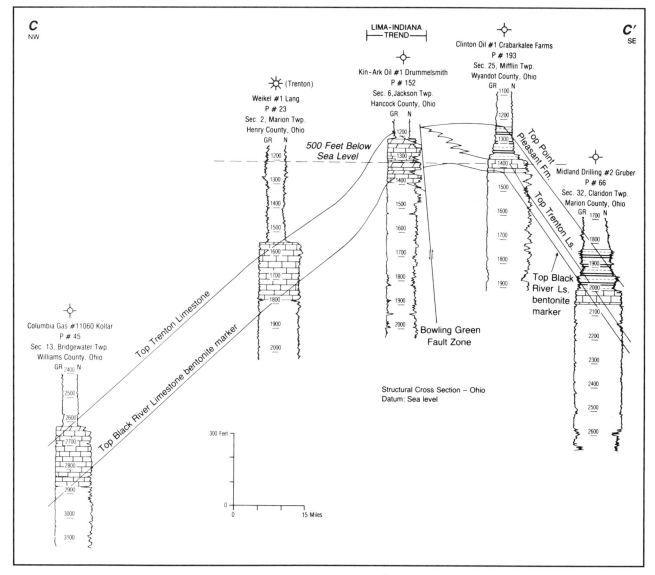

Figure 11. Structural cross section C-C' across the Lima-Indiana trend from northwestern to central Ohio. The northern end of the section is at the edge of the Michigan basin and the southern end at the edge of the Appalachian basin. The northern two wells (Kollar and Lang) contain the cap dolomite. Several zones of saddle dolomite are present in the Drummelsmith well along the Bowling Green fault zone. The relatively abrupt facies change from Trenton Limestone to Point Pleasant Formation can be seen southeast of the fault zone. (See Figure 4 for location.)

complex (Fara and Keith, 1988), formed initially on the open marine shelf but reached their greatest thickness in the platform interior northward in Indiana. This facies was replaced for the remainder of Trenton deposition by a higher energy platform facies of skeletal packstones and grainstones.

The limestones of the Trenton were subsequently dolomitized, and three types of dolomite have been described (see Keith, 1988b, for a review). The upper few feet of the Trenton are consistently a nonporous, generally ferroan dolomite, called the cap dolomite, which has a wider distribution than the regional dolomite. As implied by its name, the regional dolomite extends broadly across southern Michigan, northern Indiana, and a small part of northwestern Ohio. This dolomite occurs only in the upper part of the Trenton below the cap dolomite, but the thickness of regional dolomite is highly variable locally. In some wells, the regional dolomite can be seen throughout the Trenton section and even into the upper part of the Black River rocks. This dolomite is pervasive, generally obliterating much of the original detailed texture of the limestone, although commonly the gross texture is remarkably well preserved (Figure 13). The saddle dolomite is a coarsely crystalline white dolomite that is found

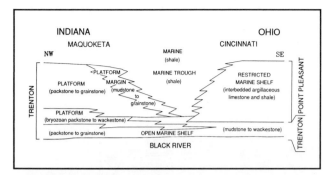

Figure 12. Schematic diagram of facies relationships and general depositional environments for Trenton, Point Pleasant, and Lower Maquoketa sediments. General line of section is from north-central Indiana to southwestern Ohio. By showing the presence of a body of shale between the Trenton and Point Pleasant, this figure is in contrast to Figure 11. The shale represents fill in the Sebree trough that is not present further to the northeast in the area of Figure 11.

lining vugs and is particularly prevalent along solution zones associated with fractures and faults. The overall distribution of dolomite in the Trenton forms a complex pattern (Figure 8) controlled by the separate distributions of the three different types of dolomite.

Reservoir Characteristics

Throughout the Lima-Indiana trend, reservoir characteristics are highly variable. Hydrocarbons are generally found in porous dolomite within the upper 100 ft (30 m) of the Trenton. In Ohio, however, along the Bowling Green fault zone, the entire Trenton and Black River section is dolomite with multiple individual pay zones that are generally less than 16 ft (5 m) thick (Wickstrom et al., in preparation). These zones are highly discontinuous both horizontally and vertically. Proprietary core-analysis data from wells along the fault zone indicate average porosities of only 4 to 6%, with individual values ranging from 1.5 to 14%. Permeabilities are highly variable, from 0.3 to 9000 md. Most producing zones have a range of 100 to 400 md. Core reports and visual inspection of cores indicate that in the area of the Bowling Green fault zone there is a dual porosity system present in the Trenton reservoir consisting of a relatively fine intercrystalline pore network connecting macroscopic vugs (Figure 14). The ratio of the two types of porosity in any given zone is highly variable and directly affects production behavior. Where the intercrystalline porosity is dominant, production rates follow a fairly typical progression of good initial production succeeded by a slow decline in production and reservoir pressure. These areas had very high recoveries, on the order of 12,000 bbl/ac (Wickstrom and Gray, 1988). Reservoirs dominated by macrovugs tend to have very high initial production rates, but unless these vugs are connected to a good intercrys-

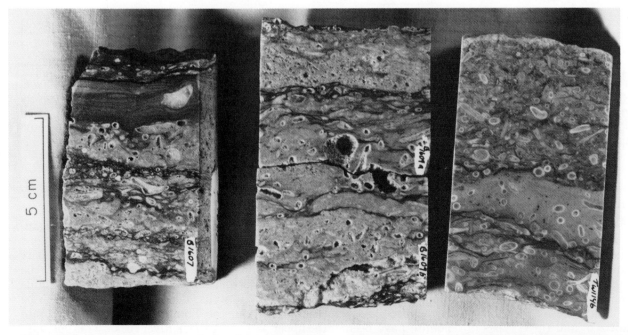

Figure 13. Core-slab photograph showing preservation of primary limestone texture in regional dolomite in Indiana. Sample on right (TW1146) is limestone from the Trenton field. Slabs in the center and on the left represent the equivalent facies that have been totally dolomitized north of the field. The bryozoan packstone texture has been preserved as moldic porosity (B1609); the pores are filled with gypsum in some examples (B1607). (From Fara and Keith, 1988.)

Figure 14. Porous regional dolomite exhibiting intercrystalline to microvug porosity. (From Fara and Keith, 1988.) (A) Photomicrograph showing pores (p) lined with dead oil. (B) SEM photomicrograph of typical pore system.

talline network, production rates fall rapidly to uneconomical levels. In zones composed almost entirely of the macrovugs, "flush" production might reach the uneconomical limit in only a matter of days. Away from the Bowling Green fault zone, elsewhere in Ohio and in Indiana, the reservoir typically is composed of discontinuous zones of the intercrystalline porosity and very little macrovug development, although microvugs are common in some places (Figure 14). Estimated recoveries in these areas ranged from 1000 bbl/ac in Ohio to less than 500 bbl/ac in Indiana. In extreme examples, individual productive zones are only inches thick and are separated by totally impermeable zones (Figure 15). Late-stage pore filling by gypsum, anhydrite, or calcite (Figure 16) is common in nonproductive areas.

Figure 15. Core photograph illustrating example of individual thin productive zones in the Trenton. Porous dolomite is oil stained. Nonporous dolomite is light colored. Core is from the Peru field in Indiana and is the only known core from a productive well in the Lima-Indiana trend.

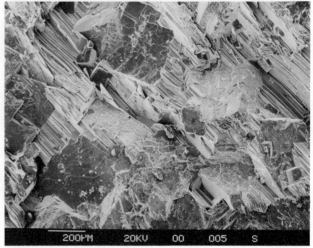

Figure 16. Pore-filling gypsum in regional dolomite from northern Indiana. (From Fara and Keith, 1988.) (A) Photomicrograph (crossed nicols). (B) SEM photomicrograph.

In the early 1970s, Husky Oil Company evaluated the Trenton field in Indiana for its potential for tertiary recovery. Under the operational name of Mitchell Inc., Husky drilled six wells to the rocks of the Knox Supergroup (Dolomite). A full suite of conventional logs was run, and the upper part of the Trenton was cored in each well. In addition to conventional core analysis, a number of flow tests were reportedly run on the cores. This evaluation program provided more sophisticated reservoir information than was previously available.

A porosity/permeability cross plot of the whole-core analysis of these six cores was made (Figure 17). Of the 203 values plotted, 90 fall in the less than 0.1 md permeability and less than 3.5% porosity area of the graph. The plot indicates the overall low reservoir quality as only 20% of the points fall outside of the field defined by 10% porosity and 10 md permeability for all six cores. Beyond this area of the plot, the points fall into two data clusters: (1)

a small number of points indicating good porosity and permeability (upper diagonal line) that are probably indicative of well-interconnected vugs; and (2) a larger number of points indicating relatively high permeability but with porosity still less than 10% (lower line). This latter field probably represents enhancement of permeability by fractures. The project was abandoned by Husky without any field testing.

Low permeability, lack of a good water drive, and wasteful production practices probably account for the low recovery in the initial drilling of the Trenton field in Indiana and the general lack of success in subsequent drilling and attempts at enhanced recovery.

Source Rocks

It is interesting to note that Orton (1889) observed that organic matter was present in the Cincinnatian

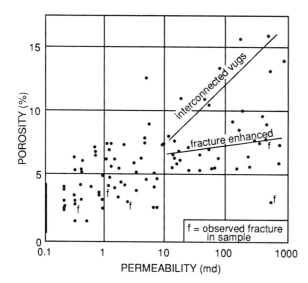

Figure 17. Porosity/permeability crossplot of whole core-analysis data from six wells in the Trenton field in Indiana. Vertical bar on lower vertical axis represents 90 points with less than 0.1 md permeability and 3.5% or less porosity.

shales (referred to as Utica shale) as well as in the Trenton Limestone, and that the organic matter was the source of the petroleum in the Trenton reservoir. Contrary to the opinion of others at the time, Orton did appear to favor the Trenton as the source rather than the overlying shales (see Owen, 1975, for concise summary of Orton's discussions on this subject).

The produced oil from the trend has essentially the same composition as other Ordovician oils from the Mid-Continent of the United States (Longman and Palmer, 1987) and shows a typical Ordovician signature of an odd-carbon dominance in the *n*-alkane fraction (Figure 18). Interpretations of the source of the oil differ for Ohio and Indiana. The general assumption in both areas for many years was that the overlying dark-gray to brownish-gray shales of the Maquoketa served as the source. However, Cole et al. (1987) suggested that shales of the Point Pleasant Formation are a more likely source for the oils in the trend in Ohio, because the Point Pleasant is in a favorable structural position for migration of expelled hydrocarbons into the reservoirs of the trend (Figure 11). Burial-history modeling (Figure 19) suggests that peak oil-generating maturity in northwestern Ohio was attained in the Point Pleasant (Cole et al., 1987).

Preliminary work by Guthrie (1989) suggests that, for Indiana at least, the Maquoketa is the probable source of oil in the Trenton, and that burial depths significantly greater than the present 1000 ft (305 m) were attained. Although burial-history modeling has not been done for the Maquoketa in Indiana, this preliminary analysis indicates that these shales did reach peak oil generation in the area of the Lima-

Indiana trend in Indiana (J. M. Guthrie, personal communication, 1990).

EXPLORATION AND DEVELOPMENT CONCEPTS

The heterogeneous nature of Trenton reservoirs throughout the trend and elsewhere indicates that no single strategy for effective exploration and development may be best. Attempts at secondary and enhanced recovery in the lower-quality reservoirs of the trend have been uniformly unsuccessful. The presence of large amounts of water from the reservoir, much of which may be from shallow aquifers, and its generally low permeability present as yet unsurmountable problems. The low initial recoveries of infill drilling attempts also present very unfavorable economics. Horizontal drilling technology has recently been used with success in Michigan at the Albion-Scipio trend, which has very similar reservoir properties to those around the Bowling Green fault zone. In areas where fractures play a key role in reservoir permeability and the potential for water production is low, this technique might breathe new life into certain plays.

The solution-enhanced reservoir development seen at Albion-Scipio and similar features offer exciting exploration targets, but exploration for these solution-enhanced fracture zones is difficult at best. Detailed seismic surveys and surface geochemistry techniques have been tried with varying degrees of reported success.

ACKNOWLEDGMENTS

We have benefitted from numerous discussions of parts of the Lima-Indiana trend with many different individuals over a number of years. In addition, BDK would like to acknowledge previous collaborative work by Dan Fara, and LHW the earlier work of Jack Gray and Ron Stieglitz. The manuscript was enhanced through the input from reviewers Bob Shaver, Charly Zuppann, Ted Beaumont, and an anonymous AAPG reviewer. We also appreciate the patience and dedication of the Treatise editors Ted Beaumont and Norm Foster. This contribution was prepared with the assistance of the staffs of the Indiana and Ohio Geological Surveys and published with the permission of Norman C. Hester, Indiana State Geologist, and Thomas M. Berg, Ohio State Geologist.

REFERENCES CITED

Carmalt, S. W., and B. St. John, 1986, Giant oil and gas fields, *in* M. T. Halbouty, ed., Future petroleum provinces of the world: AAPG Memoir 40, p. 11–54.

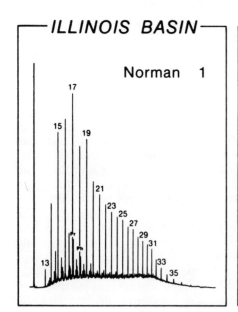

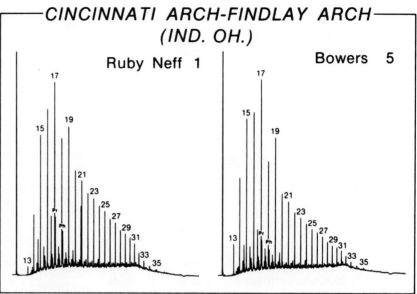

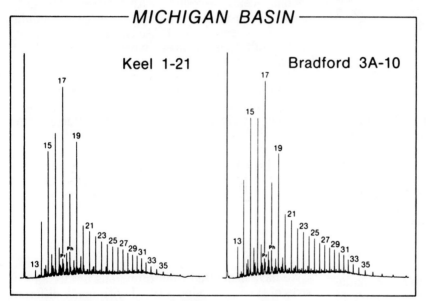

Figure 18. Gas chromatograms for oil produced from Ordovician reservoirs in the region. Note dominance of odd-numbered *n*-alkanes typical of many Ordovician oils. (From Longman and Palmer, 1987.)

Cole, G. A., R. J. Drozd, R. A. Sedivy, and H. I. Halpern, 1987, Organic geochemistry and oil-source correlations, Paleozoic of Ohio: AAPG Bulletin, v. 71, p. 788–809.

Debrosse, T. A., and J. C. Vohwinkle, 1974, Oil and gas fields of Ohio: Ohio Division of Geological Survey, map.

Droste, J. B., and R. H. Shaver, 1983, Atlas of early and middle Paleozoic paleogeography of the southern Great Lakes area: Indiana Geological Survey Special Report 32, 32 p.

Fara, D. R., and B. D. Keith, 1988, Depositional facies and diagenetic history of the Trenton Limestone in northern Indiana, *in* B. D. Keith, ed., The Trenton Group (Upper Ordovician Series) of eastern North America: AAPG Studies in Geology 29, p. 277–298.

Guthrie, J., 1989, Organic geochemistry and correlation of Paleozoic source rocks and Trenton crude oils, Indiana (abstr.): AAPG Bulletin, v. 73, p. 1032.

Halbouty, M. T., A. A. Meyerhoff, R. E. King, R. H. Dott, Sr., H. D. Klemme, and T. Shabad, 1970, World's giant oil and gas fields, geologic factors affecting their formation, and basin classification, Part I, *in* M. T. Halbouty, ed., Geology of giant petroleum fields: AAPG Memoir 14, p. 502–528.

Kahle, C. D., and J. D. Floyd, 1968, Structure and fabrics of some Middle and Upper Silurian dolostones, northwestern Ohio: Guide to 43d Annual Field Conference of the Section of Geology: Ohio Academy of Science, 40 p.

Keith, B. D., 1985, Map of Indiana showing thickness, extent, and oil and gas fields of Trenton and Lexington Limestones: Indiana Geological Survey Miscellaneous Map 45.

Keith, B. D., 1988a, Regional facies of Upper Ordovician Series of eastern North America, *in* B. D. Keith, ed., The Trenton Group (Upper Ordovician Series) of eastern North America: AAPG Studies in Geology 29, p. 1–16.

Keith, B. D., 1988b, Reservoirs resulting from facies-independent dolomitization: case histories from the Trenton and Black River carbonate rocks of the Great Lakes area, *in* B. D. Keith, ed., The Trenton Group (Upper Ordovician Series) of eastern North America: AAPG Studies in Geology 29, p. 267–276.

Longman, M. W., and S. E. Palmer, 1987, Organic geochemistry of Mid-Continent Middle and Late Ordovician oils: AAPG Bulletin, v. 71, p. 938–950.

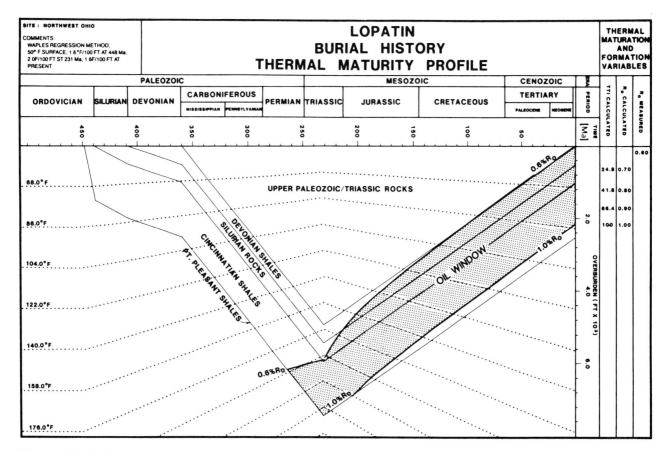

Figure 19. Burial history plot for northwestern Ohio. (From Cole et al., 1987.)

Moody, J. D., J. W. Mooney, and J. Spivak, 1970, Giant oil fields of North America, *in* M. T. Halbouty, ed., Geology of giant petroleum fields: AAPG Memoir 14, p. 502–528.

Orton, E., 1889, The Trenton Limestone as a source of petroleum and inflammable gas in Ohio and Indiana: U.S. Geological Survey 8th Annual Report, pt. 2, p. 477–662.

Owen, E. W., 1975, Trek of the oil finders: a history of exploration for petroleum: AAPG Memoir 6, 16,476 p.

Phinney, A. J., 1891, The natural gas field of Indiana: U.S. Geological Survey 11th Annual Report, pt. 1, p. 617–742.

Rarick, R. D., 1980, The petroleum industry—its birth in Pennsylvania and development in Indiana: Indiana Geological Survey Occasional Paper 32, 36 p.

Wickstrom, L. H., 1990, A new look at Trenton (Ordovician) structure in northwestern Ohio: Northeastern Geology, v. 12, p. 103–113.

Wickstrom, L. H., and J. D. Gray, 1988, Geology of the Trenton Limestone in northwestern Ohio, *in* B. D. Keith, ed., The Trenton Group (Upper Ordovician Series) of eastern North America: AAPG Studies in Geology 29, p. 159–172.

Wickstrom, L. H., J. D. Gray, and R. D. Stieglitz, in preparation, The Trenton Limestone (Ordovician) of northwestern Ohio: Ohio Geological Survey.

Appendix 1. Field Description

Field name .... Lima-Indiana Trend

Ultimate recoverable reserves .... 485+ million bbl of oil

Field location:

    Country .... U.S.A.

    State .... Ohio and Indiana

    Basin/Province .... Indiana-Ohio platform, Findlay arch

Field discovery:

    Year field discovered .... Trenton Limestone (Ohio) gas 1884

    Year second pay discovered .... Trenton Limestone (Ohio) oil 1885

    Year third pay discovered .... Black River Limestone (Ohio) oil 1903

Discovery well name and general location:

    First pay .... Eagle Creek, Hancock County, first well in the city of Findlay, Ohio

    Second pay .... Matthias No. 1, Allen County, Ohio

    Third pay .... Michael No. 1, Sec. 15, T21N, R11E, Delaware County, Indiana

Discovery well operator .... Findlay Natural Gas Company

    Second pay .... Findlay Gas-Light Company

    Third pay .... Unknown

IP:

    First pay .... 200–300 Mcf

    Second pay .... 300 BOPD

    Third pay .... 160 BOPD

All other zones with shows of oil and gas in the field:

Age	Formation	Type of show
Upper Ordovician	Undifferentiated Cincinnatian rocks	Gas and Oil
Lower Ordovician	Knox Dolomite (Supergroup)	Gas and Oil

Geologic concept leading to discovery and method or methods used to delineate prospect

Gas seepages were first noted in water wells near Findlay, Ohio, in 1836. Random drilling in search for a gas supply for the City of Findlay in 1884 resulted in the discovery well.

Structure:

    Province/basin type .... Cincinnati arch/Bally Cratonic Arch, Klemme I-Arch

Tectonic history

Trend is on flank of positive area between basins that was relatively quiet tectonically throughout its history. Minor local faulting and flexuring occurred late in the Paleozoic, but precise timing is not known.

Regional structure

The Lima-Indiana trend lies principally in the Arches province. It is southeast of the Michigan basin, west-northwest of the Appalachian basin, and northeast of the Illinois basin. Most of the trend is situated upon the Indiana-Ohio platform and the Findlay arch.

Local structure

Various local structures are associated with this trend and include: western (downthrown) side of Bowling Green fault zone; closure on top of arches; small anticlinal terraces, down-to-the-basin; updip facies change (probably growth fault related).

LIMA-INDIANA

364

Trap:

Trap type(s)

Multiple porosity-permeability pinch-out traps (Ohio and Indiana), large- and small-scale anticlinal traps and faulted anticlinal traps (both in Ohio), and local fracture-system traps.

Basin stratigraphy (major stratigraphic intervals from surface to deepest penetration in field):

Chronostratigraphy	Formation	Depth to Top in ft (m)
Pleistocene	*Glacial drift*	*0*
Silurian	*Multiple carbonate rocks*	*50 (15)*
Ordovician	*Undifferentiated Cincinnati rocks*	*450 (137)*
	Trenton-Black River Limestone (Group)	*1000–1320 (300–400)*
	Knox Dolomite (Supergroup)	*1250–1620 (380–494)*

Reservoir characteristics:

Number of reservoirs .... *Multiple discontinuous pay zones*

Formations .... *Trenton Limestone, Black River Limestone Group*

Ages .... *Ordovician*

Depths to tops of reservoirs .... *Depths ranged from 1000 to 2000 ft (305–610 m) and average around 1300 ft (400 m)*

Gross thickness (top to bottom of producing interval) .... *Avg. 180 ft (55 m), max. 260 ft (80 m)*

Net thickness—total thickness of producing zones

    Average .... *15 ft (5 m)*

    Maximum .... *50 ft (15 m)*

Lithology .... *Dolomitized skeletal packstone and grainstone*

Porosity type .... *Secondary—intercrystalline to vuggy and local fracture-solution*

Average porosity .... *6–8% estimated*

Average permeability .... *Unknown*

Seals:

Upper

    Formation, fault, or other feature .... *Undifferentiated Cincinnatian rocks*

    Lithology .... *Shale*

Lateral

    Formation, fault, or other feature .... *Point Pleasant Fm. (PP), nonporous Trenton Limestone (T), and local faults*

    Lithology .... *Interbedded limestone and shale (PP) and limestone (T)*

Source:

Formation and age .... *Point Pleasant Formation, basal Cincinnati Group in Ohio, lower Maquoketa Group in Indiana*

Lithology .... *Shale and carbonaceous limestone*

Average total organic carbon (TOC) *1.3%*

Maximum TOC *4.23%*

Kerogen type (I, II, or III) .... *II (Longman and Palmer, 1987)*

Vitrinite reflectance (maturation) .... $R_0 = 0.6$

Time of hydrocarbon expulsion .... *Late Pennsylvanian (Cole et al, 1987, for Ohio); possibly Late Silurian (Indiana)*

Present depth to top of source .... *4000 ft (1220 m) in Ohio, 1000 ft (305 m) in Indiana*

Thickness .... *200 ft (60 m)*

Potential yield .... *Unknown*

Appendix 2. Production Data

Field name .... *Lima-Indiana Trend*

Field size:

Proved acres .... *Unknown*
Number of wells all years .... *100,000 (est.)*
Current number of wells .... *A few hundred at most*
Well spacing .... *Varied from town lot to 10 or 20 ac/well*
Ultimate recoverable .... *Unknown*
Cumulative production .... *485 million bbl*
Annual production .... *Peak production in 1897 with 20.5 million bbl*
Present decline rate .... *Field depleted*
    Initial decline rate .... *NA*
    Overall decline rate .... *NA*
Annual water production .... *NA*
In place, total reserves .... *Unknown*
In place, per acre foot .... *Variable; ranges from 540–12,000 bbl/ac (0.02–0.47 m³/m²)*
Primary recovery .... *485 million bbl*
Secondary recovery .... *None successful*
Enhanced recovery .... *None*
Cumulative water production .... *Unknown*

Drilling and casing practices:

Amount of surface casing set .... *Approximately 500 ft (150 m)*
Casing program

Drive pipe through glacial drift and landed in bedrock; approximately 500 ft of surface casing, mudded or cemented; tubing set for production

Drilling mud .... *None*
Bit program .... *Cable tool bits*
High pressure zones .... *Fractured Ordovician shales (rare) and Trenton gas zones*

Completion practices:

Interval(s) perforated .... *Open-hole completions*
Well treatment .... *Most wells were shot or torpedoed with explosives*

Formation evaluation:

Logging suites .... *Entire trend was developed prior to the existence of wireline logging methods*
Testing practices .... *Open-flow measurements*
Mud logging techniques ... *Entire trend was developed prior to the existence of mud-logging techniques*

Oil characteristics:

Type .... *Paraffinic-naphthenic*
API gravity .... *38°*
Base .... *Intermediate*
Initial GOR .... *Unknown*
Sulfur, wt% *0.1–0.4%*
Viscosity, SUS .... *NA*
Pour point .... *NA*
Gas-oil distillate .... *NA*

Field characteristics:

Average elevation .... *–250 ft (–76 m)*
Initial pressure .... *220–450 psi (1517–3100 kPa)*

Present pressure	*0 (depleted)–125 psi (862 kPa)*
Pressure gradient	*0.22–0.33 psi/ft (5–7.5 kPa/m)*
Temperature	*72°F*
Geothermal gradient	*0.016°F/ft*
Drive	*Not known; possibly combination of solution gas and water*
Oil column thickness	*Highly variable*
Oil-water contact	*Highly variable*
Connate water	*Unknown*
Water salinity, TDS	*Unknown*
Resistivity of water	*Unknown*
Bulk volume water unknown (%)	*Unknown*

Transportation method and market for oil and gas:

Oil transportation by horse and wagon, truck, and other means to refineries in Toledo and Findlay; gas was marketed to local communities and vented to the atmosphere (flared)

LIMA-INDIANA

Elkhorn Ranch Field—U.S.A.
Williston Basin, North Dakota

WILLIAM D. DeMIS
Marathon Oil Company
Houston, Texas

FIELD CLASSIFICATION

BASIN: Williston
BASIN TYPE: Cratonic Sag
RESERVOIR ROCK TYPE: Dolomite
RESERVOIR ENVIRONMENT
   OF DEPOSITION: Tidal Flat to Shallow Marine

RESERVOIR AGE: Mississippian
PETROLEUM TYPE: Oil
TRAP TYPE: Anticlinal Nose and
   Hydrodynamics

LOCATION

The Elkhorn Ranch/Anderson Coulee area (which will be called simply Elkhorn Ranch field) is located in northern Billings County, North Dakota, in the south-central portion of the Williston basin (Figure 1). The field is part of the Mississippian Mission Canyon dolomite trend and is located at the northern end of the Billings Nose anticline. Elkhorn Ranch field produces from the Mississippian Mission Canyon and Mississippian/Devonian Bakken formations. Other significant Mission Canyon hydrocarbon accumulations of the region are in Rough Rider field, 5 mi (8 km) to the north, Little Knife field, 15 mi (24 km) to the east, and the Billings Nose complex, located 10 mi (16 km) to the south-southeast (Figure 2).

Total area of the field is approximately 10,800 ac (4374 ha) or 16.9 mi² (43.3 km²). Estimated primary recoverable reserves for the Mission Canyon reservoirs are 17.5 million bbl of oil (MMBO) and 23 BCFG. Elkhorn Ranch field has produced 15.5 MMBO and 21 BCFG from 70 Mission Canyon wells since the reservoir was discovered in 1974. Total field monthly production is now 75 MBO from 64 wells. Average well production is 220 MBO and 3 MMCFG. The average well has been producing for 6.8 years. Although the first Mission Canyon production was in 1974, most of the field was not developed until the 1980s. Seventy-two percent of the Mission Canyon wells in the field were completed after 1981.

HISTORY OF DISCOVERY

Elkhorn Ranch field exemplifies a field that has been rediscovered several times in its life. The field underwent three cycles of development as understanding of the nature of the trap was refined.

In the mid-1950s, Shell geologists were inspired by the very active Mississippian stratigraphic play underway in the Canadian portion of the Williston basin. They undertook a regional stratigraphic study of the Mississippian strata in south-central North Dakota to look for analogous traps. Using electric logs, well cuttings, and cores, they defined a stratigraphic play in the Mission Canyon Formation (Figure 3) consisting of porosity zones (Figure 4) that terminate updip in tight anhydritic facies. Using seismic data, a broad, regional anticline was mapped that they called the Medora nose (later to be known as the Billings Nose anticline), and a series of wells were drilled in the late 1950s and early 1960s, looking for these pinch-out traps across the anticline.

Their early attempt at defining a stratigraphic play is a classic example of the interplay of insightful, ground-breaking geology applied to a large, undrilled anticline—and bad luck. A dozen wells were drilled using a play concept that years later would be confirmed as basically correct for several of the large fields; and only one small, then marginally economic Mission Canyon field (Rough Rider) was discovered. The greater Billings Nose area today has on the order of 250 MMBO in place. All of the major oil fields of the Billings Nose area have at least one old Shell well offsetting them, if not drilled in them, and Elkhorn Ranch is no exception.

Elkhorn Ranch field was first "discovered" in 1961 when Shell Oil Company drilled the #41X-5-1 in Section 5 of T143N,R101W. This well was drilled to 13,018 ft (3970 m) in the Ordovician Red River Formation (Well #1, Figure 5). Two drill-stem tests (DSTs) were made in the Mission Canyon Formation. The first test was across the Sherwood and Mohall zones. The test had a strong blow and gas to the surface in 44 minutes. Pipe recovery was 94 ft (28.7 m) of gassy, sulfur-water cut mud and 745 ft (227 m) of highly oil, gas, and sulfur-water cut mud. The second DST recovered all water from the

369

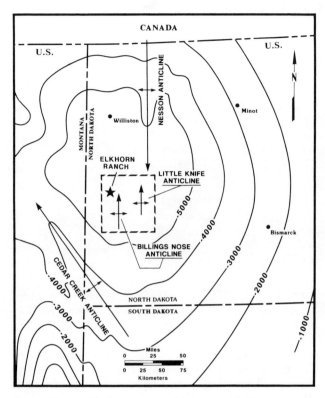

Figure 1. Location of the Williston basin and major structural features with Figure 2 located. Structure top Mississippian. Contour interval, 1000 ft (305 m).

PERIOD	GROUP			FORMATION /INTERVAL	
MISSISSIPPIAN		BIG SNOWY GROUP		OTTER	
				KIBBEY	
	MADISON GROUP	CHARLES FORMATION	INFORMAL INTERVALS	POPLAR	
				RATCLIFF	
		MISSION CANYON FORMATION		FROBISHER ALIDA	●
				TILSTON	
		LODGEPOLE FORMATION		BOTTINEAU	
DEVONIAN				BAKKEN	●
				THREE FORKS	●
				BIRDBEAR	●
				DUPEROW	●
				SOURIS RIVER	
				DAWSON BAY	
				PRAIRIE	
				WINNIPEGOSIS	
SILURIAN				INTERLAKE	
ORDOVICIAN	BIG HORN GROUP			STONEWALL	
				STONY MTN.	
				RED RIVER	● ☼
	WINNIPEG GROUP				
CAMBRIAN				DEADWOOD	

● **OIL PRODUCTION**
☼ **GAS PRODUCTION**

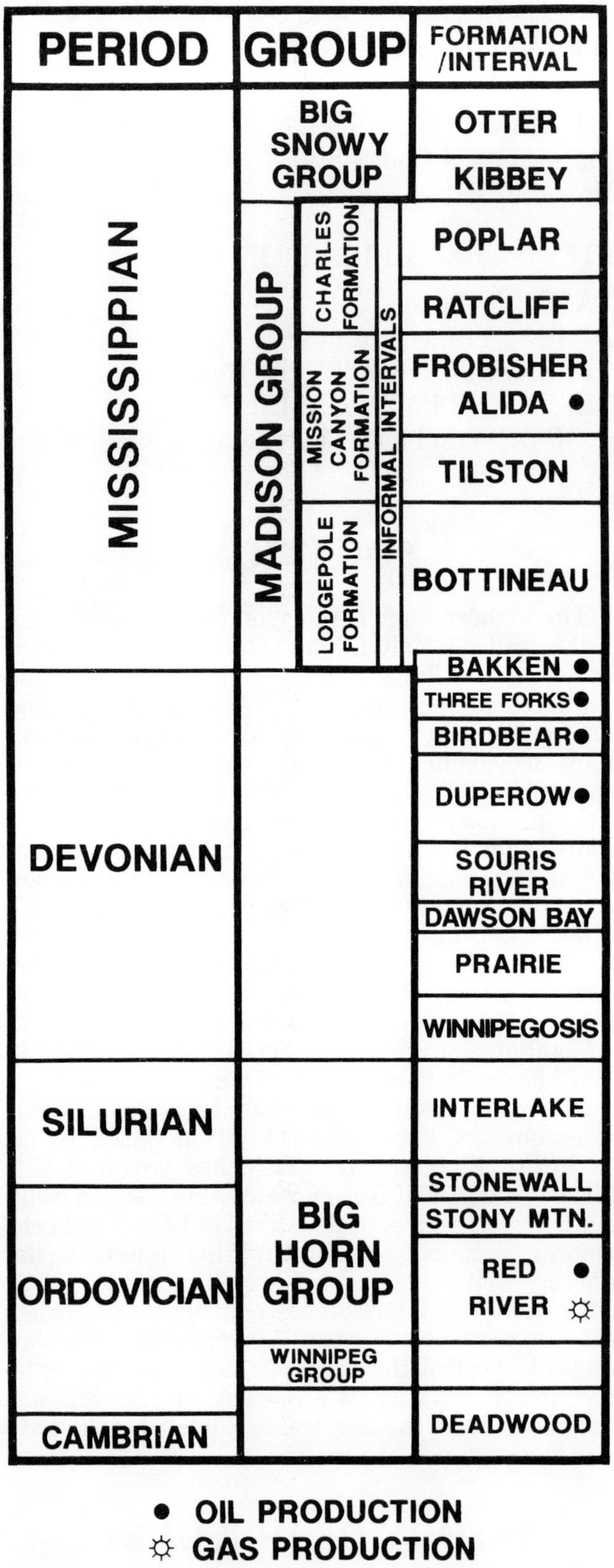

Figure 3. Stratigraphic column for pre-Pennsylvanian rocks with significant producing intervals in the area of Elkhorn Ranch field shown. (See Figure 4 for Mission Canyon Formation subdivisions.)

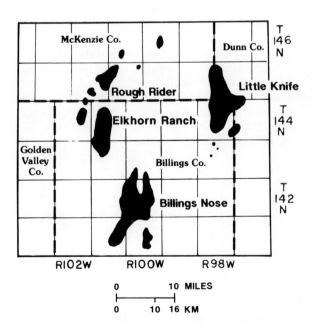

Figure 2. Location of Elkhorn Ranch field and major Mission Canyon oil fields in the immediate area.

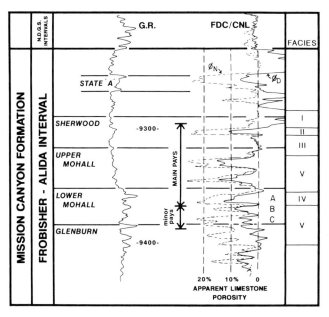

Figure 4. Type electric log, showing subdivisions within the Mission Canyon and porosity subdivisions used in this report and facies as defined by Petty (1988). See text for discussion. N.D.G.S., North Dakota Geological Survey.

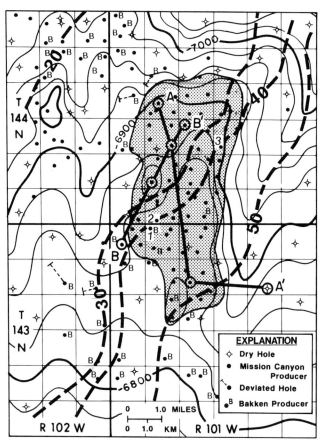

Figure 5. Mission Canyon structure, Elkhorn Ranch field area. Contour interval, 25 ft (7.6 m). Only Mission Canyon production at Elkhorn Ranch field is shaded. Dashed lines are net anhydrite isopachs (State "A" marker to base anhydrite); contour interval, 10 ft (3.1 m). Note that depositional facies, as defined by evaporite isopachs, strike at a low angle to the structure.

Glenburn zone. The well was completed in the fractured shale reservoir of the Mississippian/Devonian Bakken–Three Forks interval (Figure 3). Initial production was 136 BOPD. The well ultimately produced 50,832 bbl of oil and 20,830 bbl of water and was still making about 100 bbl of fluid per day when the casing collapsed in 1965. At the time, Shell management was becoming disillusioned with the area, and no offset wells were ever drilled. The well was plugged and abandoned.

For the next nine years, there was no further drilling activity in the area; however, at least one geologist had speculated about the possibility of significant oil occurring in this area. Bruno Hansen, past president of AAPG and a North Dakota native son, recounted that in the late 1960s, he came across the old Shell well on a hunting trip. A few feet of pipe had been left standing above the ground and somebody had shot the pipe with a high-powered rifle, puncturing the casing. A stain on the ground showed where a stream of oil had spewed out of the bullet hole. Perhaps Shell had overlooked something!

In 1974, Ted Zagurski, an ex-Shell geologist working at the Farmer Union Oil Company (also known as Cenex), proposed a "sure-bet" Bakken test to offset the original Shell well. Moreover, Ted had concluded that, based on calculated fluid volumes, the first DST of the Mission Canyon in the Shell well had probably recovered excessive quantities of mud as the result of mud filtration into the formation. The total volume of recovered drilling mud in the

pipe was greater than the annular volume between the drill-stem test packer and the bottom of the hole. Drilling mud had infiltrated into the reservoir, thereby making the recoveries of non-hydrocarbon fluids spuriously large. The large volume of mud recovered on the DST, Zagurski reasoned, masked a good oil show.

Elkhorn Ranch field was discovered the second time in 1974 when the Farmer's Union Oil Company drilled the #14-32 Federal in Sec. 32, T144N, R101W, about 0.25 mi (0.4 km) northeast from the original Shell well (Well #2, Figure 5). The well was drilled to total depth without a geologist or mud logger present, and pipe was ordered for the completion before the well reached total depth. The well was completed for 294 bbl of oil and 81 bbl of water per day from the Mission Canyon.

Following its second discovery, Elkhorn Ranch field was developed with little enthusiasm by several companies, the companies probably using a stratigraphic reservoir model. The tilted oil-water contact (OWC) was not yet recognized. Development was localized along the crest of the structure where it was thought most of the oil was located. A dry hole drilled in 1975 on the west side of the field in Sec. 31, T144N, R101W (Farmer's Union Central Exchange #14-31 Federal) had probably convinced operators that the OWC was flat at about the –6850 ft (2089 m) contour.

Elkhorn Ranch field was discovered for the third time in 1980, when the tilted OWC became apparent. Up to that time, two dozen wells had been completed in the crestal portion of the structure, mostly south of T144N, and the principal producing zones of the Mission Canyon were established. In late 1980, geophysicists at Koch Exploration Company mapped a small, seismically defined structure northeast of the field. It was thought to be separated from Elkhorn Ranch field by a structural low.

The Koch Exploration Company #13-22 Federal well was drilled in Sec. 22, T144N, R101W as an Ordovician Red River test to 13,183 ft (4021 m) (Well #3, Figure 5). The Red River and Duperow formations were not productive. The inferred intervening structural low did not exist; it was a velocity sag. The well was completed in the same Mission Canyon zones (Sherwood and upper Mohall) that were already productive on the crest of the structure. This well is 50 ft (15 m) structurally low and on the northeast side of the crest of the structure. A tilted oil column was obvious to operators, and in a few years the field was developed to roughly its present size in a frenzy of drilling driven by peaking oil prices of the early 1980s.

ANATOMY OF THE FIELD

Structure

The Williston basin encompasses approximately 250,000 mi² (647,500 km²) and is located in North Dakota, western Montana, southern Saskatchewan, and parts of South Dakota and Manitoba. It is underlain by rigid lithosphere and is classified as a cratonic basin (121) under the system of Balley and Snelson (1980).

The basin is characterized by gentle basinward dips and by a relatively uneventful tectonic history. During latest Cambrian time, the area was transgressed and the Deadwood Formation was deposited across irregular hills, but a basin shape was not established. At that time it was a large embayment of the western Cordilleran shelf. During the Middle Ordovician, the basin became a discrete depression and the basic shape of the basin persisted onward through Tertiary time (Gerhard et al., 1982).

Structural features of the basin appear to have been active episodically in the Phanerozoic and may have been the result of reactivation of pre-Phanerozoic faults (Gerhard et al., 1982). Gerhard et al. (1982) have proposed that left-lateral shearing was responsible for the formation of basement-rooted faults within the Williston basin. Movement of faults and structures of the basin appears to have occurred sporadically through Paleozoic and Mesozoic time.

Major episodes of movement on most of the structures appear to be in Late Devonian–Early Mississippian, Pennsylvanian (during the Ancestral Rocky Mountain orogenic event), and latest Cretaceous–early Tertiary during the Laramide (Gerhard et al., 1982). LeFever et al. (1987) demonstrated in a 55 township study comprising the Nesson anticline that major tectonic activity was in the latest Devonian–earliest Mississippian and that some areas had maximum uplift in the Pennsylvanian. However, they also noted that each of the nine subareas of their study had a history of movement independent of the others. Thus, any generalization about the timing of structural growth across the basin is a simplification.

Major structural features of the basin are the northwest-trending Cedar Creek anticline in the southwest portion of the basin and the south-trending Nesson anticline in the north-central basin (Figure 1). Structural features in the vicinity of Elkhorn Ranch field are the north-plunging Little Knife anticline and Billings Nose, a broad, north-plunging, low relief anticline. Elkhorn Ranch field is located north-northwest of the Billings Nose.

The field is located on a typical Mission Canyon structure, a low-relief anticline with crestal closure of about 10 ft (3 m). The asymmetric structure plunges north at about 0.5°. Dip of the east flank of the structure is about 1.5°, and dip of the west flank is about 1° to the west-northwest (Figure 5).

Stratigraphy

Sedimentary rocks of the Williston basin are up to 16,000 ft (4875 m) thick and range from uppermost Cambrian to Eocene. The pre-Pennsylvanian section is composed almost entirely of limestones and dolomites, with significant amounts of anhydrite and salt. The remainder of the Paleozoic, Mesozoic, and Tertiary section is mostly terrigenous clastics.

The Upper Cambrian Deadwood is a transgressive sandstone, followed by repeated series of carbonate to evaporite cycles representing transgression, sedimentation, and progradation until the Pennsylvanian. Sedimentation patterns changed in the Pennsylvanian to dominantly terrigenous clastics in response to the Ancestral Rocky Mountain tectonics (Gerhard et al., 1982).

Much of the Mississippian strata of the Williston basin belongs to the Madison Group (Figure 3). The Madison Group contains the vast majority of the oil and gas in the Williston basin. It has been variously (and differently) subdivided into formations, intervals, and beds. The North Dakota Geological Survey subdivides the Madison into five intervals (Carlson and LeFever, 1987); however, the term *Mission Canyon Formation* has been extensively used over the years for the middle part of the Madison Group and is so used here.

The Mission Canyon Formation is a series of carbonate shoaling-upward sequences that formed during a major regressive event. These sequences consist of open-marine, skeletal packstones that grade upward into subtidal dolomitized (porous), skeletal mudstones and wackestones. Sequences culminate with intertidal algal stromatolitic mudstones. Intertidal deposits grade laterally updip into supratidal facies infilled with generally nodular anhydrite (Altschuld and Kerr, 1982; Lindsey and Roth, 1982; Kupecz, 1984; Petty, 1988). These sequences are repeated several times in the upper Mission Canyon and form the succession of porous intervals at Elkhorn Ranch field. Individual sequences lack an evaporite facies except that during the last part of the major cycle, thick anhydrite was deposited.

All the cores in the field were studied, but the author did not come to any substantially different conclusions about the facies of the Mission Canyon than those presented by other workers (Altschuld and Kerr, 1982; Lindsey and Roth, 1982; Kupez, 1984; Petty, 1988).

Elkhorn Ranch field is a recently discovered field, and therefore most of the wells were logged with modern tools. The neutron-density suite of petrophysical logs allows easy identification of high density anhydrite which, when corroborated with sedimentary textures in cores, documents the extent of the sabkha/salina facies tract within the Mission Canyon. Isopachs of the Mission Canyon anhydrite delineate trends in the sabkha/salina facies and therefore time-equivalent rocks such as the subtidal mudstones that form the reservoir rocks. Trends of the Mission Canyon anhydrite isopach (State "A" marker to base anhydrite, Figure 4), derived from petrophysical logs, are superimposed on Figure 5. The Mission Canyon sabkha/salina facies strikes across the structure at a small angle with the structural axis.

The upper Mission Canyon is subdivided into intervals using the nomenclature of Elliot (1982). Three intervals are productive at Elkhorn Ranch field: lower Mohall, upper Mohall, and Sherwood. The lower Mohall is further subdivided into "A," "B," and "C" to reflect variations in the production. The "A" interval is the main pay in the lower Mohall. The "B" and "C" intervals are only productive in scattered places in association with the "A" interval production.

The facies defined by Petty (1988) are also shown on the type log (Figure 4). He has shown that six major facies occur in the Frobisher-Alida interval of the Mission Canyon Formation in south-central North Dakota. Five of these facies are present at Elkhorn Ranch field, and three are reservoir facies. The significant aspects of each facies in the Elkhorn Ranch area are listed below.

Facies I is composed of anhydrite, stromatolitic mudstone, and boundstone. It is easily identified on modern neutron-density petrophysical logs by the low-density anhydrite and is interpreted to represent a mosaic of sabkha/salina depositional environments. Facies II is a burrowed mudstone-wackestone with stromatolitic mudstone that was deposited in lagoons just downdip of the supratidal facies. This facies comprises the Sherwood interval reservoir at Elkhorn Ranch field. Facies III rocks are peloidal pisolitic-intraclastic packstones to peloidal-oolitic-skeletal grainstones that were deposited in shallow, subtidal shoals. This facies is tight at Elkhorn Ranch field and can sometimes form a local seal. Facies IV rocks are burrowed mudstones interpreted to have been deposited in a shallow, restricted marine environment. These sediments were extensively dolomitized, forming secondary intercrystalline porosity. Facies IV is the principal reservoir facies at Elkhorn Ranch field. Facies V is a burrowed skeletal wackestone or mudstone deposited in an open-marine environment. This facies has also undergone extensive dolomitization and is also an important reservoir facies. Facies VI consists of skeletal grainstones deposited in an open-marine environment. This is a minor facies at Elkhorn Ranch and is not a reservoir.

Cross sections A–A' and B–B' (Figure 6) show the Mission Canyon stratigraphy as defined by electric logs. Cross section A–A' is drawn parallel to depositional dip and shows the overall regressive nature of the upper Mission Canyon. Individual porosity zones grade updip into tight carbonate or anhydrite, a configuration that can be misinterpreted as creating a stratigraphic trap.

Cross section B–B' (Figure 6) is drawn parallel to depositional strike as determined from anhydrite isopach trends. Note that there is little change in the facies in this view, based on electric log response. This strike section corroborates the observations derived from the anhydrite isopachs on Figure 5: the facies trend southwest across the structure at a low angle to the structural axis.

The structurally highest well on cross section B–B', Nucorp 6-1 Federal, tested the Sherwood interval and recovered 280 bbl of mud-cut salt water. A test of the porous part of the upper Mohall also recovered a high percentage of water and mud. The Tenneco 1-29 Hamilton well was completed in these two zones, but with a high percentage of water. Successive wells to the north on this cross section are completed in successively lower zones, even though they are downdip, which indicates that the entire oil column is tilted to the northeast.

TRAP

Elkhorn Ranch field is a hydrodynamically trapped oil accumulation. An apparently tilted oil-water contact (OWC) can be a function of either changes in reservoir quality or of hydrodynamics (Jennings,

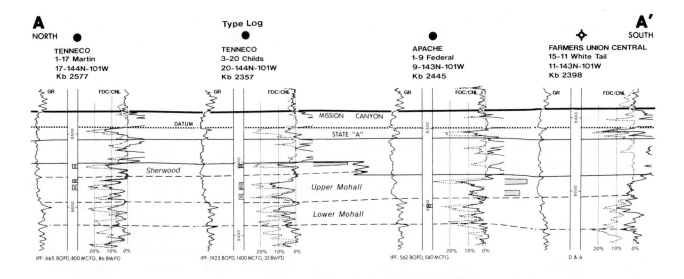

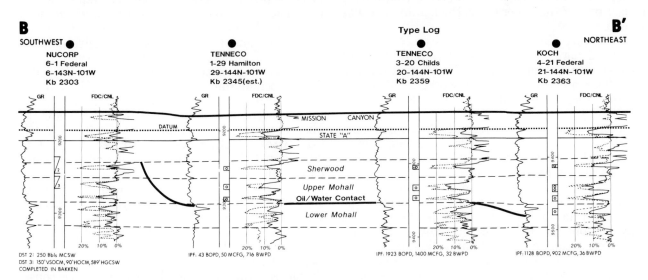

Figure 6. Cross sections across Elkhorn Ranch field. The locations of the cross sections are shown on Figure 5. Stipple pattern shows porosity pinch-out. Cross section A-A' drawn parallel to depositional dip shows porosities pinching out updip into tight carbonate and anhydrite. Cross section B-B' drawn parallel to depositional strike shows very little facies change.

1987). One may argue that the apparent tilt to the OWC at Elkhorn Ranch field is merely an artifact of a judiciously drawn cross section and changes in reservoir quality. The effects of changes in reservoir quality and hydrodynamics can be distinguished by mapping each productive unit in Elkhorn Ranch field separately.

Figures 7, 8, and 9 show the distribution of Mission Canyon hydrocarbon production for each respective zone as determined from perforations or drill-stem tests. The effective tight line of each productive interval is also superimposed on the structure map. Maps of the lower and upper Mohall production show dramatically that the oil column is tilted off the structure and that the porosity is "open" up the axis of the structure. The "A" zone of the lower Mohall

(Figure 7) is uniformly porous across the field, yet production is located on the east side only, far downdip to the north and northeast. The "tight" zone in the upper Mohall (Figure 8) could trap oil on the east side of the field, but oil in the north part of the field should drain out updip and out of the structure.

Even production from the Sherwood porosity, which pinches out across the structure, cannot be explained by a stratigraphic trap under hydrostatic conditions. The oil should migrate updip and out of the structure to the southwest (Figure 9).

Viewed in total, the productive limits of each of the zones show a single oil column tilted about 25 ft/mi (4.7 m/km) to the northeast. Note that the western limit of production for each successively

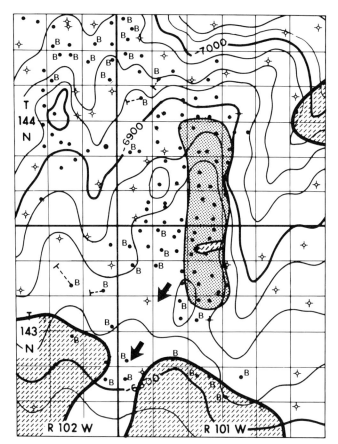

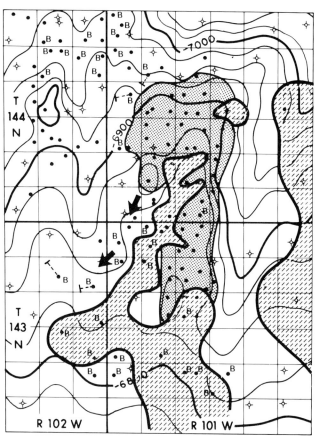

Figure 7. Map of lower Mohall "A" porosity production (shaded) superimposed on the Mission Canyon structure with tight regions indicated by diagonal dash pattern (from Figure 12). Note that production is tilted to the east and down the anticline to the north. Arrows show potential leak points if the system were hydrostatic. Scales and other symbols same as Figure 5.

Figure 8. Map of upper Mohall porosity production (shaded) superimposed on Mission Canyon structure, with tight region indicated by diagonal dash pattern (from Figure 13). The tight region might trap hydrocarbons on the east side of the field, but oil in the north end of the field would leak out (arrows) under hydrostatic conditions. Scales and symbols same as Figure 5.

lower porosity zone is shifted to the east-northeast, a confirmation in three dimensions of the tilted oil column shown on cross section B–B' (Figure 6).

A map of the actual OWC (Figure 10) is based on DSTs and well completions. In rocks with low permeability, the transition from oil-free water to water-free oil is gradational (Arps, 1964), so the map is only an approximation of the oil-water contact. Capillary pressure data from cores and pressure data could better resolve the OWC, but this information is not available. These facts, compounded by the lack of a vertically continuous reservoir, makes picking the actual OWC difficult.

Some generalizations about the tilted OWC can be made. The OWC is broadly convex and tilts to the east-northeast. Dip of the contact varies, but appears to be about 25 to 35 ft per mile (5–7 m/km). The field appears to have one common oil column.

Reservoir

For this study, the porous zones within each interval in the upper Mission Canyon were mapped separately. The facies and petrophysical characteristics and the criteria for determining the appropriate porosity cutoff for each zone are outlined below. The interested reader is referred to the excellent work by Petty (1988) for a more detailed discussion of Mission Canyon rock properties.

The lower Mohall A porosity zone at Elkhorn Ranch field is composed of burrowed skeletal mudstones with rare skeletal wackestones. Broken crinoid parts and gastropod fragments are the most common grains. Burrowing of original sediments is common. Secondary dolomitization is pervasive in this facies, but like all the reservoir facies in this part of the Williston basin, it is fabric selective.

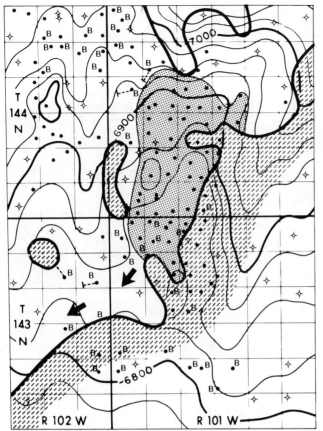

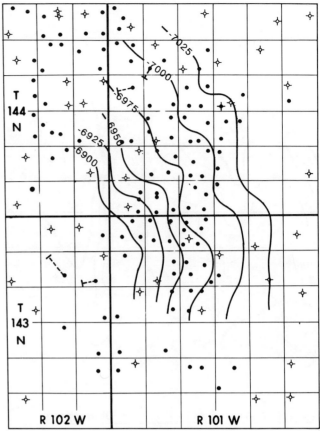

Figure 9. Map of Sherwood porosity production (shaded) superimposed on Mission Canyon structure map, with tight region, diagonal dash pattern (from Figure 14). The configuration of the structure cannot explain the accumulation. Oil would leak out (arrows) under hydrostatic conditions. Scales and symbols same as Figure 5.

Figure 10. Map of the oil-water contact showing tilt to the east-northeast. Contour interval, 25 ft (7.5 m).

Dolomitization generally creates a porosity inversion, with the least porous mudstones becoming the most porous dolomites. The mudstones are more dolomitized than the skeletal grainstones. The uniformity and fine size of the original mud leads to the formation of dolomite crystals that are all about 25 microns in size, and porosity is secondary intercrystalline (Petty, 1988).

The upper Mohall porosity zone at Elkhorn Ranch field is composed of burrowed skeletal wackestones to grainstones. Crinoid-brachiopod wackestone is the dominant lithology with minor mudstone. Extensive dolomitization produced secondary intercrystalline porosity. Some leaching of skeletal fragments also produced fossil-moldic porosity where it was not occluded by anhydrite. Dolomite crystals range from about 13 to 26 microns (Petty, 1988).

A plot of porosity versus permeability for the upper and lower Mohall porosity zones is based on all cores cut through these zones (Figure 11). These data show a linear relation between porosity and permeability above about 12% porosity. Most rocks with less than

12% porosity have very little permeability (<1.0 md). Rocks with less than 12% porosity are in what is termed "the waste zone" of the reservoir (Arps, 1964). Even though such porosity zones may be in the oil column, they will only produce water or small volumes of oil and water.

Pore-throat sorting also affects the ability of a reservoir to produce oil (Jennings, 1987), but no mercury injection profile data are available to determine the sorting of the pore throats. However, empirical observations within the field substantiate a minimum of 12% porosity limit to oil production. Rocks with less than 12% porosity in the lower Mohall "A" and upper Mohall are not capable of production, even where they are in the oil column.

Figure 12 shows an isopach of the lower Mohall "A" zone with porosity 12% or greater. This zone is porous across the field. The "A" porosity zone pinches out 15 mi (24 km) to the south at Big Stick field (Altschuld and Kerr, 1982, their Figure 16; Kupecz, 1984; Mitsdarffer, 1985).

Figure 13 shows the isopach of the upper Mohall porosity zone with porosity of 12% or greater. This zone has a peculiar "tight" region that extends across the field, parallel to the structure. Core-to-log calibrations indicate that the "tight" region corre-

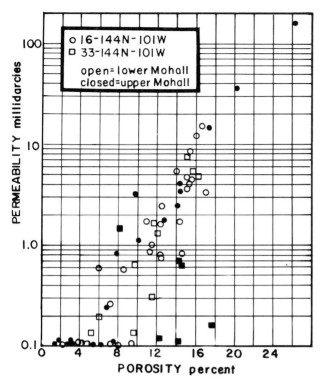

Figure 11. Relationship of porosity to permeability in the upper and lower Mohall intervals based on cores from Elkhorn Ranch field. Permeability generally becomes linear with respect to porosity above about 10 to 12%.

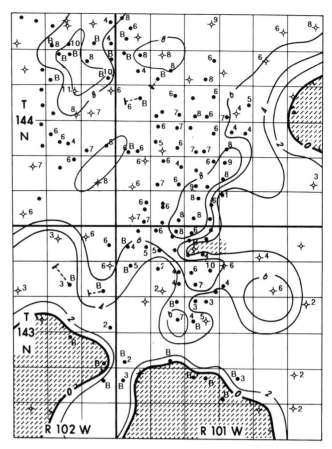

Figure 12. Isopach map of the lower Mohall "A" porosity ≥ 12%. Contour interval, 2 ft. Diagonal dash pattern is effective tight region. Note that porosity does not pinch out near the field. Scales and symbols same as Figure 5.

sponds to a skeletal grainstone facies with reduced porosity and permeability and a higher percentage of limestone. Rocks in this zone are porous but not capable of significant oil production. The "tight" region is merely an artifact of a high cutoff: a >6% porosity isopach map would not show the "tight" region. At Billings Nose field the interval isopach from the top of the Mississippian to the base of the Bakken shows a "thin" (Kupecz, 1984), and this might imply that the Billings Nose was high during Mississippian time. Although not enough deep penetrations are available to prove this, Elkhorn Ranch field also might have been a paleohigh. Therefore, the "tight" region at Elkhorn Ranch field might be the result of a subtle winnowing of muds along the crest of a paleohigh and deposition of grainstones that are less susceptible to dolomitization.

The Sherwood porosity zone is composed of burrowed mudstones and wackestones grading to burrowed stromatolites and to layered stromatolites, which grade updip directly into the evaporatic facies (see cross section A-A', Figure 6). Rocks of the Sherwood zone were deposited in shallow lagoons just downdip of the supratidal facies. This zone is locally infilled with anhydrite that is generally nodular and poikilotopic. Porosity is intercrystalline, with some fossil-moldic porosity formed by leaching

of calispheres. Average dolomite crystal size is 14 microns (Petty, 1988).

Only one core is available for the Sherwood porosity zone. The data are summarized in Table 1. These data show that there is a very significant "thin-bed" effect on the electric logs. On the logs, the zone appears to be 3 ft thick with 13% porosity, but core-derived data show higher porosity, up to 22%, and 4 ft of porous rock. Owing to the large discrepancy between the core and log-derived porosities, a mappable core-derived porosity cutoff cannot be established. An empirical cutoff of 8% was established by review of the field production. A porosity isopach map was constructed using this cutoff with the understanding that the true porosity and permeability is higher due to the "thin bed" effect.

The Sherwood zone isopach map (Figure 14) shows a southwest trend roughly parallel to the anhydrite isopach. This zone does pinch out across the plunge of the structure but trends at such a low angle that it should not hold oil.

Neither Figure 12 nor 13 shows an effective pinch-out that could trap hydrocarbons. In the case of the

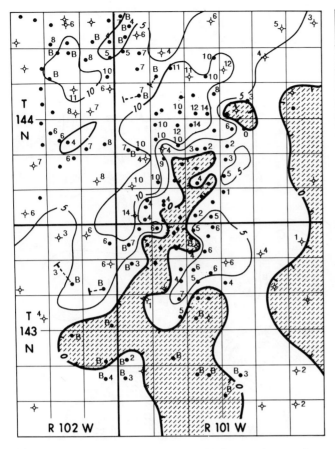

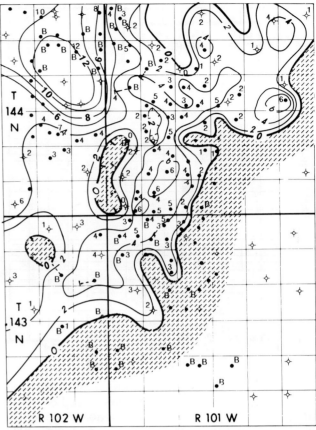

Figure 13. Isopach of upper Mohall porosity ≥ 12%. Contour interval, 5 ft. Diagonal dash pattern is effective tight region. Scales and symbols same as Figure 5.

Figure 14. Isopach of Sherwood porosity ≥ 8%. Contour interval, 2 ft. Diagonal dash pattern is tight region. Note that porosity trends to the southwest, roughly parallel to anhydrite contours. Scales and symbols same as Figure 5.

Table 1. Log- and core-derived porosities and core-derived permeabilities of Sherwood zone from Tenneco 1-33 USA-UVI well.

Depth (corrected)	Porosity (%)		Permeability (md)
	Log	Core	
9297	7.5	20.4	0.75
9298	5.25	0.5	8.5
9299	3.5	4.3	0.17
9300	13.5	19.8	2.8
9301	13.0	16.5	9.9
9302	7.5	22.8	27.0

lower Mohall "A," the actual facies change to tight evaporites is 15 mi (24 km) to the south. Although the Sherwood porosity zone apparently does pinch out in the vicinity of the field, the geometry of the porosity cutoff and the structure cannot result in oil entrapment under hydrostatic conditions; hydrodynamic trapping appears to be the trap on the field.

Hydrodynamics

Hydrodynamic theory has been discussed by Hubbard (1953) and refined by Berg (1975). The theory can be applied to the trap at Elkhorn Ranch field.

A map of the apparent formation water resistivity (R_{wa}) is shown in Figure 15. The data are for the lower Glenburn interval below the production at Elkhorn Ranch, Rough Rider, and Billings Nose fields. The values were derived by setting the Archie equation equal to 1 (assuming 100% water saturation) and solving for the resistivity of the water. This map shows that apparent resistivity of the formation water varies across the field range from 0.058 ohm-m to less than 0.011 ohm-m and implies that a plume of fresher waters is invading the Mission Canyon from the southwest.

A map of the salinities of recovered formation water from drill-stem tests taken in the Mission Canyon Formation around Elkhorn Ranch field is shown in Figure 16 (data from Table 2). No distinction was made as to the stratigraphic location of the sample within the Mission Canyon Formation. In general, there is a wide range in the data. Salinities range by more than 50,000 ppm within one township, and by more than 50,000 ppm in one well. The variation

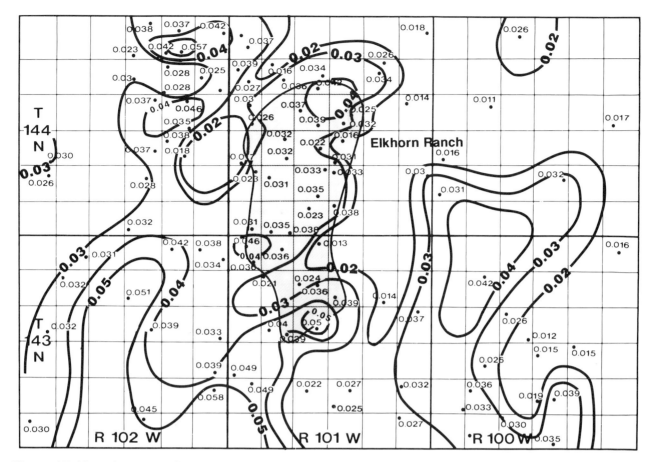

Figure 15. Map of apparent formation water resistivity for the lower Glenburn interval. Note the sharp contrast in resistivities across Elkhorn Ranch field. Contour interval, 0.01 ohm-m.

in the data is ascribed to lateral discontinuity between and heterogeneity within Mission Canyon porosities. Overall there is a trend in the data from lower salinity in the southwest to higher salinity in the northeast, and the salinity data corroborate the apparent water resistivity map. Fresher water is invading the Mission Canyon from the southwest, and there is a sharp contrast in water salinity across the field. The salient of low salinity in T143N, R102W is interpreted to indicate fresher water invasion along the more interconnected depositional strike orientation of the porosities.

DST pressure data were compiled for the region around the field and are shown in Table 2 (Figure 17). Recorded pressures were extrapolated to a true pressure using Horner plot analysis. The pressure data show a wide range of values even when the data were filtered for bad tests, as well as for tests that showed draw-down near the field. However, there is an overall gradient from higher pressures in the southwest to lower pressures in the northeast. From these data, a map of the potentiometric surface was constructed using a constant pressure gradient of 0.433 psi/ft and the equations described in Hubbard (1953).

This map shows that the potentiometric surface is inclined 20 ft/mi (3.8 m/km) in the region of

Elkhorn Ranch field. Using subsurface oil and water densities of 0.625 g/cm[3] and 1.028 g/cm[3], respectively, the tilt amplification is 2.55. The calculated tilt of the OWC is 50 ft/mi (9.5 m/km). This is twice the observed tilt of 25 ft/mi (4.7 m/km).

Tilt of the oil column at Elkhorn Ranch is approximately the same amount and direction as that derived for Billings Nose (Berg and Mitsdarffer, 1986) and Knutson fields (Bogle and Hanson, 1987). Mitsdarffer (1985) shows that there is a plume of fresher water invading the Mission Canyon south and west of the Billings Nose field, based on the salinity of recovered waters from DSTs and maps of apparent water resistivity. Mitsdarffer (1985) also shows the tilt of the oil column at Billings Nose is 25 ft/mi. Berg and Mitsdarffer (1986) show that the potentiometric surface is inclined to the northeast at Billings Nose field and that the calculated tilt of the oil column is about five times greater than the observed oil column tilt. Mitsdarffer (1985) concluded that the oil at the Billings Nose field was originally stratigraphically trapped and later tilted under a regime of lower potentiometric gradient. The hydrocarbons have not yet equilibrated to the higher tilt of the present day. The same explanation might be true for the discrepancy between the observed and calculated tilt at Elkhorn Ranch field.

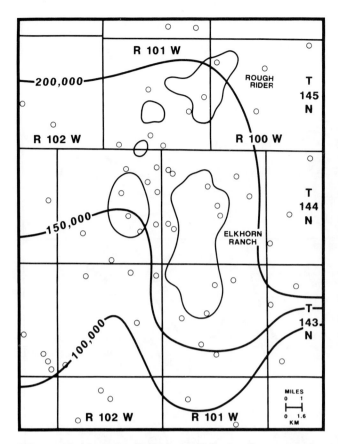

Figure 16. Map of salinity data of Mission Canyon water recovered from drill-stem tests showing strong change in salinity across the structure from southwest to northeast. Contour interval, 50,000 ppm. Circles are data points in Table 2.

Bogle and Hanson (1987) showed that Knutson field has a tilted oil column. Based on material balance and water production histories, they also show that the Mission Canyon waters are active and providing a water drive to the field.

Downey (1984) has shown that the Mission Canyon aquifer is active across the northern plains and across the Williston basin. In the Billings County portion of the Williston basin, Downey shows that the potentiometric surface is tilted to the east. Both Mitsdarffer (1985) and this study document that the potentiometric surface is inclined to the northeast. The small difference in orientation is probably due to the scale of the maps and resolution of the data.

Changes in reservoir quality, that is, in the capillary properties of reservoir rock, also can create an apparent tilt to an oil column. An alternative interpretation for the unique oil production at the Elkhorn Ranch field is that it is the result of subtle and unmappable changes in pore throat sorting and geometry in the reservoir rocks, similar to the traps reported by Schowalter and Hess (1982). Such an explanation for Elkhorn Ranch field is improbable because: (1) the apparent tilt of hydrocarbon production for each porosity zone in the field is

approximately the same amount and direction; (2) each sucessively lower zone in the field is productive farther to the northeast, as would be predicted with a single, tilted oil column; (3) tilt of the oil column at the Elkhorn Ranch field is similar to the tilt reported for Billings Nose and Knutson fields; (4) observed oil column tilt is the same direction and approximately the same amount as that predicted by the potentiometric map for both Billings Nose and Elkhorn Ranch fields; and (5) the local potentiometric surface calculated by Mitsdarffer (1985) and again by the author is tilted approximately the same amount and direction as the regional potentiometric surface calculated by Downey (1984). In light of these independent data, it is very unlikely that the similar tilts reported for Billings Nose, Elkhorn Ranch, and Knutson fields are a chance artifact of capillary changes.

One of the implications of this research is that hydrodynamic flow must have occurred during oil migration. The time of maximum oil maturation and migration is early Tertiary (Dembicki and Prickle, 1985). Berg and Mitsdarffer (1986) conclude that hydrodynamics only assisted the stratigraphic trapping ability of the facies change and accounts for a thicker than predicted oil column than would occur if the trap were only stratigraphic. On the basis of the data presented herein, it would appear that a hydrodynamic regime existed at the time of oil migration. If oil migration occurred at Elkhorn Ranch field under hydrostatic conditions, most of the oil would have migrated through the Elkhorn Ranch structure because there is no effective stratigraphic or structural trap for over half of the oil.

Source Rocks

The source for most of the Mission Canyon oils is believed to be the Bakken Formation (Price et al., 1984; Webster, 1984; Dow, 1974) (Figure 3). The Bakken Formation is a black, organic-rich, oil-prone shale that lies at about 10,600 ft (3230 m) depth at Elkhorn Ranch field. It is composed of two shale members and a middle siltstone member. Thickness of the formation ranges up to 145 ft (44 m) in western Mountrail County, North Dakota, decreasing to a knife edge at its erosional limit elsewhere. Total thickness of the two shale members ranges from 10 ft (3 m) to 60 ft (18 m) in the east-central portion of the basin, just east of the Nesson anticline. Percent organic carbon values (TOC) range from over 22% in Saskatchewan to under 2% near the erosional/depositional limit in Montana (Dembicki and Prickle, 1985). In the Elkhorn Ranch area, average TOC is about 10% and has a vitrinite reflectance value (R_o) of about 1.0, showing that the source rock is well into the oil generation window (Dembicki and Prickle, 1985).

Dow (1974) showed that Mississippian oils of the central Williston basin can be correlated to the Mississippian–Devonian Bakken Formation shale. While there has been no direct typing of the produced

Table 2. Salinities from drill-stem tests of Mission Canyon Formation.

Operator	Well No.	Section	Salinities (ppm)	K. B. Elevation (ft)	Interval (ft)	Shut-in Pressure (psi)
T142N,R101W						
Conoco	8-1	8	148,000	2523	9284-9334	4411
Conoco	15-1	14	65,000	—	9309-9377	—
T142N,R102W						
Diamond Shamrock	34-4	4	80,000	2556	9170-9229	4330
			155,000	4402	9390-9504	4402
Diamond Shamrock	21-9	9	190,000	—	9395-9427	—
Diamond Shamrock	11-10	10	50,000	—	9365-9373	—
			60,000	2338	9433-9441	—
Coastal	1-J	29	—	2641	9435-9469	—
T142N,R103W						
Shell	24-31	24	68,000	—	9498-9594	—
T143N,R100W						
Al Aquitaine	1-8	8	200,000	2461	9410-9450	2645
			200,000	2461	9452-9490	2645
Gulf	1-18-1A	18	—	2750	9742-9822	4533
Coastal	Y-23-1	23	140,000	—	9582-9636	—
Tenneco	G-1-30	30	—	2612	9489-9571	4440
T143N,R101W						
Samson	1-2	2	160,000	2373	9438-9464	4450
Cenex	12-10	10	165,000	—	9432-9445	—
Apache	4-16	16	130,000	—	9477-9495	—
Chambers	3-19	19	210,000	2375	9300-9369	4408
Chambers	2-27	27	131,000	2480	9365-9425	4435
Chambers	1-28	28	160,000	2416	9244-9340	4438
T143N,R102W						
Cenex	5-1	1	96,000	—	9237-9244	—
Cenex	6-2	2	100,000	2278	9188-9255	4391
			110,000		9253-9280	
Apache	1-5	5	160,000	2155	9092-9142	4390
Al Aquitaine	1	23	107,000	2339	9230-9337	4502
Al Aquitaine	2-31	31	146,000	—	9180-9203	—
T143N,R103W						
Grace	32-22	22	141,000	2471	9295-9331	4338
Diamond Shamrock	24-25	25	128,000	2595	9395-9415	4429
Gas Production	36-1	36	140,000	2524	9334-9360	4451
Gas Production	2	36	—	2470	9267-9283	4352
T144N,R100W						
Patrick	1-4	4	190,000	2472	9818-9864	4512
Amoco	1	20	200,000	2558	9540-9608	4482
Koch	13-30	30	200,000	2615	9599-9633	4422
Jordan	1-1	36	200,000	2592	9730-9763	4509
T144N,R101W						
Florida	7-2	7	142,000	—	9372-9396	—
Florida	1-F	7	142,000	—	9322-9350	—
Cenex	15-9	9	95,000	—	9334-9350	—
Koch	6-11	11	145,000	2328	9412-9441	4412
Amoco	13-1	13	187,000	—	9330-9370	—
Apache	15-13	15	146,000	—	9373-9385	—
Florida	19-2	19	172,000	—	9222-9246	—
Tenneco	1-30	30	150,000	—	9180-9235	—
T144N,R102W						
MGF	44-1	1	—	2308	9325-9345	4358
Apache	2-5	2	120,000	—	9440-9486	

381

Table 2. Continued

Operator	Well No.	Section	Salinities (ppm)	K. B. Elevation (ft)	Interval (ft)	Shut-in Pressure (psi)
Supron	1-F	10	128,000	—	9544-9588	—
Unit Drilling	11-12	11	125,000	—	9570-9590	—
Florida	13-1	13	180,000	—	9654-9685	—
Apache	16-3	16	132,000	—	9112-9148	—
Apache	2-23	23	140,000	—	9136-9156	—
Petroleum Inc.	1	24	110,000	—	9260-9297	—
Nance Petroleum	1-26	26	26,000	—	9392-9407	—
			120,000	—	9393-9428	—
Axem	1-29	29	90,000	—	9379-9418	—
Apache	14-34	34	65,000	—	9334-9380	—
T144N,R103W						
Coastal	1-13	13	175,000	—	9420-9481	—
Terra	2-18	18	181,000	—	9200-9300	—
T145N,R100W						
Amoco	1	1		2442	9679-9687	4519
Belco	2-1	1	172,000	2445	9633-9712	4390
Belco	3-5	7	200,000	—	9790-9806	—
Meridian	13-10	10	190,000	—	9470-9523	—
Gulf	1-21-30	21	200,000	—	9550-9617	—
T145N,R101W						
Belco	1-16	16	167,000	2424	9520-9556	—
Koch	16-23	23	215,000	—	9426-9452	—
Milestone	44-23	23	190,000	—	9528-9578	—
Union	24-1	24	170,000	2441	9540-9596	—
Sage	44-31	31	200,000	—	9420-9461	—
Milestone	33-33	33	172,000	—	9160-9230	—
Belco	14-34	34	171,000	—	9268-9306	—
T145N,R102W						
Milestone	34-19	19	178,000	2655	9652-9742	4433
T146N,R100W						
Pennzoil	28-14	28	215,000	—	9711-9800	—
T146N,R101W						
Basic E.S.	1-34	34	200,000+	2171	9336-9364	4471
Belco	2-36	36	130,000	2256	9458-9490	4498

oil in Elkhorn Ranch field to this source rock, it overlies one of the most mature regions of the Bakken in the Williston basin (Price et al., 1987; Dembicki and Prickle, 1985), and the Bakken shale itself is a fractured shale reservoir in this area.

Maturation of the Bakken shale began in the Late Cretaceous (Webster, 1984) and reached a maximum in late Eocene (40 m.y.) in the northern Billings County area (Dembecki and Prickle, 1985, their Figure 14). Oil expulsion was enhanced by fluid overpressuring from hydrocarbon generation, which created fractures in the Bakken Formation (Meissner, 1978). Oil migrated vertically through microfractures until it reached the evaporite seal of the Mission Canyon anhydrite (Dow, 1974).

EXPLORATION CONCEPTS

Incorporation of hydrodynamic concepts into the Mission Canyon play, even as only a modifier of traditional play concepts, does have significant implications for exploration and production geologists. First, primary recoveries of hydrocarbons are much higher with a strong water drive than with a gas-depletion recovery factor. Second, exploration prospects need not demonstrate a porosity pinch-out that cuts across an anticlinal fold axis at 90° to be assured of hydrocarbon trapping. Hydrodynamic flow can provide an assist to the pinch-out play. Third, production prospects can be proposed that are not possible with horizontal oil-water contacts. Downdip

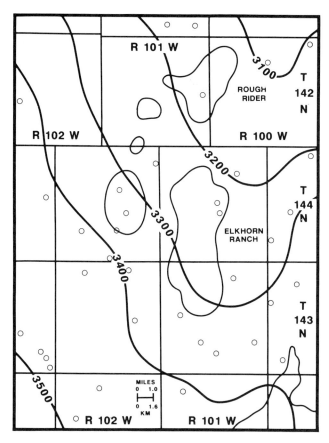

Figure 17. Map of potentiometric surface across Elkhorn Ranch field showing tilt to the northeast. Contour interval, 100 ft. Circles are data points in Table 2.

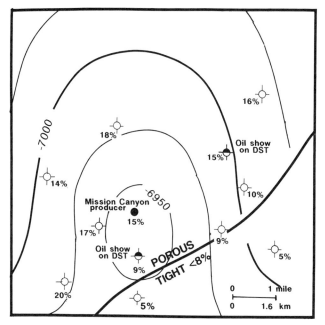

Figure 18. Hypothetical map of Mission Canyon structure and producing wells with porosity values for one producing horizon next to wells. Using an 8% porosity cutoff and assuming a hydrostatic system, the relationship between production, structure, and hydrocarbon shows makes no sense.

offsets on the northeast side of producing Mission Canyon wells in areas where the potentiometric surface is tilted might offer low-risk development prospects.

This paper also demonstrates that for each Mission Canyon porosity zone, a unique porosity value is required for effective permeability. The Mohall and Sherwood zones each have their own effective limit, which may be much higher than a "traditional" 6% or 8% porosity commonly used in carbonates. Stratigraphic prospects that call upon 6% porosity as the trap and 9% porosity as the reservoir will only define "the waste zone" of the reservoir (Figures 18 and 19).

ACKNOWLEDGMENTS

This paper is based on research initiated at Pennzoil Exploration and Production Campany. I would like to thank Pennzoil for permission to publish the ideas developed by this research. James Clement of Shell Oil Company, Dale Holyoak of Koch Exploration Company, Ted Zagurski, and Bruno Hanson provided colorful stories of the history of

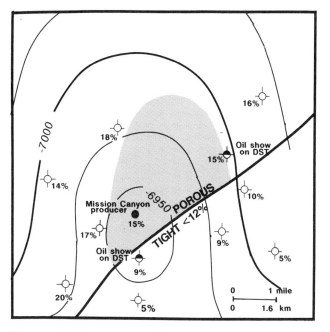

Figure 19. Same map as Figure 18, but instead a 12% porosity cutoff is used and a tilt of 25 ft/mi (4.7 m/km) is applied to the oil column. The trap and areal extent of the hydrocarbon accumulation are now apparent, and additional development wells are possible.

development of the area. Paul D. Hess made many helpful changes to the manuscript. Mary K. Nelis and Tim T. Schowalter reviewed an earlier version of this paper. Ted Beaumont assisted by encouragement of the writing of the paper, by his patience during its progress, and by his many suggestions for its improvement. Marathon Oil Company generously assisted with drafting the figures.

REFERENCES CITED

Altschuld, N., and S. D. Kerr, Jr., 1982, Mission Canyon and Duperow reservoirs of the Billings Nose, Billings County, North Dakota, *in* J. E. Christopher and J. Kaldi, eds., Fourth International Williston Basin Symposium: Saskatchewan Geological Society Special Publication 6, p. 103–112.

Arps, J. J., 1964, Engineering concepts useful in oil finding: American Association of Petroleum Geologists Bulletin, v. 48, p. 157–165.

Bally, A. W., and S. Snelson, 1980, Realms of subsidence, *in* Facts and principles of world petroleum occurrence: Canadian Society of Petroleum Geologists Memoir 6, p. 9–94.

Berg, R. R., 1975, Capillary pressure in stratigraphic traps: American Association of Petroleum Geologists Bulletin, v. 59, p. 939–956.

Berg, R. R., and A. R. Mitsdarffer, 1986, Effects of hydrodynamic flow on carbonate stratigraphic traps, Mission Canyon Formation, Billings Nose fields, North Dakota (abs.): American Association of Petroleum Geologists Bulletin, v. 70, p. 564.

Bogle, R. W., and W. B. Hansen, 1987, Knutson field and its relationship to the Mission Canyon oil play, south-central Williston Basin, *in* C. G. Carlson and J. E. Christopher, eds., Fifth International Williston Basin Symposium: Saskatchewan Geological Society Special Publication 9, p. 242–252.

Carlson, C. G., and J. A. LeFever, 1987, The Madison, a nomenclature review with a look to the future, *in* C. G. Carlson and J. E. Christopher, eds., Fifth International Williston Basin Symposium: Saskatchewan Geological Society Special Publication 9, p. 77–82.

Dembicki, H., Jr., and R. L. Prickle, 1985, Regional source rock mapping using potential rating index: American Association of Petroleum Geologists Bulletin, v. 69, n. 4, p. 567–581.

Dow, W. G., 1974, Application of oil-correlation and source rock data to exploration in Williston Basin: American Association of Petroleum Geologists Bulletin, v. 58, n. 7, p. 1253–1262.

Downey, J. S., 1984, Geology and hydrology of the Madison Limestone and associated rocks in parts of Montana, Nebraska, North Dakota, South Dakota, and Wyoming: U.S. Geological Survey Professional Paper 1273-G, 152 p.

Elliot, T. L, 1982, Carbonate facies, depositional cycles, and the development of secondary porosity during burial diagenesis:

Mission Canyon Formation, Haas Field, North Dakota, *in* J. E. Christopher and J. Kaldi, eds., Fourth International Williston Basin Symposium: Saskatchewan Geological Society Special Publication 6, p. 131–151.

Gerhard, L. C., S. B. Anderson, J. A. LeFever, and C. G. Carlson, 1982, Geological development, origin, and energy and mineral resources of Williston Basin, North Dakota: American Association of Petroleum Geologists Bulletin, v. 66, p. 989–1020.

Hubbard, M. K., 1953, Entrapment of petroleum under hydrodynamic conditions: American Association of Petroleum Geologists Bulletin, v. 37, p. 1954–2026.

Jennings, J. B., 1987, Capillary pressure techniques: applications to exploration and development geology: American Association of Petroleum Geologists Bulletin, v. 71, p. 1196–1209.

Kupecz, J. A., 1984, Depositional environments, diagenetic history, and petroleum entrapment in the Mississippian Frobisher-Alida interval, Billings anticline, North Dakota: Colorado School of Mines Quarterly, v. 79, n. 3, 53 p.

LeFever, J. A., R. D. LeFever, and S. B. Anderson, 1987, Structural evolution of the central and southern portions of the Nesson Anticline, North Dakota, *in* C. G. Carlson and J. E. Christopher, eds., Fifth International Williston Basin Symposium: Saskatchewan Geological Society Special Publication 9, p. 147–156.

Lindsay, R. F., and M. S. Roth, 1982, Carbonate and evaporite facies, dolomitization and reservoir distribution of the Mission Canyon Formation, Little Knife field, North Dakota, *in* J. E. Christopher and J. Kaldi, eds., Fourth International Williston Basin Symposium: Saskatchewan Geological Society Special Publication 6, p. 153–179.

Meissner, F. F., 1978, Petroleum geology of the Bakken Formation, Williston basin, North Dakota and Montana, *in* The economic geology of the Williston basin: Williston Basin Symposium, Montana Geological Society, p. 207–227.

Mitsdarffer, A. R., 1985, Hydrodynamics of the Mission Canyon Formation in the Billings nose area, North Dakota: Master's Thesis, Texas A & M University, College Station, Texas, 162 p.

Petty, D. M., 1988, Depositional facies, textural characteristics, and reservoir properties in the Frobisher-Alida interval in southwest North Dakota: American Association of Petroleum Geologists Bulletin, v. 72, p. 1229–1253.

Price, L. C., T. Ging, T. Daws, A. Love, M. Pawlewicz, and D. Anders, 1984, Organic metamorphism in the Mississippian-Devonian Bakken shale, North Dakota portion of the Williston Basin, *in* J. Woodward, F. F. Meissner, and J. L. Clayton, eds., Hydrocarbon source rocks of the Greater Rocky Mountain region: Rocky Mountain Association of Geologists, Denver, p. 83–134.

Schowalter, T. T., and P. D. Hess, 1982, Interpretation of subsurface hydrocarbon shows: American Association of Petroleum Geologists Bulletin, v. 66, p. 1302–1327.

Webster, R. L., 1984, Petroleum source rocks and stratigraphy of the Bakken Formation in North Dakota, *in* J. Woodward, F. F. Meissner, and J. L. Clayton, eds., Hydrocarbon source rocks of the greater Rocky Mountain Region: Rocky Mountain Association of Geologists, Denver, CO, p. 57–81.

ELKHORN RANCH

Appendix 1. Field Description

Field name .... *Elkhorn Ranch field*

Ultimate recoverable reserves .... *22 million bbl oil; 30 bcf gas*

Field location:

    Country .... *U.S.A.*

    State .... *North Dakota*

    Basin/Province .... *Williston basin*

Field discovery:

    Year first pay discovered .... *Mississippian–Devonian Bakken 1961*

    Year second pay discovered .... *Mississippian Mission Canyon Limestone 1974*

Discovery well name and general location:

    First pay .... *41X-5-1 Sec. 5, T143N, R101W, Billings County, North Dakota*

    Second pay .... *14-32 Federal Sec. 31, T144N, R101W*

Discovery well operator .... *Shell*

    Second pay .... *Farmer's Union Central Exchange (Cenex)*

IP:

    First pay .... *136 BOPD*

    Second pay .... *294 BOPD, 81 BWPD*

All other zones with shows of oil and gas in the field:

Age	Formation	Type of Show
Mississippian	*Charles (Midale)*	*Minor gas*
Devonian	*Duperow*	*Gas, sample shows*
Ordovician	*Red River*	*Gas, sample shows*

Geologic concept leading to discovery and method or methods used to delineate prospect

Regional stratigraphic play in Mission Canyon of porosity pinch-outs on nonclosing anticlines based on subsurface stratigraphy and seismic, but well was never completed in Mission Canyon. Second well based on show of oil in DST of first well.

Structure:

    Province/basin type .... *Bally 121; Klemme I*

    Tectonic history

    The region is part of a cratonic basin typified by very subtle uplift throughout Phanerozoic time. Minor uplifts in Devonian, Mississippian, and Pennsylvanian and reactivation in early Eocene.

    Regional structure

    The field is located on the south-southwest flank of the Williston basin, near the center. Elkhorn Ranch field is located north of the Billings Nose anticline.

    Local structure

    Elkhorn Ranch field is on a north-plunging nose with very low dips (<1°).

Trap:

    Trap type(s)

    Elkhorn Ranch field is a hydrodynamic trap. Structure only assists in localizing the accumulation. A stratigraphic pinch-out in the highest of three zones assists the trap at the south.

Basin stratigraphy (major stratigraphic intervals from surface to deepest penetration in field):

Chronostratigraphy	Formation	Depth to Top in ft (m)
Cretaceous	*Greenhorn*	*4641 (1416)*
	Dakota	*5536 (1688)*

Jurassic	Piper Limestone	6709 (2046)
Permian	Minnekahta	7368 (2247)
Mississippian	Kibbey Limestone	8589 (2620)
	Charles	8741 (2666)
	Mission Canyon	9461 (2886)
Mississippian-Devonian	Bakken	10,718 (3269)
Devonian	Nisku	10,974 (3347)
	Duperow	11,065 (3375)
	Souris River	11,384 (3472)
Silurian	Interlake	11,945 (3643)
Ordovician	Red River	12,894 (3933)

Reservoir characteristics:

Number of reservoirs .... *3 principal zones with up to 7 separate reservoirs*
Formations .... *Mission Canyon*
Ages .... *Mississippian*
Depths to tops of reservoirs .... *9300 ft (2840 m)*
Gross thickness (top to bottom of producing interval) .... *75 ft (23 m)*
Net thickness—total thickness of producing zones
    Average .... *40 ft (12 m)*
    Maximum .... *60 ft (18 m)*
Lithology .... *Dolomitized skeletal mudstones and wackestones*
Porosity type .... *Secondary intercrystalline with minor vuggy*
Average porosity *16%*
Average permeability .... *25 md*

Seals:

Upper
    Formation, fault, or other feature .... *Mission Canyon formation*
    Lithology .... *Anhydrite facies of Mission Canyon*
Lateral
    Formation, fault, or other feature .... *Downdip flow of formation waters with minor assists from structural flexure and stratigraphic pinch-outs*

Source:

Formation and age .... *Bakken (Mississippian-Devonian)*
Lithology .... *Shale*
Average total organic carbon (TOC) *11%*
Maximum TOC *22%*
Kerogen type (I, II, or III) .... *II*
Vitrinite reflectance (maturation) .... $R_o = 1.0$
Time of hydrocarbon expulsion .... *Early Tertiary*
Present depth to top of source .... *10,600 ft (3230 m)*
Thickness .... *80 ft (24 m)*
Potential yield .... *NA*

Appendix 2. Production Data

Field name .... *Elkhorn Ranch field*

Field size:

    Proved acres .... *10,856 ac (4397 ha)*

    Number of wells all years *70*

    Current number of wells *64*

    Well spacing .... *160 ac (64.8 ha)*

    Ultimate recoverable .... *22 MMBO; 30 bcf gas*

    Cumulative production .... *15.5 MMBO; 21 bcf gas*

    Annual production .... *900 MBO (gas NA)*

    Present decline rate .... *NA*

        Initial decline rate .... *NA*

        Overall decline rate .... *NA*

    Annual water production .... *NA*

    In place, total reserves .... *50 million bbl*

    In place, per acre foot .... *65 bbl/ac-ft*

    Primary recovery .... *17.5 million bbl*

    Secondary recovery .... *4.5 million bbl*

    Enhanced recovery .... *NA*

    Cumulative water production .... *NA*

Drilling and casing practices:

    Amount of surface casing set .... *50–100 ft (15–30 m)*

    Casing program .... *9⅝-in. at 2000 ft (610 m); 5½-in. at total depth*

    Drilling mud .... *Salt saturated muds*

    Bit program

    High pressure zones ...... *Bakken shale has anomalously high pressure due to hydrocarbon generation*

Completion practices:

    Interval(s) perforated .... *Varies from 2 to 25 ft (0.6–7.6 m)*

    Well treatment .... *Acidize perforations with 1000 gallons (3780 L) of 15% HCl*

Formation evaluation:

    Logging suites .... *GR, FDC, CNL, BHCS, induction, microlog*

    Testing practices .... *Drill-stem test drilling breaks during drilling*

    Mud logging techniques .... *FID continuous gas monitoring from Minnekahta formation down*

Oil characteristics:

    Type .... *NA*

    API gravity .... *46°*

    Base .... *NA*

    Initial GOR .... *450 ft³ gas/bbl oil (79 m³ gas/m³ oil)*

    Sulfur, wt% .... *NA*

    Viscosity, SUS .... *NA*

    Pour point .... *NA*

    Gas-oil distillate .... *NA*

Field characteristics:

    Average elevation .... *2300 ft (702 m)*

    Initial pressure .... *4490 psi (30,958 kPa)*

    Present pressure .... *NA*

    Pressure gradient .... *0.433 psi/ft (9.8 kPa/m)*

    Temperature .... *216°F (102.2°C)*

ELKHORN RANCH

Geothermal gradient .... Approx. 0.02°F/ft (approx. 0.036°C/m)
Drive .... Active water
Oil column thickness .... 100 ft (30.5 m)
Oil-water contact .... Tilted 25 ft/mi (4.7 m/km)
Connate water 35%
Water salinity, TDS .... 50,000 to 200,000 ppm; varies across field
Resistivity of water .... NA
Bulk volume water (%) .... NA

Transportation method and market for oil and gas:
Pipeline

Stanley Field—U.S.A.
Williston Basin, North Dakota

DAVID K. BEACH
Marathon Petroleum Ireland, Ltd.
Cork, Ireland

JON W. GIFFIN
Marathon Oil Company
Cody, Wyoming

FIELD CLASSIFICATION

BASIN: Williston
BASIN TYPE: Cratonic Sag
RESERVOIR ROCK TYPE: Limestone
RESERVOIR ENVIRONMENT OF DEPOSITION: Carbonate Islands and
   Subtidal Sand Bodies

RESERVOIR AGE: Mississippian
PETROLEUM TYPE: Oil
TRAP TYPE: Pinch-Out

TRAP DESCRIPTION: Updip pinch-out due to facies change from porous
   intertidal/subtidal grainstone to tight subtidal mudstone

LOCATION

Stanley field, in Mountrail County, North Dakota, is an isolated, stratigraphically trapped hydrocarbon accumulation in the east-central Williston basin (Figure 1). It has both provided a new exploration play and established a measure of the significance of early physical compaction in shallow water carbonate sediments. The nearest commercial production to Stanley field occurs more than 20 mi (32 km) to the north, west, south, and east (Figure 1). The estimated ultimate recoverable reserves from the field are 3.3 million barrels of oil (MMBO) from 33 wells (Figure 2). Total area of the field is 4000 ac. Stanley field is not currently unitized. Principal operators are Marathon Oil Company, Brooks Exploration, and BWAB Incorporated.

HISTORY

Pre-Discovery

The Williston basin was a relative latecomer to the ranks of important oil- and gas-producing basins. Although oil had been discovered as early as 1936 along the Cedar Creek anticline in Montana in the southwestern portion of the basin, it was not until the 1950 discovery of oil in Manitoba and the 1951 discovery of oil at Beaver Lodge field on the Nesson anticline (Figure 1) in North Dakota that the central and eastern portions of the basin were opened to extensive exploration (Anderson et al., 1982).

Subsequent activity during the 1950s defined three major plays in the Mississippian of the central and eastern portions of the basin (Figure 1). In the center of the basin, drilling proceeded north and south along the Nesson anticline. While multiple pay zones were discovered, the Mississippian Madison Group (Mission Canyon and Charles formations) remained the primary objective (Figure 3). Additional important fields located on the Nesson include Tioga, Charleson, and Antelope fields. To the northeast, especially in Canada, the play was for porous Mississippian units truncated beneath the pre-Mesozoic unconformity (Edie, 1958). Fields of this type include Midale, Steelman, and Carnduff. Further south, along the eastern side of the basin in North Dakota, the play was for porosity reentrants in various units of the Mission Canyon downdip of tight carbonate and evaporate facies (Johnson, 1956; Malek-Aslani, 1971). Examples of these fields include Mohall, Bluell, and Haas fields. Haas field was described in detail by Elliott (1982). The eventual discovery of Stanley field in large part resulted from exploration for this type of porous reentrant into updip tight carbonates and evaporates.

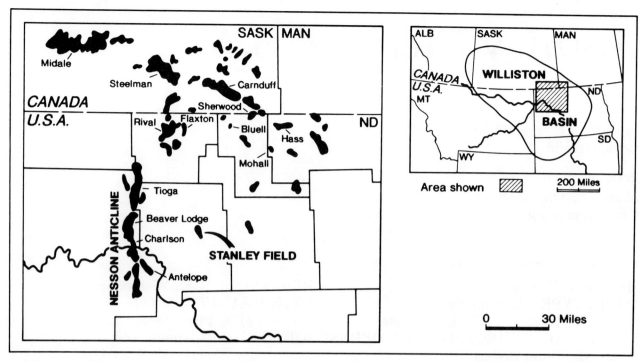

Figure 1. Location of Stanley field in west-central North Dakota. The nearest production to Stanley field is over 20 mi (32 km) away. Fields near Stanley referenced in the text are indicated.

Discovery

In 1974, John D. Trout, an independent geologist in Casper, Wyoming, conceived of a possible porous carbonate reentrant downdip of massive anhydrite and tight carbonate in the Rival zone (Figure 4) of the Mississippian Mission Canyon Formation located south of the town of Stanley, North Dakota (Figure 5). He compared his prospect to Rival production found at Rennie Lake and Rival pools 35 and 40 mi (56 and 64 km) to the north. Trout was able to get support for his prospect from John Kerns and Dick Loudon, two independent oilmen, also from Casper, who purchased the necessary acreage. After a long search for outside investors, the prospect was finally turned to Thompson Petroleum of London, England. Because the possibility existed for multiple pays, the first well, the Thompson #1 Harstad located in NE SW Sec. 10, T155N, R91W (1, Figure 2), was drilled to a depth of 13,246 ft (4037 m) into the Ordovician Red River Formation (Figure 3). The well was nonproductive below the Mission Canyon Formation. However, a drill-stem test of the interval between 8130 and 8210 ft (2478 and 2502 m) in the upper Mission Canyon recovered nearly 800 ft (244 m) of mud and gas-cut oil and 95 ft (29 m) of slightly oil-cut salt water. The sample chamber held 2 ft³ of gas and 1520 cm³ of oil. After logging, the well was perforated between 8170 and 8210 ft (2490 and 2502 m) and was completed on pump for an initial potential (IP) of 120 BOPD on 18 November 1977.

Post-Discovery

While pleased with the results of the #1 Harstad discovery well, Trout was perplexed: "We didn't know what was going on but we knew we had something different." What was different was that oil was being produced not simply from the Rival zone, which would be the case if the trap was a simple porous reentrant in anhydrite, but was also being produced from the underlying Bluell zone. Lacking a better model, and fearing drilling into a tight evaporitic updip section, Thompson Petroleum drilled three offset wells downdip of the discovery well (#2 Harstad, SW SE Sec. 10; #1-9 Corpron, E½ NE Sec. 9; #1 Corpron-State, NE NE Sec. 16, T155N, R91W). Results from these wells were disappointing and included one subeconomic producer and two dry holes. All were water wet in the Bluell. Thompson Petroleum subsequently turned its untested acreage east of the #1 Harstad discovery to Marathon Oil Company through a farm-out. Marathon drilled its #1 Jellesed (SW NW Sec. 13, T155N, R91W) well (5, Figure 2), believing at this point that an evaporite reentrant, including not only the Rival but also the Bluell intervals, existed south and east of the #1 Harstad.

In spite of the successful completion of the #1 Jellesed for an IP of 136 BOPD, this concept was once again proven wrong by two lines of evidence. First, BWAB completed a producing well (#30-41 Orville Harstad NE NE Sec. 30, T155N, R90W, IP

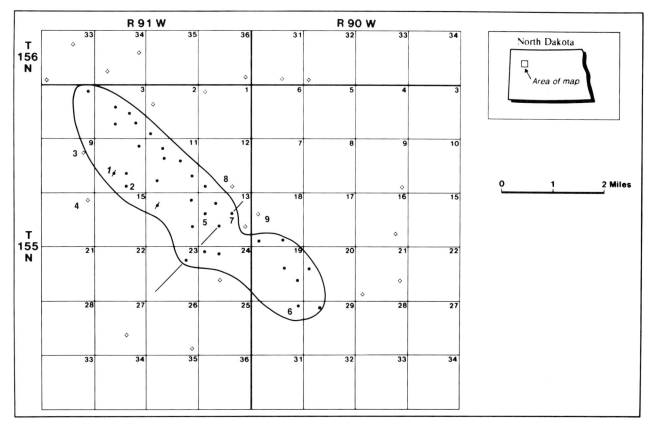

Figure 2. Map of Stanley field showing the locations of field wells and location of seismic line (Figure 28). Numbered wells are key wells mentioned in the text and include the following: 1, Thompson #1 Harstad, the discovery well for the field; 2, Thompson #2 Harstad; 3, Thompson #1-9 Corpron; 4, Thompson #1 Corpron-State; 5, Marathon #1 Jellesed; 6, BWAB #30-41 Orville Harstad; 7, Marathon #13-32 State, located in the northeast quarter of Sec. 13, offered for farm-out but subsequenty drilled and completed for an initial potential flowing of 1080 BOPD; 8, Gulf #1-12-3D Korterud; 9, Terra #1-18 Armour.

84 BOPD) south and east of the supposed barrier (6, Figure 2). Second, the #1 Jellesed produced oil not only from the Bluell interval but also from the underlying Sherwood zone. During this time, BWAB was exploring the Stanley area following the concept that Thompson may have discovered a productive fractured reservoir similar to that concurrently being developed at Mondak field located to the west on the North Dakota–Montana border.

At this point, interest in Stanley field was beginning to wane. Ten wells had been drilled in and near the field. Five were dry, three were subcommercial, and only two appeared to be moderately commercial. None of the wells had penetrated any section containing good porous and permeable rocks. Most of the pay section appeared tight but fractured. Marathon thus decided to farm out the NE ¼ of Sec. 13, T155N, R91W, because this lease was about to expire (Figure 2). Finding no takers, Marathon spudded the #13-32 State (SW NE Sec. 13, T155N, R91W) in May 1979 against its better intentions (7, Figure 2). This well flowed at an initial rate of 1080 BOPD from perforations in the Bluell

and Sherwood intervals and consequently generated the first real excitement and interest in the field. Log calculations and core analysis showed 66 ft (20 m) of net pay with porosity ranging from 6 to 12% and permeabilities from 10 to 100 md.

By the end of 1979, an additional seven wells had been drilled in the field. Two wells (8 and 9, Figure 2) located along the northeast side of the field were dry (Gulf #1-12-3D Korterud, SW SE Sec. 12, T155N, R91W, and Terra #1-18 Armour, SW NW Sec. 18, T155N, R90W) and encountered a thin upper Mission Canyon interval (Rival to top Glenburn). This led some to speculate that a fault existed along the northeast side of the field upthrown to the southwest. Other ideas suggested possible wrench faults or local unconformities affecting the upper Mission Canyon. While each concept had its proponents, each also suffered major shortcomings.

The concept finally accepted by Marathon and presented here and in previous papers (Beach and Schumacher, 1982a, b, c) is that Stanley field is a stratigraphic oil accumulation. The distribution of different depositional facies and their subsequent

391

PERIOD	EPOCH	GROUP / FORMATION	
QUATERNARY	Pleistocene	COLE HARBOR	
TERTIARY	Oligocene	WHITE RIVER GROUP	BRULE, CHADRON
	Eocene	GOLDEN VALLEY	
	Paleocene	FORT UNION GROUP	SENTINEL BUTTE, BULLION CREEK, SLOPE, CANNONBALL, LUDLOW
CRETACEOUS	Late	HELL CREEK	
		MONTANA GROUP	FOX HILLS, PIERRE
		COLORADO GROUP	NIOBRARA, CARLILE, GREENHORN, BELLE FOURCHE
	Early	DAKOTA GROUP	MOWRY, NEWCASTLE, SKULL CREEK, INYAN KARA
JURASSIC	Late	MORRISON	
		SWIFT	
	Middle	RIERDON	
		PIPER	
TRIASSIC	Early / Late	SPEARFISH	
PERMIAN	Early	MINNEKAHTA	
		OPECHE	
PENNSYLVANIAN		MINNELUSA GROUP	BROOM CREEK, AMSDEN, TYLER
MISSISSIPPIAN		BIG SNOWY GROUP	OTTER, KIBBEY
		MADISON GROUP	CHARLES, MISSION CANYON, LODGEPOLE
DEVONIAN	Late	BAKKEN	
		THREE FORKS	
		BIRDBEAR	
		DUPEROW	
		SOURIS RIVER	
	Middle	DAWSON BAY	
		PRAIRIE	
		WINNIPEGOSIS	
SILURIAN	Late / Early	INTERLAKE	
		STONEWALL	
ORDOVICIAN	Late	STONEY MOUNTAIN	
		RED RIVER	
		WINNIPEG GROUP	ROUGHLOCH, ICEBOX, BLACK ISLAND
CAMBRIAN	Late	DEADWOOD	
PRECAMBRIAN		IGNEOUS BASEMENT	

Figure 3. Stratigraphic column for the central Williston basin. Stanley field produces from the upper Mission Canyon Formation of the Mississippian Madison Group. (After Bluemle et al., 1981.)

diagenesis provide the trap and control the quality of the reservoir. Variation in thickness of the upper Mission Canyon section resulted primarily from the differential effect of mechanical compaction on the various depositional facies.

DISCOVERY METHOD

As can be discerned from the preceding discussion, the discovery of Stanley field resulted from one person, John Trout, having an idea upon which to

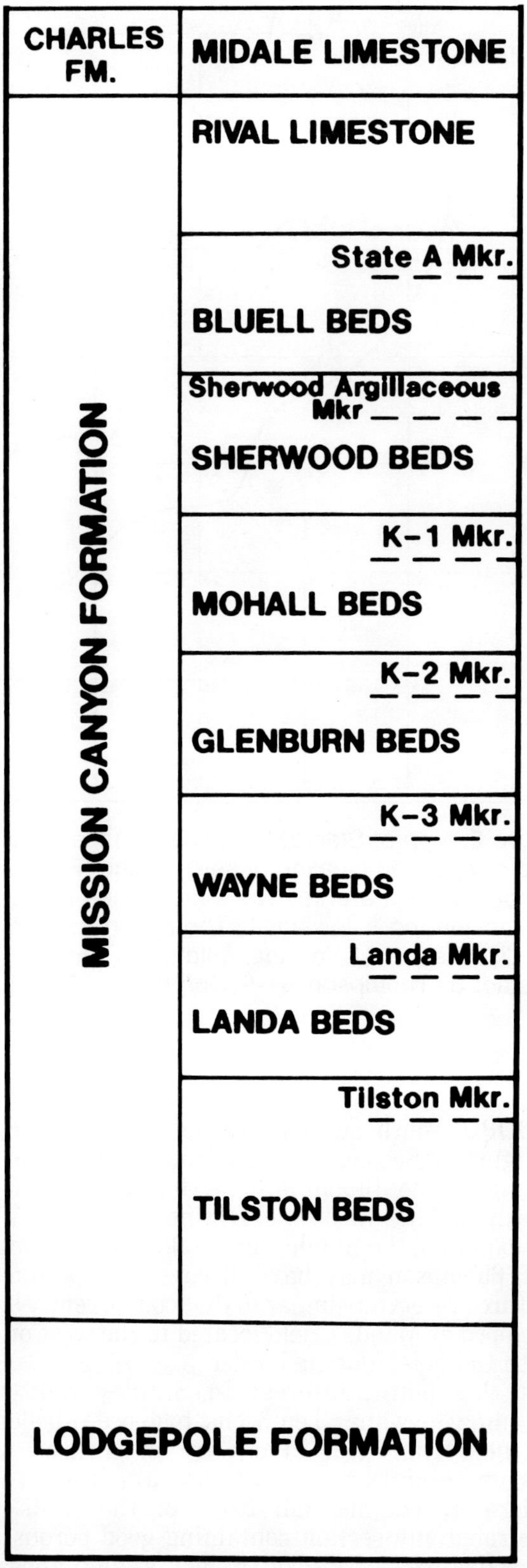

Figure 4. Detailed stratigraphic column of northeastern Williston basin. (After Harris et al., 1966.) In this paper, Mission Canyon usage includes the Rival zone. The reservoirs occur principally in the Bluell and Sherwood zones. Key marker beds used in mapping and correlations are the State "A" at the top of the Bluell and the K-2 at the top of the Glenburn.

sell a well, and then being able to sell it. As is so often the case, the original idea was subsequently found errant but success followed the drill bit. Exploration methods employed by Trout included stratigraphic mapping of upper Mission Canyon facies belts using regional subsurface well control, and structural mapping on the top of the Mission Canyon and on deeper horizons using a combination of well control and a limited amount of available seismic. Development of the field required persistence and detailed study. Development of a play based on Stanley field would occur only after the field was understood. Then subsurface well control aided by seismic could be incorporated to aid the search for analogous fields.

STRUCTURE

The Williston basin is an irregular-shaped basin located on the western side of the Canadian shield. Based on the summary compilation of sedimentary provinces by St. John et al. (1984), the Williston basin is a "cratonic basin" (121) under the modified classification scheme of Bally and Snelson (1980), or a "craton interior basin" (type I) under the basin classification of Klemme (1971).

Subsidence alternating with periods of uplift and/or exposure began by Late Cambrian and continued through the Paleocene. Periods of most active subsidence coupled with sedimentation occurred from 470 to 410 Ma (Middle Ordovician to Late Silurian), 370 to 290 Ma (Middle Devonian through Pennsylvanian–Missourian), and 115 to 55 Ma (Early Cretaceous through Paleocene). During these periods, the shape of the basin changed (Gerhard et al., 1982). From the Middle Ordovician to Late Silurian, the basin was a well-defined depression open to the southwest. During the Middle Devonian, the basin formed the southern extent of the much larger Elk Point basin. By the Mississippian, the basin was closed on all sides except for a seaway open to the west across central Montana. This seaway persisted through the Triassic. During the Cretaceous, the basin was a part of the western interior seaway. Major unconformities with associated erosion are found overlying the Cambrian Deadwood, Silurian Interlake, Pennsylvanian Amsden, Triassic Spearfish, Jurassic Swift, and Paleocene Fort Union formations (Bluemle et al., 1981).

The two largest structural features in the basin are the Nesson and Cedar Creek anticlines. The Nesson anticline trends north-south and roughly divides the basin into eastern and western sides. The Cedar Creek anticline trends northeast-southwest on the southwest side of the basin. Both features have had multiple stages of movement with development of the basin (Gerhard et al., 1982).

Stanley field occurs east of the Nesson anticline on the gently dipping east side of the basin. In the area of the field, the regional dip is less than 1° to the southwest. At the time of deposition of the reservoir and trap facies for Stanley field, the basin likewise showed only a very gradual slope into the deeper basin to the west. The gentle nature of this slope is reflected in the sedimentary facies observed over this region. This was depicted by Steed (1983) (Figure 6) who noted that maximum water depths between Stanley field and the Nesson anticline may only have been on the order of 50 ft (15 m).

Figure 7 shows structure maps on (A) the top Kibbey anhydrite (700–800 ft; 213–244 m, above the reservoir), (B) base State "A" (top of the reservoir), and (C) top Glenburn (just below the reservoir), at Stanley field, respectively (Figure 8). Figure 7C reveals gentle southwesterly regional dip on Glenburn sediments. Only subtle structural noses are evident on this map. There is no evidence of faulting or other major structural complications. The structure on the top of the reservoir (Figure 7B, base State "A") shows three structural highs across the field separated by northeast–southwest-trending lows. A significant low trends northwest-southeast updip of the field. The overlying structure map on the Kibbey anhydrite (Figure 7A) reveals a return to a much simpler nearly homoclinal structure. This pattern results from the distribution of the upper Mission Canyon (Mohall, Sherwood, and Bluell zones) depositional facies (Figure 9) and the subsequent differential effect of physical compaction on them with resultant compensation during deposition of overlying units (Beach and Schumacher, 1982b, c).

STRATIGRAPHY

A generalized stratigraphic column is shown in Figure 3. Mississippian and older rocks are predominantly carbonates. Post-Mississippian units are mostly clastics. Rocks from the Ordovician through the Pennsylvanian have been proven productive in the Williston basin. The principal exploration targets have included carbonates of the Ordovician Red River, Silurian Interlake, Devonian Winnipegosis, Devonian Duperow, and Mississippian Mission Canyon and Charles formations, as well as sandstone in the Pennsylvanian Tyler Formation (Anderson et al., 1982). Oil is produced from structural, stratigraphic, and combination structural-stratigraphic traps. The premier producing formations are the Mission Canyon and Charles formations of the Mississippian Madison Group.

Stanley field produces from the upper Mission Canyon Formation. The Mission Canyon is the middle unit of the Mississippian Madison Group in the Williston basin. It lies between the underlying Lodgepole Formation and the overlying Charles Formation and is transitional in depositional facies between them (Wilson, 1975). Composed mostly of limestone, the Lodgepole accumulated in an open marine setting across most of the basin (Lineback and Davidson, 1982). It is thickest in the center of the basin.

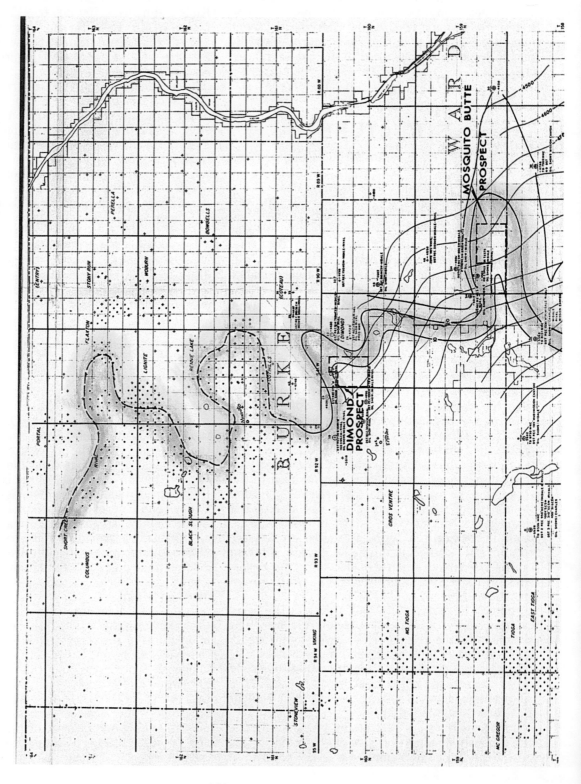

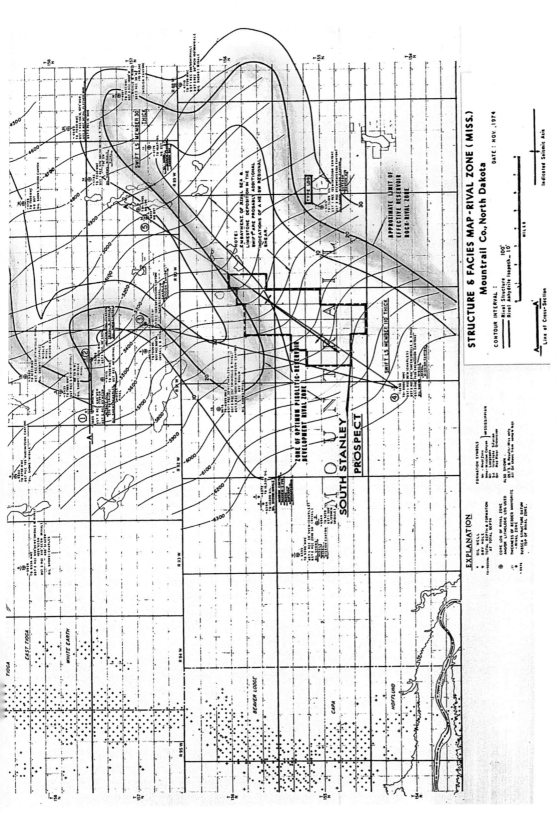

Figure 5. Reproduction of the original prospect map by John Trout, who convinced Thompson Petroleum to drill the #1 Harstad discovery well in 1977. The map shows both structural contours on and facies in the Rival interval. The concept used by Trout to sell the South Stanley prospect was a porous reentrant in nonporous anhydrite and carbonate of the Rival interval of the upper Mission Canyon. Models for this concept are Rennie Lake and Rival fields located on trend to the north in Burke County.

395

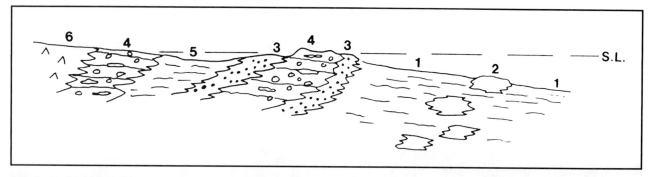

Figure 6. Idealized cross section after Steed (1983) showing facies belts of the upper Mission Canyon across the east side of the Williston basin (no scale). By the time of upper Mission Canyon deposition, water depths across the east side of the basin may only have been about 50 ft (15 m). The basin had low depositional relief and shoaled upward during Mission Canyon deposition. Numbered facies are the following: 1, crinoid, brachiopod wackestone facies—open basin sediments; 2, carbonate sand facies—crinoidal sand bodies; 3, carbonate sand facies—sand bodies, tidal deltas, channels, etc.; 4, fenestrate, coated grain facies—island build-ups; 5, wackestone, patterned carbonate facies—lagoon; 6, anhydritic facies—sabkha, related environments.

During Mission Canyon time, relatively deep-water open-marine carbonate sediments continued to accumulate in more central portions of the basin, while shallow water near-shore, lagoonal, and tidal-flat carbonates and sabkha evaporites accumulated along the margins (Malek-Aslani, 1971). Harris et al. (1966) observed the cyclical nature of the Mission Canyon deposits along the eastern side of the basin, with cycles commonly bounded by evaporitic or dolomitic "arenaceous" marker beds. Malek-Aslani (1971) and Elliott (1982) infer that the marker beds represent a regressive cap unit for each cycle. Eight major cycles were recognized by Harris et al. (1966), including the Glenburn, Mohall, Sherwood, Bluell, and Rival zones. These are present at Stanley field (Figure 4). Two marker beds are important: the top of the Glenburn (K-2 marker of Harris et al., 1966; at Stanley field a dolomitic bed), and the State "A" at the top of the Bluell (a massive anhydrite and dolomite, Figure 8). The entire Mission Canyon shoals upward, the carbonate to evaporite transition shifting more basinward with each succeeding depositional cycle.

The Charles Formation, continuing the trend of overall shoaling of the entire Madison Group, contains shallow marine and tidal flat deposited limestone and dolomite interbedded with massive anhydrite and salt (Figure 8). Three massive salt units punctuate the Charles Formation at the Stanley field and provide key markers to compare various isopach maps and cross sections (Beach and Schumacher, 1982a, b, c).

At the Stanley field, no significant shows of hydrocarbons occurred above the Mission Canyon. Five field wells have been drilled through the Mission Canyon to the underlying Lodgepole Formation (approximate depth from ground level 8650–8700 ft; 2637–2652 m). Three of these wells reached total depth in the Silurian Interlake (one well, TD 12,025 ft; 3665 m), and Ordovician Red River (two wells, TD 13,246 and 13,025 ft; 4037 and 3970 m) formations. While numerous shows were recorded in these deeper wells, no commercial quantities of hydrocarbons were found.

The prolific production from Mississippian strata in the Williston basin in part reflects the richness and maturity of the underlying source beds of the Devonian–Mississippian Bakken Formation (Figure 3). Dow (1974) describes three organic-rich shales as being principal source beds for liquid hydrocarbons in the Williston basin. In order of their importance these are the Devonian–Mississippian Bakken Formation, Ordovician Winnipeg shale, and Pennsylvanian Tyler shale. We believe, however, along with other workers (Williams, 1974; Anderson et al., 1982), that dark organic-rich carbonates in various Ordovician, Devonian, and Mississippian formations could also source large quantities of liquid hydrocarbons.

Depositional Facies

Descriptions here of the different lithologic facies at Stanley field are modified only slightly and updated from those described by Beach and Schumacher (1982c). The various lithologies and depositional facies in and near the field were described and defined in cores from 20 wells (Figure 9). Cored intervals were then calibrated to wireline logs and seismic data to determine the extent of the important facies.

At Stanley field, below the top of the Glenburn, the Mission Canyon is composed of dark, compacted, and stylolitic carbonate wackestones containing beds of clean, partially cemented skeletal (crinoidal and bryozoan) grainstone (Figure 10A). They are inferred to have accumulated in a relatively deep open marine setting. Pore filling syntaxial overgrowth and spar cements partially occlude primary porosity.

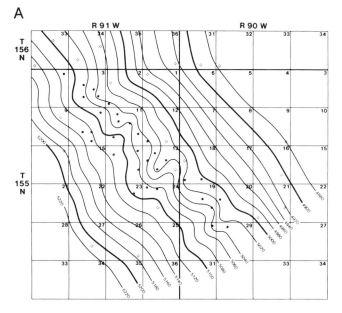

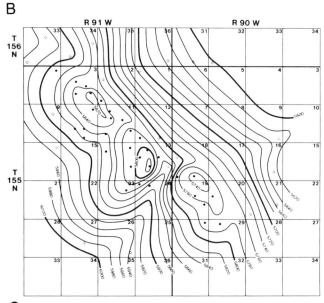

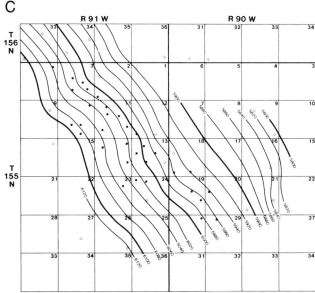

Above the Glenburn, the Bluell, Sherwood, and Mohall zones are composed of three principal rock types: (l) skeletal and peloidal grainstone and clean packstone (Figure 10B); (2) peloidal muddy packstone, wackestone, and mudstone (Figure 10C); and (3) pisoidal, fenestral grainstone and packstone interbedded with laminated mudstone (Figures 11A, B). These correspond respectively to three gross depositional facies: (1) high-energy subtidal sand bodies, (2) low-energy subtidal, and (3) restricted intertidal-supertidal. These facies (Figure 9) define a depositional system of low-relief intertidal-supratidal islands separated by marine channels, bordered on the northeast by a shallow subtidal lagoon, and on the southwest by the open sea covering the central Williston basin. It was a situation not unlike that found along the Trucial Coast of the Persian Gulf today (Purser and Evans, 1973; Butler et al., 1982). Prevailing wind direction was from the present-day northeast (paleo east) (Habicht, 1979). The climate appears to have been hot and arid. This system developed on a very low depositional slope on the leeward side of the sea. Once established at the start of Mohall deposition (Figure 4), this system of islands, channels, and lagoon was remarkably persistent in this area. At the end of Bluell sedimentation, maximum depositional relief across this system appears to have been no more than 15 ft (4.6 m, Figure 12). The Bluell is overlain by the anhydrite and carbonates of the State "A" and Rival, believed to have been deposited in an arid sabkha-like environment.

Post-Depositional History

Deposition of the evaporites of the State "A" interval atop the Bluell zone essentially entombed the underlying upper Mission Canyon deposits, isolating them from further leaching or cementation that would have been the result of continued meteoric exposure.

Following deposition of the Rival, the basin continued to subside. The entire system was subsequently overlain by 850 to 1000 ft (259 to 305

Figure 7. A series of three structure maps arranged in descending stratigraphic order on the following horizons: (A) top Kibbey anhydrite, about 750 ft (230 m) above the top of the pay; (B) base State "A" marker, just above the top of the pay; (C) top of the Glenburn interval, about 200 ft (60 m) below the top of the pay. Observe in C the gradual homoclinal dip toward the basin center with no dip reversals, only subtle plunging structural noses. This compares to B where there are three separate structures with up to 40 ft (12 m) of closure. The pay extends at least 80 ft (24 m) below the lowest closing contour. In A the structural contours again show no closure and a return toward homoclinal dip. Depths are subsea. Contour interval, 20 ft (6 m). Squares 1 mi (1.6 km) on a side.

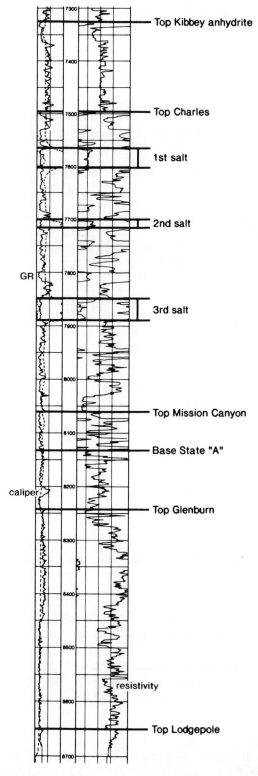

Figure 8. Typical log response showing units from the top of the Kibbey anhydrite down through the top of the Lodgepole. Log is from the Marathon #13-43 Ogden Armour, NE SE Sec. 13, T155N, R91W. Upper Mission Canyon in this well is compacted subtidal carbonate rock. Compacted section between the State "A" and top Glenburn were compensated for by deposition during the Charles. Log depths about 2225 to 2555 m.

m) of additional Mississippian deposits. The effect of this overburden was to physically compact uncemented upper Mission Canyon sediments. As described by Beach and Schumacher (1982a, b, c,), this included only the subtidal facies as is diagrammatically shown in Figure 13. The evidence for this physical compaction is summarized in Table 1 (see also Figures 14 and 15).

Near the end of Mississippian deposition, with nearly 1000 ft (300 m) of overburden, physical compaction had reached a stage where its progressive effect was diminishing (Figures 16, 17, 18, and 19). With additional overburden, chemical compaction and other deep burial processes would become more important than physical compaction to the ongoing diagenesis of the upper Mission Canyon at Stanley field.

TRAP

Stanley field is a stratigraphic accumulation of oil. The closure on the top of the reservoir (Figure 7B) results from the distribution of upper Mission Canyon depositional facies and their post-depositional susceptibility to mechanical compaction. The top seal for the field is massive anhydrite in the State "A" interval (Figure 4) at the top of the Bluell zone.

The structural closure over the field provides only a portion of the updip trap. The remaining lateral and updip seal for the field are the impervious limestone and dolomite mudstones, wackestones, and muddy packstones (Figures 10C and 16B), in the subtidal lagoonal deposits. The oil-water contact occurs at a depth of about –5925 ft (–1806 m) subsea. Its position relative to depositional facies across the field is shown in structural cross sections in Figure 16.

Mudstones are primarily aphanocrystalline dolomite and are commonly mottled light and dark gray (Figure 15B). Mottles frequently show a preferred horizontal attitude and occasionally contain fossil fragments. Mudstone intervals often grade into fossiliferous wackestones. Porosity within mudstones is generally between 10 and 20%. Permeability measured from permeability plugs is between 0.02 and 0.30 md. In spite of the relatively high porosity, measured water saturations are 70% or higher, while oil saturations are 0 to 3%, indicating that these rocks are impermeable to oil. Mudstone intervals commonly grade into wackestone and muddy packstone intervals.

The wackestones and muddy packstones (Figures 10C, 15D) are primarily limestone. Fossils and fossil fragments are common to abundant, including ostracods, trilobites, and calcispheres. Microstylolitic seams and wispy laminations are common (Figure 15C). These rocks are tighter and less permeable than the dolomitic mudstone. Porosity varies from less than 1 to 4% but averages less than 2%. Permeability ranges between less than 0.01 to 0.04 md, only occasionally exceeding 0.10 md. Water saturations

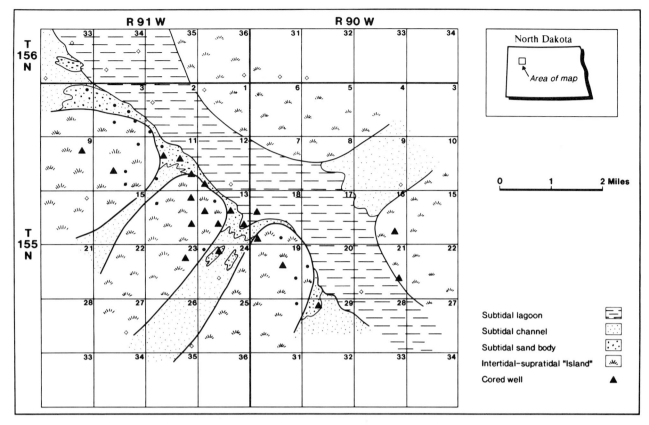

Figure 9. Map showing the generalized distribution of sedimentary environments in the upper Mission Canyon at Stanley field. During the upper Mission Canyon, the area around Stanley was characterized by low banks or islands separated by marine channels passing shoreward (eastward) into a shallow muddy lagoon. Reservoir facies at Stanley field include marine sand bodies (tidal delta, channel, and nearshore bars) and intertidal-supratidal bank or island sediments. The eastern (updip) compacted lagoonal muds provide the lateral trap for the field. Massive anhydrite of the Rival zone overlies these sediments and provides the top seal. The distribution of the sedimentary facies is based on core control from 20 wells (indicated in this figure) and log analysis of all wells in and near the field.

Figure 10A. Photomicrograph in plane light of crinoid and bryozoan grainstone from the lower Mission Canyon in Stanley field. Note presence of primary porosity (a) only partially occluded by syntaxial overgrowths around crinoid columnals (b). Cement is of a deep burial origin. Thin section is from Ogden Armour 13-43, NE SE Sec. 13, T155N, R91W, 8490 ft (2587.8 m) below KB. Bar scale, 2 mm.

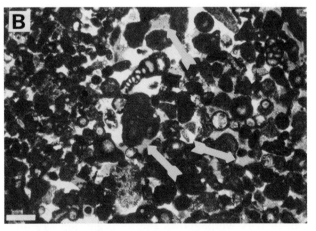

Figure 10B. Photomicrograph in plane light of peloidal and skeletal grainstone retaining a high percentage (approximately 10%) of open primary porosity (light gray in photograph, indicated by arrows). Endothyrid foraminifers are present in center and upper right of photograph. Cement is of late deep burial origin. Thin section is from Marathon #13-32 State, SW NE Sec. 13, T155N, R91W, 8133.8 ft (2479.2 m) below KB. Bar scale, 0.5 mm. (After Beach and Schumacher, 1982c.)

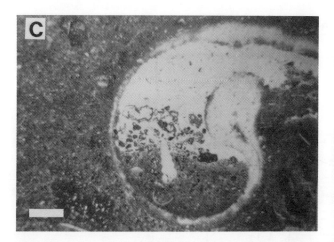

Figure 10C. Photomicrograph in plane light of skeletal wackestone typical of lagoonal sediment. Gastropod shell was only partially filled with internal sediment. Sheltered porosity is cemented by coarse spar of deep-burial origin. Gastropod shell has been recrystallized to calcite and shows no evidence of leaching. Internal sediment was sheltered from physical compaction while external sediment was not. Thin section is from Marathon #13-43 Ogden Armour, NE SE Sec. 13, T155N, R91W, 8145 ft (2482.6 m) below KB. Bar scale, 2 mm.

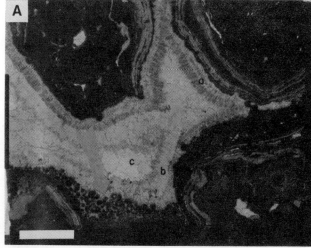

Figure 11A. Photomicrograph in plane light of pisoidal grainstone containing internal sediment (arrow) and at least three generations of cement: (a) pore-rimming fibrous to bladed cement of inferred marine (beach-rock-like) origin; (b) pore-rimming bladed cement of inferred meteoric origin; (c) later phase deep-burial coarse equant spar. Thin section is from Marathon #1 Jellesed, NE SE Sec. 13, T155N, R91W, 8058.4 ft (2456.2 m) below KB. Bar scale, 1 mm. (Photo modified from Beach and Schumacher, 1982c.)

measured from perm plugs are generally 60% or greater; oil saturations are less than 3%. Like the mudstones, the wackestones and muddy packstones are interpreted to have accumulated in a shallow subtidal environment. Together these sediments appear to have occurred as channel fill and in the protected subtidal lagoon.

The typical log responses of these facies are shown in Figure 20. The dolomitic mottled mudstone usually has a relatively dirty gamma ray signature of between 20 and 35 API units; a resistivity of 0.6 to 1.0 ohm-m showing little or no separation of deep and shallow curves; and a neutron-density response showing moderate porosity with significant separation between neutron porosity and density porosity. The mud-rich limestones also typically have a gamma ray response of 20 to 35 API units; a much higher resistivity of 10 to 50 ohm-m with virtually no separation of curves; and porosity of 3% or less with little separation between neutron and density curves. Analysis of natural gamma-ray spectroscopy logs from nearby wells shows the total gamma ray and variations in it to be largely caused by uranium, with only minor variations in the thorium or potassium contributions.

RESERVOIR

The reservoir in Stanley field is estimated to contain 16 MMBO of which 3.3 MMBO are expected

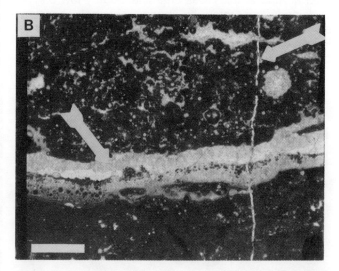

Figure 11B. Photomicrograph in plane light of a sheet crack (arrow) in a fenestral peloidal wackestone. The sheet crack contains peloidal internal sediment deposited on and within fibrous and bladed cements. This association of cement and internal sediment dates the cement as syndepositional. Vertical fracture (upper arrow), cutting both grains and early cements, is filled with later stage deep-burial cement. Thin section is from #1 Corpron State, NE NE Sec. 16, T155N, R91W, 8233 ft (2509.4 m) below KB. Bar scale, 1 mm. (Photo modified from Beach and Schumacher, 1982c.)

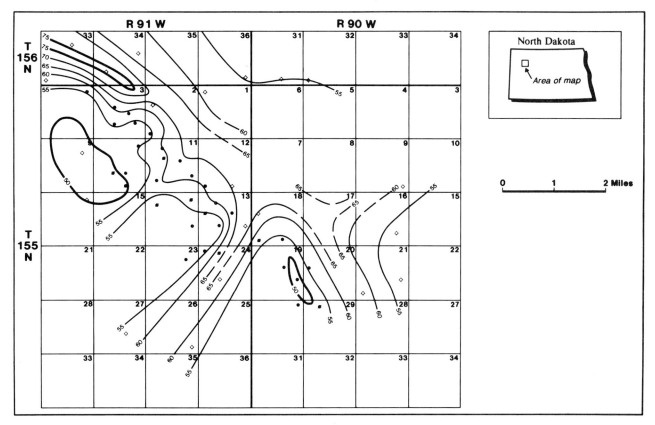

Figure 12. Isopach map of the Rival interval. Deposition of the Rival acted to infill preexisting relief. Thus, it provides some measure of depositional relief between islands and marine locations at the end of Bluell deposition. Some of the inferred relief may also be caused by ongoing compaction in the underlying upper Mission Canyon. Therefore, this map provides only a minimum measure. Contour interval, 5 ft (1.5 m).

to be recovered. The field covers approximately 4000 ac (1620 ha) with a maximum oil column of 120 ft (37 m). Depth from ground level to the top of the pay averages 8098 ft (2468 m). The average thickness of net pay is 8 ft (2.5 m); maximum is 72 ft (22 m).

Stratigraphy and Facies

The reservoir is composed of limestone from both the intertidal-supratidal "island" and the high-energy subtidal depositional facies. The intertidal-supratidal rocks are peloidal, ooidal, and pisoidal grainstone-packstone containing fenestral porosity (birds eye vugs and sheet cracks) interbedded with thin irregularly laminated mudstone (Figures 11A, B). While not abundant, occasional fossil remains occur within these rocks. Porosity within these rocks is usually occluded by multiple generations of calcite cement and occasionally anhydrite. Cements include dirty appearing inclusion-rich bladed and recrystallized fibrous cement rimming grains and sheet cracks with associated internal sediment and/or peloidal cement (Figure 11B). A later generation of cleaner pore-rimming cement is also locally present. The early generations of cements are interpreted to be mostly marine (beachrock-like) in origin. The occasional clear bladed spar may represent a meteoric (phreatic) cement. The final generation of cement, a coarse pore- and fracture-filling equant spar, along with stylotization and fracturing, developed under deep burial conditions (Beach and Schumacher, 1982c).

This facies, while productive, is generally tight but often fractured. In most wells, porosity averages less than 2%, with permeability, measured from permeability plugs, less than 0.01 md. Occasionally, however, a well penetrates a relatively porous "island" section with porosity 5 to 8% or better, permeability up to several tens of millidarcys, and correspondingly better production.

The log response of this facies (Figure 21) is characterized by a very low uniform gamma ray (10–20 API units), low neutron and density porosity, and resistivity of 10 to 100 ohm-m with little separation between deep and shallow curves. Fracture logs highlight fractured intervals.

The second reservoir facies, deposited as submarine sand bodies, is of smaller areal extent but is of greater importance economically. It is composed of peloidal and skeletal grainstone and relatively clean packstone (Figure 10B). Skeletal remains

401

1. MISSION CANYON DEPOSITION NEAR END OF BLUELL TIME

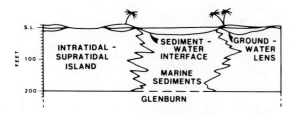

2. END OF RIVAL DEPOSITION

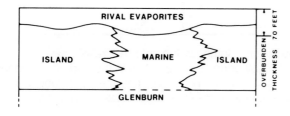

3. END OF DEPOSITION OF 3rd CHARLES SALT

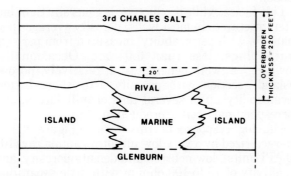

4. END OF DEPOSITION OF 1 st CHARLES SALT

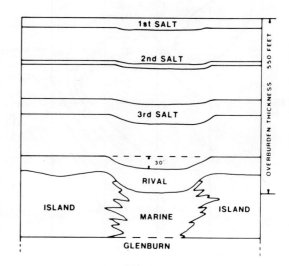

5. END OF DEPOSITION OF KIBBEY ANHYDRITE

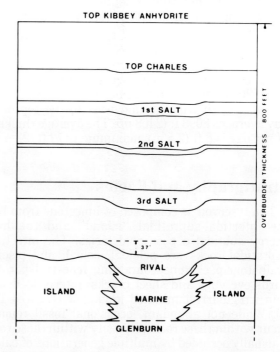

Figure 13. Diagrammatic representation showing the sequential physical compaction of upper Mission Canyon marine sections with the addition of overburden during Charles and Kibbey deposition. Island sections did not compact. Total section compensation, in overlying units, to the end of deposition of the 3rd Charles salt is 20 ft (6 m); by the end of deposition of the 1st Charles salt it is 30 ft (9 m); and by the end of deposition of the Kibbey anhydrite it is 37 ft (11.3 m). While the cumulative effect increases with increasing overburden, the incremental effect decreases as should be expected (Weller, 1959; Shinn and Robbin, 1983). This effect was demonstrated graphically by Beach and Schumacher (1982b).

402

Table 1. Evidence for mechanical compaction observed at Stanley field, North Dakota. (Numbers in parentheses beneath evidence items indicate references cited at the end of the table.)

Direct Evidence (References)	Figure
Crushed and broken fossils (1, 2, 3, 4, 5, 6, 7, 8, 9)	14A, B, C
Preferred horizontal orientation of fossil fragments (5, 6, 7, 8, 9)	14A, 15A
Preferred horizontal orientation of mottling (burrows) (6, 7, 8, 9)	15B
Tighter packing of matrix sediment versus internal sediment (1, 5, 7, 9)	10C
Microstylolitic "horsetail" swarms (2, 6, 7, 9)	15C
Penetration and drag effects (1, 5, 7)	15D
Indirect Evidence (References)	
Lack of syndepositional or early post-depositional cements (4, 7, 9)	10A, B
Widespread preservation of primary interparticle porosity (1, 4, 7, 8, 9)	10A, B
Cross sections (7, 10, 11)	16A, B, 17
Isopach maps (7, 10, 11)	18A, B, 19A, B, C
Structure maps (7, 10, 11)	7A, B, C

References: 1, Pray, 1960; 2, Shinn et al., 1977; 3, Bhattacharyya and Friedman, 1979; 4, Bathurst, 1980; 5, Meyers, 1980; 6, Shinn et al., 1980; 7, Beach and Schumacher, 1982c; 8, Shinn and Robbin, 1983; 9, Choquette and James, 1987; 10, Terzaghi, 1940; 11, Weller, 1959.

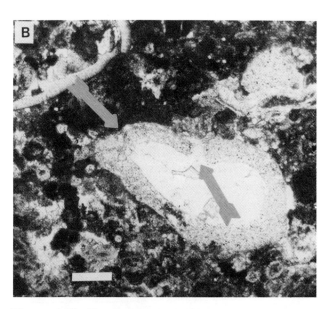

Figure 14B. Photomicrograph in plane light through a crushed crinoid columnal. A normal cross section is nearly circular. Breaks occur at both ends of the columnal and along the upper surface (arrows). Cement within the columnal postdates compaction. Thin section is from Terra #1-18 Armour, SW NW Sec. 18, T155N, R9OW, 8132.3 ft (2478.7 m) below KB. Bar scale, 0.5 mm. (Photo modified from Beach and Schumacher, 1982c.)

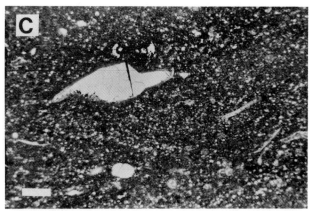

Figure 14C. Photomicrograph in plane light of crushed ostracod in skeletal wackestone. Coarse spar filling sheltered pore within the ostracod postdates compaction and is from a deep-burial origin. Thin section is from Marathon #13-32 State, SW NE Sec. 13, T155N, R91W, 8128 ft (2477 m) below KB. Bar scale, 0.5 mm.

Figure 14A. Photomicrograph in plane light of crushed rugose horn coral. Septa normally radiate from the coral center. Here septa are obviously distorted, many with a near horizontal orientation. Thin section is from Terra #1-18 Armour, SW NW Sec. 18, T155N, R90W, 8180 ft (2493.3 m) below KB. Bar scale, 0.5 mm.

include endothyrid foraminifers, ostracods, trilobites, crinoid columnals, brachiopods, rugose horn corals, and molluscs. Primary interparticle porosity is commonly preserved. Cementation as pore-filling equant spar and as syntaxial overgrowths around crinoid columnals is light to moderate and originated from a late phase, deep-burial source.

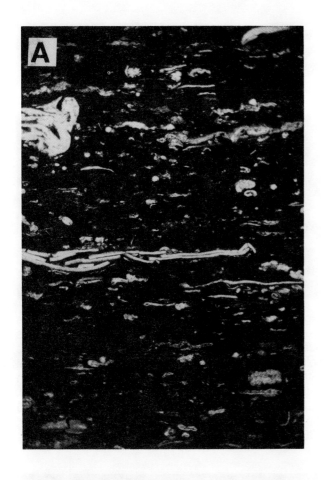

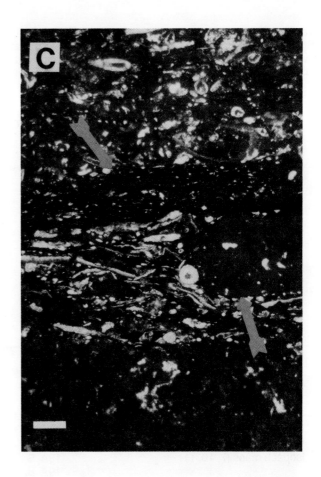

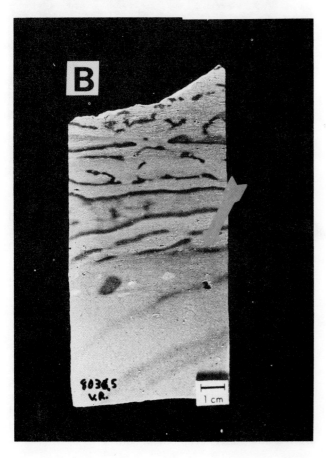

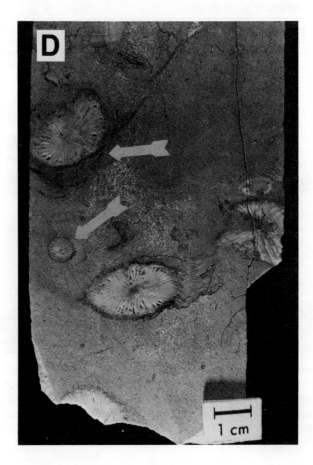

404

Porosity typically ranges from 5 to 12%, averaging about 9%. Permeability is 10 to 100 md. Logs of this facies reflect its clean porous characteristics (Figure 22). The gamma ray is usually 10 to 20 API units but is not as consistent as that seen in the "island" facies. Porosity logs indicate the good primary porosity. Resistivity logs read between 6 and 20 ohm-m with good separation between shallow and deep curves. Water saturation in reservoir sections is higher in zones of lower porosity.

Oil and Field Characteristics

A total of 33 wells have been drilled in Stanley field with 24 currently producing. Well spacing is 160 ac. The average ground elevation for the field is 2211 ft (674 m). The initial pressure of the field was 3600 psi with a pressure gradient of 0.44 psi/ft. Reservoir temperature is 180°F with a geothermal gradient of 0.01°F/ft. The field has a natural water drive with the original oil water content at –5925 ft (–1806 m) subsea. Formation water is saline (200,000 ppm solids) with a resistivity of 0.02 ohm at bottom hole temperature.

The oil is 33° API. Sulfur content is 0.5 wt. %. Oil viscosity is 0.8 cp. The field had an initial GOR of 280 MCFG/BO. A representative gas chromatogram of Stanley field oil is shown in Figure 23. Oil is transported via pipeline to the central United States.

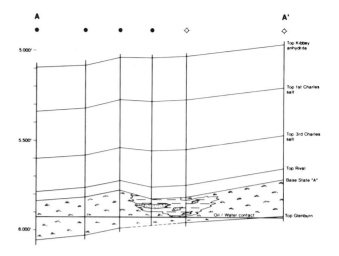

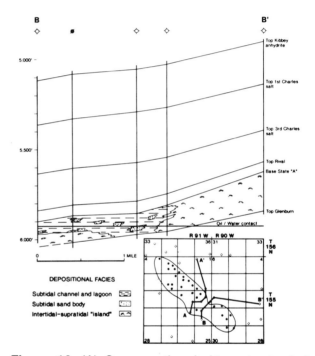

Figure 15. (A) Photomicrograph in plane light of compacted skeletal wackestone showing broken fossils, especially ostracods and trilobites, having horizontal orientation. Thin section is from Terra #1-18 Armour, SW NW Sec. 18, T155N, R90W, 8093 ft (2466.7 m) below KB. Bar scale, 0.5 mm. (B) Slabbed section of core showing mottled dolomite and limestone. Top half is dolomitic mudstone that grades down into fossiliferous wackestone. Arrow indicates approximate contact between dolomite and limestone. Mottling is most evident in the dolomite but is also present in the limestone. Mottling is believed to be due to burrowing. The horizontal aspect is in large part resultant from physical compaction. Core section is from Marathon #21-43 Vernon Rolfe, NE SE Sec. 21, T155N, R90W, 8036.5 ft (2449.5 m) below KB. (Photo after Beach and Schumacher, 1982c.) (C) Photomicrograph in plane light of compacted skeletal wackestone with wispy micro-stylolitic swarms (upper arrow). Microstylolites surround filled burrow (lower arrow) to right of center. Thin section is from Terra #1-18 Armour, SW NW Sec. 18, T155N, R90W, 8104 ft (2470.1 m) below KB. Bar scale, 1.0 mm. (D) Slabbed section of core containing coral-bearing marine packstone. Coral at upper left (upper arrow) is underlain by apparent penetration effect with a drag feature tailing upward to the right. Septa in larger corals have been distorted from the normal radial pattern seen in small coral (lower arrow). Section is from Marathon #21-43 Vernon Rolfe, NE SE Sec. 21, T155N, R90W, 8042 ft (2451.2 m) below KB. (Photo after Beach and Schumacher, 1982c.)

Figure 16. (A) Cross section A-A', a structural dip section trending from island wells in the southwest through subtidal sand body (reservoir) into the lagoon and back to island facies. Depositional facies are based on cores and logs. Island wells contain a thick Glenburn to State "A" interval and a thin overlying Charles interval. This relationship is reversed in marine wells. Correlation between wells on the top of the Glenburn shows regional dip. On the base of the State "A" there is over 40 ft (12 m) of closure. Through the Charles and lower Kibbey formations there is a gradual return to regional dip. Total thickness from top Glenburn to Kibbey anhydrite is about 1000 ft (300 m). (B) Cross section B-B', a structural dip section trending from marine wells (west) to island wells. This section roughly parallels A-A'. It shows the upper Mission Canyon interval thickening markedly in the island section located east of Stanley field. The inverse relationship of thick-thin intervals is preserved in the overlying Charles.

405

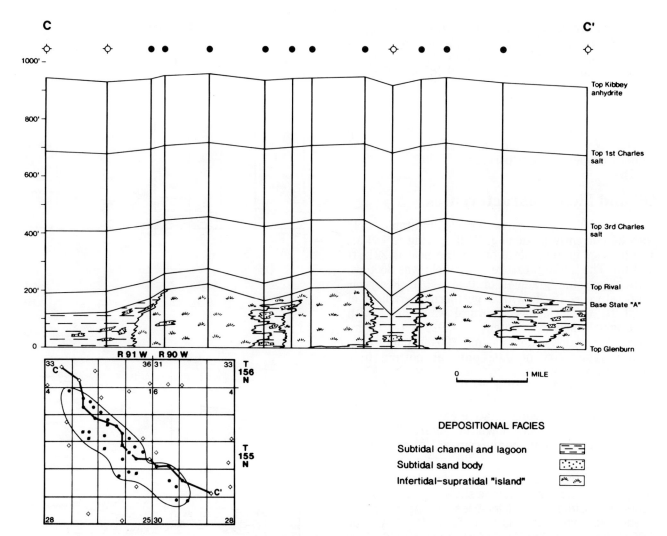

Figure 17. Cross section C-C', a strike section flattened on the top of the Glenburn. Correlations of log markers below the Glenburn (not shown; see Beach and Schumacher, 1982c) remain essentially flat (thickness from top Glenburn to top Lodgepole is about 400 ft, or 120 m). Relief develops in the upper Mission Canyon between wells containing island deposits (thick) and those containing marine deposits (thin). The opposite is observed in the Charles and lower Kibbey formations with thick intervals overlying upper Mission Canyon marine intervals and thins overlying island intervals. In the upper Charles and Kibbey intervals, there is a return to nearly flat correlation between wells. Charles deposits accumulating over marine sections in the upper Mission Canyon have compensated for compaction of the underlying marine sediments.

Because of the highly variable nature of the reservoir and the minor structural relief across the field, development was slow and based largely on subsurface geology. Seismic was of only limited value. When tied to closely spaced well control, time structure mapping on the top Mission Canyon was used to infer gross facies changes from "island" (structural high) to "marine" (structural low) sections. Gross isochron maps from the Bakken to the top of the Mission Canyon and the top of the Mission Canyon to the top of the Charles, also tied to well control, were used in a similar fashion, with

Figure 18. Gross isopach maps in descending stratigraphic position. Map A includes the gross interval of the Rival zone, the entire Charles Formation, and the lower Kibbey Formation. The pattern and magnitude of thickness variation in this map is essentially a mirror image to that shown in B. Thicks correspond to underlying marine facies, thins to island facies shown in Figure 9. Isopach map B is from the base of State "A" to top of Glenburn and includes the Mohall, Sherwood, and Bluell intervals. Thicks correspond to island facies in Figure 9, thins to marine facies. Contour interval for both maps is 10 ft (3 m).

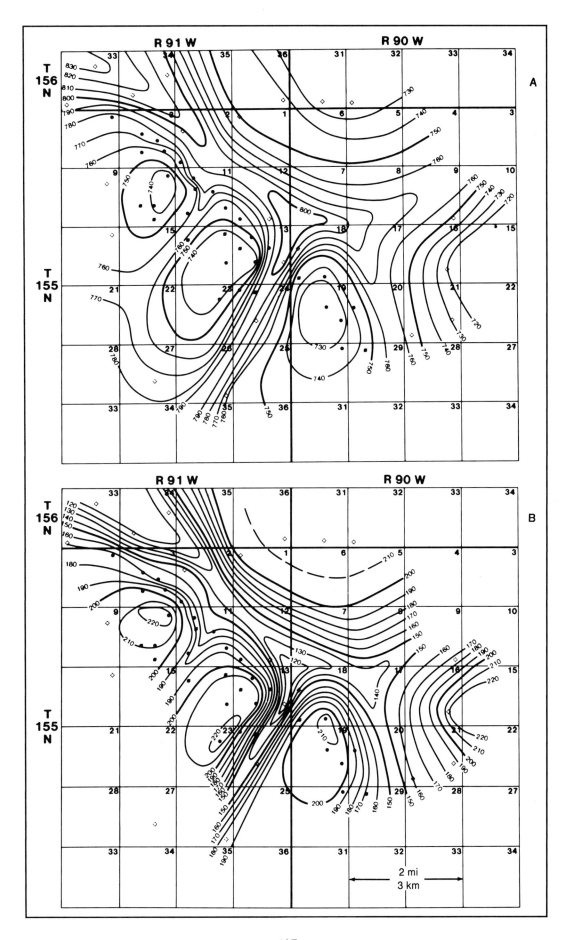

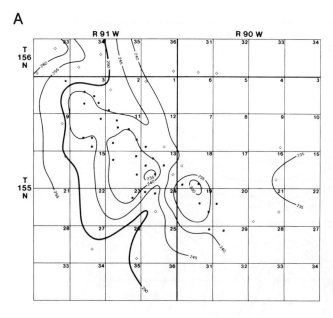

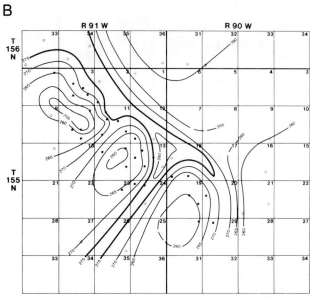

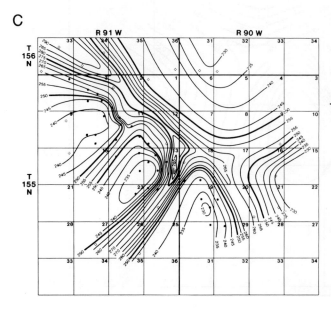

Mission Canyon thicks coupled with Charles thins indicating "island" section and the inverse indicating "marine" section. Application of secondary recovery techniques in the field has been discouraged by the heterogeneity of the reservoir rocks.

Volumetrically, the marine packstone-grainstone reservoir facies is much more productive than the island reservoir facies. When encountered, the former provides prolific production. This is apparent not only by comparing a map showing initial potential of the wells (Figure 24) to a map showing the distributions of depositional facies (Figure 9), but also by comparing decline curves from wells from the two facies (Figure 25A, B). The decline curve for the field is shown in Figure 25C.

Source

The source for the oil at Stanley field is the organic-rich black shale of the underlying Bakken Formation. Some oil also may have been sourced from Lodgepole and lower Mission Canyon carbonates. Depth to the Bakken at Stanley field is 9500 ft (2900 m). It is 90 ft (27 m) thick and includes a middle siltstone unit. Average total organic carbon within the black shale members is 11.5% with a maximum of 22%. The kerogen is type I and II. Vitrinite reflectance values are 0.4 to 1.1%. At Stanley field, based on burial history curves (Figure 26), the Bakken was estimated to have entered the oil window during the Late Cretaceous, about 70 Ma. Emplacement of oil into the reservoir appears to have occurred by combination of upward vertical migration of oil through fractures and lateral migration beneath impermeable carbonates and evaporites of the Rival.

EXPLORATION CONCEPTS

The importance of the Stanley field to exploration concepts is twofold. The first is local and pertains to the definition of a new play and the means to explore for similar fields in the Mission Canyon of

Figure 19. A series of three isopach maps of approximately equal intervals between the top Kibbey anhydrite and the base of the State "A." Maps are arranged in descending stratigraphic order to show the decreasing magnitude of compensation with increased overburden. This reflects diminishing impact of physical compaction with increased burial. Maps correspond to the following intervals: (A) top Kibbey anhydrite to top 3rd Charles salt (Figure 7); (B) top 3rd Charles salt to top 1st Charles salt; (C) top 1st Charles salt to base State "A." Maximum difference in thickness for A is 10 ft (3 m); B is 20 ft (6 m); and C is 30 ft (9 m). Contour interval for all maps is 5 ft (1.5 m).

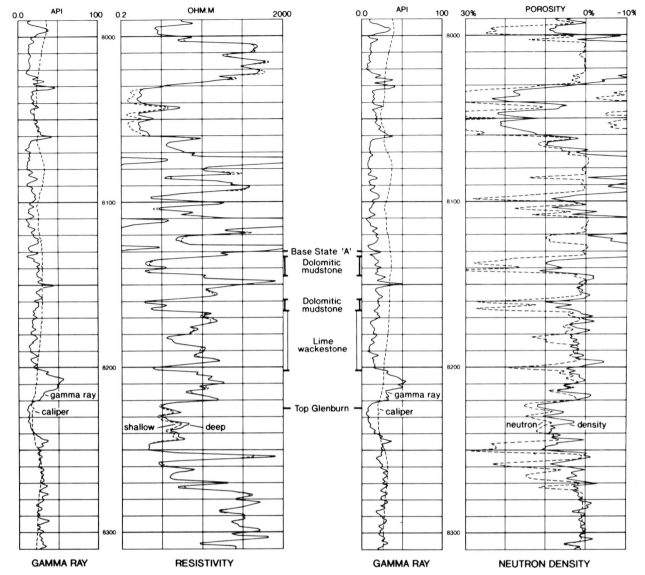

GAMMA RAY   RESISTIVITY   GAMMA RAY   NEUTRON DENSITY

Figure 20. Wireline logs from Marathon #13-43 Ogden Armour (NE SE Sec. 13, T155N, R91W) showing response to nonproductive muddy dolomite and limestone facies. The gamma ray curve is usually erratic with values between 20 and 35 API units for both limestone and dolomite. For the dolomite, resistivity is usually 0.6 to 1.0 ohm-m with little or no separation of deep and shallow curves; neutron-density response shows wide separation between neutron porosity and density porosity. The mud-rich limestones have a much higher resistivity of 10 to 50 ohm-m with no separation of curves; neutron-density reads tight, also with no separation of curves.

the Williston basin. The other is more general and underscores the recognition and potential significance of physical compaction of carbonate sediments. Both of these points were emphasized by Beach and Schumacher (1982a, b, c).

The importance of the Stanley field relative to a more regional play concept is that the associations of intertidal-supratidal sediments observed in the upper Mission Canyon at Stanley field are common within the Mission Canyon throughout much of the Williston basin (Edie, 1958; Lindsay and Kendall,

1980; Elliot, 1982). Locally, the Mission Canyon sediments were exposed to early meteoric diagenesis (Kaldi, 1982; Gerhard et al., 1978); however, this exposure was not ubiquitous. Sediments deposited in subtidal environments would certainly have been less prone to alteration by meteoric processes. Mission Canyon sediments are often capped by sealing evaporites (Malek-Aslani, 1971, 1977). In such situations, underlying uncemented sediments would physically compact as the basin subsided and overburden accumulated. Compacted mud-rich

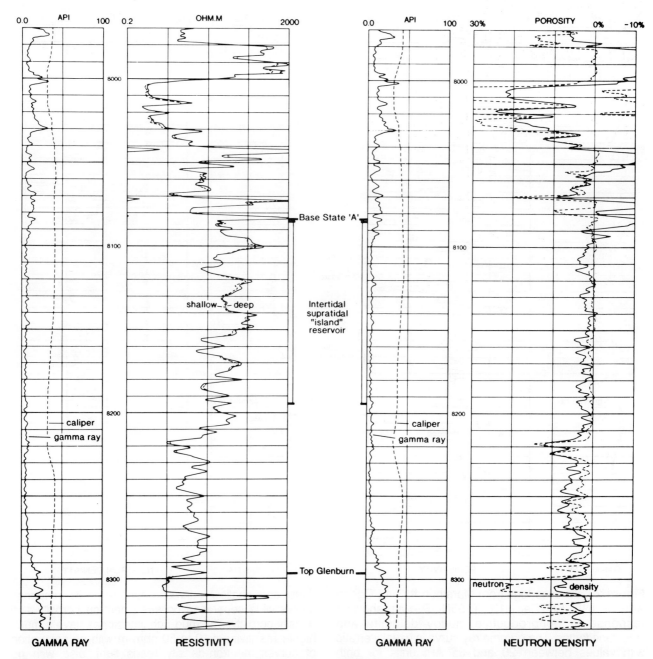

Figure 21. Wireline log from typical "island" well (Marathon #13-23 Armour, NE SW Sec. 13, T155N, R91W) showing clean (10 to 20 API units) even nature of gamma ray curve, resistivity of 10 to 100 ohm-m with no separation between deep and shallow curves. Neutron density logs show low porosity. Fracture logs would show the presence of occasional fractures.

sediments would form effective barriers to hydrocarbon migration. Porous grain-rich sediments, having avoided meteoric diagenesis, would stand to preserve primary porosity and thus retain the potential to serve as hydrocarbon reservoirs. Cemented sediments would have resisted this compaction.

Fields near Stanley that appear to have the same association of compacted updip subtidal facies and uncompacted intertidal-supratidal facies in the upper Mission Canyon are the Sherwood field in Renville County and the Flaxton field in Burke County. Flaxton field has an added benefit resulting from the differential compaction of upper Mission Canyon (Bluell) facies. Beds overlying the Bluell drape across resistant "island" intervals into updip compacted marine intervals. This drape created structural highs and allowed hydrocarbons to accumulate not only stratigraphically in the Bluell interval but also

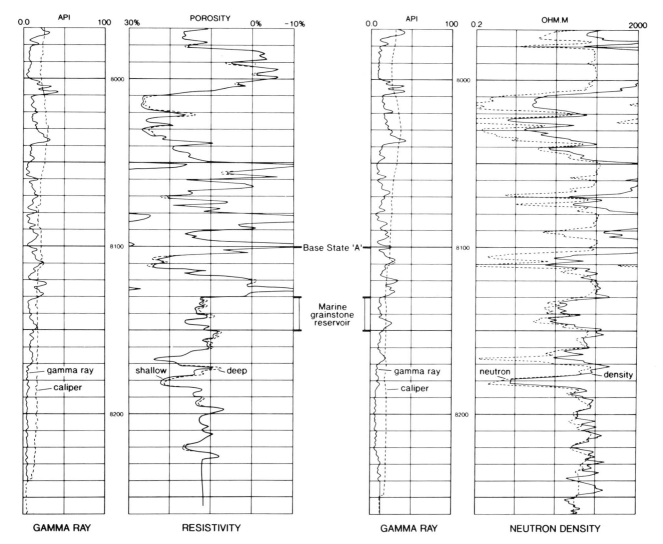

Figure 22. Wireline log from the subtidal grainstone reservoir facies in the Marathon #13-32 State (SW NE Sec. 13, T155N, R91W). The gamma ray reads relatively clean rock (10 to 20 API units); resistivities are 6 to 20 ohm-m with good separation between shallow and deep curves; and neutron-density response shows both neutron porosity and density porosity with some separation in curves. Dolomitic intervals underlying the porous grainstone are not productive reservoir rock.

structurally in overlying porous Midale beds. Such a situation was predicted by Shinn et al. (1977).

An application of the differential compaction of marine versus island facies lies in the use of isopach maps to predict and map upper Mission Canyon depositional facies. Because many of the older wells only tagged the top of the Mission Canyon, isopachs of the upper Mission Canyon usually lack sufficient detail to permit their use for exploration. However, all wells drilled to the Mission Canyon must necessarily drill through the Charles Formation. Therefore, because the Charles isopach also reflects the underlying Mission Canyon facies, it may be used to provide a much better regional picture of the distribution of these facies. Such maps are very accurate. Log picks in the Charles are also very straightforward.

The second fundamental exploration concept learned from the study of Stanley field lies in the recognition of the occurrence, timing, and magnitude of physical compaction and its relative importance to potential reservoirs and seals. Squeezing acts to reduce porosity, as has been shown in both carbonate and noncarbonate sediments (Weller, 1959; Shinn and Robbin, 1983). This improves the ability of muddy sediments to trap hydrocarbons but reduces porosity in reservoir rock. One should expect to see evidence of physical compaction in any situation where

411

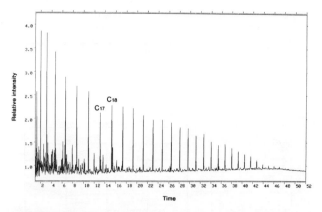

Figure 23. Representative gas chromatogram of oil from the upper Mission Canyon reservoir at Stanley field.

Seismic has thus far proven to be of limited value in the exploration for additional Stanley fields. This mostly reflects the subtle nature of isopach and structural differences between the compacted versus uncompacted upper Mission Canyon facies (Figure 28). Time differences of 2 to 5 milliseconds can be significant in both structural and isochron mapping, therefore "pushing" the limits of resolution of the data. Difficulty also results from the fact that there are, unfortunately, no consistent, reliable mappable reflectors within either the Mission Canyon, Charles, or Lodgepole formations. The most reliable seismic-based tools are structural maps near the top of the Mission Canyon combined with isochron maps from the Bakken to the Mission Canyon and Mission Canyon to the top of the Charles. When possible, all mapping with seismic should be closely tied to subsurface well control.

carbonate sediments, for whatever reason, escape subjection to processes resulting in early pervasive cementation, including both meteoric or submarine derived cements. In the case of meteoric cementation, it is envisioned that such criteria could be met by (1) entombment under an impermeable seal such as a shale or evaporite, as at Stanley field, (2) through rapid subsidence of a basin or shelf edge, or (3) deposition in a deep-sea environment (Figure 27).

ACKNOWLEDGMENTS

The authors are grateful to Marathon Oil Company for permission to publish this paper. We would especially like to thank our co-workers in Marathon's exploration, production, and petroleum technology groups for their help, stimulating discussions, and

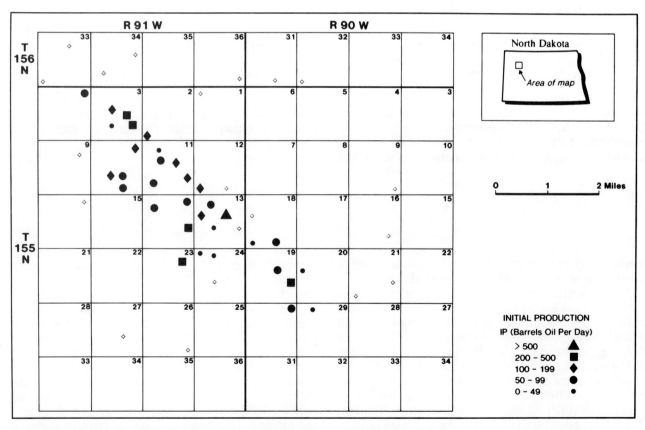

Figure 24. Map showing initial production (IP) values for wells in Stanley field. The better wells in the field generally contain porous marine grainstone (compare to Figure 9).

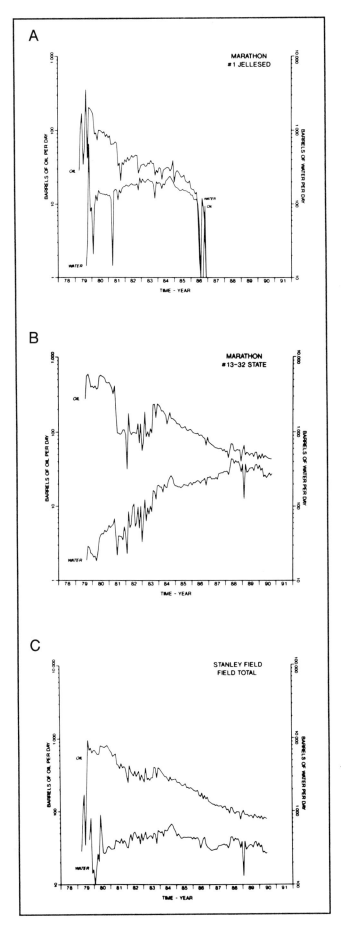

support. H. Dembicki, Jr., provided the chromatogram and B. J. Russell assisted in preparing the burial history plot. T. J. McCutcheon and D. R. Sneed provided Marathon file information. Permission from the Saskatchewan Geological Society to use parts from a earlier paper is acknowledged.

REFERENCES CITED

Anderson, S. B., J. P. Bluemle, and L. C. Gerhard, 1982, Oil exploration and development in the North Dakota Williston basin, *in* J. E. Christopher and J. Kaldi, eds., Fourth International Williston Basin Symposium: Saskatchewan Geological Society Special Publication 6, Regina, Saskatchewan, p. 3-10.

Bathurst, R. G. C., 1980, Deep crustal diagenesis in limestones: Revista del Instituto de Investigaciones Geologicas Diputacion Provincial, Universidad de Barcelona, v. 34, p. 89-100.

Bally, A. W., and S. Snelson, 1980, Realms of subsidence, *in* Facts and principles of world petroleum occurrence: Canadian Society of Petroleum Geologists Memoir 6, p. 9-94.

Beach, D. K., and A. L. Schumacher, 1982a, Stanley field, North Dakota—new model of stratigraphically trapped oil, Mission Canyon Formation, Central Williston basin (abstr.): AAPG Bulletin, v. 66, p. 547.

Beach, D. K., and A. L. Schumacher, 1982b, Stanley field, North Dakota—economic and quantitative significance of mechanically compacted shallow-water limestone (abstr.): AAPG Bulletin, v. 66, p. 547-548.

Beach, D. K., and A. Schumacher, 1982c, Stanley field, North Dakota: a new model for a new exploration play, *in* J. E. Christopher and J. Kaldi, eds., Fourth International Williston Basin Symposium: Saskatchewan Geological Society Special Publication 6, Regina, Saskatchewan, p. 235-243.

Bhattacharyya, A., and G. M. Friedman, 1979, Experimental compaction of ooids and lime mud and its implication for lithification during burial: Journal of Sedimentary Petrology, v. 49, p. 1279-1286.

Bluemle, J. P., S. B. Anderson, and C. G. Carlson, 1981, Williston basin stratigraphic nomenclature chart: North Dakota Geological Survey Miscellaneous Series No. 61.

Butler, G. P., P. M. Harris, and C. G. St. C. Kendall, 1982, Recent evaporites from the Abu Dhabi coastal flats, *in* C. R. Hanford, R. G. Loucks, and G. R. Davies, eds., Depositional and diagenetic spectra of evaporites—a core workshop: SEPM Core Workshop No. 3, p. 33-64.

Choquette, P. W., and N. P. James, 1987, Diagenesis #12. Diagenesis in limestones—3. The deep burial environment: Geoscience Canada, v.14, p. 3-35.

Dow, W. G., 1974, Application of oil-correlation and source-rock data to exploration in Williston basin: AAPG Bulletin, v. 58, p. 1253-1262.

Edie, R. W., 1958, Mississippian sedimentation and oil fields in southeastern Saskatchewan: AAPG Bulletin, v. 42, p. 94-126.

Elliott, T. L., 1982, Carbonate facies, depositional cycles, and the development of secondary porosity during burial diagenesis: Mission Canyon Formation, Haas field, North Dakota, *in* J. E. Christopher and J. Kaldi, eds., Fourth International Williston

Figure 25. Comparison of decline curves for two wells from Stanley field. The curve on the top (A) is from an "island" well (Marathon #1 Jellesed, NE NW Sec. 13, T155N, R91W) characterized by a tight but fractured reservoir; below that, B is from a well containing productive porous marine grainstone reservoir (Marathon #13-32 State, SW NE Sec. 13, T155N, R91W). Note the initial rapid decline from the island well versus more sustained production from the marine reservoir. At the bottom, C is the decline curve for the total field.

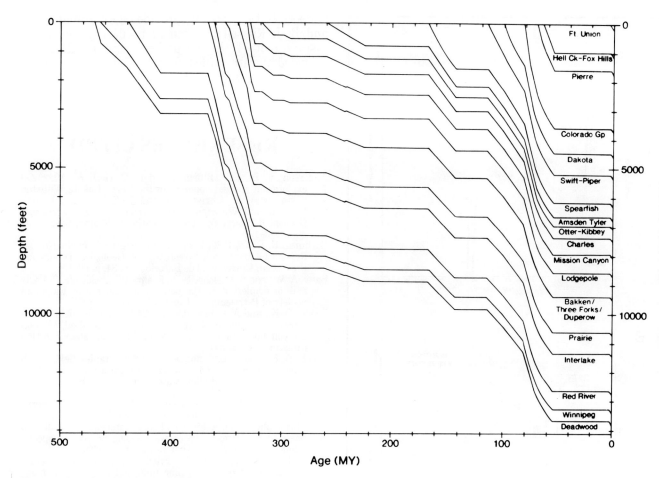

Figure 26. Geohistory diagram for Stanley field. The shales of the Bakken Formation are estimated to have entered the oil window about 70 Ma.

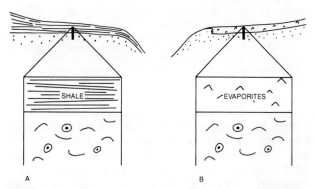
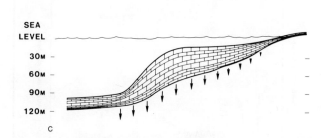

Figure 27. Schematic representations of possible depositional and early post-depositional settings that would allow shallow water carbonate sediments to avoid early meteoric diagenesis, thus being susceptible to subsequent physical compaction upon burial. Sketches A and B show core representations of isolation via entombment under impermeable seals such as shales or evaporites; C depicts deposition on a rapidly subsiding shelf or in a deep sea setting.

414

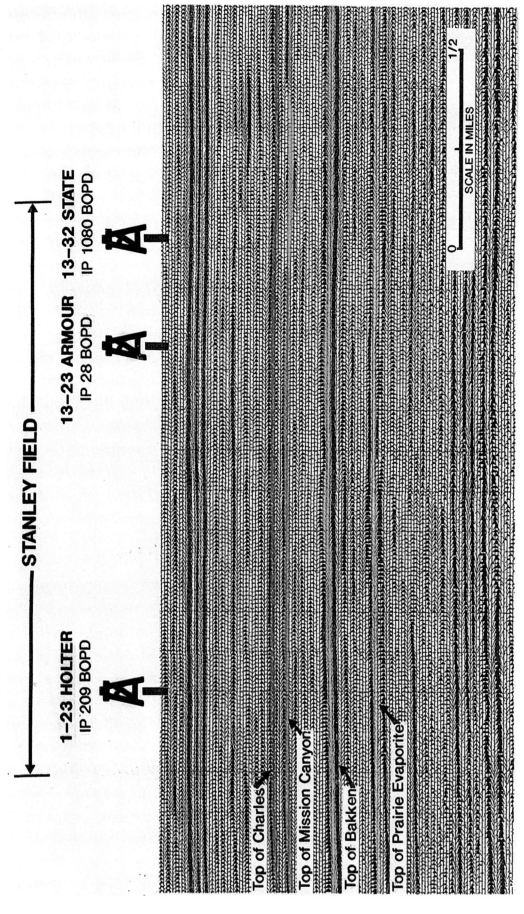

Figure 28. Vibroseis (24-fold) line trending southwest-northeast across Stanley field from island facies (orange) to marine reservoir and trap facies (blue). Location shown in Figure 2.

Basin Symposium: Saskatchewan Geological Society Special Publication 6, Regina, Saskatchewan, p.131-151.

Gerhard, L. C., S. B. Anderson, and J. Berg, 1978, Mission Canyon porosity development, Glenburn field, North Dakota Williston basin, *in* The economic geology of the Williston basin: Montana Geological Society 24th Annual Conference, p. 177-188.

Gerhard, L. C., S. B. Anderson, J. A LeFeuer, and C. G. Carlson, 1982, Geological development, origin, and energy mineral resources of Williston basin, North Dakota: AAPG Bulletin, v. 66, n. 8, p. 989-1020.

Habicht, J. K. A., 1979, Paleoclimate, paleomagnetism, and continental drift: AAPG Studies in Geology 9, 31 p.

Harris, S. H., C. B. Land, Jr., and J. H. McKeever, 1966, Relation of Mission Canyon stratigraphy to oil production in north-central North Dakota: AAPG Bulletin, v. 50, p. 2269-2276.

Johnson, W., 1956, Mississippian oil fields of northeastern Williston basin (abstr.): First International Williston Basin Symposium, p. 52.

Kaldi, J., 1982, Reservoir properties, depositional environments and diagenesis of the Mississippian Midale beds, Midale field, southeastern Saskatchewan, *in* J. E. Christopher and J. Kaldi, eds., Fourth International Williston Basin Symposium: Saskatchewan Geological Society Special Publication 6, Regina, Saskatchewan, p. 211-216.

Klemme, H. D., 1971, What giants and their basins have in common: Oil and Gas Journal, v. 69, n. 9, 10, 11; pt. 1, p. 85-90; pt. 2, p. 103-110; pt. 3, p. 96-100.

Lindsay, R. F., and C. G. St. C. Kendall, 1980, Depositional facies, diagenesis and reservoir character of the Mission Canyon Formation of the Williston basin at the Little Knife field, Billings, Dunn, and McKenzie Counties, North Dakota, *in* R. B. Halley and R. G. Loucks, eds., Carbonate reservoir rocks, Notes for SEPM Core Workshop No. 1: Denver, Colorado, p. 79-104.

Lineback, J. A., and M. L. Davidson, 1982, The Williston basin—sediment starved during the early Mississippian, *in* J. E. Christopher and J. Kaldi, eds. Fourth International Williston Basin Symposium: Saskatchewan Geological Society Special Publication 6, Regina, Saskatchewan, p. 125-130.

Malek-Aslani, M., 1971, Depositional environment of Mission Canyon (Mississippian) oil fields in north-central North Dakota (abstr.): AAPG Bulletin, v. 55, p. 351.

Malek-Aslani, M., 1977, Plate tectonics and sedimentary cycles in carbonates: Gulf Coast Association Geological Societies Transactions, v. 27, p. 125-133.

Meyers, W. J., 1980, Compaction in Mississippian skeletal limestones, southwestern New Mexico: Journal of Sedimentary Petrology, v. 50, p. 457-474.

Pray, L. C., 1960, Compaction in calcilutites (abstr.): GSA Bulletin, v. 71, p. 1946.

Purser, B. H., and G. Evans, 1973, Regional sedimentation along the Trucial Coast, southeast Persian Gulf, *in* B. H. Purser, ed., The Persian Gulf: New York, Springer-Verlag, p. 211-231.

St. John, B., A. W. Bally, and H. D. Klemme, 1984, Sedimentary provinces of the world, hydrocarbon productive and nonproductive: AAPG Map Series, 35 p.

Shinn, E. A., and D. M. Robbin, 1983, Mechanical and chemical compaction in fine-grained shallow-water limestones: Journal of Sedimentary Petrology, v. 53, p. 595-618.

Shinn, E. A., R. B. Halley, J. H. Hudson, and B. H. Lidz, 1977, Limestone compaction: an enigma: Geology, v. 5, p. 21-24.

Shinn, E. A., D. M. Robbin, and R. P. Steinen, 1980, Experimental compaction of lime sediment (abstr.): AAPG Bulletin, v. 64, p. 783.

Steed, R. W., 1983, The depositional environment and stratigraphy of the Mississippian Mission Canyon formation, east central Williston basin, North Dakota: Unpublished M.S. Thesis, Duke University, p. 163.

Terzaghi, R. D., 1940, Compaction of lime mud as a cause of secondary structure: Journal of Sedimentary Petrology, v. 10, p. 78-90.

Weller, J. M., 1959, Compaction of sediments: AAPG Bulletin, v. 43, p. 273-310.

Williams, J. A., 1974, Characterization of oil types in Williston basin: AAPG Bulletin, v. 58, p. 1243-1252.

Wilson, J. L., 1975, Carbonate facies in geologic history. New York, Springer-Verlag, 471 p.

Appendix 1. Field Description

Field name .... *Stanley field*

Ultimate recoverable reserves .... *3,300,000 BO*

Field location:

    Country .... *U.S.A.*

    State .... *North Dakota*

    Basin,Province .... *Williston basin*

Field discovery:

    Year first pay discovered .... *Mississippian upper Mission Canyon Formation 1977*

Discovery well name and general location:

    First pay .... *No. 1 Harstad, NE SW Sec. 10, T155N, R91W, Mountrail County, North Dakota*

Discovery well operator .... *Thompson Petroleum*

IP .... *120 BOPD*

All other zones with shows of oil and gas in the field:

Age	Formation	Type of Show
Mississippian	*Midale-Rival interval*	*Stain and DST show*
	Lower Mission Canyon	*Stain in core*

Geologic concept leading to discovery and method or methods used to delineate prospect

Concept for initial play was dual objective. Shallow objective, based on subsurface well control, was porosity zone in Rival interval downdip of tight carbonate and anhydrite. Deep objective, based on seismic, was Devonian Winnipegosis reef. Discovery well cored Bluell interval and recovered 1500 ft (457 m) of oil on DST. Subsequent drilling and seismic led to concept of cemented intertidal-supratidal islands dissected by marine channels entering an updip lagoon. Marine grainstones were deposited as tidal delta and channel sands. Marine sediments avoided early cementation and were subsequently compacted; island sediments were not. Marine grainstones provide the best reservoir, marine wackestone and mudstone the updip trap. This concept was confirmed through further drilling.

Structure:

    Province/basin type .... *Cratonic basin; Bally 121, Klemme I*

    Tectonic history

The Williston basin is a broad depression situated on the western edge of the Canadian shield. The basin was a well-defined structural depression by the Middle Ordovician. During the Devonian the basin was tilted to the north and was part of the large Elk Point basin. By the Mississippian, a seaway connection existed through the central Montana trough that persisted through the Triassic. Jurassic-Cretaceous sediments were deposited as a result of the basin being incorporated into the western interior Cretaceous seaway.

    Regional structure

Stanley field is situated along the gently dipping, eastern flank of the Williston basin, approximately 25 mi (40 km) east of the Nesson anticline.

    Local structure

Stanley field comprises a northwest-trending terrace development along the gently dipping (1°) eastern flank of the Williston basin. Three discrete structural highs, with up to 50 ft of structural closure, are present at the top of the pay and reflect underlying depositional facies.

STANLEY

417

Trap:

Trap type(s)

Stanley field is largely a stratigraphic trap comprising an updip facies change from fractured intertidal-supratidal rock having scattered fenestral porosity and porous subtidal grainstone and packstone with preserved primary interparticle porosity to tight subtidal wackestone and mudstone. Overlying anhydrite forms the top seal.

Basin stratigraphy (major stratigraphic intervals from surface to deepest penetration in field):

Chronostratigraphy	Formation	Depth to Top in ft (m)
Cretaceous	*Greenhorn*	*4297 (1310)*
	Dakota	*5022 (1531)*
Permian	*Minnelusa*	*6788 (2069)*
Mississippian	*Charles (Madison)*	*7584 (2312)*
	Mission Canyon	*8114 (2473)*
Mississippian-Devonian	*Bakken*	*9508 (2898)*
Silurian	*Interlake*	*11,572 (3527)*
Ordovician	*Red River*	*12,890 (3929)*

Reservoir characteristics:

Number of reservoirs *1*

Formations .... *Mission Canyon Formation*

Ages .... *Mississippian*

Depths to tops of reservoirs .... *8908 ft (2715 m) average*

Gross thickness (top to bottom of producing interval) .... *120 ft (37 m)*

Net thickness—total thickness of producing zones

    Average .... *8 ft (2.4 m)*

    Maximum .... *72 ft (22 m)*

Lithology

Limestone: pisolitic-oolitic intertidal-supratidal grainstone and packstone and locally developed skeletal marine grainstone

Porosity type

Fenestral with additional fracture porosity; also, primary interparticle and intraparticle porosity in marine skeletal grainstones

Average porosity *8%*

Average permeability .... *25 md (excluding fractures)*

Seals:

Upper

    Formation, fault, or other feature .... *Rival member*

    Lithology .... *Anhydrite*

Lateral

    Formation, fault, or other feature .... *Facies change*

    Lithology .... *Updip compacted subtidal wackestones/mudstones*

Source:

Formation and age .... *Bakken, Mississippian-Devonian*

Lithology .... *Organic-rich laminated black shale with middle siltstone unit*

Average total organic carbon (TOC) *11.5%*

Maximum TOC *22%*

Kerogen type (I, II, or III) .... *I and II*

Vitrinite reflectance (maturation) .... $R_o = 0.4$–1.1%

Time of hydrocarbon expulsion .... *Cretaceous-Tertiary*
Present depth to top of source .... *9500 ft (2896 m)*
Thickness .... *90 ft (27 m)*
Potential yield .... *102.3 × 10⁹ bbl (16.3 × 10⁹ m³) oil, North Dakota and Montana;*
little mature Bakken present in Canada

Appendix 2. Production Data

Field name .... *Stanley field*

Field size:

    Proved acres .... *4000 ac (1620 ha)*

    Number of wells all years *33*

    Current number of wells *24*

    Well spacing .... *160 ac*

    Ultimate recoverable .... *3,300,000 bbl*

    Cumulative production .... *2,450,580 bbl*

    Annual production .... *228,072 bbl*

    Present decline rate *30%*

        Initial decline rate *75%*

        Overall decline rate *38%*

    Annual water production .... *265,855 bbl*

    In place, total reserves .... *16 million bbl*

    In place, per acre foot .... *400 bbl*

    Primary recovery .... *3,300,000 bbl*

    Secondary recovery .... *NA*

    Enhanced recovery .... *NA*

    Cumulative water production .... *3,032,054 bbl*

Drilling and casing practices:

    Amount of surface casing set .... *80 ft (207 m)*

    Casing program

    8⅝-in. surface casing run to approx. 675 ft (205 m)

    Drilling mud

    Commonly drill with pit water to Cretaceous Greenhorn (4600 ft, 1400 m); drill with salt-base mud (average weight 10.5 lb/gal) to TD

    Bit program .... *NA*

    High pressure zones .... *NA*

Completion practices:

    Interval(s) perforated .... *Bluell and Sherwood members, Mission Canyon Formation*

    Well treatment .... *Low volume (less than 1000 gallons) 15% MCA acid stimulation*

Formation evaluation:

    Logging suites .... *FD/CCNL. BHC Sonic, DLL MSFL*

    Testing practices .... *60 ft (18 m) core in Bluell-Sherwood members of the Mission Canyon followed by DST of interval*

    Mud logging techniques .... *Gas chromatograph; hot wire gas detector from Mississippian Charles-Mississippian Mission Canyon*

Oil characteristics:

Type .... *NA*
API gravity .... *33°*
Base .... *NA*
Initial GOR .... *280.1 (mcfg/bbl oil)*
Sulfur, wt% .... *0.5 wt.%*
Viscosity, SUS *0.8cp*
Pour Point .... *NA*
Gas-oil distillate .... *NA*

Field characteristics:

Average elevation .... *2210 ft (674 m)*
Initial pressure .... *3600 psi (24.8 × 10³ kPa)*
Present pressure .... *1000–2000 psi (6.9 × 10³–13.8 × 10³ kPa)*
Pressure gradient .... *0.44 psi/ft (995 kPa/m)*
Temperature .... *180°F (82°C)*
Geothermal gradient .... *0.01°F/ft (0.018°C/m)*
Drive .... *Water, decline rates indicate that the drive is only a partial water drive at best*
Oil column thickness .... *l20 ft (36m) maximum*
Oil-water contact .... *−5925 ft (−1806 m) (possibly higher oil-water contact at south end of field,*
−5885 ft, −1794 m)

Connate water .... *NA*
Water salinity, TDS .... *2,000,000 ppm*
Resistivity of water .... *0.02 ohm at BHT*
Bulk volume water (%) .... *NA*

Transportation method and market for oil and gas:

Pipeline, central United States

Richardton/Taylor Fields— U.S.A.
Williston Basin, North Dakota

P. J. CHIMNEY
Chevron Overseas Petroleum
San Ramon, California

C. E. TRESKA
Chevron U.S.A.
Houston, Texas

C. A. WOLOSIN
Consultant
Casper, Wyoming

FIELD CLASSIFICATION

BASIN: Williston
BASIN TYPE: Cratonic Sag
RESERVOIR ROCK TYPE: Sandstone
RESERVOIR ENVIRONMENT
  OF DEPOSITION: Marine Shelf

RESERVOIR AGE: Ordovician
PETROLEUM TYPE: Gas and Condensate
TRAP TYPE: Combination Faulted
  Anticline and Porosity Loss

TRAP DESCRIPTION: Sandstone draped across anticline on upthrown block; lateral closure by structure and porosity changes in sandstone

LOCATION

Richardton and Taylor are both single-well gas fields located in Stark County, North Dakota. The fields are situated on the south-central flank of the Williston basin (Figures 1 and 10) along the north–south-trending Heart River fault.

The single-well Buffalo Creek field, producing from the Ordovician Red River carbonate, is located 5 mi (8 km) south of the Richardton field (Figure 2). To date, no other production has been established along the Heart River fault trend (Figures 2 and 11).

The total combined productive areas of Richardton and Taylor fields comprise approximately 1200 ac (486 ha) with an estimate of ultimate recoverable reserves from the Ordovician Winnipeg sandstones of 9 bcf gas and 250 thousand bbl of condensate. No other horizons have been proven productive within the current field outlines.

Both fields are operated by Chevron USA as part of the Southwest Williston Basin Partnership, a joint venture with CONOCO, Inc.

HISTORY

Pre-Discovery

In 1957, Pan American Petroleum (now AMOCO) drilled the first deep test on the Heart River fault trend area, the #1 Raymond Vetter, Sec. 27, T139N, R90W, Stark County, North Dakota (Figure 2). The well was drilled to a total depth of 11,212 ft (3417 m) into the Ordovician Winnipeg Formation (Figure 9) before being plugged and abandoned. No significant shows of oil or gas were reported during drilling.

The first production on the Heart River fault trend was established by Texaco at the #1 Adam Schank NCT-1, Sec. 15, T137N, R92W, Stark County, North Dakota (Figure 2). The Schank well, drilled in 1966, bottomed in the Ordovician Red River carbonates (Figure 9) at 10,426 ft (3177 m). The well was subsequently completed in the Red River flowing 265 BOPD and 30 BWPD. Cumulative production for the well is in excess of 490 MBO. Several offsets to the Schank well were drilled but all were unsuccessful;

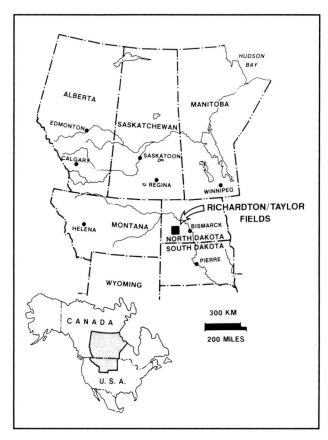

Figure 1. Regional map of the Northern Great Plains showing the general location of the Richardton/Taylor gas fields.

it remains the only producer in the Buffalo Creek field.

Prior to the discovery of the Richardton and Taylor gas fields, in the 22 townships (800 mi²; 2100 km²) contiguous to the prospects, seven wells were drilled to the Ordovician Red River carbonates and only one well to the Winnipeg sandstone, the gas reservoir in the fields (Figure 2).

With the well control available prior to drilling the initial prospect, it was not possible to define regional porosity or permeability trends in the Winnipeg sandstone. It was possible to map the regional southward thinning of the Black Island Member sandstone (Figures 16 and 17). The discovery of oil in the Cambrian Deadwood Formation at the Newporte field in north-central North Dakota in 1978 increased Gulf's interest in exploring the Cambrian and Lower Ordovician section (Clement and Mayhew, 1979). Anderson (1982) provides a summary of exploration for Winnipeg sandstone reservoirs in the Williston basin.

Discovery

Based on the above information Gulf decided to drill the initial deep test (1-21-1B Leviathan, Figure 2) past the Ordovician Red River and into the Winnipeg-Deadwood interval. Two discovery wells were drilled based on regional and detailed seismic mapping. Regional "spec" surveys were purchased to identify large time-structural highs. Several closed time-highs were mapped along the structural trend bounded by the Heart River fault trend. The time-highs were then shot out with a detailed 600% CDP seismic survey, with lines generally oriented north-south and east-west in an orthogonal grid. Line spacing of the detailed seismic program was frequently 0.5 mi (800 m) or less.

Based on the regional and detailed seismic mapping, Gulf acquired a large acreage position on the Heart River fault trend (Figure 3). Acreage was acquired without firm drillable prospects in order to gain a competitive advantage over other operators in the play.

The Richardton gas field (Figure 6) was opened with the completion of the Gulf Oil 1-21-1B Leviathan, Sec. 21, T138N, R92W, Stark County, North Dakota. The well was completed in November 1980 flowing 3500 MCFGPD and 1 BCPD. The Leviathan prospect, discovery well for the Richardton field, was mapped in fashion similar to the Ogre prospect, described below.

Figures 4 and 5 illustrate, respectively, the time-structure from the Ordovician Winnipeg reflector and the Mississippian Mission Canyon to Winnipeg isochron for the Ogre prospect. The Taylor gas field (Figure 6) was discovered with the completion of the Gulf Oil 1-24-1C Ogre, Sec. 24, T139N, R93W, Stark County, North Dakota. This well was potentialed in September 1981 flowing 3230 MCFGPD and 120 BCPD.

It is interesting to note that the location for the Ogre well was not selected solely at a position on the crest of the time structural high, but rather as a compromise between the time high and the isochron thin. A deep time high without a corresponding isochron thin was rejected as a valid prospect.

Post-Discovery

The development drilling following the two wildcat discoveries was concentrated on extending production along the strike of the Heart River fault. Figure 6 illustrates the number of step-out wells Gulf drilled as part of the development of the Winnipeg sandstone play. Unfortunately, none of the step-out development wells were successful in establishing commercial production.

A wildcat well, the Mobil #1 Bernhardt, drilled in late 1980 in Sec. 28, T141N, R93W, Stark County, North Dakota, did test significant quantities of gas from the Winnipeg sandstone (Figure 6). Flow rates in excess of 2000 MCFGPD were reported. However, subsequent fracturing and acidizing operations may have severely damaged the reservoir and inhibited gas flow to subeconomic rates. A further discussion

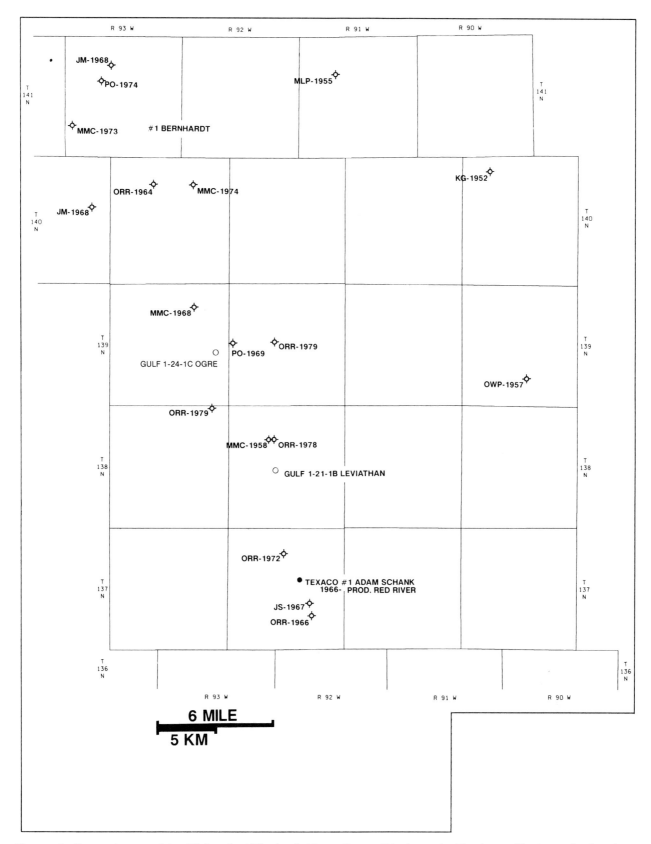

Figure 2. General area of the Richardton/Taylor fields showing well control prior to the discovery of the Richardton/Taylor gas fields. Code to formations at total depth: OWP, Ordovician Winnipeg; ORR, Ordovician Red River; MLP, Mississippian Lodgepole; MMC, Mississippian Mission Canyon; PO, Pennsylvanian Otter; JM, Jurassic Morrison; JS, Jurassic Sundance; KG, Cretaceous Greenhorn. See Figure 9 for a generalized columnar section of the Williston basin. The location of Richardton field is at the 1-21-1B Leviathan; the Taylor field is at the 1-24-1C Ogre.

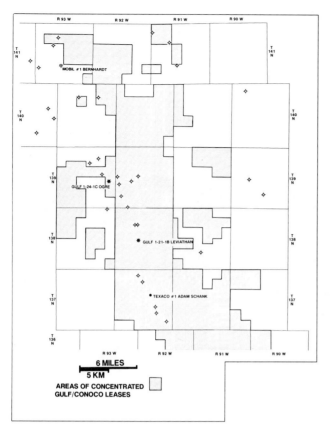

Figure 3. Map showing Gulf/CONOCO leases.

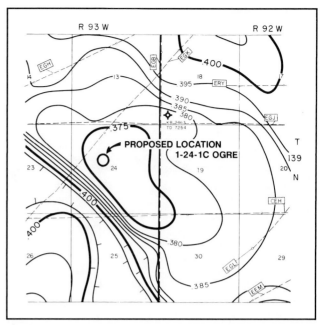

Figure 5. Time isochron for Mississippian Mission Canyon to Ordovician Winnipeg for Ogre prospect.

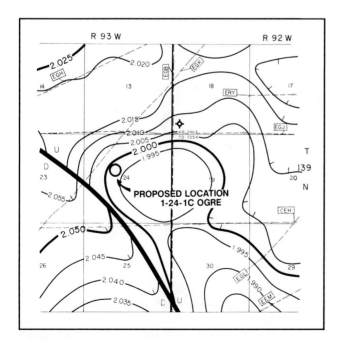

Figure 4. Time structure map of the top of Winnipeg for Ogre prospect.

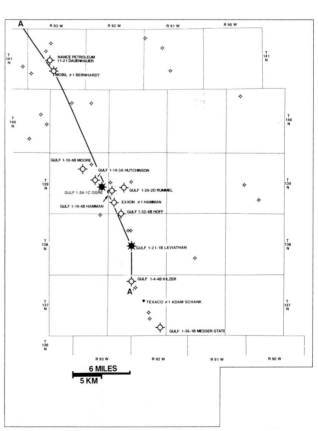

Figure 6. Map showing post-discovery drilling in the area of the Richardton/Taylor fields. Cross section A–A′ marked on map is shown in Figure 19.

of problems with clays found in the Winnipeg sandstone is found in the reservoir geology section.

No additional development drilling in the fields occurred after the end of 1983. Rapid, lateral variations in reservoir quality are the major risk factor in the failure of the development program to extend production and prove additional reserves.

DISCOVERY METHOD

The Williston basin has several good to excellent seismic reflectors for use in time-structural mapping. One of these is the Ordovician Winnipeg Shale (Figure 9). Depth conversions were generally not attempted because of severe near-surface velocity variations.

Standard practice for exploring in the Williston basin includes time-structure maps combined with "thinning" on selected isochron maps. The isochrons found to be most useful are the Mississippian-Devonian Bakken-Winnipeg or the Devonian Prairie Salt-Winnipeg (Figure 9). Many years of exploration experience have shown that without a "deep thin" coincident with a deep time-structure, it is either a near-surface velocity pull-up or a young structure.

Many oil and gas fields within the Williston basin are located over Precambrian basement structural highs. Recurrent movement of basement structural blocks during the Phanerozoic resulted in less deposition over the high as opposed to adjacent areas. Brown (1978) and Brown and Brown (1987) interpreted regional lineaments as basement block boundaries and applied these interpreted boundaries to mapping of sedimentary facies.

STRUCTURE

Tectonic History

The Williston basin (Figure 10) is the largest intracratonic basin in North America, covering approximately 300,000 mi² (777,000 km²). The basin is characterized by gentle flanks with dips generally less than 1°. Several large, basement-fault-controlled anticlinal structures (Nesson anticline) are located in the central portions near the basin near the city of Williston, North Dakota, from which the basin takes its name. Seismic line ADZ (Figures 7 and 8) covers approximately 150 mi (240 km) in an east-west direction and illustrates the overall geometry of the basin.

The deepest part of the basin is located in west-central North Dakota where over 16,000 ft (4900 m) of sedimentary section, ranging in age from Cambrian to Tertiary, is represented. Figure 9 is a generalized columnar section typical of the middle of the Williston basin. Erosion along the flanks of the basin on several

regional unconformities has removed much of the sedimentary section. Carlson and Anderson (1965) subdivided the basin's depositional history into the Sauk, Tippecanoe, Kaskaskia, Absaroka, Zuni, and Tejas sequences based on major unconformities within the section.

Transgression from the west during the Sauk sequence (Lower Cambrian–Lower Ordovician) flooded the eroded Precambrian crystalline basement. The sandstones and shales of the Deadwood-Flathead sequence record the initial sedimentary deposition upon this crystalline surface. The Tippecanoe sequence (Middle Ordovician–Silurian) was deposited during a second marine cycle. The cycle begins with the sandstones and shales of the Winnipeg Formation, the pay sands in the Richardton and Taylor fields, and ends with the carbonates of the Red River, Stony Mountain, Stonewall, and Interlake formations. A major erosional unconformity at the top of the Interlake Formation closed the Tippecanoe sequence.

By the end of the Tippecanoe sequence, the Williston basin was a well-defined structural basin. Marine connections existed to the west and southwest. Further deposition during later stages buried the Tippecanoe sequence to its present depth. Major periods of erosion at the end of subsequent stages have removed various thicknesses of the record of prior deposition, especially along the southern, eastern, and northern flanks of the Williston basin.

Regional Structure

Brown (1978), Brown and Brown (1987), Gerhard et al. (1982), and Thomas (1974) have suggested that the Williston basin and its subsidence is part of a wrench-fault tectonic system. According to this concept, a system of fault blocks has been periodically realigned as the result of regional tectonic stresses. The major axes of shearing are oriented northwest-southeast and northeast-southwest. The northwest-southeast structural grain is more pronounced in the basin, with many fields oriented along structures on this trend.

Fields oriented along northwest-southeast trends include the Cedar Creek anticline complex and Mondak field of Montana. In North Dakota, major fields with the same orientation include the extension of the Mondak structure, the Bicentennial, and the Antelope (Figure 10). No significant accumulations of hydrocarbons are present along the northeast-southwest direction of proposed shearing.

Several major north-south structures have developed in the basin. The most important of these are the Billings Nose, Little Knife, and Nesson anticlinal features (Figure 10). Compressive orogenic forces during the late Mesozoic–early Cenozoic Laramide event constituted the latest orogenic episode and caused basement blocks to readjust, forming large folds in the overlying section. The Nesson anticline is visible on seismic line ADZ (Figure 7).

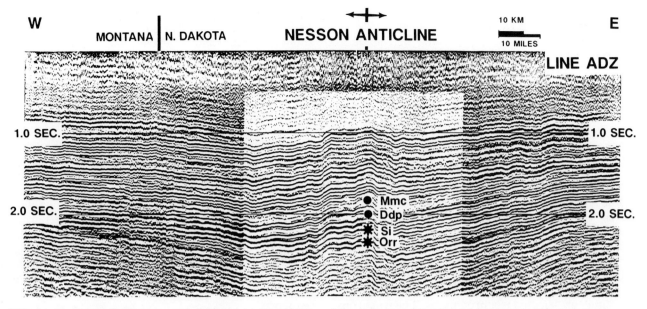

W   MONTANA | N. DAKOTA   NESSON ANTICLINE   10 KM / 10 MILES   E

LINE ADZ

1.0 SEC.   1.0 SEC.

2.0 SEC.   Mmc / Ddp / Si / Orr   2.0 SEC.

Figure 7. Compressed east-west seismic line ADZ. Total length of section approximately 150 mi (240 km). Seismic horizons labeled Orr, Ordovician Red River; Si, Silurian Interlake; Ddp, Devonian Duperow; Mmc, Mississippian Mission Canyon. See Figure 9 for general columnar section of the Williston basin. See Figure 8 for location of seismic line ADZ.

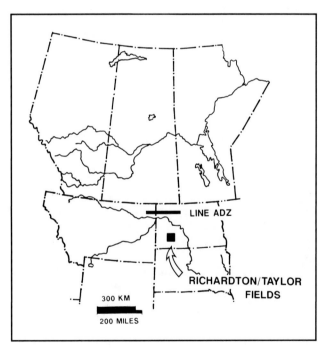

Figure 8. Map showing general location of seismic line ADZ in relation to Richardton/Taylor fields.

A structure map drawn on the top of the Ordovician Red River Formation (Figure 10) shows the large area and gentle dips along the flanks of the Williston basin. The large Cedar Creek anticline, oriented along a northwest-southeast structural trend, is evident as well as the north-south structural trend of the Nesson anticline. At the scale of the map and the contour interval selected, the Heart River fault trend is visible as a minor flexure in the Ordovician structure on the southeast flank of the basin.

Figure 11 is a detailed time-structure map, drawn on the Winnipeg seismic reflector, over the Heart River fault area. The Heart River fault is a north–south-trending sinuous feature with minor structural throw (less than 400 ft; 125 m). Small closures, developed along the crest of the upthrown or eastern block, coupled with stratigraphic aspects, provide the trapping conditions for the gas accumulations in the Winnipeg sandstones in the Richardton and Taylor fields.

STRATIGRAPHY

The Williston basin is a prolific producer of hydrocarbons. Oil was first discovered in commercial quantities in the early 1950s and is produced in reservoirs from Cambrian to Triassic in age. Natural gas is produced from many of the same reservoirs as well as Cretaceous-age sandstones (Figure 9).

Initial deposition in the basin during the Cambrian was of sands and shales onto the eroded Precambrian crystalline basement (Gerhard et al., 1982). By the Middle Ordovician, the deposition of siliciclastics was replaced by carbonate and evaporite deposition. The middle and late Paleozoic sections of the Williston basin are almost completely carbonate with only thin intervals of clastics, chiefly near the top of the Paleozoic. Several thin organic-rich shale intervals

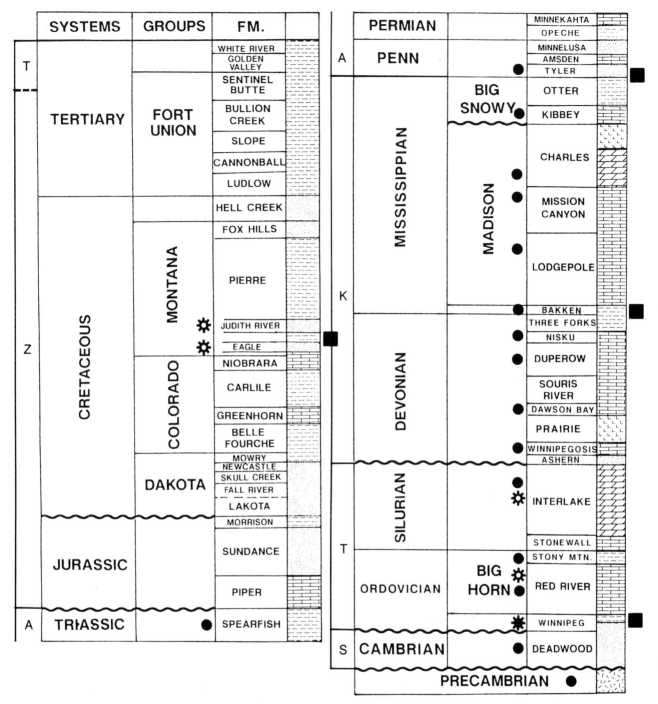

Figure 9. General columnar section for Richardton/Taylor field area, Stark County, North Dakota. Black squares indicate source rock intervals. Sequences: S, Sauk; T, Tippecanoe; K, Kaskaskia; A, Absaroka; Z, Zuni; T, Tejas. Productive zones shown by standard symbols.

have acted as source rocks for the hydrocarbons, notably the Ordovician Winnipeg shale, the Devonian–Mississippian Bakken shale, and shales within the Pennsylvanian Tyler Formation.

The majority of the oil produced in the basin is from Paleozoic-age reservoirs. Minor oil production is noted from the Mesozoic Spearfish sandstone, but this oil is believed to be Paleozoic oil that leaked updip across an angular unconformity.

The end of the Paleozoic in the Williston basin is also the end of predominantly marine deposition. The Mesozoic is characterized by mixed marine-nonmarine deposition with limestones and evaporites interbedded with continental red beds and shales (Shurr et al., 1989). During the Cretaceous, the Williston basin was again the site for marine deposition predominated by shales with interbedded thin sandstones and chalky marls.

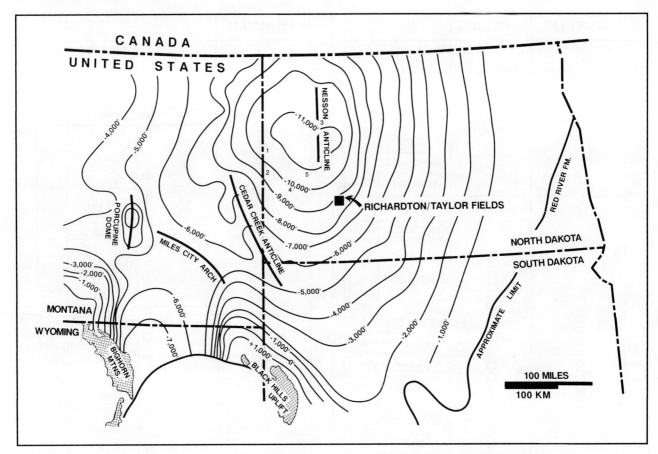

Figure 10. Regional structure map on the top of the Ordovician Red River. Contour interval is 1000 ft. Approximate location of: 1, Mondak; 2, Bicentennial; 3, Antelope; 4, Billings Nose; 5, Little Knife.

A lack of mature source rocks has left the Mesozoic section essentially barren of hydrocarbon accumulations. Shallow biogenic gas is produced from the Upper Cretaceous along the Cedar Creek anticline and on the north-plunge end of the Black Hills Uplift.

The Cenozoic section in the Williston basin is almost entirely nonmarine with shales predominant. Thin limy and shaly sands and volcanic ash deposits are widespread in the section. Extensive deposits of low-grade lignites are economically important (Rehbein, 1978; U.S. Geological Survey, 1974). Aboveground gasification of the lignites presently is underway but is marginally economic.

As mentioned above, the three main source rock intervals in the Williston basin are the Ordovician Winnipeg shale, the Mississippian–Devonian Bakken, and the shales within the Tyler Formation. It is believed that the source of the gas and condensate in the Richardton and Taylor fields is from the Winnipeg shales, specifically the Roughlock and Ice Box members (Figure 16).

TRAP

The Richardton and Taylor fields are structurally and partly stratigraphically trapped gas and condensate reservoirs. The structural element of trapping is shown in Figures 12 through 15. The Heart River trend is developed along a fault that involves blocks of the Precambrian basement. Thinning along the crest of the trend (Figure 5) suggests that the fault has experienced movement at least during the early Paleozoic. Flexure of the Cretaceous Niobrara reflector on line 3022 (Figures 12–15) indicates that movement occurred until at least middle Cretaceous time.

The Heart River fault is interpreted on line 3022 as a high angle reverse fault, based upon mapped structures and the overall compressive nature of the Williston basin. Throw on the fault is minor, and it appears to be a single fault without intermediate fault blocks.

The isochron interval mapped in Figure 5 is illustrated on the sections by the arrows between the MMC and OWP reflectors (Figures 13 and 15), the Mississippian Mission Canyon and Ordovician Winnipeg, respectively. Note that the Precambrian crystalline basement is a weak reflector, probably near 2.1 seconds two-way time at the crest of the structure.

Minor structural closures on the upthrown side of the fault provide the trap for the Richardton and Taylor fields, with the overlying Roughlock and Ice

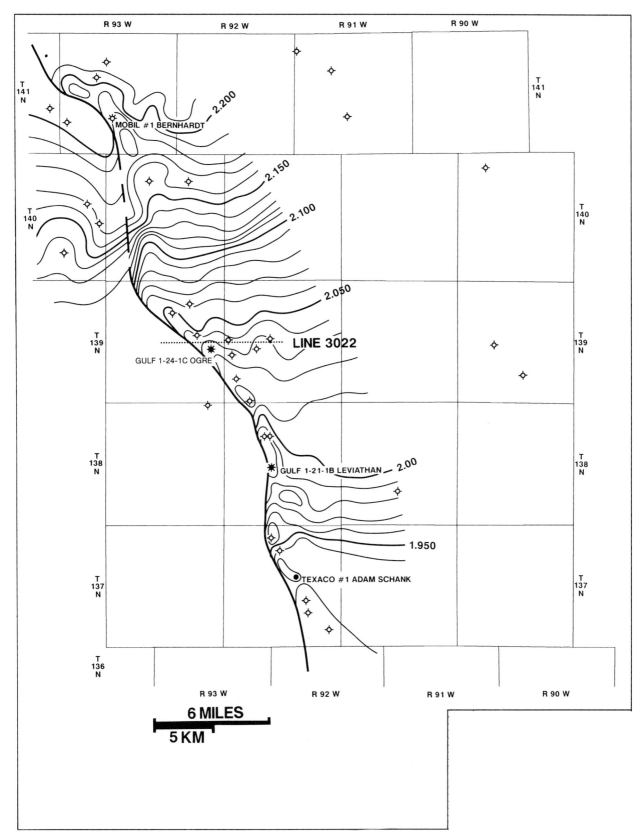

Figure 11. Time structure map Heart River trend. Seismic line 3022 location is shown. See Figures 12–15 for line.

429

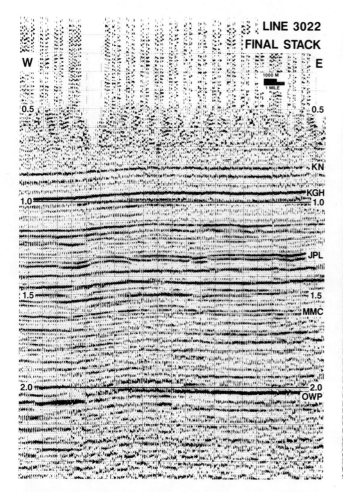

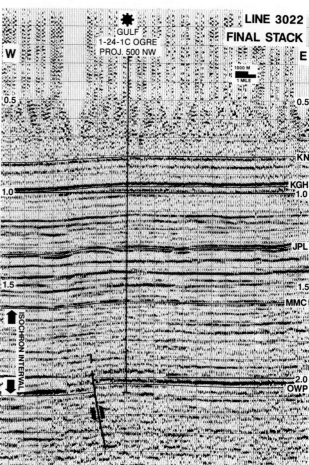

Figure 12. Seismic line 3022. Uninterpreted final stack, 600% CDP, dynamite source. Location of line shown on Figure 11. Seismic horizon code: OWP, Ordovician Winnipeg; MMC, Mississippian Mission Canyon; JPL, Jurassic Piper Lime; KGH, Cretaceous Greenhorn; KN, Cretaceous Niobrara. See Figure 9 for generalized columnar section. Vertical scale in seconds two-way time.

Figure 13. Seismic line 3022. Interpreted final stack. Projected position of Gulf 1-24-1C Ogre shown. Heavy black arrows define isochron interval mapped in Figure 5. See Figure 12 for key to names of seismic reflectors.

Box members of the Winnipeg Formation (Figure 16) providing the vertical seal. The stratigraphic component of trapping is provided by lateral changes in reservoir porosity and permeability (discussed in more detail under the *Reservoir* section). It is believed that the Richardton and Taylor gas accumulations are on separate closures. The time structure as mapped in Figures 4 and 11, as well as several wells with nonreservoir rock in the Black Island between the Ogre and Leviathan wells, support the belief in separate gas accumulations.

RESERVOIR

Depths to the top of the Winnipeg sandstone reservoirs in the Richardton and Taylor fields are

in excess of 11,000 ft (3350 m). The gas pay sands within the Black Island Member of the Winnipeg Formation tend to be thin and in places rich in clay (Figure 16). The regional isopach of the Black Island Member shows that it is less than 50 ft (15 m) in the field area (Figure 17). Individual sand units are less than 10 ft (3 m) thick, with shale interbeds.

Stratigraphy and Facies

The stratigraphic relationships of the Winnipeg Formation in the southern portion of the Williston basin have been detailed by Carlson (1958, 1960, 1964), Fuller (1961), and LeFever et al. (1985). The reader is referred to these for more detailed information.

The Winnipeg Formation unconformably overlies the Cambrian Deadwood Formation (Figure 9) in most of the Williston basin. In the extreme southeast flank of the basin, the Cambrian is truncated and

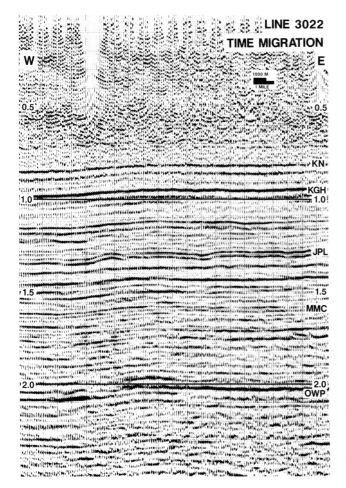

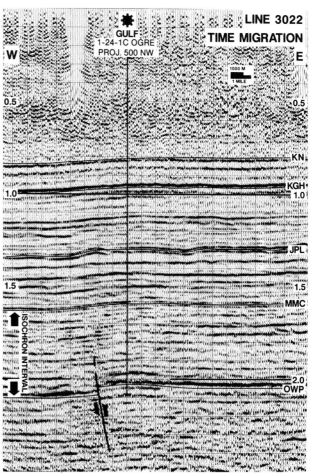

Figure 14. Seismic line 3022. Uninterpreted time migration. See Figure 12 for key to names of seismic reflectors.

Figure 15. Seismic line 3022. Interpreted time migration. See Figure 12 for key to names of seismic horizons.

the Winnipeg lies unconformably on the Precambrian crystalline basement. The Winnipeg attains a maximum thickness in excess of 300 ft (90 m) in the central portion of the basin, north of the Richardton and Taylor field areas (Figure 18).

The Winnipeg is divided into three members, the Black Island, Ice Box, and Roughlock members (Figure 16). The gas/condensate pays in the Richardton and Taylor fields are contained within the quartz-rich sandstones of the Black Island Member.

A north-south stratigraphic cross section of the Winnipeg, using the top of the Black Island Member as a datum, shows the thinning of the Winnipeg section from north to south (Figure 19). The majority of the thinning is in the Black Island Member, which was the initial unit deposited during the Tippecanoe transgression over the Deadwood Formation.

The gas reservoirs are typically well sorted and well rounded and may be fine- to coarse-grained sandstones. Feldspar and detrital clay masses are

seen in cores but are not evenly distributed throughout the pay intervals; rather, they are most abundant in thin, shaly laminae within sand intervals.

Sandstones of the Black Island Member were deposited in a nearshore marine environment. LeFever et al. (1985) have interpreted the environment of deposition as a zone that lies between the shallow water beach and foreshore area and the offshore marine shelf. Water depths may have ranged from less than 30 to 100 ft (10 to 30 m). Wave processes of sediment reworking were dominant over tidal influences.

The general lack of significant macrofauna within the Black Island sandstones suggests a higher energy environment with a mobile substrate. Salinity, temperature, and oxygen levels are believed to have been normal or near normal for marine waters. The Ice Box Shale Member, which conformably overlies the Black Island sandstones, is interpreted as an offshore transgressive marine shale.

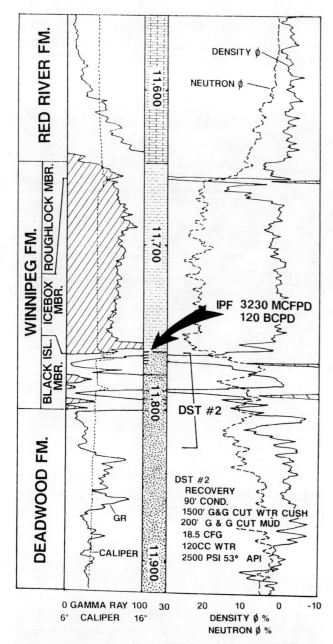

Figure 16. Type log, Winnipeg Formation Gulf Oil 1-24-1C Ogre. Well location Sec. 24, T139N, R93W, Stark County, North Dakota.

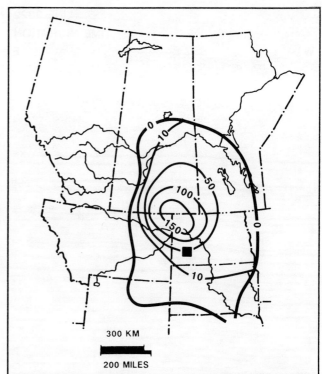

Figure 17. Regional isopach map of Black Island Member, Winnipeg Formation. Contour interval, 10 ft (3 m) and 50 ft (15 m). See type log in Figure 16 for stratigraphy of Winnipeg Formation.

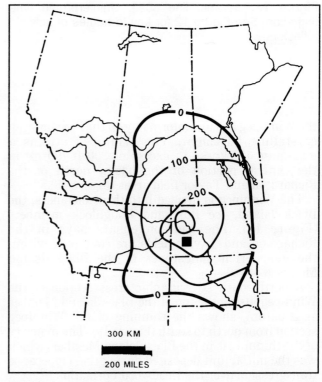

Figure 18. Regional isopach map of Winnipeg Formation. Contour interval, 100 ft (30 m). See Figure 9 for general columnar section of Williston basin.

Diagenesis

Primary interstitial porosity within the quartz sandstones of the Black Island Member is partially to totally occluded by a variety of cements. The distribution of porosity occluding cements is not predictable and thus was the primary cause for the lack of success in development drilling. In addition to porosity occlusion by cementation, the existence of acid-reactive clays, mostly iron-rich chlorite, and delicate clay fibers combine to require precautions

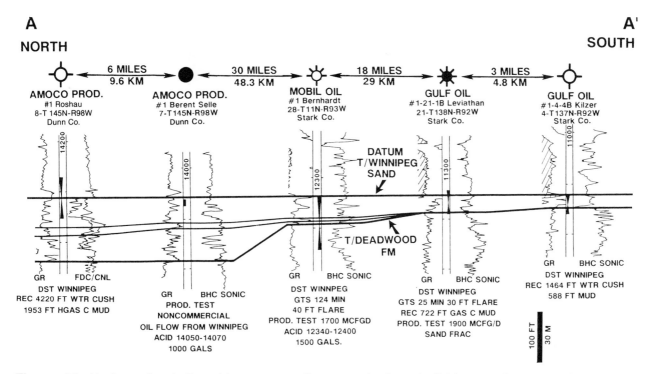

Figure 19. North-south stratigraphic cross section A-A'. See Figure 6 for location of wells on cross section. Note thinning of Black Island Member from north to south through field area. Amoco wells are to the northwest of Figure 6.

during drilling and subsequent completion operations to prevent reservoir damage.

Full diameter cores were cut in several wells drilled by Gulf, and the samples were subjected to a variety of analytical techniques, including thin-section petrography, X-ray diffraction (XRD) on both bulk samples and separated clay fractions, scanning electron microscopy (SEM), energy dispersive analysis (EDA), and cation exchange capacities (CEC).

The sandstones studied exhibit considerable variation in clay content, cement mineralogy, and matrix constituents. Quartz content varies from 44 to nearly 100% of the matrix (Figures 20, 21, and 22). Feldspars are dominantly potash feldspar (orthoclase, microcline, and perthite) and content ranges from none up to 16%. Secondary porosity is observed as dissolution voids in partially dissolved feldspar grains (Figures 23 and 24). Rock fragments are rare, and minor amounts of heavy minerals are observed (tourmaline, rutile, zircon, pyrite, and other unidentified opaques) (Figures 25 and 26).

Detrital clay fragments are concentrated in thin laminae and range in abundance from none up to 43% (Figure 27). Diagenetic, secondary clays are an even more important element and act both to occlude porosity and elsewhere to effectively preserve some primary porosity by inhibiting quartz overgrowths on individual quartz sand grains. Other minor phyllosilicate minerals include muscovite and glauconite.

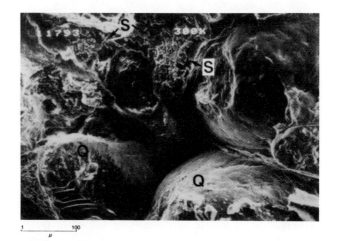

Figure 20. SEM photomicrograph from Gulf 1-19-4B Hamman, depth 11,793 ft (3594 m). Well-rounded detrital quartz grains (Q) showing little cementation. Salt masses (S) are crystallized from connate waters after drying of core.

Paragenesis is useful for determining porosity-cement relationships and timing, especially in reference to periods of peak hydrocarbon generation and charging of reservoirs. Three main cement types are recognized in the sandstones of the Black Island Member.

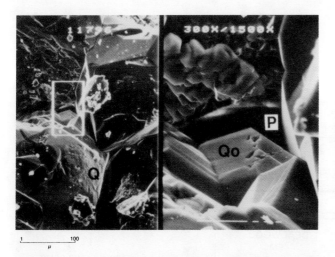

Figure 21. SEM photomicrograph from Gulf 1-19-4B Hamman, depth 11,796 ft (3595 m). Partial to complete covering by quartz overgrowths (Qo) on detrital quartz (Q) reducing porosity (P). On detail note pitting/corrosion of quartz overgrowths. Small rectangle at left is magnified at right.

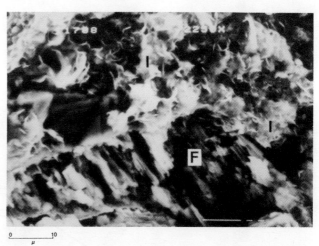

Figure 23. SEM photomicrograph from Gulf 1-19-4B Hamman, depth 11,788 ft (3592 m). Dissolved feldspar grain (F) and authigenic illite (I).

Figure 22. SEM photomicrograph from Gulf 1-21-1B Leviathan, depth 11,356 ft (3461 m). Nearly complete cementation of quartz sandstone by euhedral quartz overgrowths (Qo).

Figure 24. SEM photomicrograph from Gulf 1-21-1B Leviathan, depth 11,356 ft (3461 m). Secondary porosity developed in partially dissolved feldspar grain (F).

The first type is clay overgrowths and is widespread. Clays are noted coating quartz sand grains (Figures 28 and 29) and lining pores (Figures 30 and 31). Generally the clay overgrowths and masses do not completely block porosity, but rather reduce the size of pores and restrict pore throats, thus effectively limiting storage capacity and reservoir permeability. Clay particles lining pores are fragile, resulting in the migration of dislodged fines by turbulent action of invaded drilling and completion fluids. In addition, illitic, mixed-layer clays swell in contact with sodium-rich fluids, which also reduces porosity and pore-throat size. Potassium chloride brines were used in the completions of the reservoirs. It is possible that damage to the sandstone reservoir in the Mobil #1 Bernhardt, as discussed earlier, was the result of completion fluids interacting with reservoir clays, almost completely restricting gas flow from the reservoir to the well bore.

Iron-rich chlorites are also observed in the reservoir. These clays are reactive to acids used in completion of the wells. The released iron tends to

434

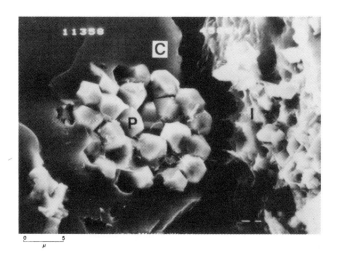

Figure 25. SEM photomicrograph from Gulf 1-21-1B Leviathan, depth 11,358 ft (3461 m). Pore lined with clay, probably illite (I), with pyrite crystals (P) within voids of carbonate cement (C). Note illite "hairs" associated with pyrite.

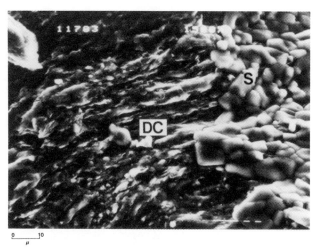

Figure 27. SEM photomicrograph from Gulf 1-19-4B Hamman, depth 11,783 ft (3591 m). Detrital clay matrix (DC) showing laminated structure. Salt crystal masses (S) are precipitated from connate water after drying of core.

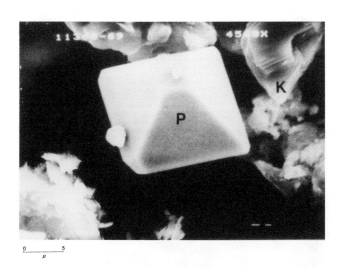

Figure 26. SEM photomicrograph from Gulf 1-21-1B Leviathan, depth 11,369 ft (3465 m). Authigenic pyrite (P) and kaolinite "books" (K) line pore.

form iron hydroxides that precipitate in pore throats and reduce reservoir permeability. Iron chelating agents in the completion fluids scavenge free iron and reduce the formation of iron hydroxides.

The second type of porosity occlusion is by quartz overgrowths on individual sand grains. Euhedral overgrowths may lead to partial to total restriction of porosity. Complete cementation by quartz forms a quartzite with no reservoir potential (Figures 21 and 22).

The final type of cement observed is carbonate, chiefly calcite. Carbonate cements range in abun-

dance from 8 to 34% (Figure 32). Other carbonate minerals (i.e., dolomite, siderite) were detected in trace amounts.

Oil and Field Characteristics

Richardton and Taylor are gas/condensate fields. Condensates are in excess of 50° API at 60°F and have a light straw yellow color. Tests indicate that no H_2S is present in either the gas or the condensate.

Gas analysis from the 1-21-1B Leviathan is listed in Table 1. The gas is predominantly methane (86.4%) with a significant proportion of nitrogen (N_2, 7.7%). The gas analysis for the 1-24-1C Ogre is listed in Table 2. The gas from the Ogre is much higher in methane (88.4%) and lower in nitrogen (N_2, 1.7%) than the gas from the Leviathan well.

Initial reservoir pressures were 5122 psia (35,316 kPa) for the 1-21-1B Leviathan (Richardton) and 5368 psia (37,012 kPa) for the 1-24-1C Ogre (Taylor). Pressure gradients at original reservoir conditions were calculated at 0.45 psi/ft (10.18 kPa/m) for the 1-21-1B Leviathan and 0.46 psi/ft (10.37 kPa/m) for the 1-24-1c Ogre, both considered to be normally pressured.

After the two initial discovery wells had been drilled, it was recognized that log analysis frequently gave erroneous values as a result of hole washout. Another frequent method for open-hole evaluation was drill-stem testing (DST) immediately after the Black Island sandstone had been drilled.

The pressure build-up curve from the Black Island sandstone, DST #2, in the 1-24-1C Ogre (Figure 33) shows a rapid pressure increase during both the initial and final flow periods and the sharp breaks at the end of both flow periods into the initial and

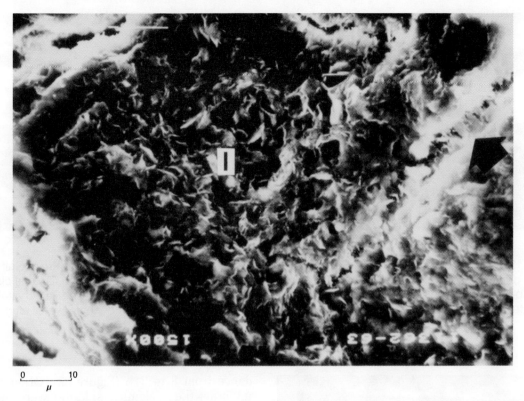

Figure 28. SEM photomicrograph from Gulf 1-21-1B Leviathan, depth 11,362 ft (3463 m). Authigenic clay coating grains, platy habit suggests illite (I). Arrow points to closure of sheet pore by clay overgrowths.

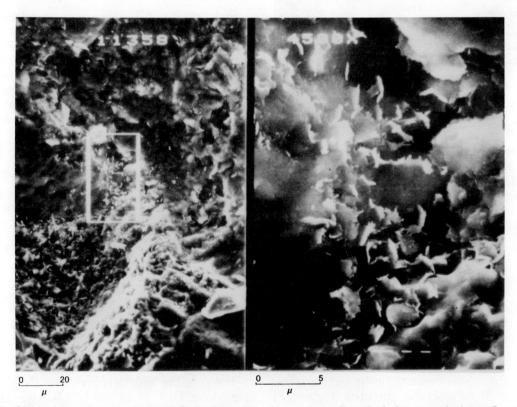

Figure 29. SEM photomicrograph from Gulf 1-21-1B Leviathan, depth 11,358 ft (3462 m). Irregular "feathered" edges of clay platelets, typical of illitic mixed-layer clays. Detail of clay morphology. Small rectangle left is magnified at right.

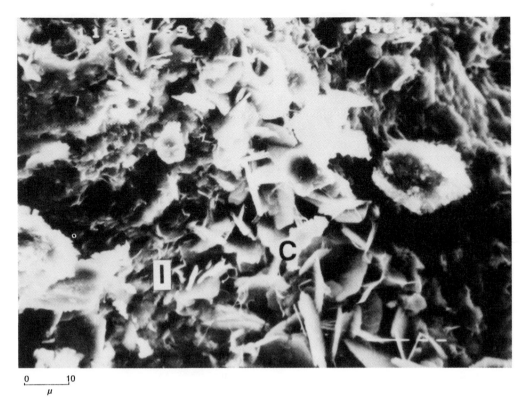

0 _____ 10
μ

Figure 30. SEM photomicrograph from Gulf 1-21-1b Leviathan, depth 11,369 ft (3465 m). Authigenic illite (I) as fragile hairs and chlorite (C) in bladed form line pore.

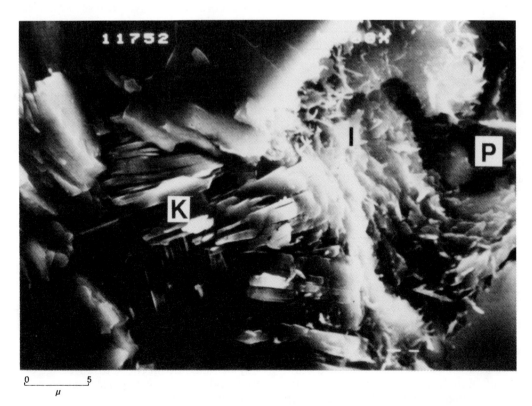

0 _____ 5
μ

Figure 31. SEM photomicrograph from Gulf 1-21-1B Leviathan, depth 11,752 ft (3581 m). Pore (P) lined with books of authigenic kaolinite (K) and hair-like illite (I), both occluding porosity and reducing permeability.

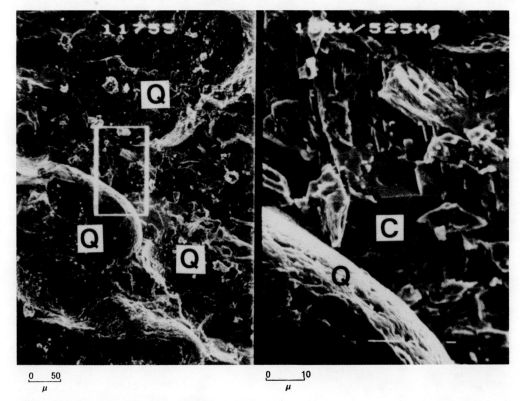

Figure 32. SEM photomicrograph from Gulf 1-21-1B Leviathan, depth 11,346 ft (3458 m). Carbonate cement (C) coats detrital quartz grains (Q) and occludes porosity. Detail of carbonate cement morphology. Small rectangle (left) shows area enlarged at right.

Table 1. Gas analysis of 1-21-1B Leviathan well.

Component	Separator Gas (mol. %)
Methane	86.360
Ethane	3.70
Propane	0.56
Iso-butane	0.16
n-Butane	0.12
Iso-pentane	0.07
n-Pentane	0.04
Hexane	0.01
Heptane plus	0.00
Hydrogen sulfide	0.00
Carbon dioxide	1.33
Nitrogen	7.65
	100.00

final shut-in periods indicating good reservoir permeability.

Contrast the pressure build-up curve from the Ogre well with the curve from the Gulf 1-10-4B Moore (Figure 34), a dry hole with no pay in the Black Island sandstone. Note the lack of pressure increase during the flow period and the rather slow pressure build-up at the end of both flow periods into the initial and final shut-in periods. As a further comparison, the Ogre test recovered 90 ft (27 m) of condensate and 18 ft^3 of gas during the drill-stem test, while the Moore well recovered less than 100 ft (30 m) of mud with no shows of condensate or gas during the drill-stem test. Other appraisal wells drilled by Gulf had similar recoveries from poor quality, tightly cemented sands in the Black Island Member. These wells were plugged and abandoned.

A lack of market has hampered production and neither gas field has been as prolific as expected (Figures 35 and 36).

Source

Williams (1974), Dow (1974), and Longman and Palmer (1987) characterized the source rocks of the Williston basin and interpreted the Winnipeg shales as the probable source of hydrocarbons in the Ordovician through Lower Devonian reservoirs. Limited data indicate that the Winnipeg shale is a rather lean source rock with less than 1.0% average TOC. Analysis of the kerogen present in the shales shows it to be marine-algal type I in nature.

Estimation of the level of thermal maturity indicates that the central portion of the basin is in the wet gas-condensate window. The Richardton and Taylor fields lie on the southern edge of the wet gas area and were probably sourced from the north as hydrocarbons migrated updip to the south (Figure 37). Dow (1974) suggests that peak generation and migration occurred during the Permian.

438

Table 2. Gas analysis of 1-24-1C Ogre well.

Component	Separator Liquid (mol. %)	Separator Gas (mol. %)	Well Stream (mol. %)
Methane	8.31	91.02	88.44
Ethane	1.90	3.72	3.66
Propane	1.73	1.04	1.06
Iso-butane	0.69	0.19	0.21
n-Butane	2.49	0.47	0.53
Iso-pentane	1.42	0.12	0.16
n-Pentane	3.73	0.25	0.36
Hexanes	7.15	0.18	0.40
Heptanes plus	72.36	0.08	2.34
Hydrogen sulfide	0.00	0.00	0.00
Carbon dioxide	0.19	0.00	0.00
Nitrogen	0.03	1.80	1.74
	100.00	100.00	100.00

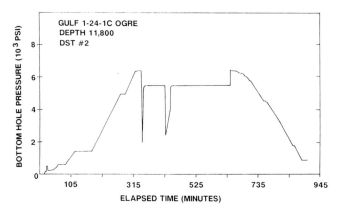

Figure 33. Pressure build-up curve, DST #2, depth 11,800 ft (3596 m), Gulf 1-24-1C Ogre. Tested Black Island sandstone.

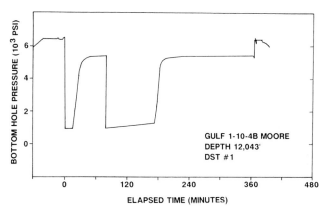

Figure 34. Pressure build-up curve, DST #1, depth 12,043 ft (3671 m), Gulf 1-10-4B Moore. Tested Black Island sandstone.

EXPLORATION AND DEVELOPMENT CONCEPTS

In evaluating the overall success of the Winnipeg sandstone play, it is obvious that the principal exploratory and development risk is in defining the limits of the effective reservoir. Despite an aggressive development program, Gulf was unable to extend production of either field beyond the initial two wells.

Since fewer than 300 Winnipeg tests have been drilled in the basin (approximately one well per 1000 mi^2 (2600 km^2), it seems reasonable that additional reservoir and play trends will be found. Anderson (1982) in his review cites numerous tests of the Winnipeg and Deadwood where free oil and/or gas were recovered during testing of the Winnipeg sandstones. Unfortunately, none of these zones were developed because other uphole pays in the wells were more attractive.

From an economic standpoint, it is unfortunate that the two original prospects drilled by Gulf (i.e., Leviathan and Ogre) were discoveries. The initial success led to the drilling of nine additional development, step-out, and new field wildcats, none of which, other than the Mobil #1 Bernhardt, were capable of production. The unsuccessful development program has had a severe negative impact on the overall economic return for this play.

The Richardton and Taylor fields are not large accumulations of gas. They are unique because they represent the only fields that produce significant quantities of gas from the Winnipeg sandstones in the Williston basin. They also hint at the possibility of further discoveries that might be found below the Ordovician Red River. The challenge of exploring in the Lower Ordovician–Cambrian section hinges on being able to predict reservoir porosity. Only with

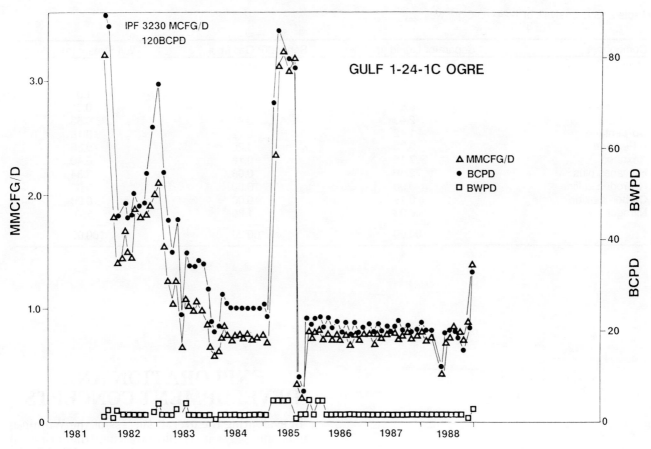

Figure 35. Monthly average production history, Gulf 1-24-1C Ogre.

additional work to understand the intricacies of reservoir development will the Winnipeg sandstones become a viable exploration target.

ACKNOWLEDGMENTS

The authors wish to thank Chevron USA and CONOCO for permission to publish this field study. The staff of the Drafting Department at the Gulf Oil office in Casper, Wyoming, and at Chevron Overseas Petroleum in San Ramon, California, aided in preparation of the illustrations.

REFERENCES CITED

Anderson, T. C., 1982, Exploration history and hydrocarbon potential of the Ordovician Winnipeg Formation in the southern Williston basin, *in* J. E. Christopher and J. Kaldi, eds., Fourth International Williston Basin Symposium: Saskatchewan Geological Society Special Publication 6, Regina, Saskatchewan, p. 19–26.

Brown, D. L., 1978, Wrench-style deformational patterns associated with a meridional stress axis recognized in Paleozoic rocks in parts of Montana, South Dakota, and Wyoming, *in* Williston Basin Symposium: Montana Geological Society, Billings, Montana, Twenty-fourth Annual Conference, p. 17–31.

Brown, D. L., and D. J. Brown, 1987, Wrench-style deformation and paleostructural influence on sedimentation in and around a cratonic basin, *in* M. W. Longman, ed., Williston basin, anatomy of a cratonic oil province: Rocky Mountain Association of Geologists, p. 57–70.

Carlson, C. G.,1958, The stratigraphy of the Deadwood-Winnipeg interval in North Dakota and Saskatchewan, *in* Second International Williston Basin Symposium, Regina, Saskatchewan: Saskatchewan and North Dakota Geological Societies, p. 20–36.

Carlson, C. G., 1960, Stratigraphy of the Winnipeg and Deadwood Formations in North Dakota: North Dakota Geological Survey Bulletin 35, 149 p.

Carlson, C. G., 1964, Facies relationships of the Winnipeg Group in eastern North Dakota, *in* Third International Williston Basin Symposium: Billings Geological Society, North Dakota Geological Society, and Saskatchewan Geological Society, p. 45–50.

Carlson, C. G., and S. B. Anderson, 1965, Sedimentary and tectonic history of North Dakota part of the Williston Basin: AAPG Bulletin, v. 49, p. 1833–1846.

Clement, J. H., and T. E. Mayhew, 1979, Newporte discovery opens new pay: Oil and Gas Journal, v. 77, n. 27, p. 165–172.

Dow, W. G, 1974, Application of oil-correlation and source-rock data to exploration in Williston basin: AAPG Bulletin, v. 58, p. 1253–1262.

Fuller, J. G. C. M., 1961, Ordovician and contiguous formations in North Dakota, South Dakota, Montana, and adjoining areas of Canada and the United States: AAPG Bulletin, v. 45, p. 1334–1363.

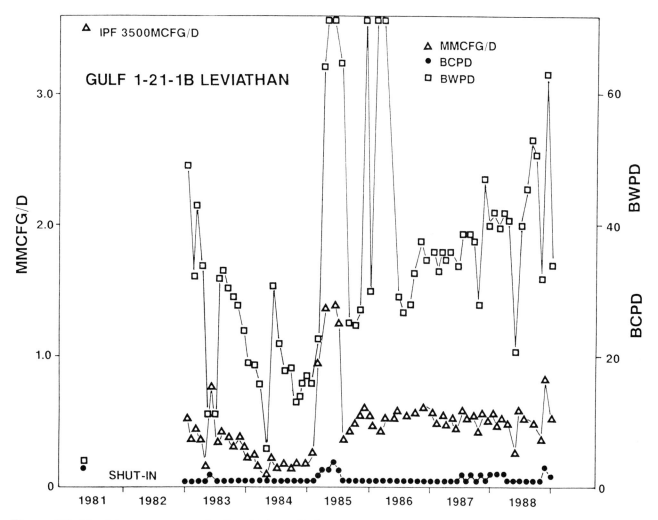

Figure 36. Monthly average production history, Gulf
1-21-1B Leviathan.

Figure 37. Regional map showing area of effective
mature source rock in Winnipeg Shales. Winnipeg
enters top of oil window at approximately -5000 ft.
Stippling shows area where Winnipeg is in wet gas
condensate generative window.

Gerhard, L. C., S. B. Anderson, J. A. LeFever, and C. G. Carlson,
1982, Geological development, origin, and energy mineral
resources of the Williston Basin, North Dakota: AAPG
Bulletin, v. 66, p. 989–1022.

LeFever, R. D., S. C. Thompson, and D. B. Anderson, 1985, *in*
Fifth International Williston Basin Symposium, p. 22–36.

Longman, M. W., and S. E. Palmer, 1987, Organic geochemistry
of Mid-continent Middle and Late Ordovician oils: AAPG
Bulletin, v. 71, p. 938–950.

Rehbein, E. A., 1978, Depositional environments and lignite
resources of the Fort Union Formation, west-central North
Dakota, *in* Williston Basin Symposium: Montana Geological
Society, Twenty-fourth Annual Conference, p. 295–305.

Shurr, G. W., L. O. Anna, and J. A. Peterson, 1989, Zuni sequence
in Williston basin—evidence for Mesozoic paleotectonism:
AAPG Bulletin, v. 73, p. 68–87.

Thomas, G. E., 1974, Lineament-block tectonics: Williston–Blood
Creek basin: AAPG Bulletin, v. 58, p. 1305–1322.

U.S. Geological Survey, 1974, Stripping coal deposits of the
Northern Great Plains, Montana, Wyoming, North Dakota,
and South Dakota: U.S. Geological Survey Miscellaneous Field
Studies Map MF-590.

Williams, J. A., 1974, Characterization of oil types in Williston
basin: AAPG Bulletin, v. 58, p. 1243–1252.

Appendix 1. Field Description

Field Name .... *Richardton/Taylor fields*

Ultimate recoverable reserves .... *9.0 BCFG, 250 MB condensate*

Field location

    Country .... *U.S.A.*

    State .... *North Dakota*

    Basin/Province .... *Williston/Great Plains*

Field discovery

    Year first pay discovered .... *Ordovician Winnipeg sandstone, Richardton and Taylor 1980*

Discovery well name and general location:

    First pay .... *Richardton, Gulf 1-21-1B Leviathan, Sec. 21, T138N, R92W, Stark County, North Dakota*
                     Taylor, Gulf 1-24-1C Ogre, Sec. 24, T139N, R93W, Stark County, North Dakota

Discovery well operator .... *Gulf Oil Exploration and Production Company*

IP .... *Richardton 3500 MCFGPD, 1 BCPD; Taylor, 3230 MCFGPD, 120 BCPD*

All other zones with shows of oil and gas in the field:

Age	Formation	Type of Show
Ordovician	*Red River*	*Gas cut mud, Ogre well*

Geological concept leading to discovery and method or methods used to delineate prospect

A regional north-south structural trend was found by utilizing a speculative seismic survey grid. Detailed seismic was acquired over leads developed from the interpretation of the speculative survey. The detailed surveys were used to define closures at the prospect level. The primary target for prospecting was the Ordovician Red River carbonates. The initial discovery well was drilled 800 ft (243 m) deeper to test a poorly defined pinch-out of the Ordovician Winnipeg sandstone on the south flank of the basin. The Ordovician Red River carbonates were found to be nonproductive but the deeper Winnipeg sandstone was found to be gas-bearing in two small accumulations, i.e., Richardton and Taylor fields.

Structure:

    Province/basin type .... *Williston/cratonic; Bally 121, Klemme I*

    Tectonic history

The Williston basin is a cratonic type basin which has undergone nearly continuous subsidence and deposition since early Paleozoic time. The subsidence and deposition has been punctuated by several episodes of low intensity uplift and erosion. The most recent tectonic episode occurred during the Late Cretaceous-early Tertiary Laramide orogeny that formed many of the larger structures present in the basin today.

Regional structure

The Richardton/Taylor fields are situated on the south flank of the Williston basin along the north-south-trending Heart River fault. The down-to-the-west fault is seated in the Precambrian crystalline basement and has involved rocks up through the Upper Ordovician-Lower Silurian level. Seismic data show rocks above the Lower Silurian level flexed but not offset by the fault.

Local structure

The Richardton/Taylor fields are located on small structural closures at the Ordovician Winnipeg shale level along the large north-south-trending Heart River fault.

Trap:

Trap type(s)

The Richardton/Taylor field area has one basic type of trap in the Ordovician Winnipeg sandstone, i.e., small (640 ac) structural closures on the regionally upthrown Heart River fault block. The fault may partially seal the fields on their western flanks. Rapid lateral changes in reservoir quality play a major role in trapping of hydrocarbons. The limits of the stratigraphic trap are unknown.

Basin Stratigraphy (major stratigraphic intervals from surface to deepest penetration in field):

Chronostratigraphy	Formation	Depth to Top in ft (m)
Cretaceous	*Greenhorn*	*4000 (1219)*
	Mowry	*4466 (1361)*
	Dakota	*4882 (1488)*
Jurassic	*Piper Lime*	*5784 (1763)*
Triassic	*Spearfish*	*5976 (1821)*
Pennsylvanian	*Minnelusa*	*6436 (1961)*
	Tyler	*6746 (2056)*
Mississippian	*Charles*	*7500 (2285)*
	Mission Canyon	*8078 (2462)*
	Lodgepole	*8436 (2571)*
	Bakken	*9170 (2794)*
Devonian	*Nisku*	*9328 (2843)*
	Duperow	*9392 (2862)*
Silurian	*Interlake*	*10,163 (3097)*
Ordovician	*Red River*	*10,972 (3344)*
	Winnipeg	*11,644 (3549)*

Reservoir characteristics:

Number of reservoirs *1*

Formations .... *Black Island Member, Winnipeg Formation*

Ages .... *Upper Ordovician (Blackriverian-Caradocian)*

Depths to top of reservoirs .... *11,800 ft (3596 m) average*

Gross Thickness (top to bottom of producing interval) .... *20 ft (6 m)*

Net thickness—total thickness of producing zones

Average .... *16 ft (4.8 m)*

Maximum .... *16 ft (4.8 m)*

Lithology

The Black Island Member of the Winnipeg Formation is a fine- to coarse-grained subrounded to well-rounded quartz sandstone deposited in a nearshore marine environment. Carbonate cements and authigenic clays degrade overall reservoir quality. Secondary porosity due to leaching of feldspars and carbonate grains enhances porosity locally.

Porosity type

Interparticle porosity with secondary carbonate cements and authigenic clays. Some secondary porosity due to leaching of carbonate grains enhances reservoir quality locally.

Average porosity *10–12%*

Average permeability .... *15.3 md (to gas)*

Seals:

Upper

Formation, fault, or other feature .... *Winnipeg shale*

Lithology .... *Dark gray shale*

Lateral

Formation, fault, or other feature

Structure on overlying Winnipeg shale; possible sealing of shale against reservoir sand at Heart River fault; stratigraphic component due to porosity/permeability changes not known

443

Source:

Formation and age .... *Roughlock and Ice Box members of Winnipeg shale*
Lithology .... *Dark gray shale*
Average total organic carbon (TOC) .... *0.40% (38 wells)*
Maximum TOC *1.34%*
Kerogen type (I, II, or III) .... *I*
Thermal alternation (TAI) .... *2–2.5 locally, 3.5 basin maximum*
Time of hydrocarbon expulsion .... *Permian*
Present depth to top of source .... *11,200 ft (3413 m)*
Thickness .... *130 ft (40 m)*
Potential yield .... *Unknown*

Appendix 2. Production Data

Field Name .... *Richardton/Taylor fields*

Field size:

Proven acres .... *1220 (493 ha)*
Number of wells all years *2*
Current number of wells *2*
Well spacing .... *640 ac (259 ha)*
Ultimate recoverable .... *9.0 BCFG; 250 MBC*
Cumulative production .... *2.9 BCFG; 73 MBC*
Annual production .... *1.51 BCFG; 8.2 MBC*
Present decline rate .... *Less than 2%*
    Initial decline rate *10%*
    Overall decline rate .... *Approximately 8%*
Annual water production .... *450 BW*
In place, total reserves .... *11 BCFG; 397 MBC*
In place, per acre foot .... *563 MCFG; 20 BC*
Primary recovery .... *9.0 BCFG; 250 MBC*
Secondary recovery .... *NA*
Enhanced recovery .... *NA*
Cumulative water production .... *65 MBW*

Drilling and casing practices:

Amount of surface casing set .... *3200 ft (975 m)*
Casing program

9⅝-in. surface casing; 5½-in. production casing set to TD; 2⅞-in. production tubing

Drilling mud .... *Salt-starch*
Bit program

12¼-in. sealed journal mill tooth to 3200 ft; 8¾-in. sealed journal mill tooth to 5000 ft (Dakota sandstone); 8¾-in insert (medium to soft formation) button to TD

High pressure zones .... *None*

Completion practices:

Interval(s) perforated .... *Black Island member, Winnipeg Formation*
Well treatment

Perforate with 4 JPF, acidize with 5000 gal. (18,900 L) 15% HCl acid in KCl brine; add Fe-chelating agent to scavenge free Fe from Fe-rich clays and to avoid formation of Fe-hydroxides

Formation evaluation:

Logging suites

Dual laterolog with micro SFL, BHC sonic, compensated neutron-formation density, all with gamma ray; casing collar and cement bond for engineering and completion data

Testing practices

Open-hole drill-stem test, shut-in tool if gas or oil flows to surface; typical drill-stem test procedure, initial open 15 minutes, initial shut-in 60 minutes, final flow 90 minutes, final shut-in 120 minutes, water cushion up to 9000 ft level, retrieve tool

Mud logging techniques

Log wills with two-man, 24 hour supervision from base of surface casing to TD; catch 30 ft ditch samples to top of Mississippian, then 10 ft samples to TD; log gases with hot-wire and gas chromatograph (to C_4)

Oil characteristics:

Type	*Retrograde condensate*
API gravity	*53.1°*
Base	*14.65 psia*
Initial GOR	*26,916:1 Gulf 1-24-1C Ogre*
Sulfur, wt%	*None*
Viscosity, SUS	*Unknown*
Pour point	*Unknown*
Gas-oil distillate	*Unknown*

Field characteristics:

Average elevation	*2380 ft (725 m)*
Initial pressure	*5368 psi (377 kg/cm²)*
Present pressure	*3795 psi (266 kg/cm²)*
Pressure gradient	*0.40 psi/ft (0.104kg/cm²/m)*
Geothermal gradient	*1.5°F/100 ft (2.7°C/100 m)*
Drive	*Gas expansion*
Oil column thickness	*None*
Oil-water thickness	*None*
Connate water	*30%*
Water salinity, TDS	*177,000 ppm Cl, TDS 262,000 ppm*
Resistivity of water	*0.055 ohm-m at 68°F*

Transportation method and market for oil and gas:

Natural gas sold by pipeline to Williston Basin Inc./Montana-Dakota Utilities; condensate sold by truck to Permian Corp.; overall production rates curtailed due to limited gas purchases by pipeline